Algorithms, Data Structures, and Problem Solving with C++

Mark Allen Weiss
Florida International University

Addison-Wesley Publishing Company, Inc.
Menlo Park, California • Reading, Massachusetts • New York • Don Mills, Ontario
Wokingham, U.K. • Amsterdam • Bonn • Paris • Milan • Madrid • Sydney
Singapore • Tokyo • Seoul • Tapei • Mexico City • San Juan, Puerto Rico

Acquisitions Editor: J. Carter Shanklin
Executive Editor: Dan Joraanstad
Developmental/Copyeditor: Barbara Conway
Editorial Assistant: Christine Kulke
Senior Production Editor: Teri Holden
Composition and Film Coordinator: Vivian McDougal
Manufacturing Coordinator: Janet Weaver
Proofreader: Holly McLean-Aldis
Text Designer: Lisa Jahred
Film Preparation/Printer: The Maple-Vail Book Manufacturing Group
Cover Designer: Yvo Riezebos

Library of Congress Cataloging-in-Publication Data

```
Weiss, Mark Allen.
    Algorithms, data structures, and problem solving with C++ / Mark
  A. Weiss
        p. cm.
    Includes index.
    ISBN 0-8053-1666-3
    1. C++ (Computer program language)  2. Data structures (computer
  science)  3. Computer Algorithms.   I. Title
QA76.73.C153W455 1995
005.13'3--dc20                                              95-37755
                                                               CIP
```

ISBN 0-8053-1666-3

1 2 3 4 5 6 7 8 9 10 MA 99 98 97 96 95

Addison-Wesley Publishing Company, Inc.
2725 Sand Hill Road
Menlo Park, CA 94025

To my father Dr. David Weiss, of blessed memory.

Contents

Part I: Objects and C++

Part II: Algorithms and Building Blocks

Chapter 8   Sorting Algorithms   263

Part III: Applications

Part IV: Implementations

Chapter 20   A Priority Queue: The Binary Heap   639

Part V: Advanced Data Structures

Appendices

Appendix A Basic C++ 759

Appendix D Modifications for Exceptions 801

Preface

This book was designed for a second course in computer science, which has typically been known as CS-2 Data Structures. The content of CS-2 has been evolving over some time, but there is general agreement that topics such as structures, pointers, and data structures should be taught, along with an introduction to algorithm analysis and a general scaling up of the complexity of programming projects.

Although the general topics of CS-2 are to some extent uniformly accepted, the language of expression has clearly not been and indeed invokes quite spirited debate among computer science educators. We use C++ in this text. C++ has a host of both benefits and disadvantages but is clearly gaining support as a preferred language in industry and academic circles.

My goal in writing this text is to provide a practical introduction to data structures and algorithms, from the viewpoint of abstract thinking and problem solving, as well as to the use of C++. I try to cover all important details concerning the data structures, the analyses, and their C++ implementations, and have stayed away from data structures that are theoretically interesting but not widely used. I have designed the textbook to allow flexibility in topic coverage for the instructor. It is impossible to cover all the C++ details, all the different data structures, and all the mathematics described in the text in a single course. The instructor will need to decide on an appropriate balance between practice, theory, and level of C++ detail.

Approach

The most unique aspect of the text is the clear separation of the interface and implementation. In C++ the class mechanism allows the programmer to write the interface and implementation separately, to place them in separate files and compile separately, and to hide implementation details. In this textbook we take this a step further: The interface and implementation are discussed in separate parts of the book. Parts I, II, and III lay the groundwork, discussing basic concepts and tools and providing some practical examples, but implementation of the basic data structures are not shown until Part IV. This is the first CS-2 textbook to take this approach.

The separation of interface and implementation provides several benefits. Generally, it promotes abstract thinking: Class interfaces are written and used before the implementation is known, and it forces the reader to think about the functionality and potential efficiency of the various data structures. For example, programs that use a hash table are written hundreds of pages before the hash table is implemented. The proposed standard template library (STL) for C++ (which is likely to be mimicked in Ada and other languages) provides classes for stacks, queues, and almost all the fundamental data structures. We believe it will hasten the shift in emphasis of data structures courses from implemention to use.

Prerequisites

The prerequisite is a working knowledge of small C or a C-like subset of C++, including basic data types, operators, control structures, functions, and input and output. Appendix A contains a review of this material. Students that have had a first course using C++ should be able to start at Chapter 1. Students that have had a first course using C should scan Appendix A to see the differences between C and C++. Students whose first course was neither C nor C++ will need to read Appendix A carefully. In any event, this textbook is not about C++; it is about data structures and algorithm design, which is the proper focus of a CS-2 course. Readers who are not fluent C++ programmers should have a C++ refcrence book available; some recommendations are listed in Chapter 1.

Discrete math is not a prerequisite. Mathematical proofs are relatively rare (except towards the end of the text), and when done they are usually preceded by a brief math review. However, establishing some of our claims requires proof; Chapters 7 and 18 through 23 require some degree of mathematical sophistication. The instructor may elect to skip mathematical aspects of the proofs by presenting only the results. All proofs in the text are clearly marked and are separate from the body of the text.

C++

Using C++ presents both advantages and disadvantages. The C++ class allows the separation of interface and implementation, as well as the hiding of internal details of the implementation. It cleanly supports the notion of abstraction. However, other languages support this also, notably Turbo Pascal and Ada. The advantage of C++ is that it is widely used in industry. Students perceive that the material they are learning is practical and will help them find employment, which provides motivation to persevere through the course. The disadvantage of C++ is that it is far from a perfect language pedagogically, especially in a second course, and thus additional care needs to be expended to avoid bad programming practices. A second disadvantage is that C++ is still not a stable language, so the various compilers behave differently.

It might have been preferable to write the book in a language-independent fashion, concentrating only on general principles such as the theory of the data structures and referring to C++ code only in passing, but that is impossible. C++ code is complex, and readers will need to see complete examples to understand some of the finer points. As mentioned earlier, a brief review of the simpler parts of C++ is provided in Appendix A. Part I of the book describes some of C++'s more advanced features relevant to data structures.

Three parts of the language stand out as requiring special pedagogical consideration: templates, inheritance, and exceptions. The approach to this material is as follows:

- *Templates*: Templates are used extensively. Some readers may have reservations with this approach because it complicates the code, but I have included them because they are fundamental concepts in any sophisticated C++ program.

- *Inheritance*: Inheritance is used relatively sparingly because it adds complications, and data structures are not a strong application area for it. The main instance in which it is used is to derive implementations of data structures from abstract specifications.

- *Exceptions*: At the time of this writing, development of exceptions is several years behind that of templates. They are not universally implemented, and the exact semantics have yet to be standardized. Eventually they will be standardized, they will work, and they will be widely used. In recognition of this, my preference would have been to include them, but except for the handling of memory exhaustion, this is not possible right now. Consequently, exceptions are not otherwise used in the code. However, throughout the text we use the function EXCEPTION, described in Appendix D, to signal points at which an exception could be used. Appendix D also describes how to incorporate exceptions into the code should they be available on your compiler.

Text Organization

This text introduces C++ and object-oriented programming (particularly abstraction) in Part I. We discuss pointers, arrays, and some other C++ topics and then go on to discuss the syntax and use of classes, templates, and inheritance.

Part II discusses Big-Oh and algorithmic paradigms, including recursion and randomization. Sorting is covered in a full chapter, and basic data structures are described in another chapter. The interfaces and running times of the data structures are presented *without* giving the implementations. The instructor then may take several approaches to present the remaining material. Two of these are:

1. Use the corresponding implementations in Part IV as each data structure is described. The instructor can ask students to extend the classes in various ways, as suggested in the exercises.

2. Show how the interface is used and cover implementation at a later point in the course. The case studies in Part III can be used to support this approach. Since complete implementations will be available on the internet, the instructor can provide a library of classes for use in programming projects. Details on using this approach are given below.

Part V describes advanced data structures such as splay trees, pairing heaps, and the disjoint set data structure that can be covered if time permits.

Chapter-by-Chapter Text Organization

Part I consists of four chapters describing some advanced features of C++ that are used throughout the text. Chapter 1 describes pointers, arrays, and structures and also contains a short study that describes how a profiling tool is used to measure the running time of a program. Chapter 2 begins the discussion of object-oriented programming by describing the class mechanism in C++. Chapter 3 continues this discussion by examining templates, and Chapter 4 illustrates the use of inheritance. Several components, including strings and vectors, are written in these chapters.

Part II is about the basic algorithms and building blocks. In Chapter 5 a complete discussion of time complexity and Big-Oh notation is provided. Binary search is discussed and analyzed here. Chapter 6 is a crucial chapter that discusses the interface to the data structures and argues intuitively what the running time of the supported operations should be for each data structure. However, implementation of these data structures is not provided until Part IV. Chapter 7 describes recursion by first introducing the notion of proof by induction. This chapter also discusses divide-and-conquer, dynamic programming, and backtracking. One section describes several recursive numerical algorithms that are used to implement the RSA cryptosystem. Chapter 8 describes, codes, and analyzes several basic sorting algorithms, including the insertion sort, Shellsort, mergesort, and quicksort, as well as indirect sorting. It also proves the classic lower bound for sorting and discusses the related problems of selection. Finally, Chapter 9 is a short chapter that discusses random numbers, including their generation and use in randomized algorithms.

Part III provides several case studies, and each chapter is organized along a general theme. Chapter 10 illustrates several important techniques by examining games. Chapter 11 discusses the use of stacks in computer languages by examining an algorithm to check for balanced symbols and the classic operator precedence parsing algorithm. Complete implementations with code are provided for both algorithms. Chapter 12 discusses the basic utilities of file compression and cross-reference generation, and a complete implementation of the cross-reference generator is provided. Chapter 13 broadly examines simulation by looking at one problem that can be viewed as a simulation and then the more classic event-driven simulation. Finally, Chapter 14 illustrates how data structures are used to implement several shortest path algorithms efficiently for graphs.

The data structure implementations that correspond to the interfaces in Chapter 6 are presented in Part IV. Some mathematics is used in this part, especially in Chapters 18 to 20, and can be skipped at the discretion of the instructor. Chapter 15 provides implementations for both stacks and queues. First these data structures are implemented using a dynamic array; then they are implemented using linked lists. In Chapter 16 general linked lists are described. Extensions such as doubly linked lists, circular linked lists, and cursor implementations are left as exercises. Chapter 17 describes trees and illustrates the basic traversal schemes. Chapter 18 is a detailed chapter that provides several implementations of binary search trees. Initially, the basic binary search tree is shown, and then a binary search tree that supports order statistics is derived. AVL trees are discussed but not implemented; however, the more practical red black trees and AA-trees are implemented. Finally, the B-tree is examined. Chapter 19 discusses hash tables, and the quadratic probing scheme is implementated after examination of a simpler alternative. In Chapter 20 we describe the binary heap and examine heapsort and external sorting.

Part V contains material that is suitable for use in a more advanced course or for general reference. The algorithms are accessible even at the first-year level; however, for completeness we have included sophisticated mathematical analyses that are almost certainly beyond the reach of a first-year student. Chapter 21 describes the splay tree, which is a binary search tree that seems to perform extremely well in practice and is also competitive with the binary heap in some applications that require priority queues. Chapter 22 describes priority queues that support merging operations and provides an implementation of the pairing heap. Finally, Chapter 23 examines the classic disjoint set data structure.

Course Organization

Ignoring factors such as the balance between theory and practice, the crucial issue in teaching the course is deciding how the materials in Parts II to IV are to be used. The material in Part I should be covered in depth, and the student should write one or two programs that illustrate the design, implementation, and testing of classes and template classes, and depending on how much C++ is desired to be taught, inheritance. Next, Chapter 5 discusses Big-Oh, and an exercise in which the student writes a short program and compares the running time with an analysis can be given to test comprehension.

In the separation approach, the key concept of Chapter 6 is simply the fact that different data structures support different access schemes with different efficiency. Students can be asked first to write an inefficient data structure. Any case study (except the tic-tac-toe example that uses recursion) can be used to test their programs, and the students can compare their inefficient data structures with an efficient library routine (provided by anonymous ftp, as discussed below). In this scheme all the case studies (except tic-tac-toe) can be examined to see how each of the particular data structures is used. In this way we see the interface for each data structure, and we see how it is used, but we do not see how it is efficiently implemented. This is truly a separation, and viewing things this way will greatly enhance the ability of students to think abstractly. Students can be asked to extend the case study but, once again, do not have to know any of the details of the data structures.

The implementation of the data structures can be discussed afterward, and recursion can be introduced whenever the instructor feels it is appropriate (but prior to binary search trees). The details of sorting can be discussed at any point after recursion. At this point the course can continue by using the same case studies and experimenting with modifications to the implementations of the data structures. For instance, the student can experiment with various forms of balanced binary search trees.

Instructors opting for a more traditional approach can simply discuss a case study in Part III after discussing a data structure implementation in Part IV. The book chapters are meant to be as independent of each other as possible.

Exercises

Exercises come in various flavors. The basic *In Short* exercise asks a simple question or requires hand-drawn simulations of an algorithm described in the text. The *In Theory* section asks questions that either require mathematical analysis or perhaps ask for theoretically interesting solutions to problems. The *In Practice* section contains simple programming questions, including questions about syntax or particularly tricky lines of code. The *Programming Projects* section contains ideas for extended assignments.

Pedagogical Features

- The code in the text is fully functional and has been tested on the following compilers: $g++$ 2.6.2, Sun 3.0.1, and Borland 4.5. The code is available by anonymous ftp, as discussed below. This code will be updated as the language evolves, and a version that uses exceptions is provided.
- Margin notes are used to highlight important topics.
- At the end of each chapter, a list of common errors is provided in the *Common Errors* section.
- The *Objects of the Game* section lists important terms along with definitions and page references.
- References for further reading are provided at the end of most chapters.

Supplements

Code Availability

The example program code in the book is available via anonymous ftp at aw.com. It is also accessible through the World Wide Web; the URL is http://www.aw.com/cseng/ (follow the links from there). **The exact location of this material may change.**

Instructor's Resource Guide

A guide that illustrates several approaches to the material is available to instructors on a disk. These approaches vary from a strong focus on theory to an emphasis on C++, to a more balanced approach. Each approach is outlined with sample test questions, sample assignments, and sample syllabi. Answers to select exercises are also provided.

Acknowledgments

Many, many people have helped me in the preparation of this book. First, I would like to thank all the folks at Addison-Wesley. My editor Carter Shanklin helped me refine my thinking and his assistant Christine Kulke kept everything flowing smoothly. Craig Johnson, Production Technology Supervisor, was especially helpful with my Frame questions. I would especially like to thank the people involved in the production of the text: Barbara Conway did a wonderful job of copyediting the manuscript and suggesting improvements throughout; Teri Holden was a fantastic production editor; Holly McLean Aldis did a great job proofreading; and Lisa Jahred wrote the templates for the book design.

Some of the material in this text is adapted from my textbook *Efficient C Programming: A Practical Approach* (Prentice-Hall, 1995) and is used with permission of the publisher. I have attempted to place end-of-chapter references where appropriate.

I would like to thank the reviewers, who provided valuable comments, many of which have been incorporated into the text.

Owen Astrachan	Duke University
Joe Faletti	University of California, San Diego
K. M. George	Oklahoma State University
Jim Heliotis	Rochestor Institute of Technology
Jim Levenick	Willamette University
George Novacky	University of Pittsburgh
John Russo	Indiana University
Laurie White	Armstrong State College of Georgia

Edward Wright	Western Oregon State University
Alan Zaring	Ohio Weslyan University

As usual, I had help from my friends at FIU. Thanks to Diane Kelly for handling all my other work and leaving me with enough time to work on the text. I would also like to thank Catherine Hernandez, Steve Luis, and Cory Tsang for their help installing Frame and keeping the printers up and running.

Most of all, I thank Becky, whom I love more than she can imagine, for her support during my book writing, especially in the last year.

Part I: Objects and C++

Chapter 1

Pointers, Arrays, and Structures

This chapter discusses three features found in many programming languages: *pointers*, *arrays*, and *structures*. Sophisticated C++ programming makes heavy use of pointers to access objects. Arrays and structures store several objects in one collection. An array stores only one type of object, while a structure can hold a collection of several distinct types.

In this chapter we will see

- why these features are important
- basic syntax and *dynamic memory allocation*
- the special C++ relationship between pointers and arrays
- how pointers, arrays, and structures are passed as parameters to functions
- an introduction to the measurement of program running time through the use of *profiling* tools

1.1   What Are Pointers, Arrays, and Structures?

A *pointer* is an object that can be used to access another object. A pointer provides *indirect* access rather than *direct* access to an object. People use pointers in real-life situations all the time. Let us look at some examples.

- Suppose a stranger in town asks you for directions. If you do not know the answer, you may give the indirect answer, "Go to the gas station and ask them for directions."
- If someone asks you for a phone number, rather than giving an immediate, direct reply, you may say, "Let me look it up in the phone book."
- When a professor says "Do problem 1.1 in the textbook," the actual homework assignment is being stated indirectly.
- A classic example of indirect access is looking up a topic in the index of a book. The index tells you where a full description can be found.

- A street address is a pointer: It tells you where someone resides. A forwarding address is a pointer to a pointer.

A *pointer* stores an address where other data reside.

In all these cases information is given out indirectly by providing a pointer to the information. In C++ a pointer is an object that stores an address (that is, a location in memory) where other data are stored. Since an address is expected to be an integer, a pointer object can usually be represented internally as an unsigned int or unsigned long, depending on the particular machine. What makes a pointer object more than just a plain integer is that we can access the datum that is being pointed at. This is known as *dereferencing* the pointer.

An *array* stores a collection of identically typed objects.

An *aggregate* is a collection of objects stored in one unit. The *array* is the basic mechanism for storing a collection of identically typed objects. A different type of aggregate type is the *structure*. The structure stores a collection of objects that need not be of the same type. As a somewhat abstract example, consider the layout of an apartment building. Each floor might have a one-bedroom unit, a two-bedroom unit, a three-bedroom unit, and a laundry room. Thus each floor is stored as a structure, and the building is an array of floors.

1.2   Pointer Syntax in C++

The unary *address-of operator* & returns the address of an object.

To have a pointer point at an object, we need to know the target object's memory address (that is, where it is stored). For (almost) any object Obj, its memory address is given by applying the unary *address-of operator* &. Thus &Obj is the memory location that stores Obj.[1]

We can declare that an object Ptr points at another int object by saying

```
int *Ptr;
```

The value represented by Ptr is an address. As with integer objects, this declaration does not initialize Ptr to any particular value, so using Ptr before assigning to it invariably produces bad results (such as a program crash). Suppose we also have the following declarations:

```
int X = 5;
int Y = 7;
```

We can make Ptr point at X by assigning to Ptr the memory location where X is stored. Thus

```
Ptr = &X;                  // LEGAL
```

sets Ptr to point at X. Figure 1.1 illustrates this in two ways. On the left a memory model shows where each object is stored. The figure on the right uses an arrow to indicate pointing.

---

1. Objects stored using the register storage class cannot be the target of the address-of operator.

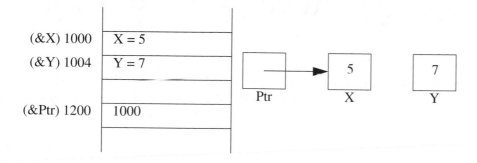

Figure 1.1   Pointer illustration

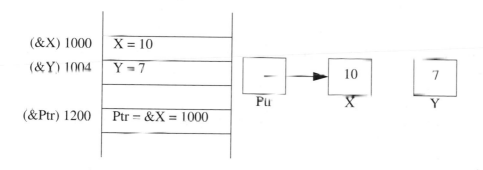

Figure 1.2   Result of *Ptr=10

The value of the data being pointed at is obtained by the unary *dereferencing operator* *. In Figure 1.1 *Ptr will evaluate to 5, which is the value of the pointed-at variable X. It is illegal to dereference something that is not a pointer. The * operator is the opposite of &. Dereferencing works not only for reading values from an object but also for writing new values to the object. Thus, if we say

```
*Ptr = 10;                 // LEGAL
```

we have changed the value of X to 10. Figure 1.2 shows the changes that result. This shows the problem with pointers: Unrestricted alterations are possible, and a runaway pointer can overwrite all sorts of variables unintentionally.

The unary dereferencing operator * accesses data through a pointer.

We could also have initialized `Ptr` at declaration time by having it point to X:

```
int X = 5;
int Y = 7;
int *Ptr = &X;           // LEGAL
```

The declaration says that X is an `int` initialized to 5, Y is an `int` initialized to 7, and `Ptr` is a pointer to an `int` and is initialized to point at X. Let us look at what could have gone wrong. The following declaration sequence is incorrect:

```
int *Ptr = &X;           // ILLEGAL: X is not declared yet
int X = 5;
int Y = 7;
```

Here we are using X before it has been declared, so the compiler will complain. Here is another common error:

```
int X = 5;
int Y = 7;
int *Ptr = X;            // ILLEGAL: X is not an address
```

In this case we are trying to have `Ptr` point at X, but we have forgotten that a pointer holds an address. Thus we need an address on the right side of the assignment. The compiler will complain that we have forgotten the &, but its error message may initially appear cryptic.

Continuing with this example, suppose that we have the correct declaration but with `Ptr` uninitialized:

```
int X = 5;
int Y = 7;
int *Ptr;                // LEGAL but Ptr is uninitialized
```

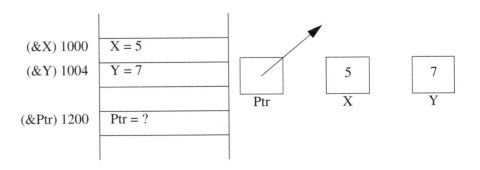

Figure 1.3   Uninitialized pointer

What is the value of `Ptr`? As Figure 1.3 shows, the value is undefined because it was never initialized. Thus the value of `*Ptr` is also undefined. However, it is more undefined because `Ptr` could hold an address that makes absolutely no sense at all, thus causing a program crash if it is dereferenced. Alternatively, `Ptr` could be pointing at an address that is accessible, in which case the program will not immediately crash but will be erroneous. If `*Ptr` is the target of an assignment, then we would be accidentally changing some other data, which could result in a crash at a later point. This is a tough error to detect because the cause and symptom may be widely separated in time.

Pointers must be pointing at an object before dereferencing.

We have already seen the correct syntax for the assignment:

```
Ptr = &X;                  // LEGAL
```

Suppose that we forget the address-of operator. Then the assignment

```
Ptr = X;                   // ILLEGAL: X is not an address
```

rightly generates a compiler error. There are two ways to make the compiler shut up. One is to take the address on the right side, as in the correct syntax. The other method is erroneous:

```
*Ptr = X;                  // Semantically incorrect
```

The compiler is quiet because the statement says that the `int` to which `Ptr` is pointing should get the value of `X`. For instance, if `Ptr` is `&Y`, then `Y` is assigned the value of `X`. This assignment is perfectly legal, but it does not make `Ptr` point at `X`. Moreover, since `Ptr` is uninitialized, dereferencing it is likely to cause a run-time error, as discussed above. This error is obvious from Figure 1.3. The moral is always draw a picture at the first sign of pointer trouble.

This is a common error for two reasons. First, since it makes the compiler quiet, programmers feel comfortable about using the incorrect semantics. Second, it looks somewhat like the syntax used for initialization at declaration time. The difference is that the `*` at declaration time is not a dereferencing ^ but rather just an indication that the object is a pointer type.

Some final words before we get to some substantive uses. First, sometimes we want to state explicitly that a pointer is pointing nowhere, as opposed to an undefined location. The *NULL pointer* points at a memory location that is guaranteed to be incapable of holding anything. Consequently, a `NULL` pointer cannot be dereferenced. The symbolic constant `NULL` is defined in several header files, and either it or an explicit zero can be used. The choice is a matter of preference, although some programmers can get surprisingly testy when someone's choice does not agree with theirs. Pointers are best initialized to the `NULL` pointer because in many cases they have no default initial values (these rules apply to other predefined types as well).

The NULL pointer has value 0 and should never be dereferenced. It is used to state that a pointer is pointing nowhere.

Second, a dereferenced pointer behaves just like the object that it is pointing at. Thus, after the following three statements, the value stored in `X` is 15:

```
X = 5;
Ptr = &X;
*Ptr += 10;
```

However, we must be cognizant of precedence rules because, as we will see in Section 1.6, it is possible to perform arithmetic not only on the dereferenced values but also on the (un-dereferenced) pointers themselves. As an example, the following two statements are very different:

```
*Ptr += 1;
*Ptr++;
```

In the first statement the += operator is applied to *Ptr, but in the second statement the ++ operator is applied to Ptr. The result of applying the ++ operator to Ptr is that Ptr will be changed to point at a memory location one memory unit larger than it used to. We will discuss this in Section 1.6.

Third, if Ptr1 and Ptr2 are pointers to the same type, then

```
Ptr1 = Ptr2;
```

sets Ptr1 to point to the same location as Ptr2, while

```
*Ptr1 = *Ptr2;
```

When you use pointers, you must know whether you are working with addresses or objects.

assigns the dereferenced Ptr1 the value of the dereferenced Ptr2. Figure 1.4 shows that these statements are quite different. Moreover, when the wrong form is used mistakenly, the consequences might not be obvious immediately. In the previous examples, after the assignment, *Ptr1 and *Ptr2 are both 7. Similarly, the expression

```
Ptr1 == Ptr2
```

is true if the two pointers are pointing at the same memory location, while

```
*Ptr1 == *Ptr2
```

is true if the values stored at the two indicated addresses are equal. It is a common mistake to use the wrong form.

The requirement that Ptr1 and Ptr2 point to the same type is a consequence of the fact that C++ is strongly typed: We cannot mix different types of pointers without an explicit type conversion, unless the user has provided an implicit type conversion.

Finally, when pointers are declared, the placement of the * and the white space that surrounds it are unimportant to the compiler. Pick a style that you like.

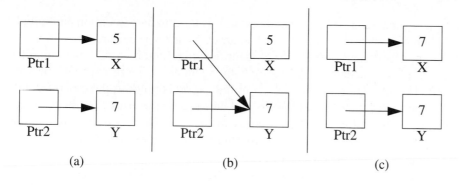

Figure 1.4   (a) Initial state; (b) `Ptr1=Ptr2` starting from initial state;
(c) `*Ptr1=*Ptr2` starting from initial state

```
1   // Generate lottery numbers (from 1-49)
2   // Print number of occurrences of each number
3
4   #include <iostream.h>
5   #include <stdlib.h>
6
7   main( )
8   {
9       const int DifferentNumbers = 49;
10      const int NumbersPerGame = 6;
11
12          // Prompt for and read number of games
13      int Games;
14      cout << "How many games to simulate?: ";
15      cin >> Games;
16
17          // Generate the numbers
18      int Numbers[ DifferentNumbers + 1 ] = { 0 },
19
20      for( int i = 0; i < Games; i++ )
21          for( int j = 0; j < NumbersPerGame; j++ )
22              Numbers[ rand( ) % DifferentNumbers + 1 ]++;
23
24          // Output the summary
25      for( int k = 1; k <= DifferentNumbers; k++ )
26          cout << k << " occurs " << Numbers[ k ] << " time(s)\n";
27
28      return 0;
29  }
```

Figure 1.5   Simple demonstration of arrays

1.3   Arrays

The *array indexing operator* [ ] provides access to any object in the array.

Just as a variable must be declared before it is used in an expression and initialized before its value is used, so must an array. An array is declared by giving it a name, in accordance with the usual identifier rules, and by telling the compiler what type the elements are. If we are defining an array, a size must also be provided. The size can be omitted if an initialization is present; the compiler will then count the number of initializers and take that as the array size. Each object in the collection of objects that an array denotes can be accessed by use of the *array indexing operator* [ ]. We say that the [ ] operator *indexes* the array, meaning that it specifies which of the objects is to be accessed.

Arrays are indexed starting at zero.

In C++, arrays are always indexed starting at zero. Thus the declaration

```
int A[ 3 ];   // Three int objects: A[0], A[1], and A[2]
```

has the compiler allocate space to store three integers, namely A[0], A[1], and A[2]. As we will see later in this text, no index range checking is performed in C++, so an access out of the array index bounds is not caught by the compiler. No explicit run-time error will be generated, but undefined and occasionally mysterious behavior occurs. Furthermore, if the array is passed as an actual argument to a function, the function has no idea how large the array is unless an additional parameter is passed. Finally, arrays cannot be copied by the = operator. Although all this may seem terribly restrictive, especially for a modern programming language, the C++ *class* allows us to define safe arrays that avoid all these problems. This is discussed in Section 3.3.3. In this section we will stick with the core language features of arrays and pointers and discuss why these restrictions come into play.

Figure 1.5 illustrates the use of arrays in C++. In the Florida lottery six different numbers between 1 and 49 (inclusive) are selected each week. The program in Figure 1.5 repeatedly chooses numbers. The output is the number of times that each number has occurred.

We must always be sure to declare the correct array size. Off-by-one errors are common and very difficult to spot.

Line 18 declares an array of integers that keep count of the occurrences of each number. Because arrays are indexed starting at zero, the + 1 is crucial. Without it we would have an array whose indexible range was 0 to 48, and thus any access to index 49 might be to memory that was assigned to another object. Incorrect results could occur, depending on the machine and the compiler; we might find that the program would work perfectly on some machines but give wrong answers on others. The initialization on line 18 uses a C++ shorthand: When the number of initializers is short (here there is one initializer instead of 50), the remaining initializers are set to zero (even if the first initializer is non-zero). Again, if no initialization was given, then the results would be machine specific. Some compilers might always initialize memory to 0, in which case the program would appear to work.

&A[0] (1000)	A[0]
&A[1] (1004)	A[1]
&A[2] (1008)	A[2]
&i (1012)	i
	...
&A (5620)	A=1000

Figure 1.6   Memory model for arrays (assumes 4 byte `int`); declaration is `int A[3]; int i;`

The rest of the program is relatively straightforward. The routine `rand`, declared in `stdlib.h` gives a (somewhat) random number; the manipulation at line 22 places it in the range 0 to 49. The results are output at lines 25 and 26.

1.3.1   The C++ Implementation: An Array Name Is a Pointer

When a new array is allocated, the compiler multiplies the size in bytes of the type in the declaration by the array size (the integer constant between the [ ]) to decide how much memory it needs to set aside. This is essentially the only use for the size component. In fact, after the array is allocated, with minor exceptions, the size is irrelevant because the name of the array represents a pointer to the beginning of allocated memory for that array. This is illustrated in Figure 1.6.

The name of an array represents a pointer to the beginning of allocated memory for that array.

Suppose we have the declarations

```
int A[ 3 ];
int i;
```

The compiler allocates memory as follows: First, three integers are set aside for the array object. These are referenced by `A[0]`, `A[1]`, and `A[2]`. The objects in the array are guaranteed to be stored in one contiguous block of memory. Thus if `A[0]` is stored at memory location 1000 and integers require four bytes, it is guaranteed that `A[1]` is located at memory location 1004 and `A[2]` at memory location 1008. Finally, the compiler allocates storage for the object `i`. One possibility is shown in Figure 1.6, where `i` is allocated the next available memory slot.

Array items are stored in contiguous, increasing memory locations.

For any i, we can deduce that A[i] would be stored at memory location 1000 + 4i. The value stored in A is exactly equal to &A[0]; this equivalence is always guaranteed and tells us that A is actually a pointer. Note also that &A is not the same as &A[0]. Now we can see that to access the item A[i], the compiler needs only to fetch the value of A and add to it 4i.

Now that we have seen how arrays are manipulated in C++, we can see why some of the limitations discussed earlier occur, and we can also see how arrays are passed as function parameters.

C++ has no built-in index range checking for arrays.

First we have the problem of checking that the index is in range. Performing the bounds check would require that we store the array size in an additional parameter. Certainly this is feasible, but it does incur both time and space overhead. In a common application of arrays (short strings), the overhead could be significant. As we mentioned earlier, if the user wants to perform the range check, an array class that performs bounds checks could be written and used just as if it were a predefined array. Thus we need not debate the wisdom of the language designer's decision not to mandate the range checks. We will point out, however, that the lack of range checking can cause serious problems. Consider the following code fragment that uses the previous declarations of A and i:

```
for( i = 0; i <= 3; i++ )
    A[ i ] = 0;
```

The programmer has made the common error of referencing A[3], forgetting that an array of size 3 represents indices 0 through 2 only. When i is 3 the compiler dutifully executes the statement A[3]=0 without checking that the index is valid. Suppose memory is allocated as in Figure 1.6. Then the effect is that memory location 1012 is overwritten with 0, thus clobbering i. The result, namely resetting i to 0, creates an infinite loop. On the other hand, if the compiler decided (as some do) to leave memory location 1012 empty and place i elsewhere, the program appears to work. Thus off-by-one errors in array indexing can lead to bugs that are very difficult to spot. In our example the loop is infinite, but i was never directly changed.

Arrays cannot be copied or compared using = and ==, respectively.

The second limitation of the basic array (which can also be fixed by a user-defined class) is array copying. Suppose that A and B are arrays of the same type. In many languages, if the arrays are also the same size, the statement A=B would perform an element-by-element copy of the array B into the array A. In C++ this statement is illegal because A and B represent constant pointers to the start of their respective arrays, specifically &A[0] and &B[0]. Then A=B is an attempt to change where A points, rather than copying the contents of array B into array A. What makes the statement illegal, rather than legal but wrong, is that A cannot be reassigned to point somewhere else because it is essentially a constant object. The only way to copy two arrays is to do it element by element; there is no shorthand. A similar argument shows that the expression A==B does not evaluate to 1 if and only if each element of A matches the corresponding element of B. Instead, this expression is legal. It evaluates to 1 if and only if A and B represent the same memory location (that is, they refer to the same array).

Finally, an array can be used as a parameter to a function, and the rules follow logically from our understanding that an array name is little more than a pointer. Suppose we have a function FunctionCall that accepts one array of int as its parameter. The caller/callee views are

```
FunctionCall( ActualArray );         // Function Call
FunctionCall( int FormalArray[ ] )  // Function Declaration
```

Note that in the function declaration, the brackets serve only as a type declaration, in the same way that int does. In the function call only the name of the array is passed; there are no brackets. In accordance with the call-by-value conventions of C++, the value of ActualArray is copied into FormalArray. Because ActualArray represents the memory location where the entire array ActualArray is stored, FormalArray[i] accesses ActualArray[i]. This means that the variables represented by the indexed array are modifiable. Thus an array, *when considered as an aggregate*, is passed *by reference*. Furthermore, any size component in the FormalArray declaration is ignored, and the size of the actual array is unknown. If the size is needed, it must be passed as an additional parameter.

The address of an array is passed by value. Consequently, the contents of an array are passed by reference.

Note that passing the aggregate by reference means that FunctionCall can change elements in the array. We can use the const directive to attempt to disallow this (but this technique is not foolproof):

Use a const to disallow changes to the aggregate. The size of the formal array is unknown.

```
FunctionCall( const int FormalArray[ ] );
```

1.3.2 Multidimensional Arrays

Sometimes arrays need to be accessed based on more than one index. A common example of this is a matrix. A *multidimensional array* is an array that is accessed by more than one index. It is allocated by specifying the size of its indices, and each element is accessed by placing each index in its own pair of brackets. As an example, the declaration

A *multidimensional array* is an array that is accessed by more than one index.

```
int X[ 2 ][ 3 ];       // X has two rows and three columns
```

defines the two-dimensional array X, with the first index ranging from 0 to 1 and the second index ranging from 0 to 2 (for a total of six objects). The compiler sets aside six memory locations for these objects.

1.3.3 The char * Type, const Pointers, and Constant Strings

An important use of pointers and arrays is the C++ implementation of strings. The C++ base language provides some minimal support for strings, based entirely on the conventions of C and the C library. The result is too minimal to be useful in a modern language, so as they do with arrays, C++ programmers tend to rely on user-defined string libraries rather than the predefined language features. Nonetheless, it is still important to know how strings are implemented in the basic C library because they form the basis of the fancier user-defined strings.

In C++ as well as C, a *string* is an array of characters. As a result, when passed to a function, the string has type `char *` or `const char *`. At first glance we might assume that the string `"Nina"` is an array of four characters: `'N'`, `'i'`, `'n'`, and `'a'`. The problem with this assumption is that if we pass this array to any routine, that routine would not know how many characters are in the array because, as we have seen, a function that receives an array only receives a pointer and thus has no idea how large the actual array is. One solution to this problem is to use a slightly larger array with an end marker.

The *null terminator* is the special character that ends a string. It is represented by `'\0'`. You must allocate an extra spot for the null terminator.

For instance, we can declare an array of five elements, placing a blank in the last spot to signal that only the first four positions represent significant characters. If all routines are written to reflect this convention, we have a solution to our problem that requires little alteration of the language. Because we might actually want to use a blank in the string (for example, to store a street address), we need to pick an end marker that is not likely to appear elsewhere in the string. In C++ this special character is the *null terminator* `'\0'`. The escape sequence indicates that the null terminator is always represented internally as zero, which, as we shall see, leads to some shorthands when the controlling expression is written in an `if` statement or a loop. (A common error is to forget the `\`; this leaves `'0'`, which is the character representation for the digit 0). Therefore, if an array of six characters has `'N'`, `'i'`, `'n'`, `'a'`, and `'\0'`, it represents the string `"Nina"`, no matter what is in the sixth character.

So far, what has C++ provided us in the way of string support? The answer is absolutely nothing! Furthermore, there are some things it does not directly provide in the language. Suppose we declare two strings `Str1` and `Str2`:

```
char Str1[ 10 ]; // Max length is nine
char Str2[ 10 ]; // Max length is nine
```

Then the following statements cannot be correct:

```
Str1 = Str2;                 // Wrong!
Cond = ( Str1 == Str2 );     // Wrong!
```

```
1 size_t strlen( const char *Str );
2 char * strcpy(       char *Lhs, const char *Rhs );
3 char * strcat(       char *Lhs, const char *Rhs );
4 int    strcmp( const char *Lhs, const char *Rhs );
```

Figure 1.7   Some of the string routines in `<string.h>`

This follows directly from the facts that `Str1` and `Str2` are arrays and array assignment and comparison are not supported directly by the language. Almost all of the support, in fact, is provided by the C++ library, which specifies routines that work for null-terminated strings. The prototypes for these routines are given in the `<string.h>` include file. Some routines of interest are shown in Figure 1.7.[2]

`strlen(Str)` gives the length of the string represented by `Str` (not including the null terminator); the length of `"Nina"` is four. In this and all routines, if a `NULL` pointer is passed, you can expect a program crash. Notice that this is different from passing a pointer to a memory cell that contains the `'\0'` character, which represents the empty string of length 0. `strcpy(Lhs,Rhs)` performs the assignment of strings; characters in the array given by `Rhs` are copied into the array given by `Lhs` until the null terminator is copied. If the string represented by `Lhs` is not large enough to store the copy, then somebody else's memory gets overwritten.

`strcpy` does not check if the target is large enough to store the copy.

`Lhs` and `Rhs` stand for *left-hand side* and *right-hand side*, respectively. The order of parameters is easy to remember if you keep in mind that

`Lhs` and `Rhs` stand for left-hand side and right-hand side, respectively.

```
strcpy( Lhs, Rhs )
```

is meant to mimic the statement

```
Lhs = Rhs;
```

The return type `char *` allows `strcpy` calls to be chained in the same way as assignments: `strcpy(A,strcpy(B,C))` is much like `A=B=C`. `strcat(Lhs,Rhs)` appends a copy of the string represented by `Rhs` to the end of `Lhs`. As with `strcpy`, it is the programmer's responsibility to assure that `Lhs` is pointing at sufficient memory to store the result. `strcmp` compares two strings returning a negative number, zero, or a positive number, depending on whether the first string is lexicographically less than, equal to, or greater than the second.

C++, as described so far, provides library routines for strings but no language support. In fact, the only language support is provided by a *string constant*. A string constant provides a shorthand mechanism for specifying a sequence of characters. It automatically includes the null terminator as an invisible last character. Any character (specified with an escape sequence if necessary) may appear in the string constant. Thus `"Nina"` represents a five-character array. Additionally, a string constant can be used as an initializer for a character array. Thus:

A string constant is a sequence of characters enclosed in double quotes. The null terminator is automatically included.

---

2. The proposed C++ standard specifies that `<string.h>` will also declare a mechanism for supporting a `string` class, in which operations on strings mimic operations on predefined types, but the exact semantics is still under consideration.

```
char Name1[   ] = "Nina"; // Name1 is an array of five char
char Name2[ 9 ] = "Nina"; // Name2 is an array of nine char
char Name3[ 4 ] = "Nina"; // Name3 is an array of four char
```

In the first case the size of the array allocated for `Name1` is determined implicitly, while in the second case we have over-allocated (which is necessary if we intend later to copy a longer string into `Name2`). The third case is wrong because we have not allocated enough memory for the null terminator. Initialization by a string constant is a special exemption; we cannot say

```
char Name4[ 8 ] = Name1;    // ILLEGAL!
```

A string constant can be used in any place that *both* a string and a constant object can.

A string constant can be used in any place that *both* a string and a constant object can. For instance, it may be used as the second parameter to `strcpy` but not as the first parameter. This is because the declaration for `strcpy` does not disallow the possibility that the first parameter might be altered (indeed, we know that it will). Because a string constant can be stored in read-only memory, allowing it to be used as a target of `strcpy` could result in a hardware error. Note carefully that we can always send a nonconstant string to a parameter that expects a constant string. Thus we have

```
strcpy( Name2, "Mark" );    // LEGAL
strcpy( "Mark", Name2 );    // ILLEGAL!
strcpy( Name2, Name1 );     // LEGAL
```

The prototypes for the string routines indicate that the parameters are pointers. This follows from the fact that the name of an array is a pointer. The second parameter to `strcpy` is a *constant string*, meaning that any string can be passed and it is guaranteed to be unchanged. The first parameter is merely a *string*, and might be changed. Consequently, a constant string cannot be passed; this includes string constants.

Beginners tend to take the equivalence of arrays and pointers one step too far. Recall that the fundamental difference between an array and a pointer is that an array definition allocates enough memory to store the array, while a pointer points to memory that is allocated elsewhere. Because strings are arrays of characters, this distinction applies to strings. A common error is declaring a pointer when an array is needed. As examples, consider the following declarations:

```
char Name[ ] = "Nina";
char *Name1  = "Nina";
char *Name2;
```

The first declaration allocates five bytes for `Name`, initializing it to a copy of the string constant `"Nina"` (including the null terminator). The second declaration states merely that `Name1` points at the zeroth character of the string constant `"Nina"`. In fact, the declaration is wrong because we are mixing pointer types: the right side is a `const char *`, while the left side is merely a `char *`.

Some compilers will complain. The reason for this is that a subsequent

```
Name1[ 3 ] = 'e';
```

is an attempt to alter the string constant. Since a string constant is supposed to be constant, this action should not be allowed. The easiest way for the compiler to do this is to follow the convention that if A is a constant array, then A[i] is a constant also and cannot be assigned to. If the statement

```
char *Name1   = "Nina";
```

were allowed, this would be hard to enforce. By enforcing constness at each assignment, the problem becomes manageable.[3] It is legal to use

```
const char *Name1 = "Nina";
```

but that is hardly the same as declaring an array to store a copy of the actual string; furthermore, Name1[3]='e' is easily seen by the compiler to be illegal in this case. A common example where this would be used is

```
const char *Message = "Welcome to FIU!";
```

Another common consequence of declaring a pointer instead of an array object is the following statement (in which we assume that Name2 is declared as above):

```
strcpy( Name2, Name );
```

Here the programmer expects to copy Name into Name2 but is fooled because the declaration for strcpy indicates that two pointers are to be passed. The call fails because Name2 is just a pointer rather than a pointer to sufficient memory to hold a copy of Name. If Name2 is a NULL pointer, points at a string constant stored in read-only memory, or points at an illegal random location, strcpy is certain to attempt to dereference it, generating an error. If Name2 points at a modifiable array (for instance, Name2=Name is executed), there is no problem.

Although all this sounds very restrictive and tricky, in C++ we can define our own String type and make it look just like any predefined type, such as an int. Consequently, once this is done (and many compilers already provide some version of a String type in their libraries), we do not have to worry about the limitations implied in the C++ base language because we will have hidden them. It is important to understand these fine details so that we can use them to implement safer constructs.

---

3. It is possible to type cast away the constness, but at this point the programmer is forfeiting the protection C++ offers.

1.4   Dynamic Allocation of Arrays: `new[ ]` and `delete[ ]`

Dynamic array alloca-tion allows us to allo-cate arbitrary-sized arrays and make them larger if needed.

Suppose we want to read a sequence of numbers and store them in an array for processing. The fundamental property of an array requires us to declare a size so that the compiler can allocate the correct amount of memory, and we must make this declaration prior to the first access of the array. If we have no idea how many items to expect, then it is difficult to make a reasonable choice for the array size. In this section we show how to allocate our arrays dynamically and expand them if our initial estimate is too small. This technique, *dynamic array allocation*, allows us to allocate arbitrary-sized arrays and make them larger or smaller as the program runs. It also allows us to allocate single instances of other objects as the program runs.

The allocation method for arrays that we have seen thus far is

```
int A1[ Size ];      // Size is a compile-time constant
```

We also know we can use

```
int *A2;
```

The new operator dynamically allocates memory.

like an array, except that no memory is allocated by the compiler for the array. The `new` operator allows us to obtain memory from the system as the program runs. We can use the expression

```
new int [ Size ]
```

to allocate enough memory to store `Size` int objects. The expression evaluates to the address where the start of that memory resides. It may be assigned only to an `int  *` object, as in

```
int *A2 = new int [ Size ];
```

As a result, `A2` is virtually indistinguishable from `A1`. The `new` operator is type-safe, meaning that

```
int *A2 = new char[ Size ];
```

would be detected at compile time as a type mismatch error.

So what is the difference, if any, between the two forms or array memory allocation? A technical difference is that the memory for `A1` is taken from a different source than `A2`. This, however, is transparent to the user. A second difference is that `A1` cannot appear on the left side of an assignment operator because the array name is a constant, while `A2` can. This also is a relatively minor difference, and if we declared

```
const int *A2 = new int [ Size ];
```

this is not a difference. More importantly, Size does not have to be a compile-time constant when we use new.

On the other hand a problem does occur when A1 is a local variable. When the function in which it is declared returns (that is, when A1 exits scope), the memory associated with the array is reclaimed automatically by the system. A1 exits scope when the block in which it is declared is exited. For example, in Figure 1.8 A1 is a local variable in a function F. When F returns, the entire contents of the A1 object, including the memory associated with the array, is freed. In contrast, when A2 exits scope only the memory associated with the pointer is freed; the memory allocated by new is now unreferenced, and we have what is known as a *memory leak*. The memory is claimed as used, but unreferenced, and will not be used to satisfy future new requests. The situation is shown graphically in Figure 1.9.

Memory allocated by new is not automatically recycled. Failure to recycle causes a *memory leak*.

```
1  void
2  F( int i )
3  {
4      int A1[ 10 ];
5      int *A2 = new int [ 10 ];
6
7      ...
8      G( A1 );
9      G( A2 );
10
11     // On return, all memory associated with A1 is freed
12     // On return, only the pointer A2 is freed;
13     // 10 ints have leaked
14     // delete [ ] A2;   // This would fix the leak
15 }
```

Figure 1.8   Two ways to allocate arrays; one leaks memory

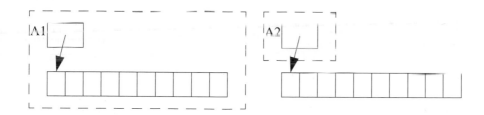

Figure 1.9   Memory reclamation in Figure 1.8

The *delete* operator recycles dynamically allocated memory that is no longer needed.

To recycle the memory, we must use the *delete operator*. The syntax is

```
delete [ ] A2;
```

The `[]` is absolutely necessary here to ensure that all of the objects in the allocated array are recycled. Without the `[]` it is possible that only `A2[0]` is recycled, which is hardly what we intend. With `new` and `delete` we have to manage the memory ourselves rather than allow the compiler to do it for us. Why then, would we be interested in this? The answer is that by managing memory ourselves, we can build expanding arrays. Suppose, for example, that in Figure 1.8 we decide, after the declarations but before the calls to `G` at lines 8 and 9, that we really wanted 12 `int`s instead of 10. In the case of `A1` we are stuck, and the call at line 8 cannot work. However, with `A2` we have an alternative, as illustrated by the following maneuver:

```
int *Original = A2;        // 1. Save pointer to the original
A2 = new int [ 12 ];       // 2. Have A2 point at more memory
for( int i = 0; i < 10; i++ ) // 3. Copy the old data over
    A2[ i ] = Original[ i ];
delete [ ] Original;       // 4. Recycle the original array
```

Always expand the array to a size that is some multiplicative constant times as large. Doubling is a good choice.

Figure 1.10 shows the changes that result. A moment's thought will convince you that this is an expensive operation, because we copy all of the elements from `Original` to `A1`. If, for instance, this array expansion is in response to reading input, it would be inefficient to re-expand every time we read a few elements. Thus when array expansion is implemented, we always make it some *multiplicative* constant times as large. For instance, we might expand to make it twice as large. In this way, when we expand the array from N items to $2N$ items, the cost of the N copies can be apportioned over the next N items that can be inserted into the array without an expansion.

To make things more concrete, Figure 1.11 shows a program that reads an unlimited number of integers from the standard input and stores the result in a dynamically expanding array. The function declaration for `GetInts` tells us that it returns the address where the array will reside, and it sets a reference parameter `ItemsRead` to indicate how many items were actually read. The `&` in the function declaration before `ItemsRead` specifies that it is a reference to, rather than a copy of, the actual parameter. Thus all changes in the formal parameter are reflected in the actual argument. We will discuss reference parameters in more detail in Section 1.7.

At the start of `GetInts`, `ItemsRead` is set to 0, as is the initial `ArraySize`. We repeatedly read new items at line 16. If the array is full, as indicated by a successful test at line 18, then the array is expanded. Lines 20 to 24 perform the array doubling. At line 20 we save a pointer to the currently allocated block of memory. We have to remember that the first time through the loop, the pointer will be `NULL`. At line 21 we allocate a new block of memory, roughly twice the size of the old. We add one so that the initial doubling converts a zero-sized array to an array of size one. At line 25 we set the new array size. At line 27, the actual input item is assigned to the array, and the number of items read is incremented. When the input fails (for whatever reason), we merely return the pointer to the dynamically allocated memory. Note carefully that

- We do not `delete` the array.
- The memory returned is somewhat larger than is actually needed. This can be easily fixed (see Exercise 1.10).

The `main` routine calls `GetInts`, assigning the return value to a pointer. The complications have to do with error handling and are discussed in the next section.

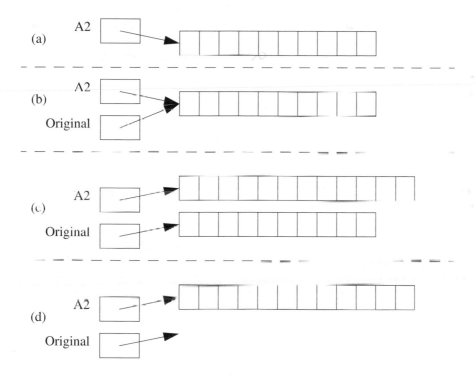

Figure 1.10   Array expansion: (a) starting point: `A2` points at 10 integers; (b) after step 1: `Original` points at the 10 integers; (c) after steps 2 and 3: `A2` points at 12 integers, the first 10 of which are copied from `Original`; (d) after step 4: the 10 integers are freed

```
1  #include <iostream.h>
2  #include <stdlib.h>
3
4  // Read an unlimited number of ints with no attempts at error
5  // recovery; return a pointer to the data, and set ItemsRead
6
7  int *
8  GetInts( int & ItemsRead )
9  {
10     int ArraySize = 0;
11     int InputVal;
12     int *Array = 0;    // Initialize to NULL pointer
13
14     ItemsRead = 0;
15     cout << "Enter any number of integers: ";
16     while( cin >> InputVal )
17     {
18         if( ItemsRead == ArraySize )
19         {        // Array doubling code
20             int *Original = Array;
21             Array = new int[ ArraySize * 2 + 1 ];
22             for( int i = 0; i < ArraySize; i++ )
23                 Array[ i ] = Original[ i ];
24             delete [ ] Original; // Safe if Original is NULL
25             ArraySize = ArraySize * 2 + 1;
26         }
27         Array[ ItemsRead++ ] = InputVal;
28     }
29     return Array;
30 }
31
32 main( )
33 {
34     int *Array;
35     int NumItems;
36
37     // The actual code
38   try
39   {
40     Array = GetInts( NumItems );
41     for( int i = 0; i < NumItems; i++ )
42         cout << Array[ i ] << '\n';
43   }
44    // Exception handler; ... used because standard is evolving
45   catch( ... )
46   {
47     cerr << "Out of memory!!" << endl; exit( 1 );
48   }
49     return 0;
50 }
```

Figure 1.11   Code to read an unlimited number of `int`s and write them out

1.5   Memory Exhaustion

When performing a new, we always have a problem: What do we do if the call to new fails because we have run out of memory. In early versions of C++, if new failed, it returned 0 (a NULL pointer). Consequently, the result of each call to new needed to be compared with 0 to see if the memory allocation was successful. This was similar to the treatment in C and was error prone because programmers tended to forget to perform the test in every instance.

Checking new's return value is no longer worthwhile.

On newer systems set_new_handler was used to specify a function that should have been called prior to the return of a failed new. The intent of the installed new handler function was that a programmer could have attempted to find memory elsewhere, and thus new either returned successfully or the program aborted. By placing an unconditional abort statement in this function, in principle we avoided checking the return value of new. On older versions of the g++ compiler, this was essentially what would happen: If new failed, we would get the error message "virtual memory exceeded" and the program would terminate, making the test of new's return value meaningless.

With the advent of exceptions, the behavior of new was further altered. Exceptions handle exceptional occurrences, and fewer things are more exceptional than running out of memory. Thus it was a logical necessity that new use the exception features. In a nutshell what happened was this: On error new threw the exception xalloc. It was the responsibility of some routine, presumably main, to catch the exception and then generally print an error message[4] and terminate the program. The exception xalloc was declared in the header file new.h.

new throws an exception if the allocation failed.

Exceptions represent information that is transmitted outside the normal return sequence. They are propagated back through the calling sequence until some routine *catches* the exception. Exceptions are discussed in more detail in Appendix D, in which we describe some of the syntax.

In C++ things change quickly: The thrown exception is currently named bad_alloc and is declared in exception.h. We now have the uncomfortable situation in which no compiler available at the time of this writing follows the most recent proposed standard, and further it appears that the standard is still evolving. Since all this is defined in the library, it is particularly unstable. What shall we do?

The name of the exception thrown when new fails is still in flux.

In this text we do not test the return value of new. We use exceptions only to catch errors in new. Rather than trying to catch bad_alloc, we catch . . . so that both xalloc and bad_alloc are handled. The . . . matches all exceptions; when things are stabilized . . . can be replaced with whatever the C++ committees decide to go with. To make the code work, we may have to include an appropriate header file.

In this text we use exceptions only to test for memory exhaustion.

In Figure 1.11 we have a simple illustration of how exceptions are pro-

---

4. Note that if the printing routine requires dynamically allocated memory, this may not be possible!

cessed. Code that might result in an exception being propagated is enclosed in a `try` block. The `try` block extends from lines 38 to 43. Immediately following the `try` block are the exception handlers. This part of the code is jumped to only if an exception is raised; at the point the exception is raised, the `try` block in which it came from is considered terminated. Each `catch` block is attempted in order until a matching handler is found. Since . . . matches everything, it will match whatever exception `new` generates. The code in the `catch` block, in this case lines 45 to 48, is executed, and then the `catch` block and the block containing the `try/catch` combination is considered terminated (one of our compilers complains that `return` statements are not allowed in catch blocks, so we use `exit` instead).

1.6   Pointer Arithmetic and Pointer Hopping

Many programmers spend lots of time attempting to hand-optimize their code. One common myth is that pointers can be used to access arrays more quickly than the usual indexing method. While this is occasionally true and sometimes leads to better or simpler code, in this section we will show that this is not universally true (and in fact is frequently false). First we look at how arithmetic applies to pointers. We have two issues to consider. First, in an expression such as `*X+10` or `*X++`, is the operator (`+` or `++`) being applied to `X` or `*X`? The answer to this question is determined by normal precedence rules. In the first case 10 is added to `*X`, while in the second case the increment is applied to `X` (after the value of `*X` is used). The second issue, then, is to decide what it means to increment or apply various operations to a pointer. Then we will see an application that shows how pointer math is typically used and whether or not it is a good idea.

1.6.1   Implications of the Precedence of *, &, and [ ]

Postfix operators have higher precedence than **prefix operators**.

The dereferencing operator `*` and the address-of operator `&` are grouped together in a class of *prefix operators*. These operators include the unary minus (`-`), the not operator (`!`), the bitwise complement operator (`~`), and the prefix increment and decrement operators (`++` and `--`), as well as `new`, `delete`, and `sizeof`. The prefix unary operators have higher precedence than almost all other operators, except for the scope operators and the *postfix operators*, such as the postfix increment and decrement operators (`++` and `--`), the function call operator (`)`, and the array access operator `[]`. Consequently, the only arithmetic operators that have higher precedence than a dereferencing operator are the postfix increment and decrement operators. In all of the following expressions, the operator is applied to the dereferenced value:

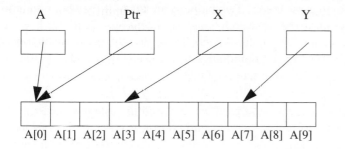

Figure 1.12   Pointer arithmetic: X=&A[3]; Y=X+4

```
*X + 5        // Adds 5 to *X
*X == 0       // True if *X is 0
*X / *Y       // Divide *X by *Y
```

Notice carefully that because of precedence rules, *X++ is interpreted as *(X++), not (*X)++. The precedence of the array indexing operator tells us that if X is a pointer, all of the following operators are applied to the indexed value of X:

> Because of precedence rules, ***X++** applies the ++ operator to **X** and then dereferences the original **X**.

```
5 + X[ 0 ]    // Add X[0] and 5
0 == X[ 0 ]   // True if X[0] is 0
++X[ 0 ]      // Increment X[0]. Same as ++*X (why?)
X++[ 0 ]      // Same as *X++ (why?)
X == &X[ 0 ]  // Always true
```

In the last example we reiterated that X always stores the memory location of X[0]. The precedence rules are convenient here because we do not need to parenthesize, as in &(X[0]).[5]

1.6.2   What Pointer Arithmetic Means

Suppose that X and Y are pointer variables. Now that we have decided on precedence rules, we need to know what the interpretation is for arithmetic performed on pointers. For instance, what does it mean to multiply X by 2? The answer in most cases is that arithmetic on pointers would be totally meaningless and is therefore illegal. Most other languages allow only comparison, assignment, and dereferencing of pointers. C++ is somewhat more lenient.

Looking at the various operators, we see that none of the multiplicative operators makes sense. Therefore, a pointer may not be involved in a multiplication. Note carefully that the dereferenced value can, of course, be multiplied, and that what we are restricting is computations involving addresses.

---

5. Appendix B provides a table of all C++ operators and their precedences.

Two pointers are equal if they both point to NULL or they both point to the same address.

Equality and logical operators all make sense for pointers, so they are allowed and have obvious meanings. Two pointers are equal if they both point to `NULL` or they both point to the same address. Assignment by = is allowed, as we have seen, but `*=`, `/=`, and `%=` are disallowed. Therefore, the questionable operators are the additive operators (including `+=`, `-=`, `++`, `--`) and the relational operators (`<`, `<=`, `>=`, `>`). To make sense, all these operators need to be viewed in the context of an array.

Figure 1.12 shows an array `A`, a pointer `Ptr`, and the assignment `Ptr=A`. The figure reinforces the idea that the value stored in `A` is just the memory location where the zeroth element of the array is stored and that elements of an array are guaranteed to be stored in consecutive and increasing memory locations. If the array `A` is an array of characters, `A[1]` is stored in memory location `A+1` because characters use one byte. Thus the expression `++Ptr` would increase `Ptr` by one, which would equal the memory location of `A[1]`.

If P is a pointer and X is in integer type, then P+X evaluates to an address P objects past X. This is also the memory location of P[X].

We see from this example that adding an integer to a pointer variable can make sense in an array of characters. If `A` was an array of four-byte integers, adding 1 to `Ptr` would make only partial sense under our current interpretation. This is because `Ptr` would not really be pointing at an integer but somewhere in the middle and would be misaligned, generally leading to a hardware fault. Since that interpretation would give erroneous results, C++ uses the following interpretation: `++Ptr` adds the size of the pointed at object to the address stored in `Ptr`.

This interpretation carries over to other pointer operations. The expression `X=&A[3]` makes `X` point at `A[3]`. Parentheses are not needed, as mentioned earlier. The expression `Y=X+4` makes `Y` point at `A[7]`. We could thus use a pointer to traverse an array instead of using the usual index iteration method. We will discuss this in Sections 1.6.3 and 1.6.4.

Although it makes sense to add or subtract an integer type from a pointer type, it does not make sense to add two pointers. It does, however, make sense to subtract two pointers: `Y-X` evaluates to 4 in the example above (since subtraction is the inverse of addition). Thus pointers can be subtracted but not added.

Do not use relational operators on pointers unless both pointers are pointing to parts of the same array.

Given two pointers `X` and `Y`, `X<Y` is true if the object `X` is pointed at is at a lower address than the object `Y` is pointing at. Assuming that neither is pointing at `NULL`, this expression is almost always meaningless unless both are pointing at elements in the same array. In that case `X<Y` is true if `X` is pointing at a lower-indexed element than `Y` because, as we have seen, the elements of an array are guaranteed to be stored in increasing and contiguous parts of memory. This is the only legitimate use of the relational operator on pointers, and all other uses should be avoided.

To summarize, we have the following pointer operations:

- Pointers may be assigned, compared for equality (and inequality), and dereferenced in C++, as well as almost all other languages. The operators are `=`, `==`, `!=`, and `*`.

- We can apply the prefix or postfix increment operators to a pointer, can add an integer, and can subtract either an integer or pointer. The operators are ++, --, +, -, +=, and -=.
- We can apply relational operators to pointers, but the result makes sense only if the pointers point to parts of the same array, or one pointer points to NULL. The operators are <, <=, >, and >=.
- We can test against NULL by applying the ! operator (because the NULL pointer has value 0).
- We can subscript and delete pointers via [] and delete.
- We can apply trivial operators, such as & and sizeof, to find out information about the pointer (not the object it is pointing at).
- As we will see later, we can apply some other operators, such as ->.

1.6.3   A Pointer-Hopping Example

Figure 1.13 illustrates how pointers can be used to traverse arrays. We have written two versions of strlen. The first version, Strlen1, uses the normal indexing mechanism to step through the array of characters. When the for loop ends, the value of i is the index of the null terminator. But since the array starts at zero, this is exactly equal to the length of the string and can thus be used as the return value at line 11. Note that some C++ programmers would omit the explicit test for the null terminator that is coded on line 8. This is because '\0' is identical to zero, so the value of Str[i] is nonzero if and only if it is not the null terminator.

The *pointer-hopping* version is Strlen2. At line 19, we declare a second pointer Sp that is initialized to point at the start of the string. The const is necessary here because we are having Sp point where Str, which is itself a const, points. We continually advance Sp, breaking the loop only after it is pointing at the null terminator. This is written concisely at line 21: the value of the expression is what Sp points at, and immediately after the test is completed, Sp is advanced to point at the next character in the string.

> **Pointers can be used to traverse arrays. This is called *pointer hopping*.**

When the while loop terminates, Sp is pointing at the position after the null terminator (because the ++ is applied even if the test indicates that a null terminator has been seen). The length of the string is thus given by the formula at line 24 as one less than the difference between the final and initial positions of Sp.[6]

---

6. It is tempting to initialize Sp to Str-1 and use a prefix ++ operator in an attempt to simplify the return statement. This is undefined behavior in C++ because a pointer must either point at NULL, an object, or if an array, part of the array or perhaps one cell following the end of the array. It may not point to the cell prior to the start of the array. The resulting code will run correctly on almost all platforms but is nonetheless in technical violation of C++ rules.

```
1  // strlen implemented with usual indexing mechanism
2
3  unsigned int
4  Strlen1( const char Str[ ] )
5  {
6      unsigned int i;
7
8      for( i = 0; Str[ i ] != '\0'; i++ )
9          ;
10
11     return i;
12 }
13
14 // strlen implemented with pointer hopping
15
16 unsigned int
17 Strlen2( const char *Str )
18 {
19     const char *Sp = Str;
20
21     while( *Sp++ )
22         ;
23
24     return Sp - Str - 1;
25 }
```

Figure 1.13   The `strlen` routine coded two ways: first by using indexing, second by using pointer hopping

1.6.4   Is Pointer Hopping Worthwhile?

Why might a pointer implementation be faster than an array implementation? Let
us consider a string of length 3. In the array implementation we access the array
via `S[0]`, `S[1]`, `S[2]`, and `S[3]`. `S[i]` is accessed by adding one to the previous value `i-1` and then adding `S` and `i` to get the required memory location. In
our pointer implementation, `S[i]` is accessed by adding one to `Sp`, and we
never keep a counter `i`. Thus we save an addition for each character, paying only
an extra two subtractions during the return statement.

**Pointer hopping used
to be an important
technique. Optimizing
compilers have made it
generally unnecessary.**

The next question is whether or not the trickier code is worth the time savings. The answer is that in most programs a few subroutines dominate the total
running time. Historically, the use of trickier code for speed has been justified
only in those routines that actually account for a significant portion of the program's running time, or in routines used in enough different programs to make
the optimization worthwhile. Thus in the old days C programs that used pointer
hopping judiciously had a large speed advantage over programs written in other
high-level languages. However, good modern compilers can, in many cases, perform this optimization. Thus the use of pointers to traverse arrays will help some
compilers, will be neutral for others, or may even generate slower code than the
typical index addressing mechanism.

As a concrete example, we coded the routine in Figure 1.14 for testing purposes. It falls very short in terms of error handling. The program merely reads strings from the standard input and verifies that the string lengths computed by the two routines in Figure 1.13 are identical. Presumably there should be no output. We compiled the program on a Sun SPARCstation, running SunOS, and using the Sun C++ compiler. Here was the command we issued:

```
CC -p ShowProf.cpp
```

The -p option specifies that the compiler should generate extra code that can be used to count the total amount of time spent executing each function. This information can be obtained by running the program and then issuing the command prof:

A profiler determines how a program is spending its time.

```
a.out < /usr/dict/words
prof
```

```
1  // Test that Strlen1 and Strlen2 give same answer
2  // Source file is ShowProf.cpp
3
4  #include <iostream.h>
5
6  main( )
7  {
8      char Str[ 512 ];
9
10     while( cin >> Str )
11     {
12         if( Strlen1( Str ) != Strlen2( Str ) )
13             cerr << "Oops!!!!" << endl;
14     }
15
16     return 0;
17 }
```

Figure 1.14   Routine to test that Strlen1 and Strlen2 are consistent and also to see which is faster

%time	cumsecs	#call	ms/call	name
26.6	0.34	25145	0.01	___rs__7istreamFPc
22.7	0.63	25144	0.01	_Strlen2__FPCc
14.8	0.82			mcount
12.5	0.98	25144	0.01	_Strlen1__FPCc
8.6	1.09	25145	0.00	_do_ipfx__7istreamFi
6.2	1.17	25145	0.00	_eatwhite__7istreamFv
4.7	1.23	204	0.29	_read
3.1	1.27	1	40.00	_main

Figure 1.15   First eight lines from prof for program in Figure 1.14.

```
%time    cumsecs    #call    ms/call    name
 34.4      0.31                          mcount
 26.7      0.55     25145       0.01     ___rs__7istreamFPc
  8.9      0.63     25145       0.00     _do_ipfx__7istreamFi
  6.7      0.69     25144       0.00     _Strlen1__FPCc
  6.7      0.75     25144       0.00     _Strlen2__FPCc
  6.7      0.81     25145       0.00     _eatwhite__7istreamFv
  6.7      0.87       204       0.29     _read
  3.3      0.90         1      30.00     _main
```

Figure 1.16   First eight lines from `prof` with highest optimization for program in Figure 1.14

C++ *mangles* names to include type information. This allows linking of several object files to be type safe.

A portion of the output from `prof` is shown in Figure 1.15. The last column indicates the names of some of the functions that are called; these names are *mangled* in some cases to include information related to the parameter types. This allows type-safe linkage across different source files. According to `prof`, 22.7 percent of the time (a total of 0.29 seconds, obtained by subtraction of 0.34 from 0.63) was spent executing the 25,144 calls to `Strlen2`, while only 12.5 percent of the time was spent executing the 25,144 calls to `Strlen1`. (14.8 percent was spent in the function `mcount`, which is the routine inserted by the `-p` option to do all the counting). Most of the other time was spent in I/O related affairs. What this tells us is that, in this case, pointer hopping was actually detrimental to program performance.

The *optimizer* is used to generate better code.

This is only half the story however. The *optimizer* can do a better job generating code for both `Strlen1` and `Strlen2`, and if we compile with the highest optimization setting, we find that `Strlen1` and `Strlen2` give equivalent performance that is significantly better than what was previously generated. For our compiler, the command is

```
CC -p -O4 tester.cc
```

and the resulting output from `prof` is shown in Figure 1.16. The optimizer is not the default because it takes longer to compile with optimization. Thus we should use the optimizer only after we are done debugging.

Optimizing compilers are quite good these days. Stick to algorithmic issues for speed improvements, and leave code generation to the compiler.

The moral of the story is that, in many cases, it is best to leave minute coding details to the compiler and concentrate on the larger algorithmic issues and on writing the clearest code possible. Most systems have a *profiler* tool that is similar to `prof` and will allow you to decide where a program is spending most of its running time. This will tell you where to apply algorithmic improvements, so it is important to learn how to use the optimizer and profiler on your system.

```
 1  #include <iostream.h>
 2
 3  // Does not work
 4  void
 5  SwapWrong( int A, int B )
 6  {
 7      int Tmp = A;
 8      A = B;
 9      B = Tmp;
10  }
11
12  // C Style -- using pointers
13  void
14  SwapPtr( int *A, int *B )
15  {
16      int Tmp = *A;
17      *A = *B;
18      *B = Tmp;
19  }
20
21  // C++ Style -- using references
22  void
23  SwapRef( int & A, int & B )
24  {
25      int Tmp = A;
26      A = B;
27      B = Tmp;
28  }
29
30  // Simple program to test various Swap routines
31  main( )
32  {
33      int X = 5;
34      int Y = 7;
35
36      SwapWrong( X, Y );
37      cout << "X=" << X << " Y=" << Y << '\n';
38      SwapPtr( &X, &Y );
39      cout << "X=" << X << " Y=" << Y << '\n';
40      SwapRef( X, Y );
41      cout << "X=" << X << " Y=" << Y << '\n';
42
43      return 0;
44  }
```

Figure 1.17   Call-by-reference parameters vs. call-by-pointer parameters

1.7   Reference Variables

A *reference type* is a pointer constant that is always dereferenced implicitly and may be viewed as an alias.

In addition to the pointer type, C++ has the *reference type*. A reference type is a pointer constant that is always dereferenced implicitly. A reference type can be viewed as an alias for another object. For instance, in the following code, `Cnt` becomes a synonym for a longer, hard-to-type variable:

```
int LongVariableName = 0;
int & Cnt = LongVariableName;

Cnt += 3;
```

Reference variables must be initialized at declaration time. Reference parameters are used to achieve call by reference instead of call by value.

Reference variables must be initialized when they are declared and cannot be changed to reference another variable. This is because an attempted reassignment via

```
Cnt = SomeOtherObject;
```

assigns to the object `LongVariableName` the value of `SomeOtherObject`. This is a poor use of reference variables but accurately reflects how they are used in a more general setting in which the scope of the reference variable is different than that of the object being referenced. One important case is that a reference variable can be used as a formal parameter, which acts as an alias for an actual argument.

As an illustration, Figure 1.17 shows a `SwapWrong` procedure that does not work because of call-by-value restrictions. The figure shows two correct alternatives: first is a routine that uses the traditional C method of passing pointers to avoid call-by-value restrictions, and then a functionally identical routine that uses C++ reference parameters.

The differences between reference and pointer types are summarized as follows:

- In the function heading, reference parameters are used instead of pointers.
- In the function body, reference parameters are implicitly dereferenced, so no * operators are needed (their placement would generate a syntax error).
- In the function call, no & is needed because an address is implicitly passed by virtue of the fact that the corresponding formal parameters are references.
- The code using reference parameters is much more readable.

Reference variables are like pointer constants in that the value they store is the address of the object they refer to. They are different in that an automatic invisible dereference operator is applied to the reference variable. This difference translates into a notational convenience, especially because it allows parameters to be passed by reference without the excess baggage of the & operator on the actual arguments and the * operator that tends to clutter up C programs.

By the way, an array is already passed by reference, so it is illegal to insert an & to indicate this explicitly. Pointers, however, can be passed by reference. This is used to allow a function to change *where* a pointer, passed as a parameter, is pointing at. A pointer that is passed using call by value cannot be changed to point to a new location (because the formal parameter stores only a copy of the *where* value).

Arrays are always passed by reference. Arrays of references are illegal.

An important issue is the choice between passing parameters by value or by reference. In Section 1.8.2 we will discuss parameter-passing mechanisms in more detail and see a third option, the *constant reference.*

1.8   Structures

As we have seen, an array is a collection of identically typed objects. The array has two major benefits. First, we can index, and thus loop over, each item in the array. Second, when using functions, we can pass the name of the array, thus using only one parameter to send the aggregate.

A different type of aggregate type is the *structure*. The structure is used to store a collection of objects that need not be of the same type. Because the objects in the collection are not constrained to be of the same type, we cannot simply loop over them as we would in an array.

A *structure* stores a collection of generally dissimilar objects.

Each object in the structure is a *member* and is accessed by applying the . *member operator*. The basic structure declaration is given by using the keyword `struct`, providing the name of the structure type, and giving a brace-enclosed list of its members. For example,

Each member of the structure can be accessed by applying the . *member operator*.

```
struct Student
{
    char FirstName[ 40 ];
    char LastName[ 40 ];
    int StudentNum;
    double GradePointAvg;
};
```

Figure 1.18 shows that Student is a structure that consists of four different objects. If we have the declaration

```
Student S;
```

the grade point average is given by `S.GradePointAvg`. Note that the member operator applies to `S` and is thus a postfix operator. This means that it has very high precedence.

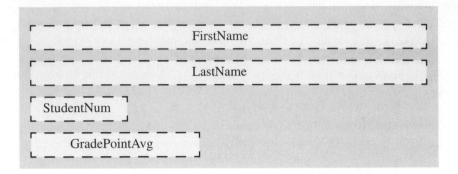

Figure 1.18 `Student` structure

The structure in C++ has been extended from its C counterpart.

The structure in C++ has been greatly extended from its C counterpart to allow functions as members, as well as restrictions on access to the members. This is perhaps the biggest difference between C and C++ because it represents a philosophical change. We will discuss this in the next chapter. For now we will stick with the basics of structures.

1.8.1 Pointers to Structures

In our discussion of advanced programming techniques, we will see that frequently we need to declare a pointer to a structure and access the members of the pointed at structure. Suppose we have

```
Student *Ptr = &S;   // Ptr points at structure S
```

The -> operator is used to access members of a pointed at structure.

Then we can access the grade point average by `(*Ptr).GradePointAvg`. The parentheses are absolutely necessary because the member operator, being a postfix operator, has higher precedence than the prefix dereferencing operator. The parentheses become annoying after awhile, so C++ provides an additional postfix operator that accesses the member of a pointed at structure. This is the `->` operator. Thus `Ptr->GradePointAvg` gives the same access as before.

1.8.2 Parameter-Passing Mechanisms

Suppose we want to pass the `Student` structure to a printing routine. The natural declaration for the routine would be

```
void PrintInfo( Student TheStudent );
```

This function declaration has a fundamental problem: the default parameter-passing mechanism is *call by value*, and call-by-value semantics dictate that a copy is made of the actual argument into the formal parameter for every call to PrintInfo. Because Student is a rather large structure, this is an expensive operation, and thus call by value is unsuitable. An alternative is to pass the parameter by *reference*:

> ***Call by value* is the default parameter-passing mechanism. The actual argument is copied into the formal parameter.**

```
void PrintInfo( Student & TheStudent );
```

Now we can avoid the overhead of a copy. This routine is still not perfect, however, because the declaration tells the reader, and also the compiler, that the actual argument might be changed as result of the call to PrintInfo. When the parameter was passed by value, we were guaranteed that the actual parameter would not be altered. To obtain equivalent behavior, we use a third form of parameter passing, the *constant reference*:

> ***Call by reference* is used to avoid a copy. However, it allows changes to the parameters.**

```
void PrintInfo( const Student & TheStudent );
```

The constant reference guarantees that

> ***Call by constant reference* is used to avoid a copy and guarantees that the actual parameter will not be changed.**

- The overhead of a copy is avoided.
- The actual parameter is unchanged by the function call.

Choosing a parameter-passing mechanism is an easily overlooked chore of the programmer. After all, the program is often correct no matter which mechanism is used. Nevertheless, it is important for both efficiency, readability, and program maintenance to choose a parameter-passing mechanism carefully:

- Call by value is appropriate for small objects that should not be altered by the function.
- Call by constant reference is appropriate for large objects that should not be altered by the function.
- Call by reference is appropriate for objects that may be altered by the function.

As we will see later, in some more complex cases, it is absolutely crucial that call by value be avoided. The program can crash if a wrong decision is made.

1.8.3   Exogenous vs. Indigenous Data and Shallow vs. Deep Copying

C++ allows the user to define operators on structures. For instance the user can write the routine with the declaration

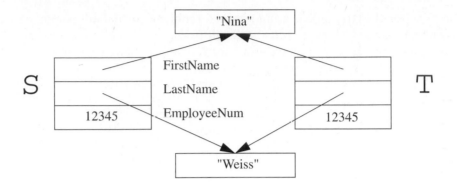

Figure 1.19   Illustration of a shallow copy in which only pointers are copied

```
int operator<( const Student & Lhs, const Student & Rhs );
```

which returns 1 if the first (left side) Student is less than the second, according to some user-defined criterion. Using the class mechanism that is discussed throughout the text, this function could be included as a structure member, much like a data member.

The copy assignment operator = and the equality operator == can also be defined, but if the programmer does nothing, then a default definition is used for copying and equality comparisons become illegal. Specifically, by default a structure copy is implemented as a member-by-member copy. In other words, each member is copied from one structure to the other. Once again, character arrays are completely copied; the null terminator does not signal the end of the array.

A problem with this mechanism is illustrated by the following declaration:

```
struct Teacher
{
    char *FirstName;
    char *LastName;
    int EmployeeNum;
};
```

Suppose we have

```
Teacher S, T;
```

Assume T has been initialized. Then the assignment S=T is a member-by-member copy. The first two members are merely pointers, however, so only the addresses are copied. The result is that S.FirstName is now sharing memory with T.FirstName; these are not independent copies of the string. If the call

```
delete [] T.FirstName
```

is made later to recycle the dynamically allocated memory, S is in serious trouble. This is illustrated in Figure 1.19. This illustrates the difference between indigenous and exogenous data.

Indigenous data are data completely represented inside the structure. For instance, in the Student structure, the FirstName and LastName members are 40-byte arrays and are completely self-contained. The disadvantage of representing an object indigenously is that the size of the object is fixed. Thus we must make an estimate of the largest instance of the object that we are prepared to handle. Often this means wasted space for smaller instances of the object.

Indigenous data are completely contained by the structure.

Exogenous data, by contrast, reside outside of the structure and are accessed only through a pointer. The advantage of exogenous data is that the amount of space required can be determined dynamically. However, using exogenous data introduces a problem. When the default assignment operator is used, the copy is only a copy of pointers and not the pointed-at values.

Exogenous data are not part of the structure but are accessed through a pointer.

A copy of pointers rather than the data being pointed at is known as a *shallow copy*. Similarly, the equality comparisons for exogenous data are shallow by default, because they only compare addresses. Although there are occasions when a shallow copy is appropriate, in general it is not, and allowing a shallow copy when it is unwarranted can lead to havoc.

A *shallow copy* is a copy of pointers rather than data being pointed at.

To get a *deep copy*, in which the pointed-at values are also copied over, we generally need to allocate some additional memory and then copy the dereferenced pointers. This requires rewriting the copy assignment operator. Details on how this is done will be presented in the next few chapters. Normally, we also need to supply a deep comparison operator to implement a deep test.

A *deep copy* is a copy of the data being pointed at rather than the pointers.

1.8.4   Noncontiguous Lists: Linked Lists

We close this chapter by discussing, in very general terms, one of the techniques we will use when we discuss data structures. Earlier we saw that, by using the dynamically expanding array, we can read in an arbitrary number of input items. The technique has one serious problem.

Suppose we are reading 1000-byte records and we have 1,000,000 bytes of memory available. Suppose at some point the array holds 400 records and is full. Then to double, we create an array of 800 records, copy over 400 records, and then delete the 400 records. The problem is that in this intermediate step, we have both a 400- and an 800-record array in use, and the total of 1200 records exceeds our memory limit. In fact, we can run out of memory after using only roughly one third of the available memory.

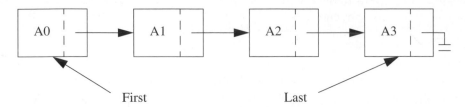

Figure 1.20   Illustration of a simple linked list

A *linked list* stores data with a cost of one pointer per item.

A solution to this problem is to allow the list of records to be stored noncontiguously. For each record we maintain a structure that stores the record and a pointer, Next, to the next structure in the list. The last structure has a NULL Next pointer. We keep a pointer to both the first structure in the list and the last structure in the list. A basic example is shown in Figure 1.20. The resulting structure is the classic *linked list*. The structure definition is

```
struct Node
{
    Etype Record;    // Some element
    Node *Next;
};
```

At any point we can print the list by using the iteration

```
for( Node *P = First; P != NULL; P = P->Next )
    PrintItem( P->Record );
```

and at any point we can add a new last item X by

```
Last->Next = new Node;    // Attach a new Node
Last = Last->Next;        // Adjust Last
Last->Record = X;         // Place X in the node
Last->Next = NULL;        // It's the last, so make Next NULL
```

An arbitrary item can no longer be found in one access. Instead, we must scan down the list. This is similar to the difference between accessing an item on a compact disk (one access) or a tape (sequential).

This is only a quick introduction; a more detailed description of the linked list will be forthcoming in Chapters 15 and 16.

Summary

In this chapter, we have examined the basics of pointers, arrays, and structures. The pointer variable emulates the real-life indirect answer. In C++ it is an object that stores the address where some other data reside. Although any sufficiently large integer could do this, the pointer is special because it can be dereferenced, thus allowing access to those other data. The NULL pointer holds the constant 0, indicating that it is not currently pointing at valid data. A reference parameter is like a pointer constant except that the compiler implicitly dereferences it on every access. Thus it behaves much like an alias. Reference variables allow three forms of parameter passing: call by value, call by constant reference, and call by reference. Choosing the best form for a particular application is a very important part of the design process.

An array is a collection of identically typed objects. In C++ these objects are stored, starting at a memory location given by the array name, in contiguous and increasing locations. The array size tells the compiler how much memory to set aside. Arrays are indexed starting at 0 and ending at one less than the array size. Because the name of the array is just a pointer, no index range checking is performed, and out-of-bounds array accesses can corrupt other objects. Additionally, arrays cannot be copied using the assignment operator but instead must be copied element by element. Dynamically expanding arrays can be implemented by using a combination of new and delete to allocate larger amounts of memory as needed.

Structures are also used to store several objects, but unlike arrays, the objects need not be identically typed. Each object in the structure is a member, and is accessed by the . member operator. The -> operator is used to access a member of a structure that is accessed indirectly through a pointer.

We also saw that a list of items can be stored noncontiguously by using a linked list. The advantage is that less space is used for large objects than in the array-doubling technique. The penalty is that access of the ith item is no longer constant but requires examination of i structures.

Objects of the Game

-> operator Allows access to members of a pointed at structure. (34)

address-of operator & Returns the address of an object. (4)

aggregate A collection of objects stored in one unit. (4)

array Stores a collection of identically typed objects. (4)

array indexing operator [] Provides access to any object in the array. (10)

call by constant reference Parameter-passing mechanism that avoids a copy and guarantees that the actual parameter will not be changed. (35)

call by reference Parameter-passing mechanism that avoids a copy but allows changes to the actual parameter. (35)

call by value The default parameter-passing mechanism in which the actual argument is copied into the formal parameter. (35)

deep copy A copy of the data being pointed at rather than the pointers. (37)

delete operator Recycles dynamically allocated memory that is no longer needed. (20)

dereference Accessing the data that a pointer is pointing at. (5)

dereferencing operator * Used to dereference a pointer. (5)

dynamic array allocation Allows us to allocate arbitrary-sized arrays and make them larger if needed. (18)

exogenous data Not part of the structure, but instead accessed through a pointer. (37)

indigenous data Completely contained by the structure (37)

Lhs and Rhs Throughout the text, we use Lhs and Rhs for left-hand side and right-hand side, respectively. (15)

linked list Stores data with a cost of one pointer per item. (38)

member An object contained in a structure. (33)

member operator . Allows access to each member of the structure. (33)

memory leak Memory allocated by new is not automatically recycled. Failure to recycle causes a memory leak. (19)

multidimensional array An array that is accessed by more than one index. (13)

name mangling C++ mangles names to include type information. This allows linking of several object files to be type safe. (30)

new operator Dynamically allocates memory. (18)

NULL pointer Has value 0 and should never be dereferenced. It is used to state that a pointer is pointing nowhere. (7)

null terminator The special character that ends a string. It is represented by '\0'. (14)

optimizer Used to generate better code. (30)

pointer Stores an address where other data resides. (4)

pointer hopping Using pointers to traverse arrays. (27)

postfix operator A general class of operators that are unary and are placed after their operand. Includes the function call operator, the array indexing operator, the structure member operators, and the postfix increment and decrement operators. (24)

prefix operator A general class of operators that are unary and are placed prior to their operand. Includes the address-of operator, the dereferencing operator, the unary minus, the not operator, the bitwise complement operator, and the prefix increment and decrement operators, as well as new, delete, and sizeof. (24)

profiler Determines how a program is spending its time. (29)

reference type A pointer constant that is always dereferenced implicitly and may be viewed as an alias. (32)

shallow copy A copy of pointers rather than the data being pointed at. (37)

string A null-terminated array of characters. You must allocate an extra spot for the null terminator. (14)

string constant A sequence of characters enclosed in double quotes. They automatically include the null terminator. (15) A constant string can be used in any place that both a string and a constant object can. (16)

structure Stores a collection of objects that are generally dissimilar. (33)

Common Errors

1. If `Ptr` is uninitialized, the assignment `*Ptr=X` is likely to cause problems. Always make sure that a pointer is pointing at an object before attempting to dereference the data.

2. In a declaration, `*Ptr=&X` initializes `Ptr` to point at `X`. In an assignment statement, `*Ptr=&X` is wrong (unless `Ptr` is a pointer to a pointer) because the left side is the dereferenced value rather than the pointer. The `*` in the declaration is not a dereferencing operator but rather part of the type.

3. A common error is mixing up the pointer and the value being pointed at. `Ptr1==Ptr2` is true if both pointers are pointing at the same memory location, while `*Ptr1==*Ptr2` is true if the values stored at the indicated addresses are equal.

4. `*Ptr++` increments `Ptr`, not `*Ptr`, because of precedence rules.

5. In C++, arrays are indexed from 0 to `N-1`, where `N` is the array size. However, range checking is not performed.

6. In C++, arrays cannot be copied or compared because the array name is merely an address.

7. In the declaration `int *A = new int[100]`, the `sizeof` operator gives a misleading result. The size of `A` is equal to `sizeof(int*)`.

8. To define an array, the array size must be a compile-time constant expression. Some compilers (notably g++) relax this rule, but this is not portable.

9. Two dimensional arrays are indexed as `A[i][j]`, not `A[i,j]`.

10. When an array is deleted, you must use `delete[]`, not merely `delete`. Use the following general rules: Anything allocated by `new` requires `delete`, anything allocated by `new[]` requires `delete[]`, and anything else does not require `delete`.

11. Continuing the previous rule, the sequence `int A[10]; delete[] A;` is almost certain to cause problems because `A` was not allocated by `new[]`.

12. It is an error to dereference a pointer immediately after `delete` has been applied to it (even though it will usually appear to work).

13. Programmers must make arrangements to handle memory (and other) errors.

14. On many personal computers you must make additional arrangements if you want to use large arrays. Read the documentation supplied with the compiler.

15. Large objects should not be passed using call by value. Use call by constant reference instead.

16. To avoid double deletion, beware of shallow copies when deep copies are needed.

17. Do not return a reference to a local (automatic) variable. This has the same effect as error 12.

18. A common programming error is over-optimizing. If you want optimized code, compile with the highest optimization supplied by the compiler, and be careful about parameter passing.

On the Internet

The available files for this chapter are listed below. Everything is self-contained, and nothing is used later in the text.

GetInts.cpp   Contains the source code for the example in Figure 1.11.
ShowProf.cpp Contains the source code for the profiling tests.
Swap.cpp   Contains the source code for the swap examples in Figure 1.17.

Exercises

In Short

1.1. Name and illustrate five operations that can be applied to pointers.

1.2. Consider

```
int A, B;
int *Ptr;      // A pointer
int **PtrPtr;  // A pointer to a pointer

Ptr = &A;
PtrPtr = &Ptr;
```

a. Is this legal?

b. What are the values of `*Ptr` and `**PtrPtr`?

c. Using no other objects besides those declared above, how can we alter `PtrPtr` so that it points at a pointer to B without directly touching `Ptr`?

d. Is the following legal?

```
PtrPtr = Ptr;
```

1.3.

      a. Is `*&X` always equal to X? If not, give an example.

      b. Is `&*X` always equal to X? If not, give an example.

1.4.   For the declarations

```
int A = 5;
int *Ptr = &A;
```

What are the values of the following?

      a. `Ptr`

      b. `*Ptr`

      c. `Ptr == A`

      d. `Ptr == &A`

      e. `&Ptr`

      f. `*A`

      g. `*&A`

      h. `**&Ptr`

1.5.   Give the types of all the identifiers declared here and the types of the expressions. Is any expression illegal?

      a. `struct S { int A; S *B; };`

      b. `S Z;`

      c. `S *X;`

      d. `S Y[10];`

      e. `S *U[10];`

      f. `X->A`

      g. `X->B`

      h. `Z.B`

      i. `Z.A`

      j. `*Z.A`

      k. `(*Z).A`

      l. `X->B-Z.B`

      m. `Y->A`

      n. `Y[1]`

      o. `Y[1].A`

      p. `Y[1].B`

      q. `U[2]`

      r. `*U[2]`

      s. `U[2]->A`

    t. `U[2]->B`

    u. `U[10]`

    v. `&Z`

    w. `&X`

    x. `U`

    y. `Y`

1.6. Draw a picture that illustrates the results after each of the following statements, which are executed sequentially:

    a. `int A = 3;`

    b. `int & B = A;`

    c. `int & C = B;`

    d. `B = 5;`

    e. `C = 2;`

1.7. Do you think the following is legal? Why or why not?

```
int A = 3;
const int & B = A;
```

1.8. What is wrong with omitting spacing in `*X/*Y`?

In Theory

1.9. Exactly how long do `Strlen1` and `Strlen2` take per call in Figures 1.15 and 1.16?

In Practice

1.10. In Figure 1.11 the final block of memory used is larger than needed. Add code to shorten the array down to size.

1.11. Write `strcpy` using both pointers and arrays. Test your routine on many cases, including the following:

```
strcpy( Str + 1, Str );
```

Does the library's routine work on this case?

1.12. Perform the profiling test done in Section 1.6.4 on your system. If you are not running UNIX, you will need to find out if your system has a profiler.

1.13. Use a linked list to read an arbitrary number of strings. After the strings are read, output all strings that are lexicographically larger than the last string read from the input.

1.14. A *checksum* is the 32-bit integer that is the sum of the ASCII characters in a file. Two identical files have the same checksum. Write a program to compute the checksum of a file that is supplied as a command-line argument.

1.15. Write a program that outputs the number of characters, words, and lines in the files that are supplied as command-line arguments.

References

The base C++ language is described in [5] but is currently undergoing revision. The most recent draft is available by anonymous ftp *for noncommercial use only* at `research.att.com` in the directory `dist/stdc++/WP`. A description of the thinking behind the design of C++ as well as the proposed extensions is discussed in Stroustrup's book [13].

A host of C++ books are now available at various levels. For those with little programming experience, a good choice is [4]. Books appropriate for readers with background in another programming language include [7], [10], [11], [12], and my particular favorite, [9]. Advanced features of C++, including more details on some of the issues discussed in future chapters, can be found in [1], [3], and [8]. Answers to many C++ questions can be found in [2]. Answers to the questions in [12] can be found in [6].

Much of the material in this chapter is adapted from the presentation in [14].

1. T. Cargill, *C++ Programming Style*, Addison-Wesley, Reading, MA, 1992.

2. M. P. Cline and G. A. Lomow, *C++ FAQs*, Addison-Wesley, Reading, MA, 1995.

3. J. O. Coplien, *Advanced C++*, Addison-Wesley, Reading, MA, 1992.

4. H. M. Deitel and P. J. Deitel, *C++: How to Program*, Prentice-Hall, Englewood Cliffs, NJ, 1994.

5. M. A. Ellis and B. Stroustrup, *Annotated C++ Reference Manual*, Addison-Wesley, Reading, MA, 1990.

6. T. Hansen, *C++ Answer Book*, Addison-Wesley, Reading, MA, 1991.

7. S. Lippman, *C++ Primer*, 2d ed., Addison-Wesley, Reading, MA, 1991.

8. S. Meyers, *Effective C++*, Addison-Wesley, Reading, MA, 1992.

9. E. Nagler, *Learning C++: A Hands-On Approach*, West, St. Paul, MN, 1993.

10. I. Pohl, *Object-Oriented Programming Using C++*, Benjamin/Cummings, Redwood City, CA, 1993.

11. I. Pohl, *C++ for C Programmers,* 2d ed., Benjamin/Cummings, Redwood City, CA, 1995.

12. B. Stroustrup, *The C++ Programming Language*, 2d ed., Addison-Wesley, Reading, MA, 1991.

13. B. Stroustrup, *The Design and Evolution of C++*, Addison-Wesley, Reading, MA, 1994.

14. M. A. Weiss, *Efficient C Programming: A Practical Approach*, Prentice-Hall, Englewood Cliffs, NJ, 1995.

Chapter 2

Objects and Classes

This chapter begins our discussion of object-oriented programming and shows why C++ is more than just C with a few bells and whistles. The basic mechanism for accomplishing object-oriented programming in C++ is the *class* mechanism.

In this chapter we will see

- how C++ uses the class to achieve *encapsulation* and *information hiding*
- how classes are implemented
- several examples of classes, including classes to manipulate bit arrays, rational numbers, and strings

2.1   What Is Object-Oriented Programming?

Object-oriented programming appears to be emerging as the dominant paradigm of the nineties. In this section we will discuss some of the things that C++ provides in the way of object-oriented support and mention some of the principles that are seen in object-oriented programming.

At the heart of object-oriented programming is the *object*. An object is a data type that has structure and state. Each object defines operations that may access or manipulate that state. One feature of object-oriented programming is that user-defined types should behave the same way as predefined (or built-in) types. When we work with any of the basic data types in a language, such as the integer, character, or floating point number, we take certain things for granted:

Objects are entities that have structure and state. Each object defines operations that may access or manipulate that state.

- We can declare new objects, possibly with initialization.
- We can copy or test for equality.
- We can perform input and output on these objects.

- If the object is an automatic variable, then when the function it is declared in terminates, the object goes away.

- We can perform type conversions when appropriate, and the compiler complains when they are inappropriate.

An object is an *atomic unit*. Its parts cannot be dissected by the general users of the object.

Additionally, we view the object as an *atomic unit* that the user ought not to dissect. Most of us would not even think about fiddling around with the bits that represent a floating point number and would find it completely ridiculous to try to increment some floating point object by altering its internal representation ourselves.

Information hiding makes implementation details, including components of an object, inaccessible.

The atomicity principle is known as *information hiding*. The user does not get direct access to the parts of the object nor their implementations; they can only be accessed indirectly by functions supplied with the object. We can view each object as coming with the warning "Do not open — no user-serviceable parts inside." In real life most people who try to fix things that have such a warning wind up doing more harm than good. In this respect programming mimics the real world. The grouping of data and the operations that apply to them to form an aggregate, while hiding implementation details of the aggregate is known as *encapsulation*.

Encapsulation is the grouping of data and the operations that apply to them to form an aggregate, while hiding the implementation of the aggregate.

A second important goal of object-oriented programming is the support of code reuse. Just as engineers use components over and over in their designs, programmers should be able to reuse objects rather than repeatedly re-implementing them. When we have an implementation of the exact object that we need to use, it is a simple matter. The challenge is to use an existing object when the object that is needed is not an exact match but is merely very similar.

C++ provides several mechanisms to support this goal. One is the *template* mechanism: If the implementation is identical except for the basic type of the object, a template can be used to describe the basic functionality. For instance, a procedure can be written to swap two items; the logic is independent of the types of objects being swapped, and so a template could be used. Templates will be discussed in Chapter 3.

The *inheritance* mechanism allows us to extend the functionality of an object; in other words, we can create new types with restricted (or extended) properties of the original type. Inheritance goes a long way toward our goal of code reuse. Another important object-oriented principle is known as *polymorphism*. A polymorphic object can hold objects of several different types. When operations are applied to the polymorphic type, the operation that is appropriate to the actual stored type is automatically selected. In C++ this is implemented as part of inheritance. We will discuss inheritance and polymorphism in Chapter 4.

A *class* is the same as a structure except that, by default, all members are inaccessible.

In this chapter we describe how C++ uses classes to achieve encapsulation and information hiding. A *class* is the same as a structure except that, by default, all members are inaccessible to the general user of the class. Because functions that manipulate the object's state are members of the class, they are accessed by the . member operator, just like any other structure member. Thus these are called *member functions*. In object-oriented terminology, when we make a call to a member function, we are passing a message to the object. As we will see, besides syntax and improved support for principles such as information hiding, the most obvious difference between object-oriented programming in C++ and typical C procedural programming is philosophical: In C++ the object is in charge.

2.2 A Simple Example

In C++ the basic structure has been extended in two ways. We normally consider a structure to be a collection of data members. Because we would like to hide these members from the user, we can specify that they are stored in a *private* section. The compiler will enforce (to the best of its ability) the rule that members in the private section are inaccessible to the user of the object. As mentioned in the previous section, the second extension is that a structure can also declare (and define) functions as members. Some of these member functions would describe how an instance of the structure is created and initialized, how it is destroyed, and how assignment and equality tests are to be performed. Other functions would be specific to the particular structure.

Functions can be supplied as additional members; these *member functions* manipulate the object's state.

Figure 2.1 illustrates a class declaration for a MemoryCell object. The declaration consists of two parts. The *public* section represents the portion that is visible to the user of the object. Since we expect to hide data, generally only member functions would be placed in the public section. In our example, we have member functions that read and write to the MemoryCell object. The private section contains the data, and this is invisible to the user of the object. The StoredValue member must be accessed through the publicly visible routines Read and Write; it cannot be accessed directly by main. Another way of viewing this is shown in Figure 2.2.

```
1  // MemoryCell class
2  //    int Read( )           -->  Returns the stored value
3  //    void Write( int X ) -->  X is stored
4
5  class MemoryCell
6  {
7    public:
8          // Public member functions
9      int Read( )              { return StoredValue; }
10     void Write( int X )      { StoredValue = X; }
11   private:
12         // Private internal data representation
13     int StoredValue;
14 };
```

Figure 2.1   A complete declaration of a MemoryCell class

Figure 2.2   `MemoryCell` members: `Read` and `Write` are accessible, but `StoredValue` is hidden

```
1  // Exercise the MemoryCell class
2
3  main( )
4  {
5      MemoryCell M;
6
7      M.Write( 5 );
8      cout << "Cell contents are " << M.Read( ) << '\n';
9          // The next line would be illegal if uncommented
10 //   cout << "Cell contents are " << M.StoredValue << '\n';
11     return 0;
12 }
```

Figure 2.3   A simple test routine to show how `MemoryCell` objects are accessed

Figure 2.3 shows how `MemoryCell` objects are used. Since `Read` and `Write` are members of the `MemoryCell` class, they are accessed using the `.` member operator. The `StoredValue` member could also be accessed using the `.` member operator, but since it is private, the compiler will complain.

If a class had many function members and these functions were nontrivial, it would be unreasonable to write all the function definitions inside the class declaration. Figure 2.4 shows the more typical mechanism: The member function declarations are provided in the class declaration, and then they are defined later, using a normal function syntax augmented with the class name and *scope operator* `::`. This reflects a separation of the class *interface* from the class *implementation*, which will be a recurring theme throughout the text.

> The *interface* describes what can be done to an object. The *implementation* represents the internals of how the interface specifications are met.

The *interface* represents the class design and tells us what can be done to an object. The syntax of C++ allows the class declaration to specify the properties of its member functions, and in conjunction with good naming conventions, this can greatly reduce the amount of commenting that is necessary. Even so, the interface should be accompanied by comments that specify what may be done to objects of the class. The *implementation* represents the internals of how this is accomplished. As far as the class user is concerned, these internal details are not important.

```
 1  // MemoryCell interface
 2  //   int Read( )        --> Returns the stored value
 3  //   void Write( int X ) -->  X is stored
 4
 5  class MemoryCell
 6  {
 7    public:
 8      int Read( );
 9      void Write( int X );
10    private:
11      int StoredValue;
12  };
13
14
15
16  // Implementation of the MemoryCell class members
17
18  int
19  MemoryCell::Read( )
20  {
21      return StoredValue;
22  }
23
24  void
25  MemoryCell::Write( int X )
26  {
27      StoredValue = X;
28  }
```

Figure 2.4   A more typical `MemoryCell` declaration in which interface
and implementation are separated

In the rest of this chapter, we will describe some of the typical member functions that are provided by classes and examine some additional C++ syntax rules.

2.3   A More Substantial Class: the Bit Array

In this and the next few sections, we examine some details that must be considered for typical classes. To do this, we begin by considering the following problem:

INDEPENDENT SELECTION
*THE INPUT IS N PEOPLE AND N ITEMS. EACH PERSON RANDOMLY AND
INDEPENDENTLY WRITES THE NAME OF K ITEMS THEY WANT ON A PIECE
OF PAPER. HOW MANY ITEMS ARE UNWANTED? (FOR SIMPLICITY, A
PERSON MAY WRITE AN ITEM MORE THAN ONCE).*

It can be shown mathematically that as N gets large, the answer is well approximated by Ne^{-K}, where e is the constant $2.71828\dots$. Thus for $N = 1,000,000$ and $K{=}10$, we still expect 45 unwanted items. We would like to write a program to verify this.

The implementation is simple if we use an array of characters (or integers) to represent the items. We mark the item selected when a corresponding random number is drawn, and at the end of the algorithm we count how many items have never been marked. For a large N, using an array of N characters (or integers) is wasteful because we only need an array of bits. Consequently, we need a new type: the bit array.

The *bit array* is an object on which the basic operations are `SetBit`, `ClearBit`, and `GetBit`, which turn a specified bit on or off, or returns its current status. Note that we can also provide other operations such as `ClearAllBits`, which initializes the entire bit array to 0s.[1]

2.3.1   Using the Bit Array

As far as the class user is concerned, this is not important.

Before we see how the bit array is implemented, it helps to see how it is used. This is shown in Figure 2.5 (a sample run is shown in Figure 2.6). We assume that the interface to the `BitArray` class is given in the header file specified at line 2. The interface tells us *what* can be done to an object, although (except as discussed later) it need not tell us *how* the implementor of the class has done it. The actual implementation could be in an inaccessible file and, as we will see later, the source code for it does not need to be supplied.

After reading N and K at line 14, we declare on line 15 a `BitArray` object B that holds N bits. At line 16 we output the number of bits that B is prepared to hold. Presumably this is the same as N, unless N was unreasonably large (or small), in which case the `BitArray` class may have elected to use a default value or even 0. In any case N is set to the actual value that was allotted. At line 19 we turn on a randomly selected bit, assuming the use of a random number generator.[2] This is done by sending a `SetBit` message to object B. Notice that the `SetBit` function is a member of the object and thus is selected with the . operator. Similarly, at line 22 we call the `GetBit` member function, incrementing the count of zero-bit entries if appropriate. The rest of the code uses no new features.

The program shown in Figure 2.5 is so trivial that you might suspect there is nothing but a syntactical difference between it and a C program. After all, by using C we can replace line 15 with a call to a function that allocates an appropriate amount of memory, and rewrite lines 19 and 22 to pass B, N, and i as parameters to a function. Certainly it appears that nothing has been gained except that we use an object syntax instead of a procedural syntax. However, even in this simple routine, using an object-oriented approach does get us something.

---

1. The proposed C++ standard library will contain a somewhat different `Bit` class; the exact details are still under consideration.
2. Random numbers are discussed in more detail in Chapter 9.

```
1  #include <iostream.h>
2  #include "BitArray.h"
3
4  // Simple main program to use BitArray class
5
6  main( )
7  {
8      int StillEmpty = 0;
9      int N;
10     int K = 1;
11     int i;
12
13     cout << "Enter N and K: ";
14     cin >> N >> K;            // Error check omitted for brevity
15     BitArray B( N );          // Declare the BitArray B
16     cout << "B holds " << ( N = B.NumItems( ) ) << " bits\n";
17
18     for( i = 0; i < K * N; i++ )
19         B.SetBit( RandInt( 0, N - 1 ) ); // RandInt not shown
20
21     for( i = 0; i < N; i++ )
22         if( !B.GetBit( i ) )
23             StillEmpty++;
24
25     cout << "After " << K * N << " random inserts, "
26          << StillEmpty << " slots are still empty\n";
27
28     return 0;
29 }
```

Figure 2.5   A sample `main` using the `BitArray` class


```
Enter N and K: 100000 2
B stores 100000 bits
After 200000 random inserts, 13555 slots are still empty
```

Figure 2.6   Output from `main` in Figure 2.5 (boldface items are user
                  input)

Imagine that the code in Figure 2.5 is a procedure and that the real `main` calls this procedure several times to prompt for different values of N and K. The C version of the routine dynamically allocates memory for B. When the procedure returns to `main`, the allocated memory must be freed. In the C version we would need to remember to issue the call `free(B)` (that is, `delete[]B` in C++). If we were to forget, then we would have a memory leak. It is very easy to forget to free up memory. In C++, when the procedure returns, B goes out of scope and a routine known as the *destructor* is called. We can arrange to have the destructor free the memory. The differences between the two approaches are clear:

A *destructor* can be used to free memory automatically when an object exits scope.

- In C++ we need to write the disposal routine once, when implementing the class. The class user never has to worry about managing the memory.
- In C users of the class must free the memory themselves. Each call to allocate memory must also have arrangements made to free the memory. Thus we have to write the disposal routine and then count on the user remembering to call the disposal routine every time objects leave scope. Otherwise, memory leaks.

Now that we have seen how a class is used, and we have also seen that, even in the most trivial cases, an object-oriented approach is beneficial, let us see how the interface to the object is specified. The class interface tells us what we can do to our objects. In some sense it is like an advertisement, and it is up to the implementor of the class interface to meet the specifications set forth in the interface.

The interface, in principle, is a simple piece of code. The complications arise from the host of const and & directives that are present to ensure efficiency. Recall from Section 1.8.2 that we do not like to pass large objects by value but prefer to use a const &. It is safe to ignore these technicalities until they are discussed later in the text. For the BitArray class the interface is shown in Figure 2.7. Let us look at some of the details.

2.3.2   Public and Private Class Members Revisited

Only members in the public section are visible to nonclass routines.

The simplest parts of the class interface are the directives public and private. There is also a third directive, protected, which we will discuss in Chapter 4. Only members that are in the public section are visible to the user of the class. Members in the private section are inaccessible to the class user and can only be accessed by the class routines themselves. Because class members are private by default, everything from the beginning of the class interface until the public label is private. Public and private directives can be intermixed arbitrarily. As a result, each of the following statements in main would be illegal:

```
cout << B.N;                // ILLEGAL
cout << B.IsInRange( 10 );  // ILLEGAL
C = B;                      // ILLEGAL, if C is a BitArray
```

Members in the private section are not visible to nonclass routines.

The first statement is illegal because N is a private member of class BitArray; the user of the class is not allowed to access it. This prohibition applies to all members, not just the data members. Thus the second statement is illegal too: The IsInRange member function can only be used internally by the class and is not available to the users of the class. The third statement is illegal because of line 41 in the interface. As we will see later, this represents the declaration for the copy assignment operator. By placing it in the private section, we have made it inaccessible to the class user. An attempt by the class user to perform an assignment would generate a compiler error.

```
1  // BitArray class: support access to an array of bits
2  //
3  // CONSTRUCTION: with (a) no initializer or (b) an integer
4  //       that specifies the number of bits
5  // All copying of BitArray objects is DISALLOWED
6  //
7  // *****************PUBLIC OPERATIONS********************
8  // void ClearAllBits( )   --> Set all bits to zero
9  // void SetBit( int i )   --> Turn bit i on
10 // void ClearBit( int i ) --> Turn bit i off
11 // int GetBit( int i )    --> Return status of bit i
12 // int NumItems( )        --> Return capacity of bit array
13
14 #include <iostream.h>
15
16 class BitArray
17 {
18   public:
19     // Constructor
20     BitArray( int Size = 320 );          // Basic constructor
21
22     // Destructor
23     ~BitArray( ) { delete [ ] TheArray; }
24
25     // Member Functions
26     void ClearAllBits( );
27     void SetBit( int i );
28     void ClearBit( int i );
29     int  GetBit( int i ) const;
30     int  NumItems( ) const { return N; }
31   private:
32       // 3 data members
33     int *TheArray;                       // The bit array
34     int N;                               // Number of bits
35     int ArraySize;                       // Size of the array
36
37     enum { IntSz = sizeof( int ) * 8 };
38     int IsInRange( int i ) const;// Check range with error msg
39
40         // Disable operator= and copy constructor
41     const BitArray & operator=( const BitArray & Rhs );
42     BitArray( const BitArray & Rhs );
43 };
```

Figure 2.7   Interface for `BitArray` class

Thinking about what to do with the copy assignment operator is an important class decision that we will discuss in Section 2.4.2. For now we can point out why copying has been disabled. By default, a copy is done data member by data member. In our case this means that we would copy each of the three members, `TheArray`, `N`, and `ArraySize`, from one object to another. The problem is that since `TheArray` is only a pointer, we would not be copying the array, just the pointer. Put another way, we would have two objects *sharing* the one allocated array. This is one case where sharing is not good. Consequently, we have to do one of two things: Either we write our own version of the assignment operator (which we will discuss in Section 2.4.2), or we do not allow copying at all. We cannot allow the incorrect semantics of the default to apply in this case. Line 42, which we will discuss in the next section, disables a similar routine for the same reason.

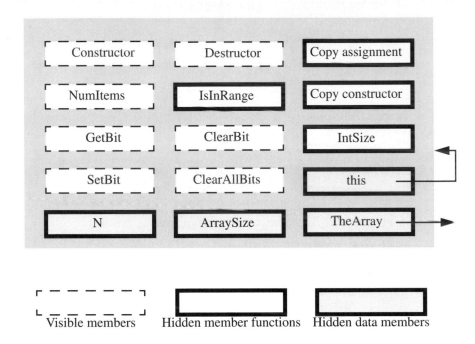

Figure 2.8   `BitArray` members

```
1 BitArray A;              // Call with Size = 320
2 BitArray B( 50 );        // Call with Size = 50
3 BitArray C = 50;         // Same as above
4 BitArray D[ 50 ];        // Calls 50 constructors, with Size 320
5 BitArray *E = new BitArray; // Allocates BitArray of Size 320
6 E = new BitArray( 20 );// Allocates BitArray of size 20; leaks
7 BitArray F = "wrong";    // Does not match basic constructor
8 BitArray G( );           // This is wrong!
```

Figure 2.9   Construction examples

Figure 2.8 gives another view of the public/private interface. Dashed rectangles are public, solid rectangles are private, and thus inaccessible. We have also shaded those members that require storage for each object instance. These are the data members. There is one data member in Figure 2.8 that is not listed in the class interface: the pointer `this`. For every object, the private data member `this` is a pointer to the object. It is not modifiable. We discuss the `this` class member in more detail in Section 2.4.2.

2.3.3   Constructors and Destructors

As we mentioned earlier, a basic property of objects is that they can be defined, possibly with initialization, and deleted, especially when they are out of scope. In C++ the function that controls how an object is allocated and initialized is the *constructor*. The function that controls how it is deleted is the *destructor*. It is expected, among other things, that a destructor will `delete` any memory that was allocated by calls to `new` in the constructor.

A *constructor* tells how an object is declared and initialized. The *destructor* tells how an object is destroyed when it exits scope.

Basic Constructor

The declaration for the basic `BitArray` constructor is shown on line 20 in the interface. In this case the constructor takes a single optional parameter (which is an `int`). This means that when an object is created with an initial value given by an `int`, the constructor is called. The action is specified by the implementor when the definition of the constructor is written (which we do later in this section). Because the single parameter is optional, this constructor is also called if no initialization is given; in that case the parameter `Size` defaults to 320. It is possible to write two separate constructors: one for the no-parameter case, and one for the single-parameter case; however, in this case it is redundant. Figure 2.9 summarizes the situations in which the constructor might be called.

The first two cases shown in Figure 2.9 are what we expect with the constructor. The third case is equivalent to the second because 50 represents an initial value and thus is treated as a parameter to the constructor. = operators that are not in declaration statements, however, are treated as copy assignment operators. The fourth case defines an array of 50 `BitArrays`. A constructor is called for each `BitArray`, and since no size can be specified, the default is used (unfortunately, we cannot specify an initial value for each of the `BitArrays`). The next two examples create a `BitArray` object through a call to `new`. The constructor is called in both cases. However the memory allocated in line 5 is leaked because at line 6 E is no longer pointing at it.

The last two cases do not call the basic constructor. The declaration in line 7 does not match the basic constructor declaration. Here, because the single initial value is not the `int` specified at line 20 in the interface, the compiler issues a complaint. To allow this form of initialization, we need to specify an additional constructor. Finally, line 8 shows a common error: The declaration states that G

If the initialization does not match any constructors, the compiler complains.

is the name of a function that returns a `BitArray`; needless to say, that is not the same as declaring a `BitArray` object.

The *scope operator* `::` is used to refer to the scope. In a class member function the scope is the class.

The body of the constructor function is shown in Figure 2.10. It uses the binary class *scope operator* `::`.[3] The class scope operators have the highest precedence, winning out even over postfix operators. All line 3 says is that the function we are defining is a member function for the class `BitArray`. A consequence of this is that objects in the body of the function have class scope. Put another way, the variable `TheArray` represents the `TheArray` member of the *current object* (that is, the object for which this function was called). Similarly, `N` and `ArraySize` represent their respective members of the current object. Consequently, line 6 dynamically allocates the array for the object while setting the `ArraySize` member. Likewise, line 7 sets the `N` member for the current object. Line 8 calls the `ClearAllBits` member function (on the current object) to initialize the array. Strictly speaking this is not needed, but it does illustrate that other member functions can be called.

The default constructor is a member-by-member application of a no-parameter constructor.

If no constructor is provided, as in the case for the `MemoryCell` class in Figure 2.1, a default constructor is generated that initializes each data member, using the data member's construction method. In the case of `MemoryCell`, since the `int` type is by default uninitialized, the `StoredValue` component is uninitialized.

Destructor

The destructor frees up resources that were allocated by the constructor or other member functions.

The destructor is called whenever an object goes out of scope or is subjected to a `delete`. Typically, the only responsibility of the destructor is to free up any resources that were allocated by the constructor. This includes calling `delete` for any corresponding `new`s, closing any files that were opened, and so on. The destructor is generally sufficiently short that we can include its body in the interface. We have done that at line 23 of our example. Looking at the examples of constructors in Figure 2.9, in cases 1 through 3, a destructor is called when the scope of B is not active (that is, the function it is declared in returns). In case 4, 50 destructors are called. In cases 5 and 6, explicit calls to `delete E` must be made to activate the destructor; otherwise, memory leaks.

The default destructor is a member-by-member application of destructors.

If a destructor is not provided, then a default is generated. The default is to apply a destructor to each data member. In our case this would be unacceptable because the dynamically allocated array would not be destroyed.

---

3. There is also a unary class scope operator that allows us to refer to global variables. Specifically, `::X` refers to object X that is global, even if there is a local or more visible X in scope.

```
1  // Definition for the basic constructor
2
3  BitArray::BitArray( int Size )
4  {
5      ArraySize = ( Size + IntSz - 1 ) / IntSz;
6      TheArray = new int[ ArraySize ];
7      N = Size;
8      ClearAllBits( );
9  }
```

Figure 2.10   Basic constructor for `BitArray` class

Copy Constructor

There is a special constructor that is required to construct a new object, initialized to a copy of the same type of object. This is the *copy constructor*. For any object, such as a `BitArray` object, a copy constructor is called in the following instances:

The *copy constructor* is called when an object is passed or returned by value.

- a declaration with initialization, such as

```
BitArray B = C;
BitArray B ( C );
```

  but not

```
B = C;        // Assignment operator
```

- an object passed using call by value (instead of by & or const &)
- an object returned by value (instead of by & or const &)

The first case is the simplest to understand because the constructed objects were explicitly requested. The second and third cases construct temporary objects that are never seen by the user. Even so, a construction is a construction, and in both cases we are copying an object into a newly created object. Consequently, the copy constructor is called for. For any type `ClassType`, the declaration of the copy constructor is given as

```
ClassType( const ClassType & );
```

This says that the initialization is with another `ClassType` object. That object is passed by constant reference not only for efficiency but also because passing by value would force the invocation of copy constructors ad infinitum. You have the right to a copy constructor, and if you cannot afford to write it yourself, one will be provided for you. However, it will default to applying copy constructors to each member in turn, which, as was the case for the assignment operator, may not be what you want. Like the assignment operator, we can disable the copy constructor by placing its declaration in the `private` section of the class inter-

By default, the copy constructor is a member-by-member application of copy constructors. Placing the declaration in the private section disables the copy constructor.

face. This also means that attempts to pass the object by value will generate a compile-time error. This is clearly needed here. Consider the result if call by value were allowed on `BitArray`:

1. A temporary object is created, and its `TheArray` member will point at the original object.
2. Eventually, the function exits.
3. At this point the temporary object goes out of scope and its destructor is called.
4. The destructor calls `delete` on the `TheArray` member.
5. Consequently, the original object's `TheArray` pointer points at memory that has been returned to the system for possible reallocation. At this point we have undefined behavior.

Either implement a good copy constructor or disable it.

Another possibility would be to write the copy constructor so that it actually allocates new memory and does the copy. The problem with this is that it is expensive: A call by value done this way would consume huge resources if done several times. We could use a third strategy, which is not only to do the allocation and copy but also to issue a warning message that would be printed whenever the copy constructor executed. Presumably, this would be used when an occasional copy is desired, and we are certain that it is not a frequent event. In our case we have decided to play it safe and disallow it for the `BitArray` class.

2.3.4   Member Functions

Now that we have seen how objects are created and destroyed, we can look at the member functions. In addition to constructors, destructors, and the copy assignment operator, our interface specifies five member functions that are public plus an additional member function that is private. The `NumItems` member function is so simple that we can write it in the interface.[4] The remaining functions are shown separately in Figure 2.11.[5] Every member function must be listed in the interface. Otherwise, the compiler will generate an error.

Do not forget the `::` operator when writing the member functions.

First, the scope resolution operator `::` comes after the class name. Thus the return type goes before the class name. View the result of the scope resolution operator as just a simple name. If you forget the scope resolution operator, then the function is interpreted as just a normal global scope function. In the case of `IsInRange`, for example, `N` will be reported as undefined, unless by some horrible coding practice you have made a global variable named `N`. In the unlikely case that all the class variables happen to have global counterparts, then the program may fail to link because you have not provided the body for a class func-

---

4. In order to achieve a strict separation of interface and implementation, some programmers prefer to avoid placing any implementations in the class interface. This is a reasonable decision. We provide implementations for one-liners in the interface mostly for the purpose of convenience.
5. We use the C++ bitwise operators which are reviewed in Appendix A.

tion. The link will fail if there is a call to that function (although when this occurs depends on the particular system).

If the member function is never called, your program may compile and run without incident, which means that you can do debugging without writing empty functions, as would be required in most other languages. This can be a powerful development tool, but some compilers might warn you that you have forgotten a member function because, in a final production program, that is always an error.

```
1  void
2  BitArray::ClearAllBits( )
3  {
4      for( int i = 0; i < ArraySize; i++ )
5          TheArray[ i ] = 0;
6  }
7
8  inline int
9  BitArray::IsInRange( int i ) const
10 {
11     if( i < 0 || i >= N )
12     {
13         cerr << "Bit " << i << " exceeds size (" << N << ")\n";
14         return 0;
15     }
16     return 1;
17 }
18
19 void
20 BitArray::SetBit( int i )
21 {
22     if( IsInRange( i ) )
23         TheArray[ i / IntSz ] |= ( 1 << ( i % IntSz ) );
24 }
25
26 void
27 BitArray::ClearBit( int i )
28 {
29     if( IsInRange( i ) )
30         TheArray[ i / IntSz ] &= ~( 1 << ( i % IntSz ) );
31 }
32
33 int
34 BitArray::GetBit( int i ) const
35 {
36     if( !IsInRange( i ) )
37         return 0;
38
39     return ( TheArray[ i / IntSz ] & ( 1 << ( i % IntSz ) ) ) != 0;
40 }
```

Figure 2.11   Implementation of the basic member functions for the BitArray class

The function *signature* includes the types of parameters, including `const` and & directives, but not the return type.

Note also that the *signature* of the function body, which includes the types of the parameters (but not default values, which are only in the declaration, and not return values), must exactly match that of the function declaration, including the placement of the `const` and & directives. If the signatures match but the return types do not, the compiler will complain.

The `BitArray` implementation uses the reserved word `inline` to implement `IsInRange`. This is a request to the compiler to expand the code inline, thus avoiding the overhead of the function call. It is guaranteed that any function whose body is written in the interface is inline. The trade-off is usually time vs. space: Expanding the code inline makes for more code. A second trade-off is that any code that calls an inline function must be recompiled if the definition of the function changes. This can be very painful in some cases. If we use an inline function for a public member function, we essentially require that it be in the interface header file, so it will be scanned when changed. Also note that unlike default parameters, the `inline` directive appears in the function body and not the declaration. Generally speaking, we will avoid use of the `inline` directive throughout the text because it blurs the separation of interface and implementation, is easy to abuse, and rarely delivers the performance increase that justifies the blemishes. A reasonable exception is for private inline functions because those can be placed in the implementation file.

2.4   Exploring More Details of the Class Interface

The description in the previous section left some mysteries unresolved:

- What do the `const` directives that are at the end of some of the member functions mean?
- How do we write a copy constructor and a copy assignment operator when we need to?

We discuss these issues in this section.

2.4.1   The `const` Directives

The `const` directive at the end of the function signature (as shown for all the member functions) specifies that the member function is a *constant member function* (sometimes abbreviated `const` *member function*), which means it does not change the object. If such a function attempts to change the object by altering any class data members, the compiler will complain. Here are some examples of a violation:

- an attempt to alter N, `ArraySize`, or `TheArray`
- implementing a constant member function by calling a non-constant member function (because that function could alter the object)

In theory, we can write a C++ program using no `const` directives at all. However this is poor programming style that leads to errors. Once we start using a couple of `const` directives, continued proper use of the `const` directive is imperative. Consider, for instance, the routine in Figure 2.12.

A constant member function is a function that does not change any class data members.

If `NumItems` and `GetBit` are not declared as constant member functions, then the compiler will issue an error message. To see why, note that B is declared at line 2 to be a `const`. If `NumItems` and `GetBit` are not constant member functions, then the compiler has no assurance that they will not try to change B, violating B's `const` directive. Since the implementation details are not guaranteed to be available, it is impossible for the compiler to do anything but complain. Of course, we can remove the error message by removing the `const` directive at line 2. But that is not good programming (and may itself generate messages from routines that call `PrintAllBits`).

On the other hand, altering `ArraySize[0]` does not violate the constant member rule because it is not a direct alteration of the data member `ArraySize`. Consequently, all the member functions could be written as constant members. But that does not express things conceptually. Therefore, we adopt the rule that we use the constant member notation to indicate that a member function does not *logically* change the state of an object.

By the way, the `const` that indicates a constant member function must be used consistently if both a declaration and a definition are given. If you use it in the declaration but not the definition, you will get an error message at the function body telling you that there is no matching declaration in the interface. Novices get quite perplexed with this message until they realize that `const` is part of the signature.

`const` member function declarations are part of the signature.

```
1  void
2  PrintAllBits( const BitArray & B )
3  {
4      for( int i = 0; i < B.NumItems( ); i++ )
5          cout << B.GetBit( i );
6  }
```

Figure 2.12   Example of a routine that breaks if `const` directives are missing

```
1  BitArray::BitArray( const BitArray & Rhs )
2  {
3      ArraySize = ( Size + IntSz - 1 ) / IntSz;
4      TheArray = new int[ ArraySize ];
5      N = Size;
6
7      for( int i = 0; i < ArraySize; i++ )
8          TheArray[ i ] = Rhs.TheArray[ i ];
9  }
```

Figure 2.13   Copy constructor for `BitArray`

2.4.2   Allowing Copying: Copy Constructors and `operator=`

The *copy assignment operator `operator=`* is used to copy objects. There are important differences between the copy constructor and the copy assignment operator.

Suppose we want to allow copying. In C++ there are two distinct forms of copying, namely the copy constructor (which is a copy on construction) and the copy assignment operator `operator=` which is a copy into an already existing object.[6] In this section we write a copy constructor and a copy assignment operator. For these to be used, the prototypes must be moved to the public section. Let us also recall the basic difference between the copy constructor and the copy assignment operator:

- For the copy constructor, the target object (which is the current object) does not exist: `TheArray` has never been allocated.
- For the copy assignment operator, the target object does exist; `TheArray` may or may not be sufficiently large to store a copy.

Let us look at the copy constructor first. The code is shown in Figure 2.13. After the array is allocated and all of the other members are set, we can perform the copy.

The copy assignment operator `operator=` is similar but a bit more complicated. If the target object is large enough to store the copy, we can just do the copy. If it is not, we have to allocate a larger array, do the copy, and only then free the original `Lhs` array. Alternatively, we could free the original array and allocate an exact size in all circumstances, thus guaranteeing minimum memory use. However memory allocation is not cheap, and it may be worth avoiding excessive calls. The object-oriented view of the copy assignment operator is as follows: the expression

```
Lhs = Rhs;
```

is semantically equivalent to

6. We use the term *copy assignment operator* to differentiate `operator=` from other assignment operators such as `operator+=`.

```
Lhs.operator=( Rhs );
```

Let us examine more carefully what this means. C++ considers the assignment operators (including +=, -=, and so on) to be no different than functions, except that they can be written in a shorthand form that we are accustomed to. Consequently, to define a nondefault behavior for the copy assignment operator, we must write the body for a member function whose

- name is operator= (white space is allowed before the =)
- single parameter is a BitArray object, which we pass as a const &, for efficiency
- return value is a const &, to allow A=B=C but not (A=B)=C.

The last point is probably the most confusing. In C++ every operator evaluates to an expression. This means that for integers, A=5 assigns the value of 5 to A but also evaluates as an expression to 5 and can thus be used in a larger expression for nested assignments, testing, addition, or essentially anything. This means that operator= should not have return type void. Once we accept the fact that there is a return type, the issue becomes how we return: by value, reference, or constant reference. Return by value will call a copy constructor to create a temporary and thus is a bad idea in general, especially for the BitArray. The BitArray's copy constructor is either disabled, making this illegal, or is enabled but time-consuming. Thus a reference is returned. The only issue is whether or not the reference should (or must) be const. If the result is a reference, then the function call can appear as the target of an assignment: (A=B)=C becomes legal but not meaningful.[7] Although there are operators for which this is desirable, operator= is not one of them ([], for example, is one operator in which this behavior might be needed). Consequently, the return type is a constant reference to the object.

Assignment operators generally return constant references.

The **this** Pointer

In C++, the pointer *this* is defined to point at the current object. this is an additional keyword in C++. Think of the this pointer as a homing device that, at any instant in time, tells you where you are. Consequently, *this is the current object, and returning *this achieves the desired result. Under no circumstances will the compiler knowingly allow you to modify this. The copy assignment operator is shown in Figure 2.14. As we see, the return uses *this. The other use of this is at line 4.

*The pointer **this** points at the current object. It is used to return a constant reference for assignment operators and also to test for aliasing.*

---

7. The effect of executing this is to assign C to the reference A, without ever assigning to B.

```
1   const BitArray &
2   BitArray::operator=( const BitArray & Rhs )
3   {
4       if( this != &Rhs )          // Do not copy to yourself!!!
5       {
6           if( ArraySize < Rhs.ArraySize )
7           {   // Not enough space: extend BitArray
8               delete [ ] BitArray;
9               ArraySize = Rhs.ArraySize;
10              N = Rhs.N;
11              BitArray = new int [ ArraySize ];
12          }
13
14          for( int i = 0; i < ArraySize; i++ )
15              BitArray[ i ] = Rhs.BitArray[ i ];
16      }
17
18      return *this;
19  }
```

Figure 2.14   The copy operator for `BitArray`

Aliasing **is a special case that occurs when the same object appears in more than one role.**

The expression A=A is logically a non-operation (no-op). In some cases, although not here, failing to treat this as a special case can result in the destruction of A. As an example, consider a program that copies one file to another. A normal algorithm begins by truncating the target file to zero length. If no check is performed to make sure the source and target file are indeed different, then the source file will be truncated, hardly a desirable feature. When performing copies, the first thing we should do is check for this special case, known as *aliasing*. The rest of the routine is straightforward (although the syntax may still take some getting used to). The difficult part is that, if the current object is not prepared to hold as many items as Rhs, we have to expand the array. This involves a `delete` of the original and a call to `new`.

2.5   Additional C++ Class Features

Now that we have seen the basics of classes, we will examine some additional related issues, including

- a second look at the distinction between the initialization and assignment
- implicit type conversions for classes
- additional examples of operator overloading
- input and output, including the friend concept
- private global variables (known as private static class members)

```
1  #include <iostream.h>
2  #include "Rational.h"
3
4  // Rational number test program
5
6  main( )
7  {
8      Rational X;
9      Rational Sum = 0;
10     Rational Max = 0;
11     int N = 0;
12
13     cout << "Type as many rational numbers as you want\n";
14
15     while( cin >> X )
16     {
17         cout << "Read " << X << '\n';
18         Sum += X;
19         if( X > Max )
20             Max = X;
21         N++;
22     }
23     cout << "Read " << N << " rationals\n";
24     if( Max > IntType( 0 ) )
25         cout << "Largest positive number is " << Max << '\n';
26     if( N > 0 )
27         cout << "Average is " << Sum / IntType( N ) << '\n';
28
29     return 0;
30 }
```

Figure 2.15   Simple `main` routine to use rational numbers

To illustrate these concepts, we will design a class called `Rational` that manipulates rational numbers. A properly designed rational number class will allow us to use rational numbers as easily as any of the built-in types, such as integers, doubles, or characters. Extending the types for which an operator can be applied to is known as *operator overloading*. Figure 2.15, which reads a sequence of rational numbers and outputs their average and maximum, shows that this is certainly the case. If we replace the word `Rational` with `double` (and use `int` for `IntType` at lines 24 and 27), the program requires no other changes to compile and run.

> Extending the types for which an operator can be applied to is known as *operator overloading*.

Examining `main`, we see the use of an explicit type conversion (the comparison at line 24 and the division at line 27, in which an `IntType` is converted to a `Rational`). The other notable feature is the overloading of the input and output stream operators on lines 15, 17, 25, and 27.

Figures 2.16 and 2.17 show the interface for the `Rational` class. We have attempted to give a complete listing of the operations that might be expected, although providing an actual implementation of all these operations could require a substantial amount of coding.

```
1  // Rational class interface: support operations for rationals
2  //
3  // CONSTRUCTION: with (a) no initializer, or (b) an integer
4  //      that specifies the numerator, or (c) two integers
5  //      specifying numerator and denominator, or
6  //      (d) another Rational
7  //
8  // ******************PUBLIC OPERATIONS*********************
9  // =, +=, -=, /=, *=       --> Usual assignment
10 // +, -, /, *              --> Usual binary arithmetic
11 // <, <=, >, >=, ==, !=    --> Usual relational and equality
12 // ++, --, +, -, !         --> Usual prefix, postfix, unary
13 // >> and <<               --> Input and output
14 // double LongDecimal( )   --> Return double equivalent
15
16 #include <iostream.h>
17 typedef IntType long;     // Better method is in Chapter 3
18
19 class Rational
20 {
21   public:
22         // Constructors
23     Rational( const IntType & Numerator = 0 ) :
24         Numer( Numerator ), Denom( 1 ) { }
25     Rational( const IntType & Numerator,
26             const IntType & Denominator ) :
27         Numer( Numerator ), Denom( Denominator )
28             { FixSigns( ); Reduce( ); }
29     Rational( const Rational & Rhs ) :
30         Numer( Rhs.Numer ), Denom( Rhs.Denom ) { }
31
32         // Destructor
33     ~Rational( ) { }
34
35     // Assignment Ops (implementation in Figure 2.19)
36     const Rational & operator= ( const Rational & Rhs );
37     const Rational & operator+=( const Rational & Rhs );
38     const Rational & operator-=( const Rational & Rhs );
39     const Rational & operator/=( const Rational & Rhs );
40     const Rational & operator*=( const Rational & Rhs );
41
42     // Mathematical Binary Ops (implementation in Figure 2.20)
43     Rational operator+( const Rational & Rhs ) const;
44     Rational operator-( const Rational & Rhs ) const;
45     Rational operator/( const Rational & Rhs ) const;
46     Rational operator*( const Rational & Rhs ) const;
```

Figure 2.16   Rational class interface (part 1)

```
47      // Relational & Equality Ops (implemented in Figure 2.21)
48      int operator< ( const Rational & Rhs ) const;
49      int operator<=( const Rational & Rhs ) const;
50      int operator> ( const Rational & Rhs ) const;
51      int operator>=( const Rational & Rhs ) const;
52      int operator==( const Rational & Rhs ) const;
53      int operator!=( const Rational & Rhs ) const;
54
55      // Unary Operators (implemented in Figures 2.22 and 2.23)
56      const Rational & operator++( );        // Prefix
57      Rational operator++( int );            // Postfix
58      const Rational & operator--( );        // Prefix
59      Rational operator--( int );            // Postfix
60      const Rational & operator+( ) const;
61      Rational operator-( ) const;
62      int operator!( ) const;
63
64          // Member Function
65      double LongDecimal( ) const    // Do the division
66          { return double( Numer ) / double( Denom ); }
67
68      // I/O friends: privacy is waived (see Figure 2.24)
69      friend ostream & operator<<
70              ( ostream & Out, const Rational & Value );
71      friend istream & operator>>
72              ( istream & In,  Rational & Value );
73  private:
74          // A rational number is represented by a numerator and
75          // denominator in reduced form
76      IntType Numer;                 // The numerator
77      IntType Denom;                 // The denominator
78
79      void FixSigns( );              // Ensures Denom >= 0
80      void Reduce( );                // Ensures lowest form
81  };
```

Figure 2.17   Rational class interface (part 2)

Recall that a rational number consists of a numerator and a denominator. The data members of the class are Numer and Denom, representing the numerator and denominator. We use IntType to represent their type. IntType could be an int, although that restricts the range of rationals that can be represented, especially since intermediate calculations could easily overflow an int. (Exercise 2.30 asks you to implement a general IntType, which is a lot more work than it seems.) Some systems come with an equivalent class.[8]

---

8. *libg++*, for instance, implements the Integer type. Include the <Integer.h> header file.

```
 1 void
 2 Rational::FixSigns( )
 3 {
 4     if( Denom < 0 )
 5     {
 6          Denom = -Denom;
 7          Numer = -Numer;
 8     }
 9 }
10
11 void
12 Rational::Reduce( )
13 {
14     IntType D = 1;
15
16     if( Denom != 0 && Numer != 0 )
17          D = Gcd( Numer, Denom );
18
19     if( D > 1 )
20     {
21          Numer /= D;
22          Denom /= D;
23     }
24 }
```

Figure 2.18   Private member routines to keep `Rational`s in normal-ized format

We will maintain the invariant that the denominator is never negative and that the rational number is expressed in the lowest form. Thus, the result of 8/–12 would be represented with a numerator of –2 and a denominator of 3. We allow `Denom` to be 0, to represent either `infinity` or `-infinity` (even if `Numer` is also 0). These invariants are maintained internally by applying `FixSigns` and `Reduce` as appropriate. Those routines are shown in Figure 2.18. The `Gcd` routine computes the greatest common divisor of two integers (the first of which might be negative). For instance `Gcd(35,45)` is 5. Computing the greatest common divisor is an interesting problem in its own right, and is discussed in Section 7.4.

The remainder of this section is devoted to examining C++ features that are used in this class, namely initialization lists, type conversions, overloading of operators, and input and output.

2.5.1   Initialization vs. Assigning in the Constructor

Line 23 of the `Rational` class interface (Figure 2.16) initializes as follows:

```
Rational( const IntType & Numerator = 0 ) :
    Numer( Numerator ), Denom( 1 ){ }
```

The sequence prior to the braces is known as the *initializer list*. Alternatively, the constructor could be written as

```
Rational( const IntType & Numerator = 0 )
    { Numer = Numerator; Denom = 1; }
```

The difference is as follows: The form in the class interface, which uses an *initializer list* to specify data member initialization, initializes Numer and Denom using the one int-parameter constructor. Because the body of the constructor is empty, no further operations are performed. The alternative form initializes Numer and Denom using the no-parameter constructor. This is because any member that is not specified in the initializer list is initialized using a zero-parameter constructor. The copy assignment operator is then called to perform the two assignments that are in the body of the Rational constructor. In the case where the members being initialized are simply integers, there is no difference because the no-parameter int constructor does not do anything (which is why automatic ints are uninitialized). Imagine, however, that IntType is itself a class that represents arbitrary precision integers. In that case the alternative form is wasteful because it first initializes Numer and Denom to 0s, only to overwrite them with assignment copies. This could have important repercussions, such as requiring the costly expansion of a dynamically allocated block of memory (we will see this in the String class in Section 2.6).

> Simple initialization of class members using *initializer lists* is preferable to assignment in the constructor.

Because initialization of each class member should usually be done using its own constructor, when possible you should use explicit initializer lists. Note however, that this form is intended for simple cases only. If the initialization is not simple (for instance if it allocates memory), use an assignment. Among other things, the order of evaluation of the initializer list is given by the order in which class data members are listed. In our case, Numer is initialized before Denom only because it appears earlier in the listing of data members (of course this does not apply to assignments in the body of the constructor). If the initialization of Numer depended on the initialization of Denom being done first, we would have to switch their declaration order. If we were to do this, we would need to comment that there is an order dependency. If possible, we should avoid order dependencies.

> Members are initialized in the order they are declared, not in the order they are encountered in the initialization list. Generally, it is best to avoid writing code that depends on this fact.

2.5.2   Type Conversions

C has extravagant rules that allow the mixing of types. For instance, if I is an int and D is a double, D=I is allowed. This is known as an *implicit type conversion* because it is performed without the use of an explicit type conversion operator. A temporary T is created from I and then is used as the right side of the assignment. Some languages do not allow implicit type conversion because of the danger of accidental usage: It weakens the notion of strong typing. On the other hand, forcing all type conversions to be explicit tends to make code laden with conversions, sometimes unnecessarily.

> A *type conversion* creates a temporary object of a new type.

A constructor defines an automatic type conversion.

In C++ the rules for type conversion follow this general principle: If you can construct an object of type T1 by providing an object of another type T2, then a type conversion from T2 to T1 is guaranteed to follow the same semantics. In the case of the Rational class, any appearance of an IntType object will be implicitly converted to a (temporary) Rational when needed, as was done in the previously cited examples in main. The temporary is created by executing the constructor. If you do not like implicit type conversions, you are in trouble: There is no way to turn this feature off.

Conversions are not transitive.

A technical point: In our case, even though a conversion is defined for int to IntType and one is defined from IntType to Rational, transitivity does not hold. Thus these two conversions do not imply a third conversion from int to Rational. This is why the type conversion from int to IntType is performed in Figure 2.15 at lines 24 and 27. We could attempt to provide a constructor for Rational that takes an int. This would solve our problems by providing the third type conversion. However, if IntType is an int, then this provides two identical constructors, and the compiler will complain about the ambiguity.

Conversions can also be defined as member functions, but do not overdo it or ambiguity can result.

We can also define a type conversion by overloading operator( ). For instance, we can specify a type conversion from Rational to int by writing the member function

```
operator int ( ) const
    { Denom == 1 ? Numer : int( LongDecimal( ) ); }
```

Too many implicit conversions can easily get you in trouble; again, ambiguity can result.

2.5.3   Operator Overloading

We examine the operators in the same order as they are given in the class interface. Many of the operators, such as the assignment operators, use no new principles. Two of these are shown in Figure 2.19. However, we do have to be careful. For example, lines 15 and 16 cannot be interchanged. For the corresponding /= operator, we need to use temporaries.

A binary operator usually returns an object by value because the result is stored in a temporary. They also can be implemented by calling the corresponding assignment operator.

The next group of operators are the binary arithmetic operators. A binary operator usually returns an object by value because the result is stored in a temporary. It also can be implemented by calling the corresponding assignment operator. A simple implementation is provided in Figure 2.20 for the addition operator. Notice how we use a previously defined operator. This is an excellent general technique to master.

```
 1  const Rational &
 2  Rational::operator=( const Rational & Rhs )
 3  {
 4      if( this != &Rhs )
 5      {
 6          Numer = Rhs.Numer;
 7          Denom = Rhs.Denom;
 8      }
 9      return *this;
10  }
11
12  const Rational &
13  Rational::operator+=( const Rational & Rhs )
14  {
15      Numer = Numer * Rhs.Denom + Rhs.Numer * Denom;
16      Denom = Denom * Rhs.Denom;
17      Reduce( );
18
19      return *this;
20  }
```

Figure 2.19   Assignment operators (two of five) for `Rational` class

```
1  Rational                     // Return a copy of Answer temporary
2  Rational::operator+( const Rational & Rhs ) const
3  {
4      Rational Answer( *this );  // Initialize Answer with *this
5      Answer += Rhs;             // Add the second operand
6      return Answer;             // Return Answer by copy
7  }
```

Figure 2.20   Mathematical binary operators (1 of 4) for `Rational` class

An interesting technical issue here is the return type. As usual we have three choices: We can return by value, by reference, or by constant reference. A return by reference is certainly wrong: We cannot allow expressions like (A+B)=C because A+B is not a named object; the assignment could at best be meaningless.

Since the += operator returns a `const` &, and since a copy takes more time than a constant reference return, it appears that we are doing the wrong thing. Why not return a constant reference? The answer is that the reference would refer to an automatic object, and when the procedure returns, the object is destroyed (by the destructor). Thus `Answer` cannot be referenced. Returning a pointer to an automatic variable is a very common C mistake. Analogously, returning a reference to an automatic variable would be a common C++ mistake except that most C++ compilers will flag the error at compile time.

What if we use a `static` variable for `Answer`? There are two problems, one easy to fix, one not. The easy-to-fix problem is that the initialization is only performed once (since the object is only created once). We can fix this with an additional assignment statement. The real problem is that for any four rationals, an expression such as

```
( R1 + R2 ) == ( R3 + R4 )
```

will always be true, since the values being compared are references to the same `static` object. Thus we see that what we have done is the only correct approach. This means that a statement such as

```
R1 = R2 + R3;
```

will have to call a copy constructor to copy `Answer` into a temporary variable and then a copy assignment operator to copy the temporary into `R1`. Many compilers will optimize out the temporary and thus the copy constructor.

The next group of operators are the equality and relational operators. A typical routine is shown in Figure 2.21. For the equality operators `==` and `!=`, we can do better by avoiding the expensive (and potentially overflowing) multiplication and directly comparing numerators and denominators. We leave this as an exercise (see Exercise 2.19), with a warning that you have to be careful when the numerator or denominator is 0.

```
1  int
2  Rational::operator==( const Rational & Rhs ) const
3  {
4      return Numer * Rhs.Denom == Denom * Rhs.Numer;
5  }
```

Figure 2.21   Relational and equality operators (1 of 6) for `Rational` class

```
1  const Rational &  // Prefix form
2  Rational::operator++( )
3  {
4      Numer += Denom;
5      return *this;
6  }
7
8  Rational          // Postfix form
9  Rational::operator++( int )
10 {
11     Rational Tmp = *this;
12     Numer += Denom;
13     return Tmp;
14 }
```

Figure 2.22   Prefix and postfix operators (2 of 4) for `Rational` class

We continue with the ++ and -- operators. We will examine the incrementing operator. In C++ there are two flavors: prefix (before the operand) and postfix (after the operand). Both add 1 to an object, but the result of the expression (which is meaningful if used in a larger expression) is the new value in the prefix form and the original value in the postfix form. They are completely different in semantics and precedence. Consequently, we need to write separate routines for each form. Since they have the same name, they must have different signatures to be distinguished. This is done by specifying an empty parameter list for the prefix form and a single (anonymous) int parameter for the postfix form. ++X calls the zero-parameter operator++; X++ calls the one-parameter operator++. This int parameter is never used; it is present only to give a different signature.

The prefix and postfix forms shown in Figure 2.22 add 1 by increasing Numer by the value of Denom. In the prefix form we can then return *this by constant reference, as done for the assignment operators. The postfix form requires that we return the initial value of *this, and thus we use a temporary. Because of the temporary, we have to return by value instead of reference. Even if the copy constructor for the return is optimized away, the use of the temporary suggests that, in many cases, the prefix form will be faster than the postfix form.

The three remaining unary operators have straightforward implementations, as shown in Figure 2.23. operator! returns true if the object is zero; this is done by applying ! to the numerator. Unary operator+ evaluates to the current object; a constant reference return can be used here. operator- returns the negative of the current object by creating a new object whose numerator is the negative of the current object. The return must be by copy because the new object is a local variable. However, there is a trap lurking in operator-. If the word Rational is omitted on line 16, then the comma operator evaluates (-Numer, Denom) as Denom, and then an implicit conversion gives the rational Denom/1, which is returned.

> **Prefix and postfix ++ and -- operators have different semantics. The prefix member function is specified by an empty parameter list. The postfix form has an unused int parameter.**

What Can Be Overloaded?

In C++ all but four operators can be overloaded. The four nonoverloadable operators are ., .*, ?:, and sizeof. Precedence cannot be changed. This means that a+b*c is always a+(b*c). Arity cannot be changed so, for example, we cannot write a unary / operator or a binary ~ operator. Finally, only existing operators can be overloaded. You cannot create new operators.

2.5.4 Input and Output and Friends

The remaining operators in the Rational class are << and >> which, as discussed in Appendix A, are used for output and input. When we make the call

```
cout << R1;   // Output Rational R1
```

```
 1  int
 2  Rational::operator!( ) const
 3  {
 4      return !Numer;
 5  }
 6
 7  const Rational &
 8  Rational::operator+( ) const
 9  {
10      return *this;
11  }
12
13  Rational
14  Rational::operator-( ) const
15  {
16      return Rational( -Numer, Denom );
17  }
```

Figure 2.23   Additional unary operators (3 of 3) for `Rational` class

we see that `operator<<` takes an `ostream` and a `Rational` as parameters. Both parameters are passed by reference. The `operator<<` returns a reference to an `ostream` so that output calls can be concatenated. A similar situation occurs for the `operator>>`, the only significant difference being that the `Rational` parameter is not a constant reference.

Input and output can be defined by over-loading << and >>.

Consequently, we arrive at the following prototypes for `operator<<` and `operator>>`:

```
ostream & operator<<( ostream & Out, const Rational & );
istream & operator>>( istream & In,        Rational & );
```

These are not member functions because, when they are called, a `Rational` is not the controlling object. The only class that these could possibly be members of would be the `ostream` or `istream` class, in which case the first parameter would not be present. For example, `ostream` has a member function for `int` output:

```
ostream & operator<<( int Value );
```

Needless to say, we cannot add member functions to `ostream` every time we design a new class. Consequently, the input and output functions for `Rational` are stand-alone functions and are not members of any class. They are declared in global scope and are used just like any other function.

Figure 2.24 shows the implementation of these functions. Notice again that there is no scope resolution operator attached to their names. The input routine reads a fraction or a single integer, as appropriate. It then normalizes the fraction.

We have not attempted any of the error checking that would be required in a serious implementation. Likewise, the output routine is fairly simple and works by calling the pre-existing output routines as needed.

```
1  istream &
2  operator>>( istream & In, Rational & Value )
3  {
4      In >> Value.Numer;
5
6      char Ch;
7      In >> Ch;
8      if( Ch == '/' )
9
10         In >> Value.Denom;
11         Value.FixSigns( );
12         Value.Reduce( );
13     }
14     else
15     {
16         Value.Denom = 1;
17         In.putback( Ch );
18     }
19
20     return In;
21 }
22
23 ostream &
24 operator<<( ostream & Out, const Rational & Value )
25 {
26     if( Value.Denom != 0 )
27     {
28         Out << Value.Numer;
29         if( Value.Denom != 1 )
30             Out << '/' << Value.Denom;
31         return Out;
32     }
33
34         // Messy code for Denom == 0
35     if( Value.Numer == 0 )
36         Out << "indeterminate";
37     else
38     {
39         if( Value.Numer < 0 )
40             Out << '-';
41         Out << "infinity";
42     }
43     return Out;
44 }
```

Figure 2.24   I/O friends for `Rational` class

Friends are functions that are exempt from private restrictions.

The alert reader may have noticed something fishy in Figure 2.24: If `Numer` and `Denom` are private data members, how is a nonmember function able to access it? Under normal circumstances it cannot. To get around that restriction, the class interface has specified (at lines 69 to 72) that these functions are *friends* and so are exempt from the usual access restrictions. Notice that only the class can give additional access, and so this does not violate information-hiding principles. In general, classes should not have too many friends.

2.5.5   Static Class Members

Static class members are essentially global variables visible only to class members.

Suppose we have an object that we want all of the members of class `Rational` to share. For instance, suppose we want to keep track of the number of `Rational` objects that are currently active. What we need is essentially a global variable because any class member will be local to the instance of each object. A single global variable allows access to all of the objects. Unfortunately, it also allows access to everyone else, violating information-hiding principles. In C++ we can declare a *static class member*. A static class member is not a data member but rather is essentially a reference to a global variable whose scope is the same as a class member. In other words, there is one data member per class instead of one per object.

Our example would work as follows. In the `Rational` class, in the private section, we declare

```
static int ActiveInstances;
```

we could then increment `ActiveInstances` in the constructor and decrement it in the destructor. In the program, where we normally place definitions of global objects, we need to place the defining declaration

```
int Rational::ActiveInstances = 0;
```

An example of this is shown in the next section.

2.6   Implementing a String Class

The built-in string mechanism has lots of limitations. The **String** class attempts to overcome some of these.

In C the string is not a predefined type but rather is implemented by using a null-terminated array of characters and well-defined routines in `<string.h>`, such as `strcpy` and `strcmp`, which operate on the `char*` type. This implementation has several limitations that can be addressed by designing a `String` class.

First, copying and comparing strings looks different from copying and comparing integers. Indeed, if the = and == operators are used, they mean something quite different from a copy assignment and equality comparison, generally leading to errors. This can be fixed by overloading these operators in the `String` class.

Second, there is a storage issue. When a string is dynamically allocated (rather than using a predetermined array size), the user has to remember to `free` the memory when the string is no longer needed; otherwise, a memory leak can result. In C++ we implement this with the `String` destructor.

Another severe limitation is error handling. If the target of `strcpy` is not pointing to sufficiently large memory, disaster may strike silently. We can fix that by including the current size in a `String` class and adding an additional test to the copy assignment operator. If needed to store a larger string, we can extend the size of the string array by calling `new` and `delete` in combination.

In C, indexing an array out of bounds generally results in no warning messages, and thus if it is not sufficient to crash the program, the programmer will never realize an error has occurred. For instance, in a short string `S` the access `S[10000]` should at least generate a run-time warning that something might be amiss. We can do this in C++ by overloading the `operator[]`.

Some other more subtle issues deal with a lack of safety. In C, consider the result of

```
char S[ 10 ] = "Hello";
char *T = S;
T[ 0 ] = 'M';
```

Here the string `S` has been altered to `"Mello"` indirectly. This should not be allowed. We can prohibit this by using information hiding, prohibiting sharing of data items, and only granting access to internal members through the use of `operator[]`. We will see how this is done later.

The proposed C++ standard will contain a `string` class (note that `string` is all lower case) with scores of features. The standard will attempt to consolidate many of the popular string classes already in existence. Unfortunately, the semantics of the proposed class seem to change quickly, and as a result `string` is unusable until the standard is adopted. Many compilers come with their own string class, perhaps using a different name, but for now, if we expect to write a portable program, we need to implement our own string class.

There are lots of string libraries around. `string` will be a standard class.

```
 1  // String class interface: support operations for strings
 2  //
 3  // CONSTRUCTION: with (a) no initializer, or (b) a
 4  //      const char * (or char *), or (c) another String
 5  //
 6  // *****************PUBLIC OPERATIONS***********************
 7  // =                    --> Usual assignment
 8  // [ ]                  --> Indexing with bounds check
 9  // == != < <= > >=      --> Usual relational and equality
10  // >> and <<            --> Input and output
11  // double Length( )     --> Return strlen equivalent
```

Figure 2.25   Class interface for `String` (part 1)

```
 1  #include <iostream.h>
 2  #include <string.h>
 3
 4  class String
 5  {
 6    public:
 7      // Constructors (implementation in Figure 2.27)
 8      String( ) : BufferLen( -1 ), Buffer( NullString ) { }
 9      String( const char * Value );
10      String( const String & Value );
11
12      // Destructor
13      ~String( ) { if( BufferLen != -1 ) delete [ ] Buffer; }
14
15      // Assignment operators (implementation in Figure 2.28)
16      const String & operator=( const String & Rhs );
17      const String & operator=( const char *   Rhs );
18
19      // Get a single character (implementation in Figure 2.29)
20      // Access to the null terminator is allowed
21      char operator[]( int Index ) const;
22      char & operator[]( int Index );
23
24      // Type cast to char *; Commented out -- see text.
25      // operator const char * ( ) const { return Buffer; }
26
27      // Get the length
28      unsigned int Length( ) const { return strlen( Buffer ); }
29
30      // Friends for comparison (implementation in Figure 2.30)
31      friend int operator==  // !=, <, >, <=, >= are similar
32          ( const String & Lhs, const String & Rhs );
33
34      // Friend for output (implementation in Figure 2.31)
35      friend ostream & operator<<( ostream & Out,
36                                      const String & Value );
37    private:
38      char *Buffer;                 // Stores the chars
39      int BufferLen;                // Max strlen for Buffer
40      static char *NullString;// Member for uninitialized case
41      void GetBuffer( int MaxStrLen );
42  };
43  istream & operator>>( istream & In, String & Value );
44
45  // Place this defining declaration in the implementation file
46  char *String::NullString = "";     // Defining declaration
```

Figure 2.26   Class interface for `String` (part 2)

Because the string is such a fundamental object, a careful implementation would be expected for any serious application. We will provide the simplest implementation that meets the objectives above and point out how a library class might improve our design. We leave these improvements as an exercise (see Exercise 2.33). When we use a String class later in the text, you can assume the semantics of the String class in this chapter.

2.6.1   Interface

Figures 2.25 and 2.26 illustrate the class interface for String. The simplest mechanism for representing a string is to use two data members. First, we have a char* variable Buffer that stores the array of characters. We also maintain an integer BufferLen that represents the largest string that we are prepared to store. For efficiency, an uninitialized String is represented with BufferLen equal to −1 and Buffer pointing at the static class member NullString (lines 40 and 46). When performing a copy, we can check if BufferLen is sufficiently large; if not, we expand Buffer by a new[]/delete[] combination. A serious implementation would require additional data members. For instance, range checking requires that we know the length of the actual string being stored (that is, the position of the null terminator). This can be determined by calling strlen, but the overhead of a strlen for every string access is prohibitive. Exercise 2.33 asks you to improve this aspect of the implementation.

String objects may be defined three ways (not including syntactical equivalents):

Constructors for the String class allow several forms of initialization.

```
String S1;            // Does not allocate memory
String S2( "Hello" ); // Length 5, with a copy of "Hello"
String S3( S2 );      // Length 5, with a copy of S2
```

The fact that we can use = to initialize helps readability:

```
String S2 = "Hello";  // Length 5, with a copy of "Hello"
String S3 = S2;       // Length 5, with a copy of S2
```

Because constructors define implicit type conversions, any occurrence of a const char *, such as "100", can and will be converted to a temporary String, if necessary. As an example, consider the copy assignment operator whose declaration is shown at line 16. Suppose the copy assignment operator at line 17 was not present. In that case, only a String could be assigned to a String.

This has important ramifications. In the case of the char *, the copy assignment statement

```
Str = "junk";
```

would still work but would be inefficient. This is because a temporary String is created using the constructor at line 9, the assignment operator is performed using the member declared at line 16, and then the destructor for the temporary String is called. Clearly it is much more efficient to provide an additional operator=, overloaded to accept a `const char *` parameter, as shown at line 17. This is true for all of the operators: We can mix and match `String` and `char *` parameters in most instances, but the cost is the creation and destruction of a temporary (which involves a call to `new` and `delete`). For all these operators we need many more routines to cover the possibilities.

operator[] has a reference return type.

Lines 21 and 22 give the declarations for the overloaded `operator[]`. The first is for constant strings objects, while the second, with the return type `char &` allows expressions such as `Str[0]='M'` to make sense. Our implementation will allow access to the `NULL` terminator. Note carefully that not all libraries take this viewpoint, and in particular this means that many `String` implementations are incompatible with each other. Line 25 gives a function to perform a type conversion from a `String` to a `const char *`. We just return a pointer to the internal memory. Note carefully the return type: We do not want to convert to a plain `char*` because that would allow a `char *` object to alter the internal buffer. As a result of the type conversion, the statement

```
cout << Str;
```

is defined for the `String` type: `Str` is converted to a `char *`, and output. We have commented out this conversion because, on some compilers, it creates problems with the comparison operators, as discussed below.

```
1  void
2  String::GetBuffer( int MaxStrLen )
3  {
4      BufferLen = MaxStrLen;
5      Buffer = new char[ BufferLen + 1 ];
6  }
7
8  String::String( const char *Value )
9  {
10     if( Value == NULL )        // Use "" if Value is NULL
11     {
12         GetBuffer( 0 );
13         Buffer[ 0 ] = '\0';
14     }
15     else
16     {
17         GetBuffer( strlen( Value ) );
18         strcpy( Buffer, Value );
19     }
20 }
21
22 String::String( const String & Value )
23 {
24     GetBuffer( strlen( Value.Buffer ) );
25     strcpy( Buffer, Value.Buffer );
26 }
```

Figure 2.27   Constructors for `String` class

The remaining routines in the interface are the comparison operators. For brevity we only include == in the text (the online code has all the others). Besides the direct String comparisons, we would like to allow both S=="mark" and "mark"==S. We would like to take advantage of the implicit type conversion rules, at least for our quick and dirty implementation. As a consequence, the comparison operators cannot be member functions because the left side of a member function would have to be a String (and not the result of a type conversion). Consequently we make these nonmember functions. In that case, they must be friends of the class. In practice, we would write three functions for each operator: One would compare two String objects, one would compare a String and a char *, and one would be a friend that compares a char * and a String. On at least one of our compilers, however, if the type conversion to const char * is defined, an ambiguity develops: The compiler can (implicitly) convert to an operator== that accepts two Strings or another one that is predefined and accepts two char *s. That is why we disabled it.

> The comparison operators use implicit type conversions for flexibility. The price is the construction of lots of temporary objects. We also disable the const char * conversion to avoid possible ambiguities.

2.6.2   Implementation

The constructors are implemented in Figure 2.27. The private member function GetBuffer is used for dynamic memory allocation and to initialize BufferLen. Each of the constructors calls GetBuffer and then copies an appropriate initial value. The constructor for char * tests that the initial value is not NULL because the C string library routines are not defined for NULL pointers. The default constructor does not allocate memory because we do not want to waste space, and we do not want to incur the overhead of memory management until it is clear how much memory will be needed for the string.

The copy assignment operators use no new features. As Figure 2.28 shows, if the source String is too large, we free Buffer's memory (assuming some had been allocated) and obtain a larger chunk. Figure 2.29 shows that the indexing operator is a simple routine. We only provide the constant member version; the other is identical. Note once again that, for a serious implementation, a call to strlen is much too expensive to accompany each String access, and we would have to keep the length of the string as an additional data member. The function EXCEPTION is described in Appendix D. If the first parameter is true, the second parameter is output, and then the program is aborted. This is a temporary fix until the exception-handling mechanisms are stable.

> operator[] is grossly inefficient.

The comparison operators, one of which is given in Figure 2.30, are also very simple. Finally, in Figure 2.31, we show the input and output operations for the String class. Output is completely trivial. For input we declare a large array of chars, read into it, and assign it to the String. A serious implementation would ensure that the 1024-byte limit on input of char * objects is observed.

```
1 const String &
2 String::operator=( const String & Rhs )
3 {
4     const int Len = strlen( Rhs.Buffer );
5
6     if( this != &Rhs )          // Don't copy to yourself
7     {
8         if( Len >= BufferLen )
9         {
10            if( BufferLen != -1 )
11                delete [ ] Buffer;
12            GetBuffer( Len );
13        }
14        strcpy( Buffer, Rhs.Buffer );
15    }
16
17    return *this;
18 }
19
20 const String &
21 String::operator=( const char * Rhs )
22 {
23     if( Rhs == NULL )
24         Rhs = "";
25
26     const int Len = strlen( Rhs );
27     if( Len >= BufferLen )
28     {
29         if( BufferLen != -1 )
30             delete [ ] Buffer;
31         GetBuffer( Len );
32     }
33     strcpy( Buffer, Rhs );
34
35     return *this;
36 }
```

Figure 2.28   Copy assignment operator for String class

```
1 char
2 String::operator[]( int Index ) const
3 {
4     EXCEPTION( Index < 0 || Index > strlen( Buffer ),
5                "Index out of range" );
6     return Buffer[ Index ];
7 }
```

Figure 2.29   Overload of [ ] for String class to perform bounds check
              (nonconstant version is omitted)

```
1  int
2  operator==( const String & Lhs, const String & Rhs )
3  {
4      return strcmp( Lhs.Buffer, Rhs.Buffer ) == 0;
5  }
```

Figure 2.30   Equality test for `String` class; others are all similar and omitted

```
1  istream &
2  operator>>( istream & In, String & Value )
3  {
4      static char Str[ 1024 ];     // Internal buffer
5
6      In >> Str;
7      Value = Str;
8      return In;
9  }
10
11 ostream &
12 operator<<( ostream & Out, const String & Value )
13 {
14     return Out << Value.Buffer;
15 }
```

Figure 2.31   Simplistic I/O for `Strings`; only the output routine is a friend

2.7   Recap: What Gets Called and What Are the Defaults?

In this section we summarize what gets called in various circumstances. First, for initialization we have the following examples:

```
String R;            // String( )
String S = "Hello";  // String( const char * )
String T = S;        // String( const String & )
```

Next, we have cases where there are exact matches:

```
R = T;               // operator=( const String & )
S = "world";         // operator=( const char * )
R[0] = 'J';          // operator[] followed by character copy
```

In the last case, the nonconstant `operator[]` is used. Here is an example that involves an implicit call to a constructor to create a temporary object:

```
if( R == "Jello" ) // String( const char * ) to
                   // create temporary; then operator==
```

Note, however, that newer versions of the compiler will not perform this conversion if the corresponding formal parameter is a (nonconstant) reference. In other words, if we have

```
int operator==( const String & Lhs, String & Rhs );
```

`"Jello"` fails to match `Rhs`. This is because the declaration of `==` is stating that `Rhs` may be altered, which does not make sense if `Rhs` is merely a temporary copy of `"Jello"`. Furthermore, for operators that are class members, the first actual parameter must be an exact match.

The copy constructor is also called if a `String` is passed by value to a function expecting a string, or returned by copy. Thus if the declaration for `==` was

```
int operator==( String Lhs, String Rhs );
```

then `S` would be copied to `Lhs` by a call to the `String` copy constructor, and `"Jello"` would be copied to `Rhs` by a call to the `String(const char *)` constructor.

Other examples in which a `String` constructor is called are the following:

```
String Array[ 100 ];                       // 100 calls
String *Ptr1 = new String;                 // 1 call
String *Ptr2 = new String( "junk" ); // 1 call
String *Ptr3 = new String( S );      // 1 call
String *Ptr4 = new String[ 100 ];    // 100 calls
```

but not

```
String *Ptr = new String( 100 );     // No String(int)
String & Ref = S;                          // 0 call: reference
```

If any of the members required above is placed in the private section, then the corresponding operations become illegal. The most common operators for which this is done are the copy constructor and `operator=`.

It is also important to understand what happens when you fail to provide a default constructor, copy constructor, destructor, or `operator=`.

If no constructor is provided, then a default zero-parameter constructor is created. It will perform a member-by-member construction of the class data members. This happens only when no constructors are provided, so if you provided a `String( const char * )` constructor but no `String( )` constructor, then you have merely disallowed uninitialized `String` definitions.

If no copy constructor is provided, then a default copy constructor is created. It will perform member-by-member copy construction. Note that if the copy constructor is disabled for some member, then this will generate a compiler error.

If no destructor is provided, then a default destructor is created that performs member-by-member destruction (in inverse order of the member declarations).

Finally, if no `operator=` is provided, then a default is created that performs member-by-member copying using each member's `operator=`. As with the copy constructor, if `operator=` is disabled for some member, then a compiler error will be generated.

2.8   Separate Compilation

Most but not all compilers support separate compilation. We can place class declarations (that is, interfaces) in a file that ends in `.h`. If we use public inline functions, those definitions must also be in the interface. Any nonmember functions that are not friends should have a declaration in the interface file (and an implementation if they are inline). The class implementation should be in a `.cpp` file that includes the interface.

We need to be sure that files that are the target of multiple `#include` directives are only processed once. We can do this by using additional preprocessing directives. Specifically, for each file, which we will call `FileName`, use the following method:

> **Use `#ifndef` and `#endif` to enclose the contents of a header file and prevent multiple inclusion.**

```
#ifndef  FileName_
#define _FileName_
     // normal contents of FileName
#endif
```

The first time `FileName` is processed, the symbol `_FileName_` is not defined. Thus the `#ifndef` is true, `_FileName_` is defined, and then the contents of `FileName` are read. If there is a second attempt to `#include File-Name`, then the `#ifndef` will be false, and we will skip to the matching `#endif`. Note that this practice should always be adhered to. Some systems require it to avoid double reading during linking stages.

The normal procedure for separate compilation should then be used. Not all compilers support separate compilation, especially when the features in the next chapter are used. If the compiler is limited in this way, then we will have to make it appear that everything is in one file by using lots of `#include` statements.

Summary

This chapter has described the C++ class construct. The class is the C++ mechanism that is used to create new types. Through it we can

- define construction and destruction of objects
- define copy semantics
- define input and output operations

- overload almost all operators
- define implicit and explicit type conversion operations (sometimes a bad thing)
- provide for information hiding and atomicity

The class consists of two parts: the interface and the implementation. The interface tells the user of the class what the class does. The implementation does it. The implementation frequently contains proprietary code and in some cases is only distributed in precompiled form.

Information hiding can be enforced by using the `private` directive in the interface. Initialization of objects is controlled by the constructor functions, and the destructor function is called when an object goes out of scope. The destructor typically cleans up after the constructor, closing files and freeing memory. Finally, we saw that the use of the `const` directive and references, as well as the decision on whether to accept a default copy, provide our own, or completely disallow it is crucial for not only efficiency but also in some cases, correctness.

Objects of the Game

#endif and #ifndef Are used to enclose the contents of a header file and prevent multiple inclusion. (87)

aliasing A special case that occurs when the same object appears in more than one role. (66)

atomic unit In reference to an object, its parts cannot be dissected by the general users of the object. (48)

bit array Stores an array of bits and provides basic operations to turn bits on or off and return their current status. (52)

class The same as a structure except that, by default, all members are inaccessible. (48)

constant member function A function that does not change any class data members. (63)

constructor Tells how an object is declared and initialized. The default constructor is a member-by-member application of a no-parameter constructor. (57)

copy assignment operator operator= Used to copy objects. (64)

copy constructor Called when an object is passed or returned by value, or initialized with an object of the same class. By default, the copy constructor is a member-by-member application of copy constructors. Placing the declaration in the private section disables the copy constructor. (59)

destructor When an object exits scope, the destructor is called. It should free up resources allocated by the constructor or other member functions. The default destructor is member-by-member application. (58)

encapsulation The grouping of data and the operations that apply to them to form an aggregate while hiding the implementation of the aggregate. (48)

friend Functions that are exempt from private restrictions. (78)

implementation Represents the internals of how the interface specifications are met. As far as the class user is concerned, the implementation is not important. (50)

implicit type conversion A type conversion performed without the use of an explicit type conversion operator. (71)

information hiding Makes implementation details, including components of an object, inaccessible. (48)

initializer list Specifies non-default initialization of each data member in an object. (71)

input and output Can be defined by overloading << and >>. (76)

interface The class interface describes the functionality, but not the implementation. (50)

member function Functions supplied as additional members that operate on an instance of the structure. (49)

object Entities that have structure and state. Each object defines operations that may access or manipulate that state. (47)

operator overloading Extending the types for which an operator can be applied to. (67)

private Members in the private section are not visible to nonclass routines. (54)

public Only members in the public section are visible to nonclass routines. (54)

scope operator : : Used to refer to the scope. In a class member function, the scope is the class. (58)

signature Includes the types of parameters in the function, including `const` and & directives, but not the return type. (62)

static class member Essentially a global variable visible only to class members. (78)

this A pointer that points at the current object. It is used to return a constant reference for assignment operators and also to test for aliasing. (65)

type conversion Creates a temporary object of a new type. A constructor defines an automatic type conversion. (71)

Common Errors

1. The class interface ends with a semicolon.
2. The declaration `Rational R( );` does not call the zero-parameter constructor. Instead it is a declaration that function R accepts no parameters and returns a `Rational`.
3. The default copy is a shallow copy. If data members are pointers to

dynamically allocated objects, then generally the default is unacceptable and should either be changed or disabled.

4. Failure to test for aliasing in assignment operators can lead to errors.

5. The class member function definitions must be preceded by a class name and scope operator. Otherwise, they will not be recognized as class members. Exported class objects (such as `ios::in`) also require the class name and scope operator.

6. A common programming error is using the incorrect parameter-passing mechanism.

7. Forgetting to free memory in a destructor can lead to memory leaks.

8. Several errors are associated with the input and output routines (`>>` and `<<`) for classes. First, in many cases they must be friends. If they are not friends, the declarations must be placed in the interface file after the interface. A stream reference should be returned in both cases. It is a common error to return `cin` or `cout` instead of the stream that is passed as a parameter.

9. The interface should be enclosed by an `#ifndef #endif` pair to avoid double scanning.

10. Constant class members can be initialized only in the constructor initializer list (since they cannot be assigned to). This means that constant arrays cannot be placed in the class as data members. Make them static class members instead. Furthermore, constant integer types can be specified by using the `enum` trick.

11. Reference class members can only be initialized in the constructor initializer list.

12. All instances of `const` are parts of the signature. If you specify a function as a constant member in the interface but not in the implementation, you will get an error that the nonmember function was not declared in the interface. Similar rules apply with parameters.

13. Private members cannot be accessed outside of the class. Remember that, by default, class members are private.

14. Type conversions can lead to troubles. One problem is that they can lead to ambiguities when exact matches are not found and approximate matches are examined. Additionally, in some cases there is substantial overhead that is required when accepting implicit conversions.

15. Exact matches are needed for reference parameters. Some compilers will give only cryptic warnings.

16. If you provide a declaration for a constructor or destructor, you must provide an implementation. Otherwise, the compiler will complain when you try to declare the object. If you provide a declaration for a member function, the implementation may be omitted if no attempt is made to use the member function. This allows incremental implementation of the class.

17. Functions that return new objects (such as `operator+`) must return them by copy. Functions that return existing objects (such as `operator+=`) should use constant reference returns unless a reference return is warranted.

18. `this` is a pointer constant and may not be altered.

19. Using inline functions can lead to many errors. Public inline functions must be defined in the interface file, and some compilers will not allow them in certain cases (for instance if they throw an exception). Avoid public inline functions unless you can prove that they yield a substantial speed benefit.

20. Prefix and postfix ++ are different operators. It is an error to use one form when only the other form is implemented by the class.

21. For static class members, in addition to the class declaration, a single definition must be provided outside of the class.

22. Relying on a library string class is dangerous practice until a standard is adopted. Use your own class for now.

On the Internet

The `String` class is used in several other routines. Consequently there is no `main` to test it. The files that are available are

BitArray.h   Interface file for the `BitArray` class, as shown in Figure 2.7.

BitArray.cpp Implementation of the `BitArray` class.

BitMain.cpp   Test routine for the `BitArray` class, as shown in Figure 2.5.

Rational.h   Interface file for the `Rational` class.

Rational.cpp Implementation of the `Rational` class.

RatMain.cpp   Test routine for the `Rational` class, as shown in Figure 2.15.

String.h   Interface file for the `String` class, as shown in Figure 2.26.

String.cpp   Casual implementation of the `String` class.

Exercises

In Short

2.1.   What is information hiding? What is encapsulation? How does C++ support these concepts?

2.2.   Explain the public and private sections of the class.

2.3.   Describe the roles of the constructor and destructor.

2.4.   What is the difference between a copy constructor and a copy assignment operator?

2.5.   If a class provides no constructor and no destructor, what is the result?

2.6.   When is it acceptable not to provide a destructor? `operator=`? copy constructor?

2.7.   Explain the benefits and liabilities of inline functions.

2.8.   What restrictions are placed on operator overloading?

2.9.   What is a friend function?

2.10.   For a class `ClassName`, what declarations are needed to perform input and output? Where are the function definitions placed?

2.11.   In the following piece of code, what functions get called at each line, and what is the semantic meaning?

```
Rational A;
Rational B = 3;
Rational C( 4, 3 );
Rational D( 0 );
Rational E = ( 4, 3 );
Rational F( );
Rational *G = new Rational( 4, 3 );
Rational *H = new Rational( 5 );
Rational *I = new Rational[ 5 ];
```

2.12.   For the last three definitions in Exercise 2.11, what needs to be done to avoid a memory leak?

2.13.   Some compilers complain if a class has no public members and no friends. Why?

2.14.   What does the `sizeof` operator do when applied on a class that has private members?

In Theory

2.15.   A complete set of baseball cards consists of 750 cards. Five kids each purchase 750 cards randomly, expecting to trade away duplicates so that each can have a complete set. Use the results in Section 2.3 to determine if this strategy will succeed.

2.16. Why can't the following be used to indicate the copy constructor for class `Rational`?

```
Rational( Rational Rhs );
```

In Practice

2.17. Add the `Flip` member function to the `BitArray` class. The expression `B.Flip(i)` toggles bit `i` in `BitArray B`.

2.18. The expression `1<<(i%IntSz)` appears repeatedly in the `BitArray` implementation shown in Figure 2.11. Write a private inline member function to implement this code, and have the appropriate `BitArray` members call it. Experiment with a profiler to determine if an inline directive yields a performance improvement.

2.19. Add the following improvements to the `Rational` class:

a. Rewrite `operator==` and `operator!=` to avoid multiplications.

b. Implement $\dfrac{N1}{D1} \times \dfrac{N2}{D2}$ as $\dfrac{N1}{D2} \times \dfrac{N2}{D1}$. Reduce $\dfrac{N1}{D2}$ and then $\dfrac{N2}{D1}$ prior to the multiplication. The result need not be reduced. Why? What is the advantage of this scheme?

c. What other operations are affected by this rearrangement?

d. Overload `^` to perform exponentiation. What are some of the problems that can occur? What is `1+2^3`?

2.20. Additional routines are required for the `String` class so that temporaries are not created when a `char *` is involved:

a. For the class interface in Figure 2.26, how many additional routines are needed?

b. Implement some subset of these.

2.21. Define `operator()` (with two parameters) to return a substring. For example, the output resulting from

```
String S = "abcd";
cout << S(1,2);
```

is `bc` (after all of the implicit conversions are applied).

a. What is the return type?

b. Implement the substring operator.

c. Is there a substantial difference between the following two alternatives?

```
      // Alternative 1
String SubStr = S( 1, 2 );

      // Alternative 2
String SubStr;
SubStr = S( 1, 2 );
```

2.22. If S is a `String`, is the typical C mistake `S='a'` caught by the compiler? Why or why not?

2.23. Add operations to allow the copy assignment of a single `char`, concatenation of `char`, and initialization with a `char`.

2.24. A *combination lock* has the following basic properties: the combination (a sequence of three numbers) is hidden; the lock can be opened by providing the combination; the combination can be changed but only by someone who knows the current combination. Design a class with public member functions `Open` and `ChangeCombo` and private data members that store the combination. The combination should be set in the constructor. Disable copying of combination locks.

Programming Projects

2.25. Implement a simple `Date` class. You should be able to represent any date from January 1, 1800, to December 31, 2500, subtract two dates, increment a date by a number of days, and compare two dates using <. A `Date` is represented internally as the number of days since some starting time, which here is the start of 1800. This makes all operations except for I/O trivial.

The rule for leap years is: A year is a leap year if it is divisible by 4, and not divisible by 100 unless it is also divisible by 400. Thus 1800, 1900, and 2100 are not leap years, but 2000 is. The input operation must check the validity of the input. The output operation must check the validity of the `Date`. The `Date` could be bad if a + or − operator caused it to go out of range.

Figure 2.32 gives a class specification skeleton for the `Date` class. Several items are missing, including `public` and `private` keywords, `const` and `&`, and I/O interfaces. Before you begin coding the interface, you must make some decisions:

- where to use `const` and/or `&` (think about this very carefully)
- whether you are willing to accept the defaults for the copy assignment and copy constructor operators
- how you will interface for input and output
- what should and should not be private

```
 1  #include <iostream.h>
 2
 3  class Date
 4  {
 5      enum { FirstYear = 1800, MaxYear = 2500 };
 6
 7      int TotalDays;                      // Days since 1/1/1800
 8
 9      // Constructor.
10      Date( int Y = FirstYear, int M = 1, int D = 1 );
11
12      // Assignment Operator (instead of +)
13      Date operator+=( int Days );
14
15      // Binary Operators.
16      int operator-( Date Right );
17      int operator<( Date Right );
18  };
```

Figure 2.32   Class specification SKELETON for Date (Exercise 2.25)

Once you have decided on the interface, you can do an implementation. The difficult part is converting between the internal and external representations of a date. What follows is a possible algorithm. Set up two arrays that are static data members (the defining declarations below are placed where globals would be):

```
static int Date::DaysTillFirstOfMonth[ ] =
    { 0, 31, 59 ,... }
static int*Date::DaysTillJan1 = NULL;
```

The first array, DaysTillFirstOfMonth, will contain the number of days until the first of each month in a nonleap year. Thus it contains 0, 31, 59, 90, and so on. The second array, DaysTillJan1, will contain the number of days until the first of each year, starting with FirstYear. Thus it contains 0, 365, 730, 1095, 1460, 1826, and so on because 1800 is not a leap year but 1804 is. You should have your program initialize this array once. If you choose this algorithm, you will need to add corresponding static class declarations in the interface. In any of the member functions, you will be able to access these arrays as you would any member. For nonmember friends, you will have to use the scope resolution operator. For nonmember nonfriends, these items will not be visible. You can then use the array to convert from the internal to external representations.

2.26.   Implement an INT class. Use a single int as the private data. Support all the operations that can be applied to an int, and allow both initialization by an int and no initialization. Explain whether you need or can accept the default copy constructor, destructor, and copy assignment operator.

2.27. Continue Exercise 2.26:

a. Modify the += operator (and by inference the binary + operator) to detect overflow. To do this, change the internal representation to an `unsigned int`, and store a sign bit separately. Print a warning message if an overflow is detected (or throw an exception if you can).

b. Modify the -= operator to detect overflow.

c. Modify the /= operator to detect division by 0.

d. Modify the unary minus operator to detect overflow (there is only one case where this happens).

e. Modify the bit shift operators to print an illegal message if the second parameter is either negative or not smaller than the number of bits in an `unsigned int`.

2.28. Suppose we want to modify the *= operator to detect overflow. Redo Exercise 2.27 by changing the internal representation to use two data members: one stores the leading bits and the other stores the trailing bits. As an example, for 32 bit integers, we have $X = 2^{16}H + L$, where H and L are 16 bits each.

2.29. Redo Exercise 2.26 by changing the internal representation to a single pointer (there is no compelling reason to do this except to illustrate pointers as data members). How does this change the class; specifically, are some defaults no longer applicable?

2.30. Implement a complete `IntType` class. Maintain an `IntType` as a sufficiently large array. For this class the difficult operation is division, followed closely by multiplication. Begin by writing the class interface. Once again, you need to decide on an internal representation, what operations will be supported, how to pass parameters, whether you are willing to accept the default for copy assignment and copy construction, how you will provide I/O, how you will provide an implicit conversion from an `int` to an `IntType`, and what should and should not be private. Do not even think about writing an actual implementation until you have thought through the interface design. Only then should you begin the task of writing the actual algorithms that implement the class.

2.31. Implement a `Complex` number class. Recall that a complex number consists of a real and an imaginary part. Support the same operations as the `Rational` class, when meaningful (for instance operator< is not meaningful). Add member functions to extract the real and imaginary parts.

2.32. Implement a `Boolean` class. Define constants `Boolean::True` and `Boolean::False`, support `&&`, `||`, `^`, `~` (for *NOT*), and I/O operations. Also provide a type conversion to `int` so that the `Boolean` can be used to express a condition (in an `if`, `while`, and so on).

2.33. Implement some of the following improvements to the `String` class:

    a. Add a data member to store the current string length, thus avoiding repeated calls to `strlen` for [ ].

    b. Add `!` (which is false if the string is zero length).

    c. Add the `+` and `+=` operators to perform string concatenation.

    d. Add the `*` and `*=` operators to expand into multiple copies. For instance, if `S = "ab";` then `S*=3` turns S into `"ababab"`.

    e. Add the left shift operator, which shifts the string over by X positions. Can you think of a way to alter the class implementation to make shifting a fast operation?

    f. Add `LowerCase` and `UpperCase` member functions.

    g. Add I/O routines that are more robust.

2.34. Index range checking costs the user time and space but greatly improves software reliability. Write a program that reads a large dictionary storing each word in a `String`. Then access each character in the array of strings (assuming you have implemented the extra data member required to avoid repeated calls to `strlen`). Measure the time cost of range checking by running the program twice: once with range checking on and again with it disabled. Also measure the difference in space usage. Use a preprocessor conditional to disable range checking on access.

References

More information on implementation of the `IntType` class can be found in [2]. An example of a production quality `String` class is given in [1]. Tips on the correct use of `const` and references as well as many advanced topics are discussed in [3].

1. B. Flamig, *Practical Data Structures in C++*, John Wiley and Sons, New York, 1993.

2. D. E. Knuth, *The Art of Computer Programming, Vol. 2: Seminumerical Algorithms* 2d ed., Addison-Wesley, Reading, MA, 1981.

3. S. Meyers, *Effective C++*, Addison-Wesley, Reading, MA, 1992.

Chapter 3

Templates

An important goal of object-oriented program is to support code reuse. This chapter introduces one mechanism that is used to further this goal, the C++ *template*. The template allows us to write routines that work for arbitrary types, without knowing, as we write the routines, what these types will be. Although this is supported somewhat by the use of the typedef facility, the template is more powerful than the typedef.

In this chapter, we will see

- what a template is and how it differs from the typedef
- how to write some useful template functions
- how to write template classes
- the limitations of templates

3.1   What Is a Template?

Suppose we want to write a Swap routine in Figure 1.17 for doubles instead of ints. The logic is identical; we just need to change the type declarations. One way to do this is to write the Swap routine for an arbitrary Etype and then issue the appropriate typedef. The typedef is a simple mechanism to allow generic routines. This is shown in Figure 3.1.

The typedef is a simple mechanism to allow generic routines. However it is unsuitable if we want routines with two different types.

Suppose, however, that we want to use Swap for both int and double. Certainly this would be acceptable because the two Swap routines would have different signatures. The typedef would not work because Etype cannot assume both int and double simultaneously. C++ provides templates that make it possible to write a routine that can be used for both types.

```
1 typedef double Etype;
2
3 // Standard Swap routine
4
5 void
6 Swap( Etype & Lhs, Etype & Rhs )
7 {
8     Etype Tmp = Lhs;
9
10    Lhs = Rhs;
11    Rhs = Tmp;
12 }
```

Figure 3.1   Swap routine using typedefs

A *template* function is a design for a function.

A *template* function is not an actual function but instead is a pattern for what could become an actual function. For example, a template for a Swap routine is shown in Figure 3.2. This design is expanded (much like a preprocessor macro) as needed to provide an actual routine. If a call to Swap with two int parameters is made, the compiler will generate a routine from the template shown in Figure 3.2, using lines 5 through 11, with int replacing Etype.

When the template is *instantiated* with a particular type, a new function is logically created.

This expansion *instantiates* the template function. The compiler must now check that the instantiation is legal C++. Some of the checking may have been performed when the template was defined. For example, missing semicolons and unbalanced parentheses are easy to check. Some checks cannot be performed that early. For instance, operator= might be disallowed for the instantiated type, and that check could only be performed at the point of instantiation. In that case the Swap operation could not work. If the instantiated type does not have a copy constructor but does have operator=, we could rewrite the template Swap routine in Figure 3.2 to avoid the copy constructor. Thus there is occasionally a trade-off between requiring more operations to be supported by the template parameter and code compactness (and/or efficiency).

Only one instantiation is created for each parameter type combination.

Figure 3.3 shows the template Swap routine in use. Each call to Swap with previously unseen parameter types generates new instantiations. Thus if there are two calls to Swap(int,int) and one call to Swap(double,double), then there are two instantiations of the template Swap: one with Etype of int and another with Etype of double.

3.2   Template Functions

Swapping is a classic example of a routine that is type independent and thus well suited for a template implementation. In this section we will give two more routines that use templates and show how a main routine uses them.

```
1   // Template Swap routine
2   // Etype: must have copy constructor and operator=
3
4   template <class Etype>
5   void
6   Swap( Etype & Lhs, Etype & Rhs )
7   {
8       Etype Tmp = Lhs;
9       Lhs = Rhs;
10      Rhs = Tmp;
11  }
```

Figure 3.2   Template Swap routine

```
1   // Exercise the template Swap routine
2
3   main( )
4   {
5       int X = 5;
6       int Y = 7;
7       double A = 2;
8       double B = 4;
9
10      Swap( X, Y );    // Instantiates Swap with int
11      Swap( X, Y );    // Uses already instantiated Swap with int
12      Swap( A, B );    // Instantiates Swap with double
13      cout << X << Y << A << B << '\n';
14  //  Swap( X, B );    // Illegal: no match
15
16      return 0;
17  }
```

Figure 3.3   Using the template Swap routine.

Our simple program will read a sequence of integers (until the end of input or bad input is detected), and will sort and output them. If we change our minds and decide that we want a sequence of floating point numbers or String objects, then we expect only a one-word change (in one location) to the entire program.[1] Sorting will be accomplished by a simple template sort routine. The other template routine performs the array-doubling that is needed because the number of input items is not known in advance. That routine is shown in Figure 3.4. As we can see, its first line indicates it is a template. Otherwise, it is very similar to lines 18 to 25 in the routine shown in Figure 1.11. However, this routine exposes a template limitation in some compilers (which is mentioned in Section 3.5).

The array-doubling template might not be instantiated by some compilers because of a technicality concerning the pointer being passed by reference.

---

1. Of course this would be true of the typedef, too. If our program were more complex and required two types of sorts, then the typedef would be inadequate.

```
1   // Array doubling: Exapand Array and double CurrentSize
2   // Etype: must have zero-parameter constructor and operator=
3
4   template <class Etype>
5   void
6   DoubleArray( Etype * & Array, int & CurrentSize )
7   {
8       Etype * OldArray = Array;
9       const int MinSize = 5;
10      int NewSize  = Array ? 2 * CurrentSize : MinSize;
11
12      Array = new Etype [ NewSize ];
13      for( int i = 0; i < CurrentSize; i++ )
14          Array[ i ] = OldArray[ i ];
15      CurrentSize = NewSize;
16
17      delete [ ] OldArray;        // Safe even if OldArray is NULL
18  }
```

Figure 3.4   Templated array doubling

```
1   // InsertionSort: sort first N items in array A
2   // Etype: must have copy constructor, operator=, and operator<
3
4   template <class Etype>
5   void
6   InsertionSort( Etype A[ ], int N )
7   {
8       for( int P = 1; P < N; P++ )
9       {
10          Etype Tmp = A[ P ];
11          int j;
12
13          for( j = P; j > 0 && Tmp < A[ j - 1 ]; j-- )
14              A[ j ] = A[ j - 1 ];
15          A[ j ] = Tmp;
16      }
17  }
```

Figure 3.5   Templated insertion sort

Insertion sort is a simple sorting algorithm that is appropriate for small inputs.

Sorting is implemented by an algorithm known as *insertion sort*. Insertion sort is generally considered a good solution if only a few elements need sorting because it is such a short algorithm. If we are dealing with a large amount of data, however, then insertion sort is a poor choice because it is too time consuming. In that case better algorithms should be used, as discussed in Chapter 8. The insertion sort algorithm is coded in Figure 3.5.

Insertion sort works as follows. The initial state is that the first element, considered by itself, is sorted. The final state that we need to attain is that all elements, considered as a group, are sorted. Figure 3.6 shows that the basic action of insertion sort is to arrange that elements in positions 0 through P (where P ranges from 1 to N−1) are sorted. In each stage P increases by 1. That is what the outer loop at line 8 in Figure 3.5 is controlling.

When the body of the for loop is entered at line 10, we are guaranteed that the elements in array positions 0 through P−1 are already sorted, and we need to extend this to positions 0 to P. Figure 3.7 gives a closer look at what has to be done, detailing only the relevant part of the array. At each step the element in boldface type needs to be added to the previously sorted part of the array. This is easily done by placing it in a temporary variable and sliding all of the elements that are larger than it over one position to the right. After that is done we can copy the temporary variable into the former position of the leftmost relocated element (indicated by lighter shading on the following line). We keep a counter j, which is the position where the temporary variable should be written back to. j decreases by 1 every time an element is slid over. Lines 10 to 15 implement this.

Array position	0	1	2	3	4	5
Initial State:	8	5	9	2	6	3
After A[0..1] is sorted:	5	8	9	2	6	3
After A[0..2] is sorted:	5	8	9	2	6	3
After A[0..3] is sorted:	2	5	8	9	6	3
After A[0..4] is sorted:	2	5	6	8	9	3
After A[0..5] is sorted:	2	3	5	6	8	9

Figure 3.6   Basic action of insertion sort (shaded part is sorted)

Array position	0	1	2	3	4	5
Initial State:	8	5				
After A[0..1] is sorted:	5	8	9			
After A[0..2] is sorted:	5	8	9	2		
After A[0..3] is sorted:	2	5	8	9	6	
After A[0..4] is sorted:	2	5	6	8	9	3
After A[0..5] is sorted:	2	3	5	6	8	9

Figure 3.7   Closer look at action of insertion sort (dark shading indicates sorted area; light shading is where new element was placed)

It is important to check that this insertion sort works in two boundary cases. First, in Figure 3.7, if the boldface element already is the largest in the group, then it is copied out to the temporary variable and then back immediately, and thus is correct. If the boldface element is the smallest in the group, then the entire group moves over, and the temporary is copied into array position zero. We just need to be careful that we do not run past the end of the array. Thus we can be sure that when the outer `for` loop terminates, the array is sorted.

Now that we have the support functions done, we can write `main`. This is shown in Figure 3.8. Using template functions is very easy. At line 17 we make a call to `DoubleArray`. There is no `DoubleArray` explicitly defined to take an `int *` and an `int` as parameters. However, there is a template `DoubleArray`, so the compiler tries to see if the template can be instantiated to provide a match. It finds that the template function `DoubleArray` using `int` for `Etype` will match. Note carefully that if the compiler finds more than one match, it will complain.[2] In this case you can explicitly tell it to expand the template function using the `<>` syntax. You would write

```
DoubleArray<int>( Array, MaxSize );
```

We will see that in many cases the `<>` is needed for template classes. Likewise, the compiler's matching algorithm will convert line 21 to

```
InsertionSort<int>( Array, ItemsRead );
```

and the `InsertionSort` template will be expanded to generate a function with `Etype` of `int`. *Warning*: This is a recent language addition and some compilers will generate errors when you instantiate a function call explicitly. They should not.

We can use templates to have array doubling and sorting at our fingertips for any type. However, it does not always make sense. Let us look at a couple of different types:

1. `double`: No problem; a one-line change in `main` and everything works well.

2. `Rational`: No problem; a one-line change in `main` and everything works well.

3. `char *`: Serious problem; the `operator=` and `operator<` do not make sense, so the program will not work. Specifically, we cannot just read into a `char *` object without first setting aside memory. Assuming we have done that, then the sort will not work because `operator<` for two `char *` objects compares their memory locations.

---

2. If the compiler finds several approximate matches (that is, matches that require a type conversion), then there are elaborate and ever-changing rules that govern which match (if any) should be used.

4. String: Efficiency problem; the algorithm will work, but the cost is overly expensive because of repeated calls to operator=. The result will be that we will do excessive String copies, which are very expensive. A solution to this problem is discussed in Chapter 8 (it involves moving pointers rather than the actual String objects).

5. A type for which operator<, or some needed operator is not defined: This will generate an error at link time. At that point, the linker will notice that operator< is not implemented. Note that this occurs even if operator> is implemented.

6. A type for which operator= is disallowed via placement in the private section: This will generate an error at compile time when the template is instantiated.

As a result, it is good practice to place in a comment a listing of the conditions that must be satisfied by the template parameter.

```
1  #include <iostream.h>
2  #include <stdio.h>
3
4  // Read an arbitrary number of items, sort and print them.
5
6  main( )
7  {
8      int *Array = NULL;       // The array
9      int X;                   // An item to read
10     int ItemsRead = 0;       // Number of items read so far
11     int MaxSize = 0;         // Number of items Array can hold
12
13     cout << "Enter items to sort: " << endl;
14     while( cin >> X )
15     {
16         if( ItemsRead >= MaxSize )
17             DoubleArray( Array, MaxSize ); // See text warning
18         Array[ ItemsRead++ ] = X;
19     }
20
21     InsertionSort( Array, ItemsRead );
22
23     cout << "Sorted items are: " << endl;
24     for( int i = 0; i < ItemsRead; i++ )
25         cout << Array[ i ] << '\n';
26
27     return 0;
28  }
```

Figure 3.8 main routine to read some integers, sort them, and output them

```
 1  // MemoryCell template class interface: simulate one Etype RAM
 2
 3  // Etype: must have zero-parameter constructor and operator=
 4  // CONSTRUCTION: with (a) no initializer or
 5  //                     (b) another MemoryCell
 6  // ****************PUBLIC OPERATIONS********************
 7  // Etype Read( )           --> Return stored value
 8  // void Write( Etype X )   --> Place X as stored value
 9
10  template <Class Etype>
11  class MemoryCell
12  {
13    public:
14          // Public member functions
15      const Etype & Read( ) const      { return StoredValue; }
16      void Write( const Etype & X )    { StoredValue = X; }
17    private:
18          // Private internal data representation
19      Etype StoredValue;
20  };
```

Figure 3.9   Complete declaration of a `MemoryCell` class

```
 1  // Exercise the MemoryCell class
 2
 3  main( )
 4  {
 5      MemoryCell<int> M;
 6
 7      M.Write( 5 );
 8      cout << "Cell contents are " << M.Read( ) << '\n';
 9
10      return 0;
11  }
```

Figure 3.10   A simple test routine to show how `MemoryCell` objects are accessed.

3.3   Template Classes

Classes can be templated. The syntax is onerous.

In Section 2.5 we implemented a class to handle rational numbers. The class assumed that the numerator and denominator were represented by two objects of some type `IntType`. Presumably, the class user issued a typedef statement that made `IntType` a synonym for either the `int` or a library class such as `Integer`. Our discussion in the last section suggests that a template would be a better mechanism than a typedef. In this section we show how we can template and use classes. First, we show how to template the `MemoryCell` class from Section 2.2. Next, we describe the changes needed to make `Rational` a template class. Finally, we implement a new class, `Vector`, which is a safe array (that is, it supports index bounds checking) and will have some additional useful member functions such as `Double`.

3.3.1 Templating `MemoryCell`

Figure 3.9 shows a template version of the `MemoryCell` class previously depicted in Figure 2.1. The template class syntax is similar to the template function syntax; we merely add a template specification (shown on line 10). There are two other differences between Figure 3.9 and Figure 2.1. First, `Read` is a constant member function (it should have been a constant member function in Figure 2.1, but we had not yet introduced the concept). The second difference is more significant: `Write` accepts a parameter passed by constant reference, and `Read` returns its parameter by constant reference. When possible, constant references should be used instead of call/return by value because, if `Etype` is a large object, making a copy could be inefficient (or illegal if the copy constructor for `Etype` is either disabled or not defined). Do not use constant reference returns blindly, however. Remember that you cannot return a reference to an automatic variable. Figure 3.10 shows a simple `main` that uses the template class. We need to take note of two features of this routine. First, in the commented description of the interface, we do not specify whether a function is a constant member or how parameters are passed. This would merely duplicate information that is clearly specified in the interface code. Second, `Etype` must have a zero-parameter constructor because the default constructor is used for `MemoryCell`, and it is a member by member call of the zero-parameter constructors.

As we saw in Chapter 2, the class interface and implementation should be separate. Figure 3.11 shows the simplest example of how this is done: In the member function definitions, the class name is now `MemoryCell<Etype>`. Note carefully that every function in the interface for which a separate body is supplied must have the template line. That line only extends for one function. Once again, failure to follow the rules leads to compiler diagnostics that are sometimes very cryptic. Other than that, nothing is new. Figure 3.12 gives a layout of the general format that is used. Boldface items are typed exactly as shown.

3.3.2 Templating `Rational`

There are three general changes that need to be applied to template `Rational`:

1. The interface must be specified as a template (we have already seen this).
2. The `main` routine must explicitly instantiate the `Rational` template (we have already seen this).
3. The member functions must all be specified as templates (we have seen part of this, but there are some additional syntax requirements for this more complicated case).

```
1  // Memory cell interface; same as in Figure 3.9
2
3  template <class Etype>
4  class MemoryCell
5  {
6    public:
7      const Etype & Read( ) const;
8      void Write( const Etype & X );
9    private:
10     int StoredValue;
11 };
12
13
14 // Implementation of the class members
15
16 template <class Etype>
17 const Etype &
18 MemoryCell<Etype>::Read( ) const
19 {
20     return StoredValue;
21 }
22
23 template <class Etype>
24 void
25 MemoryCell<Etype>::Write( const Etype & X )
26 {
27     StoredValue = X;
28 }
```

Figure 3.11   A more typical `MemoryCell` declaration in which interface and implementation are separated

```
1  // Typical template interface
2  template <class Etype>
3  class ClassName
4  {
5    public:
6      // Public members
7    private:
8      // Private members
9  };
10
11
12 // Typical member implementation
13 template <class Etype>
14 ReturnType
15 ClassName<Etype>::MemberName( Parameter List  ) /* const */
16 {
17     // Member body
18 }
```

Figure 3.12   Typical layout for template interface and member functions

```
1  #include <iostream.h>
2
3  template <class IntType>
4  class Rational
5  {
6      // Remainder of the interface is completely identical
7  };
```

Figure 3.13   Templated `Rational` interface

```
1  #include <iostream.h>
2  #include "Rational.h"
3
4  main( )
5  {
6      Rational<long> X;
7      Rational<long> Sum;
8      Rational<long> Max = 0;
9
10     // Most of main is completely identical
11     // Changes are the type conversions near the bottom
12 }
```

Figure 3.14   `main` routine altered for template `Rational` class

```
1  template <class IntType>
2  const Rational<IntType> &
3  Rational<IntType>::operator=( const Rational<IntType> & Rhs )
4  {
5      if( this != &Rhs )
6      {
7          Numer = Rhs.Numer;
8          Denom = Rhs.Denom;
9      }
10     return *this;
11 }
12
13 template <class IntType>
14 const Rational<IntType> &
15 Rational<IntType>::operator+=( const Rational<IntType> & Rhs )
16 {
17     Numer = Numer * Rhs.Denom + Rhs.Numer * Denom;
18     Denom = Denom * Rhs.Denom;
19     Reduce( );
20
21     return *this;
22 }
```

Figure 3.15   Some member functions for the template `Rational` class

A template class must have the template specification prior to the interface. Objects of a template class type must be instantiated with the template parameters.

The first item is the easiest, as we have seen; the appropriate segment is shown in Figure 3.13. The only change is the addition at line 3 of the template specification. The second item is also completely straightforward, as we have seen. Because `Rational` is now only a template and not an actual class, when we declare objects, we must give an instantiation with the template parameters. Thus the `main` routine in Figure 2.15 needs to be slightly altered, as shown in Figure 3.14. The changes to Figure 2.15 are

- Lines 8 to 10: An instantiation of the template `Rational` is needed.
- Lines 24 and 27: A different type conversion is needed.

Each member must be declared as a template.

The final change is in the member functions. There are two changes that we must make for each member function body. First, each member function is now a template function rather than an actual function; this requires the addition of the usual template line. Second, `Rational` is no longer an actual class. Instead, the actual class is `Rational<IntType>`. Thus instead of `Rational` we must use the form `Rational<IntType>`. As Figure 3.15 shows, this leads to very cumbersome syntax, but that is the way it is. If we forget the instantiation, we will get an error message, which is sometimes as cryptic as "parse error."

3.3.3   Templating a `Vector` Class

We can use templates to design a safe, dynamically expanding array.

Our final example is a complete class that supports arrays in the manner of most programming languages: It provides index range checking and allows copying between identically sized (and typed) arrays. We also support dynamically changing array sizes. Given the fact that the `String` class in Section 2.6 supported very similar operations, the only new item is the use of templates in this class.

The interface for the template `Vector` class is shown in Figure 3.16. As with the `String` class we have two data members: a pointer to a dynamically allocated array, and the number of items that the array is prepared to store. The constructor requires an array size, as for C++ arrays. The copy constructor is disabled because we do not want to allow call by value for `Vector`s but rather insist that the user pass every `Vector` by reference. If we did not disable the copy constructor, then we would have to write our own (to avoid sharing pointers), and that would be expensive. The only possible use for it would be to perform an explicit initialization of the form

```
Vector<int> A = B;       // Initialize A to be a copy of B
```

However, we can always replace these occurrences with

```
Vector<int> A( B.Length( ) );
A = B;
```

thus rendering the copy constructor expendable. The remaining single constructor is shown in Figure 3.17.

Figure 3.18 shows the member functions. Nothing is particularly remarkable here except the painful syntax caused by explicitly providing a template type whenever `Vector` is mentioned. Also, for efficiency purposes, it might be worth making `operator[]` an inline function. Many compilers will do it even without the inline directive.

```
1  // Vector class interface: support bounds-checked arrays
2  //
3  // Etype: must have zero-parameter constructor and operator=
4  // CONSTRUCTION: with (a) an integer size only
5  //
6  // ******************PUBLIC OPERATIONS********************
7  // =                        --> Copy if sizes are identical
8  // [ ]                      --> Indexing with bounds check
9  // int Length( )            --> Return # elements in Vector
10 // void Resize( int NewSize ) --> Change bounds
11 // void Double( )           --> Double Vector capacity
12
13 template <class Etype>
14 class Vector
15 {
16   public:
17     // Constructors
18     Vector( int Size );
19
20     // Destructor
21     ~Vector( ) { delete [ ] Array; }
22
23     // Index the Array
24     const Etype & operator[]( int Index ) const;
25     Etype & operator[]( int Index );
26
27     // Copy Identically Sized Arrays
28     const Vector & operator=( const Vector & Rhs );
29
30     // Get the Length
31     int Length( ) const { return ArraySize; }
32
33     // Resize the Array
34     void Resize( int NewSize );
35     void Double( ) { Resize( ArraySize * 2 ); }
36   private:
37     Etype *Array;
38     int ArraySize;
39
40     void GetArray( );       // Call new
41
42     // Disable Copy Constructor
43     Vector( const Vector & Rhs );
44 };
```

Figure 3.16   Interface for template `Vector` class

```
 1  template <class Etype>
 2  void
 3  Vector<Etype>::GetArray( )
 4  {
 5      Array = new Etype [ ArraySize ];
 6  }
 7
 8  template <class Etype>
 9  Vector<Etype>::Vector( int Size )
10  {
11      ArraySize = Size;
12      GetArray( );
13  }
```

Figure 3.17   Constructor for template `Vector` class

The range checking provided by this class can be a valuable debugging tool. This is almost always important for program development and maintenance. On the other hand, in some places the overhead of testing the index is excessive. For instance, in the inner loop of a finely tuned sorting algorithm that we are absolutely certain works, these range checks consume valuable time. Every program might have one or two tiny fragments of code for which elimination of range checking might improve performance. But those lines of code are the exception rather than the rule, and besides the sorting example mentioned above, you are not likely to run into such an example too often.

3.4   Fancy Templates

Our discussion of templates has only scratched the surface. The proposed template facility allows multiple instantiation parameters, such as

```
template <class Etype, class Dtype>
```

When instantiating, we can have several layers of templates. For instance, the following declares that V is a `Vector` of a `Vector` of `int`:

```
Vector< Vector<int> > V;
```

Make sure you have space between > and > when instantiating layers of templates. Note carefully that white space must separate the two > characters; otherwise, the compiler will interpret the >> token as a shift operation.

These two features are used in the case studies. There are a host of other features that we do not use.

```
 1  template <class Etype>
 2  const Etype &
 3  Vector<Etype>::operator[]( int Index ) const
 4  {
 5      EXCEPTION( Index < 0 || Index >= ArraySize,
 6                  "Index out of range" );
 7      return Array[ Index ];
 8  }
 9
10  template <class Etype>
11  const Vector<Etype> &
12  Vector<Etype>::operator=( const Vector<Etype> & Rhs )
13  {
14      if( this != &Rhs )
15      {
16          EXCEPTION( ArraySize != Rhs.ArraySize,
17                      "Incompatible array sizes" );
18
19          for( int i = 0; i < ArraySize; i++ )
20              Array[ i ] = Rhs.Array[ i ];
21      }
22      return *this;
23  }
24
25  template <class Etype>
26  void
27  Vector<Etype>::Resize( int NewSize )
28  {
29      Etype *OldArray = Array;          // Original array
30      const int MinOfOldAndNew = Min( ArraySize, NewSize );
31
32      ArraySize = NewSize;
33      GetArray( );
34      for( int i = 0; i < MinOfOldAndNew; i++ )
35          Array[ i ] = OldArray[ i ];
36      delete [ ] OldArray;
37  }
```

Figure 3.18   Indexing (one of two), copying, and resizing member functions for template class `Vector`

3.5   Bugs Associated with Templates

We close our discussion of templates with some warnings. Templates are a relatively recent addition to the language, and not all of the details have been completely worked out. Many compilers have bugs or unimplemented features that are a direct consequence of templates. We will describe some of the bugs that were noticed in the preparation of this text (note that some, or possibly none, might apply in your case).

Bad Error Messages and Inconsistent Rules

The rules on when templates need instantiation seem to change frequently, and the compiler writers are having a hard time keeping up. You may find that your compiler is accepting old syntax, and when you port to another system it will complain that you have forgotten an explicit instantiation or, in some cases, provided an instantiation that you should not have. Some compilers do not accept current syntax, such as the explicit instantiation of a template function call.

Template-Matching Algorithms

Sometimes, the matching algorithm breaks when templates are involved. The most common example of this is when a template stand-alone function (that is, one that is not part of a class) has a parameter that is a reference to a pointer. For example, `DoubleArray`, shown in Figure 3.4, has a parameter like this. On some compilers, the call at line 17 in Exercise 3.8 does not match. If yours does not, rewrite the routine in a C style: have `DoubleArray` return the new value of `Array` and pass `Array` by value. The declaration becomes

```
Etype *DoubleArray( Etype *Array, int & CurrentSize );
```

Nested Templated Classes

Not all compilers support the nesting of template classes. If yours does not, you will have to unnest the classes and make the original outer class a friend of the original inner class.

Separate Compilation

Some compilers do not support separate compilation of template classes. If yours does not, use lots of include statements to make it appear that everything is in one file.

Summary

This chapter has provided a brief discussion of the C++ template facilities. Templates allow us to write general classes and functions, thus helping us achieve the goal of code reuse. We will see templates used throughout the text.

In Chapter 4 we will look at another important mechanism for code reuse: inheritance.

Objects of the Game

insertion sort A simple sorting algorithm that is appropriate for small inputs. (102)

instantiation When a template is instantiated with a particular type or types, a new function or class is logically created. (100)

template A template is a design for code and allows us to write routines that work for arbitrary types without knowing what these types will be. (100)

typedef A simple mechanism to allow generic routines. However it is unsuitable if we want routines with two different types simultaneously. (99)

Common Errors

1. The template line must precede the template class interface and each member function definition.

2. A common error is forgetting an instantiation of a template. This occurs frequently in member function definitions. The definition shown in Figure 3.15 is typical of the instantiations that are required.

3. When instantiating a template class with an object that is itself a template class, white space must be used to separate successive >s. Otherwise, >> is interpreted as a shift operator. For instance, use `Vector<Rational<int> >`.

4. When writing template classes, we must be especially careful about parameter passing mechanisms. Avoid passing unknown types by copying. Use either reference or constant reference types. Always assume that you are working with a large object.

5. Sometimes when a template is instantiated, an ambiguity develops. For instance, if we have two constructors: `T(int)` and `T(Etype)`, for template class `T` and `Etype` is an `int`, we have an ambiguity. When designing classes, be sure that no ambiguities can develop.

6. When a template class is instantiated, all operations that are needed must be available. For instance, the template insertion sort needs to have `operator<` defined for whatever `Etype` is instantiated. Otherwise, an error will be detected at link time. Clearly state what conditions must be satisfied by the template parameters.

7. If a template class uses call by value and the instantiated type has a disabled copy constructor, a compile-time error will be detected.

8. All of the errors that occur for classes occur for template classes.

9. Be aware of the limitations of your compiler. Many compilers have buggy template implementations.

On the Internet

The available files are:

InsSort.cpp   Contains `DoubleArray`, `InsertionSort`, and `main` shown in Figure 3.4 to Figure 3.8.

Vector.h   Contains `Vector` class interface shown in Figure 3.16.

Vector.cpp   Contains `Vector` class implementation.

Exercises

In Short

3.1. Write a template function to sort three `Etype` objects.

3.2. When templates are used, what types of errors are detected when the template function is scanned, and what errors are detected when the function is instantiated?

3.3. Describe the syntax for template classes.

In Practice

3.4. Rewrite `DoubleArray` in C style to avoid template-matching problems. Specifically, return `Array` and accept `Array` by value (instead of by reference).

3.5. Write a template function `Min` and `Max`, each of which accepts two parameters.

3.6. Write a template function `Min` and `Max`, each of which accepts an array and an array size.

3.7. Write a template function `Min` and `Max`, each of which accepts a `Vector`.

3.8. In many situations `operator<` is defined for an object, but we also need `operator>`. Explore the possibility of writing a template `operator>` that calls `operator<`.

3.9. Add `Min` and `Max` as members of the `Vector` class.

3.10. Rewrite the `BitArray` class in Chapter 2 to accept the (initial) size as a template parameter. Is there any advantage to this approach?

3.11. A `SingleBuffer` class supports `Get` and `Put`: The `SingleBuffer` stores a single item and a data member that indicates whether or not the `SingleBuffer` is logically empty. A `Put` may be applied only to an empty buffer and inserts an item to the buffer. A `Get` may only be applied to a nonempty buffer and deletes and returns the contents of the buffer. Write a template class to implement `SingleBuffer`. Use `EXCEPTION` to signal errors. What is the return type of `Get`, and why?

3.12. Adjust Figure 3.18 so that if the preprocessor symbol `NoCheck` is defined, then the call to `EXCEPTION` is not made.

Programming Projects

3.13. Implement an insertion sort that takes a `Vector` as a single parameter.

3.14. Implement a routine that reads an arbitrary number of `Etype` items and stores them in a `Vector`.

3.15. Use class `Vector` to show how to implement a two-dimensional bounded vector. A two-dimensional vector can be viewed as a vector of vectors.

Chapter 4

Inheritance

As we have mentioned earlier, an important goal of object-oriented programming is code reuse. Just as engineers use components over and over in their designs, programmers should be able to reuse objects rather than repeatedly reimplementing them. In Chapter 3 we saw one mechanism for reuse provided by C++, the template. Templates are appropriate if the basic functionality of the code is type independent. The other mechanism for code reuse is *inheritance*. Inheritance allows us to extend the functionality of an object; in other words, we can create new types with restricted (or extended) properties of the original type. Inheritance goes a long way toward our goal for code reuse. Another important goal is *polymorphism*. Polymorphism allows an object to hold several different types of objects.

In this chapter we will see

- how inheritance and the related object-oriented concept of polymorphism is implemented in C++
- how a new class `BoundedVector` can be derived from `Vector`
- how a collection of classes can be derived from a single abstract class
- how run-time binding decisions, rather than compile time linking decisions, can be made for these classes

4.1   What Are Polymorphism and Inheritance?

An important object-oriented principle is known as *polymorphism*. A polymorphic object can hold objects of several different types. When operations are applied to the polymorphic type, the operation that is appropriate to the actual stored type is automatically selected. Function and operator overloading is one example of polymorphic behavior; however, the overloading that we have seen so far is static. The function selection is made at compile time, and this limits the polymorphic behavior. In C++ it is possible to have the function selection

A *polymorphic* object can hold objects of several different types. When operations are applied to the polymorphic type, the operation appropriate to the actual stored type is automatically selected.

deferred until the program is running. The basic mechanism in C++ uses inheritance. So what is inheritance?

When we need to design a new class, we frequently find that we have a similar class already written. Code reuse requires that we not start from scratch but implement the new class by basing it on the already existing class, with some new routines added, some deleted, and some altered. When we are designing a collection of similar classes, polymorphism suggests that we should attempt to design an abstract polymorphic class that can store objects of these similar classes. Consider the following examples:

- Vectors: In Section 3.3 we showed how to implement a `Vector` class that supports index range checking for arrays. Suppose we want to implement a `BoundedVector` class that allows the user to specify the range of indices.
- Dates: A `Date` object can be read, output, and operated on using several operators. For example, subtraction of two `Date` objects yields an elapsed time. Similarly, comparison of two `Dates` makes sense. An example (skeleton) interface was shown in Figure 2.32. Suppose we want to implement the `Date` class for various calendar systems (such as Gregorian, Hebrew, and Chinese).
- Taxes: Suppose we want to write a class that computes income taxes. We may have several classes of taxpayers: `SinglePayer`, `MarriedPayer`, `SeparatePayer`, `HeadPayer`.
- Shapes: A graphics system must deal with many kinds of shapes, such as circles, squares, and so on. We might want to define a separate class for each type of shape.

In these scenarios we have three basic options. The first possibility is to define each class completely independently. The problem with this approach is that we may have to rewrite many similar pieces of code. This leads to much more work than is necessary. For example, math for the `Date` class is independent of any particular calendar system. More code means more chance for errors and makes maintenance difficult because any change in the basic implementation must be reflected in the code for each class.

A second alternative is to use a single class and have each function controlled by `if/else` or `switch` statements. This solves the redundancy problem that complete independence exhibits. However, maintenance is still difficult. Each new `Shape`, for example, requires alteration and recompilation of the entire collective's code. This means that the user cannot just extend library classes, unless source code is available. It is also error-prone because it leads to very long routines, and it is possible to unintentionally alter code for some other `Shape`. Furthermore, nested `if/else` statements incur a substantial run-time overhead, even though the result of the `if/else` may be known at compile time. Finally, there is the issue of type safety. If every shape is contained in one class, then assignment of a circle to a square makes sense, in principle, unless additional code is provided to disallow it. Thus these types of mismatches might not be detected or, if so, would only be detected at run time. If each shape were a separate class, then the type checks would be done automatically at compile time.

The first two approaches are typical of procedural programming. The third alternative, inheritance, is the topic of this chapter. In *inheritance* we have a *base class* from which other classes are derived. A *derived class* inherits all the properties of a base class. It can then add data members, disable functions, alter functions, and add new functions. Each derived class is a completely new class. However the base class is completely unaffected by any changes that are made in the derived class; thus, in designing the derived class, it is impossible to break the base class. The base class is the class on which the inheritance is based.

Inheritance **allows us to derive classes from a *base class* without disturbing the implementation of the base class.**

A derived class is type compatible (in some ways) with its base class, but not vice versa. Sibling classes (that is, classes derived from a common class) are not type compatible. This is simple enough it seems, but a powerful feature such as inheritance raises many questions:

Each *derived class* **is a completely new class that nonetheless has some compatibility with the class it was derived from.**

- What is the syntax used to derive a new class from an existing base class?
- What about constructors and destructors?
- How does this affect public or private status?
- What about friends: Are they friends of the new class too?
- Is there a limit to how deep we can derive classes?

There are also some deeper questions that require examination:

- How do we factor out common differences into an abstract class and then create a hierarchy?
- Given a pointer to a class, is overloading resolved at compile time or run time?
- Can we derive a new class from more than one class (*multiple inheritance*)?

To answer these questions, we will implement the `BoundedVector` class and a `Shape` class that derives `Circle`, `Square`, and `Rectangle`. In doing so we will see how C++ implements run-time polymorphism. Recall that a polymorphic object can hold objects of several different types. When operations are applied to the polymorphic type, the operation that is appropriate to the actual stored type is selected automatically.

```
1  class Derived : public Base
2  {
3      // Any members that are not listed are inherited unchanged
4      // except for constructor, destructor,
5      // copy constructor, and operator=
6   public:
7      // Constructors, and destructors if defaults are not good
8      // Base members whose definitions are to change in Derived
9      // Additional public member functions
10  private:
11      // Additional data members (generally private)
12      // Additional private member functions
13      // Base members that should be disabled in Derived
14  };
```

Figure 4.1   General layout of public inheritance

4.2   A Derived Class: `BoundedVector`

A derived class inherits all data members from the base class and may add additional data members.

Recall that a derived class inherits all the properties of a base class. It can then add data members, disable functions, alter functions, and add new functions. Each derived class is a completely new class. A typical layout for inheritance is shown in Figure 4.1. C++ tokens are set in boldface. The form of inheritance described here and used almost exclusively throughout the text is *public inheritance*. This and other forms of inheritance are discussed in Section 4.3. Let us briefly describe a derived class:

The derived class inherits all member functions from the base class. It may accept them, disallow them, or redefine them. Additionally, it can define new functions.

- Generally all data is private, so we just add additional data members in the derived class by specifying them in the private section.
- Any base class member functions that are not specified in the derived class are inherited unchanged, with the following exceptions: constructor, destructor, copy constructor, and `operator=`. For those the typical defaults apply, with the inherited portion considered as a member. Thus by default a copy constructor is applied to the inherited portion (considered as a single entity) and then member by member. We will be more specific in Section 4.3.5.
- Any base class member function that is declared in the derived class' private section is disabled in the derived class.
- Any base class member function that is declared in the derived class' public section requires an overriding definition that will be applied to objects of the derived class.
- Additional member functions can be added in the derived class.

Figure 4.2 shows how simple it is (in principle) to derive a `BoundedVector` class from a `Vector` class. Let us examine the basics of this process; in subsequent sections we will look at some options that we could have used.

A bounded vector is an array that supports index range checking and allows the user to specify upper and lower bounds on the array. This feature was added to the `Vector` class we saw in Section 3.3 because `Vector` requires that indexing commence at position zero. However, that is the only operational difference between the two classes. `BoundedVector` is a templated class, and thus the code carries all of the baggage associated with the template syntax. Line 11 states that `BoundedVector` inherits everything from `Vector`. The keyword `public`, signifying *public inheritance*, means that any public members of the base class are also public in the derived class. From this basis the rest of the interface can then add, delete, or alter these inherited semantics in the derived class. In our case `BoundedVector` has the data member `Low` in addition to the data members in the `Vector` class. Notice carefully that this means that `BoundedVector` now has three data members, `Array`, `ArraySize`, and `Low`, but it does not say anything about whether or not the two inherited members are visible to the derived class. Indeed, because they are private in the `Vector` class, they are not visible to `BoundedVector`. If our class required direct access to these members, we would have to make additional arrangements.

```
1  // BoundedVector class interface: Vectors with arbitrary range
2  //
3  // Etype: same requirements as Vector class Etype
4  // CONSTRUCTION: with (a) two integers that specify the
5  //       lower and upper range
6  //
7  // ******************PUBLIC OPERATIONS********************
8  // All Vector operations are supported
9
10 template <class Etype>
11 class BoundedVector : public Vector<Etype>
12 {
13   public:
14       // Constructor
15     BoundedVector( int L, int H ) :
16         Vector<Etype>( H - L + 1 ), Low ( L ) { }
17
18       // Index the Array
19     const Etype & operator[]( int Index ) const;
20     Etype & operator[]( int Index );
21   private:
22     int Low;              // Low index
23 };
24   // Overriding Definition (constant member omitted for brevity)
25 template <class Etype>
26 Etype &
27 BoundedVector<Etype>::operator[]( int Index )
28 {
29     return Vector<Etype>::operator[]( Index - Low );
30 }
```

Figure 4.2   Simple inheritance for vectors

The `BoundedVector` class also inherits all of the functions defined in `Vector`. Specifically, `Resize`, `Double`, and `Length` are now defined exactly as in the `Vector` class (`operator=` is special, as we will see in the next section). If we are not happy with this, we must provide a new definition for an inherited function. Thus `operator[]`, which would be defined incorrectly if the inherited definition was used, must be redefined. As we see from Figure 4.2, a new declaration is provided for it at lines 19 and 20, and one of the new definitions is specified at lines 25 to 30. We merely call the base class `operator[]` (offset to reflect indexing starting at zero). Three points are worth noting. First, as mentioned earlier, we cannot directly access the array because it is private. Second, we must use the scope resolution operator to obtain the `Vector` class' `operator[]` because the default scope is the `BoundedVector` class. If we do not use the scope operator, the result is that `operator[]` calls itself repeatedly. Third, we do not have to test if the index is out of range; this is done in the `Vector` class.

The inherited data members must be constructed using the base class constructor.

The other detail is the constructor at lines 15 and 16. As we see, it calls the `Vector` constructor with an appropriate size to initialize the inherited members, and then it initializes `Low`. We would not initialize the inherited members separately, even if they were public. The inherited data members must be constructed using the base class constructor. When viewed from an object-oriented perspective, requiring initialization of the inherited portion as an atomic group seems logical because it is consistent with encapsulation principles.

4.3   Public, Private, and Protected Members and Inheritance

Line 11 in Figure 4.2 indicates that `BoundedVector` is derived from `Vector` using public inheritance. In this section we describe how the public or private status of a class member is affected by inheritance, and examine a third access specifier, `protected`.

In an *IS-A relationship*, we say the derived class *is a* (variation of the) base class.

First, let us look at the kinds of relationships that warrant inheritance. The most common is an *IS-A relationship*. In an IS-A relationship we say the derived class *is a* (variation of the) base class. For example, a circle IS-A shape, and a car IS-A vehicle. However, an ellipse IS-NOT-A circle.

In a *HAS-A relationship*, we say the derived class *has a* (property of the) base class.

Another type of relationship is a *HAS-A* (or IS-COMPOSED-OF) *relationship*. This type of relationship does not possess the properties that would be natural in an inheritance hierarchy. Though inheritance can be used for a HAS-A relationship, it is often a result of a poor design decision. Generally speaking, inheritance should be used only when an IS-A relationship exists. An example of a HAS-A relationship is that a car HAS-A steering wheel.

4.3.1   Public Inheritance

The most common form of inheritance is *public inheritance*. In public inheritance all public members of the base class remain public, and all private members of the base class remain private. Public inheritance also defines a standard type conversion from a pointer to the derived class to the pointer to the base class; this is important, as we will see later on. Public inheritance typifies an *IS-A* relationship.

In *public inheritance*, all public members of the base class remain public. Public inheritance models an IS-A relationship.

In public inheritance, private member functions that are not redefined remain private in the derived class. (The zero-parameter constructor, destructor, and `operator=` are technical exceptions to this rule but, as discussed in Section 4.3.5, this rule does, in effect, apply to them also.)

Private members of the base class remain private by default.

4.3.2   Private Inheritance

Private inheritance means that even public members of the base class are hidden. Seems like a silly idea, doesn't it? In fact it is, if we are talking about implementing an IS-A relationship. Private inheritance is thus generally used to implement a HAS-A relationship (that is, a derived class B has or uses a base class A).

Private inheritance means that even public members of the base class are hidden.

In many cases we can get by without using inheritance: We can make an object of class A a member of class B and, if necessary, make B a friend of A. This is known as *composition*. Composition is the preferred mechanism, but occasionally private inheritance is more expedient or slightly faster (because it avoids a layer of function calls). In general, it is best to avoid private inheritance unless it greatly simplifies some coding logic or can be justified on performance grounds.

***Composition* is preferred to private inheritance. In composition, we say that class *B* is composed of class *A* (and other objects).**

By default, *private inheritance* is used. If the keyword `public` were omitted on line 11 of Figure 4.2, we would have private inheritance. In that case the public member functions of `Vector` would still be inherited, but they would be private members of `BoundedVector` and they could not be called by users of `BoundedVector`. The type conversion of pointers described earlier does not apply for nonpublic inheritance.

The default is private inheritance but it should be avoided.

4.3.3   Protected Members

We know that any member that is declared in the private section of a class interface is accessible only to the implementation of the class. Thus the `Array` and `ArrayLen` members, which are declared private to the `Vector` class, are inaccessible to the `BoundedVector` class. As our implementation shows, access is not necessarily needed by a derived class. But what if it were?

We would have two choices for accessibility. One possibility is to have the `Vector` class make `BoundedVector` a friend. This solution is problematic for two reasons. First, the base class may have to issue a friend declaration for all its derived classes, which could be considerable. Second, each new derived class requires a modification (via a friend declaration) and subsequent recompilation of the base class. This can be time consuming and lead to errors (accidental alterations of the interface), or it may even be impossible (a user cannot change a library specification).

Protected class members *are accessible by the publicly derived class but private to everyone else.*

The alternative is that the base class can make certain members protected. A *protected class member* is private to everyone except a publicly derived class. `Vector` could declare that `Array` and `ArrayLen` are protected, thus granting access to `BoundedVector` (and any other class that is derived from `Vector`). This is an all-or-nothing declaration: All derived classes have direct access to the protected members; consequently, the decision to make a member protected should not be made lightly. Figure 4.4 shows the visibility of the members in certain situations.

Declaring data members as protected or public violates the spirit of encapsulation and is generally done only as a matter of programming expediency; however, if a protected declaration allows you to avoid convoluted code, then it is not unreasonable to use it.

4.3.4   Friends

Friendship is not inherited.

Are friends of a class still friends in a derived class? The answer is no. For example, suppose *F* is a friend of class *A*, and *B* is derived from *A*. Suppose *B* has nonpublic member *M*. Then in class *B*, *F* does not have access to *M*. However, the inherited portion of *A* is accessible to *F* in class *B*. Figure 4.4 summarizes the results. *B* can declare that *F* is also a friend, in which case all of *B*'s members would be visible.

Public inheritance situation	Public	Protected	Private
Base class member function accessing *M*	Yes	Yes	Yes
Derived class member function accessing *M*	Yes	Yes	No
`main`, accessing *B.M*	Yes	No	No
`main`, accessing *D.M*	Yes	No	No
Derived class member function accessing *B.M*	Yes	No	No
B is an object of the base class; *D* is an object of the publicly derived class; *M* is a member of the base class.			

Figure 4.3   Access rules that depend on what *M*'s visibility is in the base class

4.3.5   The Default Constructor, Copy Constructor, and Copy Assignment Operator

There are two issues surrounding the default constructor, copy constructor, and copy assignment operator: first, if we do nothing, are these operators private or public? Second, if they are public, what are their semantics?

> The public/private status of the default constructor, copy constructor, and copy assignment operator, like all other members is inherited.

We assume public inheritance. We also assume that these functions were public in the base class. What happens if they are completely omitted from the derived class? We know that they will be public, but what will their semantics be? We know that for classes there are defaults for the simple constructor, the copy constructor and the copy assignment operator. Specifically, the default is to apply the appropriate operation to each member in the class. Thus if a copy assignment operator is not specified in a class, we have seen that it is defined as a member-by-member copy. The same rules apply to inherited classes. This means, for instance, that

```
const BoundedVector & operator=( const BoundedVector & Rhs );
```

since it is not explicitly defined, is implemented by a call to `operator=` for the base class (in effect copying the contents of the array and the length) and then a copy of the `Low` member. This is not necessarily the correct action (see Exercise 4.11).

> If a default destructor, copy constructor, or copy assignment operator is publicly inherited but not defined in the derived class, then by default the operator is applied to each member.

What is true for any member function is in effect true for these operators when it comes to visibility. Thus, if `operator=` is disabled by being placed in the private section in the base class, then it is still disabled. The same holds true for the copy constructor and default constructor. The reasoning, however, is slightly different. `operator=` is in effect disabled because a public default `operator=` is generated. However, by default `operator=` is applied to the inherited portion and then member by member. Since `operator=` for the base class is disabled, the first step becomes illegal. Thus placing default constructors, copy constructors, and `operator=` in the private section of the base class has the effect of disabling them in the derived class (even though technically they are public in the derived class).

Public inheritance situation	Public	Protected	Private
F accessing B.MB	Yes	Yes	Yes
F accessing D.MD	Yes	No	No
F accessing D.MB	Yes	Yes	Yes

B is an object of the base class; D is an object of the publicly derived class; MB is a member of the base class. MD is a member of the derived class. F is a friend of the base class (but not the derived class)

Figure 4.4   Friendship is not inherited

```
1     const VectorSize = 20;
2     Vector<int> V( VectorSize );
3     BoundedVector<int> BV( VectorSize, 2 * VectorSize - 1 );
4       ...
5     BV[ VectorSize ] = V[ 0 ];
```

Figure 4.5   Vector and BoundedVector classes with calls to
                  operator[] that are done automatically and correctly

```
1     Vector<int> *Vptr;
2     const int Size = 20;
3     cin >> Low;
4     if( Low )
5         Vptr = new BoundedVector<int>( Low, Low + Size - 1 );
6     else
7         Vptr = new Vector<int>( Size )
8
9       ...
10    (*Vptr)[ Low ] = 0;          // What does this mean?
```

Figure 4.6   Vector and BoundedVector classes

4.3.6   Base Objects in Member Function Declarations

Avoid placing base objects as parameters or return types.

Return types present an important difficulty. Consider the following operator, defined in a base class:

```
const Base & operator++( );
```

The derived class inherits it,

```
const Base & operator++( );
```

but that is not really what we want. If we have a return type in the derived class, it ought to be a constant reference to the derived type and not the base type. Thus the operator++ that is inherited is not the one we want. Unfortunately, we are stuck here. We cannot disable the Base::operator++ and then enable a Derived::operator++ because the function signature includes only the name and parameter types, and not the return type. Thus the compiler will see a conflict.

In any base class, therefore, member functions that return objects of the base class should be avoided. In our case it is probably safest to have `operator++` return a `void`. In some cases it is fine, but in others it is a bad idea. Thus, in some examples, we will implement `operator++` with a `void` return type.[1] Care also needs to be taken to avoid using the base type as a parameter to a member function.

4.4   Static and Dynamic Binding

Figure 4.5 illustrates that there is no problem in declaring `Vector` and `BoundedVector` objects in the same scope because the compiler can deduce which `operator[]` to apply. `V` is a `Vector` and `BV` is a `BoundedVector`, so the determination of which `operator[]` is used in the two calls at line 5 is computable at compile time. We call this *static binding* or *static overloading*.

> In *static binding*, the decision on which function to use to resolve an overload is made at compile time.

On the other hand, the code in Figure 4.6 is more complicated. If `Low` is zero, we use a plain `Vector` class (to avoid the run-time overhead of subtracting zero meaninglessly); otherwise, we use a `BoundedVector`. Because public inheritance automatically defines a type conversion from a pointer to a derived class to a pointer to the base class, we can declare that `Vptr` is a pointer to the base class `Vector` and then dynamically allocate either a `Vector` or `BoundedVector` object for it to point at. When we get to line 10, which `operator[]` gets called?[2]

The decision of which `operator[]` to use can be made at compile time or at run time. If the decision is made at compile time (static binding), then we must use `Vector`'s `operator[]` because that is the type of `*Vptr` at compile time. If `Vptr` is actually pointing at the `BoundedVector`, this is the wrong decision; for example, if `Low` is 30, it causes an out-of-bounds array access. Because the type of object that `Vptr` is actually pointing at can only be determined once the program has run, this decision must be made at run time. This is known as *dynamic binding*. However a run-time decision incurs some run-time overhead because it requires that the program maintain extra information and that the compiler generate code to perform the test. This overhead was once thought to be significant, and thus although other languages, such as Smalltalk and Objective C, use dynamic binding by default; C++ does not.

> If a member function is declared to be virtual, *dynamic binding* is used. The decision on which function to use to resolve an overload is made at run time, if it cannot be determined at compile time.

---

1. As a practical matter, this causes problems in some implementations of the `istrstream` class, which is derived from `istream`. Specifically, if `InStr` is an `istrstream`, then `InStr>>X>>Y` is supposed to read from it into `X` and then into `Y`. However, this requires that the first call to `operator>>` return a reference to the `InStr`. Unfortunately, unless carefully implemented (it is not on either of our two compilers) it returns a reference to an `istream` object because the return type is inherited. This requires a workaround later in the text (in Figure 14.18).
2. The parentheses are necessary because `[]` has higher precedence than `*`.

In general, if a function is redefined in a derived class, it should be declared virtual in the base class.

Instead, the C++ programmer must ask for it by specifying that the function is virtual. A *virtual function* will use dynamic binding if a compile-time binding decision is impossible to deduce. A non-virtual function will always use static binding. The default, as we implied above, is that functions are non-virtual. This is unfortunate because we now know that the overhead is relatively minor. Virtualness is inherited, so it can be indicated in the base class. Thus if the base class declares that a function is virtual (in its declaration), then the decision is made at run time; otherwise, it is made at compile time. Consequently, in the code we have written so far, a compile-time decision would be made at line 10. To make this a run-time decision, we would have to place the keyword `virtual` at the start of line 24 of the `Vector` class interface (Figure 3.16). As a general rule, if a function is overwritten in a derived class, it should be declared `virtual` in the base class to ensure that the correct function is selected when a pointer to an object is used. An important exception is discussed in Section 4.5.

To summarize: Static binding is used by default, and dynamic binding is used for virtual functions if the binding cannot be resolved at compile time. However, a run-time decision is only needed when an object is accessed through a pointer to a base class.

4.5   Constructors and Destructors: Virtual or not Virtual?

In an inheritance hierarchy the destructor is always virtual and the constructors are never virtual.

The short answer to the question of whether constructors and destructors should be virtual or not is that constructors are never virtual, and destructors should always be made virtual if they are being used in a base class and should be non-virtual otherwise. Let us explain the reasoning.

For constructors a `virtual` label is meaningless. We can always determine at compile time what we are constructing. For destructors we need `virtual` to ensure that the destructor for the actual object is called. Otherwise, if the derived class consists of some additional members that have dynamically allocated memory, that memory will not be freed by the base class destructor. In a sense the destructor is no different than any other member function. For example, in Figure 4.7 suppose that the constructor for the base class dynamically allocates strings `Name1` and `Name2`. Presumably, its destructor will free up the memory associated with these strings. In the derived class we have an additional string `NewName`. If the destructor for the base class is used for an object of the derived class, only those items that are inherited are destroyed. The dynamically allocated memory associated with `NewName` cannot possibly be deleted because the destructor for the base class is oblivious to `NewName`'s existence.

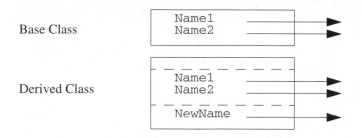

Base Class

Derived Class

Figure 4.7   Calling the base class destructor does not free memory
associated with `NewName`

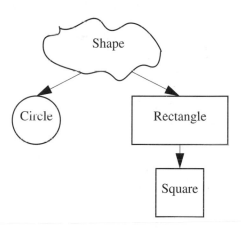

Figure 4.8   The hierarchy of shapes used in an inheritance example

4.6   Abstract Classes: A Shape Class

Our vector example showed how we can use inheritance to derive a new class
from an existing class. In this section we consider the related problem of designing a collection of classes that share basic properties. As an example, a CAD
(computer-aided design) system needs to represent objects such as lines, squares,
circles, an so on. Although these objects appear differently when drawn, all have
fundamental commonality. For instance, the location (that is, the center) of an
object is represented by coordinates in all cases. We could use the `Draw` operation for all of these objects, as well as `Place`, `Shade`, an so on. Each of these
operations requires a different implementation for each object, but some functions might not. For instance, the `Distance` function might return the distance
between the centers of any two objects. Clearly, we need to write only one distance function rather than a function for each possible combination of objects.

**Polymorphism with
dynamic binding is
achieved in C++ by fac-
toring out common dif-
ferences among a
collection of abstrac-
tions. The commonal-
ity is absorbed into a
base class.**

The factoring out of the differences among a collection of abstractions so that we can write programs in terms of their common properties allows us to use polymorphism.

To implement the polymorphic behavior of shapes, we introduce an *abstract base class* Shape. Specific shapes, such as Circle and Rectangle, are derived from Shape. We can then derive a Square as a special Rectangle. Figure 4.8 shows the class hierarchy that results.

A *pure virtual function* has no meaningful definition and is thus always defined in the derived class.

The Shape class can have data members that are common to all classes. In the CAD example, this would include the coordinates of the center of an object. It declares and provides a definition for member functions, such as PositionOf, that are independent of the actual type of object. It also declares virtual member functions that apply for each particular type of object. Some of the virtual functions make no sense for the abstract class Shape. For instance it is difficult to compute the area of an abstract object. When there is no meaningful way to implement the virtual function in the abstract base class, we specify that the function is a *pure virtual function* by appending =0 to its declaration in the interface. A pure virtual function has no meaningful definition and is thus always defined in the derived class.

```
1  // Shape class interface: abstract base class for shapes
2  //
3  // CONSTRUCTION: is not allowed; Shape is abstract
4  //      zero-parameter constructor provided for derived classes
5  //
6  // ******************PUBLIC OPERATIONS*******************
7  // double Area( )          --> Return the area (pure virtual)
8  // <                       --> Compare to Shape objects by area
9  // <<                      --> Output of Shape objects
10
11 #include <iostream.h>
12 #include "String.h"
13
14 class Shape
15 {
16   public:
17     virtual ~Shape( ) { }                    // Destructor
18     virtual double Area( ) const = 0;        // Area function
19
20     int operator<( const Shape & Rhs ) const // < function
21             { return Area( ) < Rhs.Area( ); }
22
23     friend ostream & operator<<               // Output
24             ( ostream & Output, const Shape & S );
25   protected:
26     String Name;                              // Shape ID
27 };
```

Figure 4.9   Abstract base class Shape

```
1  ostream & operator<<( ostream & Output, const Shape & S )
2  {
3      Output << S.Name << " of area " << S.Area( ) << '\n';
4      return Output;
5  }
```

Figure 4.10   Output routine for `Shape` that includes its name and area

The existence of at least one pure virtual function makes the base class abstract and disallows instantiation of it. Thus a `Shape` object cannot itself be created. Only the derived objects can. However, a `Shape*` object can be created, because we can have it point at a concrete derived object such as a `Circle` or `Rectangle`.

> **A class with at least one pure virtual function is an *abstract base class*.**

To make this discussion more concrete, we will consider the following problem:

SORTING SHAPES
READ N SHAPES (CIRCLES, SQUARES, OR RECTANGLES) AND OUTPUT THEM SORTED BY AREA.

Figure 4.9 shows the interface for the abstract base class `Shape`. At line 26 we declare a `String` that stores the type of shape. This is used only for the derived classes. The member is protected to allow the inherited classes to have access to it. The rest of the interface specifies a collection of functions.

The constructor never actually gets called directly because `Shape` is an abstract base class. We need a constructor, however, so we can accept the default. The reason we need a `Shape` constructor is that construction of the derived type requires construction of the base type. We also know that the destructor never gets called either. However, we cannot omit its declaration, even though the default semantics appear to be reasonable. This would be wrong for the destructor because, as we saw in Section 4.5, destructors in base classes should be virtual. Consequently, we declare a virtual destructor and provide an implementation that can be meaningfully inherited by the derived classes.

> **An abstract base class can never be created. However, we must still provide a constructor and destructor. In our case we accept the default constructor.**

Line 18 declares the pure virtual function `Area`. A run-time decision will select the appropriate `Area` in a derived class. `Area` is a pure virtual function because there is no meaningful default that could be specified to apply for an inherited class that chose not to define its own.

The comparison function shown at line 20 is not virtual because it can be meaningfully applied for all derived classes. In fact, in the form it is written, it need not be a member function; it can be rewritten as a two-parameter function outside of the class. However, we might want to add extensions that would require it to be a member function (or friend). For example, we might want to break ties in the area alphabetically by the `Name` member. Notice that, after inheritance, both the left and right sides of `operator<` can be any of three shapes; this implies that this operator overloads into nine possible operators. If we had many shapes, it would be incredibly tedious to cover all of the possibilities without inheritance.

The output function, declared at line 23 and 24 and whose body is shown in Figure 4.10, prints out the name of the shape and its area. Like the comparison function, it works for all of the derived classes.

Before continuing, let us summarize the three types of functions in the interface:

Static binding is used for a nonvirtual function when the function is invariant over the inheritance hierarchy.

1. *Nonvirtual functions*: Overloading is resolved at compile time. To ensure consistency when pointers to objects are used, we generally use a nonvirtual function only when the function is invariant over the inheritance hierarchy (that is, when the function is never redefined). The exception to this rule is that constructors are always nonvirtual, as mentioned in Section 4.5.

2. *Virtual functions*: Overloading is resolved at run time. The base class provides a default implementation that may be overridden by the derived classes. Destructors should be virtual functions, as mentioned in Section 4.5.

3. *Pure virtual functions*: Overloading is resolved at run time. The base class provides no implementation. The absence of a default requires that the derived classes provide an implementation.

The implementation of the derived classes, as shown in Figure 4.11, is then completely straightforward and illustrates almost nothing that we have not already seen. The only new item is that `Square` is derived from `Rectangle`, which itself is derived from `Shape`. This derivation is done exactly like all the others. In implementing these classes, we must do the following:

1. Provide a new constructor.
2. Examine each virtual function to decide if we are willing to accept its defaults; for each virtual function whose defaults we do not like, we must write a new definition.
3. Write a definition for each pure virtual function.
4. Write additional member functions if appropriate.

For each class we provide a simple constructor. Because none of these constructors allocates memory, we accept the default destructor provided by the `Shape` class. Each class is required to provide an `Area` function because `Shape` has declared that it is a pure virtual function. If the `Area` function is not provided for some class and an attempt to call it is made by an object in that class, then an error will be detected either at compile time if static binding is used or at run time if dynamic binding is used. Note that the `Square` is willing to inherit the `Area` function from the `Rectangle`, so it does not provide a redefinition.

```
1  // Circle, Square, Rectangle class interfaces;
2  //      all based on Shape
3  //
4  // CONSTRUCTION: with (a) no initializer or (b) radius (for
5  //      circle), side length (for square), length and width
6  //      (for rectangle)
7  // ******************PUBLIC OPERATIONS*********************
8  // double Area( )        --> Implements Shape pure virtual Area
9
10 const double Pi = 3.1415927;
11
12 class Circle : public Shape
13 {
14   public:
15     Circle( double R = 0.0 ) : Radius( R )
16            { Name = "circle"; }
17     double Area( ) const  { return Pi * Radius * Radius; }
18   private:
19     double Radius;
20 };
21
22 class Rectangle : public Shape
23 {
24   public:
25     Rectangle( double L = 0.0, double W = 0.0 ) :
26            Length( L ), Width( W )  { Name = "rectangle"; }
27     double Area( ) const  { return Length * Width; }
28   private:
29     double Length;
30     double Width;
31 };
32
33 class Square : public Rectangle
34 {
35   public:
36     Square( double S = 0.0 ) : Rectangle( S, S )
37            { Name = "square"; }
38 };
```

Figure 4.11   Complete Circle, Rectangle, and Square classes

```
1  #include <iostream.h>
2
3  // main: read shapes and output increasing order of area
4  // Error checks omitted for brevity
5
6  main( )
7  {
8      int NumShapes;
9      cin >> NumShapes;
10     Shape *Array[ NumShapes ];   // Array of pointers to shapes
11
12         // Read the shapes
13     for( int i = 0; i < NumShapes; i++ )
14     {
15         cout << "Enter a shape: ";
16         cin >> Array[ i ];
17     }
18
19     InsertionSort( Array, NumShapes );
20
21     cout << "Sorted by increasing size:" << endl;
22     for( int j = 0; j < NumShapes; j++ )
23         cout << *Array[ j ];
24
25     return 0;
26 }
```

Figure 4.12   `main` routine to read shapes and output them in increasing order of area

We can only declare arrays of pointers to base classes because the size of the base class is usually smaller than the size of the derived class. It can never be larger.

Now that we have written the classes, we are ready to solve the original problem. What we would like to do is declare an array of Shapes. But we cannot declare one Shape, much less an array of them. There are two reasons for this. First, Shape is an abstract base class, so a Shape object does not exist. Even if Shape was not abstract, which would be the case if it defined an Area function, we still could not reasonably declare an array of Shapes. This is because the basic Shape has one data member, Circle adds a second data member, Rectangle adds a third data member, and so on. The basic Shape is not large enough to hold all of the possible derived types. Consequently, we need an array of pointers to Shape. Figure 4.12 uses this approach. First we read the objects. At line 16 we are actually reading a character and then the dimensions of some shape, creating a shape, and finally assigning a pointer to point at the newly created shape. Figure 4.13 shows a bare bones implementation.

We then call InsertionSort to sort the shapes. Recall that we already have a template InsertionSort. Since Array is an array of pointers to shapes, we expect that it will work as long as we provide a comparison routine with the declaration

```
int operator<( const Shape * Lhs, const Shape * Rhs );
```

```
1   // Read a pointer to a shape
2   // Bare bones, with no error checking
3
4   istream & operator>>( istream & Input, Shape * & S )
5   {
6       char Ch;
7       double D1, D2;
8
9       Input.get( Ch );        // First character represents shape
10      switch( Ch )
11      {
12        case 'c':
13          Input >> D1;
14          S = new Circle( D1 );
15          break;
16
17        case 'r':
18          Input >> D1 >> D2;
19          S = new Rectangle( D1, D2 );
20          break;
21
22        case 's':
23          Input >> D1;
24          S = new Square( D1 );
25          break;
26
27        default:
28          cerr << "Needed one of c, r, or s" << endl;
29          S = new Circle;        // Radius is 0
30          break;
31      }
32
33      return Input;
34  }
```

Figure 4.13   Simple input routine for reading a pointer to a Shape

Unfortunately, that does not work. InsertionSort uses the operator< that already exists for pointers. That operator compares the addresses being pointed at, which guarantees that the array will be unaltered (because A[i] is always stored at a lower address than A[j] if i<j). Therefore, we modify InsertionSort to work for an array of arbitrary pointers. This minor change is illustrated in Figure 4.14. operator< defined for Shape and its derivations is used when InsertionSort is instantiated with Shape as Etype. Lines 21 to 23 of main (see Figure 4.12) write the resulting sorted array of shapes to the standard output.

If a class is instantiated with pointer types, shallow operations are used.

```
1   // InsertionSort: sort first N items in array A of pointers
2   // Etype: must have operator<
3
4   template <class Etype>
5   void
6   InsertionSort( Etype *A[ ], int N )
7   {
8       for( int i = 1; i < N; i++ )
9       {
10          Etype *Tmp = A[ i ];
11          int j;
12
13          for( j = i; j > 0 && *Tmp < *A[ j - 1 ]; j-- )
14              A[ j ] = A[ j - 1 ];
15          A[ j ] = Tmp;
16      }
17  }
```

Figure 4.14   Templated `InsertionSort` for pointer types

Deep comparison semantics can be obtained by designing a class to store the pointer.

A better solution than rewriting `InsertionSort` is to define a new class that hides the fact that the objects we are storing and sorting are pointers. This is shown in Figure 4.15. The `PtrToShape` structure stores the pointer to a `Shape` and provides a meaningful comparison function. It also overloads the unary * operator, so that a `PtrToShape` object looks just like a pointer to a `Shape`. We certainly can add more members to hide information better, but we prefer to keep things as short as possible. Note that in either implementation we make excessive calculations to compute areas. Avoiding this is left as Exercise 4.12.

4.7   Multiple Inheritance

Multiple inheritance is used to derive a class from several base classes. We do not use multiple inheritance in this book.

All the inheritance examples seen so far derived one class from a single base class. In *multiple inheritance* a class may be derived from more than one base class. As an example, in the `iostream` library, an `fstream` (which allows both reading and writing) is derived from both an `ifstream` and an `ofstream`. As a second example, a university has several classes of people, including: students and employees. But some people are both students and employees. The `StudentEmployee` class could be derived from both the `Student` class and the `Employee` class; each of those classes could be derived from the abstract base class `UniversityPerson`.

In multiple inheritance the new class inherits members from all of its base classes. This leads to some immediate problems that the user will need to watch out for:

```
1   struct PtrToShape
2   {
3       Shape *Ptr;
4
5       int operator < ( const PtrToShape & Rhs ) const
6               { return *Ptr < *Rhs.Ptr; }
7
8       const Shape & operator*( ) const { return *Ptr; }
9   };
10
11  // main: read shapes and output increasing order of area
12  // Error checks omitted for brevity
13
14  main( )
15  {
16      int NumShapes;
17      cin >> NumShapes;
18      PtrToShape Array[ NumShapes ];
19
20          // Read the shapes
21      for( int i = 0; i < NumShapes; i++ )
22      {
23          cout << "Enter a shape: ";
24          cin >> Array[ i ].Ptr;
25      }
26
27      InsertionSort( Array, NumShapes );
28
29      cout << "Sorted by increasing size:" << endl;
30      for( int j = 0; j < NumShapes; j++ )
31          cout << *Array[ j ];
32
33      return 0;
34  }
```

Figure 4.15   main routine to read shapes and output them in increasing order of area

- Suppose UniversityPerson has class members Name and SSN. Then these are inherited by Student and Employee. However, since StudentEmployee inherits the data members from both Student and Employee, we will get two copies of Name and SSN unless we use *virtual inheritance*, as in the following:

```
class Student : virtual public UniversityPerson {...}
class Employee :virtual public UniversityPerson {...}
class StudentEmployee : public Student,
                        public Employee{...}
```

- What if Student and Employee have member functions that are augmented to Employee but have the same signatures? For instance, the

Credit function, not given in UniversityPerson, is added to
Student to mean the number of credits for which a student is currently
registered. For employees the function returns the number of vacation
days still left. Consider the following:

```
UniversityPerson *P = new StudentEmployee;
cout << P->Student::Credits( );    // OK
cout << P->Employee::Credits( )    // OK
cout << P->Credits( );             // Ambiguous
```

- Suppose UniversityPerson defines a virtual member function F,
  and Student redefines it. However, Employee and
  StudentEmployee do nothing. Then, for P defined in the previous
  example, is P->F( ) ambiguous? In the example above, the answer is no
  because UniversityPerson is a virtual base class with respect to
  Student; consequently, Student::F( ) is said to *dominate*
  UniversityPerson::F( ), and there is no ambiguity. There would
  be if we did not use virtual inheritance for Student.

Does all this make your head spin? Most of these problems tend to suggest
that multiple inheritance is a tricky feature that requires careful analysis before
use. Generally speaking, multiple inheritance is not needed as often as we might
suspect, but when it is needed it is extremely important. Although the rules for
multiple inheritance are carefully defined in the language standard, it is also an
unfortunate fact that many compilers have bugs associated with this feature
(especially in conjunction with others). Do not use multiple inheritance until you
are extremely comfortable with simple inheritance and virtual functions; many
object-oriented languages (such as Smalltalk, Object Pascal, Objective C, and
Ada) do not support multiple inheritance, so you can live without it.

Summary

Inheritance is a powerful feature that allows the reuse of code. However, make
sure that functions applied to objects created at run time through the new operator are bound at run time. This feature is known as dynamic binding, and the use
of virtual functions is required to ensure that run-time decisions are made.
Reread this chapter as often as necessary to make sure you understand the distinction between nonvirtual functions (in which the same definition applies
throughout the inheritance hierarchy, and thus compile-time decisions are correct), virtual functions (in which the default provided in the base class can be
overwritten in the derived class; run-time decisions are made if needed), and
pure virtual functions (which have no default definition).

This chapter concludes the first part of the text, which provided an overview
of C++ and object-oriented programming. We will now go on to look at algorithms and the building blocks of problem-solving programming.

Objects of the Game

abstract base class A class with at least one pure virtual function. (133)

base class The class on which the inheritance is based. (121)

composition Preferred mechanism to private inheritance. In composition, we say that an object of class *B* is composed of an object of class *A* (and other objects). (125)

derived class A completely new class that nonetheless has some compatibility with the class it was derived from. (121)

dynamic binding Used when a member function is declared to be virtual. The decision on which function to use to resolve an overload is made at run time, if it cannot be determined at compile time. (129)

HAS-A relationship In which the derived class has a (property of the) base class. (124)

inheritance Allows us to derive a class from a base class without disturbing the implementation of the base class. (121)

IS-A relationship In which the derived class is a (variation of the) base class. (124)

multiple inheritance Used to derive a class from several base classes. (138)

nonvirtual functions Used when the function is invariant over the inheritance hierarchy. Static binding is used for nonvirtual functions. (134)

polymorphism The ability of an object to hold objects of several different types. When operations are applied to the polymorphic type, the operation that is appropriate to the actual stored type is automatically selected. (119)

private inheritance In which even public members of the base class are hidden. (125)

protected class member Accessible by the derived class but private to everyone else. (126)

public inheritance In which all public members of the base class remain public in the derived class. Public inheritance models an IS-A relationship. (125)

pure virtual function Has no meaningful definition and is thus always defined in the derived class. (132)

static binding/overloading In which the decision on which function to use to resolve an overload is made at compile time. (129)

virtual functions Dynamic binding is used for virtual functions. Use it if the function is redefined in the inheritance hierarchy. (129)

Common Errors

1. Inheritance is private by default. A common error is to omit the keyword `public` that is needed to specify public inheritance.

2. If a base class member function is redefined in a derived class, it should be made virtual. Otherwise, the wrong function could be called when accessed through a pointer.

3. Base class destructors should be declared as virtual functions. Otherwise, the wrong destructor may get called in some cases.

4. Constructors should never be declared virtual.

5. Objects of an abstract base class cannot be instantiated.

6. If the derived class fails to implement any inherited pure virtual function, then the derived class becomes abstract and cannot be instantiated, even if it makes no attempts to use the undefined pure virtual function.

7. Never redefine a default parameter for a virtual function. Default parameters are bound at compile time, and this can create an inconsistency with virtual functions that are bound at run time.

8. To access a base class member, the scope resolution must be used. Otherwise, the scope is the current class.

9. Friendship is not inherited.

10. In a derived class, the inherited base class members can only be initialized as an aggregate in a constructor's initializer list. If these members are public or protected, they may later be read or assigned to individually.

11. A common error is to declare a virtual destructor in an abstract base class but not provide an implementation (`virtual~Base()` or `virtual~Base()=0`). Both are wrong because the derived class destructor needs to call the base class destructor. If there is nothing to do, then use `{ }` as the definition.

12. If a constructor declaration is provided in the base class, provide the definition, too, for the same reason that we saw in the destructor case.

13. The return type in a derived class cannot be redefined to be different from the base class. This can cause problems for cases such as `operator++`. When this happens, it may be better to use a `void` return type.

14. If the base class has a constant member function F and the derived class attempts to define a nonconstant member function F with an otherwise identical signature, the compiler will warn that the derived F hides the base F. Heed the warning and find a workaround.

On the Internet

Two self-contained files are available. They are not used anywhere else.

BndVct.h   The `BoundedVector` class interface.
BndVct.cpp   The `BoundedVector` class implementation, plus a small test routine.

```
1 class Base
2 {
3   public:
4       int Bpublic;
5   protected:
6       int Bprotect;
7   private:
8       int Bprivate;
9 };
10
11 class Derived : public Base
12 {
13  public:
14      int Dpublic;
15  private:
16      int Dprivate;
17 };
18
19 main( )
20 {
21     Base B;
22     Derived D;
23
24     cout << B.Bpublic << ' ' << B.Bprotect << ' ' << B.Bprivate
25          << ' ' << D.Dpublic << ' ' << D.Dprivate << '\n';
26
27     return 0;
28 }
```

Figure 4.16   Program to test visibility

Exercises

In Short

4.1.   Explain the rules for when to use virtual and nonvirtual functions.

4.2.   What members of an inherited class can be used in the derived class? What members become public for users of the derived class?

4.3.   What is the default type of inheritance?

4.4.   What is private inheritance? What is composition?

4.5.   Consider the program in Figure 4.16:

    a. Which accesses are illegal?

    b. Make main a friend of class Base. Which accesses are illegal?

    c. Make main a friend of both Base and Derived. Which accesses are illegal?

        d. Write a three-parameter constructor for `Base`. Then write a five-parameter constructor for `Derived`.

        e. The class `Derived` consists of five integers. Which are accessible to the class `Derived`?

        f. The class `Derived` is passed a `Base` object. Which of the `Base` object members can the `Derived` class access?

4.6.   Define polymorphism.

4.7.   Explain dynamic binding and when it is used.

4.8.   What is a pure virtual function?

4.9.   When should a constructor be virtual?

4.10.   When should a destructor be virtual?

Programming Projects

4.11.   In the `BoundedVector` class, `operator=` as implemented copies `Low` members. This alters the array bound. What changes are needed to avoid this behavior?

4.12.   Rewrite the `Shape` hierarchy to store the area as a data member, and have it computed by the constructor. Make `Area` a nonvirtual function that returns only the value of this data member.

4.13.   Add the concept of a position to the `Shape` hierarchy by including coordinates as data members. Then add a `Distance` member function.

4.14.   Write an abstract base class for `Date` and its derived class `GregorianDate`.

4.15.   Implement the taxpayer hierarchy described in Section 4.1. Implement the classes `SinglePayer` and `MarriedPayer` in addition to the interfaces for an abstract base class and the other two derived classes.

4.16.   Design a templated `Pointer` class with overloaded `operator<` and `operator*`, as was done for `PtrToShape`. Then modify the routine in Figure 4.15.

References

The usual suspects give more information on inheritance. I particularly like [1], from which the guidelines for use of virtual, pure virtual, and nonvirtual functions appears. You might also want to check out Stroustrup's book [2], which explains the design of C++. The `Shape` class is taken from [3].

1. S. Meyers, *Effective C++*, Addison-Wesley, Reading, MA, 1992.

2. B. Stroustrup, *The Design and Evolution of C++*, Addison-Wesley, Reading, MA, 1994.

3. M. A. Weiss, *Efficient C Programming: A Practical Approach*, Prentice-Hall, Englewood Cliffs, NJ, 1995.

Part II: Algorithms and Building Blocks

Chapter 5

Algorithm Analysis

In Part I we examined how object-oriented programming can help in the design and implementation of large systems. This is only half the story, however. Generally, we use a computer because we need to process a large amount of data. When we run a program on large amounts of input, we must be certain that it terminates within a reasonable amount of time. This is almost always independent of the programming language we use or even the methodology (such as procedural vs. object-oriented).

An *algorithm* is a clearly specified set of instructions the computer will follow to solve a problem. Once an algorithm is given for a problem and determined to be correct, an important next step is to determine the amount of resources, such as time and space, the algorithm will require. This process is known as *algorithm analysis*. An algorithm that requires several gigabytes of main memory is not useful for most current machines even if it is completely correct.

In this chapter we will see

- how to estimate the time required for an algorithm
- techniques that drastically reduce the running time of an algorithm
- a mathematical framework that more rigorously describes the running time of an algorithm
- how to write a simple *binary search* routine

5.1   What Is Algorithm Analysis?

The amount of time that any algorithm takes to run almost always depends on the amount of input it must process. We expect, for instance, that sorting 10,000 elements requires more time than sorting 10 elements. The running time of an algorithm is thus a function of the input size. The exact value of the function is dependent on many factors, such as the speed of the host machine, the quality of the compiler, and in some cases, the quality of the program. For a given program

More data means the program takes more time.

on a given computer, we can plot the graph that represents the running time function. Figure 5.1 illustrates such a plot for four programs; the curves represent four common functions that are encountered in algorithm analysis. The input size N ranges from 1 to 100 items, and the running times range from 0 to 10 milliseconds.

Of the common functions encountered in algorithm analysis, linear is the best.

A quick glance at Figure 5.1 and its companion, Figure 5.2, suggests that the linear, O(N log N), quadratic, and cubic curves represent running times in order of decreasing preference: Linear is much better than cubic. We will address several important questions:

- What do these terms mean?
- Is it always important to be on the most preferable curve?
- How much better is one curve than another?
- How do we decide which curve a particular algorithm lies on?

A cubic function is a function whose dominant term is some constant times N^3. As an example, $10N^3 + N^2 + 40N + 80$ is a cubic function. Similarly, a quadratic function has a dominant term that is some constant times N^2, and a linear function has a dominant term that is some constant times N. $O(N \log N)$ represents a function whose dominant term is N times the logarithm of N. The logarithm is a slowly growing function; for instance, the logarithm of 1,000,000 (with the typical base 2) is only 20. The logarithm grows more slowly than a square or cube (or any) root. We will discuss the logarithm in more depth in Section 5.5.

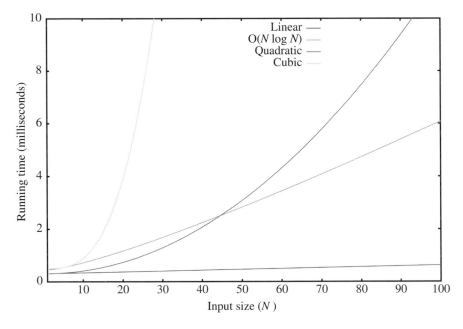

Figure 5.1   Running times for small inputs

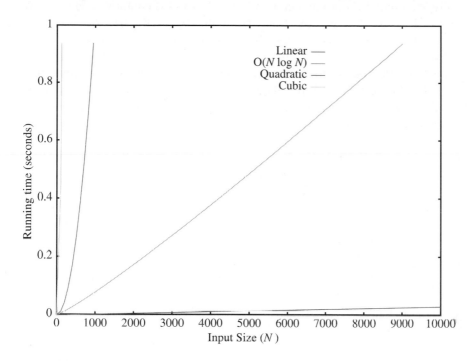

Figure 5.2   Running time for moderate inputs

Given two functions, either may be smaller than the other at any given point, so it does not make sense to claim, for instance, that $F(N) < G(N)$. Instead, we measure the functions' rates of growth. This is justified for three reasons. First, for cubic functions such as the one shown in Figure 5.2, we see that when N is 1000, the value of the cubic function is almost entirely determined by the cubic term. If we were to use only the cubic term to estimate the entire function, an error of about 0.01 percent would result. For sufficiently large N, the value of a function is largely determined by its dominant term. The meaning of the term *sufficiently large* varies from function to function. Second, the exact value of the leading constant of the dominant term is not meaningful across different machines (although the relative values of the leading constant for identically growing functions might be). For instance, as we saw in Section 1.6, the optimizer could have a large influence on the leading constant. Third, small values of N generally are not important.

The growth rate of a function is most important when *N* is sufficiently large.

We use *Big-Oh* notation to represent growth rate. For instance, the running time of a quadratic algorithm is specified as $O(N^2)$ (pronounced "order N-squared"). Big-Oh notation allows us to establish a relative order among functions by comparing dominant terms. We will discuss Big-Oh notation more fully in Section 5.4.

***Big-Oh* notation is used to capture the most dominant term in a function.**

For small values of N (for instance, those less than 30), Figure 5.1 shows that there are points where one curve is initially better than another, even though eventually this does not prove true. For example, initially the quadratic curve is better than the $O(N \log N)$ curve, but as N gets sufficiently large, the quadratic algorithm loses its advantage. For small amounts of input, it is difficult to make comparisons between functions because leading constants become very significant. The function $N + 2500$ is larger than N^2 when N is less than 50. Eventually, the linear function will always be less than the quadratic function. Most importantly, for small input sizes the running times are generally inconsequential, and we need not worry about them. For instance, Figure 5.1 shows that when N is less than 25, all the algorithms that we describe for this problem run in less than 10 milliseconds. Consequently, when input sizes are very small, a good rule of thumb is to use the simplest algorithm.

Quadratic algorithms are impractical for input sizes exceeding a few thousand.

Figure 5.2 clearly demonstrates the differences between the various curves for large input sizes. A linear algorithm solves a problem of size 10,000 in a small fraction of a second. The $O(N \log N)$ algorithm uses roughly ten times as much time. Note that the actual time differences would depend on the constants involved and thus might be more or less. Depending on these constants, it is possible that an $O(N \log N)$ algorithm might be faster than a linear algorithm for fairly large input sizes. For equally complex algorithms, however, linear algorithms tend to win over $O(N \log N)$ algorithms in practice.

Cubic algorithms are impractical for input sizes exceeding a few hundred.

This is not true, however, for the quadratic and cubic algorithms. Quadratic algorithms are almost always impractical when the input size is more than a few thousand, and cubic algorithms are impractical for input sizes as small as a few hundred. Just try to run the `InsertionSort` algorithm given in Section 3.2 for 50,000 items. Be prepared to wait a long time because an insertion sort is a quadratic algorithm. The sorting algorithms discussed in Chapter 8 run in *subquadratic* time (that is, better than $O(N^2)$), making sorting large arrays practical.

The most striking feature of these curves is that the quadratic and cubic algorithms are not competitive with the others for reasonably large inputs. We can code the quadratic algorithm in highly efficient machine language, do a poor job coding the linear algorithm, and the quadratic algorithm still loses badly. Even the most clever programming tricks cannot make an inefficient algorithm fast. Thus, before we waste effort attempting to optimize code, we need to optimize the algorithm. Figure 5.3 arranges functions that commonly describe algorithm running times in order of increasing growth rate.

Function	Name
c	Constant
$\log N$	Logarithmic
$\log^2 N$	Log-squared
N	Linear
$N \log N$	$N \log N$
N^2	Quadratic
N^3	Cubic
2^N	Exponential

Figure 5.3   Functions in order of increasing growth rate

5.2   Examples of Algorithm Running Times

In this section we will examine three problems and, without providing detailed programs, we will sketch possible solutions and determine what kind of running times the algorithms will exhibit. Our goal in this section is to provide some intuition about algorithm analysis. In the next section we will provide more details on the process, and then in Section 5.4 we will formally approach an algorithm analysis problem.

The problems we will look at in this section are:

MINIMUM ELEMENT IN AN ARRAY
GIVEN AN ARRAY OF N ITEMS, FIND THE SMALLEST.

CLOSEST POINTS IN THE PLANE
GIVEN N POINTS IN A PLANE (THAT IS, AN X-Y COORDINATE SYSTEM), FIND THE PAIR OF POINTS THAT ARE CLOSEST TOGETHER.

COLINEAR POINTS IN THE PLANE
GIVEN N POINTS IN A PLANE (THAT IS, AN X-Y COORDINATE SYSTEM), DETERMINE IF ANY THREE FORM A STRAIGHT LINE.

The minimum element problem is fundamental in computer science. It can be solved as follows: Maintain a variable Min that stores the minimum element. Initialize Min to the first element. Make a sequential scan through the array and update Min as appropriate. The running time of this algorithm will be $O(N)$, or linear, because we will repeat a fixed amount of work for each element in the array. A linear algorithm is as good as we can hope for because we have to examine every element in the array, a process that requires linear time.

The closest points problem is a fundamental problem in graphics that can be solved as follows: Calculate the distance between each pair of points, and retain the minimum distance. This is an expensive calculation, however, because there are $N(N-1)/2$ pairs of points.[1] Thus there are roughly N^2 pairs of points, and examining all these pairs and finding the minimum distance among those pairs will take quadratic time. There is an improved algorithm that runs in $O(N \log N)$ time and works by avoiding the computation of all distances. There is also an algorithm that is expected to take $O(N)$ time. These last two algorithms use subtle observations to provide faster results.

The colinear points problem is important for many graphics algorithms because the existence of colinear points introduces a degenerate case that requires special handling. It can be directly solved by enumerating all groups of three points. This solution is even more computationally expensive than the closest points problem because the number of different groups of three points is $N(N-1)(N-2)/6$ (using reasoning similar to that used for the closest points problem). This tells us that the direct approach will yield a cubic algorithm. There is also a more clever strategy that solves the problem in quadratic time (and further improvement is an area of continuously active research).

In the next section we will look at a problem that illustrates the differences between linear, quadratic, and cubic algorithms, and we will see how the performance of these algorithms compares to a mathematical prediction. After discussing the basic ideas, we will examine Big-Oh notation more formally.

5.3   The Maximum Contiguous Subsequence Sum Problem

In this section, we will consider the following problem:

MAXIMUM CONTIGUOUS SUBSEQUENCE SUM PROBLEM
GIVEN (POSSIBLY NEGATIVE) INTEGERS $A_1, A_2, ..., A_N$, FIND (AND IDENTIFY THE SEQUENCE CORRESPONDING TO) THE MAXIMUM VALUE OF $\sum_{k=i}^{j} A_k$. THE MAXIMUM CONTIGUOUS SUBSEQUENCE SUM IS ZERO IF ALL THE INTEGERS ARE NEGATIVE.

As an example, if the input is {-2, **11**, **-4**, **13**, -5, 2}, then the answer is 20, representing the contiguous subsequence encompassing items 2 through 4. As a second example, for the input { 1, -3, **4**, **-2**, **-1**, **6** }, the answer is 7 for the subsequence encompassing the last four items.

---

1. To see this, note that each of *N* points can be paired with $N-1$ points, for a total of $N(N-1)$ pairs. However, this double counts pairs *A*, *B* and *B*, *A*, so we must divide by two.

In C++, arrays begin at zero, so a C++ program would represent the input as a sequence A_0 to A_{N-1}. Alternatively, we could use the `BoundedVector` class from Section 4.2. This is a programming detail and not part of the algorithm.

Programming details are considered after the algorithm design.

Before beginning our discussion of the algorithms for this problem, it is worth commenting on the degenerate case where all input integers are negative. The problem statement gives a maximum contiguous subsequence sum of zero for this case. One might wonder why we do this, rather than just returning the largest (that is, the smallest in magnitude) negative integer in the input. The reason for this is that the empty subsequence, consisting of zero integers, is also a subsequence, and its sum is clearly zero. Since the empty subsequence is contiguous, we see that there is always a contiguous subsequence whose sum is zero. This is analogous to the empty set being a subset of any set. It is important to be cognizant of the fact that emptiness is always a possibility and that in many instances it is not a special case at all.

Always consider emptiness.

```
1   // Cubic maximum contiguous subsequence sum algorithm
2   // Etype: must have constructor from int, must have
3   //        += and > defined, must have copy constructor
4   //        and operator=, and must have all properties
5   //        needed for Vector
6
7   template<class Etype>
8   Etype
9   MaxSubsequenceSum( const Vector<Etype> & A, int N,
10                      int & SeqStart, int & SeqEnd )
11  {
12      Etype MaxSum = 0;
13
14      for( int i = 0; i < N; i++ )
15          for( int j = i; j < N; j++ )
16          {
17              Etype ThisSum = 0;
18              for( int k = i; k <= j; k++ )
19                  ThisSum += A[ k ];
20
21              if( ThisSum > MaxSum )
22              {
23                  MaxSum = ThisSum;
24                  SeqStart = i;
25                  SeqEnd = j;
26              }
27          }
28
29      return MaxSum;
30  }
```

Figure 5.4   Cubic maximum contiguous subsequence sum algorithm

The maximum contiguous subsequence sum problem is interesting mainly because there are so many algorithms to solve it, and the performance of these algorithms varies drastically. In this section we will discuss three algorithms. The first algorithm is an obvious exhaustive search algorithm, but it is also very inefficient. We will go on to improve this algorithm by a simple observation. We close by providing a very efficient but not obvious algorithm and prove that its running time is linear. In Chapter 7 we will present a fourth algorithm, which has $O(N \log N)$ running time. That algorithm is not as efficient as the linear algorithm, but it is much more efficient than the other two and is typical of the kinds of algorithms that result in $O(N \log N)$ running times. The graphs shown in Figures 5.1 and 5.2 are representative of these four algorithms.

5.3.1   The Obvious $O(N^3)$ Algorithm

The simplest algorithm is a direct exhaustive search, or brute force algorithm, as shown in Figure 5.4. Lines 14 and 15 control a pair of loops that iterate over all possible subsequences. For each possible subsequence, the value of its sum is computed at lines 17 to 19. If it is the best sum seen, then we update the value of `MaxSum`, which is eventually returned at line 29. Two reference parameters, `SeqStart` and `SeqEnd`, are also updated whenever a new best sequence is encountered.

The exhaustive search algorithm has the merit of extreme simplicity; the less complex an algorithm is, the more likely it is to be programmed correctly. However, it is usually the case that the exhaustive search algorithm is not as efficient as possible. In the remainder of this section, we show that the running time of the algorithm is cubic. To do this, we will count how many times (as a function of the input size) the expressions in Figure 5.4 are evaluated. Since we only require a Big-Oh result, we can ignore lower-order terms and leading constants once we find a dominant term.

We will show that the running time of the algorithm is entirely dominated by the innermost `for` loop in lines 18 and 19. Four expressions there are repeatedly executed:

1. The initialization `k = i`
2. The test `k <= j`
3. The increment `ThisSum += A[ k ]`
4. The adjustment `k++`

The number of times that expression 3 is executed makes it the dominant term among the four expressions. To see this, first notice that each initialization is accompanied by at least one test. We are ignoring constants, so we may disregard the cost of the initializations: The initializations cannot be the single dominating cost of the algorithm. Because the test given by expression 2 is unsuccessful exactly once per loop, the number of unsuccessful tests performed by expression 2 is exactly equal to the number of initializations and consequently is not dominant. The number of successful tests at expression 2, the number of increments performed by expression 3, and the number of adjustments at expression 4 are all identical. Thus the number of increments (that is, the number of times that line 19 is executed) is a dominant measure of the work performed in the innermost loop.

The number of times line 19 is executed is exactly equal to the number of ordered triplets (i, j, k) that satisfy $1 \leq i \leq k \leq j \leq N$.[2] This is because the index i runs over the entire array, j runs from i to the end of the array, and k runs from i to j. We can compute the exact number of ordered triplets by evaluating the sum $\sum_{i=1}^{N} \sum_{j=i}^{N} \sum_{k=i}^{j} 1$. We can evaluate this sum inside out (see Exercise 5.9), but instead we will use an alternative approach.

The number of integer ordered triplets (i, j, k) that satisfy   ***Theorem 5.1***
$1 \leq i \leq k \leq j \leq N$ *is* $N(N+1)(N+2)/6$.

Place the following $N+2$ *balls in a box: N balls numbered 1 to N, one*   ***Proof***
unnumbered red ball, and one unnumbered blue ball. Remove three balls
from the box. If a red ball is drawn, number it as the lowest of the num-
bered balls drawn, and if a blue ball is drawn, number it as the highest of
the numbered balls drawn. Notice that if we draw both a red and blue
ball, then the effect is to have three balls identically numbered. Order the
three balls. Each possible order corresponds to a triplet solution to the
equation in Theorem 5.1. The number of possible orders is the number of
distinct ways to draw three balls without replacement from a collection of
$N+2$ *balls. This is similar to the problem of selecting three points from a*
group of N that we evaluated in Section 5.2, so we immediately obtain the
stated result

The result of Theorem 5.1 is that the innermost `for` loop accounts for cubic running time. The remaining work in the algorithm is inconsequential because it is done at most once per iteration of the inner loop. Put another way, the cost of lines 21 to 26 is inconsequential because it is done only as often as the initialization of the inner `for` loop, rather than as often as the repeated body of the inner `for` loop. Consequently, the algorithm is $O(N^3)$.

---

2. In C++ the indices run from 0 to $N-1$; we use the algorithmic equivalent 1 to N in the analysis.

```
1    // Quadratic maximum contiguous subsequence sum algorithm.
2    // Etype: must have constructor from int, must have
3    //        += and > defined, must have copy constructor
4    //        and operator=, and must have all properties
5    //        needed for Vector
6
7    template<class Etype>
8    Etype
9    MaxSubsequenceSum( const Vector<Etype> & A, int N,
10                                    int & SeqStart, int & SeqEnd )
11   {
12       Etype MaxSum = 0;
13
14       for( int i = 0; i < N; i++ )
15       {
16           Etype ThisSum = 0;
17           for( int j = i; j < N; j++ )
18           {
19               ThisSum += A[ j ];
20
21               if( ThisSum > MaxSum )
22               {
23                   MaxSum = ThisSum;
24                   SeqStart = i;
25                   SeqEnd = j;
26               }
27           }
28       }
29
30       return MaxSum;
31   }
```

Figure 5.5   Quadratic maximum contiguous subsequence sum algorithm

We do not need precise calculations for a Big-Oh estimate. In many cases we can use the simple rule of multiplying the size of all the nested loops. Note carefully that consecutive loops do not multiply.

The combinatoric argument used above allows us to obtain precise calculations on the number of iterations in the inner loop. For a Big-Oh calculation, this is not really necessary; we only need to know that the leading term is some constant times N^3. Looking at the algorithm, we see a loop that is potentially of size N inside a loop that is potentially of size N inside another loop that is potentially of size N. This tells us that the triple loop has the potential for $N \times N \times N$ iterations. This potential is only about six times higher than what our precise calculation shows actually occurs. Since constants are ignored anyway, we can adopt the general rule that when we have nested loops, we should multiply the cost of the innermost statement by the size of each loop in the nest to obtain an upper bound. In most cases the upper bound will not be a gross overestimate.[3] Thus a program with three nested loops, each running sequentially through large por-

---

3. Exercise 5.16 illustrates a case where the multiplication of loop sizes yields an overestimate in the Big-Oh result.

tions of an array, is likely to exhibit $O(N^3)$ behavior. Note that three consecutive (nonnested) loops exhibit linear behavior; it is nesting that leads to a combinatoric explosion. Consequently, to improve the algorithm, we will need to remove a loop.

5.3.2 An Improved $O(N^2)$ Algorithm

If we could remove a loop from the algorithm, we could lower the running time. How can we remove a loop? Obviously this is not always possible, but this algorithm has many unnecessary computations. The inefficiency that the improved algorithm corrects can be seen by noticing that $\sum_{k=i}^{j} A_k = A_j + \sum_{k=i}^{j-1} A_k$, so that computation in the inner for loop in Figure 5.4 is unduly expensive. Put another way, if we have just calculated the sum for the subsequence extending from i to $j-1$, then computing the sum for the subsequence extending from i to j should not take long because we need only one more addition. However the cubic algorithm throws this information away. If we use this observation, we obtain the improved algorithm shown in Figure 5.5. We have two rather than three nested loops, and the running time is $O(N^2)$.

> When we remove a deeply nested loop from an algorithm, we generally lower the running time.

5.3.3 A Linear Algorithm

To move from a quadratic algorithm down to a linear algorithm, we need to remove yet another loop. However, unlike the reduction illustrated in Figures 5.4 and 5.5, where loop removal was simple, it is not so easy to get rid of another loop. The problem is that the quadratic algorithm is still an exhaustive search: We are trying all possible subsequences. The only difference between the quadratic and cubic algorithms is that the cost of testing each successive subsequence is a constant $O(1)$ instead of linear $O(N)$. Because a quadratic number of subsequences are possible, the only way we can attain a subquadratic bound is to find a clever way to eliminate from consideration a large number of subsequences, without actually computing their sum and testing to see if that sum is a new maximum. In this section we show how that is done.

> If we remove another loop, we are down to a linear algorithm.

We begin by showing one method that allows us to eliminate a large number of possible subsequences from consideration. Let $A_{i,j}$ be the subsequence encompassing elements from i to j, and let $S_{i,j}$ be its sum.

> The algorithm is tricky; it uses a clever observation to step quickly over large numbers of subsequences that cannot be the best.

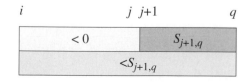

Figure 5.6 The subsequences used in Theorem 5.2

Theorem 5.2   *Let $A_{i,j}$ be any sequence with $S_{i,j} < 0$. If $j < q$, then $A_{i,q}$ is not the maximum contiguous subsequence.*

Proof   *The sum of A's elements from i to q is the sum of A's elements from i to j added to the sum of A's elements from $j + 1$ to q. Thus we have $S_{i,q} = S_{i,j} + S_{j+1,q}$. Since $S_{i,j} < 0$, we know that $S_{i,q} < S_{j+1,q}$. We can thus see that $A_{i,q}$ is not a maximum contiguous subsequence.*

If we detect a negative sum, we can move *i* all the way past *j*.

     An illustration of the sums generated by i, j, and q is shown on the first two lines in Figure 5.6. Theorem 5.2 demonstrates that it is possible to avoid examination of several subsequences by incorporating an additional test: If `ThisSum` is less than zero, then we can `break` from the inner loop in Figure 5.5. Intuitively, if we see a subsequence whose sum is negative, then it cannot be part of the maximum contiguous subsequence, because we can get a large contiguous subsequence by not including it. This observation by itself is not sufficient to reduce the running time below quadratic. A similar observation also holds: All contiguous subsequences that border the maximum contiguous subsequence must have negative (or zero) sums (otherwise, we would include them). This also does not reduce the running time to below quadratic. However a third observation, illustrated in Figure 5.7, does. We can formalize this with the following theorem:

Theorem 5.3   *For any i, let $A_{i,j}$ be the first sequence, with $S_{i,j} < 0$. Then, for any $i \leq p \leq j$ and $p \leq q$, $A_{p,q}$ is either not a maximum contiguous subsequence or is equal to an already seen maximum contiguous subsequence.*

Proof   *If $p = i$, then Theorem 5.2 applies. Otherwise, as before, we have $S_{i,q} = S_{i,p-1} + S_{p,q}$. Since j is the lowest index for which $S_{i,j} < 0$, it follows that $S_{i,p-1} \geq 0$. Thus $S_{p,q} \leq S_{i,q}$. If $q > j$ (shown on the left in Figure 5.7), then Theorem 5.2 implies that $A_{i,q}$ is not a maximum contiguous subsequence, so neither is $A_{p,q}$. Otherwise, as shown on the right in Figure 5.7, the subsequence $A_{p,q}$ has a sum equal to, at most, that of the already seen subsequence $A_{i,q}$.*

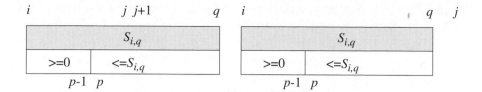

Figure 5.7   The subsequences used in Theorem 5.3. The sequence from p to q has sum at most that of the subsequence from i to q. On the left, the sequence from i to q is itself not the maximum (by Theorem 5.2). On the right, the sequence from i to q has already been seen.

Theorem 5.3 tells us that when a negative subsequence is detected, not only can we `break` the inner loop, but also we can advance i to j+1. Figure 5.8 shows that we can rewrite the algorithm using only a single loop. Clearly the running time of this algorithm is linear: At each step in the loop we advance j, so the loop iterates at most N times. The correctness of this algorithm is much less obvious than for the previous algorithms. This is typical: Algorithms that use the structure of a problem to beat exhaustive search generally require some sort of correctness proof. We have proven that the algorithm (though not the resulting C++ program) is correct using a short mathematical argument. Our purpose is not to make the discussion entirely mathematical but rather to give a flavor of the techniques that might be required in advanced work.

5.4   General Big-Oh Rules

Now that we have given the basic ideas of algorithm analysis, we can adopt a slightly more formal approach. In this section we will outline the general rules for using Big-Oh notation. Although we use Big Oh notation almost exclusively throughout the book, we also define three other types of algorithm notation that are related to Big-Oh and used occasionally later on.

> **If an algorithm is complex, a correctness proof is required.**

DEFINITION: (Big-Oh) $T(N) = O(F(N))$ if there are positive constants c and N_0 such that $T(N) \le cF(N)$ when $N \ge N_0$.

DEFINITION: (Big-Omega) $T(N) = \Omega(F(N))$ if there are positive constants c and N_0 such that $T(N) \ge cF(N)$ when $N \ge N_0$.

DEFINITION: (Big-Theta) $T(N) = \Theta(F(N))$ if and only if $T(N) = O(F(N))$ and $T(N) = \Omega(F(N))$.

DEFINITION: (Little-Oh) $T(N) = o(F(N))$ if there are positive constants c and N_0 such that $T(N) < cF(N)$ when $N \ge N_0$.

Big-Oh is similar to less than or equal to, when considering growth rates.

The first definition, *Big-Oh* notation, states that there is a point N_0 such that for all values of N that are past this point, $T(N)$ is bounded by some multiple of $F(N)$. This is the sufficiently large N that we mentioned earlier. Thus, if the running time $T(N)$ of an algorithm is $O(N^2)$, then, ignoring constants, we are guaranteeing that at some point we can bound the running time by a quadratic function. Notice that if the true running time is linear, then the statement that the running time is $O(N^2)$ is technically correct because the inequality holds. However, $O(N)$ would be the more precise claim.

If we use the traditional inequality operators to compare growth rates, then the first definition says that the growth rate of $T(N)$ is less than or equal to that of $F(N)$.

```
1    // Linear maximum contiguous subsequence sum algorithm
2    // Etype: must have constructor from int, must have
3    //        += and > defined, must have copy constructor
4    //        and operator=, and must have all properties
5    //        needed for Vector
6
7    template<class Etype>
8    Etype
9    MaxSubsequenceSum( const Vector<Etype> & A, int N,
10                              int & SeqStart, int & SeqEnd )
11   {
12       Etype MaxSum = 0;
13       Etype ThisSum = 0;
14
15       for( int i = 0, j = 0; j < N; j++ )
16       {
17           ThisSum += A[ j ];
18
19           if( ThisSum > MaxSum )
20           {
21               MaxSum = ThisSum;
22               SeqStart = i;
23               SeqEnd = j;
24           }
25           else if( ThisSum < 0 )
26           {
27               i = j + 1;
28               ThisSum = 0;
29           }
30       }
31
32       return MaxSum;
33   }
```

Figure 5.8   Linear maximum contiguous subsequence sum algorithm

The second definition, $T(N) = \Omega(F(N))$, called *Big-Omega*, says that the growth rate of $T(N)$ is greater than or equal to that of $F(N)$. For instance we might say that any algorithm that works by examining every possible subsequence in the maximum subsequence sum problem must take $\Omega(N^2)$ time because a quadratic number of subsequences are possible. This is a lower-bound argument that is used in more advanced analysis. Later in the text we will see one example of this: We will show that any general-purpose sorting algorithm requires $\Omega(N \log N)$ time.

Big-Omega is similar to greater than or equal to when considering growth rates.

The third definition, $T(N) = \Theta(F(N))$, called *Big-Theta*, says that the growth rate of $T(N)$ equals the growth rate of $F(N)$. For instance, the maximum subsequence algorithm shown in Figure 5.5 runs in $\Theta(N^2)$ time. This means that the running time is bounded by a quadratic function, and that this bound cannot be improved because it is also lower-bounded by another quadratic function. When we use Big-Theta notation, we are not only providing an upper bound on an algorithm but also providing assurances that the analysis that leads to the upper bound is as good (tight) as possible. In spite of the additional precision offered by Big-Theta, Big-Oh is more commonly used, except by researchers in the algorithm analysis field.

Big-Theta is similar to equal to when considering growth rates.

The final definition, $T(N) = o(F(N))$, called *Little-Oh*, says that the growth rate of $T(N)$ is strictly less than the growth rate of $F(N)$. This is different from Big-Oh because Big-Oh allows the possibility that the growth rates are the same. For instance, if the running time of an algorithm is $o(N^2)$, then it is guaranteed to be growing at a slower rate than quadratic (that is, it is *subquadratic*). Thus a bound of $o(N^2)$ is a better bound than $\Theta(N^2)$. Figure 5.9 illustrates the meaning of these four definitions.

Little-Oh is similar to less than when considering growth rates.

A couple of stylistic notes are in order. First, it is bad style to include constants or low-order terms inside a Big-Oh. Do not say $T(N) = O(2N^2)$ or $T(N) = O(N^2 + N)$. In both cases the correct form is $T(N) = O(N^2)$. Remember that in any analysis that requires a Big-Oh answer, all sorts of shortcuts are possible. Lower-order terms are ignored, and leading constants and relational symbols are thrown away.

Throw out leading constants, lower-order terms, and relational symbols when using Big-Oh.

Mathematical expression	Relative rates of growth
$T(N) = O(F(N))$	Growth of $T(N)$ is $\leq$ growth of $F(N)$
$T(N) = \Omega(F(N))$	Growth of $T(N)$ is $\geq$ growth of $F(N)$
$T(N) = \Theta(F(N))$	Growth of $T(N)$ is $=$ growth of $F(N)$
$T(N) = o(F(N))$	Growth of $T(N)$ is $<$ growth of $F(N)$

Figure 5.9   Meanings of the various growth functions

Now that we have formalized the mathematics, we can relate it to the analysis of algorithms. The most basic rule is that *the running time of a loop is at most the running time of the statements inside the loop (including tests) times the number of iterations.* As we saw earlier, the initialization and testing of the loop condition is usually no more dominant than the statements encompassing the body of the loop.

A *worst-case bound* is a guarantee over all inputs of some size.

The running time of statements inside a group of nested loops is the running time of the statements (including tests in the innermost loop) multiplied by the sizes of all the loops. The running time of a sequence of consecutive loops is equal to the running time of the dominant loop. The time difference between a nested loop in which both indices run from 1 to N and two consecutive loops that are not nested but run over the same indices is the same as the space difference between a two-dimensional array and two one-dimensional arrays. The first case is quadratic, and the second case is linear because $N+N$ is $2N$, which is still $O(N)$. Occasionally, this simple rule can overestimate the running time, but in most cases it does not, and even if it does, Big-Oh does not guarantee an exact asymptotic answer, just an upper bound.

In an *average-case bound*, the running time is measured as an average over all of the possible inputs of size *N*.

The analyses we have performed thus far are *worst-case bounds*, which are guarantees over all inputs of some size. Another form is the *average-case bound*, in which the running time is measured as an average over all of the possible inputs of size N. The average might differ from the worst case if, for example, a conditional statement that depends on the particular input causes an early exit from a loop. Average-case bounds are discussed in more detail in Section 5.8. For now we note that the fact that one algorithm has a better worst-case bound than another algorithm does not imply anything about their relative average-case bounds. However, in many cases average-case and worst-case bounds are closely correlated. When they are not we will discuss the bounds separately.

N	Figure 5.4 $O(N^3)$	Figure 5.5 $O(N^2)$	Figure 7.12 $O(N \log N)$	Figure 5.8 $O(N)$
10	0.00103	0.00045	0.00066	0.00034
100	0.47015	0.01112	0.00486	0.00063
1,000	448.77	1.1233	0.05843	0.00333
10,000	NA	111.13	0.68631	0.03042
100,000	NA	NA	8.01130	0.29832

Figure 5.10   Observed running times (in seconds) for various maximum contiguous subsequence sum algorithms

The last Big-Oh item we examine is how the running time grows for each type of curve. We have already seen this in the graphs in Figures 5.1 and 5.2. We want a more quantitative answer to the question, if an algorithm takes $T(N)$ time to solve a problem of size N, how long does it take to solve a larger problem? For instance, how long does it take to solve a problem with ten times as much input? The answers are shown in Figure 5.10, but we would like to answer the question without running the program. We hope our analytical answers will agree with the observed behavior.

We begin by examining the cubic algorithm. By assumption, we may assume that the running time is reasonably approximated by $T(N) = cN^3$. Consequently, $T(10N) = c(10N)^3$. Mathematical manipulation yields

$$T(10N) = 1000cN^3 = 1000T(N)$$

If the size of the input increases by a factor of 10, a cubic program takes 1,000 times as long to run.

Thus the running time of a cubic program increases by a factor of 1000 (assuming N is sufficiently large) when the amount of input is increased by a factor of 10. This is roughly confirmed by examining the increase in running time from N = 100 to 1000 in Figure 5.10. Remember that we do not expect an exact answer, just a reasonable approximation. We would also expect that for N = 10,000 there would be another 1000-fold increase in running time. The result would be that using a cubic algorithm would require roughly two weeks of computation time.

We can perform similar calculations for quadratic and linear algorithms. For the quadratic algorithm, we assume $T(N) = cN^2$. It follows that $T(10N) = c(10N)^2$. When we expand, we obtain

$$T(10N) = 100cN^2 = 100T(N)$$

If the size of the input increases by a factor of f, the running time of a quadratic program increases by a factor of roughly f^2.

so we can see that, when the input size increases by a factor of ten, the running time of a quadratic program increases by a factor of approximately 100. This is also confirmed in Figure 5.10.

Finally, for a linear program a similar calculation will show that a tenfold increase in input size results in a tenfold increase in running time. Once again, this is confirmed experimentally. Notice, however, that for a linear program the term *sufficiently large* means a somewhat higher input size than for the other programs. This is because of the overhead of 0.0003 second that is used in all cases. For a linear program this term is still significant for moderate input sizes.

If the size of the input increases by a factor of f, then the running time of a linear program also increases by a factor of f. This is the preferential running time for an algorithm.

The analysis used here does not work when there are logarithmic terms. When an $O(N\log N)$ algorithm is presented with ten times as much input, the running time increases by a factor that is slightly larger than ten. Specifically, we have $T(10N) = c(10N)\log(10N)$. When we expand we obtain

$$T(10N) = 10cN\log(10N) = 10cN\log N + 10cN\log 10 = 10T(N) + c'N$$

Here $c' = 10c\log 10$. As N gets very large, the ratio $T(10N)/T(N)$ gets closer and closer to ten because $c'N/T(N) \approx (10\log 10)/\log N$ gets smaller and smaller with increasing N. Consequently, if the algorithm is competitive with a linear algorithm for very large N, it is likely to remain competitive for slightly larger N.

Does all this mean that quadratic and cubic algorithms are useless? The answer is no. In some cases the most efficient algorithms known are quadratic or cubic, and in others the most efficient algorithm is even worse (exponential). Furthermore, when the amount of input is small, any algorithm will do, and frequently the algorithms that are not asymptotically efficient are nonetheless easy to program. For small inputs, that is the way to go. Finally, it should be pointed out that a good way to test a complex linear algorithm is to compare its output with an exhaustive search-type algorithm. Section 5.8 discusses some other limitations of the Big-Oh model.

5.5   The Logarithm

The *logarithm* of *N* (to the base 2) is the value *X* such that 2 raised to the power of *X* equals *N*.

Our list of typical growth rate functions includes several entries containing the *logarithm*. In this section we will look at the mathematics behind the logarithm in more detail. In the next section we will see how it shows up in a simple algorithm. We begin with the formal definition, which we will follow with more intuitive viewpoints:

DEFINITION: For any $B, N > 0$, $\log_B N = K$ if $B^K = N$.

By default the base of the logarithm is 2.

In this definition, B is the base of the logarithm. In computer science, when the base is omitted, it defaults to 2. As we will see later, this is natural for several reasons. We will prove one mathematical theorem to show that, as far as Big-Oh notation is concerned, the base is unimportant, and also to show how relations that involve logarithms can be derived.

Theorem 5.4   *The base does not matter. For any constant $B > 1$, $\log_B N = O(\log N)$.*

Proof   *Let $\log_B N = K$. Then $B^K = N$. Let $C = \log B$. Then $2^C = B$. Thus $B^K = (2^C)^K = N$. Hence we have $2^{CK} = N$, which implies that $\log N = CK = C \log_B N$. Therefore, $\log_B N = \dfrac{\log N}{\log B}$, completing the proof.*

In the rest of the text, we will use base 2 logarithms exclusively. An important fact about the logarithm is that it grows slowly. Because $2^{10} = 1024$, we see that $\log 1024 = 10$. Additional calculations show that the logarithm of one million is roughly 20, and the logarithm of one billion is only 30. Consequently, performance of an $O(N \log N)$ algorithm is much closer to a linear $O(N)$ algorithm than a quadratic $O(N^2)$ algorithm for even moderately large amounts of input. Before we see a realistic algorithm whose running time includes the logarithm, let us look at a few examples of how the logarithm comes into play.

BITS IN A BINARY NUMBER

*HOW MANY BITS ARE REQUIRED TO REPRESENT N CONSECUTIVE INTE-
GERS?*

A typical 16-bit integer represents the 65,536 integers in the range –32,768 to
32,767. In general, B bits are sufficient to represent 2^B different integers. Thus
the number of bits B required to represent N consecutive integers satisfies the
equation $2^B \geq N$. Hence we obtain $B \geq \log N$. The minimum number of bits is
thus $\lceil \log N \rceil$. (Here $\lceil X \rceil$ is the ceiling function and represents the smallest integer that is at least as large as X. The corresponding floor function $\lfloor X \rfloor$ represents
the largest integer that is at least as small as X.)

The number of bits required to represent numbers is logarithmic.

REPEATED DOUBLING

*STARTING FROM $X = 1$, HOW MANY TIMES SHOULD X BE DOUBLED
BEFORE IT IS AT LEAST AS LARGE AS N?*

Starting with $1, if we can double it every year, how long would it take to save a
million dollars? In this case after one year we would have $2; after 2 years, $4;
after 3 years, $8. In general, after K years we would have 2^K dollars, and so we
want to find the smallest K satisfying $2^K \geq N$. This is the same equation as
before, so $K = \lceil \log N \rceil$. After 20 years, we would have over a million dollars.
The *repeated doubling principle* states that starting from one, we can repeatedly
double only $\lceil \log N \rceil$ times until we reach N.

Starting at one, we can repeatedly double only logarithmically many times until we reach N.

REPEATED HALVING

*STARTING FROM $X = N$, IF N IS REPEATEDLY HALVED, HOW MANY
ITERATIONS MUST BE APPLIED TO MAKE N SMALLER THAN OR EQUAL TO
1?*

If the division rounds up to the nearest integer (or is real, not integer, division),
this is the same problem as repeated doubling except that we are going the opposite direction. Once again the answer is $\lceil \log N \rceil$ iterations. If the division rounds
down, the answer is $\lfloor \log N \rfloor$. The difference can be seen by starting with $X = 3$.
Two divisions are necessary, unless the division rounds down, in which case only
one is needed.

We can halve only log-arithmically many times. This is used to obtain logarithmic routines for searching.

Many of the algorithms that we examine will have logarithms introduced
because of the *repeated halving principle*: An algorithm is $O(\log N)$ if it takes
constant ($O(1)$) time to cut the problem size by a constant fraction (which is
usually $1/2$). This follows directly from the fact that there will be $O(\log N)$
iterations of the loop. Any constant fraction will do because the fraction is
reflected in the base of the logarithm, and Theorem 5.4 tells us that the base does
not matter. All of the remaining occurrences of logarithms are introduced (either
directly or indirectly) by application of the following theorem. The proof uses
calculus, but an understanding of the proof is not needed to use the theorem.

The N th *harmonic number* is the sum of the reciprocals of the first N positive inte-gers. The growth rate of the harmonic num-ber is logarithmic.

Theorem 5.5 *Let $H_N = \sum_{i=1}^{N} \frac{1}{i}$. Then $H_N = \Theta(\log N)$. A more precise estimate is $\ln N + 0.577$.*

Proof *The intuition of the proof is that a discrete sum is well approximated by the (continuous) integral. The proof uses a construction to show that the sum H_N can be bounded above and below by $\int \frac{dx}{x}$, with appropriate limits. Details are left as Exercise 5.18. H_N is known as the Nth harmonic number.*

In the next section we will see how the repeated halving principle leads to an efficient searching algorithm.

5.6   Static Searching Problem

An important use of computers is looking up data. If the data are not allowed to change (for instance, they are stored on a CD-ROM), we say that the data are static. A *static search* accesses static data. The static searching problem is naturally formulated as follows:

> **STATIC SEARCHING PROBLEM**
> GIVEN AN INTEGER X AND AN ARRAY A, RETURN THE POSITION OF X IN A OR AN INDICATION THAT IT IS NOT PRESENT. IF X OCCURS MORE THAN ONCE, RETURN ANY OCCURRENCE. THE ARRAY A IS NEVER ALTERED.

An example of static searching is looking up a person in the telephone book. The efficiency of a static searching algorithm depends on whether or not the array being searched is sorted. In the case of the telephone book, searching by name is fast, but searching by phone number is hopeless (for humans). In this section, we will examine some solutions to the static searching problem.

5.6.1   Sequential Search

A sequential search is linear.

When the input array is not sorted, we have little choice but to do a linear *sequential search*, stepping through the array sequentially until a match is found. The complexity of the algorithm is analyzed in three ways. First, we provide the cost of an unsuccessful search. Then, we give the worst-case cost of a successful search. Finally, we find the average cost of a successful search. Analyzing successful and unsuccessful searches separately is typical. It is also typical that unsuccessful searches are more time consuming than successful searches (just think about the last time you lost something in your house). For sequential searching, the analysis is straightforward.

An unsuccessful search requires the examination of every item in the array, so the total will be $O(N)$. In the worst case a successful search also requires the examination of every item in the array, because we might not find a match until the last item. Thus the worst-case running time for a successful search is also linear. On average, however, we only search half of the array: For every successful search in position i, there is a corresponding successful search in position $N - i$ (assuming we number starting from 1). However, $N/2$ is still $O(N)$. As we mentioned earlier, all of these Big-Oh terms should correctly be Big-Theta terms. However the use of Big-Oh is more popular.

5.6.2   Binary Search

If the input array is sorted, then we have an alternative to the sequential search, the *binary search*. We perform a binary search from the middle of the array rather than the end.

If the input array is sorted, we can use the *binary search*, which we perform from the middle of the array rather than the end.

```
1  // BinarySearch: Return position of X in array A of N elements
2  //       Return NotFound if appropriate
3  // Etype: must have operator< and all properties
4  //       needed for Vector
5
6  template <class Etype>
7  int
8  BinarySearch( const Vector<Etype> & A, const Etype & X, int N )
9  {
10     int Low = 0, High = N - 1, Mid;
11
12     while( Low <= High )
13     {
14         Mid = ( Low + High ) / 2;
15         if( A[ Mid ] < X )
16             Low = Mid + 1;
17         else if( X < A[ Mid ] )
18             High = Mid - 1;
19         else
20             return Mid;
21     }
22
23     return NotFound;        // NotFound is -1
24 }
```

Figure 5.11   Basic binary search that uses three-way comparisons

At any point in time we keep track of `Low` and `High`, which delimit the portion of the array where an item, if present, must reside. Initially the range is from 0 to `N-1`. If `Low` is larger than `High`, we know that the item is not present and we return -1, which cannot be confused with the return value of a successful search. Otherwise, we let `Mid` be the halfway point of the range (rounding down if the range has an even number of elements), and compare the item we are searching for with the item in position `Mid`. If we find a match, we are done and can return. If the item we are searching for is less than the item in position `Mid`, then it must reside in the range `Low` to `Mid-1`; if it is greater, then it must reside in the range `Mid+1` to `High`. In Figure 5.11, lines 15 to 18 alter the possible range, essentially cutting it in half. By the repeated halving principle, we know that the number of iterations will be $O(\log N)$.

> **The *binary search* is logarithmic because the search range is halved in each iteration.**

For an unsuccessful search the number of iterations in the loop is $\lfloor \log N \rfloor + 1$ because we halve the range in each iteration (rounding down if the range has an odd number of elements); we add 1 because the final range encompasses zero elements. For a successful search, the worst case is $\lfloor \log N \rfloor$ iterations because in the worst case we get down to a range of only one element. The average case is only one iteration better. Intuitively, this is because half of the elements require the worst case for their search, a quarter of the elements save one iteration, and only one in 2^i elements will save i iterations from the worst case. The mathematics involves computing the weighted average by calculating the sum of a finite series. The bottom line, however, is that the running time for each search is $O(\log N)$. Exercise 5.20 asks you to complete the calculation.

For reasonably large values of N, the binary search outperforms the sequential search. For instance, if N is 1000, then on average a successful sequential search requires about 500 comparisons. The average binary search, using the formula above, requires 8 iterations for a successful search. Since each iteration uses 2 comparisons, the total is 16 comparisons for a successful search. The binary search wins by even more in the worst case or when searches are unsuccessful.

> **Optimization of the binary search can cut the number of comparisons roughly in half.**

If we want to make the binary search even faster, we need to make the inner loop tighter. A possible strategy is to remove the (implicit) test for a successful search from that inner loop and shrink the range down to one item in all cases. Then we can use a single test outside of the loop to determine if the item is in the array or is not found, as shown in Figure 5.12. If the item we are searching for in Figure 5.12 is not larger than the item in the `Mid` position, then it is in the range that includes the `Mid` position. When we break the loop, presumably the subrange is one, and we can test to see if we have a match. Exercise 5.4 asks you to explain line 21 in more detail.

In the revised algorithm the number of iterations is always $\lfloor \log N \rfloor$ because we always shrink the range in half, possibly rounding down. The number of comparisons that are used is thus always $\lfloor \log N \rfloor + 1$.

Binary search is surprisingly tricky to code. Exercise 5.6 illustrates some common errors.

```
1  // BinarySearch: Return position of X in array A of N elements
2  //       Return NotFound if appropriate
3  // Etype: must have operator< and operator== and all
4  //       properties needed for Vector
5
6  template <class Etype>
7  int
8  BinarySearch( const Vector<Etype> & A, const Etype & X, int N )
9  {
10     int Low = 0, High = N - 1, Mid;
11
12     while( Low < High )
13     {
14         Mid = ( Low + High ) / 2;
15         if( A[ Mid ] < X )
16             Low = Mid + 1;
17         else
18             High = Mid;
19     }
20
21     return ( Low == High && A[ Low ] == X ) ? Low : NotFound;
22 }
```

Figure 5.12   Binary search using two-way comparisons

Notice that for small *N*, such as values smaller than 6, the binary search might not be worth using. It uses roughly the same number of comparisons for a typical successful search but has the overhead of line 14 in each iteration. Indeed, the last few iterations of the binary search make progress slowly. One can adopt a hybrid strategy in which the binary search loop terminates when the range is small and applies a sequential scan to finish. This is similar to what people do: They search a phone book nonsequentially, but when they have narrowed the range down to a column, they perform a sequential scan. The scan of a telephone book is not sequential, but it also is not a binary search. We discuss this in the next section.

5.6.3   Interpolation Search

The binary search is a very fast method for searching a sorted static array. In fact, it is so fast that we would rarely use anything else. *Interpolation search* is a static searching method that is sometimes faster. For it to be practical, two assumptions must be satisfied:

Interpolation search has a better Big-Oh bound on average than binary search but has limited practicality and a bad worst case.

1. Each access must be very expensive compared to a typical instruction. For example, the array might be on a disk instead of in memory, and each comparison requires disk access.

2. The data must not only be sorted, but they must be fairly uniformly distributed. For example, a phone book is fairly uniformly distributed. If

the input items are { 1, 2, 4, 8, 16, … }, then the distribution is not uniform.

These assumptions are quite restrictive, so you might never actually use an interpolation sort. But it is interesting to see that there is more than one way to solve a problem and that no algorithm, not even the classic binary search, is the best in all situations.

The idea of the interpolation search is that we are willing to spend more time to make an accurate guess where the item might be. The binary search always uses the midpoint. It is silly to search for *Hank Aaron* in the middle of the phone book; somewhere near the start is clearly more appropriate. Thus, instead of Mid, we use Next to indicate the next item we will try to access.

As an example of what might be good, suppose the range contains 1000 items, the low item in the range is 1000 and the high item in the range is 1,000,000, and we are searching for an item of value 12,000. If the items are uniformly distributed, then we expect to find a match somewhere near the 12th item. The applicable formula is

$$Next = Low + \left\lceil \frac{X - A[Low]}{A[High] - A[Low]} \times (High - Low - 1) \right\rceil$$

The subtraction of 1 is a technical adjustment that has been shown to perform well in practice. Clearly this calculation is more costly then the binary search calculation: It involves an extra division (the division by 2 in the binary search is really just a bit shift, just as dividing by 10 is easy for humans), multiplication, and four subtractions. These calculations need to be done using floating point operations. One iteration may be slower than the complete binary search. However, if the cost of these calculations is insignificant when compared to the cost of accessing an item, this is immaterial; we only care about the number of iterations.

N	CPU time T (milliseconds)	T/N	T/N^2	$T/(N \log N)$
10,000	100	0.01000000	0.00000100	0.00075257
20,000	200	0.01000000	0.00000050	0.00069990
40,000	440	0.01100000	0.00000027	0.00071953
80,000	930	0.01162500	0.00000015	0.00071373
160,000	1960	0.01225000	0.00000008	0.00070860
320,000	4170	0.01303125	0.00000004	0.00071257
640,000	8770	0.01370313	0.00000002	0.00071046

Figure 5.13   Empirical running time for *N* binary searches in an *N*-item array

In the worst case, where data are not uniformly distributed, the running time could be linear, and every item might be examined. Exercise 5.19 asks you to construct such a case. However, under the assumption that the items are reasonably distributed, as is the case with a phone book, the average number of comparisons has been shown to be $O(\log\log N)$. This means that we apply the logarithm twice in succession. For $N = 4$ billion, $\log N$ is about 32 and $\log\log N$ is roughly 5. Of course, there are some hidden constants in Big-Oh notation, but we see that the extra logarithm can lower the number of iterations considerably, as long as a bad case does not crop up. Proving the result rigorously, however, is quite complicated.

5.7   Checking an Algorithm Analysis

Once we have performed an algorithm analysis, we want to see if it is correct and as good as possible. One way to do this is to code up the program and see if the empirically observed running time matches the running time predicted by the analysis. When N increases by a factor of 10, the running time goes up by a factor of 10 for linear programs, 100 for quadratic programs, and 1000 for cubic programs. Programs that run in $O(N \log N)$ take slightly more than 10 times as long to run under the same circumstances. These increases can be hard to spot if the lower-order terms have relatively large coefficients and N is not large enough. An example is the jump from $N - 10$ to 100 in the running time for the various implementations of the maximum contiguous subsequence sum problem. It also can be very difficult to differentiate linear programs from $O(N \log N)$ programs based purely on empirical evidence.

Another commonly used trick to verify that some program is $O(F(N))$ is to compute the values $T(N)/F(N)$ for a range of N (usually spaced out by factors of 2), where $T(N)$ is the empirically observed running time. If $F(N)$ is a tight answer for the running time, then the computed values converge to a positive constant. If $F(N)$ is an overestimate, the values converge to zero. If $F(N)$ is an underestimate and hence wrong, the values diverge.

As an example, suppose we write a program to perform N random searches using the binary search algorithm. Since each search is logarithmic, we expect the total running time of the program to be $O(N \log N)$. Figure 5.13 shows the actual observed running time for the routine for various input sizes on a real computer. The table shows that the last column is most likely the converging column and thus confirms our analysis, whereas the increasing numbers for T/N suggest that $O(N)$ is an underestimate and the quickly decreasing values for T/N^2 suggest that $O(N^2)$ is an overestimate. Note carefully that we do not have definitive convergence. One problem is that the clock that we used to time the program ticks only every ten milliseconds. Notice also that there is not a great difference between $O(N)$ and $O(N \log N)$. Certainly an $O(N \log N)$ algorithm is much closer to being linear than quadratic. Finally, we remark that our machine has enough memory to store 640,000 objects (in the case of this experiment, integers). If this is not true on your machine, then you will not be able to reproduce similar results.

The next section discusses some of the limitations of the Big-Oh model.

5.8   Limitations of Big-Oh Analysis

We have seen that Big-Oh analysis is a very effective tool, but it is important to be aware of its limitations. First, as we have mentioned, it is not appropriate for small amounts of input. When the amount of input is small, we use the simplest algorithm. It may also be the case that for a particular algorithm, the constant implied by the Big-Oh is too large to be practical. For example, if one algorithm's running time is governed by the formula $2N \log N$ and another has a running time of $1000N$, then we would most likely prefer the first algorithm, even though its growth rate is larger. Large constants can come into play when an algorithm is excessively complex. They also come into play because our model disregards constants and thus cannot differentiate between things like memory access (which is cheap) and disk access (which typically is many thousand times more expensive). Our model assumes infinite memory, but in applications involving large data sets, lack of sufficient memory can be a severe problem.

Worse case is sometimes uncommon and can be safely ignored. Other times it is very common and cannot be ignored.

Sometimes, even when constants and lower-order terms are considered, the analysis is shown empirically to be an overestimate. If this is the case, then either the analysis needs to be tightened (usually by a clever observation), or it may be the case that the average-case running time bound is significantly less than the worst-case running time bound and no improvement in the bound is possible. There are many complicated algorithms for which the worst-case bound is achievable by some bad input but is usually an overestimate in practice. Two examples are the sorting algorithms Shellsort and quicksort (both are described in Chapter 8).

Average-case analysis is almost always much more difficult than worst-case analysis.

Worst-case bounds are usually easier to obtain than their average-case counterparts, however. For example, a mathematical analysis of the average-case running time of Shellsort has not been obtained. Sometimes, merely defining what average means is difficult. We use a worst-case analysis because it is expedient and also because, in a large majority of instances (sorting algorithms not being one of them), the worst-case analysis is very meaningful. In the course of performing the analysis, we frequently can tell if it will apply to the average case.

Summary

This chapter introduced the broad subject of algorithm analysis and showed that algorithmic decisions generally influence the running time of a program much more than programming tricks. We showed the huge difference between quadratic and linear programs and saw that cubic algorithms are, for the most part, unsatisfactory. We also examined an algorithm that could be viewed as the basis for our first data structure. The binary search efficiently supports static operations (that is, searching but not updating), providing a logarithmic worst-case search. Later chapters in the text will examine dynamic data structures that will efficiently support updates (both insertion and deletion).

In the next chapter we will define data structures and their allowable operations. We will also look at some applications of data structures and discuss their efficiency.

Objects of the Game

average-case bound In which the running time is measured as an average over all of the possible inputs of size N. (164)

Big-Oh Notation used to capture the most dominant term in a function. Big-Oh is similar to less than or equal to when considering growth rates. (151)

Big-Omega Notation similar to greater than or equal to when considering growth rates. (163)

Big-Theta Notation similar to equal to when considering growth rates. (163)

binary search Used if the input array is sorted. Searches are performed from the middle rather than the end. The binary search is logarithmic because the search range is halved in each iteration. (169)

harmonic number The Nth harmonic number is the sum of the reciprocals of the first N positive integers. The growth rate of the harmonic number is logarithmic. (167)

interpolation search A static searching algorithm that has better Big-Oh performance on average than binary search but has limited practicality and a bad worst case. (171)

linear time algorithm The running time grows as $O(N)$. If the size of the input increases by a factor of f, then the running time also increases by a factor of f. This is the preferential running time for an algorithm. (165)

Little-Oh Notation similar to less than when considering growth rates. (163)

logarithm The logarithm of N (to the base 2) is the value X such that 2 raised to the power of X equals N. (166)

repeated-doubling principle Starting at 1, we can repeatedly double only logarithmically many times until we reach N. (167)

repeated-halving principle Starting at N, we can repeatedly halve only logarithmically many times until we reach 1. This is used to obtain logarithmic routines for searching. (167)

sequential search A linear search that steps through an array until a match is found. (168)

static search Finds an item in data that is never altered. (168)

> **subquadratic** An algorithm whose running time is strictly slower than quadratic. The running time can be written as $o(N^2)$. (163)
>
> **worst-case bound** A guarantee over all inputs of some size. (164)

Common Errors

1. For nested loops, the total time is affected by the product of the loop sizes. For consecutive loops it is not.

2. Do not just blindly count the number of loops. A pair of nested loops that each run from 1 to N^2 accounts for $O(N^4)$ time.

3. Do not write expressions such as $O(2N^2)$ or $O(N^2 + N)$. Only the dominant term, with the leading constant removed, is needed.

4. Use equalities with Big-Oh, Big-Omega, an so on. Do not write that the running time is $> O(N^2)$; this makes no sense because Big-Oh is an upper bound. Do not write that the running time is $< O(N^2)$; if the intention is to say that the running time is strictly less than quadratic, use Little-Oh notation.

5. Use Big-Omega to express a lower bound. Do not use Big-Oh.

6. Use the logarithm to describe the running time for a problem that is solved by halving its size in constant time. If it takes more than constant time to halve the problem, the logarithm does not apply.

7. The base of the logarithm is irrelevant for the purposes of Big-Oh. It is an error to include it.

On the Internet

An alternative binary search algorithm is used for the case study in Section 10.1. Consequently, the algorithm in the file is slightly different from the one in the text. The three maximum contiguous subsequence sum algorithms, as well as a fourth taken from Section 7.5, are also available, along with a `main` that conducts the timing tests. Here are the file names:

> **MaxSum.cpp** Contains four algorithms for the maximum subsequence sum problem.
>
> **BinSrch1.cpp** Contains a binary search, similar to Figure 5.12 but slightly modified.

Exercises

In Short

5.1. Balls are drawn from a box as specified in Theorem 5.1. What are the corresponding values of i, j, and k?

      a. Red, 5, 6

      b. Blue, 5, 6

      c. Blue, 3, Red

      d. 6, 5, Red

5.2. Why isn't an implementation based solely on Theorem 5.2 sufficient to obtain a subquadratic running time for the maximum contiguous subsequence sum problem?

5.3. Suppose $T_1(N) = O(F(N))$ and $T_2(N) = O(F(N))$. Which of the following are true?

      a. $T_1(N) + T_2(N) = O(F(N))$

      b. $T_1(N) - T_2(N) = O(F(N))$

      c. $T_1(N) / T_2(N) = O(1)$

      d. $T_1(N) = O(T_2(N))$

5.4. What is the purpose of the first equality tested at line 21 in Figure 5.12? Are the parentheses necessary?

5.5. Programs A and B are analyzed and found to have worst-case running times no greater than $150N \log N$ and N^2, respectively. Answer the following questions, if possible:

      a. Which program has the better guarantee on the running time for large values of N ($N > 10{,}000$)?

      b. Which program has the better guarantee on the running time for small values of N ($N < 100$)?

      c. Which program will run faster *on average* for $N = 1000$?

      d. Is it possible that program B will run faster than program A on *all* possible inputs?

5.6. For the binary search routine in Figure 5.11, show the consequences of the following replacement code fragments:

      a. Line 12: using the test `Low < High`

      b. Line 14: assigning `Mid = Low + High / 2`

      c. Line 16: assigning `Low = Mid`

      d. Line 18: assigning `High = Mid`

      e. Line 23: returning 0 instead of −1

      f. Basing the code in Figure 5.12 on the test `A[ Mid ] > X`. Assume symmetric replacements for the lines that follow.

In Theory

5.7.   For the typical algorithms that you use to perform calculations by hand, what is the running time to

a. add two N-digit integers

b. multiply two N-digit integers

c. divide two N-digit integers

5.8.   In terms of N, what is the running time of the following algorithm to compute X^N?

```
double
Power( double X, int N )
{
    for( double Result = 1; N-- > 0; Result *= X )
        ;
    return Result;
}
```

5.9.   Directly evaluate the triple summation that precedes Theorem 5.1, and verify that the answers are identical.

5.10.   For the quadratic algorithm, precisely how many times is the inner-most statement executed?

5.11.   An algorithm takes 0.5 milliseconds for input size 100. How long will it take for input size 500 if the running time is

a. linear

b. $O(N \log N)$

c. quadratic

d. cubic

5.12.   An algorithm takes 0.5 milliseconds for input size 100. How large a problem can be solved in one minute if the running time is

a. linear

b. $O(N \log N)$

c. quadratic

d. cubic

5.13.   Complete the table in Figure 5.10 with estimates for the running times that were too long to simulate. Interpolate the running times for all four algorithms, and estimate the time required to compute the maximum contiguous subsequence sum of one million numbers. What assumptions have you made?

5.14.   Order the following functions by growth rate: N, $\sqrt{N}$, $N^{1.5}$, N^2, $N \log N$, $N \log \log N$, $N \log^2 N$, $N \log (N^2)$, $2/N$, 2^N, $2^{N/2}$, 37, N^3, $N^2 \log N$. Indicate which functions grow at the same rate.

5.15.   For each of the following six program fragments:

a. Give a Big-Oh analysis of the running time.

b. Implement the code, and give the code for several values of N.

c. Compare your analysis with the actual running times.

```
// Fragment #1
for( int i = 0, Sum = 0; i < N; i++ )
    Sum++;


// Fragment #2
for( int i = 0, Sum = 0; i < N; i++ )
    for( int j = 0; j < N; j++ )
        Sum++;


// Fragment #3
for( int i = 0, Sum = 0; i < N; i++ )
    Sum++;
for( int j = 0; j < N; j++ )
    Sum++;


// Fragment #4
for( int i = 0, Sum = 0; i < N; i++ )
    for( int j = 0; j < N * N; j++ )
        Sum++;


// Fragment #5
for( int i = 0, Sum = 0; i < N; i++ )
    for( int j = 0; j < i; j++ )
        Sum++;


// Fragment #6
for( int i = 0, Sum = 0; i < N; i++ )
    for( int j = 0; j < N * N; j++ )
        for( int k = 0; k < j; k++ )
            Sum++;
```

5.16.   Occasionally, multiplying the sizes of nested loops can give an overestimate for the Big-Oh running time. This happens when an innermost loop is infrequently executed. Repeat Exercise 5.15 for the following program fragment:

```
for( int i = 0; Sum = 0; i < N; i++ )
    for( int j = 0; j < i * i; j++ )
        if( j % i == 0 )
            for( int k = 0; k < j; k++ )
                Sum++;
```

5.17. In a recent court case, a judge cited a city for contempt and ordered a fine of $2 for the first day. Each subsequent day, until the city followed the judge's order, the fine was squared (that is, the fine progressed as follows: $2, $4, $16, $256, $65536,...).

a. What would the fine be on day N?

b. How many days would it take for the fine to reach D dollars (a Big-Oh answer will do)?

5.18. Prove Theorem 5.5. *Hint*: show that $\sum_2^N \frac{1}{i} < \int_1^N \frac{dx}{x}$. Then show a similar lower bound.

5.19. Construct an example where an interpolation search examines every element in the input array.

5.20. Analyze the cost of an average successful search for the binary search algorithm.

In Practice

5.21. Give an efficient algorithm to determine if there exists an integer i such that $A_i = i$ in an array of increasing integers. What is the running time of your algorithm?

5.22. A prime number has no factors besides 1 and itself.

a. Write a program to determine if a positive integer N is prime. In terms of N, what is the worst-case running time of your program?

b. Let B equal the number of bits in the binary representation of N. What is the value of B?

c. In terms of B, what is the worst-case running time of your program?

d. Compare the running times to determine if a 20-bit and 40-bit number are prime.

5.23. An important problem in numerical analysis is finding a solution to the equation $F(X) = 0$ for some arbitrary F. If the function is continuous and has two points *Low* and *High* such that $F(Low)$ and $F(High)$ have opposite signs, then a root must exist between *Low* and *High* and can be found by either a binary search or an interpolation search. Write a function that takes as parameters F, *Low*, and *High* and solves for a zero. What must you do to ensure termination?

5.24.   A majority element in an array A of size N is an element that appears more than $N/2$ times (thus, there is at most one). For example the array

   3, 3, 4, 2, 4, 4, 2, 4, 4,

has a majority element (4), whereas the array

   3, 3, 4, 2, 4, 4, 2, 4

does not. Give an algorithm to find a majority element if one exists, or report that one does not. What is the running time of your algorithm? (There is an $O(N)$ solution.)

Programming Projects

5.25.   The Sieve of Erastothenes is a method used to compute all primes less than N. We begin by making a table of integers 2 to N. We find the smallest integer, i, that is not crossed out, print i, and cross out i, $2i$, $3i$,.... When $i > \sqrt{N}$, the algorithm terminates. The running time has been shown to be $O(N \log\log N)$. Write a program to implement the Sieve and verify that the running time is as claimed. How difficult is it to differentiate the running time from $O(N)$ and $O(N \log N)$?

5.26.   The equation $A^5 + B^5 + C^5 + D^5 + E^5 = F^5$ has exactly one integral solution that satisfies $0 < A \le B \le C \le D \le E \le F \le 75$. Write a program to find the solution. *Hint:* First precompute all values of X^5 and store them in an array. Then for each tuple (A, B, C, D, E), you only need to check that there exists some F in the array. One method is to use a binary search to check for F, but there is an even better way to check for F.

5.27.   In C++ an automatic variable or formal parameter can be declared with storage class *register*. A register declaration suggests (rather than mandates) that the compiler should place the object in a machine register rather than in main memory. Rewrite one of the maximum contiguous subsequence sum algorithms using register variables. Do you get any speed improvements? What does this tell you about implementing these kinds of optimizations?

5.28.   Implement the maximum contiguous subsequence sum algorithms to obtain data equivalent to the data in Figure 5.10. Compile the programs with the highest optimization settings.

References

The maximum contiguous subsequence sum problem is from [5]. Books [4], [5], and [6] show how to optimize programs for speed. Interpolation search was first suggested in [14] and was analyzed in [13]. Books [1], [8], and [17] provide a more rigorous treatment of algorithm analysis. The three-part series [10], [11], and [12], though somewhat dated, remains the foremost reference work on the topic. The mathematical background required for more advanced algorithm analysis is provided by [2], [3], [7], [15], and [16]. An especially good book for advanced analysis is [9].

1. A. V. Aho, J. E. Hopcroft, and J. D. Ullman, *The Design and Analysis of Computer Algorithms*, Addison-Wesley, Reading, MA, 1974.

2. M. O. Albertson and J. P. Hutchinson, *Discrete Mathematics with Algorithms*, John Wiley & Sons, New York, NY, 1988.

3. Z. Bavel, *Math Companion for Computer Science*, Reston Publishing Company, Reston, VA, 1982.

4. J. L. Bentley, *Writing Efficient Programs*, Prentice-Hall, Englewood Cliffs, NJ, 1982.

5. J. L. Bentley, *Progamming Pearls*, Addison-Wesley, Reading, MA, 1986.

6. J. L. Bentley, *More Programming Pearls*, Addison-Wesley, Reading, MA, 1988.

7. R. A. Brualdi, *Introductory Combinatorics*, North-Holland, New York, NY, 1977.

8. T. H. Cormen, C. E. Leiserson, and R. L. Rivest, *Introduction to Algorithms*, MIT Press, Cambridge, MA, 1990.

9. R. L. Graham, D. E. Knuth, and O. Patashnik, *Concrete Mathematics*, Addison-Wesley, Reading, MA, 1989.

10. D. E. Knuth, *The Art of Computer Programming, Vol 1: Fundamental Algorithms*, Addison-Wesley, Reading, MA, 1973.

11. D. E. Knuth, *The Art of Computer Programming, Vol 2: Seminumerical Algorithms,* 2d ed., Addison-Wesley, Reading, MA, 1981.

12. D. E. Knuth, *The Art of Computer Programming, Vol 3: Sorting and Searching*, Addison-Wesley, Reading, MA, 1973.

13. Y. Pearl, A. Itai, and H. Avni, "Interpolation Search - A log log N Search," *Communications of the ACM* **21** (1978), 550-554.

14. W. W. Peterson, "Addressing for Random Storage," *IBM Journal of Research and Development* **1** (1957), 131-132.

15. F. S. Roberts, *Applied Combinatorics*, Prentice-Hall, Englewood Cliffs, NJ, 1984.

16. A. Tucker, *Applied Combinatorics*, 2d ed., John Wiley & Sons, New York, NY, 1984.

17. M. A. Weiss, *Data Structures and Algorithm Analysis in C++*, Benjamin/ Cummings, Redwood City, CA, 1994.

Chapter 6

Data Structures

Many algorithms require that we use a proper representation of data to achieve efficiency. This representation and the operations that are allowed for it are known as a *data structure*. Each data structure allows arbitrary insertion. They differ in how they allow access to members in the group. Some data structures allow arbitrary access and deletions, while others impose restrictions, such as allowing access only to the most recently or least recently inserted item in the group.

In this chapter we discuss seven of the most common data structures, stacks, queues, linked lists, trees, binary search trees, hash tables, and priority queues. Our goal is to define each data structure and also to give an intuitive feel for the time complexity of efficient insertion, deletion, and access operations. An efficient implementation is deferred until later in the book.

In this chapter we will see

- descriptions of common data structures, their allowed operations, and their running times
- for each data structure, a C++ class interface containing the appropriate member functions but omitting the data members
- some applications of the data structures

The case studies in Part III of the book will use these data structures. We will implement the data structures in Part IV. As stated previously, our goal is to show that the interface, which describes the functionality, is independent of the implementation. We do not need to know *how* something is implemented as long as we know that it *is* implemented.

6.1 Why Do We Need Data Structures?

A *data structure* is a representation of data and the operations allowed on that data. Data structures allow us to achieve component reuse.

Data structures allow us to achieve an important object-oriented programming goal, component reuse. As we will see, the data structures that are described in this section (and implemented later) have recurring uses. Once we have implemented each data structure once, it can be used over and over again in various applications. In this chapter we provide only the interface and defer consideration of efficient implementation to the chapters in Part IV.

This approach based on the separation of the interface and implementation is itself part of the object-oriented paradigm. The user of the data structure does not need to see the implementation, only the available operations. This is the encapsulation and information hiding part of object-oriented programming. However, another important part of object-oriented programming is *abstraction*: We are forced to think more carefully about the design of the data structures because we are required to write programs that use these data structures without having their implementations. This in turn makes the interface cleaner, more flexible (that is, more reusable), and generally easier to implement.

All the data structures are easy to implement if we are not concerned about performance. This allows us to plug "cheap" components into our program for the purposes of debugging. The exercises at the end of this chapter ask you to write inefficient implementations that are suitable for processing small amounts of data. Later we can replace the "cheap" data structure implementations with implementations that have better time (and/or) space performance properties and are suitable for processing large amounts of data. Because the interfaces are fixed, these changes require virtually no change to the programs that use the data structures.

In this chapter we will describe data structures by using abstract base classes. In a later chapter, when we implement the abstract base class, we will derive a new class. For instance, the stack is specified by the abstract class `AbsStack`. When we implement it in Chapter 15, the resulting class will be named `Stack`. In some cases we will derive an actual class from an abstract base class presented in this chapter. In other cases we will write a new class from scratch (to avoid complications). In all cases the abstract base class will provide the same functionality as the derived class; the derived class may address minor issues such as `const`-ness and include some additional functionality.

As an example, in Figure 6.1 we see an abstract class interface for the memory cell that was described in Section 3.3.1. The abstract interface describes the available functions, takes care of making the destructor virtual, generally disables the copy constructor, and provides a default constructor. Although we could omit the default constructor we include it for symmetry with the destructor. For most of our classes, we will allow `operator=`; for the abstract class we use the default. Each of the member functions is made pure virtual, meaning that the concrete derived class must provide a definition. The interface for the derived class is shown in Figure 6.2. The `main` routine in Figure 3.10 and the implementation in Figure 3.11 can be used without change. It specifies a constructor, destructor, and `operator=`; provides overriding declarations for the inherited pure virtual functions; and declares the private data representation.

```
1  // MemoryCell abstract class interface: simulate one Etype RAM
2  //
3  // Etype: must have zero-parameter constructor and operator=
4  // CONSTRUCTION: with (a) no initializer;
5  //      copy construction of MemoryCell objects is DISALLOWED
6  //
7  // ******************PUBLIC OPERATIONS********************
8  // Etype Read( )          --> Return stored value; pure virtual
9  // void Write( Etype X )--> Store X; pure virtual
10
11 template <class Etype>
12 class AbsMemoryCell
13 {
14   public:
15     AbsMemoryCell( ) { }              // Default constructor
16     virtual ~AbsMemoryCell( ) { }    // Destructor
17
18     const Etype & Read( ) const = 0;
19     void Write( const Etype & X ) = 0;
20   private:
21         // Disable copy constructor
22     AbsMemoryCell( const AbsMemoryCell & ) { }
23 };
```

Figure 6.1   Interface for the abstract memory cell class

```
1  // MemoryCell class interface; implements AbsMemoryCell
2  // No alterations to the public interface
3
4  template <class Etype>
5  class MemoryCell : public AbsMemoryCell<Etype>
6  {
7    public:
0          // Construction, destruction, operator=
9      MemoryCell( ) { }
10     ~MemoryCell( ) { }
11     const MemoryCell & operator=( const MemoryCell & Rhs );
12
13         // Inherited pure virtual members
14     const Etype & Read( ) const;
15     void Write( const Etype & X );
16   private:
17         // Copy constructor is disabled by inheritance
18     Etype StoredValue;
19 };
```

Figure 6.2   Interface for the concrete memory cell class

6.2 Stacks

A *stack* restricts access to the most recently inserted item.

A *stack* is a data structure in which all access is restricted to the most recently inserted elements. It behaves very much like the common stack of bills, stack of plates, or stack of newspapers. The last item added to the stack is placed on the top and is easily accessible, while items that have been in the stack for a while are more difficult to access. Thus the stack is appropriate if we expect to access only the top item; all other items are inaccessible. In a stack the three natural operations of `Insert`, `Delete`, and `Find` are renamed `Push`, `Pop`, and `Top`. These basic operations are illustrated in Figure 6.3. A C++ template class interface for an abstract stack is shown in Figure 6.4. There are no new C++ features introduced there. Note however that the destructor is virtual, in accordance with the general principles described in Section 4.5, and that the member functions are pure virtual. Figure 6.5 shows how a `Stack` class is used and provides corresponding output. Notice that the stack can be used to reverse things.

Stack operations take a constant amount of time.

We expect that each stack operation should take a constant amount of time, independent of the number of items in the stack. By analogy, finding today's newspaper in a stack of newspapers is fast, no matter how deep the stack is. However, arbitrary access in a stack is not efficiently supported, and in fact we do not list it as an option.

What makes the stack useful is that there are many applications for which we need to access only the most recently inserted item. To illustrate, let us describe an important use of stacks in compiler design.

6.2.1 Stacks and Computer Languages

Compilers check your programs for syntax errors, but frequently a lack of one symbol (such as a missing comment ender `*/` or `}`) will cause the compiler to spill out a hundred lines of diagnostics without identifying the real error. Other compilers are simply quiet: `g++` will in some cases tell you that `_main` is undefined, even though the real problem is a missing closing brace.

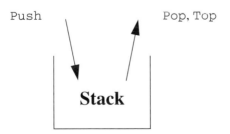

Figure 6.3   Stack model: input to a stack is by `Push`, output is by `Top`, deletion is by `Pop`

```
 1  // Stack abstract class interface
 2  //
 3  // Etype: must have zero-parameter constructor;
 4  //      implementation will require either
 5  //      operator= or copy constructor, perhaps both
 6  // CONSTRUCTION: with (a) no initializer;
 7  //      copy construction of Stack objects is DISALLOWED
 8  //
 9  // ******************PUBLIC OPERATIONS********************
10  //      All of the following are pure virtual functions
11  // void Push( Etype X ) --> Insert X
12  // void Pop( )           --> Remove most recently inserted item
13  // Etype Top( )          --> Return most recently inserted item
14  // int IsEmpty( )        --> Return 1 if empty; else return 0
15  // int IsFull( )         --> Return 1 if full;  else return 0
16  // void MakeEmpty( )     --> Remove all items
17  // ******************ERRORS*******************************
18  // Top or Pop on empty stack
19
20  template <class Etype>
21  class AbsStack
22  {
23    public:
24      AbsStack( ) { }              // Default constructor
25      virtual ~AbsStack( ) { }     // Destructor
26
27      // Basic Members
28      virtual void Push( const Etype & X ) = 0;    // Insert
29      virtual void Pop( ) = 0;                     // Remove
30      virtual const Etype & Top( ) const = 0;      // Find
31      virtual int IsEmpty( ) const = 0;
32      virtual int IsFull( ) const = 0;
33      virtual void MakeEmpty( ) = 0;
34    private:
35          // Disable copy constructor
36      AbsStack( const AbsStack & ) { }
37  };
```

Figure 6.4   Interface for the abstract stack class

A useful tool in this situation is a program that checks whether everything is balanced, thus every { corresponds to a }, every [to a], and so on. The sequence [( )] is legal but [( ]) is not, so simply counting the numbers of each symbol is insufficient. We will assume for now that we are only processing a sequence of tokens and will not worry about problems such as the character constant ' { ' not needing a matching ' } '.

```
 1  #include <iostream.h>
 2  #include "Stack.h"
 3
 4  // Simple test program for stacks
 5
 6  main( )
 7  {
 8      Stack<int> S;
 9
10      for( int i = 0; i < 5; i++ )
11          S.Push( i );
12
13      cout << "Contents:";
14      do
15      {
16          cout << ' ' << S.Top( );
17          S.Pop( );
18      } while( !S.IsEmpty( ) );
19      cout << '\n';
20
21      return 0;
22  }
```

Figure 6.5   Sample stack program; output is
                  Contents: 4 3 2 1 0

A stack can be used to check for unbalanced symbols.

A stack is useful for checking unbalanced symbols because we know that when a closing symbol such as) is seen, it matches the most recently seen unclosed (. Therefore, by placing opening symbols on a stack, we can easily check that a closing symbol makes sense. Specifically, we have the following algorithm:

> Make an empty stack. Read tokens until the end of the file. If the token is an opening symbol, push it onto the stack. If it is a closing symbol, and if the stack is empty, then report an error. Otherwise, pop the stack. If the symbol popped is not the corresponding opening symbol, then report an error. At the end of the file, if the stack is not empty, report an error.

In Section 11.1 we will develop this algorithm to work for (almost) all C++ programs. Details include error reporting, processing of comments, strings, and character constants, as well as escape sequences.

The stack is used to implement function calls in most procedural languages.

The algorithm to check balanced symbols suggests a way to implement function calls. The problem is that, when a call is made to a new function, all the variables local to the calling function need to be saved by the system; otherwise, the new function would overwrite the calling routine's variables. Furthermore, the current location in the calling routine must be saved so that the new function knows where to go after it is done. The variables have generally been assigned by the compiler to machine registers, and conflicts will certainly arise. The reason that this problem is similar to balancing symbols is that a function call and a function return are essentially the same as an open parenthesis and a closed parenthesis, so the same ideas should apply. This indeed is the case: as discussed in Section 7.3, the stack is used to implement function calls in most procedural languages.

A final important application of the stack is the evaluation of expressions in computer languages. In the expression 1+2*3, we see that at the point that the * is encountered, we have already read the operator + and the operands 1 and 2. Does * operate on 1, 2, or 1+2? Precedence rules tell us that * operates on 2, which is the most recently seen operand. After the 3 is seen, we can evaluate 2*3 as 6 and then apply the + operator. This suggests that operands and intermediate results should be saved on a stack, and also that the operators be saved on the stack (since the + is held until the higher precedence * is evaluated). An algorithm that uses this strategy is *operator precedence parsing*, and is described in Section 11.2.

> The *operator precedence parsing* algorithm uses a stack to evaluate expressions.

6.3 Queues

Another simple data structure is the *queue* (which is a British word for *line*). In many cases it is important to be able to find and/or remove the most recently inserted item, but in an equal number of cases it is not only unimportant but actually the wrong thing to do. In a multiprocessing system, for example, when jobs are submitted to a printer, we expect the least recent or more senior job to be printed first. This is not only fair but also required to guarantee that the first job does not wait forever. Thus printer queues can be expected to be found on all large systems.

> The *queue* restricts access to the least recently inserted item.

The basic operations supported by queues are Enqueue, Dequeue, and Front, representing insertion to the back of the line, removal of the item at the front of the line, and access of the item at the front of the line, respectively. Figure 6.6 illustrates these queue operations. Historically, Dequeue and Front have been combined into one operation, but we will keep them separate here. C++ allows function overloading; thus, if we wish, we could simultaneously define two forms of Dequeue: one that gives the front item and one that does not.

Enqueue → **Queue** Dequeue →
Front

Figure 6.6   Queue model: input is by Enqueue, output is by Front, deletion is by Dequeue

```
 1  // Queue abstract class interface
 2  //
 3  // Etype: must have zero-parameter constructor;
 4  //      implementation will require either
 5  //      operator= or copy constructor, perhaps both
 6  // CONSTRUCTION: with (a) no initializer;
 7  //      copy construction of Queue objects is DISALLOWED
 8  //
 9  // ******************PUBLIC OPERATIONS*********************
10  //      All of the following are pure virtual functions
11  // void Enqueue( Etype X )--> Insert X
12  // void Dequeue( )        --> Remove least recently inserted item
13  // Etype Front( )         --> Return least recently inserted item
14  // int IsEmpty( )         --> Return 1 if empty; else return 0
15  // int IsFull( )          --> Return 1 if full;  else return 0
16  // void MakeEmpty( )      --> Remove all items
17  // ******************ERRORS*******************************
18  // Front or Dequeue on empty queue
19
20  template <class Etype>
21  class AbsQueue
22  {
23    public:
24      AbsQueue( ) { }              // Default constructor
25      virtual ~AbsQueue( ) { }     // Destructor
26
27      // Basic Members
28      virtual void Enqueue( const Etype & X ) = 0;  // Insert
29      virtual void Dequeue( ) = 0;                  // Remove
30      virtual const Etype & Front( ) const = 0;     // Find
31      virtual int IsEmpty( ) const = 0;
32      virtual int IsFull( ) const = 0;
33      virtual void MakeEmpty( ) = 0;
34    private:
35          // Disable copy constructor
36      AbsQueue( const AbsQueue & ) { }
37  };
```

Figure 6.7   Interface for the abstract queue class

Queue operations take a constant amount of time.

Figure 6.7 illustrates the interface for an abstract base class, and Figure 6.8 shows how the queue is used and gives sample output. Because the queue operations are restricted in a way similar to the stack operations, we expect that they should also take a constant amount of time per query. This is indeed the case. All of the basic queue operations take $O(1)$ time. We will see several applications of queues in the case studies.

```
 1  #include <iostream.h>
 2  #include "Queue.h"
 3
 4  // Simple test program for queues
 5
 6  main( )
 7  {
 8      Queue<int> Q;
 9
10      for( int i = 0; i < 5; i++ )
11          Q.Enqueue( i );
12
13      cout << "Contents:";
14      do
15      {
16          cout << ' ' << Q.Front( );
17          Q.Dequeue( );
18      } while( !Q.IsEmpty( ) );
19      cout << '\n';
20
21      return 0;
22  }
```

Figure 6.8   Sample queue program; output is
                  Contents:0 1 2 3 4

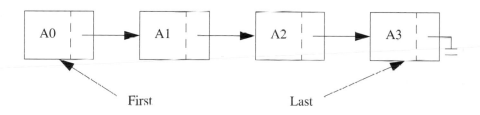

Figure 6.9   A simple linked list

6.4   Linked Lists

In Section 1.8.4 we saw a very basic linked list. In a linked list we store items noncontiguously rather than in the usual contiguous array. The advantage of doing this is twofold. First, an insertion into the middle of the list does not require moving all of the items that follow the insertion point. Data movement is very expensive in practice, and the linked list allows insertion with only a constant amount of assignment statements. Second, if the array size is not known in advance, we must use the array-doubling technique. In the course of expanding the array from size S to $2S$, we need to have $3S$ units of memory available. After the expansion is complete, we still need $2S$ units of memory, meaning that we

The linked list is used to avoid large amounts of data movement. It also stores items with only one pointer per item overhead.

have to waste lots of memory. If the data items are large, we would rather have only the overhead of a pointer per item. The basic linked list picture is shown in Figure 6.9. Notice, by the way, that if we allow access only at `First`, then we have a stack, and if we allow insertions only at `Last` and access only at `First`, we have a queue.

Access to the list is done through an iterator class. The list class has operations that reflect the state of the list. All other operations are in the iterator class.

Typically we need more general operations, such as finding or removing any named item in the list. We also need to be able to insert a new item at any point. This is far more than either a stack or a queue allows. Figure 6.10 illustrates these linked list operations.

To access items in the list, we need a pointer to the corresponding node. Clearly, however, granting this access is a violation of information-hiding principles. We need to ensure that any access to the list through a pointer is a safe. To do this, we define the list class in two parts. Figure 6.11 gives the basic abstract linked list class, supplying operators that describe only the state of the list.

Figure 6.12 defines an iterator class that is used for all access into the list. To see how it is used, let us look at the standard code to output each element in a list. If the list is stored contiguously in an array, typical code would look like this:

```
// Step through array A, outputting each item
for( int Index = 0; Index < Size; Index++ )
    cout << A[ Index ] << '\n'
```

In C, the code to iterate through the linked list is

```
// Step through List L, outputting each item, C version
for( Node *P = L; P != NULL; P = P->Next )
    cout << P->Data << '\n';
```

The iteration mechanism that C++ would use is

```
// Step through List L, using abstraction and an iterator
for( ListItr Itr = L; +Itr; ++Itr )
    cout << Itr( ) << '\n';
```

The initialization in the `for` loop is obtained by calling the constructor for `ListItr`. Presumably the initialization sets the iterator to the start of the linked list. The test uses the + operator defined for the `ListItr` class. ++Itr (or Itr++) calls the postfix increment operator for the `ListItr` to advance to the next node in the linked list. We can access the item that is "current" by making a call to `operator()` defined for `ListItr`. We can replace the operators with more readable names. The general principle is that since all access to the list is through the `ListItr` class, we have guarantees of safety. Also, we can have multiple iterators traversing a single list.

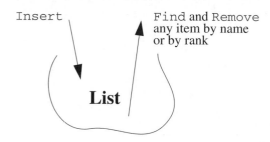

Insert

Find and Remove
any item by name
or by rank

List

Figure 6.10   Link list model: inputs are arbitrary and ordered, any item
may be output, and iteration is supported, but this data structure is not time-efficient

```
1  // List abstract class interface
2  //
3  // Etype: must have zero-parameter constructor;
4  //      implementation will require either
5  //      operator= or copy constructor, perhaps both;
6  //      implementation will require either
7  //      operator== or operator!=, perhaps both
8  // CONSTRUCTION: with (a) no initializer;
9  //      copy construction of List objects is DISALLOWED
10 //
11 // ******************PUBLIC OPERATIONS********************
12 //      All of the following are pure virtual functions
13 // int IsEmpty( )         --> Return 1 if empty; else return 0
14 // int IsFull( )          --> Return 1 if full;  else return 0
15 // void MakeEmpty( )      --> Remove all items
16
17 template <class Etype>
18 class AbsList
19 {
20   public:
21     AbsList( ) { }              // Default constructor
22     virtual ~AbsList( ) { }    // Destructor
23
24     // Basic Members
25     virtual int IsEmpty( ) const = 0;
26     virtual int IsFull( ) const = 0;
27     virtual void MakeEmpty( ) = 0;
28
29     friend class AbsListItr<Etype>;
30   private:
31     AbsList( const AbsList & ) { } // Disable copy constructor
32 };
```

Figure 6.11   Interface for the abstract linked list class

```
1  // ListItr abstract class; maintains "current position"
2  //
3  // Etype: same restrictions as for List
4  // CONSTRUCTION: with (a) List to which ListItr is permanently
5  //      bound or (b) another ListItr;
6  //      copying of ListItr objects is allowed only if both the
7  //      source and target are bound to the same List
8  //
9  // ******************PUBLIC OPERATIONS********************
10 //      All of the following are pure virtual functions
11 // void Insert( Etype X )--> Insert X after current position
12 // int Remove( Etype X ) --> Remove X
13 // int Find( Etype X )   --> Set current position to view X
14 // int IsFound( Etype X )--> Return 1 if X found else return 0
15 // void Zeroth( )   --> Set current position to prior to first
16 // void First( )        --> Set current position to first
17 // void operator++      --> Advance (both prefix and postfix)
18 // int operator+( )     --> True if at valid position in list
19 // Etype operator( )    --> Return item in current position
20 // ******************ERRORS*****************************
21 // Illegal access, advance, insertion, or First on empty list
22
23 template <class Etype>
24 class AbsListItr
25 {
26   public:
27     AbsListItr( const AbsList<Etype> & L ) { }  // Constructor
28     AbsListItr( const AbsListItr & );      // Copy constructor
29     virtual ~AbsListItr( ) { }                   // Destructor
30
31     virtual const AbsListItr & operator=( const AbsListItr& );
32
33     // Basic Members: These return success or fail
34     virtual void Insert( const Etype & X ) = 0;//after current
35     virtual int Find( const Etype & X ) = 0;   // Go to  X
36     virtual int Remove( const Etype & X ) = 0; // Remove X
37     virtual int IsFound( const Etype & X ) const = 0;
38
39     // Access operators
40     virtual int operator+( ) const = 0;   // True if in list
41     virtual const Etype & operator( ) ( ) const = 0;
42
43     // Iteration operators
44     virtual void Zeroth( ) = 0;      // Go prior to first item
45     virtual void First( ) = 0;       // Go to at first item
46     virtual void operator++( ) = 0;  // Advance
47     virtual void operator++( int ) = 0;
48   protected: // Real ListItr will have a reference to the list
49     AbsListItr( ) { }                      // Disallow default
50 };
```

Figure 6.12   Interface for the abstract linked list iterator

```
1  #include <iostream.h>
2  #include "List.h"
3
4  // Simple test program for lists
5
6  main( )
7  {
8      List<int> L;
9      ListItr<int> P = L;
10
11         // Repeatedly insert new items as first elements
12     for( int i = 0; i < 5; i++ )
13     {
14         P.Insert( i );
15         P.Zeroth( ); // Reset P to the start
16     }
17
18     cout << "Contents:";
19     for( P.First( ); +P; ++P )
20         cout << ' ' << P( );
21     cout << "end\n";
22
23     return 0;
24 }
```

Figure 6.13   Sample list program; output is Contents: 4 3 2 1 0
                   end

To make this work, the `ListItr` class must maintain two internal objects. First, it needs a pointer to the "current" node. Second, it needs a reference to the `List`; this reference is initialized once (and only once) in the constructor. Figure 6.13 shows the interaction of the list and its iterator. The details of the linked list implementation will be shown in Chapter 16.

6.5   General Trees

A *tree* is a widely used data structure that consists of a set of nodes and a set of edges that connect pairs of nodes. Throughout this book we consider only *rooted trees*. A rooted tree has the following properties:

A *tree* consists of a set of nodes and a set of edges that connect pairs of nodes.

- One node is distinguished as the root.
- Every node *c* except the root is connected by an edge from exactly one other node *p*. *p* is *c*'s parent. *c* is one of *p*'s children.
- There is a unique path from the root to each node. The number of edges that we must follow is the *path length*.

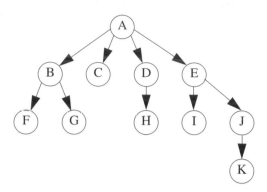

Figure 6.14   A tree

Various relationships exist between the tree nodes.

Figure 6.14 illustrates a tree. The root node is *A*. *A*'s children are *B*, *C*, *D*, and *E*. Because *A* is the root, it has no parent. All other nodes have parents. For instance, *B*'s parent is *A*. Nodes that have no children are called *leaves*. The leaves in our tree are *C*, *F*, *G*, *H*, *I*, and *K*. The length of the path from *A* to *K* is three (edges). The length of the path from *A* to *A* is zero edges. We can also define properties such as ancestor, descendant, and sibling in the usual manner. *C*'s siblings are *B*, *D*, and *E*.

Trees are used for file systems.

The tree is a fundamental data structure in computer science. Almost all operating systems store files in trees or treelike structures. Under DOS, VMS, and UNIX, for instance, directories are stored as the internal, nonleaf nodes of the tree, while all other files are each stored in a leaf. Traversing an edge is then the same as descending to a subdirectory. A special edge that connects back to the parent (namely the .. entry) allows easy traversal up the tree (although by creating a cycle, the .. entry makes the structure only treelike rather than a formal tree).

With this in mind we are able to see what kinds of operations are supported by a tree. We would like to add, search, and remove from the tree. Much like the linked list, we want to define an iterator that allows us access to do this by maintaining the notion of a current internal node. We need to provide operators that allow us to traverse the tree in an orderly manner. Thus in Figure 6.15 we define the abstract tree class and an iterator friend using the same method seen for linked lists. The operations `GotoRoot`, `FirstChild`, and `NextSibling`, are sufficient to allow us to traverse the tree in one of several methods. In Chapter 17 we describe a hierarchy of classes that supports traversal of trees using only the functions `First`, `operator()`, `operator+`, and `operator++`. This includes the classes `InOrder`, `PreOrder`, `PostOrder`, and `LevelOrder`.

```
1   // Tree abstract class interface; details are similar to List
2
3   template <class Etype>
4   class AbsTree
5   {
6     public:
7       AbsTree( ) { }                    // Default constructor
8       virtual ~AbsTree( ) { }           // Destructor
9
10      // Basic Members
11      virtual int IsEmpty( ) const = 0;
12      virtual int IsFull( ) const = 0;
13      virtual void MakeEmpty( ) = 0;
14
15      friend class AbsTreeItr<Etype>;
16    private:
17      // Implementation details
18      AbsTree( const AbsTree & ) { } // Disable copy constructor
19  };
20
21  template <class Etype>
22  class AbsTreeItr
23  {
24    public:
25      AbsTreeItr( const AbsTree & T ) { }    // Constructor
26      AbsTreeItr( const AbsTreeItr & )  { }  // Copy constructor
27      virtual ~AbsTreeItr( ) { }             // Destructor
28
29      // Access operators
30      virtual int operator+( ) const = 0;
31      virtual const Etype & operator( ) ( ) const = 0;
32      virtual void NextSibling( ) = 0;// Advance to next sibling
33
34      // Basic Members to add, remove and find a child
35      virtual void Insert( const Etype & X, int Child ) = 0;
36      virtual int Remove( const Etype & X ) = 0;
37      virtual int Find( const Etype & X ) = 0;
38      virtual int IsFound( const Etype & X ) const = 0;
39      virtual void GotoRoot( ) = 0;          // Go to root
40      virtual void FirstChild( ) = 0;        // Go to First child
41    private:
42      // Reference to tree
43      AbsTreeItr( ) { }   // Default construction disallowed
44  };
```

Figure 6.15   Interface for the abstract tree class

Expression trees are used in parsing. In an expression tree, the value of a node is the result of applying the operand at the node, using the children as operands.

A **binary tree** has at most two children per node.

A second application of trees, called the *expression tree*, is shown in Figure 6.16. In an expression tree, the value of a node is the result of applying the operand at the node, using the children as operands. Leaves evaluate to themselves. Consequently, the expression tree shown in Figure 6.16 evaluates to (a+b) * (c-d). Expression trees and the related parse tree are crucial data structures in the parsing and code-generation stages of the compiler. We will see more details in Section 11.2.

The expression tree in Figure 6.16 is a *binary tree* because the number of children is limited to at most two per node. An important use of the binary tree is examined in the next section.

6.6   Binary Search Trees

In Section 5.6 we examined the static searching problem and saw that if the items are presented to us in sorted order, then we can support the Find operation in logarithmic worst-case time. This is static searching because, once we are presented with the items, we cannot add or remove items.

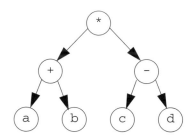

Figure 6.16   Expression tree for (a+b) * (c-d)

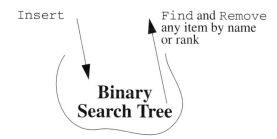

Figure 6.17   Binary search tree model; the binary search is extended to allow insertions and deletions

```
 1  // SearchTree abstract class interface
 2  //
 3  // Etype: must have zero-parameter constructor;
 4  //      must have operator< and operator==; implementation
 5  //      may require operator> and operator!=;
 6  //      implementation will require either
 7  //      operator= or copy constructor, perhaps both
 8  // CONSTRUCTION: with (a) no initializer;
 9  //      copy construction of SearchTree objects is DISALLOWED
10  //
11  // ****************PUBLIC OPERATIONS********************
12  //      All of the following are pure virtual functions
13  // void Insert( Etype X )  --> Insert X
14  // void Remove( Etype X )  --> Remove X
15  // Etype Find( )           --> Return item that matches X
16  // int WasFound( )         --> Return 1 if last Find succeeded
17  // int IsFound( Etype X )  --> Return 1 if X would be found
18  // Etype FindMin( )        --> Return smallest item
19  // Etype FindMax( )        --> Return largest item
20  // int IsEmpty( )          --> Return 1 if empty; else return 0
21  // int IsFull( )           --> Return 1 if full;  else return 0
22  // void MakeEmpty( )       --> Remove all items
23
24  template <class Etype>
25  class AbsBst
26  {
27    public:
28      AbsBst( ) { }             // Default constructor
29      virtual ~AbsBst( ) { }    // Destructor
30
31      // Basic Members
32      virtual void Insert( const Etype & X ) = 0;
33      virtual int Remove( const Etype & X ) = 0;
34      virtual const Etype & Find( const Etype & X ) = 0;
35      virtual int WasFound( ) const = 0; // If last find OK
36      virtual const Etype & FindMin( ) const = 0;
37      virtual const Etype & FindMax( ) const = 0;
38      virtual int IsFound( const Etype & X ) const = 0;
39      virtual int IsEmpty( ) const = 0;
40      virtual int IsFull( ) const = 0;
41      virtual void MakeEmpty( ) = 0;
42    private:
43      AbsBst( const AbsBst & ) { }   // Disable copy constructor
44  };
```

Figure 6.18   Interface for the abstract binary search tree class

Suppose, however, that we do want to add and remove items. One data structure that does this is known as the *binary search tree*. Figure 6.17 shows the basic operations that are allowed in a binary search tree. An abstract base class is shown in Figure 6.18.

The *binary search tree* supports insertion, removal, and searching.

The set of allowed operations is now extended to allow arbitrary `Find` (by name) as well as `Insert` and `Remove`. The `Find` by itself does not tell us if the search was successful. We will maintain an internal variable to record this; `WasFound` can be used to access that variable. Figure 6.19 shows how `Find` and `WasFound` interact. If we are performing a search in the tree and only need to view the result of the `Find`, then the result can be assigned to a constant reference variable, as in lines 22 through 26. This is appropriate if, for instance, the search tree is storing large records, we are searching by using one key, and we want to output the entire matched record but do no more to it. If, however, we need a copy of the matched record for later use (for instance, if we want to store all matched records in an array so they can be sorted on some other key), then the code must include a `String` copy, as in lines 14 through 18. In our example the constant reference is preferable.

Using a binary search tree, we can access the *K*th smallest item. The cost is logarithmic average-case time for a simple implementation and logarithmic worst-case time for a more careful implementation.

Our class also provides two additional members: one to find the smallest item and another to find the largest item. It turns out that with some additional work we can also efficiently support access of the *K*th smallest item, for any *K* provided as a parameter.

Let us summarize the running time of these operations. We are hoping that the worst-case cost of the `Find`, `Insert`, and `Remove` operations is $O(\log N)$ because that would match the bound obtained for the static binary search. Unfortunately, for the simplest implementation of the binary search tree, this is not the case. The average case is logarithmic, but the worst case is $O(N)$ and occurs quite frequently. However, by applying some algorithmic tricks, we can obtain a more complex structure that does indeed have $O(\log N)$ cost per operation.

What about `FindMin`, `FindMax`, and a general `FindKth` procedure? In the binary search these are clearly constant-time operations because we merely index an array. These operations take the same time in a binary search tree as an arbitrary `Find`: $O(\log N)$ per operation on average, although $O(N)$ in the worst-case. With sufficient care the worst-case bound can be reduced to $O(\log N)$ per operation. As the name of the data structure suggests, the binary search tree is implemented as a binary tree and thus requires the overhead of two pointers per item. A more careful variant that supports efficient worst-case access requires additional space per item. Chapter 18 will give more details on the implementation of a binary search tree.

6.7 Hash Tables

The *hash table* supports constant average-time insertions, removals, and searches.

Many applications require dynamic searching based only on a name. The classic application is the compiler's *symbol table*. As it compiles a program, the compiler must record the names (including types, scope, and memory assignment) of all declared identifiers. When it sees an identifier outside of a declaration statement, the compiler checks to see that it has been declared; if it has, the compiler looks up the appropriate information in the symbol table.

Since the binary search tree supports logarithmic time access of arbitrary named items, why do we need a new data structure? The answer is that a binary search tree could give linear-time cost per access, and ensuring logarithmic cost requires more sophisticated algorithms. The hash table will avoid this worst case and instead support operations in constant time almost certainly. Degenerative performance is possible but extremely unlikely. Thus the access time for any one item does not depend on the number of items that are in the table. We will also see that the hash table avoids pointers and thus memory management. This makes it very fast in practice. An additional benefit of the hash table is that, unlike the binary search tree, it does not require that Etype have a relational operator defined. Only equality and/or inequality is needed.

The hash table is not as susceptible to the worst case as a simple binary search tree.

```
1  #include <iostream.h>
2  #include "Bst.h"
3
4  // Simple test program for binary search trees
5
6  main( )
7  {
8      SearchTree<String> T;
9
10     T.Insert( "Becky" );
11
12         // Simple use of Find/WasFound
13         // Appropriate if we need a copy
14     String Result1 = T.Find( "Becky" );
15     if( T.WasFound( ) )
16         cout << "Found " << Result1 << ';';
17     else
18         cout << "Becky not found;";
19
20         // More efficient use of Find/WasFound
21         // Appropriate if we only need to examine
22     const String & Result2 = T.Find( "Mark" );
23     if( T.WasFound( ) )
24         cout << " Found " << Result2 << ';';
25     else
26         cout << " Mark not found; ";
27
28     cout << '\n';
29
30     return 0;
31 }
```

Figure 6.19   Sample search tree program; output is `Found Becky; Mark not found;`

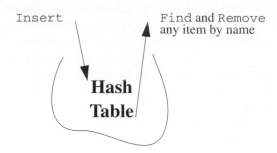

Figure 6.20   The hash table model: any named item can be accessed or deleted in essentially constant time

To use the hash table, we must provide a hash function, which converts a specific Etype to an integer.

The allowed operations are illustrated in Figure 6.20, and an abstract base class is shown in Figure 6.21. To use the hash table, we must provide a *hash function*, which converts an Etype to an integer. It has the following declaration. (Details on implementing the hash function are given in Chapter 19.)

```
// Return an integer between 0 and TableSize - 1
unsigned int Hash( const Etype & Element, int TableSize );
```

An example of the use of the hash table is shown in Figure 6.22. There we maintain a hash table of String objects, so the hash function has the following declaration:

```
unsigned int Hash( const String & Element, int TableSize );
```

A *dictionary* stores keys and definitions.

A common use of the hash table is the *dictionary*. A dictionary stores objects that consist of a key, which is looked up in the dictionary, and its definition, which is returned. We can use the hash table to implement the dictionary because we can instantiate it as follows:

1. The Etype is a class that stores both the key and the definition.
2. Equality, inequality, and the hash function are based only on the key portion of Etype.
3. A lookup is performed by constructing an Etype object E with the key and performing a hash table Find.
4. The definition is obtained by using a constant reference object F, which is assigned the return value of the Find, and by calling WasFound to see if the Find was successful.

The overhead of this scheme is the construction of the Etype object E in step 3. Consequently, in some cases we would prefer to define a Dictionary class with two templated parameters to avoid the extra construction. We would use algorithms identical to the hash table algorithms. Because the hash table is more general, we prefer to discuss it exclusively and use it to implement the dictionary. Commonly, the price paid for generality is reduced speed. However, in our examples, the reduction in speed is very small.

```
1  // HashTable abstract class interface
2  //
3  // Etype: must have zero-parameter constructor and
4  //        operator==; implementation may require operator!=;
5  //        implementation will require either
6  //        operator= or copy constructor, perhaps both
7  // unsigned int Hash( const Etype & Element, int TableSize );
8  //        must be defined
9  // CONSTRUCTION: with (a) no initializer
10 //        Copy construction of HashTable objects is DISALLOWED
11 //
12 // ******************PUBLIC OPERATIONS********************
13 //     All of the following are pure virtual functions
14 // int Insert( Etype X )    --> Insert X
15 // int Remove( Etype X )    --> Remove X
16 // Etype Find( )            --> Return item that matches X
17 // int WasFound( )          --> Return 1 if last Find succeeded
18 // int IsFound( Etype X )   --> Return 1 if X would be found
19 // int IsEmpty( )           --> Return 1 if empty; else return 0
20 // int IsFull( )            --> Return 1 if full;  else return 0
21 // void MakeEmpty( )        --> Remove all items
22
23 template <class Etype>
24 class AbsHTable
25 {
26   public:
27     AbsHTable( ) { }              // Default constructor
28     virtual ~AbsHTable( ) { }     // Destructor
29
30     // Basic Members
31     virtual int Insert( const Etype & X ) = 0;
32     virtual int Remove( const Etype & X ) = 0;
33     virtual const Etype & Find( const Etype & X ) = 0;
34     virtual int WasFound( ) const = 0;
35     virtual int IsFound( const Etype & X ) const = 0;
36     virtual int IsEmpty( ) const = 0;
37     virtual int IsFull( ) const = 0;
38     virtual void MakeEmpty( ) = 0;
39   private:
40         // Disable copy constructor
41     AbsHTable( const AbsHTable & ) { }
42 };
```

Figure 6.21   Interface for the abstract hash table class

6.8   Priority Queues

The *priority queue* supports access of the minimum item only.

Although jobs sent to a printer are generally placed on a queue, this might not always be the best thing to do. For instance, one job might be particularly important, so it might be desirable to allow that job to be run as soon as the printer is available. Conversely, when the printer finishes a job and several 1-page jobs and one 100-page job are waiting, it might be reasonable to print the long job last, even if it is not the last job submitted. (Unfortunately, most systems do not do this, which can be particularly annoying at times.)

Similarly, in a multiuser environment the operating system scheduler must decide which of several processes to run. Generally, a process is allowed to run only for a fixed period of time. One algorithm uses a queue. Jobs are initially placed at the end of the queue. The scheduler will repeatedly take the first job on the queue, run it until either it finishes or its time limit is up, and place it at the end of the queue if it does not finish. Generally, this strategy is not appropriate because short jobs must wait and thus seem to take a long time to run. Clearly, users that are running an editor should not see a visible delay in the echoing of typed characters. Thus short jobs (that is, those using fewer resources) should have precedence over jobs that have already consumed large amounts of resources. Furthermore, some resource-intensive jobs, such as jobs run by the system administrator, might be important and should also have precedence.

```
1  #include <iostream.h>
2  #include "Hash.h"
3
4  // A good hash function is given in Figure 19.1
5  unsigned int Hash( const String & Element, int TableSize );
6
7  // Simple test program for hash tables
8
9  main( )
10 {
11     HashTable<String> H;
12
13     H.Insert( "Becky" );
14
15     const String & Result2 = H.Find( "Mark" );
16     if( H.WasFound( ) )
17         cout << " Found " << Result2 << ';';
18     else
19         cout << " Mark not found; ";
20
21     cout << '\n';
22
23     return 0;
24 }
```

Figure 6.22   Sample hash table program; output is `Found Becky; Mark not found;`

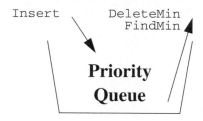

Figure 6.23   Priority queue model: only the minimum element is accessible

If we give each job a number to measure its priority, then the smaller number (pages printed, resources used) tends to indicate greater importance. Thus we want to be able to access the smallest item in a collection of items and remove it from the collection. These are the `FindMin` and `DeleteMin` operations. The data structure that supports these operations is the aptly named *priority queue*. Figure 6.23 illustrates the basic priority queue operations. Notice that `DeleteMin` comes in two forms: One form removes the smallest item, and the second form removes the smallest item but passes that item back to the caller.

The priority queue abstract base class is shown in Figure 6.24, and a sample program that illustrates its use is provided in Figure 6.25. Once again we must ask: Why not use a binary search tree? Once again the answer is that a binary search tree is overly powerful, has poor worst-case performance, and requires the overhead of two pointers per item. Using a sophisticated binary search tree allows logarithmic worst-case performance, but then the coding is excessive, leading to sluggish performance in practice.[1] Since the priority queue supports only the `DeleteMin` and `FindMin` operations, we might expect performance that is a compromise between the constant-time queue and the logarithmic time binary search tree. Indeed, this is the case. We will see that the basic priority queue supports all operations in logarithmic worst-case time, does not require the overhead of two pointers per item, supports insertion in constant average time, and is very simple to implement. The resulting structure is known as the *binary heap* and is one of the most elegant data structures known. It turns out that it is convenient to construct a binary heap with the sentinel $-\infty$ (negative infinity) and to make `FindMin` a nonconstant member function. Consequently, the binary heap class is not derived from the abstract priority queue class.

The *binary heap* implements the priority queue in logarithmic time per operation without using any extra pointers (besides the pointer used for an array).

The binary heap is constructed with a sentinel representing negative infinity.

---

1. However, the splay tree, discussed in Chapter 21, is a notable exception in some applications.

```
1   // PriorityQueue abstract class interface
2   //
3   // Etype: must have zero-parameter constructor and operator<;
4   //      implementation may require other relationals;
5   //      implementation will require either
6   //      operator= or copy constructor, perhaps both
7   //   CONSTRUCTION: with (a) no initializer
8   //      copy construction of PriorityQueue object is DISALLOWED
9   //
10  // ******************PUBLIC OPERATIONS*********************
11  //      All of the following are pure virtual functions
12  // void Insert( Etype X )--> Insert X
13  // void DeleteMin( )      --> Remove smallest item
14  // Etype FindMin( )       --> Return smallest item
15  // void DeleteMin( Etype & X )
16  //                        --> Remove smallest item, put it in X
17  // int IsEmpty( )         --> Return 1 if empty; else return 0
18  // int IsFull( )          --> Return 1 if full;  else return 0
19  // void MakeEmpty( )      --> Remove all items
20  // ******************ERRORS****************************
21  // FindMin or DeleteMin on empty priority queue
22
23  template <class Etype>
24  class AbsPrQueue
25  {
26    public:
27      AbsPrQueue( ) { }              // Default constructor
28      virtual ~AbsPrQueue( ) { }     // Destructor
29
30      // Basic Members
31      virtual void Insert( const Etype & X ) = 0
32      virtual void DeleteMin( ) = 0;
33      virtual void DeleteMin( Etype & X ) = 0;
34      virtual const Etype & FindMin( ) const = 0;
35      virtual int IsEmpty( ) const = 0;
36      virtual int IsFull( ) const = 0;
37      virtual void MakeEmpty( ) = 0;
38    private:
39      AbsPrQueue( const AbsPrQueue & ) { }  // Disabled
40  };
```

Figure 6.24   Interface for the abstract priority queue class

An important use of priority queues is *event-driven simulation*.

Chapter 20 will provide details on the implementation of priority queues. An important application of the priority queue is in the area of *event-driven simulation*. Consider, for example, a system such as a bank where customers arrive and wait in line until one of *K* tellers is available. Customer arrival is governed by a probability distribution function, as is the service time (the amount of time it takes a teller to provide complete service to one customer). We are interested in statistics such as how long on average a customer has to wait or how long a line might be.

```
 1  #include <iostream.h>
 2  #include "BinaryHeap.h"
 3
 4  // Simple test program for priority queues
 5
 6  main( )
 7  {
 8      BinaryHeap<int> PQ;
 9
10      PQ.Insert( 4 ); PQ.Insert( 2 ); PQ.Insert( 1 );
11      PQ.Insert( 5 ); PQ.Insert( 0 );
12
13      cout << "Contents:";
14      do
15      {
16          cout << ' ' << PQ.FindMin( );
17          PQ.DeleteMin( );
18      } while( !PQ.IsEmpty( ) );
19      cout << '\n';
20
21      return 0;
22  }
```

Figure 6.25   Sample program for priority queues;
output is Contents: 0 1 2 3 4

Data Structure	Access	Comments
Stack	Most recent only, Pop, $O(1)$	Very very fast
Queue	Least recent only, Dequeue, $O(1)$	Very very fast
Linked list	Any item	$O(N)$
Search Tree	Any item by name or rank, $O(\log N)$	Average case, can be made worst case
Hash Table	Any named Item, $O(1)$	Almost certain
Priority Queue	FindMin, $O(1)$, DeleteMin, $O(\log N)$	Insert is $O(1)$ on average $O(\log N)$ worst case

Figure 6.26   Summary of some data structures

With certain probability distributions and values of K, we can compute these statistics exactly. However, as K gets larger, the analysis becomes considerably more difficult, so it is appealing to use a computer to simulate the operation of the bank. In this way the bank officers can determine how many tellers are needed to ensure reasonably smooth service. An *event-driven simulation* consists of processing events. The two events here are (a) a customer arriving and (b) a customer departing, thus freeing up a teller. At any point we have a collection of events waiting to happen, and to run the simulation, we need to determine the *next* event. This is the event whose time of occurrence is minimum, hence a priority queue that extracts the event of minimum time is used to process the event list efficiently. A complete discussion and implementation of event-driven simulation is contained in Section 13.2.

Summary

In this chapter we examined the basic data structures that will be used throughout the book. We provided an abstract base class specification and explained what the running time ought to be for each data structure. In future chapters we will show how these data structures are used, and eventually we will give an implementation of each data structure that meets the time bounds we have claimed here. Figure 6.26 summarizes the results that will be obtained.

The next chapter describes an important problem-solving tool known as recursion. Recursion allows many problems to be efficiently solved using short algorithms and is central to the implementation of the binary search tree.

Objects of the Game

binary heap Implements the priority queue in logarithmic time per operation without using any extra pointers (besides the pointer used for an array). The binary heap is constructed with a sentinel representing negative infinity. (207)

binary search tree A tree that supports insertion, removal, and searching. We can also access the *K*th smallest item. The cost is logarithmic average-case time for a simple implementation and logarithmic worst-case time for a more careful implementation. (202)

binary tree A tree with at most two children per node. (200)

data structure A representation of data and the operations allowed on that data. Data structures allow us to achieve component reuse. (186)

dictionary Stores keys which are looked up in the dictionary and their corresponding definitions. (204)

expression tree Trees used in parsing in which the value of a node is the result of applying the operand at the node, using the children as operands. (200)

hash function Converts a specific `Etype` to an integer. To use the hash table, we must provide a hash function. (204)

hash table Data structure that supports constant average-time insertions, removals, and searches. (202)

iterator class Access to the list is done through an iterator class. The list class has operations that reflect the state of the list. All other operations are in the iterator class. (194)

leaf In a tree, a node with no children. (198)

operator precedence parsing Algorithm that uses a stack to evaluate expressions. (191)

path length In a tree, the number of edges the must be followed from the root to reach a node. (197)

priority queue Data structure that supports access of the minimum item only. (206)

queue Data structure that restricts access to the least recently inserted item. (191)

rooted tree A tree with a node that is designated as the root. (197)

stack Data structure that restricts access to the most recently inserted item. (188)

symbol table Data structure used by the compiler to keep track of identifiers. Generally it is implemented by a hash table. (202)

tree Widely used data structure that consists of a set of nodes and a set of edges that connect pairs of nodes. Throughout the text, we assume the tree is rooted. (197)

Common Errors

1. Failure to adequately document the characteristics of the class interface is a serious error.

2. It is an error to access or delete from an empty stack, queue, or priority queue. The class implementor must make sure that the error is detected. Access and remove operations are allowed for empty trees and hash tables because access on an empty tree or hash table is a subset of the unsuccessful search.

3. Several errors can occur during list or tree access. These must be signalled by the class.

4. The user of a hash table must supply a good hash function for the particular type the hash table is to be instantiated with. This hash function is not part of the class.

5. A priority queue is not a queue. It just sounds like it is.

On the Internet

Only header files are provided for the code in this chapter. Class derivation is used to implement the stack, queue, list, and hash table. The other classes are not used.

AbsStack.h	Contains the interface for `AbsStack` shown in Figure 6.4
AbsQueue.h	Contains the interface for `AbsQueue` shown in Figure 6.7
AbsList.h	Contains the interface for `AbsList` shown in Figure 6.11 and `AbsListItr` (in Figure 6.12)
AbsBst.h	Contains the interface for `AbsBst` shown in Figure 6.18
AbsHash.h	Contains the interface for `AbsHTable` shown in Figure 6.21
AbsPrQue.h	Contains the interface for `AbsPrQueue` shown in Figure 6.24

Exercises

In Short

6.1.   Show the results of the following sequence: `Add(4)`, `Add(8)`, `Add(1)`, `Add(6)`, `Remove`, `Remove`, when the `Add` and `Remove` operations correspond to the basic operations in a

a. Stack

b. Queue

c. Priority queue

In Theory

6.2.   Suppose we want to support the following three operations exclusively: `Insert`, `FindMax`, and `DeleteMax`. How fast do you think these operations can be performed?

6.3.   Can we support all of the following in logarithmic time? `Insert`, `DeleteMin`, `DeleteMax`, `FindMin`, and `FindMax`.

6.4.   Which of the data structures in Figure 6.26 lead to sorting algorithms that could run in less than quadratic time?

6.5.   Show that we can support the following operations in constant time simultaneously: `Push`, `Pop`, `FindMin`. Note that `DeleteMin` is not part of the repertoire. *Hint*: Maintain two stacks: One stores items, the other stores minimums as they occur.

6.6.   A double-ended queue supports insertions and deletions at both the front and end of the line. What do you think the running time is per operation?

In Practice

6.7.   Write a routine that prints out the items in a linked list in reverse order. To do this, have a `ListItr` go down the linked list, and `Push` onto a stack each item that is seen. When the end of the linked list is reached, repeatedly Pop the stack until it is empty.

6.8. A deletion in a linked list or a binary search tree leaves the following problem: If the "current" element is deleted, what becomes the new "current" element? Discuss some alternatives.

6.9. Show how to implement a Stack efficiently by using a linked list as a data member.

6.10. Show how to implement a Queue efficiently by using a linked list as a data member and maintaining a ListItr object that is fixed to the last element in the linked list.

6.11. Implement a templated class Dictionary that supports the Insert and LookUp operations. Some of the lines of the Dictionary class are shown below. Assume that you have a hash table class.

```
template <class KeyType, class DefType>
class Dictionary
{
        // Some of the member functions
    void Insert( const KeyType & Key,
                 const DefType & Definition );
    const DefType & Lookup( const KeyType & Key );
    int WasFound( );
};
```

Programming Projects

6.12. A stack can be implemented by using an array and maintaining the current and maximum sizes. The stack elements are stored in consecutive array positions, with the top item always in position 0. Note that this is not the most efficient method.

a. Give a description of the algorithms for Push, Pop, and Top.

b. What is the Big-Oh running time for each of Push, Pop, and Top, using your algorithms?

c. Write a derived class interface and an implementation that use your algorithms.

6.13. A queue can be implemented by using an array and maintaining the current and maximum sizes. The queue elements are stored in consecutive array positions, with the front item always in position 0. Note that this is not the most efficient method.

a. Give a description of the algorithms for GetFront, Enqueue, and Dequeue.

b. What is the Big-Oh running time for each of GetFront, Enqueue, and Dequeue, using your algorithms?

c. Write a derived class interface and an implementation that use your algorithms.

6.14. The operations that are supported by the search tree can also be implemented by using an array and maintaining the current size, the maximum size, and an integer that records the position where the last Find operation succeeded (or −1 if it failed). The array elements are stored in sorted order in consecutive array positions. Thus Find can be implemented by a binary search.

a. Give a description of the algorithms for Insert and Remove.

b. What is the running time for these algorithms?

c. Write a derived class interface and an implementation that use your algorithms.

6.15. A hash table can be implemented by using an array and maintaining the current size, the maximum size, and an integer that records the position where the last Find operation succeeded (or −1 if it failed). The elements are stored in consecutive locations but are not kept sorted; instead, they are inserted in the next available array position.

a. Give a description of the algorithms for Insert, Remove, Find, and WasFound.

b. What is the Big-Oh running time for each of Insert, Remove, and Find, using your algorithms?

c. Write a derived class interface and an implementation that use your algorithms.

6.16. A priority queue can be implemented by using a sorted array (as in Exercise 6.14).

a. Give a description of the algorithms for FindMin, DeleteMin, and Insert.

b. What is the Big-Oh running time for each of FindMin, DeleteMin, and Insert, using your algorithms?

c. Write a derived class interface and an implementation that use your algorithms.

6.17. A priority queue can be implemented by storing items in an unsorted array and inserting items in the next available location (as in Exercise 6.15).

a. Give a description of the algorithms for FindMin, DeleteMin, and Insert.

b. What is the Big-Oh running time for each of `FindMin`, `DeleteMin`, and `Insert`, using your algorithms?

c. Write a derived class interface and an implementation that use your algorithms.

6.18. If we add an extra member to the priority queue class in Exercise 6.17, we can implement both `Insert` and `FindMin` in constant time. The extra member will store the array position where the minimum is stored. However, `DeleteMin` will still be expensive.

a. Describe the algorithms for `Insert`, `FindMin`, and `DeleteMin`.

b. What is the Big-Oh running time for `DeleteMin`?

c. Write a derived class interface and an implementation that use your algorithms.

6.19. If we maintain the invariant that the elements in the priority queue are sorted in nonincreasing order (that is, the largest item is first, the smallest is last), we can implement both `FindMin` and `DeleteMin` in constant time. However, `Insert` will be expensive.

a. Describe the algorithms for `Insert`, `FindMin`, and `DeleteMin`.

b. What is the Big-Oh running time for `Insert`?

c. Write a derived class interface and an implementation that use your algorithms.

6.20. A double-ended priority queue allows access to both the minimum and maximum elements. In other words, all of the following are supported: `FindMin`, `DeleteMin`, `FindMax`, `DeleteMax`.

a. Give a description of the algorithms for `FindMin`, `DeleteMin`, `FindMin`, `DeleteMin`, and `Insert`.

b. What is the Big-Oh running time for each of `FindMin`, `DeleteMin`, `FindMin`, `DeleteMin`, and `Insert`, using your algorithms?

c. Write a derived class interface and an implementation that use your algorithm.

6.21. A median heap supports the following operations: `Insert`, `FindKth`, `RemoveKth`. The last two operations find and remove the kth smallest element, respectively. The simplest implementation maintains the data in sorted order.

a. Give a description of algorithms that can be used to support median heap operations.

b. What is the Big-Oh running time for each of the basic operations using your algorithms?

c. Write a derived class interface and an implementation that use your algorithms.

References

References for these data structures are provided in Part IV.

Chapter 7

Recursion

A function that is partially defined in terms of itself is called *recursive*. Like many procedural languages, C++ supports recursive functions. Recursion, which is the use of recursive functions, is a powerful programming tool that in many cases can yield both short and efficient algorithms. In order to discuss recursion, we will first examine the mathematical principle on which it is based, namely *mathematical induction*. Then we will give examples of simple recursive functions and prove that they generate correct answers. We will also explore how recursion works, thus providing some insight into its variations, its limitations, and some of its many uses.

In this chapter we will see

- the four basic rules of recursion
- numerical applications of recursion, leading to implementation of an encryption algorithm
- a general technique known as *divide and conquer*
- a general technique, known as *dynamic programming*, that is similar to recursion but uses tables instead of recursive function calls
- a general technique, known as *backtracking*, that amounts to a careful exhaustive search

7.1   What Is Recursion?

A recursive function is a function that either directly or indirectly makes a call to itself. This may seem to be circular logic: How can a function F solve a problem by calling itself? The key is that the function F calls itself on a different, generally simpler, instance. Here are some examples:

A *recursive function* is a function that directly or indirectly makes a call to itself.

- In C++ source file is processed by replacing all #include directives with the contents of the include file. However, include files may themselves have #include directives. This is easily handled with recursion: To process a file, we replace all #include directives with the contents of the recursively processed include file. Any nested includes are automatically handled. Notice that if a file attempts to include itself, either directly or indirectly, then we have an infinite loop.

- Files on a computer are generally stored in directories. Users may create subdirectories that store more files and directories. Suppose we want to examine every file in a directory D, including all files in all subdirectories (and subsubdirectories, and so on). This is done by recursively examining every file in each subdirectory and then examining all files in the directory D (this is discussed in Chapter 17).

- Suppose we have a large dictionary. Words in dictionaries are defined in terms of other words. When we look up the meaning of a word, we might not always understand the definition, so we might have to look up words in the definition. Likewise, we might not understand some of those, so we might have to continue this search for a while. As the dictionary is finite, eventually either we will come to a point where we understand all of the words in some definition (and thus understand that definition and can retrace our path through the other definitions), or we will find that the definitions are circular and we are stuck, or that some word we need to understand is not defined in the dictionary. Our recursive strategy to understand words is as follows: If we know the meaning of a word we are done; otherwise, we look the word up in the dictionary. If we understand all the words in the definition, we are done; otherwise, we figure out what the definition means by recursively looking up the words we do not know. This procedure will terminate if the dictionary is well defined but can loop indefinitely if a word is either not defined or circularly defined.

- Computer languages are frequently defined recursively. For instance, an arithmetic expression is either an object, or a parenthesized expression, or two expressions added to each other, and so on.

Recursion is a powerful problem-solving tool. Many algorithms are most easily expressed using a recursive formulation. Furthermore, there are many problems whose most efficient solutions use this natural recursive formulation. But we must be careful not to create circular logic that would result in infinite loops. In this chapter we will discuss the general conditions that must be satisfied by recursive algorithms and see several practical examples. We will also show that sometimes algorithms that are naturally expressed recursively must be rewritten without recursion.

7.2   Background: Proofs by Mathematical Induction

In this section we discuss proof by mathematical *induction*. (Throughout this chapter we will omit the word *mathematical* when describing this technique.) Induction proofs are commonly used to establish theorems that hold for positive integers. We will start by proving a simple theorem. It is easy to establish this particular theorem using other methods, but often it turns out that a proof by induction is the simplest mechanism.

Induction is an important proof technique used to establish theorems that hold for positive integers.

For any integer $N \geq 1$, the sum of the first N integers, given by **Theorem 7.1**
$\sum_{i=1}^{N} i = 1 + 2 + \ldots + N$, *is equal to* $N(N+1)/2$.

It is easy to see that the theorem is true for $N = 1$ because both the left and right sides evaluate to 1. Further checking shows that it is true for $2 \leq N \leq 10$. However, the fact that the theorem holds for all N that are easy to check by hand does not imply that it is true for all N. Consider, for instance, numbers of the form $2^{2^k} + 1$. The first five numbers (corresponding to $0 \leq k \leq 4$ are 3, 5, 17, 257, and 65537. These numbers are all prime, and indeed at one time it was conjectured that all numbers of this form are prime. This is not the case: It is easy to check by computer that $2^{2^5} + 1 = 641 \times 6700417$. In fact, no other prime of the form $2^{2^k} + 1$ is known.

A proof by induction works in two steps. First, as above, we show that the theorem is true for the smallest cases. We then show that if the theorem is true for the first few cases, then it can be extended to include the next case. For instance, we show that a theorem that is true for all $1 \leq N \leq k$ must be true for $1 \leq N \leq k + 1$. Once we show how to extend the range of true cases, we have shown that it is true for all cases, because we can extend the range of true cases indefinitely. Let us use this technique to prove Theorem 7.1.

A proof by induction shows that the theorem is true for some base case and then shows how to extend the range of true cases indefinitely.

Clearly the theorem is true for $N = 1$. Suppose that the theorem is true for all $1 \leq N \leq k$. Then **Proof** *(of Theorem 7.1)*

$$\sum_{i=1}^{k+1} i = (k+1) + \sum_{i=1}^{k} i \qquad (7.1)$$

Since by assumption the theorem is true for k, we may replace the sum on the right side of Equation 7.1 with $k(k+1)/2$, obtaining

Proof *(of Theorem*
    7.1 continued)

$$\sum_{i=1}^{k+1} i \;=\; (k+1) + k(k+1)/2 \qquad\qquad \textbf{(7.2)}$$

Algebraic manipulation of the right side of Equation 7.2 now yields

$$\sum_{i=1}^{k+1} i \;=\; (k+1)(k+2)/2$$

This confirms the theorem for the case $k+1$. Thus by induction, the theorem is true for all integers $N \geq 1$.

In a proof by induction, the *basis* is the easy case that can be shown by hand.

    Let us explain why this constitutes a proof. First we showed that the theorem is true for $N = 1$. We call this the *basis*. One can view it as being the basis for our belief that the theorem is true in general. Once we have established the basis, we hypothesize that the theorem is true for some arbitrary k. We call this the *inductive hypothesis*. We show that if the theorem is true for k, then it is true for $k + 1$. In our case, since we know the theorem is true for the basis $N = 1$, we know that it is true for $N = 2$. Since it is true for $N = 2$, it must be true for $N = 3$. And since it is true for $N = 3$, it must be true for $N = 4$. Extending this logic, we see that the theorem is true for every positive integer beginning with $N = 1$.

The *inductive hypothesis* assumes that the theorem is true for some arbitrary case and shows that, under this assumption, it is true for the next case.

    Let us apply proof by induction to a second problem, which is not quite as simple as the first. Let us examine the sequence of numbers 1^2, $2^2 - 1^2$, $3^2 - 2^2 + 1^2$, $4^2 - 3^2 + 2^2 - 1^2$, $5^2 - 4^2 + 3^2 - 2^2 + 1^2$, and so on. Each member represents the sum of the first N squares, with alternating signs. The sequence evaluates to 1, 3, 6, 10, and 15. It seems that in general the sum is exactly equal to the sum of the first N integers, which, as we know from Theorem 7.1, would be $N(N+1)/2$. Let us prove this.

Theorem 7.2

The sum $\sum_{i=N}^{1} (-1)^{N-i} i^2 = N^2 - (N-1)^2 + (N-2)^2 \ldots$ is $N(N+1)/2$.

Proof

The proof is by induction.

Basis: Clearly the theorem is true for $N = 1$.

Inductive hypothesis: First we assume the theorem is true for k:
$\sum_{i=k}^{1} (-1)^{k-i} i^2 = \dfrac{k(k+1)}{2}$. *Then we must show that it is true for $k + 1$, namely that $\sum_{i=k+1}^{1} (-1)^{k-i} i^2 = \dfrac{(k+1)(k+2)}{2}$. We write*

Proof (continued)

$$\sum_{i=k+1}^{1} (-1)^{k+1-i} i^2 = (k+1)^2 - k^2 + (k-1)^2 \ldots \qquad \textbf{(7.3)}$$

If we rewrite the right side of Equation 7.3, we obtain

$$\sum_{i=k+1}^{1} (-1)^{k+1-i} i^2 = (k+1)^2 - (k^2 - (k-1)^2 \ldots)$$

This allows a substitution to yield

$$\sum_{i=k+1}^{1} (-1)^{k+1-i} i^2 = (k+1)^2 - (\sum_{i=k}^{1} (-1)^{k-i} i^2) \qquad \textbf{(7.4)}$$

If we apply the inductive hypothesis, then we can replace the summation on the right side of Equation 7.4 obtaining

$$\sum_{i=k+1}^{1} (-1)^{k+1-i} i^2 = (k+1)^2 - k(k+1)/2 \qquad \textbf{(7.5)}$$

Simple algebraic manipulation of the right side of Equation 7.5 then yields

$$\sum_{i=k+1}^{1} (-1)^{k+1-i} i^2 = (k+1)(k+2)/2$$

which establishes the theorem for $N = k+1$. Thus, by induction, the theorem is true for all $N \geq 1$.

7.3   Basic Recursion

Proofs by induction show us that if we know that a statement is true for a smallest case, and we can show that one case implies the next case, then we know the statement is true for all cases.

Sometimes mathematical functions are defined recursively. For instance, let $S(N)$ be the sum of the first N integers. Then $S(1) = 1$, and we can write $S(N) = S(N-1) + N$. Here we have defined the function S in terms of a smaller instance of itself. The recursive definition of $S(N)$ is identical to the closed form $S(N) = N(N+1)/2$, except that the recursive definition is only defined for positive integers and is less directly computable.

A recursive function is defined in terms of a smaller instance of itself. There must be some base case that can be computed without recursion.

```
 1  // Evaluate the sum of the first N integers
 2
 3  unsigned long
 4  S( unsigned int N )
 5  {
 6      if( N == 1 )
 7          return 1;
 8      else
 9          return S( N - 1 ) + N;
10  }
```

Figure 7.1   Recursive evaluation of the sum of the first N integers

Sometimes it is easier to write a formula recursively than in closed form. Figure 7.1 shows a straightforward implementation of the recursive function. If $N = 1$, then we have the basis, for which we know $S(1) = 1$. We take care of this case at lines 6 and 7. Otherwise we follow the recursive definition $S(N) = S(N-1) + N$ precisely at line 9. It is hard to imagine that we could implement the recursive function any more simply than this, so the natural question is: Does this actually work?

The answer to the question is, Sort of. Except as noted below, this routine works. Let us see how the call to $S(4)$ is evaluated. When the call to $S(4)$ is made, the test at line 6 fails. We then execute line 9, where we evaluate $S(3)$. Like any other function, this requires a call to S. In that call we get to line 6, where the test fails, and thus we go to line 9. At this point we call $S(2)$. Once again we call S, and now N is 2. The test at line 6 still fails, and so we call $S(1)$ at line 9. Now we have N equal to 1, so $S(1)$ returns 1. At this point $S(2)$ can continue, adding the return value from $S(1)$ to 2, and thus $S(2)$ returns 3. Now $S(3)$ continues, adding the value of 3 that was returned by $S(2)$ to N, which is 3. Thus $S(3)$ returns 6. This enables the completion of the call to $S(4)$, which finally returns 10.

Notice here that although it seems that S is calling itself, in reality it is calling a clone of itself, that is simply another function with different parameters. At any instant only one clone is active; the rest are pending. It is the computer's job to handle all the bookkeeping, not yours. If there were too much bookkeeping even for the computer, then it would be time to worry. We will talk more about these details later.

The *base case* is an instance that can be solved without recursion. Any recursive call must make progress toward a base case.

What we see is that if we have a base case, and if our recursive calls make progress toward reaching the base case, then eventually we terminate. We thus have our first two fundamental rules of recursion

1. *Base cases*: Always have at least one case that can be solved without using recursion.
2. *Make progress*: Any recursive call must make progress toward a base case.

The routine does have a few problems. One problem is the call S(0), for which the function behaves poorly.[1] This is natural because the recursive definition of $S(N)$ does not allow for $N < 1$. We can fix this problem by extending the definition of $S(N)$ to include $N = 0$. Since there are no numbers to add in this case, a natural value for $S(0)$ would be 0. This makes sense because the recursive definition can apply for $S(1)$, since $S(0) + 1$ is 1. To implement this change, we just replace 1 with 0 on lines 6 and 7.

A second problem is that the return value may be too large to fit in an unsigned long, but that is not an important issue here. A third problem, however, is that if the parameter N is large, but not so large that the answer does not fit in an unsigned long, it is possible for the program to crash or hang. On our system, for instance, $N \geq 74754$ cannot be handled.

The reason is that, as we have seen, the implementation of recursion requires some bookkeeping to keep track of the pending recursive calls, and for sufficiently long chains of recursion, the computer simply runs out of memory. We will explain this in more detail later. If you implement this routine, you will also see that it is somewhat more time consuming than an equivalent loop because the bookkeeping also uses up some time.

Suffice it to say that this particular example does not demonstrate the best use of recursion, since it is so easy to solve the problem without recursion. Most of the good uses of recursion will not exhaust the computer's memory and will be only slightly more time consuming than nonrecursive implementations. However, recursion will almost always lead to more compact code.

7.3.1   Printing Numbers in Any Base

A good example of how recursion simplifies the coding of routines is number printing. Suppose we would like to print out a nonnegative number N in decimal, but we do not have a number output function available. However, we can print out one digit at a time. Consider, for instance, how we would print the number 1369. First we would need to print a 1, then 3, then 6, and then 9. The problem is that obtaining the first digit is a bit sloppy: Given a number N, we need a loop to determine the first digit of N. This is in contrast to the last digit, which is immediately available as N%10 (which is N for N less than 10).

Recursion provides a nifty solution. To print out 1369, we print out 136, followed by the last digit, 9. As we have mentioned, it is easy to print out the last digit using the % operator. Printing out all but the number represented by eliminating the last digit is also easy, because it is the same problem as printing out N/10. Thus, it can be done by a recursive call.

---

1. A call to S(-1) is made, −1 is converted to an unsigned long, and then the program eventually crashes because there will be too many pending recursive calls. If the formal parameter N was declared to be a signed long, we would have a problem of not progressing toward a base case.

```
1  // Print N as a Decimal Number
2
3  void
4  PrintDecimal( unsigned long N )
5  {
6      if( N >= 10 )
7          PrintDecimal( N / 10 );
8      cout.put( '0' + N % 10 );
9  }
```

Figure 7.2   Recursive routine to print *N* in decimal

```
1   // Print N in any base
2   // Assumes 2 <= Base <= 16
3
4   void
5   PrintInt( unsigned long N, unsigned int Base )
6   {
7       static char DigitTable[ ] = "0123456789abcdef";
8
9       if( N >= Base )
10          PrintInt( N / Base, Base );
11      cout << DigitTable[ N % Base ];
12  }
```

Figure 7.3   Recursive routine to print *N* in any base

The routine in Figure 7.2 implements this printing routine. If N is smaller than 10, then line 7 is not executed and only the one digit N%10 is printed; otherwise, all but the last digit is printed recursively, and then the last digit is printed.

Notice how we have a base case (N is a one-digit integer), and that all recursive calls make progress toward the base case because the recursive problem has one less digit. Thus we have satisfied the first two fundamental rules of recursion.

Since this printing routine is already provided, it may seem like a silly exercise. However, the iostream classes supply only octal, decimal, and hexadecimal formats. To make our printing routine useful, we will extend it to print in any base between 2 and 16. This modification is shown in Figure 7.3.

We have introduced an array of characters to make the printing of a through f easier. Each digit is now output by indexing into the DigitTable array. The PrintInt routine is not robust. If Base is larger than 16, then the index into DigitTable could be out of the DigitTable array.[2] If Base is 0, then an arithmetic error will result when a division by 0 is attempted at line 10.

---

2. Technically, since a null terminator is present, if Base is 17, the index is guaranteed to be into the array.

```
1  // Print N in any base
2
3  static char DigitTable[ ] = "0123456789abcdef";
4  static const MaxBase = sizeof( DigitTable ) - 1;
5
6  static void
7  PrintIntRec( unsigned long N, unsigned int Base )
8  {
9      if( N >= Base )
10         PrintIntRec( N / Base, Base  );
11     cout << DigitTable[ N % Base ];
12 }
13
14 void
15 PrintInt( unsigned long N, unsigned int Base )
16 {
17     if( Base <= 1 || Base > MaxBase )
18         cerr << "Cannot print in base " << Base << endl;
19     else
20         PrintIntRec( N, Base );
21 }
```

Figure 7.4   Robust number printing program

The most interesting error occurs when Base is 1. When that happens, the recursive call at line 10 fails to make progress, because the two parameters to the recursive call will be identical to the original call. Thus the system will make recursive calls until it eventually runs out of bookkeeping space (and perhaps exits less than gracefully).

Failure to make progress means the program does not work.

We can make the routine more robust by adding an explicit test for Base. The problem with that strategy is that the test would be executed during each of the recursive calls to PrintInt, and not just the first call. Once Base is valid in the first call, it is silly to retest it, since it does not change in the course of the recursion, and thus must still be valid. One way to avoid this inefficiency is to set up a *driver routine*, which tests the validity of Base and then calls the recursive routine. This is shown in Figure 7.4. The use of driver routines for recursive programs is a common technique.

A *driver routine* tests the validity of the first call and the calls the recursive routine.

7.3.2   Why It Works

Let us show, somewhat rigorously, that the PrintDecimal algorithm works. Our proof will assume that we have made no syntax errors, because our goal is to verify that the algorithm is correct.

Recursive algorithms can be proven correct with mathematical induction.

Theorem 7.3   *The algorithm* PrintDecimal *shown in Figure 7.2 correctly prints* N *in base 10.*

Proof   *Let k be the number of digits in* N. *The proof is by induction on k.*

Basis: If k = 1, then no recursive call is made, and line 8 correctly outputs the one digit of N.

Inductive Hypothesis: Assume that PrintDecimal *works correctly for all k ≥ 1 digit integers. We show that this assumption implies correctness for any k + 1 digit integer* N. *Because k ≥ 1, the* if *statement at line 6 is satisfied for a k + 1 digit integer* N. *By the inductive hypothesis, the recursive call at line 7 prints the first k digits of* N. *Then the call at line 8 prints the final digit. Thus if any k digit integer can be printed, then so can a k + 1 digit integer. By induction, we conclude that* PrintDecimal *works for all k, and thus all* N.

The proof of Theorem 7.3 illustrates an important principle. When designing a recursive algorithm, we can always assume that the recursive calls work, because when a proof is performed, this assumption will be used as the inductive hypothesis.

At first glance such an assumption seems strange. However, recall that we always assume function calls work, and thus the assumption that the recursive call works is really no different. Just like any function, a recursive routine needs to combine solutions from calls to other functions to obtain a solution. It is just that other functions may include easier instances of the original function.

This observation leads us to the third fundamental rule of recursion:

3. *"You gotta believe"*: Always assume that the recursive call works.

The third fundamental rule of recursion: Always assume that the recursive call works. Use this rule to design your algorithms.

Rule 3 tells us that when we design a recursive function, we do not have to attempt to trace the possibly long path of recursive calls. As we saw earlier, this can be a daunting task, and tends to make the design and verification more difficult. A good use of recursion makes such a trace almost impossible to understand. Intuitively, we are letting the computer handle the bookkeeping that, were we to do ourselves, would result in much longer code.

This principle is so important, that we state it again: *Always assume that the recursive call works.*

7.3.3   How It Works

We have mentioned already that the implementation of recursion requires additional bookkeeping on the part of the computer. We can state that another way by saying that the implementation of any function requires bookkeeping, and that a recursive call is not particularly special (except that it can overload the computer's bookkeeping limitations).

The bookkeeping in a procedural language is done by using a stack of *activation records*. Recursion is a natural by-product.

C++, like other procedural languages such as Pascal and Ada, implements functions using an internal stack of *activation records*. We can view an activation record as a piece of paper containing relevant information about the function. This includes, for instance, the values of the parameters and local variables. The actual contents of the activation record is system dependent.

The stack of activation records is used because functions return in reverse order of their invocation; recall that stacks are great for reversing things. In the most popular scenario, the top of the stack stores the activation record for the currently active function. When function G is called, an activation record for G is pushed onto the stack; this makes G the currently active function. When a function returns, the stack is popped and the activation record that is the new top of the stack contains the restored values.

Function calling and function return sequences are stack operations.

As an example, Figure 7.5 shows a stack of activation records that occurs in the course of evaluating S(4). At this point, we have the calls to main, S(4), and S(3) pending, and we are actively processing S(2).

The space overhead is the memory used to store an activation record for each currently active function. Thus, in our earlier example where S(74754) crashes, we see that our system has room for roughly 74,754 activation records. (Note that main generates an activation record itself). The pushing and popping of the internal stack also represents the overhead of executing a function call. This is what is saved when an inline directive is honored.

The close relation between recursion and stacks tells us that recursive programs can always be implemented iteratively with an explicit stack. Presumably our stack will store items that are smaller than an activation record, so we can also reasonably expect to use less space. The result is slightly faster but longer code. Modern optimizing compilers have lessened the costs associated with recursion to such a degree that, for the purposes of speed, it is rarely worth removing recursion from an application that uses it well.

Recursion can always be removed by using a stack. This is occasionally required to save space.

```
TOP:        S(2)
       ┌───────────┐
       │   S(3)    │
       ├───────────┤
       │   S(4)    │
       ├───────────┤
       │  main()   │
       └───────────┘
```

Figure 7.5   Stack of activation records

```
 1  // Compute the Nth Fibonacci Number
 2  // Bad algorithm
 3
 4  long
 5  Fib( int N )
 6  {
 7      if( N <= 1 )
 8          return N;
 9      else
10          return Fib( N - 1 ) + Fib( N - 2 );
11  }
```

Figure 7.6   Recursive routine for Fibonacci numbers: a bad idea

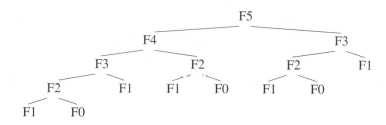

Figure 7.7   Trace of the recursive calculation of the Fibonacci numbers

7.3.4   Too Much Recursion Can Be Dangerous

Do not use recursion as a substitute for a simple loop.

In this text we will see many examples that illustrate the power of recursion. However, before we do that we must realize that recursion is not always appropriate. For instance, the use of recursion in Figure 7.1 is poor because a loop would do just as well. A practical liability is that the overhead of the recursive call takes time and limits the value of N for which the program is correct. A good rule of thumb is that you should never use recursion as a substitute for a simple loop.

The _i_ th _Fibonacci number_ is the sum of the two previous Fibonacci numbers.

A much more serious problem is illustrated by an attempt to calculate the *Fibonacci numbers* recursively. The Fibonacci numbers $F_0, F_1, ..., F_i$ are defined as follows: $F_0 = 0$ and $F_1 = 1$. The ith Fibonacci number is equal to the sum of the $(i-1)^{th}$ and $(i-2)^{th}$ Fibonacci numbers. Thus $F_i = F_{i-1} + F_{i-2}$. From this definition we can determine that the series of Fibonacci numbers continues: 1, 2, 3, 5, 8, 13, 21, 34, 55, 89, ...

Do not do redundant work recursively; the program will be incredibly inefficient.

The Fibonacci numbers have an incredible number of properties which seem to always crop up. In fact, one journal, *The Fibonacci Quarterly*, exists solely for the purpose of publishing theorems involving the Fibonacci numbers. For instance, the sum of the squares of two consecutive Fibonacci numbers is another Fibonacci number. The sum of the first N Fibonacci numbers is one less than F_{N+2} (see Exercise 7.8 for some other interesting identities).

Because the Fibonacci numbers are recursively defined, it seems natural to write a recursive routine to determine F_N. This recursive routine, shown in Figure 7.6, works but has a serious problem. This routine, on our relatively fast machine, takes over four minutes to compute F_{40}. This is an absurd amount of time considering that the basic calculation requires only 39 additions.

The underlying problem is that this particular recursive routine performs redundant calculations. To compute `Fib(N)`, we recursively compute `Fib(N-1)`. When the recursive call returns, we compute `Fib(N-2)` by using another recursive call.[3] But we have already computed `Fib(N-2)` in the process of computing `Fib(N-1)`, so the call to `Fib(N-2)` is a wasted, redundant calculation. In effect, we make two calls to `Fib(N-2)` instead of only one.

Normally making two function calls instead of one would only double the running time of a program. However, it is worse than that because each call to `Fib(N-1)` and each call to `Fib(N-2)` makes a call to `Fib(N-3)`. Thus there are actually three calls to `Fib(N-3)`. In fact, it just keeps getting worse: Each call to `Fib(N-2)` or `Fib(N-3)` results in a call to `Fib(N-4)`, so there are five calls to `Fib(N-4)`. Thus we get a compounding effect: Each recursive call does more and more redundant work.

Let $C(N)$ be the number of calls to `Fib` made during the evaluation of `Fib(N)`. Clearly $C(0) = C(1) = 1$ call. For $N \geq 2$, we make the call for `Fib(N)`, plus all the calls needed to evaluate `Fib(N-1)` and `Fib(N-2)` recursively and independently. Thus, $C(N) = C(N-1) + C(N-2) + 1$. By induction, we can easily verify that for $N \geq 3$ the solution to this recurrence is $C(N) = F_{N+2} + F_{N-1} - 1$. Thus the number of recursive calls is larger than the Fibonacci number we are trying to compute, and is exponential. For $N = 40$, $F_{40} = 102,334,155$, while the total number of recursive calls is over 300 million. No wonder the program takes forever. The explosive growth of the number of recursive calls is illustrated in Figure 7.7.

The recursive routine **Fib** *is exponential.*

This example illustrates the fourth and final basic rule of recursion:

4. *Compound interest rule*: Never duplicate work by solving the same instance of a problem in separate recursive calls.

The last fundamental rule of recursion: Never duplicate work by solving the same instance of a problem in separate recursive calls.

7.4   Numerical Applications

In this section we look at three problems drawn primarily from number theory. Number theory used to be considered an interesting but useless branch of mathematics. However, in the last 20 years, an important application for number theory has emerged: data security. We will begin our discussion by providing a small amount of mathematics background. We then show recursive algorithms to solve three problems. In conjunction with a fourth algorithm that is more complex and

---

3. Technically, C++ does not guarantee the order of evaluation, so at line 10, `Fib(N-2)` could be evaluated prior to `Fib(N-1)`. However, this does not affect the total number of recursive calls.

is described in Chapter 9, we can combine these routines to implement an algorithm that can be used to encode and decode messages. To date, nobody has been able to show that the encryption scheme we will describe is not secure.

Here are the four problems we examine:

1. *Modular exponentiation*: Compute $X^N(\bmod\ P)$.
2. *Greatest common divisor*: Compute $gcd(A, B)$.
3. *Multiplicative inverse*: Solve $AX \equiv 1(\bmod\ P)$ for X.
4. *Primality testing*: Determine if N is prime (this is deferred to Chapter 9).

The integers we expect to deal with are all large, requiring at least 100 digits each. Therefore, we must already have a way to represent the class `HugeInt`, along with a complete set of algorithms for basic operations such as addition, subtraction, multiplication, division, and so on. Implementing the `HugeInt` efficiently is no trivial matter, and in fact there is an extensive literature on the subject. Some libraries (for instance the one that comes with g++) provide the `Integer` class for this purpose.

The functions that we write will be templated to work with some `HugeInt` class, for which we assume the normal arithmetic operations are overloaded. By instantiating with `long`, the reader can test the basic algorithms. The routines that we describe will have the property that they work with large objects, but still execute in a reasonable amount of time.

7.4.1 Modular Arithmetic

The problems in this section, as well as the implementation of the hash table data structure (Section 6.7 and Chapter 19), require the use of the C++ `%` operator. The `%` operator, which we will denote as `operator%`, computes the remainder of two integral types.[4] As an example, `13%10` evaluates to 3, as does `3%10`, and `23%10`. When we compute the remainder of a division by 10, the possible results range from 0 to 9. This makes `operator%` useful when small integers need to be generated.

If two numbers A and B give the same remainder when divided by N, we say that they are congruent modulo N. This is written as $A \equiv B(\bmod\ N)$. In this case, it must be true that N divides $A - B$. Furthermore, the converse is true: If N divides $A - B$, then $A \equiv B(\bmod\ N)$. Because there are only N possible remainders — 0, 1, ..., $N - 1$ — we say that the integers are divided into congruence classes modulo N. In other words, every integer can be placed in one of N classes, and those in the same class are congruent to each other, modulo N. There are three important facts that we will use in our algorithms (we leave this as Exercise 7.9):

---

4. C++ does not specify what happens when negative numbers are involved. We assume that they are not.

- If $A \equiv B(\bmod N)$, then for any C, $A + C \equiv B + C(\bmod N)$.

- If $A \equiv B(\bmod N)$, then for any D, $AD \equiv BD(\bmod N)$.

- If $A \equiv B(\bmod N)$, then for any P, $A^P \equiv B^P(\bmod N)$.

These theorems allow certain calculations to be done with less effort. For instance, suppose we want to know the last digit in 3333^{5555}. Since this number has over 15,000 digits, it is expensive to directly compute the answer. However, what we want is to determine $3333^{5555}(\bmod 10)$. Since $3333 \equiv 3(\bmod 10)$, it suffices to compute $3^{5555}(\bmod 10)$. Since $3^4 = 81$, we know that $3^4 \equiv 1(\bmod 10)$, and raising both sides to the power of 1388 tells us that $3^{5552} \equiv 1(\bmod 10)$. If we multiply both sides by $3^3 = 27$, we see that $3^{5555} \equiv 27 \equiv 7(\bmod 10)$, completing the calculation. In the next section, we will see how this procedure is generalized.

7.4.2   Modular Exponentiation

In this section we show how to efficiently compute $X^N(\bmod P)$. This can be done by initializing `Result` to 1 and then repeatedly multiplying `Result` by X, applying the `%` operator after every multiplication. Using `operator%` after every multiplication instead of just the last multiplication makes each multiplication easier because it keeps `Result` smaller.

After N multiplications, `Result` is the answer we are looking for. However, doing N multiplications is impractical if N is a 100-digit `HugeInt`. In fact, it is impractical on all but the fastest machines if N is one billion.

```
 1  // Compute X^N ( mod P )
 2  // HugeInt: must have copy constructor, operator=,
 3  //      conversion from int, *, /, %, ==, and !=
 4  //      Assumes that P is not zero and Power( 0, 0, P ) is 0
 5
 6  template <class HugeInt>
 7  HugeInt
 8  Power( const HugeInt & X, const HugeInt & N,
 9                          const HugeInt & P )
10  {
11      if( N == 0 )
12          return 1;
13
14      HugeInt Tmp = Power( ( X * X ) % P, N / 2, P );
15
16      if( N % 2 != 0 )
17          Tmp = ( Tmp * X ) % P;
18      return Tmp;
19  }
```

Figure 7.8   Modular exponentiation routine

A faster algorithm is based on the following observation: if N is even, then $X^N = (X \cdot X)^{\lfloor N/2 \rfloor}$ and if N is odd, then $X^N = X \cdot X^{N-1} = X \cdot (X \cdot X)^{\lfloor N/2 \rfloor}$ (recall that $\lfloor X \rfloor$ is the largest integer that is smaller than or equal to X). As before, to perform modular exponentiation, we apply a % after every multiplication.

The recursive algorithm in Figure 7.8 represents a direct implementation of this strategy. Lines 11 and 12 handle the base case: X^0 is 1, by definition.[5] At line 14, we make a recursive call based on the identity stated above. If N is even, then this computes the desired answer, while if N is odd, we need to multiply by an extra X (and use `operator%`).

> **Exponentiation can be done in logarithmic number of multiplications.**

This algorithm is faster than the simple algorithm proposed earlier. If $M(N)$ is the number of multiplications that are used by `Power`, then we have $M(N) \leq M\lfloor N/2 \rfloor + 2$. This is because if N is even, we perform one multiplication, plus those done recursively, and if N is odd, we perform two multiplications, plus those done recursively. Since $M(0) = 0$, we can show that $M(N) < 2\log N$. The logarithmic factor can be seen without direct calculation by application of the halving principle (see Section 5.5), which tells us the number of recursive invocations of `Power`. Moreover, an average value of $M(N)$ is $(3/2)\log N$, because in each recursive step, N is equally likely to be even or odd. If N is a 100-digit number, then in the worst case only about 665 multiplications (and typically only 500 on average) are needed.

> **Do not over optimize. You are likely to break your program.**

A C++ note: `HugeInts` are passed by constant reference to avoid the copy. However, we return by copy. We could attempt to avoid these excessive copies, but it is not worth the effort. This is because for each return, we know we have done a multiplication and mod operation, and the costs of these operations will greatly exceed the overhead of the copy. Thus optimizing by attempting to use reference return values or global variables is not likely to achieve any significant time improvements.

7.4.3 Greatest Common Divisor and Multiplicative Inverses

> **The *greatest common divisor* (gcd) of two integers is the largest integer that divides both of them.**

Given two nonnegative integers A and B, their greatest common divisor, $gcd(A, B)$, is the largest integer D that divides both A and B. For instance, $gcd(70, 25)$ is 5.

It is easy to verify that $gcd(A, B) \equiv gcd(A - B, B)$. If D divides both A and B, it must also divide $A - B$; and if D divides both $A - B$ and B, then it must also divide A.

This observation leads to a simple algorithm in which we repeatedly subtract B from A, transforming the problem into a smaller one. Eventually A becomes less than B, and then we can switch roles for A and B and continue from there. At

---

5. We define $0^0 = 0$ for the purposes of this algorithm. We also assume that N is nonnegative and P is positive.

some point B will become 0. At that point we know that $gcd(A, 0) \equiv A$, and since each transformation preserves the gcd of the original A and B, we have our answer. This is known as Euclid's Algorithm, and was described over 2000 years ago. Though correct, it is unusable for HugeInts, because a huge number of subtractions are likely to be required.

A computationally efficient modification is that the repeated subtractions of B from A until A is smaller than B is equivalent to the conversion of A to precisely $A \bmod B$. Thus, $gcd(A, B) \equiv gcd(B, A \bmod B)$. This recursive definition, along with the base case where $B = 0$, is directly used to obtain the routine in Figure 7.9. To see how this works, note that in the example above, the following sequence of recursive calls is used to deduce that the greatest common divisor of 70 and 25 is 5: $gcd(70, 25) \Rightarrow gcd(25, 20) \Rightarrow gcd(20, 5) \Rightarrow gcd(5, 0) \Rightarrow 5$.

The number of recursive calls that are used is proportional to the logarithm of A, which is the same order of magnitude as the other routines that we have seen in this section. The reason for this is that in two recursive calls, the problem is reduced at least in half. The proof of this is left as Exercise 7.10.

> The greatest common divisor and multiplicative inverse can also be calculated in logarithmic time using a variant of Euclid's algorithm.

The greatest common divisor algorithm is used implicitly to solve a similar mathematical problem. The solution $1 \leq X < N$ to the equation $AX \equiv 1 \pmod{N}$ is known as the *multiplicative inverse* of A, mod N. We will also assume that $1 \leq A < N$. As an example, the inverse of 3, mod 13 is 9: 3*9 mod 13 yields 1.

The ability to compute multiplicative inverses is important because equations such as $3i \equiv 7 \pmod{13}$ are easily solved if we know the multiplicative inverse. These equations arise in many applications, including the encryption algorithm that we will discuss at the end of this section. In this example, if we multiply by the inverse of 3 (namely 9), we obtain $i \equiv 63 \pmod{13}$, so $i = 11$ is a solution. If

$$AX \equiv 1 \pmod{N}$$

then

$$AX + NY \equiv 1 \pmod{N}$$

is true for any Y. For some Y, the left hand side must be exactly 1. Thus, the equation

```
1  template <class HugeInt>
2  HugeInt
3  Gcd( const HugeInt & A, const HugeInt & B )
4  {
5      if( B == 0 )
6          return A;
7      else
8          return Gcd( B, A % B );
9  }
```

Figure 7.9   Computation of greatest common divisor

$$AX + NY = 1$$

is solvable if (and only if) A has a multiplicative inverse.

Given A and B, we show how to find X and Y satisfying

$$AX + BY = 1$$

We assume $0 \leq |B| < |A|$. To do this, we will extend the Gcd algorithm to compute X and Y.

First, consider the base case $B \equiv 0$. In this case we have to solve $AX = 1$, which implies both A and X are 1. In fact, if A is not 1, then there is no multiplicative inverse. A consequence of this fact is that A has a multiplicative inverse modulo N if and only if $gcd(A, N) = 1$.

Otherwise, B is not zero. Recall that $gcd(A, B) = gcd(B, A \bmod B)$. So let $A = BQ + R$. Here Q is the quotient and R is the remainder, and thus the recursive call is gcd(B,R). Suppose we can recursively solve

$$BX_1 + RY_1 = 1$$

Since $R = A - BQ$, we have

$$BX_1 + (A - BQ)Y_1 = 1$$

which means that

$$AY_1 + B(X_1 - QY_1) = 1$$

Thus $X = Y_1$ and $Y = X_1 - \lfloor A/B \rfloor Y_1$ is a solution. This is directly coded as FullGcd in Figure 7.10. Inverse just calls FullGcd, passing X and Y by reference. The only detail left is that the value given for X may be negative. If it is, line 37 of Inverse will make it positive. We leave a proof of that fact as Exercise 7.13 to the reader. The proof can be done by induction.

7.4.4   The RSA Cryptosystem

Number theory is used in cryptography because factoring appears to be a much harder process than multiplication.

For centuries, number theory was thought to be a completely impractical branch of mathematics. Recently, however, number theory has emerged as an important field because of its applicability in cryptography.

The problem we consider has two parts. Suppose Alice wants to send a message to Bob, but she is worried that the transmission may be compromised. For instance, if the transmission is over a phone line and the phone is tapped, then somebody else may be reading the message. We assume that even if there is eavesdropping on the phone line, there is no maliciousness (that is, damage to the signal): Bob gets whatever Alice sends.

```
1  // Given A and B, assume Gcd( A, B ) = 1
2  // Find X and Y such that AX + BY = 1
3  // HugeInt: must have copy constructor,
4  //     zero parameter constructor, operator=,
5  //     conversion from int, *, /, +, -, %, ==, and >
6
7  template <class HugeInt>
8  void
9  FullGcd( const HugeInt & A, const HugeInt & B,
10                 HugeInt & X, HugeInt &Y )
11 {
12     HugeInt X1, Y1;
13
14     if( B == 0 )
15     {
16         X = 1;          // If A != 1, there is no inverse
17         Y = 0;          // We omit this check
18     }
19     else
20     {
21         FullGcd( B, A % B, X1, Y1 );
22         X = Y1;
23         Y = X1 - ( A / B ) * Y1;
24     }
25 }
26
27 // Solve AX == 1 ( mod N )
28 // Assume that gcd( A, N ) = 1
29
30 template <class HugeInt>
31 HugeInt
32 Inverse( const HugeInt & A, const HugeInt & N )
33 {
34     HugeInt X, Y;
35
36     FullGcd( A, N, X, Y );
37     return X > 0 ? X : X + N;
38 }
```

Figure 7.10   Routine to determine multiplicative inverse

A solution to this problem is to use an encryption scheme, consisting of two parts. First Alice *encrypts* the message and sends the result, which is no longer plainly readable. When Bob receives Alice's transmission, he *decrypts* it, obtaining the original. The security of the algorithm is based on the fact that nobody else besides Bob should be able to perform the decryption, including Alice (if she did not save the original message).

Encryption **is used to transmit messages that cannot be read by other parties.**

Thus Bob must provide Alice with a method of encryption that only he knows how to reverse. This is an extremely challenging problem. Many proposed algorithms can be compromised by subtle code-breaking techniques. We

The *RSA cryptosystem* is a popular encryption method.

will describe one method, known as the *RSA cryptosystem* (named after the initials of its authors), that is a very elegant implementation of the strategy.

Our goal is to give only a high-level overview showing how the functions we have written in this section interact in a practical way. The references contain pointers to a more detailed description, as well as proofs of the key properties of the algorithm.

Let us first remark that a message consists of a sequence of characters, and each character is just a sequence of bits. Thus a message is a sequence of bits. If we break up the message into blocks of B bits, then we can interpret the message as a series of very large numbers. Thus, the basic problem is reduced to encrypting a large number and then decrypting the result.

Computation of the RSA Constants

The RSA algorithm begins by having the receiver determine some constants. First, two large primes p and q are randomly chosen. Typically these would be 100 or so digits each. For the purposes of this example, suppose $p = 127$ and $q = 211$. Note that Bob is the receiver and thus is performing these computations. Let us remark that primes are plentiful. Bob can thus keep trying random numbers until two of them pass the primality test (which is discussed in Chapter 9).

Next Bob computes $N = pq$ and $N' = (p-1)(q-1)$. For our example this gives $N = 26797$ and $N' = 26460$. The receiver, Bob, continues by choosing any $e > 1$ such that $gcd(e, N') = 1$. In mathematical terms, he chooses any e that is relatively prime to N'. Bob can keep trying different values of e by using the routine shown in Figure 7.9 until one is found that satisfies the property. Since any prime e would work, finding e is at least as easy as finding a prime number. In our case $e = 13379$ is one of many valid choices. Next d, the multiplicative inverse of e, modulo N' is computed using the routine in Figure 7.10. In this example $d = 11099$.

Once Bob has computed all of these constants, he does the following. First, p, q, and N' are destroyed. The security of the system is compromised if any of these values are discovered. Bob then tells anybody who wants to send him an encrypted message what the values of e and N are, and keeps d secret.

Encryption and Decryption Algorithms

To encrypt an integer M, the sender computes $M^e (\mod N)$ and sends it. In our case, if $M = 10237$, then the value sent is 8422. When an encrypted integer R is received, all Bob has to do is compute $R^d (\mod N)$. For $R = 8422$, it can be verified that he gets back the original $M = 10237$ (this is not accidental). Both encryption and decryption can thus be carried out by using the modular exponentiation routine in Figure 7.8.

Let us examine why the algorithm works. The choices of e, d, and N guarantee (via a number theory proof beyond the scope of this text) that $M^{ed} \equiv M(\bmod N)$, as long as M and N share no common factors. Since the only factors of N are two 100-digit primes, it is virtually impossible for that to occur.[6] Thus decryption of the encrypted text gets the original back.

What makes the scheme seem secure is that knowledge of d is apparently required in order to decode. Now N and e uniquely determine d. For instance, if we factor N, we get p and q, and can then reconstruct d. The caveat is that factoring is apparently very hard to do for large numbers. Thus the security of the RSA system is based on the fact that based on current knowledge it is very expensive to factor. So far it has held up well.

This general scheme is known as *public key cryptography*. Anybody who wants to receive messages publishes encryption information for anybody else to use. In the RSA system, e and N would be computed once by each enrolled person and listed in a publicly readable place.

> In *public key cryptography*, each participant publishes the code others can use to send encrypted messages, but keeps the decrypting code secret.

A problem with the system is that each person must safely hide a 200-digit key (d). Thus it must be saved somewhere (unlike a password, it is too long to be remembered). If the file where it is stored is compromised, so is the security of all incoming messages.

7.5   Divide and Conquer

An important problem-solving technique that makes use of recursion is *divide and conquer*. Divide-and-conquer algorithms consist of two parts:

> Divide-and-conquer algorithms are recursive algorithms that are generally very efficient.

- *Divide*: Smaller problems are solved recursively (except, of course, base cases).
- *Conquer*: The solution to the original problem is then formed from the solutions to the subproblems.

Traditionally, routines in which the algorithm contains at least two recursive calls are called divide and conquer algorithms, while routines whose text contains only one recursive call are not. Consequently the recursive routines seen thus far in this chapter are not divide-and-conquer algorithms. We also generally insist that the subproblems be disjoint (that is, essentially nonoverlapping), so we do not wind up with the excessive costs seen in the sample recursive computation of the Fibonacci numbers.

In this section we will see an example of the divide-and-conquer paradigm. First we show how to use recursion to solve the maximum subsequence sum problem. Then we provide an analysis to show that the running time is $O(N \log N)$. Although we have already seen a linear algorithm for this problem,

---

6. You are more likely to win a typical state lottery 13 weeks in a row. However, if this does happen, the system is compromised because the greatest common divisor will be a factor of N.

the solution that we use here is thematic of others in a wide range of applications, including sorting. Consequently the technique is important to learn. Finally, we show the general form for the running time of a wide class of divide-and-conquer algorithms.

7.5.1   The Maximum Contiguous Subsequence Sum Problem

In Section 5.3 we discussed the problem of finding, in a sequence of numbers, a contiguous subsequence of maximum sum. For convenience, we restate the problem:

> **MAXIMUM CONTIGUOUS SUBSEQUENCE SUM PROBLEM**
> *GIVEN (POSSIBLY NEGATIVE) INTEGERS $A_1, A_2, ..., A_N$, FIND (AND IDENTIFY THE SEQUENCE CORRESPONDING TO) THE MAXIMUM VALUE OF $\sum_{k=i}^{j} A_k$. THE MAXIMUM CONTIGUOUS SUBSEQUENCE SUM IS ZERO IF ALL THE INTEGERS ARE NEGATIVE.*

The maximum contiguous subsequence sum problem can be solved with a divide-and-conquer algorithm.

Three algorithms of various complexity were presented. One was a cubic algorithm that was based on an exhaustive search: We calculated the sum of each possible subsequence and selected the maximum. A quadratic improvement was described that takes advantage of the fact that each new subsequence can be computed in constant time from a previous subsequence. Since we have $O(N^2)$ subsequences, this is the best bound that can be achieved using an approach that directly examines all subsequences. We also saw a linear-time algorithm that works by examining only a few subsequences. However, its correctness is not obvious.

Let us consider a divide-and-conquer algorithm. Suppose the sample input is { 4, -3, 5, -2, -1, 2, 6, -2 }. We divide this input into two halves, as shown in Figure 7.11. Then the maximum contiguous subsequence sum can occur in one of three ways:

- *Case 1*: It resides entirely in the first half.
- *Case 2*: It resides entirely in the second half.
- *Case 3*: It begins in the first half but ends in the second half.

We will show how to find the maximums for each of these three cases more efficiently than an exhaustive search. We begin by looking at case 3. We want to avoid the nested loop that results from considering all $N/2$ starting points and $N/2$ ending points independently. The idea we use is to replace two nested loops by two consecutive loops. The consecutive loops, each of size $N/2$, combine to require only linear work. We can do this because any contiguous subsequence that begins in the first half and ends in the second half must include both the last element of the first half and the first element of the second half.

Figure 7.11 shows that we can calculate, for each element in the first half, the contiguous subsequence sum that ends at the rightmost item. We do this with a right-to-left scan, starting from the border between the two halves. Similarly, we can calculate the contiguous subsequence sum for all sequences that begin with the first element in the second half. These two subsequences can then be combined to form the maximum contiguous subsequence that spans across the dividing border. In the example in Figure 7.11, we see that the resulting sequence spans from the first element in the first half to the next to last element in the second half. The total sum is the sum of the two subsequences, $4 + 7 = 11$.

This analysis shows us that case 3 can be solved in linear time. But what about cases 1 and 2? Because there are $N/2$ elements in each half, an exhaustive search applied to each half will still require quadratic time per half; specifically, all we have done is eliminate roughly half of the work, and half of quadratic is still quadratic. What we can do in cases 1 and 2 is apply the same strategy of dividing into more halves. We can keep dividing those quarters further and further until splitting is impossible. This is succinctly stated as follows: *Solve cases 1 and 2 recursively.* As we will see later, this will lower the running time below quadratic because the savings will compound throughout the algorithm. The following is a summary of the main portion of the algorithm:

In divide and conquer, the recursion is the divide, the overhead is the conquer.

1. Recursively compute the maximum contiguous subsequence sum that resides entirely in the first half

2. Recursively compute the maximum contiguous subsequence sum that resides entirely in the second half.

3. Compute, via two consecutive loops, the maximum contiguous subsequence sum that begins in the first half but ends in the second half.

4. Choose the largest of the three sums.

A recursive algorithm requires us to specify a base case. When the size of the problem reaches one element, we must not use recursion. The C++ function that results is coded in Figure 7.12.

The general form for the recursive call is to pass the input array along with the left and right borders, which delimit the portion of the array that is being operated on. A one-line driver routine sets this up by passing the borders 0 and N-1 along with the array.

First Half				Second Half				
4	-3	5	-2	-1	2	6	-2	Values
4*	0	3	-2	-1	1	7*	5	Running Sums

Running Sum from the Center (*denotes maximum for each half)

Figure 7.11 Dividing the maximum contiguous subsequence problem into halves

```
1   // Recursive maximum contiguous subsequence sum algorithm
2   // Etype: Must have constructor from int, must have +,
3   //       +=, and > defined, must have copy constructor,
4   //       and operator=, and must have all properties
5   //       needed for Vector
6
7   template<class Etype>
8   Etype
9   MaxSumRec( const Vector<Etype> & A, int Left, int Right )
10  {
11      Etype MaxLeftBorderSum = 0, MaxRightBorderSum = 0;
12      Etype LeftBorderSum = 0, RightBorderSum = 0;
13      int Center = ( Left + Right ) / ?;
14
15      if( Left == Right )         // Base case
16          return A[ Left ] > 0 ? A[ Left ] : 0;
17
18      Etype MaxLeftSum =  MaxSumRec( A, Left, Center );
19      Etype MaxRightSum = MaxSumRec( A, Center + 1, Right );
20
21      for( int i = Center; i >= Left; i-- )
22      {
23          LeftBorderSum += A[ i ];
24          if( LeftBorderSum > MaxLeftBorderSum )
25              MaxLeftBorderSum = LeftBorderSum;
26      }
27
28      for( int j = Center + 1; j <= Right; j++ )
29      {
30          RightBorderSum += A[ j ];
31          if( RightBorderSum > MaxRightBorderSum )
32              MaxRightBorderSum = RightBorderSum;
33      }
34
35      return Max3( MaxLeftSum, MaxRightSum,
36                      MaxLeftBorderSum + MaxRightBorderSum );
37  }
38
39  // Publicly visible routine
40  template<class Etype>
41  Etype
42  MaxSubsequenceSum( const Vector<Etype> & A, int N )
43  {
44          return N > 0 ? MaxSumRec( A, 0, N - 1 ) : 0;
45
46  }
```

Figure 7.12   Divide-and-conquer algorithm for maximum contiguous subsequence sum problem

Lines 15 and 16 handle the base case. If `Left==Right`, there is one element, and it is the maximum contiguous subsequence if the element is nonnegative (otherwise, the empty sequence with sum 0 is maximum). Lines 18 and 19 perform the two recursive calls. We can see that the recursive calls are always on a smaller problem than the original, and thus we make progress toward the base case. Lines 21 to 26 and then 28 to 33 calculate the maximum sums that touch the center border. The sum of these two values is the maximum sum that spans both halves. The routine `Max3` (not shown) returns the largest of the three possibilities.

7.5.2   Analysis of a Basic Divide-and-Conquer Recurrence

The recursive maximum contiguous subsequence sum algorithm works by performing linear work to compute a sum that spans the center border and then performing two recursive calls. These recursive calls each perform their work to compute a sum that spans the center border, and then perform further recursive calls, and so on. The total work performed by the algorithm is then proportional to the scanning performed over all of the recursive calls.

> Intuitive analysis of the maximum contiguous subsequence sum divide-and-conquer algorithm: We spend $O(N)$ per level.

Figure 7.13 graphically illustrates how the algorithm works for $N = 8$ elements. Each rectangle represents a call to `MaxSubsequenceSum`, and the length of the rectangle is proportional to the size of the subarray (and hence the cost of the scanning of the subarray) being operated on by the invocation. The initial call is shown on the first line: The size of the subarray is N, and this represents the cost of the scanning for the third case. The initial call then makes two recursive calls, yielding two subarrays of size $N/2$. The cost of each scan in case 3 is half the original cost, but since there are two such recursive calls, the combined cost of these recursive calls is also N. Each of those two recursive instances themselves make two recursive calls, yielding four subproblems that are a quarter of the original size. Thus the total of all of those case 3 costs is also N. Eventually, we reach the base case. Each base case has size 1, and there are N of them. Of course, there are no case 3 costs in this case, but we charge one unit to perform the check that determines if the sole element is positive or negative. The total cost then, as we see in Figure 7.13, is N per level of recursion. Each level halves the size of the basic problem, so the halving principle tells us that there are approximately $\log N$ levels. In fact, the number of levels is $1 + \lceil \log N \rceil$ (which is 4 when N is equal to 8). Thus we expect that the total running time is $O(N \log N)$.

The above analysis gives an intuitive explanation of why the running time is $O(N \log N)$. In general, however, expanding a recursive algorithm to examine behavior is a bad idea; it violates the third rule of recursion. We now give a more formal mathematical treatment.

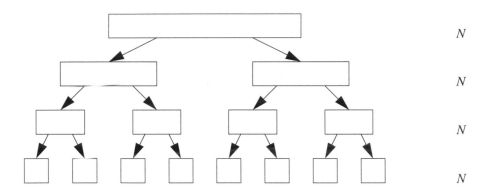

N

N

N

N

Figure 7.13   Trace of recursive calls for recursive maximum contiguous subsequence sum algorithm

A more formal analysis. Note carefully that it holds for all classes of algorithms that recursively solve two halves and use linear additional work.

Let $T(N)$ represent the time it takes to solve a maximum contiguous subsequence sum problem of size N. If $N = 1$, then the program takes some constant amount of time to execute lines 15 to 16, which we shall call one unit. Thus $T(1) = 1$. Otherwise, the program must perform two recursive calls plus the linear work involved in computing the maximum sum for case 3. The constant overhead is absorbed by the $O(N)$ term. How long do the two recursive calls take? Since they solve problems of size $N/2$, we know they must each require $T(N/2)$ units of time; consequently, the total recursive work is $2T(N/2)$. This gives the equations

$$T(1) = 1$$
$$T(N) = 2T(N/2) + O(N)$$

Of course, for the second equation to make sense, N must be a power of two. Otherwise, at some point $N/2$ will not be even. A more precise equation would be

$$T(N) = T(\lfloor N/2 \rfloor) + T(\lceil N/2 \rceil) + O(N)$$

To simplify the calculations, we assume N is a power of 2 and replace the $O(N)$ term with N. These assumptions are minor and do not affect the Big-Oh result. Consequently, assuming N is a power of 2, we need to obtain a closed form solution for $T(N)$ from

$$T(1) = 1$$

$$T(N) = 2T(N/2) + N \tag{7.6}$$

This is exactly the equation that is illustrated in Figure 7.13, so we know that the answer will be $N \log N + N$. This is easily verified by examining a few values: $T(1) = 1$, $T(2) = 4$, $T(4) = 12$, $T(8) = 32$, and $T(16) = 80$. We now prove this mathematically, using two different methods.

Assuming N is a power of 2, the solution to the equation $T(N) = 2T(N/2) + N$, with initial condition $T(1) = 1$ is $T(N) = N \log N + N$.

Theorem 7.4

For sufficiently large N, we have $T(N/2) = 2T(N/4) + N/2$, because we can use Equation 7.6 with $N/2$ instead of N. Consequently, we have

Proof (Version 1)

$$2T(N/2) = 4T(N/4) + N$$

Substituting this into Equation 7.6 yields

$$T(N) = 4T(N/4) + 2N \qquad (7.7)$$

If we use Equation 7.6 for $N/4$ and multiply by 4, we obtain

$$4T(N/4) = 8T(N/8) + N$$

which we can substitute into the right side of Equation 7.7 to obtain

$$T(N) = 8T(N/8) + 3N$$

Continuing in this manner, we obtain

$$T(N) = 2^k T(N/2^k) + kN$$

Finally, using $k = \log N$ (which makes sense since then $2^k = N$), we obtain

$$T(N) = NT(1) + N \log N = N \log N + N$$

Although this proof method appears to work well, it can be difficult to apply in more complicated cases because it tends to give very long equations. We give a second method that appears to be easier because it generates equations vertically that are more easily manipulated.

Proof (Version 2)   *We divide Equation 7.6 by N, yielding a new basic equation:*

$$\frac{T(N)}{N} = \frac{T(N/2)}{N/2} + 1$$

This equation is now valid for any N that is a power of 2, so we may also write the following equations:

$$\frac{T(N)}{N} = \frac{T(N/2)}{N/2} + 1$$

$$\frac{T(N/2)}{N/2} = \frac{T(N/4)}{N/4} + 1$$

$$\frac{T(N/4)}{N/4} = \frac{T(N/8)}{N/8} + 1 \tag{7.8}$$

$$\cdots$$

$$\frac{T(2)}{2} = \frac{T(1)}{1} + 1$$

Telescoping sums generate large numbers of cancelling terms.

Now we add up the collective in Equation 7.8. This means that we add all of the terms on the left side and set the result equal to the sum of all the terms on the right side. Observe that the term $T(N/2)/(N/2)$ appears on both sides and thus cancels. In fact, virtually all the terms appear on both sides and cancel. This is called a telescoping sum. After everything is added, the final result is

$$\frac{T(N)}{N} = \frac{T(1)}{1} + \log N$$

because all of the other terms cancel and there are $\log N$ equations. Thus all the 1s at the end of these equations add up to $\log N$. Multiplying through by N gives the final answer, as before.

Notice that if we did not divide through by N at the start of the solution, the sum would not telescope. Deciding on the division required to ensure a telescoping sum requires some experience and makes the method a little more difficult to apply than the first alternative. However, once you have found the correct divisor, the second alternative tends to produce scrap work that fits better on a standard sheet of paper, leading to fewer mathematical errors. In contrast, the first method is more of a brute force approach.

Notice carefully that whenever we have a divide-and-conquer algorithm that solves two half-sized problems with linear additional work, we will always have $O(N \log N)$ running time. The next section examines what happens in a more general setting.

7.5.3   A General Upper Bound for Divide-and-Conquer Running Times

The last analysis shows that when a problem is divided into two equal halves that are solved recursively, with $O(N)$ overhead, the result is an $O(N \log N)$ algorithm. What if we divide into three half-sized problems with linear overhead, or seven half-sized problems with quadratic overhead (see Exercise 7.16)? In this section we provide a general formula to compute the running time of a divide-and-conquer algorithm. The formula requires three parameters:

- A, which is the number of subproblems

- B, which is the relative size of the subproblems (for instance $B = 2$ represents half-sized subproblems)

- k, which is representative of the fact that the overhead is $\Theta(N^k)$.

The proof of the formula requires familiarity with geometric sums. However, knowledge of the proof is not needed to use the formula.

This section gives a general formula that allows the number of subproblems, the size of the subproblems, and the amount of additional work, to assume general forms. The result can be used without understanding of the proof.

The solution to the equation $T(N) = AT(N/B) + O(N^k)$, where $A \geq 1$ and $B > 1$, is

$$T(N) = \begin{cases} O(N^{\log_B A}) & \text{if } A > B^k \\ O(N^k \log N) & \text{if } A = B^k \\ O(N^k) & \text{if } A < B^k \end{cases}$$

Theorem 7.5

Before proving Theorem 7.5, let us see some applications. For the maximum contiguous subsequence sum problem, we have two problems, two halves, and linear overhead. The applicable values are $A = 2$, $B = 2$, and $k = 1$. Consequently, the second case in Theorem 7.5 applies, and we get $O(N \log N)$, in agreement with our previous calculations. If we recursively solve three half-sized problems with linear overhead, then we have $A = 3$, $B = 2$, and $k = 1$, and the first case applies. The result is $O(N^{\log_2 3}) = O(N^{1.59})$. Here we see that the overhead does not contribute to the total cost of the algorithm: Any overhead that is smaller than $O(N^{1.59})$ would give the same running time for the recursive algorithm. An algorithm that solved three half-sized problems but required quadratic overhead would have $O(N^2)$ running time because the third case would apply. In effect, the overhead dominates once it exceeds the $O(N^{1.59})$ threshold. At the threshold the penalty is the logarithmic factor shown in the second case. We can now prove Theorem 7.5.

Proof (of Theorem 7.5)

Following the second proof of Theorem 7.4, we will assume N is a power of B; thus let $N = B^M$. Then $N/B = B^{M-1}$ and $N^k = (B^M)^k = (B^k)^M$. Let us assume $T(1) = 1$ and ignore the constant factor in $O(N^k)$. Then we have the basic equation

$$T(B^M) = AT(B^{M-1}) + (B^k)^M$$

If we divide through by A^M, we obtain the new basic equation

$$\frac{T(B^M)}{A^M} = \frac{T(B^{M-1})}{A^{M-1}} + \left(\frac{B^k}{A}\right)^M$$

Now we can write this equation for all M, obtaining

$$\frac{T(B^M)}{A^M} = \frac{T(B^{M-1})}{A^{M-1}} + \left(\frac{B^k}{A}\right)^M$$

$$\frac{T(B^{M-1})}{A^{M-1}} = \frac{T(B^{M-2})}{A^{M-2}} + \left(\frac{B^k}{A}\right)^{M-1}$$

$$\frac{T(B^{M-2})}{A^{M-2}} = \frac{T(B^{M-3})}{A^{M-3}} + \left(\frac{B^k}{A}\right)^{M-2} \qquad \text{(7.9)}$$

$$\cdots$$

$$\frac{T(B^1)}{A^1} = \frac{T(B^0)}{A^0} + \left(\frac{B^k}{A}\right)^1$$

If we add up the collective denoted by Equation 7.9, once again virtually all of the terms on the left cancel the leading terms on the right, yielding

$$\frac{T(B^M)}{A^M} = 1 + \sum_{i=1}^{M} \left(\frac{B^k}{A}\right)^i$$

$$= \sum_{i=0}^{M} \left(\frac{B^k}{A}\right)^i$$

Thus,

$$T(N) = T(B^M) = A^M \sum_{i=0}^{M} \left(\frac{B^k}{A}\right)^i \qquad \text{(7.10)}$$

If $A > B^k$, then the sum is a geometric series with a ratio smaller than 1.   ***Proof (continued)***
Since the sum of an infinite series would converge to a constant, this finite
sum is also bounded by a constant, and thus we obtain Equation 7.11.

$$T(N) = O(A^M) = O(N^{\log_B A}) \tag{7.11}$$

If $A = B^k$, then each term in the sum in Equation 7.10 is 1. Since the sum
contains $1 + \log_B N$ terms and $A = B^k$ implies $A^M = N^k$,

$$T(N) = O(A^M \log_B N) = O(N^k \log_B N) = O(N^k \log N)$$

Finally, if $A < B^k$, then the terms in the geometric series are larger than 1.
We can compute the sum using a standard formula, obtaining

$$T(N) = A^M \frac{\left(\dfrac{B^k}{A}\right)^{M+1} - 1}{\dfrac{B^k}{A} - 1} = O\left(A^M \left(\frac{B^k}{A}\right)^M\right) = O((B^k)^M) = O(N^k)$$

proving the last case of Theorem 7.5.

7.6   Dynamic Programming

A problem that can be mathematically expressed recursively can also be
expressed as a recursive algorithm. In many cases this yields a significant performance improvement over a more naive exhaustive search. Any recursive mathematical formula could be directly translated to a recursive algorithm, but often
the compiler may not do justice to the recursive algorithm and an inefficient program results. Such is the case for the recursive computation of the Fibonacci
numbers described in Section 7.3.4. In such a case we can rewrite the recursive
algorithm as a nonrecursive algorithm that systematically records the answers to
the subproblems in a table. One technique that makes use of this approach is
known as *dynamic programming*.

Dynamic program-ming **solves subprob-lems nonrecursively by recording answers in a table.**

We will illustrate the technique with the following problem:

CHANGE-MAKING PROBLEM
  FOR A CURRENCY WITH COINS $C_1, C_2, \ldots, C_N$ (CENTS) WHAT IS THE
  MINIMUM NUMBER OF COINS NEEDED TO MAKE K CENTS OF CHANGE?

Greedy algorithms **make locally optimal decisions at each step. This is simple, but not always the correct thing to do.**

United States currency has coins in 1, 5, 10, and 25-cent denominations (we ignore the less frequently occurring 50-cent piece). We can make 63 cents by using two 25-cent pieces, one 10-cent piece, and three 1-cent pieces, for a total of six coins. Change making in this currency is relatively simple: We repeatedly use the largest coin that is available to us. One can show that for United States currency, this always minimizes the total number of coins used. This is an example of a so-called *greedy algorithm* in which, during each phase, a decision is made that appears to be good, without regard for future consequences. This "take what you can get now" strategy is the source of the name for this class of algorithms. When a problem can be solved with a greedy algorithm, we are usually quite happy: Greedy algorithms often match our intuition and make for relatively painless coding. Unfortunately, greedy algorithms do not always work. If the United States currency included a 21-cent piece, then the greedy algorithm would still give a solution that uses six coins, while the optimal solution uses three coins (all 21-cent pieces).

The question then becomes how do we solve the problem for an arbitrary coin set. We assume that there is always a 1-cent coin, so that the solution always exists. A simple strategy to make K cents in change uses recursion as follows:

1. If we can make change using exactly one coin, that is the minimum.
2. Otherwise, for each possible value i we can compute the minimum number of coins needed to make i cents in change and $K - i$ cents in change independently. We then choose the i that minimizes this sum.

A simple recursive algorithm for change making is easily written, but it is inefficient.

As an example, let us see how we can make 63 cents in change. Clearly, one coin will not suffice. We can compute the number of coins required to make 1 cent of change and 62 cents of change independently (these are 1 and 4, respectively). These results are obtained recursively, so they must be taken as optimal. It happens that the 62 cents is given as two 21-cent pieces and two 10-cent pieces. Thus we have a method that uses five coins. If we split into 2 cents and 61 cents, the recursive solutions yield 2 and 4, respectively, for a total of six coins. We continue trying all the possibilities. Some of these possibilities are shown in Figure 7.14. Eventually, we see a split into 21 cents and 42 cents, which is changeable in one and two coins, respectively, thus allowing change to be made in three coins. The last split we need to try is 31 cents and 32 cents. We can change 31 cents in two coins, and we can change 32 cents in three coins for a total of five coins. But the minimum remains the three coins. Again, each of these subproblems is solved recursively. This yields the natural algorithm shown in Figure 7.15. If we run the algorithm to make small change, it works perfectly. But like the Fibonacci calculations, there is too much redundant work. It will not terminate in a reasonable amount of time for the 63-cent case.

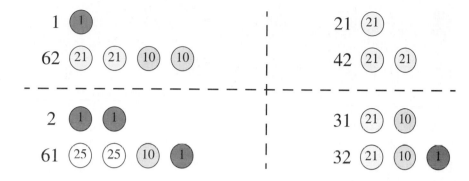

Figure 7.14   Some of the subproblems that are solved recursively in Figure 7.15

```
 1  // Return minimum coins to make change
 2  // Simple recursive algorithm that is very inefficient
 3
 4  int
 5  MakeChange( const Vector<int> & Coins, int DifferentCoins,
 6              int Change )
 7  {
 8      int MinCoins = Change;
 9
10          // Look for exact match with any single coin
11      for( int i = 0; i < DifferentCoins; i++ )
12          if( Coins[ i ] == Change )
13              return 1;
14
15          // No match; solve recursively
16      for( int j = 1; j <= Change / 2; j++ )
17      {
18          int ThisCoins = MakeChange( Coins, DifferentCoins, j )
19              + MakeChange( Coins, DifferentCoins, Change - j );
20          if( ThisCoins < MinCoins )
21              MinCoins = ThisCoins;
22      }
23
24      return MinCoins;
25  }
```

Figure 7.15   Inefficient recursive procedure to solve coin-changing problem

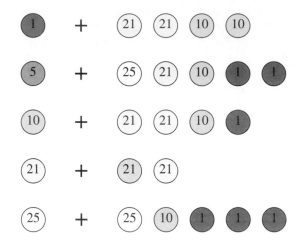

Figure 7.16   Alternative recursive algorithm for coin-changing problem

An alternative recursive change-making algorithm is still inefficient.

An alternative algorithm is to reduce the problem recursively by specifying one of the coins. For example, for 63 cents, we can give change in the following ways shown in Figure 7.16:

- One 1-cent piece plus 62 cents recursively distributed
- One 5-cent piece plus 58 cents recursively distributed
- One 10-cent piece plus 53 cents recursively distributed
- One 21-cent piece plus 42 cents recursively distributed
- One 25-cent piece plus 38 cents recursively distributed

Instead of solving 62 recursive problems, as was done in Figure 7.14, we get by with only 5 recursive calls, one for each different coin. Once again, a naive recursive implementation would be very inefficient because it would recompute answers. For example, in the first case we are left with a problem of making 62 cents in change. In this subproblem, one of the recursive calls that is made chooses a 10-cent piece and recursively solves for 52 cents. In the third case we are left with 53 cents. One of its recursive calls removes the 1-cent piece and also recursively solves for 52 cents. This redundant work again leads to a wildly large running time. If we are careful, however, we can make the algorithm reasonably fast.

The trick is to save answers to the subproblems in an array. This *dynamic programming* technique forms the basis of many algorithms. Since a large answer only depends on smaller answers, we can compute the optimal way to change 1 cent, then 2 cents, then 3 cents, and so on. This strategy is shown in the program in Figure 7.17.

```
1   // Dynamic programming algorithm for change-making problem
2   // As a result, the CoinsUsed array is filled with the
3   // minimum number of coins needed for change for each
4   // 0->MaxChange and LastCoin contains one of the Coins needed
5   // to make the change.
6
7   void
8   MakeChange( const Vector<int> & Coins, int DifferentCoins,
9               int MaxChange, Vector<int> & CoinsUsed,
10                      Vector<int> & LastCoin )
11  {
12      CoinsUsed[ 0 ] = LastCoin[ 0 ] = 0;
13
14      for( int Cents = 1; Cents <= MaxChange; Cents++ )
15      {
16          int MinCoins = i, NewCoin = 0;
17
18          for( int j = 0; j < DifferentCoins; j++ )
19          {
20              if( Coins[ j ] > Cents )    // Can't use coin j
21                  continue;
22              if( CoinsUsed[ Cents - Coins[ j ] ] + 1 < MinCoins )
23              {
24                  MinCoins = CoinsUsed[ Cents - Coins[ j ] ] + 1;
25                  NewCoin  = Coins[ j ];
26              }
27          }
28
29          CoinsUsed[ Cents ] = MinCoins;
30          LastCoin [ Cents ] = NewCoin;
31      }
32  }
```

Figure 7.17   Dynamic programming algorithm to solve change-making problem by computing optimal change for all amounts from 0 to MaxChange and maintaining information to construct the actual coin sequence

First, at line 12 we observe that 0 cents can be changed using zero coins. The LastCoin array is used to tell us which coin was last used to make the optimal change. Otherwise, we attempt to make Cents cents worth of change, for Cents ranging from 1 to the final MaxChange. To make Cents worth of change, we try each coin in succession as indicated by the for statement beginning at line 18. If the coin is larger than the amount of change we are trying to make, then of course there is nothing to do. Otherwise, we test at line 22 if the number of coins used to solve the subproblem plus the one coin combine to be fewer than the minimum number of coins we have used thus far; if so, we perform an update at lines 24 and 25. When the loop ends for the current number of Cents, the minimums can be inserted in the array. This is done at lines 29 and 30.

At the end of the algorithm, `CoinsUsed[i]` represents the minimum number of coins needed to make change for `i` cents (`i==MaxChange` is the particular solution we are looking for). By tracing back through `LastCoin`, we can figure out the coins that are needed to achieve the solution. The running time is that of two nested `for` loops, and is thus $O(NK)$, where N is the number of different denominations of coins, and K is the amount of change we are trying to make.

7.7 Backtracking

Backtracking algorithms use recursion to try all the possibilities.

As our last application of recursion, we show how to write a routine to have the computer select an optimal move in the game tic-tac-toe. The interface for a `TicTacToe` class is shown in Figure 7.18. The class has a data object `Board` that represents the current game position. A host of trivial member functions are specified, including routines to clear the board, test if a square is occupied, place something on a square, and test if a tic-tac-toe win has been achieved. We assume that the reader can fill in the implementation of these details. The challenging routine is to decide, for any position, what the best move is. This is the routine `ChooseMove`. The general strategy uses a backtracking algorithm. *Backtracking algorithms* use recursion to try all the possibilities.

The minimax strategy is used for tic tac toe. It assumes optimal play by both sides.

The basis for making this decision is `PositionValue`, which is shown in Figure 7.19. `PositionValue` returns either `HumanWin`, `Draw`, `ComputerWin`, or `Unclear`, depending on what the board represents. The idea we use is often referred to as a *minimax strategy,* which assumes optimal play by both players. The value of a position is a `ComputerWin` if optimal play implies that the computer can force a win. If the computer can force a draw but not a win, the value is `Draw`, and if the human can force a win, the value is `HumanWin`. Since we want the computer to win, we have `HumanWin < Draw < ComputerWin`.

For the computer, the value of the position is the maximum of all the values of the positions that can result from making a move. Thus, if one move leads to a winning position, two lead to a drawing position, and six lead to a losing position, the starting position is a winning position because we can force the win. Moreover, the move that leads to the winning position is the move we want to make. For the human we use minimum instead of the maximum.

This suggests a recursive algorithm to determine the value of a position. Keeping track of the best move is a matter of bookkeeping once the basic algorithm to find the value of the position is written. If the position is a terminal position (that is, we can see right away that tic-tac-toe has been achieved or the board is full without tic-tac-toe), the position's value is immediate. Otherwise, we recursively try all moves, computing the value, and choose the maximum. The recursive call will then require that the human player evaluate the value of the position. For the human the value is the minimum of all the possible next moves, since the human is trying to force the computer to lose. Thus the recursive function ChooseMove, shown in Figure 7.20 takes a parameter S, which indicates whose turn it is to move.

```
1  class TicTacToe
2  {
3    public:
4      enum Side { Human, Computer, Empty };
5      enum PositionVal { HumanWin, Draw, Unclear, ComputerWin };
6
7      TicTacToe( ) { ClearBoard( ); }      // Constructor
8
9          // Find optimal move
10     int ChooseMove( Side S, int & BestRow, int & BestColumn );
11         // Play a move, including checking legality.
12     int PlayMove( Side S, int Row, int Column );
13
14         // Simple supporting routines
15     void ClearBoard( );                  // Make the board empty
16     void GetMove( );        // Get move from human; update board
17     int BoardIsFull( ) const;  // Return true if board is full
18     int IsAWin( Side S ) const;    // True if board shows a win
19
20         // Print the board
21     friend ostream & operator<<( ostream & Out,
22                                  const TicTacToe & B );
23   private:
24     int Board[ 3 ][ 3 ];
25
26         // Play a move (possibly clearing a square). No checks
27     void Place( int Row, int Column, int Piece = Empty )
28         { Board[ Row ][ Column ] = Piece; }
29
30         // Test if a square is empty.
31     int SquareIsEmpty( int Row, int Column ) const
32         { return Board[ Row ][ Column ] == Empty; }
33
34         // Compute static value of position (win, draw, etc.)
35     int PositionValue( ) const;
36  };
```

Figure 7.18   Interface for class TicTacToe

```
1  int
2  TicTacToe::PositionValue( ) const
3  {
4      return IsAWin( Computer ) ? ComputerWin :
5             IsAWin( Human ) ? HumanWin   :
6             BoardIsFull( ) ? Draw        : Unclear;
7  }
```

Figure 7.19   Supporting routine to evaluate positions

```
 1  int
 2  TicTacToe::
 3  ChooseMove( Side S, int & BestRow, int & BestColumn )
 4  {
 5      Side Opp;              // The other side
 6      int Reply;            // Value of opponent's reply
 7      int Value;            // Value of best move, so far
 8      int Dc;               // Placeholder
 9      int SimpleEval;       // Result of an immediate evaluation
10
11      if( ( SimpleEval = PositionValue( ) ) != Unclear )
12          return SimpleEval;
13
14      if( S == Computer )
15      {
16          Opp = Human; Value = HumanWin;
17      }
18      else
19      {
20          Opp = Computer; Value = ComputerWin;
21      }
22
23          // Search for a move
24      for( int Row = 0; Row < 3; Row++ )
25          for( int Column = 0; Column < 3; Column++ )
26              if( SquareIsEmpty( Row, Column ) )
27              {
28                  Place( Row, Column, S );    // Try a move; then
29                  Reply = ChooseMove( Opp, Dc, Dc );// Evaluate;
30                  Place( Row, Column, Empty );      // then undo
31
32                      // If S gets a better position; update
33                  if( S == Computer && Reply > Value ||
34                      S == Human && Reply < Value )
35                  {
36                      Value = Reply;
37                      BestRow = Row; BestColumn = Column;
38                  }
39              }
40
41      return Value;
42  }
```

Figure 7.20   Recursive routine to find an optimal tic-tac-toe move

Lines 11 and 12 handle the base case of the recursion. If we have an immediate answer, we can return. Otherwise, we set some values at lines 14 to 21, depending on which side is moving. The code in lines 28 to 38 is executed once for each available move. We try the move at line 28, recursively evaluate the move at line 29 (saving the value), and then undo the move at line 30. Lines 33 and 34 test to see if this is the best move seen so far, and if so, we adjust Value at line 36 and record the move at line 37. At line 41 we return the value of the position; the move is stored in the parameters `BestRow` and `BestColumn`, that are passed by reference.

Although the routine in Figure 7.20 optimally solves tic-tac-toe, it performs a lot of searching. Specifically, to choose the first move on an empty board, it makes 549,946 recursive calls. By using some algorithmic tricks, we can compute exactly the same information using fewer searches. One such technique is known as *alpha-beta pruning*. This is described in detail in Chapter 10. Application of alpha-beta pruning reduces the number of recursive calls to only 18,297.

Alpha-beta pruning **is an improvement to the minimax algorithm.**

Summary

In this chapter we have examined recursion and seen that it is a powerful problem-solving tool. The fundamental rules, which you should never forget, are:

1. *Base cases*: Always have at least one case that can be solved without using recursion.
2. *Make progress*: Any recursive call must make progress toward the base case.
3. *"You gotta believe"*: Always assume that the recursive call works.
4. *Compound interest rule*: Never duplicate work by solving the same instance of a problem in separate recursive calls.

Recursion has many uses, some of which were discussed in this chapter. Three important algorithm design techniques that are based on recursion are divide and conquer, dynamic programming, and backtracking.

In the next chapter we examine sorting. The fastest known sorting algorithm is recursive.

Objects of the Game

activation record The bookkeeping in a procedural language is done by using a stack of activation records. Recursion is a natural by-product. (227)

alpha-beta pruning An improvement to the minimax algorithm. (255)

backtracking Uses recursion to try all possibilities. (252)

base case An instance that can be solved without recursion. Any recursive call must make progress toward a base case. (222)

basis In a proof by induction, the basis is the easy case that can be shown by hand. (220)

divide and conquer Recursive algorithms that are generally very efficient. The recursion is the *divide* part, and the combining of recursive solutions is the *conquer* part. (237)

driver routine Test the validity of the first case and then calls the recursive routine. (225)

dynamic programming A technique that avoids the recursive explosion by recording answers in a table. (247)

encryption Used to transmit messages that cannot be read by other parties. (235)

Fibonacci numbers The ith Fibonacci number is the sum of the two previous Fibonacci numbers. They are widely encountered. (228)

greatest common divisor (gcd) The greatest common divisor of two integers is the largest integer that divides both of them. (232)

greedy algorithm Makes locally optimal decisions at each step. This is simple but not always the correct thing to do. (248)

induction A proof technique used to establish theorems that hold for positive integers. (219)

inductive hypothesis Assumes that the theorem is true for some arbitrary case and shows that, under this assumption, it is true for the next case. (220)

minimax strategy Used for tic-tac-toe and other strategic games. It assumes optimal play by both sides. (252)

multiplicative inverse The solution $1 \le X < N$ to the equation $AX \equiv 1 (\bmod N)$. (233)

public key cryptography A type of cryptography in which each participant publishes the code others can use to send the participant encrypted messages but keeps the decrypting code secret. (237)

recursive function A function that directly or indirectly makes a call to itself. (221)

RSA cryptosystem A popular encryption method. (235)

rules of recursion 1. Base cases: Always have at least one case that can be solved without using recursion. (222); 2. Make progress: Any recursive call must make progress toward a base case. (222); 3. "You gotta believe": Always assume that the recursive call works. (226); 4. Compound Interest Rule: Never duplicate work by solving the same instance of a problem in separate recursive calls. (229)

telescoping sum Generates large numbers of cancelling terms. (244)

Common Errors

1. The most common error when using recursion is forgetting a base case.
2. Make sure that each recursive call makes progress toward a base case. Otherwise, the recursion is not correct.
3. Overlapping recursive calls must be avoided because they tend to yield exponential algorithms.
4. It is bad style to use recursion in place of a simple loop.

5. Recursive algorithms are analyzed by using a recursive formula. Do not assume that a recursive call takes linear time.

6. Violating copyright laws is another bad error. RSA is patented, but some uses are allowed. See the references for more information.

On the Internet

We provide a host of routines but few programs. We provide part of class `TicTacToe` (Exercise 7.26 asks you to finish it). The backtracking algorithm is part of a larger routine that is shown in Chapter 10. Here are the files:

RecSum.cpp The routine in Figure 7.1 with a simple `main`
PrintInt.cpp The routine in Figure 7.4 to print a number in any base, plus a `main`
Math.cpp The math routines in Section 7.4, the primality testing routine, and `main`
MaxSum.cpp The four maximum contiguous subsequence sum routines
MkChnge.cpp The routine in Figure 7.17 with a simple `main`
TicTac.cpp Routines incorporating ideas in Chapter 10, with incomplete class and no `main`

Exercises

In Short

7.1. What are the four fundamental rules of recursion?

7.2. Below are four alternatives for line 14 of routine `Power`. Why is each of them wrong?

```
HugeInt Tmp = Power( X * X, N/2, P );
HugeInt Tmp = Power( Power( X, 2, P ), N/2, P );
HugeInt Tmp = Power( Power( X, N/2, P ), 2, P );
HugeInt Tmp = Power( X, N/2, P ) * Power( X, N/2, P ) % P;
```

7.3. Show how the recursive calls are processed in the calculation $2^{63} \bmod 37$.

7.4. Compute $gcd(1995,1492)$.

7.5. Bob chooses p and q equal to 37 and 41, respectively. Determine acceptable values for the remaining parameters in the RSA algorithm.

7.6. Show that the greedy change-making algorithm fails if nickels (5-cent pieces) are not part of United States currency.

In Theory

7.7.   Prove by induction the formula for F_N:

$$F_N = \frac{1}{\sqrt{5}}\left(\left(\frac{(1+\sqrt{5})}{2}\right)^N - \left(\frac{1-\sqrt{5}}{2}\right)^N\right)$$

7.8.   Prove the following identities relating to the Fibonacci numbers:

a. $F_1 + F_2 + \ldots + F_N = F_{N+2} - 1$
b. $F_1 + F_3 + \ldots + F_{2N-1} = F_{2N}$
c. $F_0 + F_2 + \ldots + F_{2N} = F_{2N+1} - 1$
d. $F_{N-1}F_{N+1} = (-1)^N + F_N^2$
e. $F_1 F_2 + F_2 F_3 + \ldots + F_{2N-1}F_{2N} = F_{2N}^2$
f. $F_1 F_2 + F_2 F_3 + \ldots + F_{2N}F_{2N+1} = F_{2N+1}^2 - 1$
g. $F_N^2 + F_{N+1}^2 = F_{2N+1}$

7.9.   Show that if $A \equiv B(\bmod N)$, then for any C, D, and P, the following are true:

a. $A + C \equiv B + C(\bmod N)$
b. $AD \equiv BD(\bmod N)$
c. $A^P \equiv B^P(\bmod N)$

7.10.   Prove that if $A \geq B$, then $A \bmod B < A/2$. (*Hint:* Consider the cases $B \leq A/2$ and $B > A/2$ separately). How does this show that the running time of Gcd is logarithmic?

7.11.   Prove by induction the formula for the number of calls to the recursive function Fib in Section 7.3.4.

7.12.   Prove by induction that if $A > B \geq 0$ and the invocation Gcd(A, B) performs $k \geq 1$ recursive calls, then $A \geq F_{k+2}$ and $B \geq F_{k+1}$.

7.13.   Prove by induction that in the extended *gcd* algorithm, $|X| < B$ and $|Y| < A$.

7.14.   Write an alternate Gcd algorithm, based on the following observations (arrange that $A > B$):

a. $gcd(A, B) = 2gcd(A/2, B/2)$ if A and B are both even.
b. $gcd(A, B) = gcd(A/2, B)$ if A is even and B is odd.
c. $gcd(A, B) = gcd(A, B/2)$ if A is odd and B is even.
d. $gcd(A, B) = gcd((A+B)/2, (A-B)/2)$ if A and B are both odd.

7.15.   Solve the following equation: $T(N) = AT(N/B) + O(N^k \log^P N)$. Assume $A \geq 1$, $B > 1$, and $P \geq 0$.

7.16. Strassen's algorithm for matrix multiplication multiplies two $N \times N$ matrices by performing seven recursive calls to multiply two $N/2 \times N/2$ matrices. The additional overhead is quadratic. What is the running time of Strassen's algorithm?

In Practice

7.17. For $N > 0$, the factorial function $N!$ can be defined as $N((N-1)!)$. Use recursion to implement a function that evaluates $N!$.

7.18. Implement the binary search recursively.

7.19. The maximum contiguous subsequence sum algorithm in Figure 7.12 does not give any indication of the actual sequence. Modify it so that it fills reference parameters SeqStart and SeqEnd, as was done in Section 5.3.

7.20. For the coin problem, give an algorithm that computes the number of different ways to give exactly K cents in change.

7.21. One form of the *knapsack problem* is as follows: We are given N integers $A_1, A_2, ..., A_N$ and an integer K. Is there a group of integers that sums to exactly K? Give an $O(NK)$ algorithm to solve the knapsack problem.

7.22. Give an $O(2^N)$ algorithm for the knapsack problem described in Exercise 7.21. *Hint*: Use recursion.

7.23. Write the routine with declaration

```
void Permute( char *Str );
```

that prints all the permutations of the characters in the string Str. If Str is "abc", then the strings that are output are abc, acb, bac, bca, cab, and cba. Use recursion.

Programming Projects

7.24. The binomial coefficients $C(N, k)$ can be defined recursively as follows: $C(N, k) = 1$, $C(N, N) = 1$ and for $0 < k < N$, $C(N, k) = C(N, k-1) + C(N-1, k-1)$. Write a function and give an analysis of the running time to compute the binomial coefficients

a. Recursively

b. Using dynamic programming

7.25. Implement the RSA cryptosystem using a library HugeInt class.

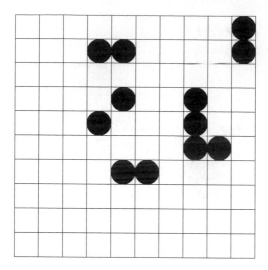

Figure 7.21   Grid for Exercise 7.28

7.26.   Complete the `TicTacToe` class.

7.27.   Let A be a sequence of N distinct sorted numbers $A_1, A_2, ..., A_N$ with $A_1 = 0$. Let B be a sequence of $N(N-1)/2$ numbers, defined by $B_{i,j} = A_i - A_j$ ($i < j$). Let D be the sequence obtained by sorting B. Both B and D may contain duplicates. *Example*: A = 0, 1, 5, 8. Then D = 1, 3, 4, 5, 7, 8.

   a. Write a program that constructs D from A. This part is easy.

   b. Write a program that constructs some sequence A that corresponds to D. Note that A is not unique. Use a backtracking algorithm.

7.28.   Consider an N-by-N grid in which some squares are occupied. Two squares belong to the same group if they share a common edge. In Figure 7.21 there is one group of four squares, three groups of two squares, and two groups of one square. Assume that the grid is represented by a two-dimensional array. Write a program that does the following:

   a. Computes the size of a group, given a square in the group.

   b. Computes the number of different groups.

   c. Lists all groups.

7.29.   Write a program that expands a C++ source file's `#include` directives (recursively).

References

Much of this chapter is based on the discussion in [3].

A description of the RSA algorithm, with proof of correctness, can be found in [1]. The text also devotes a chapter to dynamic programming. The RSA algorithm is patented, and its commercial use requires payment of a licensing fee. However, MIT's implementation of RSA, namely *PGP* (pretty good privacy), is widely available, and noncommercial use is allowed for free. More details can be found in [2].

1. T. H. Cormen, C. E. Leiserson, and R. L. Rivest, *Introduction to Algorithms*, The MIT Press, Cambridge, MA, 1990.

2. W. Stallings, *Protect Your Privacy: A Guide for PGP Users,* Prentice-Hall, Englewood Cliffs, NJ, 1995.

3. M. A. Weiss, *Efficient C Programming: A Practical Approach*, Prentice-Hall, Englewood Cliffs, NJ, 1995.

Chapter 8

Sorting Algorithms

Sorting is a fundamental application for computers. Much of the output that is eventually produced by a computation is sorted in some way, and many computations are made efficient by invoking a sorting procedure internally. Thus sorting is perhaps the most well-studied and important operation in computer science.

In this chapter we discuss the problem of sorting an array of elements. We describe and analyze the various sorting algorithms. The sorts we do in this chapter can be done entirely in main memory, so the number of elements is relatively small (less than a few million). Sorts that cannot be performed in main memory and must be done on disk or tape are also quite important. This type of sorting, known as external sorting, will be discussed in Section 20.6.

Our discussion of sorting will blend theory and practice. We will see several algorithms with different performances and show how an analysis of an algorithm's performance properties can guide us as we make decisions about implementation that are not obvious.

In this chapter we will see

- that the insertion sort, previously shown in Figure 3.5, runs in quadratic time
- how to code Shellsort, which is a simple and efficient algorithm that runs in subquadratic time
- how to write the slightly more complicated $O(N \log N)$ mergesort and quicksort algorithms
- that $\Omega(N \log N)$ comparisons are required for any general-purpose sorting algorithm
- how we can use pointers to sort large objects without incurring the excessive overhead associated with data movement

8.1   Why Is Sorting Important?

In Section 5.6 we saw that searching a sorted array is much easier than searching an unsorted array. This is especially true for people: Finding a person's name in a phone book is easy, but finding a phone number without knowing the person's name is virtually impossible. As a result, any significant amount of computer output is generally arranged in some sorted order so it can be interpreted. Here are some more examples

- Words in a dictionary are sorted (and case distinctions are ignored).
- Files in a directory are often listed in sorted order.
- The index of a book is sorted (and case distinctions are ignored).
- The card catalog in a library is sorted by both author and title.
- A listing of course offerings at a university is sorted, first by department and then by course number.
- Many banks provide statements that list checks in increasing order (by check number).
- In a newspaper, the calendar of events in a schedule is generally sorted by date.
- Musical compact disks in a record store are generally sorted by recording artist.
- In the programs that are printed for graduation ceremonies, departments are listed in sorted order, and then students in those departments are listed in sorted order.

An initial sort of the data can significantly enhance the performance of an algorithm.

It is not surprising that much of the work in computing involves sorting. However, there are also indirect uses of sorting. For instance, suppose we want to decide if an array has any duplicates. Figure 8.1 shows a simple function (for an array of N items) that is immediately seen to require quadratic worst-case time. Sorting provides an alternative algorithm: if we sort a copy of the array, then any duplicates will be adjacent and can be detected in a single linear-time scan of the array. The cost of this algorithm is dominated by the time to sort, so if we can sort in subquadratic time, we have an improved algorithm. There are many other algorithms whose performance is significantly enhanced when we initially sort the data.

The vast majority of significant programming projects use a sort somewhere, and in many cases the sorting cost determines the running time. Thus we would like to implement a fast and reliable sort.

8.2 Preliminaries

The algorithms we describe in this chapter are all interchangeable. Each will be passed an array containing the elements and an integer containing the number of elements. We could have used the `Vector` class described in Section 3.3.3 but have not. Using the `Vector` class requires only a trivial change in the sorting function declaration. However, the bounds checking performed by the `Vector` class is not needed for our sorting algorithm and in some instances could significantly decrease performance.

We do not use the `Vector` class in our sorting algorithms because range checking slows them down.

We will assume that N, the number of elements passed to our sorting routines, has already been checked and is legal. In keeping with C++ conventions, arrays start at index 0 and the items being sorted reside in positions 0 to $N-1$. We require the existence of `operator<`, which can be used to place a consistent ordering on the input. As shown in Figure 8.2, once one of the relational operators is defined, all the relational and equality operators can also be meaningfully defined. Besides the copy assignment operator, these are the only operations allowed on the input data. Algorithms that sort under these conditions are known as *comparison-based sorting algorithms*.

Comparison-based sorting algorithms make ordering decisions only on the basis of comparisons.

8.3 Analysis of the Insertion Sort and Other Simple Sorts

Because of the nested loops, each of which can take N iterations, the insertion sort algorithm is $O(N^2)$. Furthermore, this bound is achievable because input in reverse order really does take quadratic time. A precise calculation shows that the tests at line 12 in Figure 8.3 (which duplicates Figure 3.5) can be executed at most P times for each value of P. Summing over all P gives a total of

The Insertion sort is quadratic in the worst and average cases. It is fast if the input is already sorted.

$$\sum_{P=2}^{N} P = 2 + 3 + 4 + \ldots + N - O(N^2)$$

```
1  // Return true if A has duplicates, false otherwise
2  // Etype: must have == defined and must have properties
3  //        required for Vector
4
5  template <class Etype>
6  int
7  Duplicates( const Vector<Etype> & A, int N )
8  {
9      for( int i = 0; i < N; i++ )
10         for( int j = i + 1; j < N; j++ )
11             if( A[ i ] == A[ j ] )
12                 return 1;    // Duplicate found
13
14     return 0;               // No duplicates found
15 }
```

Figure 8.1   Simple quadratic algorithm to detect duplicates

Operators	Definition
operator> (A, B)	return B < A;
operator>=(A, B)	return !(A < B);
operator<=(A, B)	return !(B < A);
operator!=(A, B)	return A < B || B < A;
operator==(A, B)	return !(A < B || B < A);

Figure 8.2   Deriving the relational and equality operators from operator<

```
1  // InsertionSort: sort first N items in array A
2  // Etype: must have copy constructor, operator=, and operator<
3
4  void
5  InsertionSort( Etype A[ ], int N )
6  {
7      for( int P = 1; P < N; P++ )
8      {
9          Etype Tmp = A[ P ];
10         int j;
11
12         for( j = P; j > 0 && Tmp < A[ j - 1 ]; j-- )
13             A[ j ] = A[ j - 1 ];
14         A[ j ] = Tmp;
15     }
16 }
```

Figure 8.3   Template insertion sort

On the other hand, if the input is presorted, the running time is $O(N)$ because the test at the top of the inner `for` loop always fails immediately. Indeed, if the input is almost sorted (almost sorted will be more rigorously defined below), the insertion sort will run quickly. This means that the running time depends not only on the amount of input but also on the specific ordering of the input. Because of this wide variation, it is worth analyzing the average-case behavior of this algorithm. It turns out that the average case is $\theta(N^2)$ for the insertion sort as well as a variety of other simple sorting algorithms.

Inversions measure unsortedness.

An *inversion* in an array of numbers is any ordered pair (i, j) having the property that $i < j$ but $A[i] > A[j]$. For example, the sequence { 8, 5, 9, 2, 6, 3 } has ten inversions that correspond to the pairs (8,5), (8,2), (8,6), (8,3), (5,2), (5,3), (9,2), (9,6), (9,3), and (6,3). Notice that the number of inversions is equal to the total number of times that line 13 in Figure 8.3 is executed. This is always the case because the effect of the assignment statement is to swap the two items

A[j] and A[j-1]. (We avoid the actual excessive swapping by using the temporary variable, but nonetheless it is an abstract swap.) Swapping two elements that are out of place removes exactly one inversion, and a sorted file has no inversions. Thus, if there are I inversions at the start of the algorithm, we must have I implicit swaps. Since there is $O(N)$ other work involved in the algorithm, the running time of the insertion sort is $O(I+N)$, where I is the number of inversions in the original array. Thus the insertion sort runs in linear time if the number of inversions is $O(N)$.

We can compute precise bounds on the average running time of the insertion sort by computing the average number of inversions in a permutation. Defining *average* is a difficult proposition. We can assume that there are no duplicate elements (if we allow duplicates, it is not even clear what the average number of duplicates is). We can also assume that the input is some permutation of the first N integers (since only relative ordering is important) and that all these permutations are equally likely. Under these assumptions we can establish the following theorem:

The average number of inversions in an array of N distinct numbers is ***Theorem 8.1***
$N(N-1)/4$.

For any array A of numbers, consider A_r, which is the array in reverse ***Proof***
order. For example, the reverse of array 1, 5, 4, 2, 6, 3 is 3, 6, 2, 4, 5, 1.
Consider any two numbers (x, y) in the array, with $y > x$. In exactly one
of A and A_r, this ordered pair represents an inversion. The total number
of these pairs in an array A and its reverse A_r is $N(N-1)/2$. Thus an
average list has half this amount, or $N(N-1)/4$ inversions.

Theorem 8.1 implies that insertion sort is quadratic on average. It also can be used to provide a very strong lower bound about any algorithm that only exchanges adjacent elements.

Any algorithm that sorts by exchanging adjacent elements requires ***Theorem 8.2***
$\Omega(N^2)$ *time on average.*

The average number of inversions is initially $N(N-1)/4$. Each swap ***Proof***
removes only one inversion, so $\Omega(N^2)$ swaps are required.

This is an example of a *lower-bound proof*. It is valid not only for the insertion sort, which performs adjacent exchanges implicitly, but also for other simple algorithms such as the bubble sort and the selection sort, which we will not describe here. In fact, it is valid over an entire *class* of algorithms, including undiscovered ones, that perform only adjacent exchanges.

Unfortunately, any computational confirmation of a proof applying to a class of algorithms would require running all algorithms in the class; this is impossible because the number of possible algorithms is infinite. Any attempt at confirmation would apply only to the algorithms that are run. This makes the confirmation of the validity of lower-bound proofs more difficult than the usual single-algorithm upper bounds we are accustomed to. A computation could only *disprove* a lower-bound conjecture; it could never prove it in general.

Although this lower-bound proof is rather simple, in general proving lower bounds is much more complicated than proving upper bounds. Lower-bound arguments are much more abstract than their upper-bound counterparts.

This lower bound shows us that for a sorting algorithm to run in subquadratic or $o(N^2)$ time, it must do comparisons and, in particular, exchanges between elements that are far apart. A sorting algorithm makes progress by eliminating inversions, and to run efficiently, it must eliminate more than just one inversion per exchange.

8.4 Shellsort

The first algorithm to improve on the insertion sort substantially was *Shellsort*. Shellsort was discovered in 1959 by Donald Shell. Though it is not the fastest algorithm known, it is only two lines longer than the insertion sort (one of which is a declaration), thus making it the simplest of the faster algorithms.

Shell's idea was to avoid the large amount of data movement by first comparing elements that were far apart and then elements that were less far apart, until gradually shrinking toward the basic insertion sort. Shellsort uses a sequence $h_1, h_2, \ldots, h_t$ called the increment sequence. Any increment sequence will do as long as $h_1 = 1$, but some choices are better than others. After a phase, using some increment h_k, we will have $A[i] \leq A[i + h_k]$ for every i where this makes sense; all elements spaced h_k apart are sorted. The file is then said to be h_k-sorted. For example, Figure 8.4 shows an array after several phases of Shellsort. After a 5-sort, elements spaced five apart are guaranteed to be in correct sorted order. In Figure 8.4, elements spaced five apart are identically shaded, and as you can see, they are sorted relative to each other. Similarly, after a 3-sort, elements spaced three apart are guaranteed to be in sorted order, relative to each other. An important property of Shellsort (which we state without proof) is that an h_k-sorted array that is then h_{k-1}-sorted remains h_k-sorted. If this were not the case, the algorithm would likely be of little value because work done by early phases would be undone by later phases.

Original	81	94	11	96	12	35	17	95	28	58	41	75	15
After 5-sort	35	17	11	28	12	41	75	15	96	58	81	94	95
After 3-sort	28	12	11	35	15	41	58	17	94	75	81	96	95
After 1-sort	11	12	15	17	28	35	41	58	75	81	94	95	96

Figure 8.4   Shellsort after each pass, if increment sequence is { 1, 3, 5 }

In general, to perform an h_k-sort, for each position i in h_k, $h_k + 1$, ..., $N-1$, we place the element in the correct spot among i, $i - h_k$, $i - 2h_k$, and so on. Although this does not affect the implementation, a careful examination shows that the action of an h_k-sort is to perform an insertion sort on h_k independent subarrays (shown in different shades in Figure 8.4). Consequently, it should be no surprise that in Figure 8.6, lines 10 to 18 represent a *gap insertion sort*: After the loop is executed, we can be sure that elements separated by a distance of Gap in the array are sorted. For instance, when Gap is 1, the loop is identical, statement by statement, to an insertion sort. Thus, Shellsort is also known as *diminishing gap sort*.

A diminishing gap sort is another name for Shellsort.

It is easy to show several facts. First, as we have shown, when Gap is 1 the inner loop is guaranteed to sort the array A. If Gap is never 1, then there is always some input for which the array cannot be sorted. Thus Shellsort always sorts as long as we eventually have Gap equal to 1, and at that point we can stop. The only issue remaining, then, is to choose the increment sequence.

Shell suggested starting Gap at $N/2$ and halving it until it reaches 1, after which the program can terminate. Using these increments, Shellsort represents a substantial improvement over the insertion sort, despite the fact that it nests three for loops instead of two, which is usually inefficient. By altering the sequence of gaps, one can further improve the algorithm's performance. A summary of Shellsort's performance with three different choices of increment sequences is shown in Figure 8.5.

Shell's increment sequence is an improvement over the insertion sort, but better sequences are known.

8.4.1   Performance of Shellsort

The running time of Shellsort depends heavily on the choice of increment sequences, and in general the proofs can be rather involved. The average-case analysis of Shellsort is a longstanding open problem except for the most trivial increment sequences.

N	Insertion sort	Shellsort		
		Shell's	Odd gaps only	Dividing by 2.2
1,000	122	11	11	9
2,000	483	26	21	23
4,000	1,936	61	59	54
8,000	7,950	153	141	114
16,000	32,560	358	322	269
32,000	131,911	869	752	575
64,000	520,000	2,091	1,705	1,249

Figure 8.5   Running time (milliseconds) of the insertion sort and Shellsort with various increment sequences

In the worst case, Shell's increments give quadratic behavior.

When Shell's increments are used, the worst case can be proven to be $O(N^2)$. This bound is achievable if N is an exact power of 2, all the large elements are in even-indexed array positions, and all the small elements are in odd-indexed array positions. When the final pass is reached, all the large elements will still be in the even-indexed array positions, and all the small elements will still be in the odd-indexed array positions. A calculation of the number of remaining inversions shows that the final pass will require quadratic time. The fact that this is the worst that can happen follows from the fact that an h_k-sort consists of h_k insertion sorts of roughly N/h_k elements. Consequently, the cost of each pass is $O(h_k(N/h_k)^2)$, or $O(N^2/h_k)$. When we sum this over all the passes, we obtain $O(N^2\sum h_k)$. Since the increments are roughly a geometric series, the sum is bounded by a constant, and the result is a quadratic worst-case running time. One can also prove that, when N is an exact power of 2, the average running time is $O(N^{3/2})$. Thus, on average, Shell's increments give a significant improvement over insertion sort.

If consecutive increments are relatively prime, the performance of Shellsort is improved.

A minor change to the increment sequence can prevent the quadratic worst case from occurring. If we divide Gap by 2 and it becomes even, then we can add one to make it odd. We can then prove that the worst case is not quadratic but only $O(N^{3/2})$. Although the proof is complicated, the basis for it is that in this new increment sequence, consecutive increments share no common factors (whereas in Shell's increment sequence they do). Any sequence that satisfies this property (and whose increments decrease roughly geometrically) will have a worst-case running time of at most $O(N^{3/2})$.[1] The average performance of the algorithm with these new increments is unknown but seems to be $O(N^{5/4})$, based on simulations.

---

1. To appreciate the subtlety involved, note that subtracting one instead of adding one does not work. For instance, if N is 186, the resulting sequence is 93, 45, 21, 9, 3, 1, which all share the common factor 3.

```
1   // Shellsort: sort first N items in array A
2   // Etype: must have copy constructor, operator=, and operator<
3
4   template <class Etype>
5   void
6   Shellsort( Etype A[ ], int N )
7   {
8       for( int Gap = N / 2; Gap > 0;
9               Gap = Gap == 2 ? 1 : ( int ) ( Gap / 2.2 ) )
10          for( int i = Gap; i < N; i++ )
11          {
12              Etype Tmp = A[ i ];
13              int j = i;
14
15              for( ; j >= Gap && Tmp < A[ j - Gap ]; j -= Gap )
16                  A[ j ] = A[ j - Gap ];
17              A[ j ] = Tmp;
18          }
19  }
```

Figure 8.6   Shellsort implementation

A third alternative that performs well in practice but has no theoretical basis is to divide by 2.2 instead of 2. This appears to bring the average running time to below $O(N^{5/4})$ (perhaps to $O(N^{7/6})$), but this is completely unresolved. For 100,000 to 1,000,000 items, it typically improves performance by about 25 to 35 percent, although nobody knows why. A Shellsort implementation with this increment sequence is coded in Figure 8.6. The complicated code at line 9 is necessary to avoid setting Gap equal to 2. If that happens, then Gap/2.2 goes below 1 and the algorithm is broken because we never see a 1-sort. Line 9 ensures that, if Gap is about to be set to 2, it is reset to 1.

Dividing by 2.2 gives excellent performance in practice.

The table in Figure 8.5 compares the performance of insertion sort and Shellsort, with various gap sequences. These results were obtained on a reasonably fast machine. The test is clearly biased against the original gap sequence because N is chosen to be 125 times an exact power of 2. Rounding up to an odd number is beneficial, especially as N gets large. We could easily conclude that Shellsort, even with the simplest gap sequence, provides a significant improvement over the insertion sort, at a cost of only two lines of code. A simple change to the gap sequence can further improve performance. More improvement is possible (as you will see in Exercise 8.21). Some of these improvements have theoretical backing, but no known sequence markedly improves the program shown in Figure 8.6.

The performance of Shellsort is quite acceptable in practice, even for N in the tens of thousands. The simplicity of the code makes it the algorithm of choice for sorting up to moderately large input. It is also a fine example of a very simple algorithm with an extremely complex analysis.

Shellsort is a good choice for moderate amounts of input.

8.5 Mergesort

Mergesort **uses divide and conquer to obtain an order** *N* **log** *N* **running time.**

In Section 7.5 we saw that recursion can be used to develop subquadratic algorithms. Specifically, a divide-and-conquer algorithm in which two half-size problems are solved recursively with an $O(N)$ overhead results in an $O(N \log N)$ algorithm. Mergesort is such an algorithm. It offers a better bound, at least theoretically, than the bounds claimed for Shellsort.

The mergesort algorithm involves three steps:

1. If the number of items to sort is 0 or 1, return.
2. Recursively sort the first and second halves separately.
3. Merge the two sorted halves into a sorted group.

Merging of sorted arrays can be done in linear time.

To claim an $O(N \log N)$ algorithm, we only need to show that the merging of two sorted groups can be performed in linear time. We will show how to merge two input arrays A and B, placing the result in a third array C. We then provide a simple implementation of mergesort. As we will see in Section 20.6, the merge routine is the cornerstone of most external sorting algorithms.

8.5.1 Linear-Time Merging of Sorted Arrays

The basic merge algorithm takes two input arrays A and B, output array C, and three counters *Aptr*, *Bptr*, and *Cptr*, which are initially set to the beginning of their respective arrays. The smaller of *A[Aptr]* and *B[Bptr]* is copied to the next entry in C, and the appropriate counters are advanced. When either input array is exhausted, the remainder of the other array is copied to C. An example of how the merge routine works is provided for the following input:

If the array A contains 1, 13, 24, 26, and B contains 2, 15, 27, 38, then the algorithm proceeds as follows:

First, a comparison is done between 1 and 2, 1 is added to C, and then 13 and 2 are compared:

2 is added to *C*, and then 13 and 15 are compared:

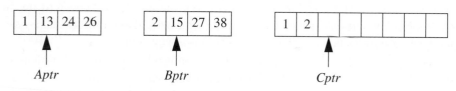

13 is added to *C*, and then 24 and 15 are compared:

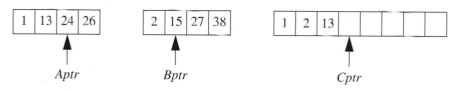

The process continues until 26 and 27 are compared:

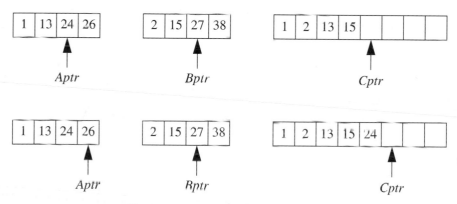

26 is added to *C*, and the *A* array is exhausted:

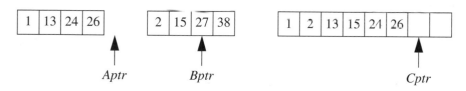

The remainder of the *B* array is then copied to *C*.

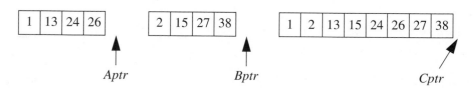

The time needed to merge two sorted arrays is linear because each comparison advances *Cptr* (thus limiting the number of comparisons). As a result, a divide-and-conquer algorithm that uses a linear merging procedure will run in $O(N \log N)$ worst-case time. This running time will also be the average-case and best-case times because the merging step is always linear.

An example of the mergesort algorithm would be sorting the eight-element array 24, 13, 26, 1, 2, 27, 38, 15. After recursively sorting the first four and last four elements, we obtain 1, 13, 24, 26, 2, 15, 27, 38. Then we merge the two halves, obtaining the final array 1, 2, 13, 15, 24, 26, 27, 38.

```
1  // MergeSort: sort first N items in array A
2  // Etype: must have zero parameter constructor,
3  //        operator=, and operator<=
4  //
5  // Recursive MergeSort and Merge are supporting routines
6
7  template <class Etype>
8  void
9  MergeSort( Etype A[ ], Etype TmpArray[ ],
10                      int Left, int Right )
11 {
12     if( Left < Right )
13     {
14         int Center = ( Left + Right ) / 2;
15         MergeSort( A, TmpArray, Left, Center );
16         MergeSort( A, TmpArray, Center + 1, Right );
17         Merge( A, TmpArray, Left, Center + 1, Right );
18     }
19 }
20
21 template <class Etype>
22 void
23 MergeSort( Etype A[ ], int N )
24 {
25    try
26    {
27      Etype *TmpArray = new Etype [ N ];
28      MergeSort( A, TmpArray, 0, N - 1 );
29      delete [ ] TmpArray;
30    }
31    catch( ... )
32    {
33      cerr << "Out of memory!! Sort fails." << endl;
34    }
35 }
```

Figure 8.7   Basic `MergeSort` routines

8.5.2   The Mergesort Algorithm

A straightforward implementation of mergesort is shown in Figure 8.7. The
externally visible MergeSort is a simple driver that declares a temporary array
and calls recursive MergeSort with the boundaries of the array. The Merge
routine follows the description given in the previous section, using the first half
of the array (indexed from Left to Center) as *A*, the second half (indexed
from Center+1 to Right) as *B*, and the temporary as *C*. Figure 8.8 implements the Merge routine. The temporary is then copied back into the original
array.

**Mergesort uses linear
extra memory, which
is a practical liability.**

```
1  // Merge routine
2  // Etype: requirements described in MergeSort
3  //
4  // LeftPos  = start of the left half
5  // RightPos = start of the right half
6
7  template <class Etype>
8  void
9  Merge( Etype A[ ], Etype TmpArray[ ], int LeftPos,
10                      int RightPos, int RightEnd )
11  {
12      int LeftEnd = RightPos - 1;
13      int TmpPos = LeftPos;
14      int NumElements = RightEnd - LeftPos + 1;
15
16      // Main loop
17      while( LeftPos <= LeftEnd && RightPos <= RightEnd )
18          if( A[ LeftPos ] <= A[ RightPos ] )
19              TmpArray[ TmpPos++ ] = A[ LeftPos++ ];
20          else
21              TmpArray[ TmpPos++ ] = A[ RightPos++ ];
22
23      while( LeftPos <= LeftEnd )      // Copy rest of first half
24          TmpArray[ TmpPos++ ] = A[ LeftPos++ ];
25
26      while( RightPos <= RightEnd )    // Copy rest of right half
27          TmpArray[ TmpPos++ ] = A[ RightPos++ ];
28
29      // Copy TmpArray back
30      for( int i = 0; i < NumElements; i++, RightEnd-- )
31          A[ RightEnd ] = TmpArray[ RightEnd ];
32  }
```

Figure 8.8   Merge routine

We can avoid excessive copying with more work, but the linear extra memory cannot be removed without excessive time penalties.

Although mergesort's running time is $O(N \log N)$, it is hardly ever used for main memory sorts. The problem is that merging two sorted lists uses linear extra memory, and the additional work involved in copying to the temporary array and back, throughout the algorithm, slows down the sort considerably. This copying can be avoided by judiciously switching the roles of A and TmpArray at alternate levels in the recursion. A variant of mergesort can also be implemented nonrecursively, but for serious internal sorting applications, the algorithm of choice is quicksort, which is described in the next section.

8.6 Quicksort

Quicksort is a fast divide-and-conquer algorithm when properly implemented. In practice it is the fastest comparison-based sorting algorithm.

As its name implies, *quicksort* is the fastest known sorting algorithm. Its average running time is $O(N \log N)$. Its speed is mainly due to a very tight and highly optimized inner loop. It has quadratic worst-case performance, but this can be made statistically impossible with a little effort. The quicksort algorithm is relatively simple to understand and prove correct because it relies on recursion. It is a tricky algorithm to implement because minute changes in the code can make significant differences in the running time. In this section we first describe the algorithm in broad terms. We then provide an analysis that shows its best-, worst-, and average-case running times and use this analysis to make decisions on how certain details, such as the handling of duplicate items, are implemented in C++.

8.6.1 The Quicksort Algorithm

The basic quicksort algorithm is recursive. Details include choosing the pivot, deciding how to partition, and dealing with duplicates. The wrong decisions will give quadratic running times for a variety of common inputs.

The basic algorithm $Quicksort(S)$ consists of the following four steps:

1. If the number of elements in S is 0 or 1, then return.
2. Pick *any* element v in S. This is called the *pivot*.
3. *Partition* $S - \{v\}$ (the remaining elements in S) into two disjoint groups: $L = \{x \in S - \{v\} \mid x \leq v\}$ and $R = \{x \in S - \{v\} \mid x \geq v\}$.
4. Return the result of $Quicksort(L)$ followed by v followed by $Quicksort(R)$.

The *pivot* divides array elements into two groups: those smaller than the pivot and those larger than the pivot.

Several things stand out when we look at these steps. First, the base case of the recursion includes the possibility that S might be an empty set. This is needed because the recursive calls could generate empty subsets. Second, the algorithm allows any element to be used as the *pivot*. The pivot divides array elements into two groups: elements that are smaller than the pivot and elements that are larger than the pivot. The analysis we will perform will show that some choices for the pivot are better than others. Thus, when we provide an actual implementation, we will not use just any pivot, but instead we will try to make an educated choice.

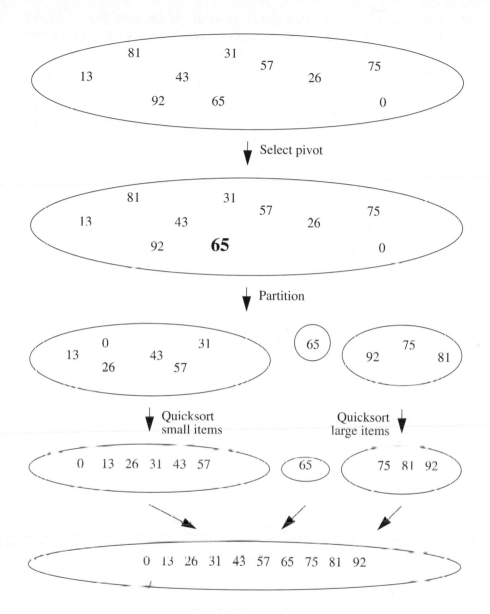

Figure 8.9   The steps of quicksort

Finally, in the *partition* step every element in *S*, except for the pivot, is placed in either *L* (which stands for the left part of the array) or *R* (which stands for the right part of the array). The intent is that elements that are smaller than the pivot go to *L*, while elements that are larger than the pivot go to *R*. The description in the algorithm, however, ambiguously describes what to do with elements equal to the pivot. It allows each instance of a duplicate to go into

The *partition* step places every element except the pivot in one of two groups.

either subset, specifying only that it must go to one or the other. Part of a good C++ implementation is handling this case as efficiently as possible. Once again, the analysis will allow us to make an informed decision.

Figure 8.9 shows the action of quicksort on a set of numbers. The pivot is chosen (by chance) to be 65. The remaining elements in the set are partitioned into two smaller subsets. Each of these groups is then sorted recursively. Recall that, by the third rule of recursion, we can assume that this step works. The sorted arrangement of the entire group is then trivially obtained. In a C++ implementation, the items would be stored in a part of an array delimited by Low and High. After the partitioning step the pivot would wind up in some array cell P. The recursive calls would then be on the parts from Low to P-1 and then P+1 to High.

Because recursion allows us to take the giant leap of faith, the correctness of the algorithm is guaranteed as follows:

- The group of small elements is sorted, by virtue of the recursion.
- The largest element in the group of small elements is not larger than the pivot, by virtue of the partition.
- The pivot is not larger than the smallest element in the group of large elements, by virtue of the partition.
- The group of large elements is sorted, by virtue of the recursion.

Quicksort is fast because the partitioning step can be performed quickly and in place.

Although the correctness of the algorithm is easily established, it is not clear why it is any faster than mergesort. Like mergesort, it recursively solves two subproblems and requires linear additional work (in the form of the partitioning step). Unlike mergesort, however, the subproblems are not guaranteed to be of equal size, which we will see is bad for performance. The reason that quicksort is faster than mergesort is that the partitioning step can be performed significantly faster than the merging step. In particular, we will see that the partitioning step can be performed without using an extra array and that the code to implement it is very compact and efficient. This makes up for the lack of equal-sized subproblems.

8.6.2   Analysis of Quicksort

The algorithm description leaves several questions unanswered: How do we choose the pivot? How do we perform the partition? What do we do if we see an element that is equal to the pivot? All these questions can have a dramatic effect on the running time of the algorithm. We will perform an analysis to help us decide how we should implement the unspecified steps in quicksort.

Best Case

The best thing that can happen for quicksort is that the pivot partitions the set into two equal-sized subsets and that this happens at each stage of the recursion. We then have two half-sized recursive calls plus linear overhead, which matches the performance of mergesort. The running time is $O(N \log N)$. (Although we have shown that for this case the running time is $O(N \log N)$, we have not actually proved that this is the best case. Such a proof is possible however.

The best case occurs when the partition always splits into equal subsets. The running time is $O(N \log N)$.

Worst Case

Since equal-sized subsets are good for quicksort, one might expect that unequal-sized subsets are bad. This is indeed the case. Let us suppose that in each step of the recursion, the pivot happens to be the smallest element. Then the set of small elements L will be empty, and the set of large elements R will have all the elements except for the pivot. We will then have to recursively call quicksort on subset R. If we let $T(N)$ be the running time to quicksort N elements and assume that the time to sort 0 or 1 element is just 1 time unit, and if we charge N units to partition a set that contains N elements, then for $N > 1$, we obtain a running time that satisfies

The worst case occurs when the partition generates an empty subset. The running time is $O(N^2)$.

$$T(N) = T(N-1) + N \qquad (8.1)$$

Let us restate how Equation 8.1 arises. The time to quicksort N items is equal to the time to recursively sort the $N - 1$ items in the subset of larger elements plus the N units of cost to perform the partition. This assumes that, in each step of the iteration, we are unfortunate enough to pick the smallest element as the pivot. To simplify the analysis, we have normalized by throwing out constant factors. We can solve this recurrence by telescoping Equation 8.1 repeatedly:

$$T(N) = T(N-1) + N$$
$$T(N-1) = T(N-2) + (N-1)$$
$$T(N-2) = T(N-3) + (N-2) \qquad (8.2)$$
$$\cdots$$
$$T(2) = T(1) + 2$$

When we add up everything in Equation 8.2, we obtain massive cancellations, yielding

$$T(N) = T(1) + 2 + 3 + \ldots + N = N(N+1)/2 = O(N^2) \qquad (8.3)$$

This analysis verifies the intuition that an uneven split is bad. Intuitively, we spend N units of time to partition and then have to make a recursive call for $N - 1$. Then we spend $N - 1$ units to partition that group, only to have to make a recursive call for $N-2$ elements. In that call we spend $N-2$ units performing the partition, and so on. The total cost of performing all the partitions throughout the recursive calls exactly matches what is obtained in Equation 8.3. This tells us that when implementing the selection of the pivot and the partitioning step, we do not want to do anything that might encourage the subsets to be unbalanced in size.

Average Case

The average case is $O(N \log N)$. Although this seems intuitive, a formal proof is required.

The first two analyses tell us that the best and worst cases are wildly different. Naturally, we would like to know what happens in the average case. We would expect that, since each subproblem is half of the original on average, the $O(N \log N)$ would now become an average-case bound. Such intuition, while correct for the particular quicksort application we will examine, does not constitute a formal proof. Averages cannot be thrown around lightly. For example, suppose we have a pivot algorithm that is guaranteed to select only the smallest or largest element, each with probability 1/2. Then the average size of the small group of elements is roughly $N/2$, as is the average size of the large group of elements (because each is equally likely to have 0 or $N-1$ elements). But the running time of quicksort with that pivot selection will always be quadratic because we always get a poor split of elements. We must be careful how we assign the label *average*. We can argue that the group of small elements is as likely to contain 0, 1, 2, ... , or $N-1$ elements. This is also true for the group of large elements. Under this assumption we can establish that the average-case running time is indeed $O(N \log N)$.

The average cost of a recursive call is obtained by averaging the costs of all possible subproblem sizes.

Since the cost of quicksort of N items is equal to N units for the partitioning step plus the cost of the two recursive calls, we need to determine the average cost of each of the recursive calls. If $T(N)$ represents the average cost to quicksort N elements, the average cost of each recursive call is equal to the average, over all possible subproblem sizes, of the average cost of a recursive call on the subproblem.

$$T(L) = T(R) = \frac{T(0) + T(1) + T(2) + \ldots + T(N-1)}{N} \tag{8.4}$$

Equation 8.4 states that we are looking at the costs for each possible subset size and averaging them. Since we have two recursive calls plus linear time to perform the partition, we obtain

$$T(N) = 2\left(\frac{T(0) + T(1) + T(2) + \ldots + T(N-1)}{N}\right) + N \tag{8.5}$$

The average running time is given by $T(N)$. We solve by removing all but the most recent recursive value of T.

To solve Equation 8.5, we begin by multiplying both sides by N, obtaining

$$NT(N) = 2(T(0) + T(1) + T(2) + \ldots + T(N-1)) + N^2 \tag{8.6}$$

we then write Equation 8.6 for the case $N-1$, with the idea being that we can perform a subtraction and greatly simplify the equation. If we do this, we obtain

$$(N-1)\,T(N-1) = 2\,(T(0)+T(1)+T(2)+\ldots+T(N-2)) + (N-1)^2 \quad \textbf{(8.7)}$$

Now if we subtract Equation 8.7 from Equation 8.6, we obtain

$$NT(N)-(N-1)\,T(N-1) = 2T(N-1)+2N-1$$

We rearrange terms and drop the insignificant -1 on the right, obtaining

$$NT(N) = (N+1)\,T(N-1)+2N \quad \textbf{(8.8)}$$

> Once we have $T(N)$ in terms of $T(N-1)$ only, we attempt to telescope.

We now have a formula for $T(N)$ in terms of $T(N-1)$ only. Again the idea is to telescope, but Equation 8.8 is in the wrong form. If we divide Equation 8.8 by $N(N+1)$, we obtain

$$\frac{T(N)}{N+1} = \frac{T(N-1)}{N}+\frac{2}{N+1}$$

Now we can telescope:

$$\frac{T(N)}{N+1} = \frac{T(N-1)}{N}+\frac{2}{N+1}$$

$$\frac{T(N-1)}{N} = \frac{T(N-2)}{N-1}+\frac{2}{N}$$

$$\frac{T(N-2)}{N-1} = \frac{T(N-3)}{N-2}+\frac{2}{N-1} \quad \textbf{(8.9)}$$

$$\ldots$$

$$\frac{T(2)}{3} = \frac{T(1)}{2}+\frac{2}{3}$$

If we add all the equations in Equation 8.9, we obtain

> We use the fact that the Nth harmonic number is $O(\log N)$.

$$\frac{T(N)}{N+1} = \frac{T(1)}{2}+2\left(\frac{1}{3}+\frac{1}{4}+\ldots+\frac{1}{N}+\frac{1}{N+1}\right)$$

$$= 2\left(1+\frac{1}{2}+\frac{1}{3}+\ldots+\frac{1}{N+1}\right)-\frac{5}{2} \quad \textbf{(8.10)}$$

$$= O(\log N)$$

The last line in Equation 8.10 follows from Theorem . When we multiply both sides by $N+1$, we obtain the final result:

$$T(N) = O(N\log N) \quad \textbf{(8.11)}$$

8.6.3 Picking the Pivot

Now that we have established that quicksort will run in $O(N\log N)$ time on average, our primary concern is to ensure that the worst case does not occur. By performing a complex analysis, we can compute the standard deviation of quicksort's running time. The result is that if a single random permutation is presented, it is almost certain that the running time used to sort it will be close to the average. Thus we must be careful that degenerate inputs do not result in bad running times. Degenerate inputs include data that are already sorted and data that contain only N completely identical elements. As we will see, sometimes it is the easy cases that give algorithms trouble.

A Wrong Way

Picking the pivot is crucial to good performance. Never choose the first element as pivot.

The popular, uninformed choice is to use the first element (that is, the element that is in position Low) as the pivot. This is acceptable if the input is random, but if the input is presorted or in reverse order, then the pivot provides a poor partition because it will be an extreme element. Furthermore, this behavior will continue recursively. As we saw earlier, we would get quadratic running time to do absolutely nothing, which needless to say is embarrassing. We must *never* use the first element as the pivot. Another popular alternative is to choose the larger of the first two distinct keys as the pivot, but this has the same bad effects as choosing the first key. Stay away from any strategy that looks only at some key near the front or end of the input group.

A Safe Choice

The middle element is a reasonable but passive choice.

A perfectly reasonable choice for the pivot is the middle element (that is, the element in array cell (Low+High)/2). When the input is already sorted, this gives the perfect pivot in each recursive call. Of course, we could construct an input sequence that forces quadratic behavior for this strategy (see Exercise 8.8), but the chances of randomly running into a case that took even twice as long as the average case is astronomically small.

Median-of-Three Partitioning

In *median-of-three partitioning*, the median of the first, middle, and last elements is used as the pivot. This simplifies the partitioning stage of quicksort.

Choosing the middle element as the pivot avoids the degenerate cases that arise from nonrandom inputs. Notice that it is passive: We do not attempt to choose a good pivot but merely try to avoid picking a bad pivot. *Median-of-three partitioning* is an attempt to pick a better than average pivot.

The median of a group of N numbers is the $\lceil N/2 \rceil$th smallest number. The best choice for the pivot would clearly be the median because it would guarantee an even split of the elements. Unfortunately, this is hard to calculate and would slow down quicksort considerably. We want to get a good estimate of the median without spending too much time. Such an estimate can be obtained by sampling: We pick a subset of these numbers and find their median. This is the classic method used in opinion polls. The larger the sample, the more accurate the estimate. However the larger sample takes longer to evaluate. It has been shown that a sample size of three gives a small improvement in the average running time of quicksort and also simplifies the resulting partitioning code by eliminating some special cases. It has also been shown that large sample sizes do not significantly improve performance and thus are not worth using.

The three elements that are used in the sample are the first, middle, and last elements. For instance, with input 8, 1, 4, 9, 6, 3, 5, 2, 7, 0, the leftmost element is 8, the rightmost element is 0, and the center element is 6; thus the pivot would be 6. Note that for already-sorted items, we keep the middle element as pivot, which is the best case.

8.6.4   A Partitioning Strategy

There are several commonly used partitioning strategies, but the one described in this section is known to give good results. We will show the simplest partitioning strategy now, and in Section 8.6.6 we will show the improvements that occur when we use median-of-three pivot selection.

The first step in the partitioning algorithm is to get the pivot element out of the way by swapping it with the last element. The result for our sample input is shown in Figure 8.10. The pivot element is shown in the darkest shade at the end of the array.

Step 1: Swap the pivot with the element at the end.

For now we will assume that all the elements are distinct. Later we will worry about what to do in the presence of duplicates. As a limiting case, our algorithm must work properly when *all* the elements are identical.

Using our partitioning strategy, we want to move all the small elements to the left part of the array and all the large elements to the right part. *Small* and *large* are relative to the pivot. In our figures, white cells are cells that we know are correctly placed. The cells that are almost as dark as the pivot are not known to be correctly placed. We will search from left to right looking for a large element. To do this we will use a counter i, initialized at position Low. We will also search from right to left looking for a small element. We do this by using a counter j, initialized to start at High-1. Figure 8.11 shows that our search for a large element stops at 8 and the search for a small element stops at 2. These cells have been lightly shaded. Notice that by skipping past 7, we know that 7 is not small and thus is correctly placed. Thus it is colored white. Now we have a large element, 8, on the left side of the array and a small element, 2, on the right side of the array. We must swap these two elements to correctly place them, as shown in Figure 8.12.

Step 2: Run i from left to right, j from right to left. When i sees a large element, stop. When j sees a small element, stop. If i and j have not crossed, swap their items and continue. Otherwise, stop this loop.

Figure 8.10   Partitioning algorithm: pivot element 6 is placed at the end

8	1	4	9	0	3	5	2	7	6

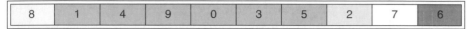

Figure 8.11 Partitioning algorithm: `i` stops at large element 8; `j` stops at small element 2

2	1	4	9	0	3	5	8	7	6

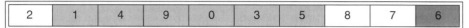

Figure 8.12 Partitioning algorithm: out-of-order elements 8 and 2 are swapped

2	1	4	9	0	3	5	8	7	6

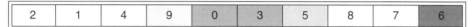

Figure 8.13 Partitioning algorithm: `i` stops at large element 9; `j` stops at small element 5

2	1	4	5	0	3	9	8	7	6

Figure 8.14 Partitioning algorithm: out-of-order elements 9 and 5 are swapped

2	1	4	5	0	3	9	8	7	6

Figure 8.15 Partitioning algorithm: `i` stops at large element 9; `j` stops at small element 3

2	1	4	5	0	3	6	8	7	9

Figure 8.16 Partitioning algorithm: swap pivot and element in position `i`

As the algorithm continues, `i` stops at large element 9 and `j` stops at small element 5. Once again, elements that `i` and `j` skip during the scan are guaranteed to be correctly placed. Figure 8.13 shows the result: The ends of the array (not counting the pivot) become filled with correctly placed elements.

We now swap the elements that `i` and `j` are indexing, as shown in Figure 8.14. The scan continues with `i` stopping at large element 9 and `j` stopping at small element 3. However, at this point i and j have crossed positions in the array. Consequently, a swap would be useless. We can see this by looking at Figure 8.15, which shows that the item being accessed by j is already correctly placed and should not move.

Figure 8.15 shows that all but two items are correctly placed. Wouldn't it be nice if we could just swap them and be done? After some reflection we can see that, indeed, all we need to do is swap the element in position i and the element in the last cell (the pivot). This is shown in Figure 8.16. The element that i is indexing was clearly large, so moving it to the last position is fine.

Step 3: Swap the element in position i with the pivot.

Notice that the partitioning algorithm requires no extra memory and that each element is compared exactly once with the pivot. When the code is written, this translates to a very tight inner loop.

8.6.5 Keys Equal to the Pivot

One important detail that we must consider is how to handle keys that are equal to the pivot. The questions are whether or not i should stop when it sees a key equal to the pivot, and whether or not j should stop when it sees a key equal to the pivot. i and j should do the same thing; otherwise, the partitioning step is biased. For instance, if i stops and j does not, then all keys that are equal to the pivot wind up on the right.

i and j must stop when they see an item equal to the pivot to guarantee good performance.

Let us consider the case in which all elements in the array are identical. If both i and j stop, there will be many swaps between identical elements. Although this seems useless, the positive effect is that i and j cross in the middle, so when the pivot is replaced, the partition creates two nearly equal subsets. Thus the best case analysis applies, and the running time is $O(N \log N)$.

If neither i nor j stops, then i winds up at the last position (assuming of course that it does stop at the boundary), and no swaps are performed. This seems great until we realize that the pivot will then be placed as the last element because that is the last cell that i touches. The result is wildly uneven subsets and a running time that matches the worst-case bound of $O(N^2)$. The effect is the same as using the first element as a pivot for presorted input. It takes quadratic time to do nothing.

We can conclude that it is better to do the unnecessary swaps and create even subsets than to risk wildly uneven subsets. Therefore, we will have both i and j stop if they encounter an element equal to the pivot. This turns out to be the only one of the four possibilities that does not take quadratic time for this input.

At first glance it may seem that worrying about an array of identical elements is silly. After all, why would anyone want to sort 5000 identical elements? However, recall that quicksort is recursive. Suppose there are 100,000 elements, of which 5000 are identical. Eventually quicksort could make the recursive call on only the 5000 identical elements. Then it really will be important to make sure that 5000 identical elements can be sorted efficiently.

Figure 8.17   Original array

Figure 8.18   Result of sorting three elements (first, middle, and last)

Figure 8.19   Result of swapping the pivot with next to last element

8.6.6   Median-of-Three Partitioning

When we do median-of-three partitioning, we can do a simple optimization that saves a few comparisons and also greatly simplifies the code. Figure 8.17 shows the original array.

Computing the median of three involves sorting three elements. Because of this, we can give the partitioning step a head start and also never worry about running off the end of the array.

Median-of-three partitioning requires that we find the median of the first, middle, and last elements. The easiest way to do this is to sort them in the array. The result is shown in Figure 8.18. Notice the resulting shading: The element that winds up in the first position is guaranteed to be smaller than (or equal to) the pivot, and the element in the last position is larger than (or equal to) the pivot. This tells us four things:

- We should not swap the pivot with the element in the last position. Instead, we should swap it with the element in the next to last position. This is shown in Figure 8.19.
- We can start i at Low+1 and j at High-2.
- We are guaranteed that, whenever i searches for a large element, it will stop because in the worst case it will encounter the pivot (and we stop on equality).
- We are guaranteed that, whenever j searches for a small element, it will stop because in the worst case it will encounter the first element (and we stop on equality).

All of these optimizations will be incorporated into the final C++ code.

8.6.7   Small Arrays

Our final optimization concerns small arrays. Is it worth using a high-powered routine like quicksort when there are only ten elements to sort? The answer is of course not. A simple routine, such as the insertion sort, will probably be faster for small arrays. The recursive nature of quicksort tells us that we will generate many calls that have only small subsets. Thus it is worthwhile to test the size of the subset. If it is smaller than some cutoff, we apply insertion sort; otherwise, we do the quicksort.

Sort ten or fewer items by insertion sort. Place this test in the recursive quicksort routine.

It has been shown that a good cutoff is ten elements, although any cutoff between 5 and 20 is likely to produce similar results. The actual best cutoff is machine dependent. Using a cutoff saves us from degenerate cases. For example, finding the median of three elements does not make much sense when there are not three elements.

In the past, it was thought that an even better alternative was to leave the array slightly unsorted by doing absolutely nothing when the subset size was below the cutoff. Because the insertion sort is so efficient for nearly sorted files, we could show mathematically that running a final insertion sort to clean up the array was faster than running all the smaller insertion sorts. The savings was roughly the overhead of the insertion sort function calls.

Now function calls are not as expensive as they used to be, and furthermore a second scan of the array for the insertion sort is expensive. Because of a technique called *caching*, we are better off doing the insertion sort on the small files. Localized memory accesses are faster than nonlocalized accesses. On many machines, touching memory twice in one scan is faster than touching memory once in each of two separate scans.

8.6.8   C++ Quicksort Routine

The actual implementation of quicksort is shown in Figure 8.20. The visible Quicksort, declared at lines 45 to 50, is merely a driver that calls the recursive Quicksort. Thus we only discuss the implementation of the recursive Quicksort.

We use a driver to set things up.

At line 8 we test for small subsets and call the insertion sort when the problem instance is below some specified value given by the external object Cutoff. Otherwise, we proceed with the recursive procedure. Lines 13 to 19 sort the low, middle, and high elements in place. In keeping with our previous discussion, the middle element is used as the pivot and is swapped with the element in the next to last position at lines 22 and 23. We then do the partitioning phase. We initialize the counters i and j to 1 past their true initial values because the prefix increment and decrement operators will immediately adjust them before the array accesses at lines 29 and 31. When the first while loop at line 29 exits, i will be indexing an element that is greater than or possibly equal to the pivot. Likewise, when the second loop ends, j will be indexing an element that is less than or possibly equal to the pivot. If i and j have not crossed, these elements are swapped and we continue scanning; otherwise, the scan is terminated and the pivot is restored at line 38. The sort is finished by making the two recursive calls at lines 40 and 41.

The inner loop of quicksort is very tight.

As we can see, the fundamental operations occur at lines 29 through 34. The scans consist of simple operations: increments, array accesses, and simple comparisons. This accounts for the *quick* in *quicksort*. To ensure that the inner loops are efficient, we want to make sure that the Swap at line 34 comprises the three assignments that we expect and does not incur the overhead of a function call. Thus we declare that the Swap routine is an inline function, or in some cases, we write the three assignments explicitly (for example, if the compiler exercises its right to ignore the inline request).

Quicksort is a classic example of using an analysis to guide the program implementation.

Although the code looks straightforward now, it is important to keep in mind that this is only because of the analysis we performed prior to coding. Additionally, there are still some traps lurking (see Exercise 8.13).

8.7   Quickselect

Selection is finding the kth smallest element of an array.

A problem closely related to sorting is *selection*: given an array of N items, finding the kth smallest. An important special case is finding the median, or the $N/2$th smallest element. Obviously, we can sort the items, but we would hope that, since selection requests less information than sorting, selection would be a faster process. It turns out that this is true. By making a small change to quicksort, we can solve the selection problem in linear time, on average. We call this algorithm *quickselect*. The steps for *Quickselect(S, k)* are as follows:

1. If the number of elements in S is 1, then presumably k is also 1, and we can return the single element in S.
2. Pick any element v in S. This is the pivot.
3. *Partition $S - \{v\}$ into L and R*, exactly as was done for quicksort.
4. If k is less than or equal to the number of elements in L, then the item we are searching for must be in L. Call *Quickselect(L, k)* recursively. Otherwise, if k is exactly equal to one more than the number of items in L, then the pivot is the kth smallest element, and we can return it as the answer. Otherwise, the *kth* smallest element lies in R, and it is the $(k - |L| - 1)$th smallest element in R. Again, we can make a recursive call and return the result.

Quickselect is used to perform a selection. It is similar to quicksort but makes only one recursive call. The average running time is linear.

Quickselect makes only one recursive call compared to quicksort's two. The worst case of quickselect is identical to that of quicksort and is quadratic: when one of the recursive calls is on an empty set. In such cases quickselect does not save much. We can show that the average time is linear, however, by using an analysis that is similar to quicksort's (see Exercise 8.9).

```
1   // Quicksort: sort first N items in array A
2   // Etype: must have copy constructor, operator=, and operator<
3
4   template <class Etype>
5   void
6   Quicksort( Etype A[ ], int Low, int High )
7   {
8       if( Low + Cutoff > High )
9           InsertionSort( &A[ Low ], High - Low + 1 );
10      else
11      {
12              // Sort Low, Middle, High
13          int Middle = ( Low + High ) / 2;
14          if( A[ Middle ] < A[ Low ] )
15              Swap( A[ Low ], A[ Middle ] );
16          if( A[ High ] < A[ Low ] )
17              Swap( A[ Low ], A[ High ] );
18          if( A[ High ] < A[ Middle ] )
19              Swap( A[ Middle ], A[ High ] );
20
21              // Place Pivot at Position High - 1
22          Etype Pivot = A[ Middle ];
23          Swap( A[ Middle ], A[ High - 1 ] );
24
25              // Begin Partitioning
26          int i, j;
27          for( i = Low, j = High - 1; ; )
28          {
29              while( A[ ++i ] < Pivot )
30                  ;
31              while( Pivot < A[ --j ] )
32                  ;
33              if( i < j )
34                  Swap( A[ i ], A[ j ] );
35              else
36                  break;
37          }
38          Swap( A[ i ], A[ High - 1 ] );   // Restore pivot
39
40          Quicksort( A, Low, i - 1 );      // Sort small elements
41          Quicksort( A, i + 1, High );     // Sort large elements
42      }
43  }
44
45  template <class Etype>
46  void
47  Quicksort( int A[ ], int N )
48  {
49          Quicksort( A, 0, N - 1 );
50  }
```

Figure 8.20   Quicksort with median-of-three partitioning and cutoff for
small files

```
1  // Quickselect: find Kth smallest of first N items in array A
2  // recursive routine finds Kth smallest in A[Low..High]
3  // Etype: must have copy constructor, operator=, and operator<
4  // Nonrecursive driver is omitted
5
6  template <class Etype>
7  void
8  QuickSelect( Etype A[ ], int Low, int High, int k )
9  {
10     if( Low + Cutoff > High )
11         InsertionSort( &A[ Low ], High - Low + 1 );
12     else
13     {
14             // Sort Low, Middle, High
15         int Middle = ( Low + High ) / 2;
16         if( A[ Middle ] < A[ Low ] )
17             Swap( A[ Low ], A[ Middle ] );
18         if( A[ High ] < A[ Low ] )
19             Swap( A[ Low ], A[ High ] );
20         if( A[ High ] < A[ Middle ] )
21             Swap( A[ Middle ], A[ High ] );
22
23             // Place Pivot at Position High - 1
24         Etype Pivot = A[ Middle ];
25         Swap( A[ Middle ], A[ High - 1 ] )
26
27             // Begin Partitioning
28         int i, j;
29         for( i = Low, j = High - 1; ; )
30         {
31             while( A[ ++i ] < Pivot )
32                 ;
33             while( Pivot < A[ --j ] )
34                 ;
35             if( i < j )
36                 Swap( A[ i ], A[ j ] );
37             else
38                 break;
39         }
40
41         Swap( A[ i ], A[ High - 1 ] );    // Restore pivot
42
43             // Recurse: only this part changes
44         if( k < i )
45             QuickSelect( A, Low, i - 1, k );
46         else if ( k > i )
47             QuickSelect( A, i + 1, High , k );
48     }
49 }
```

Figure 8.21   Quickselect with median-of-three partitioning and cutoff for small files

The implementation of quickselect is even simpler than our abstract description might imply. A complete implementation is shown in Figure 8.21. Except for the extra parameter (k) and the recursive calls, the algorithm is identical to quicksort. When it terminates, the kth smallest element is in its correct position in the array. Note that since the array begins at index 0, the fourth smallest element is in position three, which destroys the original ordering. If this situation is undesirable, we can have the driver routine pass a copy of the array instead.

Using median-of-three partitioning makes the chance of the worst case occurring almost negligible. By carefully choosing the pivot, it can be shown that the worst case never occurs and that the running time is linear even in the worst-case scenario. The resulting algorithm is entirely of theoretical interest, however, because the constant that the Big-Oh notation hides is much larger than the constant seen in the normal median-of-three implementation.

The linear worst-case algorithm is a classic result even though it is impractical.

8.8   A Lower Bound for Sorting

Although we have $O(N \log N)$ algorithms for sorting, it is not clear that this is as good as we can do. In this section we prove that any algorithm for sorting that uses only comparisons requires $\Omega(N \log N)$ comparisons (and hence time) in the worst case. Let us explain what this means *any algorithm that sorts by using element comparisons must use at least roughly N log N comparisons for some input sequence.* A similar technique can be used to show that this is also true on average.

Any comparison-based sorting algorithm must use roughly N log N comparisons on average and in the worst case.

Must every sorting algorithm work by using comparisons? The answer is no, but algorithms that do not use general comparisons are likely to work only for restricted types, such as integers. Although we may often need to sort only integers (see Exercise 8.14), a general-purpose sorting algorithm cannot make such sweeping assumptions about its input. It may only assume the given, namely that since the items need to be sorted, we can assume that any two items can be compared.

The proofs are abstract; we show the worst-case lower bound.

Let us now prove one of the most fundamental theorems in computer science. Recall first that the product of the first N positive integers is $N!$. The proof is an existence proof, which is somewhat abstract. It shows that some bad input must always exist.

Proof   *We may regard the possible inputs as any of the permutations of 1, 2, ..., N.*
This is because only the relative order of the input items matters, not their
actual values. Thus the number of possible inputs is the number of different
arrangements of N items, which is exactly N!. Let P_i be the number of per-
mutations that are consistent with the results after the algorithm has pro-
cessed i comparisons. Let F be the number of comparisons processed when
the sort terminates. We know the following: (a) $P_0 = N!$, because all per-
mutations are possible before the first comparison; (b) $P_F = 1$, because if
more than one permutation was possible, the algorithm could not terminate
with confidence that it produced the correct output; (c) there exists a permu-
tation such that $P_i \geq P_{i-1}/2$, because after a comparison, each permuta-
tion goes into one of two groups: the still-possible group and the no-longer-
possible group. The larger of these groups has at least half the permuta-
tions, and there is at least one permutation for which we can apply this
logic throughout the comparison sequence. The action of a sorting algo-
rithm is thus to go from the state P_0, in which all N! permutations are possi-
ble, to the final state P_F, in which only one permutation is possible, with the
restriction that there exists an input such that in each comparison, only half
of the permutations can be eliminated. By the halving principle, we know
that at least $\lceil \log(N!) \rceil$ comparisons are required for that input.

How large is $\lceil \log(N!) \rceil$? It is approximately $N \log N - 1.44N$.

8.9   Indirect Sorting

Although we can use templates to write sorting routines that are easily reused for
different objects, we have thus far ignored an important consideration. Recall
that large objects are very expensive to copy. Thus when writing templated routines we always pass an unknown `Etype` object by reference (or constant reference). Sorting presents a different problem: Sorting large structures is
algorithmically identical to sorting integers, but the data movement is extremely
expensive. Changes may need to be made to avoid the overhead of unnecessary
copies.

```
 1 struct Block
 2 {
 3     ...              // Data objects that use 508 bytes
 4     int Key;     // 4 more bytes.
 5
 6     int operator< ( const Block & Rhs ) const
 7             { return Key < Rhs.Key; }
 8 };
 9
10 const int NumItems = 2000;
11
12 main( )
13 {
14     Block P[ NumItems ];
15
16     ...              // Read the array P
17     Shellsort( P, NumItems );
18     ...              // Process the sorted array P
19 }
```

Figure 8.22   Shellsort is slow because of excessive data movement

To be more concrete, consider the code fragment in Figure 8.22. The Block object is to be sorted on the basis of a single integer Key. Consequently, we only need to provide a comparison member function to be able to use any of our templated sorting routines. We will use Shellsort because it is the simplest of the efficient algorithms. The objects are large, so the cost to move them dominates the algorithm's running time. While it takes only 23 milliseconds to Shellsort 2000 integers, it takes roughly 725 milliseconds to Shellsort 2000 Block objects. When we use a profiler, we see the problem: Almost all of the time is spent performing roughly 47,000 Block copies in an average run of Shellsort. Of course, since elements have to be rearranged, there must be some copies, but since there are only 2000 elements, we should expect to get by with much less than 47,000 copies. If we can reduce the number of copies (that is, assignments of Etype objects in Shellsort), we would expect a significant improvement in the running time for large objects.

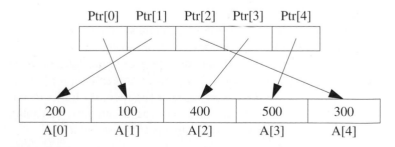

Figure 8.23   Using an array of pointers to sort

8.9.1   Using Pointers to Reduce Etype Copies to 2N

In this section we perform an *indirect sort* by using pointers. We will have an array of pointers to Etype, which we will name Ptr. Initially, each Ptr[i] will point at A[i]. All comparisons will be done through the Ptr array. Movement of items will be simulated by movement of the pointers in the Ptr array. The result, as shown in Figure 8.23, is that after the Shellsort of pointers, Ptr[0] will point at the smallest Etype in A (in this case A[1]), Ptr[1] will point at the next smallest, and so on. Of course, the array of pointers is merely an internal object. We must still rearrange the items in A. This can be done by declaring an array ACopy of Etype. We can write out the correct sorted order to ACopy by scanning through the array of pointers. We then copy back from ACopy to A.

This strategy is implemented in Figure 8.24. Let us first examine the declarations. Line 7 declares the variable Tmp. The basic operation of Shellsort is to rearrange pointers, so Tmp is a pointer to an Etype, just like Ptr[i]. We use the Vector class from Section 3.3.3 to store the Ptr and ACopy arrays.

The rest of the algorithm closely follows our description. At lines 11 and 12 we initialize the *i*th pointer to point at the *i*th Etype object. Lines 14 to 24 perform Shellsort using Ptr instead of A. Notice that at line 21 we compare dereferenced pointers; if we forget the *, we are merely comparing addresses and not Etype objects.

When we come to line 26, we have the situation shown in Figure 8.23. We can form a sorted Vector in ACopy by sequentially copying the Etypes that are referenced by Ptr[j]. We can then copy this Vector into A, as shown at lines 29 and 30.

On our machine, when instantiated with Block, this algorithm runs in 150 milliseconds, which is a large reduction from the previous case. The reason is that all Etype copies are now performed at lines 27 and 30 instead of during the actual Shellsort. It is very easy to see that this means that a total of only 2*N* Etype copies are done, which in our case is only 4000.

> Large objects are expensive to move. *Indirect sorting* constructs an array of pointers and moves the pointers during most of the algorithm. At the end of the algorithm, the array of large objects is then rearranged to match the pointers.

> The simplest rearrangement strategy uses an extra array of large objects.

8.9.2   Avoiding the Extra Array

The algorithm in Figure 8.24, although improved from the nonpointer implementation in Figure 8.6, has a potentially important problem. By using the Vector ACopy, we have doubled the space requirement. We can assume that *N* is large (otherwise, we would use an insertion sort) and that the size of an Etype object is large (otherwise we would not bother using a pointer implementation). Thus we can reasonably expect that we are operating near the memory limits of our machine. Although we can expect to use an extra Vector of integers, we cannot necessarily expect an extra Vector of Etype objects to be available.

> A more complex strategy performs the rearrangement in place and typically moves each object only once.

```
1  template <class Etype>           // Indirect Shellsort
2  void                            // Uses only 2N Etype copies
3  Shellsort( Etype A[ ], int N )
4  {
5    try
6    {
7      Etype *Tmp;
8      Vector<Etype *>  Ptr ( N ); // Vector of pointers to Etype
9      Vector<Etype>  ACopy ( N ); // The sorted vector
10
11     for( int i = 0; i < N; i++ )
12         Ptr[ i ] = &A[ i ];
13
14     for( int Gap = N / 2; Gap > 0;
15           Gap = Gap == 2 ? 1 : ( int ) ( Gap / 2.2 ) )
16         for( int i = Gap; i < N; i++ )
17         {
18             Tmp = Ptr[ i ];
19             int j = i;
20
21             for( ; j >= Gap && *Tmp < *Ptr[ j - Gap ]; j -= Gap )
22                 Ptr[ j ] = Ptr[ j - Gap ];
23             Ptr[ j ] = Tmp;
24         }
25
26     for( int j = 0; j < N; j++ )      // Make sorted array
27         ACopy[ j ] = *Ptr[ j ];
28
29     for( int k = 0; k < N; k++ )      // Copy it back
30         A[ k ] = ACopy[ k ];
31   }
32
33   catch( ... )
34   {
35     cerr << "Out of memory!! Sort fails." << endl;
36   }
37 }
```

Figure 8.24   Shellsort with pointers and only 2N Etype copies

Loc[0]	Loc[1]	Loc[2]	Loc[3]	Loc[4]
1	0	4	2	3

200	100	400	500	300
A[0]	A[1]	A[2]	A[3]	A[4]

Figure 8.25   Data structure used for in-place rearrangement

A second consequence of our decision to use ACopy is that a total of 2*N* Etype copies are used. Although this is an improvement over the original algorithm, we will show how we can improve the algorithm even more by avoiding the extra copy. In particular, we will never use more than $3N/2$ Etype copies, and on almost all inputs we will use only a few more than *N*. Not only will we save space, but also we will save time. Our modified routine will rearrange A without using an extra Vector of Etype objects. Before we step through the code, let us get a general idea of what needs to be done. Surprisingly, we have already done it before.

Figure 8.25 shows the same input as Figure 8.23. Instead of showing the Ptr array, we are showing what we shall denote as the Loc array. Loc[i] tells the index where to find the element that should be in A[i]. For instance, Loc[2] is 4 because the element that *should* be in A[2] is currently in A[4]. When Loc[i]==i, the *i*th element is correctly placed. Otherwise, the Loc array tells us exactly what elements need to be moved where. To get an idea of what we have to do, let us start with $i = 2$. Since Loc[2] is 4, we know we need to move A[4] to A[2]. First we must save A[2], or we will not be able to place it correctly. We then have Tmp=A[2], and then A[2]=A[4]. When A[4] has been moved to A[2], we can move something into A[4], which is essentially vacant. By examining Loc[4], we see that the correct statement is A[4]=A[3]. Now we need to move something into A[3]. Since Loc[3] is 2, we know that we want to move A[2] there. But A[2] has been overwritten at the start of this rearrangement; since its original value is in Tmp, we finish with Loc[3]=Tmp. This process shows that, by starting with i equal to 2 and following the Loc array, we form a cyclic sequence 2,4,3,2, which corresponds to

```
Tmp     = A[ 2 ];
A[ 2 ] = A[ 4 ];
A[ 4 ] = A[ 3 ];
A[ 3 ] = Tmp;
```

We have rearranged three elements using only four Etype copies and one extra Etype of storage. Actually we have already seen this method before. The innermost loop of the insertion sort saves the current element A[i] in a Tmp object. We then assign A[j]=A[j-1], to move lots of elements over one to the right. Finally, we assign A[j]=Tmp to place the original element. We are doing exactly the same thing here, except that instead of sliding over by one, we are using Loc to guide how the rearrangement is performed.

The algorithm is easily translated into C++ code. At lines 28 and 29 of Figure 8.26, we compute the Loc array. At line 32 we search sequentially for a position i that contains the wrong element. When we find such an i, we do the sequence of assignments that we described above. We also update the Loc array when we assign to A[j]. The order of lines 40, 41, and the update in the for loop are crucial because the value in Loc[j] indicates the location of the next position to examine. We have to save it before updating it.

```
1  template <class Etype>          // Indirect Shellsort
2  void                            // Avoids extra array
3  Shellsort( Etype A[ ], int N )
4  {
5    try
6    {
7      Etype *Tmp, ShuffleTmp;
8      Vector<Etype *> Ptr( N );  // Array of pointers to Etype
9      Vector<int>     Loc( N );  // Array w/correct final spots
10     int i;
11
12     for( i = 0; i < N; i++ )
13         Ptr[ i ] = &A[ i ];
14
15     for( int Gap = N / 2; Gap > 0;
16             Gap = Gap == 2 ? 1 : ( int ) ( Gap / 2.2 ) )
17         for( i = Gap; i < N; i++ )
18         {
19             Tmp = Ptr[ i ];
20             int j = i;
21
22             for( ; j >= Gap && *Tmp < *Ptr[ j - Gap ]; j -= Gap )
23                 Ptr[ j ] = Ptr[ j - Gap ];
24             Ptr[ j ] = Tmp;
25         }
26
27         // Determine correct final positions
28     for( i = 0; i < N; i++ )
29         Loc[ i ] = Ptr[ i ] - A;
30
31         // Shuffle it back
32     for( i = 0; i < N; i++ )
33         if( Loc[ i ] != i )
34         {
35             int j = i, NextJ;
36
37             for( ShuffleTmp=A[ i ]; Loc[ j ] != i; j = NextJ )
38             {
39                 A[ j ] = A[ Loc[ j ] ];
40                 NextJ = Loc[ j ];
41                 Loc[ j ] = j;
42             }
43             A[ j ] = ShuffleTmp;
44             Loc[ j ] = j;
45         }
46   }
47   catch( ... )
48   {
49     cerr << "Out of memory!! Sort fails" << endl;
50   }
51 }
```

Figure 8.26   Shellsort with pointers but no extra `Etype` array

The analysis requires counting the number of cycles in the permutations.

In general, what happens is that we have a collection of cycles that are rearranged. In Figure 8.25 there are two cycles: One involves two elements, and the other involves three. Rearranging a cycle of length L uses $L + 1$ `Etype` copies, as we have seen. Cycles of length 1 represent elements that are already correctly placed and thus use no copies. This improves the previous algorithm because now an array that is already sorted does not incur any `Etype` copies.

For a given array of N elements, let C_L be the number of cycles of length L. The total number of `Etype` copies, M, is given by

$$M = N - C_1 + (C_2 + C_3 + \ldots + C_N) \tag{8.12}$$

The best thing that can happen is that there are no `Etype` copies because there are N cycles of length 1 (that is, every element is correctly placed). The worst thing that can happen is that we have $N/2$ cycles of length 2, in which case Equation 8.12 tells us that $M = 3N/2$ `Etype` copies are performed. This can happen if the input is 2, 1, 4, 3, 6, 5, and so on. What is the expected value of M? We only need to compute the expected value of C_L for each L (see Exercise 8.12 which asks you to argue that this value is $1/L$). This gives the value of M:

$$M = N - 1 + \frac{1}{2} + \frac{1}{3} + \ldots + \frac{1}{N}$$

$$= N - 2 + 1 + \frac{1}{2} + \frac{1}{3} + \ldots + \frac{1}{N}$$

$$= N - 2 + H_N$$

The result obtained by using a known estimate for the term H_N (see Theorem) is that the average number of `Etype` copies is given by $N + \ln N - 1.423$. A random arrangement of the input yields only a very small number of cycles. In our case we observed 2006 `Etype` copies, averaged over 10 trials, which is in strong agreement with the theoretical answer claimed above. The sorting time was reduced to only 80 milliseconds, which is only a few times more than the ideal of sorting integers.

Summary

For most general internal sorting applications, either an insertion sort, Shellsort, or quicksort is the method of choice, and the decision of which to use depends on the size of the input.

Insertion sort is appropriate for very small amounts of input. Shellsort is a good choice for sorting moderate amounts of input. With a proper increment sequence, it gives excellent performance using only a few lines of code. Quicksort gives the best performance but is trickier to code. Asymptotically, it has almost certain $O(N \log N)$ performance with a careful implementation, and we showed that this is essentially as good as we can expect. In Section 20.5 we will see another popular internal sort, heapsort.

When sorting large objects, data movement must be minimized. We showed how to use pointers to do almost no extra moves. When sorting input that does not fit entirely in main memory, different techniques are needed. The general technique is discussed in Section 20.6. It makes use of the merge algorithm discussed in Section 8.5.

To test and compare the merits of the various sorting algorithms, we need to be able to generate random inputs. Randomness is an important topic in general and is discussed in the next chapter.

Objects of the Game

comparison-based sorting algorithms Make ordering decisions only on the basis of comparisons. (265)

diminishing gap sort Another name for Shellsort. (269)

indirect sorting Large objects are expensive to move. Indirect sorting constructs an array of pointers and moves the pointers during most of the algorithm. At the end of the algorithm, the array of large objects is then rearranged to match the pointers. (294)

inversion Measures unsortedness. (266)

lower-bound proof for sorting Confirms that any comparison-based sorting algorithm must use at least roughly $N \log N$ comparisons on the average and in the worst case. (291)

median-of-three partitioning The median of the first, middle, and last elements is used as the pivot. This simplifies the partitioning stage of quicksort. (282)

mergesort Uses divide and conquer to obtain an $O(N \log N)$ sort. (272)

partition The partition step of quicksort places every element except the pivot in one of two groups: One comprises elements that are smaller than the pivot, the other comprises elements that are larger than the pivot. (277)

pivot For quicksort, an element that splits the array into two groups: smaller than the pivot and those larger than the pivot. (276)

quickselect Algorithm used to perform a selection. It is similar to quicksort but makes only one recursive call. The average running time is linear. (288)

quicksort A fast divide-and-conquer algorithm when properly implemented. In practice it is the fastest comparison-based sorting algorithm. (276)

selection Finding the kth smallest element of an array. (288)

Shellsort A subquadratic algorithm that works well in practice and is simple to code. The performance of Shellsort is highly dependent on the increment sequence and requires a challenging (and not completely resolved) analysis. (268)

Common Errors

1. The sorts coded in this chapter begin at array position 0. The exercises ask you to make the sorts more general so they work with a `Vector` class.
2. Using the wrong increment sequence for Shellsort is a common error. Make sure the increment sequence terminates with 1, and avoid sequences that are known to give poor performance.
3. Quicksort has a host of traps. The most common errors deal with sorted inputs, duplicate elements, and degenerate partitions.
4. For small inputs an insertion sort is appropriate. But it is wrong to use it for large inputs.

On the Internet

We provide three new sorts plus an indirect Shellsort and an implementation of quickselect. We have not provided any `mains`. The files are

Shellsrt.cpp The Shellsort implementation in Figure 8.6
Mergesrt.cpp The mergesort implementation in Figure 8.7 and Figure 8.8
Quicksrt.cpp The quicksort implementation in Figure 8.20
Select.cpp The quickselect implementation in Figure 8.21
Indirect.cpp The indirect Shellsort in Figure 8.26

Exercises

In Short

8.1. Sort the sequence 8, 1, 4, 1, 5, 9, 2, 6, 5 using

    a. Insertion sort
    b. Shellsort, using the increments { 1, 3, 5 }
    c. Mergesort
    d. Quicksort, using the middle element as pivot and no cutoff (show all steps)
    e. Quicksort, using median-of-three pivot selection and a cutoff of three.

8.2. A sorting algorithm is *stable* if elements with equal keys are left in the same order as they occur in the input. Which of the sorting algorithms in this chapter are stable and which are not? Why?

8.3. Explain why the elaborate quicksort in the text is better than randomly permuting the input and choosing the middle element as pivot.

In Theory

8.4.   When all keys are equal, what is the running time of

    a. Insertion sort

    b. Shellsort

    c. Mergesort

    d. Quicksort

8.5.   When the input is already sorted, what is the running time of

    a. Insertion sort

    b. Shellsort

    c. Mergesort

    d. Quicksort

8.6.   When the input is already sorted in reverse order, what is the running time of

    a. Insertion sort

    b. Shellsort

    c. Mergesort

    d. Quicksort

8.7.   Suppose we exchange elements `A[i]` and `A[i+k]`, which were originally out of order. Prove that at least 1 and at most $2k - 1$ inversions are removed.

8.8.   Construct a worst-case input for quicksort with

    a. The middle element as pivot

    b. Median-of-three pivot partitioning

8.9.   Show that the quickselect has linear average performance. Do this by solving Equation 8.5 with the constant 2 replaced by 1.

8.10.   Using Stirling's formula, $N! \geq (N/e)^N \sqrt{2\pi N}$, derive an estimate for $\log(N!)$.

8.11.   Prove that any comparison-based algorithm used to sort four elements requires at least five comparisons for some input. Then show that an algorithm that sorts four elements using at most five comparisons does indeed exist.

8.12.   Let p be any position in the array containing N elements. For the rearrangement procedure shown in Section 8.9.2

    a. Show that the probability that p is in a cycle of length 1 is $1/N$.

b. Show that the probability that p is in a cycle of length 2 is also $1/N$.

c. Show that the probability that p is in a cycle of any length $1 \le L \le N$ is $1/N$.

d. Based on part c, deduce that the expected number of cycles of length L is $1/L$. *Hint*: Each element contributes $1/N$ to the number of cycles of length L, but a simple addition overcounts cycles.

In Practice

8.13. A student alters the Quicksort routine in Figure 8.20 by making the changes to lines 27 to 32 shown below. Is the result equivalent to the original routine?

```
for( i = Low + 1, j = High - 2; ; )
{
    while( A[ i ] < Pivot )
        i++;
    while( Pivot < A[ j ] )
        j--;
```

8.14. If we know more information about the items being sorted, we can sort them in linear time. Show that a collection of N 16-bit integers can be sorted in $O(N)$ time. *Hint*: Maintain an array indexed from 0 to 65,535.

8.15. Suppose we want to add a Sort member function to the template class Vector from Section 3.3.3. One solution is to call Quicksort with the internal data.

a. Implement this idea.

b. Would the Sort member function be inherited by the BoundedVector class shown in Section 4.2?

8.16. An alternative to Exercise 8.15 is to implement Quicksort to accept a Vector (reference) parameter.

a. Implement this idea.

b. If we want to disable the range checks, what are our options?

c. Can a BoundedVector be passed to this Quicksort routine?

d. Compare the merits of this solution with the solution in Exercise 8.15.

8.17. We are given an array that contains N numbers. We want to determine if there are two numbers whose sum equals a given number K. For instance, if the input is 8, 4, 1, 6, and K is 10, then the answer is yes (4 and 6). A number may be used twice.

a. Give an $O(N^2)$ algorithm to solve this problem.

b. Give an $O(N \log N)$ algorithm to solve this problem. *Hint*: Sort the items first. After that is done, you can solve the problem in linear time.

c. Code both solutions and compare the running times of your algorithms.

8.18. Repeat Exercise 8.17 for four numbers. Try to design an $O(N^2 \log N)$ algorithm. *Hint*: Compute all possible sums of two elements. Sort these possible sums. Then proceed as in Exercise 8.17.

8.19. Repeat Exercise 8.17 for three numbers. Try to design an $O(N^2)$ algorithm.

8.20. Exercise 5.26 asked you to find the single integral solution to the equation $A^5 + B^5 + C^5 + D^5 + E^5 = F^5$ that satisfies $0 < A \le B \le C \le D \le E \le F \le N$, where N is 75. Use the ideas explored in Exercise 8.18 to obtain a solution relatively quickly by sorting all possible values of $A^5 + B^5 + C^5$ and $F^5 - (D^5 + E^5)$, and then seeing if a number in the first group is equal to a number in the second group. In terms of N, how much space and time does the algorithm require?

Programming Projects

8.21. Compare the performance of Shellsort with various increment sequences, some of which are shown below. Obtain an average time for some input size N by generating several random sequences of N items. Use the same input for all increment sequences. In a separate test obtain the average number of Etype comparisons and Etype copies. Set the number of repeated trials to be large but doable within one hour of CPU time. The increment sequences are

a. Shell's original sequence (repeatedly divide by 2)

b. Shell's original sequence, adding 1 if the result is nonzero but even

c. Gonnet's sequence shown in the text, in which we repeatedly divide by 2.2

d. Hibbard's increments: 1, 3, 7, ... , $2^k - 1$

e. Knuth's increments: 1, 4, 13, ... , $(3^k + 1)/2$

f. Sedgewick's increments: 1, 5, 19, 41, 109, ... ; each term is of the form either $9 \cdot 4^k - 9 \cdot 2^k + 1$ or $4^k - 3 \cdot 2^k + 1$

8.22. Code both Shellsort and quicksort and compare their running times. Use the best implementations in the text. Run on the following objects:

a. Integers

b. Real numbers of type double

c. Strings (using an efficient `String` class)

8.23. Many implementations of quicksort use pointer hopping as an alternative to the normal array-indexing mechanism. In Section 1.6.4 we argued that pointer hopping is not always a good idea. Implement quicksort using both techniques, and see which is faster, on average, for sorting 100,000 integers.

8.24. Write the indirect version of quicksort using the techniques in Section 8.9.2. Answer the following questions:

a. How large does `Etype` need to be for it to be worthwhile to implement the indirect sort?

b. Compare the performance of an indirect quicksort with an indirect Shellsort for various sizes of `Etype`. Does Shellsort ever win?

8.25. Write a function that removes all duplicates in an array A of N items. Return the number of items that remain in A. Your function must run in $O(N \log N)$ average time (use quicksort as a preprocessing step).

8.26. Exercise 8.2 discussed stable sorting. Write a template function that performs a stable quicksort. To do this, create an array of records; each record contains a data item and its initial position in the array. The array of records is sorted; if two records have identical data items, use the initial position to break the tie. After the array of records is sorted, copy the data items back to the original array and delete the array of records.

8.27. Redo Exercise 8.26 by using pointers to avoid excessive data movements.

8.28. Write a simple sorting utility, `Sort`. The `Sort` command takes a file name as a parameter. The file contains one item per line. By default the lines are considered strings and are sorted by normal lexicographic order (in a case-sensitive manner). Add two options. The `-c` option means that the sort should be case insensitive. The `-n` option means that the lines are to be considered integers for the purpose of the sort.

8.29. Suppose we have K files that are each sorted.

a. Write a function `ReadFile` that reads the elements of a single file into a dynamically allocated queue. A pointer to the dynamically allocated `Queue` is returned. Notice that the elements in the queue will be sorted. The declaration is

```
template <class Etype>
Queue<Etype> *ReadFile( const char *FileName );
```

b. Write a function named `MergeTwo` that takes two pointers to queues and creates a third queue with the merged result. A pointer to the newly created queue is returned, and the originals are destroyed. The declaration is

```
template <class Etype>
Queue<Etype> *MergeTwo( Queue<Etype> *Q1,
                        Queue<Etype> *Q2 )
```

c. The algorithm to produce a sorted file is as follows. Declare (in a template function) a queue of pointers to queues:

```
Queue< Queue<Etype> * > TheItems;
```

Call `ReadFile` for each of the K files, and insert the returned result onto `TheItems`. Then $K-1$ times, remove two elements from `TheItems`, merge the two (pointers to) queues, and `Enqueue` the result. The result is that `TheItems` will contain only a single (pointer to queue) entry that has all the items in sorted order. Write the template function.

d. Write a complete program to implement the merging of K sorted files.

e. Show that declaring `TheItems` as a `Stack<Queue<Etype>*>` can lead to poor performance. *Hint*: Consider the case where the first file has N elements and all the others have one element each.

References

The classic reference for sorting algorithms is [5]. A more recent reference, complete with up-to-date results is [3]. The Shellsort algorithm first appeared in [7]. An empirical study of its running time was done in [8]. Quicksort was discovered by Hoare [4]. The paper also includes the quickselect algorithm and details many of the important implementation issues. A thorough study of the quicksort algorithm, including analysis for the median-of-three variant, appears in [6]. A detailed C implementation that includes additional improvements can be found in [1]. The $\Omega(N \log N)$ lower bound for comparison-based sorting is taken from [2]. The presentation of Shellsort and indirect sorting is adapted from [9].

1. J. L. Bentley and M. D. McElroy, "Engineering a Sort Function," *Software-Practice and Experience* **23** (1993), 1249-1265.

2. L. R. Ford and S. M. Johnson, "A Tournament Problem," *American Mathematics Monthly* **66** (1959), 387-389.

3. G. H. Gonnet and R. Baeza-Yates, *Handbook of Algorithms and Data Structures*, 2d ed., Addison-Wesley, Reading, MA, 1991.

4. C. A. R. Hoare, "Quicksort," *Computer Journal* **5** (1962), 10-15.

5. D. E. Knuth, *The Art of Computer Programming, Volume 3: Sorting and Searching*, Addison-Wesley, Reading, MA, 1973.

6. R. Sedgewick, *Quicksort*, Garland Publishing, New York, 1978. (Originally presented as the author's Ph.D. thesis, Stanford University, 1975).

7. D. L. Shell, "A High-Speed Sorting Procedure," *Communications of the ACM* **2** 7 (1959), 30-32.

8. M. A. Weiss, "Empirical Results on the Running Time of Shellsort," *Computer Journal* **34** (1991), 88-91.

9. M. A. Weiss, *Efficient C Programming: A Practical Approach*, Prentice-Hall, Englewood Cliffs, NJ, 1995.

Chapter 9

Randomization

Many situations in computing require the use of random numbers: Modern cryptography, simulation systems, and, surprisingly, even searching and sorting algorithms rely on random number generators. Yet good random number generators are difficult to implement. This chapter will discuss the generation and use of random numbers.

In this chapter we will see

- how random numbers are generated
- how random permutations are generated
- how random numbers allow us to design efficient algorithms, a general technique known as the *randomized algorithm*

9.1 Why Do We Need Random Numbers?

Random numbers are used in many applications. This section lists a few of the most common ones.

One important application of random numbers is in program testing. Suppose, for example, that we want to test if the sorting algorithms that were written in Chapter 8 work. Of course, we can provide some small amount of input, but if we want to test the algorithms for the large data sets they were designed for, we need lots of input. Providing sorted data as input tests one case, but more convincing tests would be preferable. For instance, we would want to test the program by perhaps running 5000 sorts for inputs of size 1000. This requires writing a routine to generate the test data, which in turn requires the use of random numbers.

Random numbers have many important uses including cryptography, simulation, and program testing.

Continuing this example, once we have random inputs, how do we know if the sorting algorithm works? One test is that the result of the sort is that the array is arranged in nondecreasing order. This can clearly be done in a linear-time sequential scan. But how do we know that the items present after the sort are the

A permutation of 1, 2, ..., N is a sequence of N integers that includes each of 1, 2, ..., N exactly once.

same as those prior to the sort? One method is to fix the items into an arrangement of 1, 2, ..., *N*. In other words, we start with a random *permutation* of the first *N* integers. A permutation of 1, 2, ..., *N* is a sequence of *N* integers that includes each of 1, 2, ..., *N* exactly once. Then, no matter what permutation we start with, the result of the sort will be the sequence 1, 2, ..., *N*; this is easily tested as well.

In addition to helping us generate test data to verify program correctness, random numbers are useful in helping us to compare the performance of various algorithms because, once again, they can be used to provide a host of inputs. Consequently, random numbers are useful in performance comparisons.

Another use of random numbers is in simulations. If we want to know the average time it takes a service system (such as bank tellers) to process a sequence of requests, we can model the system by using a computer. In this computer simulation the request sequence is generated using random numbers.

One more use of random numbers is in the general technique known as the *randomized algorithm*: A random number is used to determine the next step performed in the algorithm. The most common type of randomized algorithm is used when there are several possible alternatives that are more or less indistinguishable. For instance, in a commercial computer chess program, the computer generally chooses its first move randomly rather than playing deterministically (that is, rather than always playing the same move). In this chapter we will look at several problems that can be solved more efficiently by using a randomized algorithm.

9.2 Random Number Generators

Pseudorandom numbers have many properties of random numbers. Good generators are hard to find.

How are random numbers generated? True randomness is impossible to do on a computer since any numbers obtained will depend on the algorithm used to generate them and thus cannot possibly be random. Generally, it is sufficient to produce *pseudorandom numbers*, which are numbers that appear to be random. When we say they appear to be random, we mean that pseudorandom numbers should satisfy many of the properties that random numbers do. This is much easier said than done.

Suppose we only need to simulate a coin flip. One way to do this is to examine the system clock. Presumably the clock maintains the number of seconds in the current time; if this number is even, we can return 0 (for heads), and if it is odd, we can return 1 (for tails). The problem is that this strategy does not work well if we need a sequence of random numbers. One second is a long time, and the clock might not change at all while the program is running. We would expect to generate all 0s or all 1s, which is hardly a random-looking sequence. Even if the time was recorded in units of microseconds, and the program was running by itself, the sequence of numbers that would be generated would be far from random because the time between calls to the generator would be essentially identical on every program invocation.

What we really need is a *sequence* of pseudorandom numbers, a sequence with the same properties as a random sequence. Suppose we want random numbers between 0 and 999, uniformly distributed. In a *uniform distribution*, all numbers in the specified range are equally likely to occur. Other distributions are also widely used. The class interface in Figure 9.1 supports several distributions. We will see that most distributions can be derived from the uniform distribution, so that is the one we consider first. The following properties hold if the sequence 0...999 is a true uniform distribution:

> In a *uniform distribution*, all numbers in the specified range are equally likely to occur.

- The first number is equally likely to be 0, 1, 2, ..., 999.
- The *i*th number is equally likely to be 0, 1, 2, ..., 999.
- The average of all the generated numbers is 499.5.

These properties are not particularly restrictive. For instance we could generate the first number by examining a clock that was accurate to one millisecond and then using the number of milliseconds. We can generate subsequent numbers by adding one to the previous number. Clearly, after 1000 numbers are generated, all the properties above hold. However, stronger properties do not. Some stronger properties that would hold for uniformly distributed random numbers include

> Typically a random sequence, rather than one random number, is required.

- The sum of two consecutive random numbers is equally likely to be even or odd.
- If 1000 numbers are randomly generated, some will be duplicated. Roughly 368 numbers will never appear (see Section 2.3.1).

Our numbers do not satisfy these properties. Consecutive numbers always sum to an odd number, and our sequence is duplicate-free. We say then that our simple pseudorandom number generator has failed two statistical tests. All pseudorandom number generators fail some statistical tests, but the better generators fail fewer tests than the bad ones. Exercise 9.16 describes a common statistical test.

In this section we describe the simplest uniform generator that passes a reasonable number of statistical tests. By no means is it the best generator, but it is suitable for use as a reasonable generator in applications where a good approximation to a random sequence is acceptable. The method we use is the *linear congruential generator*, which was first described in 1951. Numbers X_1, X_2, ... are generated satisfying

> The *linear congruential generator* is a good algorithm to generate uniform distributions.

$$X_{i+1} = AX_i(\bmod M) \qquad\qquad \textbf{(9.1)}$$

This equation states that we can get the $(i + 1)$th number by multiplying the *i*th number by some constant A and computing the remainder when the result is divided by M. In C++ we would have

```
X[ i + 1 ] = A * X[ i ] % M;
```

```
1  // Random class interface: random number generation
2  //
3  // CONSTRUCTION: with (a) no initializer or (b) an integer
4  //      that specifies the initial state of the generator
5  // ******************PUBLIC OPERATIONS*********************
6  //      Return a random number according to some distribution
7  // unsigned long RandomLong( )          --> Uniform, 1 to 2^31-1
8  // double RandomReal( )                 --> Uniform 0..1
9  // long RandLong( long Low, Low High )  --> Uniform Low..High
10 // unsigned Poisson( double ExpectedVal )-> Poisson
11 // double NegExp( double ExpectedVal )   --> Neg exponential
12
13 class Random
14 {
15   public:
16     Random( unsigned long InitVal = 1 ) : Seed( InitVal ) { }
17
18         // Uniform distributions
19     unsigned long RandomLong( );// 1 to 2^31-1  (Coded below)
20     double RandomReal( );        // >0.0 to <1.0 (Exercise 9.8)
21     long RandLong( long Low, long High );    // (Exercise 9.8)
22
23         // Nonuniform distributions
24     unsigned Poisson( double ExpectedVal );   // (Section 9.3)
25     double NegExp( double ExpectedVal );      // (Section 9.2)
26   private:
27     unsigned long Seed;
28 };
```

Figure 9.1   Interface for random number generator class

The *seed* is the initial value of the random number generator.

The constants A and M are specified below. Notice that all generated numbers will be smaller than M. Some value X_0 must be given to start the sequence. This value is known as the *seed*. If $X_0 = 0$, then the sequence is not random because it generates all zeros, but if A and M are carefully chosen, then any other seed satisfying $1 \le X_0 < M$ is equally valid. If M is prime, then X_i is never 0. For example, if $M = 11$, $A = 7$, and the seed $X_0 = 1$, then the numbers generated are

$$7, 5, 2, 3, 10, 4, 6, 9, 8, 1, 7, 5, 2, \ldots$$

A random number generator with *period P* generates the same sequence of numbers after *P* iterations.

When we generate a number a second time, we have a repeating sequence. In our case the sequence repeats after $M - 1 = 10$ numbers; this is known as the *period* of the sequence. The period obtained with this choice of A is clearly as good as possible, since all nonzero numbers smaller than M are generated. (We must have a repeated number generated on the 11th iteration.)

A *full-period linear congruential generator* has period *M*-1.

If M is prime, several choices of A give a full period of $M - 1$. This type of generator is called a *full-period linear congruential generator*. Some choices of A do not give a full period. For instance, if $A = 5$ and $X_0 = 1$, the sequence has a short period of 5:

```
1  // Implementation of some of the Random class
2  static const long A = 48271L;
3  static const long M = 2147483647L;    // 2^31 - 1
4  static const long Q = M / A;
5  static const long R = M % A;
6
7  // RandomInt returns the next random number and updates Seed
8  unsigned long
9  Random::RandomLong( )
10 {
11     long TmpSeed = A * ( Seed % Q ) - R * ( Seed / Q );
12     if( TmpSeed >= 0 )
13         Seed = TmpSeed;
14     else
15         Seed = TmpSeed + M;
16
17     return Seed;
18 }
```

Figure 9.2   Random number generator that works if LONG_INT_MAX is at least $2^{31} - 1$

5, 3, 4, 9, 1, 5, 3, 4, ...

If M is chosen to be a large, 31-bit prime, the period should be significantly large for most applications. The 31-bit prime $M = 2^{31} - 1 = 2,147,483,647$ is a common choice. For this prime, $A = 48,271$ is one of the many values that gives a full-period linear congruential generator. Its use has been well studied and is recommended by experts in the field. We will see later that with random number generators, tinkering usually means breaking, so we are well advised to stick with this formula until told otherwise.

This seems like a simple routine to implement. If Seed represents the last value computed by the Random routine, then it would appear that the new value of Seed should be given by

Because of overflow, we must rearrange calculations.

```
Seed = ( A * Seed ) % M;    // Incorrect
```

Unfortunately, on most machines this computation is done on 32-bit integers, and the multiplication is certain to overflow. Although C++ allows overflow, and we could argue that the result is part of the randomness, it is unacceptable because we would no longer have the guarantee of a full period. It turns out that a slight reordering allows the computation to proceed without overflow. Specifically, if Q and R are the quotient and remainder of M/A, then we can rewrite Equation 9.1 as

$$X_{i+1} = A(X_i(\mod Q)) - R\lfloor X_i/Q \rfloor + M\delta(X_i) \qquad (9.2)$$

and the following are true (see Exercise 9.5):

- The first term can always be evaluated without overflow.
- The second term can be evaluated without overflow if $R < Q$.
- $\delta(X_i)$ evaluates to 0 if the result of the subtraction of the first two terms is positive, and it evaluates to 1 if the result of the subtraction is negative.

Stick with these numbers unless you know better.

For the values of M and A, we have $Q = 44{,}488$ and $R = 3399$. Consequently $R < Q$ and a direct application now gives an implementation of a random number class. The resulting code is shown in Figure 9.2. The class works as long as the `long` is capable of holding M. The routine `RandomLong` returns the value of the seed.

We also provide two additional member functions in the interface in Figure 9.1: One to generate a random real number in the open interval from 0 to 1, and a second to generate a random long integer in a specified closed interval (see Exercise 9.8). Finally, the interface provides a generator for the case where nonuniform random numbers are required. In Section 9.3 we provide the body for the member functions `Poisson` and `NegExp`.

One might be tempted to assume that all machines have a random number generator at least as good as the one in Figure 9.2. Sadly, this is not true. Many libraries have generators based on the function

$$X_{i+1} = (AX_i + C) \bmod 2^B$$

where B is chosen to match the number of bits in the machine's integer, and C is odd. These libraries, like the `RandomLong` routine in Figure 9.2, also return the newly computed `Seed` directly, instead of (for example) a value between 0 and 1. Unfortunately, these generators always produce values of X_i that alternate between even and odd, which is an obviously undesirable property. Indeed, the lower k bits cycle with a period of 2^k (at best). Many other random number generators have much smaller cycles than the one we have provided. These are not suitable for any application requiring long sequences of random numbers. Finally, it may seem that we can get a better random number generator by adding a constant to the equation. For instance, we might conclude that

$$X_{i+1} = (48271X_i + 1) \bmod (2^{31} - 1)$$

would somehow be more random. However when we use this equation, we see that

$$(48271 \cdot 179424105 + 1) \bmod (2^{31} - 1) = 179424105$$

so if the seed is 179,424,105, the generator gets stuck in a cycle of period 1. This illustrates how fragile these generators are.

Winning Tickets	0	1	2	3	4	5
Frequency	0.135	0.271	0.271	0.180	0.090	0.036

Figure 9.3   Distribution of lottery winners if expected number of winners is 2

9.3   Nonuniform Random Numbers

Not all applications require uniformly distributed random numbers. For example, grades in a large course are generally not uniformly distributed but rather satisfy the classic bell curve distribution, more formally known as the normal or Gaussian distribution. A uniform random number generator can be used to generate random numbers that satisfy other distributions.

*The **Poisson distribution** models the number of occurrences of a rare event and is used in simulations.*

An important nonuniform distribution that occurs in simulations is the *Poisson distribution*. Occurrences that happen under the following circumstances satisfy the Poisson distribution:

- The probability of one occurrence in a small region is proportional to the size of the region.
- The probability of two occurrences in a small region is proportional to the square of the size of the region and is usually small enough to be ignored.
- The event of getting k occurrences in one region and the event of getting j occurrences in another region disjoint from the first region are independent. (Technically this statement means that you can get the probability of both events simultaneously occurring by multiplying the probability of individual events.)
- The mean number of occurrences in a region of some size is known.

Then if the mean number of occurrences is the constant a, then the probability of exactly k occurrences is $a^k e^{-a}/k!$.

The Poisson distribution generally applies to events that have a low probability of a single occurrence. For example, consider the event of purchasing a winning lottery ticket in Florida, where the odds of winning the jackpot are 14 million to 1. Presumably the picked numbers are more or less random and independent. If a person buys one hundred tickets, the odds of winning become 140,000 to 1 (the odds improve by a factor of 100), so condition 1 holds. The odds of the person holding two winning tickets are negligible, so condition 2 holds. If some other person buys 10 tickets, their odds of winning are 1,400,000 to 1, and this is independent of the first person, so condition 3 holds. Suppose 28 million tickets are sold. The mean number of winning tickets in this situation is 2 (this is the number we need for condition 4). The actual number of winning tickets is a random variable with an expected value of 2, and it satisfies the Poisson distribution. Thus the probability that exactly k winning tickets have been sold is $2^k e^{-2}/k!$. This gives the distribution shown in Figure 9.3. If the expected number of winners is the constant a, then the probability of k winning tickets is $a^k e^{-a}/k!$.

```
1  #include <math.h>
2
3  unsigned
4  Random::Poisson( double ExpectedValue )
5  {
6      double Limit = exp( -ExpectedValue );
7      double Product = RandomReal( );
8
9      for( int Count = 0; Product > Limit; Count++ )
10         Product *= RandomReal( );
11
12     return Count;
13 }
```

Figure 9.4   Generation of a random number according to the Poisson distribution

```
1  double
2  Random::NegExp( double ExpectedValue )
3  {
4      return - ExpectedValue * log( RandomReal( ) );
5  }
```

Figure 9.5   Generation of a random number according to the negative exponential distribution

To generate a random unsigned integer according to a Poisson distribution that has an expected value of a, we can adopt the following strategy (whose mathematical justification is beyond the scope of this book): repeatedly generate uniformly distributed random numbers in the interval (0, 1) until their product is smaller than (or equal to) e^{-a}. This is done in Figure 9.4.

The *negative exponential distribution* has the same mean and variance. It is used to model the time between occurrences of random events.

Another important nonuniform distribution is the *negative exponential distribution*, as shown in Figure 9.5. It has the same mean and variance. The negative exponential distribution is used to model the time between occurrences of random events, as in a simulation application shown in Section 13.2.

Many other distributions are common, and our main purpose is to show that most can be generated from the uniform distribution. Consult any book on probability and statistics to find out more about these functions.

9.4   Generating a Random Permutation

Consider the problem of simulating a card game. The deck consists of 52 distinct cards, and in the course of a deal, we must generate cards from the deck, without duplicates. In effect, we need to shuffle the cards and then iterate through the deck. We want the shuffle to be fair: Each of the 52! possible orderings of the deck should be equally likely as a result of the shuffle.

```
1   // Generate a random permutation of 1..N
2
3   void
4   Permute( int A[ ], int N )
5   {
6       Random R( (int) time( ) ); // Random obj; seed set by time
7
8       for( int i = 0; i < N; i++ )
9           A[ i ] = i + 1;
10
11      for( int j = 1; j < N; j++ )
12          Swap( A[ j ], A[ R.RandLong( 0, j ) ] );
13  }
```

Figure 9.6   Permutation routine

This type of problem involves *random permutations*, which uses one distinct random number per item. In general, the problem is the following: Generate a random permutation of 1, 2, ..., N. All permutations should be equally likely. The randomness of the random permutation is, of course, limited by the randomness of the pseudorandom number generator. Thus all permutations being equally likely is contingent on all random numbers being uniformly distributed and independent. Random permutations can be generated in linear time.

Random permutations can be generated in linear time using one random number per item.

A routine to generate a random permutation is shown in Figure 9.6. Let us describe how the Permute routine works. The first loop initializes the permutation with 1, 2, ..., N. The second loop performs a random shuffling. In each iteration of the loop, we switch A[j] with some array element in positions 0 to j (it is possible to perform no Swap).

It is clear that Permute generates shuffled permutations. But are all permutations equally likely? The answer is both yes and no. We can answer yes when we notice that there are N! possible permutations, and the number of different possible outcomes of the N – 1 calls to RandLong at line 12 is also N! This is because the first call produces either 0 or 1, so it has two outcomes. The second call produces either 0, 1, or 2, so it has three outcomes. The *i*th call has N outcomes. The total number of outcomes is the product of all these possibilities because each random number is independent of the previous one. All we have to show is that each sequence of random numbers corresponds to one and only one permutation. This can be established by working backward (see Exercise 9.6). We can answer no, all permutations are not equally likely, when we realize that since there are only $2^{31} - 2$ initial states for the random number generator, there can be only $2^{31} - 2$ different permutations. This could be a problem in some situations. For instance, a program that generates 1,000,000 permutations (perhaps by splitting the work among many computers) to measure the performance of a sorting algorithm will, unfortunately, almost certainly generate some permutations twice. Better random number generators are needed to make the practice meet the theory.

The correctness or Permute is subtle.

Notice, by the way, that rewriting the call to `Swap` with the call to `R.RandLong(0,N-1)` does not work, even for three elements. We can see that there are 3! = 6 possible permutations, and that the number of different sequences that could be computed by the three calls to `RandInt` is 3^3 = 27. Since 6 does not divide 27 exactly, some permutations must be more likely than others.

9.5   Randomized Algorithms

Suppose you are a professor who is giving weekly programming assignments. You want to make sure that the students are doing their own programs or, at the very least, understand the code they are submitting. One solution is to give a quiz on the day that each program is due. On the other hand, these quizzes take time out of class, so it might be practical to do this for only roughly half of the programs. Your problem is to decide when to give the quizzes.

Of course, if you announce the quizzes in advance, that could be interpreted as an implicit license to cheat for the 50 percent of the programs that will not get a quiz. You could adopt the unannounced strategy of giving quizzes on alternate programs, but students would figure out the strategy before too long. Another possibility is to give quizzes on what seems like the important programs, but this would likely lead to similar quiz patterns from semester to semester. Student grapevines being what they are, this strategy would probably be worthless after one semester.

One method that seems to eliminate these problems is to use a coin. You make a quiz for every program (making quizzes is not nearly as time-consuming as grading them), and at the start of class, you flip a coin to decide whether the quiz is to be given. This way it is impossible to know before class whether or not the quiz will occur, and these patterns do not repeat from semester to semester. The students can expect a quiz to occur with 50 percent probability, regardless of previous quiz patterns. The disadvantage of this strategy is that you could end up giving no quizzes during an entire semester. Assuming a large number of programming assignments, however, this is not a likely occurrence unless the coin is suspect. Each semester the expected number of quizzes is half the number of programs, and with high probability, the number of quizzes will not deviate much from this.

Randomized algorithms use random numbers rather than deterministic decisions to control branching.

This example illustrates what we call *randomized algorithms*. At least once during a randomized algorithm, a random number rather than a deterministic decision is used to make a decision. The running time of the algorithm depends not only on the particular input but also on the random numbers that occur.

The worst-case running time of a randomized algorithm is almost always the same as the worst-case running time of the nonrandomized algorithm. The important difference is that a good randomized algorithm has no bad inputs but only bad random numbers (relative to the particular input). This may seem like only a philosophical difference, but actually it is quite important, as the following example shows.

Consider the following problem: Your boss asks you to write a program to determine the median of a group of 1,000,000 numbers. Your boss wants you to submit the program and then run it on an input that the boss will choose. If the correct answer is given within a few seconds of computing time (which would be expected for a linear algorithm), your boss will be very happy, and you will get a bonus. But if your program does not work or takes too much time, your boss will fire you for incompetence. Your boss already thinks you are overpaid and is hoping to be able to take the second option. What should you do?

The running time of a randomized algorithm depends on the random numbers that occur as well as the particular input.

The quickselect algorithm described in Section 8.7 might seem like the way to solve this problem. Although the algorithm (see Figure 8.21) is very fast on average, recall that it has quadratic worst-case time if the pivot is continually poor. By using median-of-three partitioning, we have guaranteed that this worst case will not occur for common inputs, such as those that are already sorted or contain a host of duplicates. However, there is still a quadratic worst case, and as Exercise 8.8 showed, the boss will read your program, realize how you are choosing the pivot and be able to construct the worst case. Consequently, you will be fired.

By using random numbers, you can statistically guarantee the safety of your job. You begin the quickselect algorithm by randomly shuffling the input, using lines 11 and 12 in Figure 9.6.[1] As a result, your boss has essentially lost control of specifying the input sequence. When you run the quickselect algorithm, it will now be working on random input, so you expect it to take linear time. Can it still take quadratic time? The answer is yes. For any original input, it is possible that the shuffling gets you to the worst case for quickselect, and thus the result would be a quadratic-time sort. If you are unfortunate enough to have this happen, you lose your job. However, this is a statistically impossible event: For a million items the chances of using even twice as much time as the average would indicate is so small, you can essentially ignore the possibility. The computer is much, much more likely to break. Your job is secure.

Randomized quickselect is statistically guaranteed to work in linear time.

Instead of using a shuffling technique, we can achieve the same result by choosing the pivot randomly instead of deterministically. We take a random item in the array and swap it with the item in position Low. We take another random item and swap it with the item in position High. We take a third random item and swap it with the item in the middle position. We then continue as usual. As before, degenerate partitions are always possible, but this now happens as a result of bad random numbers and not bad inputs.

Let us describe the differences between the randomized algorithms and nonrandomized algorithms. Thus far we have seen nonrandomized algorithms. When calculating their average running times, we assume that all inputs are

---

1. We do need to make sure that the random number generator is sufficiently random and its output cannot be predicted by the boss.

equally likely. This assumption is not true, however, because nearly sorted input, for instance, occurs much more often than is statistically expected. This can cause problems for some algorithms, such as quicksort. By using a randomized algorithm, the particular input is no longer important. The random numbers are important, and we get an *expected* running time, where we average over all possible random numbers for any particular input. Using quickselect with random pivots (or a shuffle preprocessing step) gives an $O(N)$ expected time algorithm. This means that *for any input*, including already sorted input, the running time is expected to be $O(N)$, based on the statistics of random numbers. An expected time bound is somewhat stronger than an average-case time bound because the assumptions used to generate it are weaker (random numbers vs. random input) but is weaker than the corresponding worst-case time bound. On the other hand, in many instances, solutions that have good worst-case bounds frequently have extra overhead built in to assure that the worst case does not occur. The $O(N)$ worst-case algorithm for selection, for example, is a marvelous theoretical result but is not practical.

Some randomized algorithms work in a fixed amount of time but randomly make mistakes (presumably with low probability). These mistakes are *false positives* or *false negatives*.

Randomized algorithms come in two basic flavors. The first type, as we have seen, always gives a correct answer but could take a long time, depending on the luck of the random numbers. The second type is what we examine in the remainder of this chapter. Some randomized algorithms work in a fixed amount of time but randomly make mistakes (presumably with low probability). These mistakes are *false positives* or *false negatives*. This is a commonly accepted technique in medicine: False positives and false negatives for most tests are actually fairly common; some tests have surprisingly high error rates. Furthermore, for some tests the errors depend on the individual and not random numbers, so repeating the test is certain to produce another false result. In randomized algorithms we can rerun the test on the same input using different random numbers. If we run a randomized algorithm ten times and get ten positives, and if a single false positive is an unlikely occurrence (say 1 chance in 100), then the probability of ten consecutive false positives (1 chance in 100^{10} or one hundred billion billion) is essentially zero.

9.6 Randomized Primality Testing

In Section 7.4 we described some numerical algorithms and showed how they could be used to implement an encryption scheme known as the RSA algorithm. An important step in the RSA algorithm is producing two prime numbers p and q. We can find a prime number by repeatedly trying successive odd numbers until we find one that is prime. Thus the issue boils down to testing if a given number is prime.

```
1  // Return true if odd integer N is prime
2
3  int
4  IsPrime( long N )
5  {
6      for( long i = 3; i * i <= N; i += 2 )
7          if N % i == 0 )
8              return 0;       // Not prime
9
10     return 1;               // Prime
11 }
```

Figure 9.7   Primality testing by trial division

The simplest algorithm for testing if an odd number N is prime is *trial division*: An odd number greater than 3 is prime if it is not divisible by any other odd number smaller than or equal to $\sqrt{N}$. A direct implementation of this strategy is shown in Figure 9.7.

Trial division is reasonably fast for small (32-bit) numbers, but it is unusable for larger numbers because it could require the testing of roughly $\sqrt{N}/2$ divisors, thus using $O(\sqrt{N})$ time.[2] What we would like is a test whose running time is of the same order of magnitude as the Power routine in Section 7.4.2. A well-known theorem, called *Fermat's Little Theorem*, looks very promising. (We provide a proof of this theorem for completeness, but it is not needed to understand the primality-testing algorithm).

Trial division is a simple algorithm for primality testing. It is fast for small (32-bit) numbers but cannot be used for larger numbers.

(Fermat's Little Theorem): If P is prime and $0 < A < P$, then $A^{P-1} \equiv 1 \pmod{P}$

Theorem 9.1

Consider any $1 \le k < P$. Clearly $Ak \equiv 0 \pmod{P}$ is impossible since P is prime, and less than A and k. Now consider any $1 < i < j < P$. $Ai \equiv Aj \pmod{P}$ would imply $A(j-i) \equiv 0 \pmod{P}$, which is impossible by the previous argument because $1 \le j - i < P$. Thus the sequence $A, 2A, ..., (P-1)A$, when considered $\pmod{P}$ is a permutation of $1, 2, ..., P-1$. The product of both sequences $\pmod{P}$ must be equivalent, yielding the equivalence $A^{P-1}(P-1)! \equiv (P-1)! \pmod{P}$ from which the theorem follows.

Proof

---

2. Though $\sqrt{N}$ may seem small, if N is a 100-digit number, then $\sqrt{N}$ is still a 50-digit number; tests that take $O(\sqrt{N})$ time are thus out of the question for the HugeInt type.

Fermat's Little Theorem is necessary but not sufficient to establish primality.

If the converse of Fermat's Little Theorem was true, then we would have a primality-testing algorithm that would be computationally equivalent to modular exponentiation (that is, $O(\log N)$). Unfortunately, it is not. It is easily verified that $2^{340} \equiv 1(\mathrm{mod}\ 341)$, but 341 is composite ($11*31$).

To do the primality test, we need an additional theorem:

Theorem 9.2   **If P is prime and $X^2 \equiv 1(\mathrm{mod}\ P)$, then $X \equiv \pm 1(\mathrm{mod}\ P)$**

Proof   *Since $X^2 - 1 \equiv 0(\mathrm{mod}\ P)$ implies $(X-1)(X+1) \equiv 0(\mathrm{mod}\ P)$ and P is prime, $X - 1$ or $X + 1 \equiv 0(\mathrm{mod}\ P)$.*

Let us explain why a combination of these two theorems is useful. Let A be any integer between 2 and $N - 2$. If we compute $A^{N-1}(\mathrm{mod}\ N)$ and the result is not 1, then we know that N cannot be prime; otherwise, we would contradict Fermat's Little Theorem. We say then that A is a *witness* to Ns compositeness. Every composite number N has some witnesses A, but for some numbers, known as the Carmichael numbers, these witnesses are hard to find. We need to make sure that we have a high probability of finding a witness no matter what the choice of N is. To improve our chances, we use Theorem 9.2.

In the course of computing A^i, we compute $(A^{\lfloor i/2 \rfloor})^2$. So let $X = A^{\lfloor i/2 \rfloor}$. Let $Y = X^2$. Notice that X and Y are computed automatically as part of the Power routine. If Y is 1 and if X is not $\pm 1(\mathrm{mod}\ N)$, then by Theorem 9.2, N cannot be prime. We can return 0 for the value of A^i when this is detected. N will appear to have failed the test of primality implied by Fermat's Little Theorem.

If the algorithm declares a number not to be prime, it is not prime with 100 percent certainty. Each random attempt has at most a 25 percent false positive rate.

The routine Witness, shown in Figure 9.8, computes $A^i(\mathrm{mod}\ P)$, augmented to return 0 if a violation of Theorem 9.2 is detected. If Witness does not return 1, then A is a witness to the fact that N cannot be prime. Lines 15 to 17 make a recursive call and produce X. We then compute X^2, as is normal for the Power computation. We check if Theorem 9.2 is violated, returning 0 if it is. Otherwise, we complete the Power computation.

The only remaining issue is correctness. If our algorithm declares that N is composite, then N *must* be composite. If N is composite, then is it true that all $2 \le A \le N - 2$ are witnesses? The answer, unfortunately, is no. This means that there exist some choices of A that will trick our algorithm into declaring that N is prime. In fact, if we choose A randomly, we have at most a $1/4$ chance of failing to detect a composite number and thus making an error. Note carefully that this is true for *any* N. If it were only obtained by averaging over all N, we would not have a good enough routine. In the analogy with medical tests, our algorithm generates false positives at most 25 percent of the time for any N.

```
 1  // If Witness does not return 1, N Is definitely composite
 2  // Do this by computing A^i ( mod N ) and looking for
 3  // non-trivial square roots Of 1 along the way
 4  // HugeInt: must have copy constructor, operator=,
 5  //     conversion from int, *, /, -, %, ==, and !=
 6
 7  template <class HugeInt>
 8  HugeInt
 9  Witness( const HugeInt & A, const HugeInt & i,
10                            const HugeInt & N )
11  {
12      if( i == 0 )
13          return 1;
14
15      HugeInt X = Witness( A, i / 2, N );
16      if( X == 0 )        // If N Is recursively composite, stop
17          return 0;
18
19      // N is not prime if we find A nontrivial square root of 1
20      HugeInt Y = ( X * X ) % N;
21      if( Y == 1 && X != 1 && X != N - 1 )
22          return 0;
23
24      if( i % 2 != 0 )
25          Y = ( A * Y ) % N;
26
27      return Y;
28  }
29
30  // Make NumTrials calls to witness to check if N Is prime
31
32  template <class HugeInt>
33  int
34  IsPrime( const HugeInt & N )
35  {
36      const int NumTrials = 5;
37
38      for( int Counter = 0; Counter < NumTrials; Counter++ )
39          if( Witness( RandInt( 2, N - 2 ), N - 1, N ) != 1 )
40              return 0;
41
42      return 1;
43  }
```

Figure 9.8   Randomized test for primality

Some composites will pass the test and be declared prime. It is very unlikely that a composite will pass 20 consecutive independent random tests.

This does not seem like very good odds, since a 25 percent error rate is considered very high. However, if we independently use 20 values of A, then the chances that none of these will witness a composite number is $1/4^{20}$, which is about one in a million million. Those odds are much more reasonable and can be made even better by using more trials. The routine `IsPrime`, which is also shown in Figure 9.8, uses five trials.[3]

Summary

In this chapter we described how random numbers are generated and used. The linear congruential generator is a good choice for simple applications, as long as care is taken in choosing the parameters A and M. Based on a uniform random number generator, we can derive random numbers for other distributions, such as the Poisson and negative exponential distributions. Random numbers have many uses. Some of these include the empirical study of algorithms, the simulation of real-life systems, and the design of algorithms that probabilistically avoid the worst case. We will see uses of random numbers in other parts of the book, most notably in Section 13.2 and Exercise 20.18.

This concludes Part II of the book. In Part III we look at some simple applications, beginning with a discussion of games in Chapter 10 that illustrates three important problem-solving techniques.

Objects of the Game

false positives and false negatives Mistakes randomly made (presumably with low probability) by some randomized algorithms that work in a fixed amount of time. (318)

Fermat's Little Theorem Necessary but not sufficient to establish primality. (320)

full-period linear congruential generator Has period $M - 1$. (310)

linear congruential generator A good algorithm to generate uniform distributions. (309)

negative exponential distribution Used to model the time between occurrences of random events. Has the same mean and variance. (314)

period A random number generator with period P generates the same random sequence of random numbers after P iterations. (310)

permutation A permutation of 1, 2, ..., N is a sequence of N integers that includes each of 1, 2, ..., N exactly once. (307)

Poisson distribution Models the number of occurrences of a rare event. (313)

pseudorandom numbers Have many properties of random numbers. Good

---

3. These bounds are typically pessimistic, and the analysis involves number theory that is much too involved for this book.

generators are hard to find. (308)

random permutation Can be generated in linear time using one random number per item. (315)

randomized algorithm Uses random numbers rather than deterministic decisions to control branching. (316)

seed The initial state of the random number generator. (310)

trial division A simple algorithm for primality testing. It is fast for small (32-bit) numbers but cannot be used for larger numbers. (319)

uniform distribution In which all numbers in the specified range are equally likely to occur. (309)

witness to compositeness A value of A that proves that a number is not prime using Fermat's Last Theorem. (320)

Common Errors

1. Using an initial seed of zero will give bad random numbers.

2. Inexperienced users occasionally reinitialize the seed prior to generating a random permutation. This guarantees that the same permutation will be repeatedly produced, which is probably not intended.

3. Many random numbers are notoriously bad; for serious applications in which long strings of random numbers are required, the linear congruential generator is also unsatisfactory.

4. The low-order bits of linear congruential generators are known to be somewhat nonrandom, so avoid using them. As an example, RandInt()%2 is a bad way to flip a coin.

5. When generating random numbers in some interval, it is a common error to be slightly off at the boundaries and either allow some number outside of the interval to be generated or not allow the smallest number to be generated with fair probability.

6. Many random permutation generators do not generate all permutations with equal likelihood. As discussed in the text, our algorithm is limited by the random number generator.

7. Tinkering with a random number generator is likely to weaken its statistical properties.

On the Internet

Most of the code in this chapter is available.

Random.h   Contains the class interface for Random, as shown in the first half of Figure 9.2

Random.cpp   Contains the RandomInt, Poisson, and HyperExp members

Permute.cpp Contains the `Permute` routine in Figure 9.6
Math.cpp Contains the primality-testing routine in Figure 9.8 plus the math routines from Section 7.4

Exercises

In Short

9.1. For the random number generator described in the text, what are the first ten values of `Seed`, assuming that it is initialized with a value of 1.

9.2. Show the result of running the primality-testing algorithm for $N = 561$ with values of A ranging from 2 to 5.

9.3. If 42,000,000 Florida lottery tickets are sold, what is the expected number of winners? What are the odds that there will be no winners? exactly one winner?

9.4. Why can't zero be used as a seed for the linear congruential generator?

In Theory

9.5. Prove that Equation 9.2 is equivalent to Equation 9.1 and that the resulting program in Figure 9.2 is correct.

9.6. Complete the proof that each permutation obtained in Figure 9.6 is equally likely.

9.7. Suppose you have a biased coin that comes up heads with probability p and tails with probability $1 - p$. Show how to design an algorithm that uses the coin to generate a 0 or 1 with equal probability.

In Practice

9.8. Write the remaining member function `RandomReal` and `RandLong`. Then write a program that calls `RandLong` 1000 times to generate numbers between 1 and 1000. Does it pass the stronger statistical tests given in Section 9.2?

9.9. Run the Poisson generator shown in Figure 9.4 1,000,000 times using an expected value of two. Does the distribution agree with Figure 9.3?

9.10. Consider a two-candidate election in which the winner has a fraction p of the vote. If the votes are counted sequentially, what is the probability that the winner is ahead (or tied) at every stage of the election? This is the so-called *ballot problem*. (The answer is p). Write a program that verifies this. *Hint*: Simulate an election of 10,000 voters. Generate random arrays of $10000p$ ones and $10000(1-p)$ zeros. Then verify in a sequential scan that the difference between ones and zeros is never negative.

9.11. Suppose we want to add a `PermuteVector` member function to the template class `Vector` from Section 3.3.3. One solution is to call `Permute` with the internal data.

 a. Implement this idea.

 b. Is the `PermuteVector` member function inherited by `BoundedVector` given in Section 4.2?

9.12. An alternative to Exercise 9.11 is to implement `Permute` to accept a `Vector` (reference) parameter.

 a. Implement this idea.

 b. If we want to disable the range checks, what are our options?

 c. Can a `BoundedVector` be passed to this `Permute`?

 d. Compare the merits of this solution with the solution in Exercise 9.11.

Programming Projects

9.13. An alternative permutation algorithm is to fill the array A from A[0] to A[N-1] as follows: To fill A[i], generate random numbers until you get one that has not been used previously. Use a bit array to perform that test. Give an analysis of the expected running time (this is tricky), and then write a program that compares this running time with both your analysis and the routine shown in Figure 9.6.

9.14. Suppose we want to generate a random permutation of N distinct items drawn from the range 1, 2, ... M. (The case $M - N$ is of course already discussed). Floyd's algorithm is the following: recursively generate a permutation of $N-1$ distinct items drawn from the range $M-1$. Then generate a random integer in the range 1 to M. If the random integer is not already in the permutation add it; otherwise, add M.

 a. Prove that this algorithm does not add duplicates.

 b. Prove that each permutation is equally likely.

 c. Give a recursive implementation of the algorithm.

 d. Give an iterative implementation of the algorithm.

9.15. A *random walk* in two dimensions is the following game played on the x-y coordinate system. Starting at the origin (that is, (0,0)) each iteration consists of a random step either one unit left, up, right, or down. The walk terminates when the walker returns to the origin. (It can be shown that this happens with probability 1 in two dimensions but with probability less than 1 in three dimensions.) Write a program that performs 100 independent random walks and computes the average number of steps taken in each direction.

9.16. A simple and effective statistical test is the chi-square test. Suppose we generate N positive numbers that can assume one of M values (for instance, we generate numbers between 1 and M, inclusive). The number of occurrences of each number is a random variable with mean $\mu = N/M$. For the test to work, we should have $\mu > 10$. Let f_i be the number of times i is generated. Then compute the chi-square value $V = \sum (f_i - \mu)^2 / u$. The result should be close to M; if the result is consistently (that is, more than once in ten tries) more than $2\sqrt{M}$ away from M, then the generator has failed the test. Implement the chi-square test and run it on your implementation of the `RandLong` member function (with `Low=1` and `High=100`).

References

A good discussion of elementary random number generators is provided in [3]. The permutation algorithm is due to R. Floyd, and can be found in [1]. The randomized primality-testing algorithm is taken from [2] and [4]. More information on random numbers can be found in any good book on statistics or probability.

1. J. Bentley, "Programming Pearls," *Communications of the ACM* **30** (1987), 754-757.

2. G. L. Miller, "Riemann's Hypothesis and Tests for Primality," *Journal of Computer and System Science* **13** (1976), 300-317.

3. S. K. Park and K. W. Miller, "Random Number Generators: Good Ones Are Hard to Find," *Communications of the ACM* **31** (1988) 1192-1201. (See also *Technical Correspondence* in **36** (1993) 105-110.)

4. M. O. Rabin, "Probabilistic Algorithms for Testing Primality," *Journal of Number Theory* **12** (1980), 128-138.

Part III: Applications

Chapter 10

Fun and Games

This chapter introduces three important algorithmic techniques by showing their use in the context of implementing of programs to solve recreational problems. The first problem is the *word search puzzle* and involves finding words in a two-dimensional grid of characters. The second is optimal play in the game of tic-tac-toe.

In this chapter we will see

- how to use the binary search algorithm, modified from Figure 5.12 to incorporate information from unsuccessful searches to solve large instances of a word search problem in under a second
- how to use the *alpha-beta pruning* algorithm to speed up the recursive algorithm in Section 7.7
- how to use hash tables to increase the speed of the tic-tac-toe algorithm

10.1 Word Search Puzzles

The input to the *word search puzzle* problem is a two-dimensional array of characters and a list of words. The object is to find the words in the grid. These words may be horizontal, vertical, or diagonal in any direction (for a total of eight directions). As an example, the grid shown in Figure 10.1 contains the words this, two, fat, and that. The word this begins at row 0, column 0 – the point (0,0) – and extends to (0,3); two goes from (0,0) to (2,0); fat goes from (3,0) to (1,2); and that goes from (3,3) to (0,0).

The word search puzzle requires searching for words in a two-dimensional grid of letters. Words may be oriented in one of eight directions.

10.1.1 Theory

There are several naive algorithms we can use to solve the word search puzzle problem. The most direct is the following brute force approach:

The brute force algorithm searches each word in the word list.

```
for each word W in the word list
    for each row R
        for each column C
            for each direction D
                check if W exists at row R, column C
                in direction D
```

An alternative algorithm searches from each point in the grid in each direction for each word length and looks to see if the word is in the word list.

Since there are eight directions, this algorithm requires $8WRC$ checks. For the typical puzzles published in magazines, we have 40 or so words and a 16-by-16 grid. This is roughly 80,000 checks and is certainly easy to compute on any modern machine. Suppose, however, we consider the variation where only the puzzle board is given and the word list is essentially an English dictionary. In this case the number of words might be 40,000 instead of 40, resulting in 80,000,000 checks. If the grid is doubled, we would then have 320,000,000 checks, and this is no longer a trivial calculation. We would like an algorithm that can solve a puzzle of this size in roughly a second. To do this, we consider an alternative algorithm:

```
for each row R
    for each column C
        for each direction D
            for each word length L
                check if L chars starting at row R column C
                    in direction D form a word
```

The lookups can be done by a binary search.

This algorithm rearranges the loop to avoid searching for every word in the word list. Let us assume that words are limited to 20 characters. In this case the number of checks used by the algorithm is $160RC$. For a 32-by-32 puzzle, this is roughly 160,000 checks. The problem, of course, is that we must now decide if a word is in the word list. If we use a linear search, we lose. If we use a good data structure, we can expect an efficient search. If the word list is sorted, which is to be expected for an online dictionary, then we can use a binary search (shown in Figure 5.12), and perform each check in roughly $\log W$ string comparisons. For 40,000 words, this is perhaps 16 comparisons per check, for a total of under 3,000,000 string comparisons. This can certainly be done in a few seconds and is a factor of 100 better than the previous algorithm.

	0	1	2	3
0	t	h	i	s
1	w	a	t	s
2	o	a	h	g
3	f	g	d	t

Figure 10.1   Sample word search grid

```
 1  // Binary search routine
 2  //  Etype: must have <, and all properties required for Vector
 3  //
 4  // Returns position in A[0..N-1] that contains X
 5  // If X is not found, returns last examined position
 6
 7  template <class Etype>
 8  int
 9  BinarySearch( const Vector<Etype> & A, const Etype & X, int N )
10  {
11      int Low = 0, High = N - 1, Mid;
12
13      while( Low < High )
14      {
15          Mid = ( Low + High ) / 2;
16          if( A[ Mid ] < X )
17              Low = Mid + 1;
18          else
19              High = Mid;
20      }
21      return Low;
22  }
```

Figure 10.2   Binary search modified to return ending point of search

We can further improve the algorithm with the following observation. Suppose we are searching in some direction and we see the character sequence qx. An English dictionary will not contain any words beginning with qx. So is it worth continuing the innermost loop (over all word lengths)? The answer is obviously no: If we detect a character sequence that is not a prefix of any word in the dictionary, we can immediately look in another direction. This algorithm is given by the following pseudocode:

If a character sequence is not a prefix of any word in the dictionary, we can terminate searching in that direction.

```
for each row R
    for each column C
        for each direction D
            for each word length L
                check if L chars starting at row R column
                        C in direction D form a word
                if they do not form a prefix,
                    break;    // the innermost loop
```

The only remaining algorithmic detail is the implementation of the prefix test: Assuming that the current character sequence is not in the word list, how can we decide if it is a prefix of some word in the word list? The answer turns out to be simple. The binary search algorithm in Figure 5.12 narrows down the search range to one item and then checks to see if a match is found. Suppose that instead of doing the test that verifies the match, we merely return the narrowed-down position and let the caller use that information. Then, of course, it is easy

Prefix testing can also be done by binary search.

for the caller of the binary search to check if a match is found. If a match is not found, then it is also easy to verify if the character sequence is a prefix of some word in the list, because if it is, it must be a prefix of the word in the returned position (Exercise 10.3 asks you to prove this). Thus we rewrite the BinarySearch algorithm as shown in Figure 10.2.

```
 1 // Puzzle class interface: solve word search puzzle
 2 //
 3 // CONSTRUCTION: with (a) no initializer
 4 // ******************PUBLIC OPERATIONS*********************
 5 // int SolvePuzzle( )    --> Print all words found in the
 6 //                           puzzle; return number of matches
 7
 8 #include "String.h"
 9 #include <fstream.h>
10 #include <string.h>
11 #include "Vector.h"
12
13 class Puzzle
14 {
15   public:
16     Puzzle( );
17     int SolvePuzzle( );
18   private:
19     enum { MaxRows = 20, MaxColumns = 20,
20            MaxWords = 10000, MaxWordLength = 24 };
21
22     int Rows;
23     int Columns;
24     int NumEntries;
25     char TheBoard[ MaxRows ][ MaxColumns ];
26     Vector<String> TheWords;
27     ifstream PuzzleStream;
28     ifstream WordStream;
29
30         // Private supporting routines
31     void OpenFile( const char *Message, ifstream & InFile );
32     void ReadPuzzle( );
33     void ReadWords( );
34     int SolveDirection( int BaseRow, int BaseCol,
35                         int RowDelta, int ColDelta );
36 };
```

Figure 10.3   Puzzle class interface

```
1  // Constructor for Puzzle class
2  // Prompts for and reads puzzle and dictionary files
3
4  Puzzle::Puzzle( ) : TheWords( MaxWords )
5  {
6      OpenFile( "Enter puzzle file", PuzzleStream );
7      OpenFile( "Enter dictionary name", WordStream );
8      ReadPuzzle( );
9      ReadWords( );
10 }
```

Figure 10.4 Puzzle constructor

```
1  // Print a prompt and open a file
2  // retry until open is successful
3
4  void
5  Puzzle::OpenFile( const char *Message, ifstream & InFile )
6  {
7      const int FileNameLen = 1024;
8      char Name[ FileNameLen + 1 ];
9
10     do
11     {
12         cout << Message << ": ";
13         cin.getline( Name, FileNameLen );
14         InFile.open( Name, ios::in );
15     } while( !InFile );
16 }
```

Figure 10.5 OpenFile routine to open both the grid and word list file

10.1.2   C++ Implementation

Our C++ implementation follows the algorithm description almost verbatim. We design a class named Puzzle to store the grid and word list as well as the corresponding input streams. The class interface is shown in Figure 10.3. For simplicity we assume a limit of 20 rows and columns and a maximum dictionary size of 10,000 words. We leave the problem of removing these restrictions as Exercise 10.5. The public part of the class consists of a constructor and a single member function SolvePuzzle. The private part includes the data members and supporting routines.

Our implementation follows the algorithm description.

```
 1  // Routine to read the dictionary
 2  // Error message is printed if dictionary is not sorted
 3  // Check is made to avoid exceeding MaxWords
 4
 5  void
 6  Puzzle::ReadWords( )
 7  {
 8      NumEntries = 0;
 9      while( WordStream >> TheWords[ NumEntries ] )
10      {
11          if( NumEntries != 0 && TheWords[ NumEntries ] <
12                                  TheWords[ NumEntries - 1 ] )
13          {
14              cerr << "Dictionary is not sorted... skipping\n";
15              continue;
16          }
17          else if( ++NumEntries >= MaxWords )
18              break;
19      }
20  }
```

Figure 10.6   ReadWords routine to read the word list

The constructor opens and reads the data files. We skimp on error checks for brevity.

Figure 10.4 gives the code for the constructor. It merely opens and reads the two files corresponding to the grid and the word list. The supporting routine OpenFile, shown in Figure 10.5, repeatedly prompts for a file until an open is successful. The ReadWords routine, shown in Figure 10.6, reads the word list. Most of the code is concerned with error checks: We do not want to read more than the limit MaxWords, and we make sure that the word list is sorted. Similarly, ReadPuzzle, shown in Figure 10.7, reads the grid and is also concerned with error handling. We need to make sure that we can handle missing puzzles, and we want to warn the user if the grid is not rectangular. In the interest of brevity, we have omitted a few error checks that really should have been performed. Exercise 10.1 asks you to figure out what is missing.

We use two loops to iterate over the eight directions.

SolvePuzzle, shown in Figure 10.8, nests the row, column, and direction loops and then calls the private routine SolveDirection for each possibility. The return value is the number of matches found. A direction is given by indicating a column direction and then a row direction. For instance, north is indicated by CD=0 and RD=1 and southeast by CD=1 and RD=-1. CD can range from -1 to 1 and RD from -1 to 1, except that both cannot be 0 simultaneously. All that remains is SolveDirection, and that is coded in Figure 10.9.

SolveDirection constructs a string by starting at the base row and column and extending in the appropriate direction. We assume that we have the string concatenation and assignment member functions for the String class that accept a single-character parameter, as suggested in Exercise 2.23:

```
const String & operator+=( char Ch );
const String & operator= ( char Ch );
```

```
1  // Routine to read the grid
2  // Checks are performed to ensure that the grid is rectangular
3  // and to make sure that capacity is not exceeded is omitted
4
5  void
6  Puzzle::ReadPuzzle( )
7  {
8      char FirstLine[ MaxColumns + 1 ];
9
10     if( !PuzzleStream.getline( FirstLine, MaxColumns ) )
11     {
12         Rows = 0;
13         return;
14     }
15     Columns = strlen( FirstLine );
16     for( int i = 0; i < Columns; i++ )
17         TheBoard[ 0 ][ i ] = FirstLine[ i ];
18
19     for( Rows = 1;
20             PuzzleStream.getline( FirstLine, MaxColumns );
21                                                    Rows++ )
22     {
23         if( strlen( FirstLine ) != Columns )
24             cerr << "Puzzle is not rectangular" << endl;
25         for( int i = 0; i < Columns; i++ )
26             TheBoard[ Rows ][ i ] = FirstLine[ i ];
27     }
28 }
```

Figure 10.7   ReadPuzzle routine to read the grid

```
1  // Routine to solve the word search puzzle
2  // Performs checks in all eight directions
3
4  int
5  Puzzle::SolvePuzzle( )
6  {
7      int Matches = 0;
8
9      for( int R = 0; R < Rows; R++ )
10         for( int C = 0; C < Columns; C++ )
11             for( int RD = -1; RD <= 1; RD++ )
12                 for( int CD = -1; CD <= 1; CD++ )
13                     if( RD != 0 || CD != 0 )
14                         Matches += SolveDirection( R, C, RD, CD );
15
16     return Matches;
17 }
```

Figure 10.8   SolvePuzzle routine to search in all directions from all
starting points

We also assume that one-letter matches are not allowed (because any one-letter match would be reported eight times). At lines 14 and 15, we iterate and extend the string while checking that we do not go past the boundary of the grid. At line 17 we tack on the next character using operator+= and perform a binary search at line 18. If we do not have a prefix, then clearly we can stop looking and return. Otherwise, we know that we will continue after checking at line 24 for a possible exact match. Line 32 returns the number of matches found when it is clear that the call to SolveDirection can find no more words. A simple main program is shown in Figure 10.10.

```
1  // Search the grid from a starting point and direction
2
3  int
4  Puzzle::SolveDirection( int BaseRow, int BaseCol,
5                          int RowDelta, int ColDelta )
6  {
7      static String CharSequence;
8      int NumMatches = 0;
9      int SearchResult;
10
11     CharSequence = TheBoard[ BaseRow ][ BaseCol ];
12
13     for( int i = BaseRow + RowDelta, j = BaseCol + ColDelta;
14          i >= 0 && j >= 0 && i < Rows && j < Columns;
15              i += RowDelta, j += ColDelta )
16     {
17         CharSequence += TheBoard[ i ][ j ];
18         SearchResult = BinarySearch( TheWords, CharSequence,
19                                      NumEntries );
20         if( !IsPrefix( CharSequence,
21                     TheWords[ SearchResult ] ) )
22             break;
23
24         if( TheWords[ SearchResult ] == CharSequence )
25         {
26             NumMatches++;
27             cout << "Found " << CharSequence << " at " <<
28                 BaseRow << ' ' << BaseCol << " to " <<
29                 i << ' ' << j << '\n';
30         }
31     }
32     return NumMatches;
33 }
```

Figure 10.9   Implementation of a single search

```
1  // Simple main routine for word search puzzle problem
2
3  main( )
4  {
5      Puzzle P;
6      cout << "Found " << P.SolvePuzzle() << " matches" << endl;
7
8      return 0;
9  }
```

Figure 10.10   Simple `main` routine for word search puzzle problem

10.2   The Game of Tic-Tac-Toe

In Section 7.7 we described a simple algorithm that allows the computer to select an optimal move in a game of tic-tac-toe. This recursive strategy known as the *minimax strategy* is as follows:

> The *minimax strategy* examines lots of positions. We can get by with less, without losing any information.

1. If the position is *terminal* (that is, can immediately be evaluated), return its value.

2. Otherwise, if it is the computer's turn to move, return the maximum value of all positions reachable by making one move. The reachable values are calculated recursively.

3. Otherwise, it is the human's turn to move. Return the minimum value of all positions reachable by making one move. The reachable values are calculated recursively.

10.2.1   Alpha-Beta Pruning

Although the minimax strategy gives an optimal tic-tac-toe move, it performs a lot of searching. Specifically, to choose the first move, it makes roughly a half million recursive calls. One reason for this is that the algorithm does more searching than is necessary. Suppose that the computer is considering five moves, C_1, C_2, C_3, C_4, and C_5. Suppose that the recursive evaluation of C_1 reveals that C_1 forces a draw. Now C_2 is evaluated. At this stage we have a position from which it would be the human's turn to move. Suppose that in response to C_2 the human can consider H_{2a}, H_{2b}, H_{2c}, and H_{2d}. Suppose that an evaluation of H_{2a} shows a forced draw. Automatically, C_2 is at best a draw and possibly even a loss for the computer (because the human is assumed to play optimally). Because we need to improve on C_1, we do not have to evaluate any of H_{2b}, H_{2c}, and H_{2d}. We say that H_{2a} is a *refutation*, meaning that it proves that C_2 is not a better move than what has already been seen. Thus we return that C_2 is a draw, and keep C_1 as the best move seen so far. This is shown in Figure 10.11.

> A *refutation* is a countermove that proves that a proposed move is not an improvement over moves previously considered. If we find a refutation, we do not have to examine any more moves and the recursive call can return.

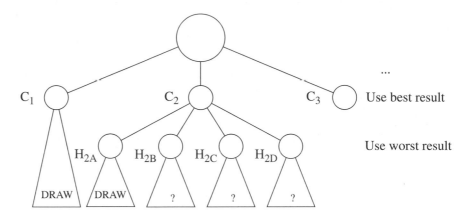

Figure 10.11 Alpha-beta pruning: After H_{2A} is evaluated, C_2, which is the minimum of the H_2's, is at best a draw. Consequently, it cannot be an improvement over C_1. We therefore do not need to evaluate H_{2B}, H_{2C}, and H_{2D}, and can proceed directly to C_3

Alpha-beta pruning **is used to reduce the number of positions that are evaluated in a minimax search. Alpha is the value that the human has to refute and beta is the value that the computer has to refute.**

We do not need to evaluate each node completely; for some nodes, a refutation suffices. This means that some loops can terminate early. Specifically, when the human evaluates a position, such as C_2, a refutation, if found, is just as good as the absolute best move. The same logic applies to the computer. At any point in the search, `Alpha` is the value that the human has to refute, and `Beta` is the value that the computer has to refute. When searching on the human side, any move less than `Alpha` is equivalent to `Alpha`, and on the computer side, any move greater than `Beta` is equivalent to `Beta`. This strategy is commonly known as *alpha-beta pruning*.

As Figure 10.12 shows, alpha-beta pruning requires only a few changes to `ChooseMove`. Both `Alpha` and `Beta` are passed as additional parameters. Initially, `ChooseMove` is started with `Alpha` and `Beta` representing `HumanWin` and `ComputerWin`, respectively. Lines 18 and 22 reflect a change in the initialization of `Value`. The move evaluation is only slightly more complex than the original in Figure 7.20. The recursive call at line 30 includes the parameters `Alpha` and `Beta`, which are adjusted at line 37 or 39 if needed. The only other change is at line 42, which provides for an immediate return when a refutation is found.

```
1    // Routine to compute optimal tic-tac-toe move
2
3    int
4    TicTacToe::ChooseMove( Side S, int & BestRow,
5                           int & BestColumn, int Alpha, int Beta )
6    {
7        Side Opp;              // The other side
8        int Reply;            // Value of opponent's reply
9        int Value;            // Value of best move, so far
10       int Dc;               // Placeholder
11       int SimpleEval;       // Result of an immediate evaluation
12
13       if( ( SimpleEval = PositionValue( ) ) != Unclear )
14           return SimpleEval;
15
16       if( S == Computer )
17       {
18           Opp = Human; Value - Alpha;
19       }
20       else
21       {
22           Opp = Computer; Value = Beta;
23       }
24
25       for( int Row = 0; Row < 3; Row++ )
26           for( int Column = 0; Column < 3; Column++ )
27               if( SquareIsEmpty( Row, Column ) )
28               {
29                   Place( Row, Column, S );
30                   Reply = ChooseMove( Opp, Dc,Dc, Alpha, Beta );
31                   Place( Row, Column, Empty );
32
33                   if( S == Computer && Reply > Value ||
34                       S == Human && Reply < Value)
35                   {       // Better move found
36                       if( S == Computer )
37                           Alpha = Value = Reply;
38                       else
39                           Beta = Value = Reply;
40
41                       BestRow = Row; BestColumn = Column;
42                       if( Alpha >= Beta )
43                           return Value;   // Refutation
44                   }
45               }
46
47       return Value;
48   }
```

Figure 10.12 ChooseMove routine to compute optimal tic-tac-toe move
using alpha-beta pruning

Alpha-beta pruning works best when it finds refutations early.

To take full advantage of alpha-beta pruning, game programs usually try to apply heuristics to place the best moves early in the search. This results in even more pruning than one would expect from a random search of positions. In practice alpha-beta pruning limits the searching to only $O(\sqrt{N})$ nodes, where N is the number of nodes that would be examined without alpha-beta pruning. This is a huge savings. Our tic-tac-toe example is not ideal because there are so many identical values, but even so, the initial search is reduced to roughly 18,000 positions.

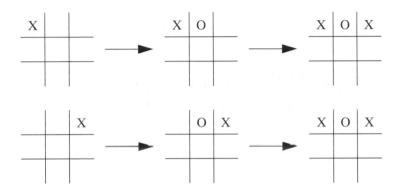

Figure 10.13   Two searches that arrive at identical positions

```
1  #include <iostream.h>
2  #include "Hash.h"
3
4  // A minimal Position class for use with transposition table
5  struct Position
6  {
7      int Board[ 3 ][ 3 ];
8      int Value;
9
10     Position( ) { }
11     Position( int TheBoard[ 3 ][ 3 ] );
12
13     const Position & operator= ( const Position & Rhs );
14
15     int operator==( const Position & Rhs ) const;
16     int operator!=( const Position & Rhs ) const
17         { return !( operator==( Rhs ) ); }
18 };
```

Figure 10.14   `Position` class interface

10.2.2   Transposition Tables

Another commonly employed practice is to use a table to keep track of all positions that have been evaluated. For instance, in the course of searching for the first move, the program will examine the positions in Figure 10.13. If the values of the positions are saved, the second occurrence of a position need not be recomputed; it essentially becomes a terminal position. The data structure that records this is known as a *transposition table*; it is implemented as a simple hash table. In many cases this can save considerable computation.

A *transposition table* stores previously evaluated positions.

To implement the transposition table we first define a `Position` class, as shown in Figure 10.14, which is used to store each position and its computed value. The hash table routines require that we define a default constructor, a copy assignment operator, and both `operator==` and `operator!=`. We also provide a constructor that can be initialized with a (two-dimensional) board array. Separately, we provide a hash function.

A hash table is used to implement the transposition table.

All of these routines are implemented in Figure 10.15. The constructors and copy operators are not particularly efficient since they require copying a two-dimensional array. For larger game problems this is a serious consideration. Note also that `operator==` and `operator!=` compare only the `Board` members. A related issue concerns whether it is worthwhile to include all positions in the transposition table. The overhead of maintaining the table suggests that positions near the bottom of the recursion ought not be saved because

We do not store positions that are at the bottom of the recursion in the transposition table.

- There are so many.
- The point of alpha-beta pruning and transposition tables is to reduce search times by avoiding recursive calls early in the game; saving a recursive call very deep in the search does not greatly reduce the number of positions that are examined, because that recursive call would only examine a few positions anyway.

We will see how this applies to tic-tac-toe when we implement the transposition table. The changes that are needed in the `TicTacToe` class interface are shown in Figure 10.16. The additions are the new data member at line 4 and the new declaration for `ChooseMove` at lines 11 to 13. We now pass `Alpha` and `Beta` (as was done for alpha-beta pruning) and also the `Depth` of the recursion, which is zero by default. Presumably, the initial call to `ChooseMove` will involve only three parameters, and these new parameters will be assigned their default values.

`ChooseMove` has three additional parameters, all of which have defaults.

```
 1  // Position class members
 2
 3  Position::Position( int TheBoard[ 3 ][ 3 ] )
 4  {
 5      for( int i = 0; i < 3; i++ )
 6          for( int j = 0; j < 3; j++ )
 7              Board[ i ][ j ] = TheBoard[ i ][ j ];
 8  }
 9
10  const Position &
11  Position::operator=( const Position & Rhs )
12  {
13      if( this != &Rhs )
14      {
15          for( int i = 0; i < 3; i++ )
16              for( int j = 0; j < 3; j++ )
17                  Board[ i ][ j ] = Rhs.Board[ i ][ j ];
18
19          Value = Rhs.Value;
20      }
21
22      return *this;
23  }
24
25  int
26  Position::operator==( const Position & Rhs ) const
27  {
28      for( int i = 0; i < 3; i++ )
29          for( int j = 0; j < 3; j++ )
30              if( Board[ i ][ j ] != Rhs.Board[ i ][ j ] )
31                  return 0;
32
33      return 1;
34  }
35
36  unsigned int
37  Hash( const Position & Key, int TableSize )
38  {
39      unsigned int HashVal = 0;
40
41      for( int i = 0; i < 3; i++ )
42          for( int j = 0; j < 3; j++ )
43              HashVal = HashVal * 4 ^ Key.Board[ i ][ j ];
44
45      return HashVal % TableSize;
46  }
```

Figure 10.15   Position class and hash function used for transposition table in tic-tac-toe algorithm

```
1  class TicTacToe
2  {
3      enum PositionVal { HumanWin, Draw, Unclear, ComputerWin };
4      HashTable<Position> Transpositions;
5
6  public:
7      enum Side { Human, Computer, Empty };
8
9      TicTacToe( ) { ClearBoard( ); }
10
11     int ChooseMove( Side S, int & BestRow, int & BestColumn,
12         int Alpha = HumanWin, int Beta = ComputerWin,
13         int Depth = 0 );
14     . . .
15 }
```

Figure 10.16   Changes to `TicTacToe` class to incorporate transposition table and alpha-beta pruning

Figures 10.17 and 10.18 show the new `ChooseMove`. At line 11, we declare a `Position` object named `ThisPosition`. When the time comes it will be placed in the transposition table. This is not the most efficient technique because it involves making a copy of the board, but it is simple, and furthermore, a profiler shows that it is not excessively time consuming. `Value` is declared as a reference to `ThisPosition.Value`; this allows much of the code to be unaltered. The constant object `TableDepth` tells us how deep in the search we will allow positions to be placed in the transposition table. By experimenting we found that 5 was optimal. Allowing positions at `Depth` 6 to be saved hurt because the extra cost of maintaining the larger transposition table was not compensated by the fewer examined positions.

Lines 18 to 26 are new. If we are in the first call to `ChooseMove`, we initialize the transposition table. Otherwise, if we are at an appropriate depth, we check if the current position has already been evaluated, and if so, we return its value. The code has two tricks. First, we can only transpose at `Depth` 3 or higher, as Figure 10.13 suggests. Second, we assign the return value of the `Find` to a constant reference to avoid the cost of a copy. The compiler might have optimized this anyway (and many argue that it should always find this optimization), but this kind of thing is best not left to chance. The only other difference is from lines 54 onward. We consolidate the two return statements originally in the code into one by using a goto. (If you are one of those who cannot stand any use of a goto, it is easy enough to unconsolidate.) Immediately before the return, we store the value of the position in the transposition table (if the table is full, this is not fatal; we merely stop adding positions into it).

> The code has a few little tricks but nothing major.

```
1    // Routine to compute optimal tic-tac-toe move
2
3    int
4    TicTacToe::ChooseMove( Side S, int & BestRow,
5                int & BestColumn, int Alpha, int Beta, int Depth )
6    {
7        Side Opp;              // The other side
8        int Reply;            // Value of opponent's reply
9        int Dc;               // Placeholder
10       int SimpleEval;       // Result of an immediate evaluation
11       Position ThisPosition = Board;
12       int & Value = ThisPosition.Value;
13       const int TableDepth = 5;  // Max depth in Trans table
14
15       if( ( SimpleEval = PositionValue( ) ) != Unclear )
16           return SimpleEval;
17
18       if( Depth == 0 )
19           Transpositions.MakeEmpty( );
20       else if( Depth >= 3 && Depth <= TableDepth )
21       {
22           const Position & LookupVal =
23                           Transpositions.Find( ThisPosition );
24           if( Transpositions.WasFound( ) )
25               return LookupVal.Value;
26       }
27
28       if( S == Computer )
29       {
30           Opp = Human; Value = Alpha;
31       }
32       else
33       {
34           Opp = Computer; Value = Beta;
35       }
36
37       for( int Row = 0; Row < 3; Row++ )
38           for( int Column = 0; Column < 3; Column++ )
39               if( SquareIsEmpty( Row, Column ) )
40               {
41                   Place( Row, Column, S );
42                   Reply = ChooseMove( Opp, Dc, Dc,
43                                   Alpha, Beta, Depth + 1 );
44                   Place( Row, Column, Empty );
```

Figure 10.17   Tic-tac-toe algorithm with alpha-beta pruning and transposition table (part 1)

```
45                      if( S == Computer && Reply > Value ||
46                          S == Human && Reply < Value )
47                      {
48                          if( S == Computer )
49                              Alpha = Value = Reply;
50                          else
51                              Beta = Value = Reply;
52                          BestRow = Row; BestColumn = Column;
53                          if( Alpha >= Beta )
54                              goto Done;    // Refutation
55                      }
56                  }
57      Done:
58        if( Depth <= TableDepth )
59        {
60            try { Transpositions.Insert( ThisPosition ); }
61            catch( ... )
62            {
63                // Transposition table is full; not fatal
64            }
65        }
66        return Value;
67  }
```

Figure 10.18   Tic-tac-toe algorithm with alpha-beta pruning and transposition table (part 2)

The use of the transposition table in this tic-tac-toe algorithm removes about half the positions from consideration with only a slight cost for the transposition table operations. We observed almost a doubling of the program speed.

10.2.3   Computer Chess

In a complex game such as chess or go, it is infeasible to search all the way to the terminal nodes; some estimates claim that there are roughly 10^{100} legal chess positions, and all the tricks in the world will not bring this down to a manageable level. In this case we have to stop the search after a certain depth of recursion is reached. The nodes where the recursion is stopped become terminal nodes. These terminal nodes are evaluated with a function that estimates the value of the position. For instance, in a chess program, the evaluation function measures such variables as the relative amount and strength of pieces and other positional factors.

Terminal positions cannot be searched in computer chess. At the upper levels considerable knowledge is built into the evaluation function.

Computers are especially adept at playing moves involving deep combinations that result in exchanges of material, because the strength of pieces is easily evaluated. However, extending the search depth merely one level requires an increase in processing speed of about 6 (because the number of positions increases by about a factor of 36). Each extra level of search greatly enhances the ability of the program, up to a certain limit (which appears to have been reached

The best computer chess programs play at grandmaster level.

by the best programs). On the other hand, computers generally are not as good at playing quiet positional games where more subtle evaluations and knowledge of the game is required. However, this is only apparent when the computer is playing very strong opposition. The best computer chess programs play at grandmaster level. Current research is focusing on incorporating knowledge into the evaluation function. The best programs have surprisingly sophisticated evaluation functions.

Summary

In this chapter we saw an application of binary search and some algorithmic techniques that are commonly used in game playing programs such as chess, checkers, and Othello. The top programs for these games are all world class. The game Go, however, appears too complex for computer searching.

Objects of the Game

alpha-beta pruning Used to reduce the number of positions that are evaluated in a minimax search. Alpha is the value that the human has to refute, and beta is the value that the computer has to refute. (338)

minimax strategy A recursive strategy that allows the computer to select an optimal move in a game of tic-tac-toe. (337)

refutation A countermove that proves that a proposed move is not an improvement over moves previously considered. If we find a refutation, we do not have to examine any more moves and the recursive call can return. (337)

terminal position Describes positions in a game that can be evaluated immediately. (337)

transposition table Stores previously evaluated positions. (341)

word search puzzle Requires searching for words in a two-dimensional grid of letters. Words may be oriented in one of eight directions. (329)

Common Errors

1. When using a transposition table, we must be careful not to fill it up prematurely.
2. It is important to check that assumptions are satisfied. For instance, in the word search puzzle we check that the dictionary is sorted. It is a common error to forget this check.

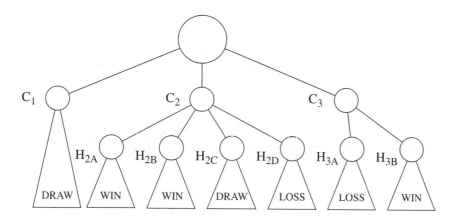

Figure 10.19   Alpha-beta pruning example for Exercise 10.2

On the Internet

Both case studies are completely coded, although the interface for the tic-tac-toe game leaves a great deal to be desired.

> **WordSrch.cpp**   Contains the word search puzzle algorithm
> **TicTac.cpp**   Contains a tic-tac-toe class, minus the basic member functions

Exercises

In Short

10.1.   What error checks are missing in Figure 10.7?

10.2.   For the situation in Figure 10.19,

a. which of the responses to move C_2 is a refutation?
b. what is the value of the position?

In Theory

10.3.   Verify that if X is a prefix of some word in A, then X is a prefix of the word that terminates the binary search.

10.4.   Explain how the running time of the word search algorithm changes when

a. the number of words doubles
b. the number of rows and columns double (simultaneously)

In Practice

10.5. Remove restrictions on the grid size and dictionary size that are present in the text implementation of the `Puzzle` class.

10.6. For the word search problem, represent the grid as a `Vector<Vector<char> >`. What changes are needed?

10.7. For the word search problem, replace the binary search with a sequential search. How does the change affect performance?

10.8. Compare the performance of the word search algorithm with and without the prefix search.

10.9. A tic-tac-toe program requires additional code to read moves and output the board. Write a user-friendly interface.

10.10. Even if the computer has a move that gives an immediate win, it may not make it if it detects another move that is also guaranteed to win. Some early chess programs had the problem that they would get into a repetition of position when a forced win was detected, allowing the opponent to claim a draw. In tic-tac-toe, this is not a problem, because the program eventually will win. Modify the tic-tac-toe algorithm so that when a winning position is found, the move that leads to the shortest win is always taken. You can do this by adding `9-Depth` to `ComputerWin`, so that a quicker win gives the highest value.

10.11. Compare the performance of the tic-tac-toe program with and without alpha-beta pruning.

10.12. Implement the tic-tac-toe algorithm and measure the performance when various depths are allowed to be stored in the transposition table. Also measure the performance when no transposition table is used. How are the results affected by alpha-beta pruning?

Programming Projects

10.13. Write a program to play 5-by-5 tic-tac-toe, where 4 in a row wins. Can you search to terminal nodes?

10.14. The game of boggle consists of a grid of letters and a word list. The object is to find words in the grid subject to the constraint that two adjacent letters must be adjacent in the grid (that is, north, south, east, or west) of each other, and each item in the grid can be used at most once per word. Write a program to play boggle.

10.15. Write a program to play MAXIT. The board is represented as an *N*-by-*N* grid of numbers randomly placed at the start of the game. One position is designated as the initial current position. Two players alternate turns. At each turn a player must select a grid element in the current row or column. The value of the selected position is added to the player's score, and that position becomes the current position and cannot be selected again. Players alternate until all grid elements in the current row and column are already selected, at which point the game ends and the player with the highest score wins.

10.16. Othello played on a 6-by-6 board is a forced win for black. Prove this by writing a program. What is the final score if play on both sides is optimal?

References

If you are interested in computer games, a good starting point is the following paper which is contained in a special issue devoted exclusively to the subject. You will find plenty of information and references to other works covering chess, checkers, and other computer games.

1. K. Lee and S. Mahajan, "The Development of a World Class Othello Program," *Artificial Intelligence* **43** (1990), 21-36.

Chapter 11

Stacks and Compilers

Stacks are used extensively in compilers. This chapter will present two simple components of a compiler: a balanced symbol checker and a simple calculator. Our goal is to show simple algorithms that use stacks and to see how the classes that were described in Chapter 6 are used.

In this chapter we will see

- how to use a stack to check for balanced symbols
- how to use a *state machine* to parse symbols in a balanced symbol program
- how to use *operator precedence parsing* to evaluate infix expressions in a simple calculator program

11.1   Balanced Symbol Checker

As we discussed in Section 6.2, compilers check your programs for syntax errors, but frequently a lack of one symbol (such as a missing comment ender * / or }) will cause the compiler to spill out a hundred lines of diagnostics without identifying the real error. A useful tool to help debug compiler error messages is a program that checks whether symbols are balanced. In other words, every { must correspond to a }, every [to a], and so on. The sequence [( )] is legal, but [( ]) is wrong, so simply counting the numbers of each symbol is insufficient. We will assume for now that we are only processing a sequence of tokens and not worry about problems such as { not needing a matching }.

11.1.1   Basic Algorithm

A stack is useful here because we know that when a closing symbol such as) is seen, it matches the most recently seen unclosed (. Therefore, by placing opening symbols on a stack, we can easily check that a closing symbol makes sense.

A stack can be used to detect mismatched symbols.

Specifically, we have the following algorithm:

> Make an empty stack. Read tokens until the end of the file. If the token is an opening symbol, push it onto the stack. If it is a closing symbol and if the stack is empty, report an error. Otherwise, pop the stack. If the symbol popped is not the corresponding opening symbol, then report an error. At the end of the file, if the stack is not empty, then report an error.

In this algorithm, illustrated in Figure 11.1, the fourth, fifth, and sixth symbols all generate errors. The } is an error because the symbol popped from the top of stack is an (, so a mismatch is detected. The) is an error because the stack is empty, so there is no corresponding (. The [is an error that is detected when the end of input is seen, and the stack is not empty.

Symbols in comments, string constants, and character constants need not be balanced.

To make this work for C++ programs, we need to consider all the contexts in which parentheses, braces, and brackets need not match. For example, we should not consider a parenthesis as a token if it occurs inside a comment, string, or character constant. We thus need routines to skip comments, strings, and character constants. A character constant in C++ can be complex to recognize because of the host of escape sequences, so we will simplify things. Our goal is to design a program that will work for the bulk of inputs likely to occur.

Line numbers are needed for meaningful error messages.

For the program to be useful, we must not only report mismatches but also attempt to identify where the mismatches occur. Consequently, we will keep track of the line numbers where the tokens are seen. When an error is seen, it is always difficult to give an accurate message: if we have an extra }, does that mean the } is extraneous, or was a { missing earlier? We will keep the error handling as simple as possible. Note, however, that once one error is reported, it is possible that the program will be confused and start flagging many errors. Thus only the first error can be considered meaningful. Even so, we will see that the program we develop is very useful.

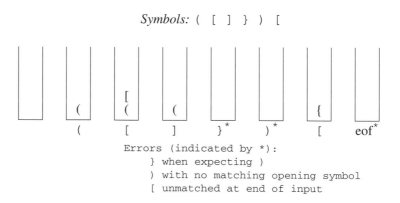

Figure 11.1   Stack operations in balanced symbol algorithm

```
 1  // Program class interface: check for balanced symbols
 2  //
 3  // CONSTRUCTION: with an istream object
 4  // ******************PUBLIC OPERATIONS*********************
 5  // int CheckBalance( )    --> Print mismatches
 6  //                            return number of errors
 7
 8  #include <fstream.h>
 9  #include "Stack.h"
10
11  // Symbol is the class that will be placed on the Stack
12  struct Symbol
13  {
14      char   Token;
15      int    TheLine;
16  };
17
18  class Program
19  {
20    public:
21      Program( istream & Input ) : Errors( 0 ),
22              CurrentLine( 1 ), InputStream( Input ) { }
23      ~Program( ) { }
24
25          // The only publicly visible member function
26      int CheckBalance( );
27    private:
28      enum CommentType { SlashSlash, SlashStar };
29
30      istream & InputStream;      // Reference to input stream
31      char Ch;                    // Current character
32      int CurrentLine;            // Current line
33      Stack<Symbol> PendingTokens;// Open symbols pending
34      int Errors;                 // Number of errors seen
35
36          // A host of internal routines
37      int NextChar( );
38      void PutBackChar( );
39      void SkipComment( CommentType Start );
40      void SkipQuote( char QuoteType );
41      char GetNextSymbol( );
42      void CheckMatch( const Symbol & OpSym,
43                       const Symbol & ClSym );
44  };
```

Figure 11.2   Class interface for balanced symbol program

```
1  // NextChar sets Ch based on the next character in InputStream
2  // and returns result of get
3  // PutBackChar puts the character back onto InputStream
4  // Both routines adjust CurrentLine if necessary
5
6  int
7  Program::NextChar( )
8  {
9      if( !InputStream.get( Ch ) )
10         return 0;
11     if( Ch == '\n' )
12         CurrentLine++;
13     return 1;
14 }
15
16 void
17 Program::PutBackChar( )
18 {
19     InputStream.putback( Ch );
20     if( Ch == '\n' )
21         CurrentLine--;
22 }
```

Figure 11.3   NextChar routine to read next character, update
CurrentLine if necessary, and return true if not at end of
file; and PutBackChar routine to put back Ch and update
CurrentLine if necessary

11.1.2   Implementation

Figure 11.2 shows the Program class that does all the work. In addition to a
constructor and destructor, the only publicly visible routine is CheckBalance,
shown at line 26. Everything else is a supporting routine or a class data member.
We begin by describing the data members.

InputStream is a reference to an istream object and is initialized at
construction. Because of the ios hierarchy, it may be initialized with an
ifstream object. The current character being scanned is stored in Ch, and
CurrentLine stores the current line number. The balanced symbol algorithm
requires that we place opening symbols on a stack. In order to print diagnostics,
we store a line number with each symbol, as shown in the Symbol struct at
lines 12 to 16. The stack itself is the data member PendingTokens declared at
line 33. Finally, an integer that counts the number of errors is declared at line 34.

The constructor, shown at lines 21 and 22, initializes the error count to 0, the
current line number to 1, and sets the istream reference. The remaining data
members, namely Ch and PendingTokens, are initialized using their default
constructors; in the case of PendingTokens, this creates an empty stack. We
accept the default destructor, which is member-by-member destruction.

```
1   // Precondition: We are about to process a comment;
2   //                have already seen comment start token
3   // Postcondition: Stream will be set immediately after
4   //                comment ending token
5
6   void
7   Program::SkipComment( CommentType Start )
8   {
9       if( Start == SlashSlash )
10      {
11          while( NextChar( ) && ( Ch != '\n' ) )
12              ;
13          return;
14      }
15          // Look for */
16      int State = 0;   // Number of chars seen in comment ender
17      while( NextChar( ) )
18      {
19          if( State == 1 && Ch == '/' )
20              return;
21          State = Ch == '*';
22      }
23      Errors++;
24      cout << "Unterminated comment!" << endl;
25  }
```

Figure 11.4   SkipComment routine to move past an already started comment

We can now examine some of the supporting routines. Much of it is concerned with keeping track of the current line and attempting to differentiate symbols that represent opening and closing tokens with those that are inside comments, character constants, and string constants. This general process is known as *lexical analysis*. Figure 11.3 shows a pair of routines, NextChar and PutBackChar. NextChar reads the next character from InputStream, assigns it to Ch, and updates CurrentLine if a newline is seen. It returns 0 only if the end of the file is reached. The complementary procedure PutBackChar puts the current character (Ch) back onto the input stream, and decrements CurrentLine if the character is a newline. Clearly PutBackChar should be called only once between calls to NextChar; since it is a private routine, we do not worry about abuse on the part of the class user. Putting back characters on the input stream is a commonly used technique in parsing. In many instances we have read one too many characters, and it is useful to undo the read. In our case this occurs after processing a /. We must see if the next character begins the comment start token, but if it has not, we cannot simply disregard it because it could be an opening or closing symbol, or a quote. Thus we pretend that it was never read.

Lexical analysis is used to ignore comments and recognize symbols.

```
 1  // Precondition: We are about to process a quote;
 2  //                have already seen beginning quote
 3  // Postcondition: Stream pointer will be set immediately
 4  //                after matching quote
 5
 6  void
 7  Program::SkipQuote( char QuoteType )
 8  {
 9      while( NextChar( ) )
10      {
11          if( Ch == QuoteType )
12              return;
13          else if( Ch == '\n' )
14          {
15              Errors++;
16              cout << "Missing closed quote at line " <<
17                      CurrentLine << endl;
18              return;
19          }
20          // If a backslash, skip next character
21          else if( Ch == '\\' )
22              NextChar( );
23      }
24  }
```

Figure 11.5   SkipQuote routine to move past an already started character or string constant

Next up is the routine SkipComment shown in Figure 11.4. The purpose is to skip over the characters in the comment, and position the input stream so that the next read will be the first character after the comment ends. Things are complicated by the fact that comments can either begin with //, in which case the line ends the comment, or /*, in which case */ ends the comment.[1] When we have the // case, we continually get the next character until either the end of file is reached (in which case the first half of the && operator fails) or we see a newline. At that point we return. Notice that the line number is updated automatically by NextChar. Otherwise, we have the /* case, which is processed starting at line 16.

The *state machine* is a common technique used to parse symbols. At any point it is in some state, and each input character takes it to a new state. Eventually the state machine reaches a state where a symbol has been recognized.

The SkipCommand routine uses a simplified *state machine*. The state machine is a common technique used to parse symbols. At any point we are in some state, and each input character takes us to a new state. Eventually, we reach a state where a symbol has been recognized. At any point we have matched either 0, 1, or 2 characters of the */ terminator, corresponding to states 0, 1, and 2. If we match two characters, we can return. This happens if we are in state 1 and see a /, and it is tested at line 19. Otherwise, we go back to either state 1 if we see a * or state zero if we do not. This is stated succinctly at line 21. If we

1. We will not consider deviant cases involving \.

never find the comment-ending token, then eventually `NextChar` returns 0 and the `while` loop terminates, resulting in an error message. `SkipQuote`, shown in Figure 11.5 is similar. Here the parameter is the opening quote character, which is either " or '. In either case we need to see that character as the closing quote. As we can see, however, we must be prepared to handle the \ character, or else our program will report errors when run on its own source. Thus we repeatedly digest characters. If the current character is the closing quote, we are done; if it is newline, we have an unterminated character or string constant, and if it is a backslash, we digest an extra character without examining it.

Once the skipping routine is written, it is easier to write `GetNextSymbol`. If the current character is a /, we read a second character to see if we have a comment. If so, we call `SkipComment`; if not, we undo the second read. If we have a quote, we call `SkipQuote`. If we have an opening or closing symbol, we can return. Otherwise, we keep reading until we eventually run out of input or find an opening or closing symbol. The entire routine is shown in Figure 11.6.

```
1  // Return the next opening or closing symbol or 0 (if EOF)
2  // Skip past comments and character and string constants
3
4  char
5  Program::GetNextSymbol( )
6  {
7      while( NextChar( ) )
8      {
9          if( Ch == '/' )
10         {
11             if( NextChar( ) )
12             {
13                 if( Ch == '*' )
14                     SkipComment( SlashStar );
15                 else if( Ch == '/' )
16                     SkipComment( SlashSlash );
17                 else
18                     PutBackChar( );
19             }
20         }
21         else if( Ch == '\'' || Ch == '"' )
22             SkipQuote( Ch );
23         else if( Ch == '(' || Ch == '[' || Ch == '{' ||
24             Ch == ')' || Ch == ']' || Ch == '}' )
25             return Ch;
26     }
27     return 0;        // End of file
28 }
```

Figure 11.6   `GetNextSymbol` routine to skip comments and quotes and return next opening or closing character

```
1  // Print error messages for unbalanced symbols
2  // Return number of errors detected
3
4  int
5  Program::CheckBalance( )
6  {
7      char LastChar;
8      Symbol LastSymbol, Match;
9
10     Errors = 0; CurrentLine = 1;
11     while( LastChar = GetNextSymbol( ) )
12     {
13         LastSymbol.Token = LastChar;
14         LastSymbol.TheLine = CurrentLine;
15
16         switch( LastChar )
17         {
18           case '(': case '[': case '{':
19             PendingTokens.Push( LastSymbol );
20             break;
21
22           case ')': case ']': case '}':
23             if( PendingTokens.IsEmpty( ) )
24             {
25                 Errors++;
26                 cout << "Extraneous " << LastChar <<
27                     " at line " << CurrentLine << endl;
28             }
29             else
30             {
31                 Match = PendingTokens.Top( );
32                 PendingTokens.Pop( );
33                 CheckMatch( Match, LastSymbol );
34             }
35             break;
36
37           default: // Can't happen
38             break;
39         }
40     }
41
42     while( !PendingTokens.IsEmpty( ) )
43     {
44         Errors++;
45         Match = PendingTokens.Top( );
46         PendingTokens.Pop( );
47         cout << "Unmatched " << Match.Token << " at line "
48                 << Match.TheLine << endl;
49     }
50     return Errors;
51 }
```

Figure 11.7   CheckBalance, the main algorithm

```
1  // Print an error message if ClSym does not match OpSym
2  // Update Error
3
4  void
5  Program::CheckMatch( const Symbol & OpSym,
6                       const Symbol & ClSym )
7  {
8      if( OpSym.Token == '(' && ClSym.Token != ')' ||
9          OpSym.Token == '[' && ClSym.Token != ']' ||
10         OpSym.Token == '{' && ClSym.Token != '}' )
11     {
12         cout << "Found " << ClSym.Token << " on line " <<
13             CurrentLine << "; does not match " << OpSym.Token
14             << " at line " << OpSym.TheLine << endl;
15         Errors++;
16     }
17 }
```

Figure 11.8   CheckMatch routine to check that close symbol matches opening symbol

CheckBalance is implemented in Figure 11.7. It follows the algorithm description almost verbatim. Opening symbols are pushed onto the stack with the current line number. When a closing symbol is seen, if the stack is empty, then the closing symbol is extraneous; otherwise, we remove the top item from the stack and check that the opening symbol that was on the stack matches the closing symbol just read. This is done by the routine CheckMatch, which is shown in Figure 11.8. Once the end of input is seen, any symbols on the stack are unmatched; these are repeatedly output in the while loop that begins at line 42. The total number of errors that were detected is then returned.

CheckBalance does all the algorithmic work.

Note that the current implementation allows multiple calls to CheckBalance, but if the input stream is not reset externally, then all that happens is that the end of the file is immediately detected and we return immediately. Figure 11.9 shows that we expect a Program object to be created and then CheckBalance to be invoked. In our example, if there are no command-line arguments, the associated istream is cin, otherwise, we repeatedly use istreams that are associated with the files given in the command-line argument list.

11.2   A Simple Calculator

Some of the techniques used to implement compilers can be used on a smaller scale in the implementation of a typical pocket calculator. Typically, calculators evaluate infix expressions, such as 1+2, which consists of a binary operator with arguments to its left and right. This format, although often fairly easy to evaluate, can be more complex. Consider the expression

```
 1  // Main routine for balanced symbol checker
 2
 3  main( int argc, const char **argv )
 4  {
 5    try
 6    {
 7      if( argc == 1 )
 8      {
 9          Program P( cin );
10          if( P.CheckBalance( ) == 0 )
11              cout << "No errors!\n";
12          return 0;
13      }
14
15      while( --argc )
16      {
17          ifstream Ifp( *++argv, ios::in );
18          if( !Ifp )
19          {
20              cerr << "Cannot open " << *argv << endl;
21              continue;
22          }
23          cout << *argv << ":\n";
24          Program P( Ifp );
25          if( P.CheckBalance( ) == 0 )
26              cout << "No errors!\n";
27      }
28    }
29    catch( ... )
30    {
31      cerr << "Out of memory!!" << endl;
32      exit( 1 );
33    }
34
35      return 0;
36  }
```

Figure 11.9   `main` routine with command-line arguments

```
1 + 2 * 3
```

In an *infix expression*, a binary operator has arguments to its left and right. When there are several operators, precedence and associativity determine how the operators are processed.

Mathematically, this evaluates to 7 because the multiplication operator has higher precedence than addition. Some calculators give the answer 9, illustrating that a simple left to right evaluation is not sufficient: We cannot begin by evaluating 1+2. Furthermore, consider the expressions

```
10 - 4 - 3
2 ^ 3 ^ 3
```

in which ^ is the exponentiation operator. Which subtraction and which exponentiation get evaluated first? Subtractions are processed left to right, meaning the result is 3. On the other hand, exponentiation is generally processed right to left, reflecting the mathematical 2^{3^3} rather than $(2^3)^3$. Thus subtraction associates left to right, while exponentiation associates from right to left. With all of these possibilities, it would then seem that evaluating an expression such as

```
1 - 2 - 3 * 4 ^ 5 * 6 / 7 ^ 2 ^ 2
```

would be quite challenging.

If the calculations are performed in integer math (that is, rounding down on division), the answer is -8. To see this, we will insert parentheses to show the calculations are ordered:

```
( 1 - 2 ) - ( ( ( 3 * ( 4 ^ 5 ) ) * 6 ) / ( 7 ^ ( 2 ^ 2 ) ) )
```

Although the parentheses make the order of evaluations unambiguous, it is difficult to argue that they make the mechanism for evaluation any clearer. It turns out that a different expression form, known as a *postfix expression*, provides a direct mechanism for evaluation. First we will examine the postfix expression form and show how postfix expressions can be evaluated in a simple left to right scan. Then we will show algorithmically how the expressions above, which are presented as infix expressions, can be converted to postfix. Finally, we will give a C++ program that evaluates infix expressions containing additive, multiplicative, and exponentiation operators as well as overriding parentheses. We use an algorithm known as *operator precedence parsing*.

11.2.1   Postfix Machines

A *postfix expression* is a series of operators and operands. It is evaluated using a *postfix machine* as follows: When an operand is seen, it is pushed onto a stack. The appropriate number of operands are popped from the stack, the operator is evaluated, and the result is pushed back onto the stack. For binary operators, which are the most common, two operands are popped. When the complete postfix expression is evaluated, the result should be a single item on the stack, representing the answer. The postfix form represents a natural way to evaluate expressions, because precedence rules are not required. Let us provide a simple example. Consider the postfix expression

> A *postfix expression* can be evaluated as follows: Operands are pushed onto a single stack. An operator pops its operands and then pushes the result. At the end of the evaluation, the stack should contain exactly one element, which represents the result.

```
1 2 3 * +
```

The evaluation proceeds as follows: 1, then 2, and then 3 are each pushed onto the stack. To process *, we pop the top two items on the stack: 3 and then 2. Note that the first item popped becomes the Rhs parameter to the binary operator, and the second item popped is the Lhs parameter; thus parameters are popped in reverse order. For multiplication, this does not matter, but for subtraction and division, it certainly does. The result of the multiplication is 6, and that is pushed back onto the stack. At this point the top of the stack is 6; below it is 1.

To process the +, these are popped, and their sum, 7, is pushed. At this point the expression has been read, the stack has only one item, and thus the final answer is 7.

Every valid infix expression can be converted to postfix form. For example the earlier long infix expression can be written in postfix notation as

```
1 2 - 4 5 ^ 3 * 6 * 7 2 2 ^ ^ / -
```

Evaluation of a postfix expression takes linear time.

Figure 11.10 shows the steps used by the postfix machine to evaluate it. Each step involves exactly one push. Consequently, since there are nine operands and eight operators, there are 17 steps and 17 pushes. Clearly the time to evaluate a postfix expression is linear. The remaining detail is an algorithm to convert from infix notation to postfix notation. Once we have one, we have an algorithm to evaluate an infix expression.

11.2.2   Infix to Postfix Conversion

The *operator precedence parsing* algorithm converts an infix expression to a postfix expression, so we can evaluate the infix expression.

The basic principle involved in the *operator precedence parsing* algorithm, which converts an infix expression to a postfix expression is the following. When an operand is seen, we can immediately output it. However, when we see an operator, we can never output it because we must wait to see the second operand. Consequently, we must save it. If we look at an expression such as

```
1 + 2 * 3 ^ 4
```

which in postfix form is

```
1 2 3 4 ^ * +
```

we see that in some cases, a postfix expression has operators in the reverse order than they appear in an infix expression. Of course, this is only true if the precedence of the involved operators is increasing as we go left to right. Even so, this suggests that a stack is appropriate for storing operators. Following this logic, we see that when we read an operator, it must somehow be placed onto a stack. Consequently, at some point the operator must get off the stack. The rest of the algorithm involves deciding when operators go on and come off the stack.

An operator stack is used to store operators that have been seen but not yet output.

Let us look again at a simple infix expression:

```
2 ^ 5 - 1
```

When we reach the − operator, 2 and 5 have been output and ^ is on the stack. Because − has lower precedence than ^, we know that ^ needs to be applied to 2 and 5. Thus we must pop the ^ and any other operands of higher precedence than − from the stack. After that is completed we push the −. The resulting postfix expression is

```
2 5 ^ 1 -
```

Postfix Expression: 1 2 – 4 5 ^ 3 * 6 * 7 2 2 ^ ^ / –

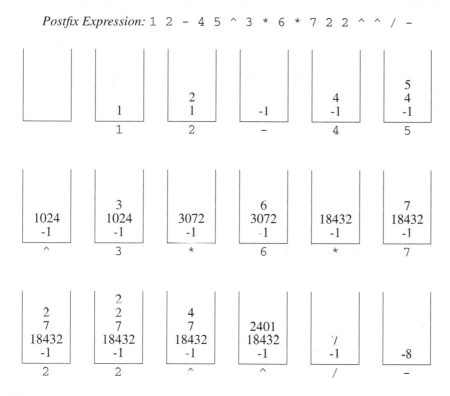

Figure 11.10   Steps in evaluation of a postfix expression

In general, when we are processing an operator from the input, we output those operators from the stack that the precedence (and associativity) rules tell us need to be processed.

As a second example, consider the infix expression

3 * 2 ^ 5 – 1

When we reach the ^ operator, 3 and 2 have been output and * is on the stack. Since ^ has higher precedence than *, nothing is popped, and ^ goes on the stack. When we see the 5, it is output immediately. Then we see a – operator. Precedence rules tell us that ^ is popped and then so is the *. At this point there is nothing left to pop, so we are done popping and – goes onto the stack. We then output 1. When we reach the end of the infix expression, we can pop the remaining operators from the stack. The resulting postfix expression is

3 2 5 ^ * 1 –

When an operator is seen on the input, operators of higher priority (or left associative operators of equal priority) are removed from the stack, signalling that they should be applied. The input operator is then placed on the stack.

Before we give a complete summary of the algorithm, we need to answer a few questions. First, if the current symbol is a + and the top of the stack is a +, should the + on the stack be popped, or should it stay? The answer is determined by deciding if the input + implies that the stack + is completed. Since + associates from left to right, the answer is yes. However, if we were talking about the ^ operator, which associates from right to left, the answer would be no. Therefore, when examining two operators of equal precedence, we look at the associativity to decide, as shown in the following examples:

Infix expression	Postfix expression	Associativity
2 + 3 + 4	2 3 + 4 +	Left associative: Input + is lower than stack +
2 ^ 3 ^ 4	2 3 4 ^ ^	Right associative: Input ^ is higher than stack ^

A left parenthesis is treated as a high precedence operator when it is an input symbol but a low precedence operator when it is on the stack. A left parenthesis is removed only by a right parenthesis.

What about parentheses? Left parentheses can be considered a high precedence operator when it is an input symbol but a low precedence operator when it is on the stack. Consequently, the input left parenthesis is simply placed on the stack. When a right parenthesis is seen on the input, we pop the operator stack until we see a left parenthesis. The operators are written, but the parentheses are not.

Let us summarize the various cases in the operator precedence parsing algorithm; everything that is popped from the stack is output, with the exception of parentheses:

- *Operands*: Immediately output.
- *Close parenthesis*: Pop stack symbols until an open parenthesis is seen.
- *Operator*: Pop all stack symbols until we see a symbol of lower precedence or a right associative symbol of equal precedence. Then push the operator.
- *End of input*: Pop all remaining stack symbols.

As an example, Figure 11.11 shows how the algorithm processes

```
1 - 2 ^ 3 ^ 3 - ( 4 + 5 * 6 ) * 7
```

Below each stack is the symbol that is read. To the right in bold is any output.

Infix: 1 - 2 ^ 3 ^ 3 - (4 + 5 * 6) * 7

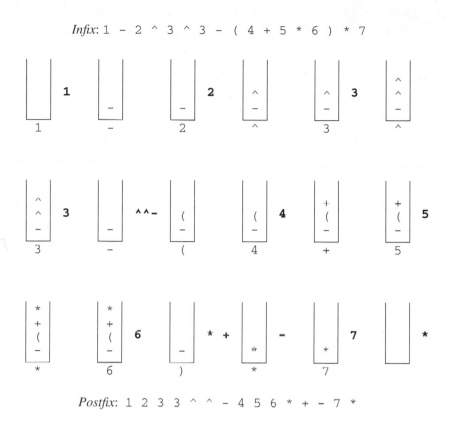

Postfix: 1 2 3 3 ^ ^ - 4 5 6 * + - 7 *

Figure 11.11   Infix to postfix conversion

11.2.3   Implementation

We now have the theoretical background required to implement a simple calculator. Our calculator supports addition, subtraction, multiplication, division, and exponentiation. We will write a template class `Evaluator` that can be instantiated with the type in which the math is to be performed (presumably `int`, `double`, or `Integer`). We make a simplifying assumption: Negative numbers are not allowed. Distinguishing between the binary minus operator and the unary minus requires extra work in the scanning routine and also complicates matters because it introduces a nonbinary operator. It is not difficult to incorporate unary and ternary operators; however, the extra code does not illustrate any unique concepts and thus is left as an exercise.

The `Evaluator` class will parse and evaluate infix expressions.

```
 1  // Evaluator class interface: evaluate infix expression
 2  // Type: Must have usual repertoire of arithmetic operators
 3  //
 4  // CONSTRUCTION: with (a) const char * or (b) another
 5  //        Evaluator object
 6  //
 7  // ******************PUBLIC OPERATIONS*********************
 8  // Type GetValue( )      --> Return value of infix expression
 9  // ******************ERRORS********************************
10  // Some error checking is performed
11
12  #include <strstream.h>
13  #include "Stack.h"
14
15      // Tokens are ordered by precedence to match PrecTable
16  enum Token { EOL, VALUE, OPAREN, CPAREN, EXP,
17                  MULT, DIV, PLUS, MINUS };
18
19  template <class Type>
20  class Evaluator
21  {
22    public:
23      Evaluator( const char *S ) : Str( S, 256 )
24          { OpStack.Push( EOL ); }
25
26          // The only publicly visible routine
27      Type GetValue( );              // Do the evaluation
28    private:
29      Stack<Token> OpStack;       // Operator stack for conversion
30      Stack<Type>  PostFixStack;// Stack for postfix machine
31
32      istrstream Str;             // The character stream
33      Type CurrentValue;          // Current operand
34      Token LastToken;            // Last token read
35
36          // Internal routines
37      Token GetToken( );       // Read next token into LastToken
38      Type GetTop( );              // Get top of postfix stack
39      void BinaryOp( Token );     // Process an operator
40      void ProcessToken( );       // Handle LastToken
41  };
```

Figure 11.12   Evaluator class interface

We need two stacks: an operator stack and a stack for the postfix machine.

Figure 11.12 shows the Evaluator class interface, which is used to read a single null terminated string of input. The basic evaluation algorithm requires two stacks. The first stack is used to evaluate the infix expression and generate the postfix expression. It is a stack of operators declared at line 29. Token is an enumerated type declared at line 16; note that the symbols are listed in order of precedence. Rather than explicitly outputting the postfix expression, we send each postfix symbol to the postfix machine as it is generated. Thus we also need a stack that stores operands. Consequently, the postfix machine stack, declared at line 30, is instantiated with `Type`. Notice that if we did not have templates, we would be in trouble because the two stacks hold items of different types. The remaining data members are an `istrstream` object that is used to step through the input line, and members to store the current token and, if the token is an operand, the value of the operand. We can now discuss the member functions.[2]

The only publicly visible member function is `GetValue`. Shown in Figure 11.13, `GetValue` repeatedly reads a token and processes it until the end of line is detected. At that point the item at the top of the stack is the answer. Figure 11.14 shows the `GetToken` routine. First we skip past any blanks. When the loop at line 12 ends, we have gone past any blanks. If we have not reached the end of line, then we check to see if we match any of the one-character operators and return the appropriate token if so. Otherwise, we reach the `default` case in the `switch` statement. We expect that what remains is an operand, so we unread the `Ch` and then use `operator>>` to get `CurrentValue`. Note that in order for the `putback` to work, we must use `get`. This is why we do not simply use `operator>>` (in place of lines 12 to 15) to skip implicitly past the blanks.

C++ note: `get` must be used so that `putback` works.

```
1   // Public routine that performs the evaluation
2   // Examine postfix machine to see if a single result is
3   // left and if so return it; otherwise print error
4
5   template <class Type>
6   Type
7   Evaluator<Type>::GetValue( )
8   {
9       do
10      {
11          LastToken = GetToken( );
12          ProcessToken( );
13      } while( LastToken != EOL );
14
15      if( PostFixStack.IsEmpty( ) )
16      {
17          cerr << "Missing operand!" << endl;
18          return 0;
19      }
20
21      Type TheResult = PostFixStack.Top( );
22      PostFixStack.Pop( );
23      if( !PostFixStack.IsEmpty( ) )
24          cerr << "Warning: missing operators!" << endl;
25
26      return TheResult;
27  }
```

Figure 11.13   `GetValue` routine to read and process tokens and then return item at the top of the stack

---

2. `istrstream` will be replaced by `istringstream` in future versions of C++.

```
1  // Return the next token, skipping blanks, and return it
2  // For VALUE token, place the processed value in CurrentValue
3  // Print error message if input is unrecognized
4
5  template <class Type>
6  Token
7  Evaluator<Type>::GetToken( )
8  {
9      char Ch;
10
11         // Skip blanks
12     while( Str.get( Ch ) && Ch == ' ' )
13         ;
14
15     if( Str.good( ) && Ch != '\n' && Ch != '\0' )
16     {
17         switch( Ch )
18         {
19           case '^': return EXP;
20           case '/': return DIV;
21           case '*': return MULT;
22           case '(': return OPAREN;
23           case ')': return CPAREN;
24           case '+': return PLUS;
25           case '-': return MINUS;
26
27           default:
28             Str.putback( Ch );
29             if( ( Str >> CurrentValue ) == 0 )
30             {
31                 cerr << "Parse error" << endl;
32                 return EOL;
33             }
34             return VALUE;
35         }
36     }
37
38     return EOL;
39  }
```

Figure 11.14 GetToken routine to return the next token in the line
stream

Figures 11.15 and 11.16 show the routines used to implement the postfix machine. GetTop returns and removes the top item in the postfix stack. The routine BinaryOp applies TopOp (which is expected to be the top item in the operator stack) to the top two items on the postfix stack and replaces them with the result. It also pops the operator stack, signifying that processing for TopOp is complete. The routine Pow is presumed to exist for Type objects; we can either use the math library routine or adapt the one in Figure 7.8.

```
1  // Top and Pop the postfix machine stack; return the result
2  // If stack is empty, print an error message
3
4  template <class Type>
5  Type
6  Evaluator<Type>::GetTop( )
7  {
8      if( PostFixStack.IsEmpty( ) )
9      {
10         cerr << "Missing operand" << endl;
11         return 0;
12     }
13
14     Type Tmp = PostFixStack.Top( );
15     PostFixStack.Pop( );
16     return Tmp;
17 }
```

Figure 11.15   GetTop routine to get the top item in the postfix stack and remove it

Figure 11.17 declares a *precedence table* which stores the operator precedences and is used to decide what is removed from the operator stack. The operators are listed in the same order as the enumeration type Token. Because enumeration types are assigned consecutive indices beginning with zero, they can be used to index an array.

We want to assign each level of precedence with a number; the higher the number, the higher the precedence. We could assign the additive operators precedence 1, multiplicative operators precedence 3, exponentiation 5, and parentheses precedence 99. However, we also need to take into account associativity. To do this, we assign each operator a number that represents its precedence when it is an input symbol, and a second number that represents its precedence when it is on the operator stack. A left associative operator has the operator stack precedence set at one higher than the odd number would indicate, while a right-associative operator has the input symbol precedence set at one higher than the odd number. Thus the precedence of the + operator that is on the stack is 2. A consequence of this rule is that any two operators that have different precedences are still correctly ordered. However, if a + is on the operator stack and is also the input symbol, it will appear that the operator that is on the top of the stack has higher precedence and thus will be popped. This is what we want for left-associative operators. Similarly, if a ^ is on the operator stack and is also the input symbol, it will appear that the operator that is on the top of the stack has lower precedence and thus will not be popped, which is correct for right-associative operators. The token VALUE never gets placed on the stack, so its precedence is meaningless. The end of line token is given lowest precedence because we will place it on the stack for use as a sentinel (this is done in the constructor). If we treat it as a right-associative operator, then it is covered under the operator case.

A *precedence table* is used to decide what is removed from the operator stack. Left-associative operators have the operator stack precedence set at one higher than the input symbol precedence. Right-associative operators go the other way.

```
1   // Process an operator by taking two items off the postfix
2   // stack, applying the operator, and pushing the result
3   // Print error if missing closing parentheses or division by 0
4
5   template <class Type>
6   void
7   Evaluator<Type>::BinaryOp( Token TopOp )
8   {
9       if( TopOp == OPAREN )
10      {
11          cerr << "Unbalanced parentheses" << endl;
12          OpStack.Pop( );
13          return;
14      }
15      Type Rhs = GetTop( );
16      Type Lhs = GetTop( );
17
18      if( TopOp == EXP )
19          PostFixStack.Push( Pow( Lhs, Rhs ) );
20      else if( TopOp == PLUS )
21          PostFixStack.Push( Lhs + Rhs );
22      else if( TopOp == MINUS )
23          PostFixStack.Push( Lhs - Rhs );
24      else if( TopOp == MULT )
25          PostFixStack.Push( Lhs * Rhs );
26      else if( TopOp == DIV )
27          if( Rhs != 0 )
28              PostFixStack.Push( Lhs / Rhs );
29          else
30          {
31              cerr << "Division by zero" << endl;
32              PostFixStack.Push( Lhs );
33          }
34      OpStack.Pop( );
35  }
```

Figure 11.16 `BinaryOp` routine to apply `TopOp` to the postfix stack

```
1       // PrecTable matches order of Token enumeration
2   struct Precedence
3   {
4       int InputSymbol;
5       int TopOfStack;
6   } PrecTable[ ] = {
7       { 0, -1 }, { 0, 0 },        // EOL, VALUE
8       { 100, 0 }, { 0,99 },       // OPAREN, CPAREN
9       { 6, 5 },                   // EXP
10      { 3, 4 }, { 3, 4 },         // MULT, DIV
11      { 1, 2 }, { 1, 2 }          // PLUS, MINUS
12  };
```

Figure 11.17 Table of precedences used to evaluate an infix expression

We can now describe the remaining member function `ProcessToken`, which is shown in Figure 11.18. When an operand is seen, it is pushed onto the postfix stack. If we see a close parenthesis, we repeatedly pop and process the top operator on the operator stack until the opening parenthesis is seen (lines 18 and 20); the open parenthesis is then popped at line 22 (the test at line 21 is used to avoid popping the sentinel in the event of a missing open parenthesis). Otherwise, we have the general operator case, which is succinctly described by the code in lines 28 to 32.

A simple main routine is given in Figure 11.19. It repeatedly reads a line of input, instantiates an `Evaluator` object, and computes its value. As written, `int` math is performed. We can change line 12 to use `double` math or perhaps the *g++* `Integer` class.

```
1  // After token is read, use operator precedence parsing
2  // algorithm to process it; missing opening parentheses
3  // are detected here
4
5  template <class Type>
6  void
7  Evaluator<Type>::ProcessToken( )
8  {
9      Token TopOp;
10
11     switch( LastToken )
12     {
13       case VALUE:
14         PostFixStack.Push( CurrentValue );
15         return;
16
17       case CPAREN:
18         while( ( TopOp = OpStack.Top( ) ) != OPAREN &&
19                                             TopOp != EOL )
20             BinaryOp( TopOp );
21         if( TopOp == OPAREN )
22             OpStack.Pop( ); // Get rid of opening parenthesis
23         else
24             cerr << "Missing opening parentheses" << endl;
25         break;
26
27       default:    // General operator case
28         while( PrecTable[ LastToken ].InputSymbol <=
29                 PrecTable[ TopOp = OpStack.Top() ].TopOfStack )
30             BinaryOp( TopOp );
31         if( LastToken != EOL )
32             OpStack.Push( LastToken );
33         break;
34     }
35  }
```

Figure 11.18   `ProcessToken` routine to process `LastToken` using operator precedence parsing algorithm

```
 1  // Simple main to exercise Evaluator class
 2
 3  main( )
 4  {
 5      const int LineLength = 80;
 6      char Str[ LineLength + 1 ];
 7
 8    try
 9    {
10      while( cin.getline( Str, LineLength ) )
11      {
12          Evaluator<int> E( Str );
13          cout << E.GetValue( ) << '\n';
14      }
15    }
16    catch( ... )
17    {
18      cerr << "Out of memory!!" << endl;
19      exit( 1 );
20    }
21
22      return 0;
23  }
```

Figure 11.19   Simple `main` to evaluate expressions repeatedly

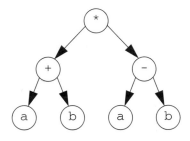

Figure 11.20   Expression tree for `(a+b) * (c-d)`

11.2.4   Expression Trees

In an *expression tree*, the leaves contain operands and the other nodes contain operators.

Figure 11.20 shows an example of an *expression tree*. The leaves of an expression tree are operands such as constants or variable names, and the other nodes contain operators. This particular tree happens to be binary because all the operations are binary, and although this is the simplest case, it is possible for nodes to have more than two children. It is also possible for a node to have only one child, as is the case with the unary minus operator. We can evaluate an expression tree T by applying the operator at the root to the values obtained by recursively evaluating the left and right subtrees. In our example the left subtree evaluates to (a+b), and the right subtree evaluates to (a-b). The entire tree therefore represents ((a+b)*(a-b)). It is evident that we can produce an (overly parenthesized) infix expression by recursively producing a parenthesized left expression, then printing out the operator at the root, and finally recursively producing a parenthesized right expression. This general strategy (left, node, right) is known as an inorder traversal; it is easy to remember because of the type of expression it produces.

If we recursively print the left subtree, then the right subtree, and then the operator (without parentheses), we obtain the postfix expression. This is known as a postorder traversal of the tree. A third strategy for evaluating a tree results in a prefix expression. These are all discussed in Chapter 17. The expression tree (and its generalizations) are useful data structures in compiler design because they allow us to see an entire expression; this makes code generation easier and in some cases greatly enhances optimization efforts.

Recursive printing of the expression tree can be used to obtain an infix, postfix, or prefix expression.

Of interest is the construction of an expression tree given an infix expression. As we have seen, we can always convert an infix expression to postfix, so it suffices to show how to construct an expression tree from a postfix expression. Not surprisingly, this is simple. We maintain a stack of pointers to trees (maintaining a stack of trees involves excessive copying). When an operand is seen, we create a single node tree and push a pointer to it onto our stack. When an operator is seen, the top two trees on the stack are popped and merged. In the new tree the node is the operator, the right child is the first tree popped from the stack, and the left child is the second tree popped. A pointer to the result is then pushed back onto the stack. This is essentially the same algorithm as postfix evaluation, with tree creation replacing the binary operator computation. Consequently, it can be easily incorporated into the infix algorithm presented above.

Expression trees can be constructed from a postfix expression in a similar manner as postfix evaluation.

Summary

This chapter examined two uses of stacks in the general area of programming language and compiler design, and illustrated that even though the stack is a simple structure, it is very powerful. Stacks can be used to decide if a sequence of symbols is well-balanced; the resulting algorithm uses linear time and, equally importantly, consists of a single sequential scan of the input. Operator precedence parsing is a technique that can be used to parse infix expressions, and also uses linear time and a single sequential scan. Two stacks are used by the operator precedence parsing algorithm, and although the stacks store different types of objects, the template mechanism allows us to use a single stack implementation for both types of objects.

Objects of the Game

expression tree A tree in which the leaves contain operands and the other nodes contain operators. (372)

infix expression An expression in which a binary operator has arguments to its left and right. When there are several operators, precedence and associativity determine how the operators are processed. (360)

lexical analysis Used to ignore comments and recognize symbols. (355)

operator precedence parsing An algorithm that converts an infix expression to a postfix expression in order to evaluate the infix expression. (362)

postfix expression An expression that can be evaluated by a postfix machine without knowing any precedence rules. (361)

postfix machine Used to evaluate a postfix expression as follows: Operands are pushed onto a stack and an operator pops its operands and then pushes the result. At the end of the evaluation, the stack should contain exactly one element, which represents the result. (361)

precedence table Used to decide what is removed from the operator stack. Left-associative operators have the operator stack precedence set at one higher than the input symbol precedence. Right-associative operators go the other way. (369)

state machine A common technique used to parse symbols. At any point the machine is in some state, and each input character takes it to a new state. Eventually, the state machine reaches a state where a symbol has been recognized. (356)

Common Errors

1. Errors in the input must be handled as carefully as possible. It is a programming error to be lax in this area.
2. For the balanced symbol routine, handling quotes incorrectly is a common error.
3. For the infix to postfix algorithm, the precedence table must reflect the correct precedence and associativity.

On the Internet

Both application programs are available. You should probably download the balancing program; it may help you debug other C++ programs.

Balance.cpp   Contains the balanced symbol program
Infix.cpp   Contains the expression evaluator, instantiated for `int`

Exercises

In Short

11.1.   Show the result of running the balanced symbol program on the following inputs

a. }

b. (}

c. [[[

d.) (

e. [ )]

11.2.   Show the postfix expression for

a. 1 + 2 - 3 ^ 4

b. 1 ^ 2 - 3 * 4

c. 1 + 2 * 3 - 4 ^ 5 + 6

d. (1 + 2) * 3 - (4 ^ (5 - 6))

11.3.   For the infix expression a + b ^ c * d ^ e ^ f - g - h / (i + j)

a. Show how the operator precedence parsing algorithm generates the corresponding postfix expression.

b. Show how a postfix machine evaluates the resulting postfix expression.

c. Draw the resulting expression tree.

In Theory

11.4.   For the balanced symbol program, explain how to print out an error message that is likely to reflect the probable cause.

11.5.   Explain, in general terms, how unary operators are incorporated into the expression evaluators. Assume that the unary operators precede their operands and have high precedence. Include a description of how they are recognized by the state machine.

In Practice

11.6.   The use of the ^ operator for exponentiation is likely to confuse C++ programs. Rewrite the program with ** as the exponentiation operator.

11.7. The infix evaluator accepts illegal expressions in which the operators are misplaced.

    a. What will 1 2 3 + * be evaluated as?

    b. How can we detect these illegalities?

    c. Modify the program to do so.

Programming Projects

11.8. Modify the expression evaluator to handle negative input numbers.

11.9. Implement a complete C++ expression evaluator. Handle all C++ operators that can accept constants and make arithmetic sense (do not implement [ ], for example).

11.10. Implement a C++ expression evaluator that includes variables. Assume that there are at most 26 variables, namely A through Z, and that a variable can be assigned to by an = operator of low precedence (as in C++).

11.11. Write a program that reads an infix expression and generates a postfix expression.

11.12. Write a program that reads a postfix expression and generates an infix expression.

References

The infix to postfix algorithm (*operator precedence parsing*) was first described in [3]. Some good books on compiler construction are [1] and [2].

1. A. V. Aho, R. Sethi, and J. D. Ullman, *Compilers: Principles, Techniques, and Tools*, Addison-Wesley, Reading, MA, 1975.

2. C. N. Fischer and R. J. LeBlanc, *Crafting a Compiler with C*, Benjamin/ Cummings, Redwood City, CA, 1991.

3. R. W. Floyd, "Syntactic Analysis and Operator Precedence," *Journal of the ACM* **10:3** (1963), 316-333.

Chapter 12

Utilities

In this chapter we discuss two utility applications of our data structures, compression and cross-referencing. Data compression is an important technique in computer science. It can be used to reduce the size of files stored on disk (in effect increasing the capacity of the disk) and also to increase the effective rate of transmission across modems (by transmitting less data). Virtually all newer modems perform some type of compression. Cross-referencing is a scanning and sorting technique that is done, for example, to make an index to a book.

In this chapter we will see

- a discussion of a file compression algorithm, known as *Huffman's algorithm*, and a description of how it can be implemented (an actual implementation is beyond the scope of this text, however)

- an implementation of a cross-referencing program that lists, in sorted order, all identifiers in a C++ program and gives the line numbers on which they occur.

12.1   File Compression

The ASCII character set consists of roughly 100 printable characters. To distinguish these characters, $\lceil \log 100 \rceil = 7$ bits are required. Seven bits allow the representation of 128 characters, so the ASCII character set adds some other "unprintable" characters. An eighth bit is added to allow parity checks. The important point, however, is that if the size of the character set is C, then $\lceil \log C \rceil$ bits are needed in a standard fixed-length encoding.

> A standard encoding of C characters uses $\lceil \log C \rceil$ bits.

Suppose we have a file that contains only the characters a, e, i, s, t, plus blank spaces (sp) and newlines (nl). Suppose further that the file has ten a's, fifteen e's, twelve i's, three s's, four t's, thirteen blanks, and one newline. As the table in Figure 12.1 shows, this file requires 174 bits to represent, since there are 58 characters and each character requires three bits.

In real life, files can be quite large. Many of the very large files are output of some program, and there is usually a big disparity between the most frequent and least frequent characters. For instance, many large data files have an inordinately large amount of digits, blanks, and newlines, but few q's and x's.

Reducing the amount of bits required for data representation is known as *compression*. **Compression consists of two phases: the encoding phase (compressing) and the decoding phase (uncompressing).**

There are many situations where reducing the size of a file is desirable. For instance, since disk space is precious on virtually every machine, decreasing the amount of space that is required for files would increase the effective capacity of the disk. When data is being transmitted across phone lines by a modem, the effective rate of transmission is increased if the amount of data that is transmitted can be reduced. Reducing the amount of bits required for data representation is known as *compression*. Actually, compression consists of two phases: the encoding phase (compression) and the decoding phase (uncompression). A simple strategy that we discuss in this chapter achieves 25 percent savings on typical large files, and as much as 50 or 60 percent savings on many large data files. Extensions provide somewhat better compression.

In a variable-length code, the most frequent characters have the shortest representation.

The general strategy is to allow the code length to vary from character to character and to ensure that the frequently occurring characters have short codes. Notice that if all characters occur with the same or very similar frequency, we cannot expect any savings.

12.1.1   Prefix Codes

In a *binary trie*, **a left branch represents 0 and a right branch represents 1. The path to a node indicates its representation.**

The binary code in Figure 12.1 can be represented by the binary tree in Figure 12.2. In that tree, characters are stored only in leaf nodes. The representation of each character can be found by starting at the root and recording the path, using a 0 to indicate the left branch and a 1 to indicate the right branch. For instance, s is reached by going left, then right, and finally right. This is encoded as 011. This data structure is sometimes referred to as a *binary trie* (pronounced "try"). If character c_i is at depth d_i and occurs f_i times, then the *cost* of the code is equal to $\sum d_i f_i$.

Character	Code	Frequency	Total Bits
a	000	10	30
e	001	15	45
i	010	12	36
s	011	3	9
t	100	4	12
sp	101	13	39
nl	110	1	3
Total			**174**

Figure 12.1   A standard coding scheme

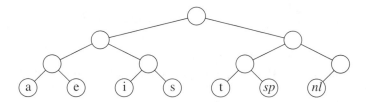

Figure 12.2   Representation of the original code by a tree

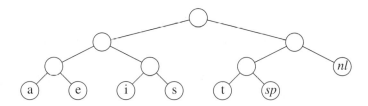

Figure 12.3   A slightly better tree

A better code than the one given in Figure 12.2 can be obtained by noticing that *nl* is an only child. By placing it one level higher (in place of its parent), we obtain the new tree in Figure 12.3. This new tree has a cost of 173 but is still far from optimal.

Notice that the tree in Figure 12.3 is a *full tree*: All nodes either are leaves or have two children. An optimal code will always have this property; otherwise, as we have already seen, nodes with only one child could move up a level. If the characters are placed only at the leaves, any sequence of bits can always be decoded unambiguously. For instance, suppose the encoded string is 0100111100010110001000111. From Figure 12.1 we know that 0 is not a character code and 01 is not a character code but 010 represents *i*, so the first character is *t*. Then 011 follows, giving a *t*. Then 11 follows, which is a newline (*nl*). The remainder of the code is *a*, *sp*, *t*, *i*, *e*, and *nl*.

> In a *full tree* all nodes either are leaves or have two children.

The character codes can be different lengths, as long as no character code is a prefix of another character code. Such an encoding is known as a *prefix code*. Conversely, if a character is contained in a nonleaf node, it is no longer possible to guarantee that the decoding will be unambiguous.

Putting these facts together, we see that our basic problem is to find the full binary tree of minimum cost (as defined above) in which all characters are contained in the leaves. The tree in Figure 12.4 shows the optimal tree for our sample alphabet. As can be seen in Figure 12.5, this code uses only 146 bits. Notice that there are many optimal codes. These can be obtained by swapping children in the encoding tree.

> In a *prefix code*, no character code is a prefix of another character code. This is guaranteed if the characters are only in leaves. A prefix code can be decoded unambiguously.

12.1.2   Huffman's Algorithm

Huffman's algorithm constructs an optimal prefix code. It works by repeatedly merging the two minimum-weight trees.

How is the coding tree constructed? The coding system algorithm was given by Huffman in 1952 and is commonly referred to as *Huffman's algorithm*.

Throughout this section we will assume that the number of characters is C. Huffman's algorithm can be described as follows: We maintain a forest of trees. The *weight* of a tree is equal to the sum of the frequencies of its leaves. $C - 1$ times, select the two trees, T_1 and T_2, of smallest weight, breaking ties arbitrarily, and form a new tree with subtrees T_1 and T_2. At the beginning of the algorithm, there are C single-node trees (one for each character). At the end of the algorithm there is one tree, and this is an optimal Huffman tree. Exercise 12.4 asks you to prove that Huffman's algorithm is correct.

Ties are broken arbitrarily.

A worked example will make the operation of the algorithm clear. Figure 12.6 shows the initial forest; the weight of each tree is shown in small type at the root. The two trees of lowest weight are merged together, creating the forest shown in Figure 12.7. We will name the new root *T*1. We have made *s* the left child arbitrarily; any tie-breaking procedure can be used. The total weight of the new tree is just the sum of the weights of the old trees and can thus be easily computed.

Now there are six trees, and we again select the two trees of smallest weight, *T*1 and *t*. They are merged into a new tree with root *T*2 and weight 8. This is shown in Figure 12.8. The third step merges *T*2 and *a*, creating *T*3, with weight $10 + 8 = 18$. Figure 12.9 shows the result of this operation.

After the third merge is completed, the two trees of lowest weight are the single-node trees representing *i* and the blank space. Figure 12.10 shows how these trees are merged into the new tree with root *T*4. The fifth step is to merge the trees with roots *e* and *T*3, since these trees have the two smallest weights. The result of this step is shown in Figure 12.11.

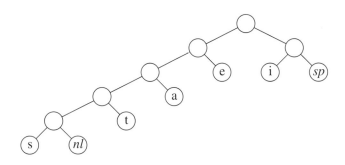

Figure 12.4   Optimal prefix code tree

Finally, an optimal tree, which was shown earlier in Figure 12.4, is obtained by merging the two remaining trees. Figure 12.12 shows the optimal tree, with root *T6*.

Character	Code	Frequency	Total Bits
a	001	10	30
e	01	15	30
i	10	12	24
s	00000	3	15
t	0001	4	16
sp	11	13	26
nl	00001	1	5
Total			**146**

Figure 12.5   Optimal prefix code

Figure 12.6   Initial stage of Huffman's algorithm

Figure 12.7   Huffman's algorithm after the first merge

Figure 12.8   Huffman's algorithm after the second merge

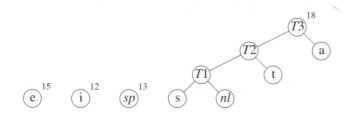

Figure 12.9 Huffman's algorithm after the third merge

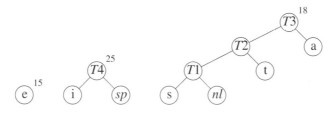

Figure 12.10 Huffman's algorithm after the fourth merge

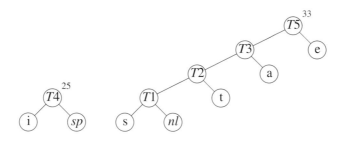

Figure 12.11 Huffman's algorithm after the fifth merge

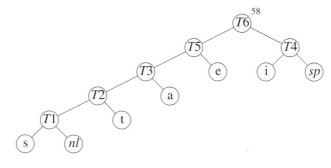

Figure 12.12 Huffman's algorithm after the final merge

	Character	Weight	Parent	Child Type
0	a	10	9	1
1	e	15	11	1
2	i	12	10	0
3	s	3	7	0
4	t	4	8	1
5	sp	13	10	1
6	nl	1	7	1
7	T1	4	8	0
8	T2	8	9	0
9	T3	18	11	0
10	T4	25	12	1
11	T5	33	12	0
12	T6	58	0	

Figure 12.13   Encoding table (numbers on left are array indices)

12.1.3   The Encoding Phase

Once a tree is built, we must decide what the code for each character is. This can be done if every node in the tree stores its parent and an indication of whether it is a left or right child. If there are C characters, then there will be $2C - 1$ nodes. We can use an array of structures containing the weight, parent, and child status.

The code can be represented in an array.

The encoding table for our Huffman tree is shown in Figure 12.13. The character is not really stored, but is used to index into the table (presumably, then 'a' would index into position 97, representing its ASCII value, 'b' into 98, and so on). The parent of *nl*, for example, is *T1*, and *nl* is a right child. We can print *nl*'s code by recursively printing *T1*'s code and then the child type. Notice that *T6* has 0 for a parent. This tells us when to stop the recursion. Since the ASCII set runs from 0 to 127, the array would run from 0 to 254, representing the fact that at most $C - 1$ internal symbols might be needed.

12.1.4   Decoding Phase

Once we have generated a compressed file, eventually we need to uncompress it. To do this, we must include extra information in the compressed file. Obviously, we would like to include as little information as possible. Let us assume that we are using the ASCII character set.

For the ASCII character set, we can store the tree in 255 bytes.

One possibility is to store the character counts. This requires 128 integers;

presumably 24-bit (that is, three-byte) integers will suffice (16-bit integers are probably not sufficient because it is possible that some characters occur more than 65,535 times if the file is large). The total storage requirement is 384 bytes.

An alternative is to store the parent and child type information. Since every parent is a newly created node, the value of the parent is a number between 128 and 254. Consequently we need 7 bits to store the parent. In fact, we can use an 8-bit character: the low 7 bits plus 128 will represent the parent (the root can use 255 as its parent). This leaves the 8th (that is, the most significant) bit free to represent the child type. Consequently, the total storage requirement for the coding information is 255 bytes.

12.1.5   Practical Considerations

A practical algorithm cannot scan the file twice. There are several alternatives.

Before we can begin compression, we need a frequency count for each character. If the file is small enough to fit in main memory we can read the file into a character array, compute the character counts, and apply the algorithm. But what if it is too large?

Certainly we do not want to read the file twice; disk I/O is extremely slow. A possibility is to break the file into chunks that can be stored in main memory and then compress each chunk separately. Most modern computers can store several megabytes at a time, so the overhead of 255 bytes for each coding table is not likely to be large.

An alternative is to assume that the input file is "typical": For instance, the distribution of characters in C++ programs is well known. An advantage of this method is that we do not need to store the coding table; this is particularly attractive if the file sizes are not huge. There are many other possibilities that have been explored, as well as more complex compression schemes that perform even better than Huffman coding. See the references for some pointers.

12.2   A Cross-Reference Generator

A *cross-reference generator* lists identifiers and their line numbers. It is a common application because it is similar to creating an index.

In this section we design a program that scans a C++ source file and outputs all identifiers, along with the line numbers on which they occur. The identifiers are sorted. This is known as a *cross reference generator*. One compiler application is to list, for each function, the names of all other functions that it directly calls.

However, this is a general problem that occurs in many other contexts. For instance, it generalizes the creation of an index for a book. Another use is described in Exercise 12.14: misspelled words in a document are gathered together with the lines on which they occur. This avoids repeatedly printing out the same misspelled word and provides an indication of where the errors are.

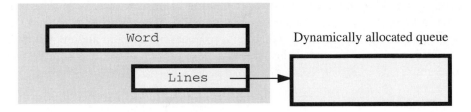

Figure 12.14   IdNode data members: Word is a String; Lines is a
pointer to a Queue

12.2.1   Outline

Each identifier and the line numbers on which it occurs is stored in an IdNode
object. We then maintain a sorted collection of IdNodes. When the source file
has been read, we can iterate over the collection, outputting identifiers and their
corresponding line numbers.

One alternative is to use a sorted linked list of IdNode objects. When an
identifier is read, we check to see if it is already in the list of IdNode objects. If
so, we add the current line number to the IdNode object referenced by a call to
Find. If not, we create a new IdNode object with the new identifier and the
current line number, and insert the IdNode into the linked list. After the entire
input is read, we can iterate over the linked list and output our answers. However, a sorted linked list has poor asymptotic performance. Consequently, we use
a binary search tree and perform an inorder traversal to obtain the final output.

> We store the line num-
> bers for each identifier
> in a queue. We place
> the identifiers in a
> binary search tree.

The only remaining detail is the IdNode object. As we mentioned already,
it stores the identifier and the line numbers on which it occurs. The identifier can
be represented by a String. The line numbers can be represented by a queue of
integers. This makes sense because, when we output the line numbers, they will
come out in the same order as they went in, namely increasing order. As we will
see however, there is an important detail: The linked list and search tree classes
use copy construction on the basic object. Copy construction is not defined for
the queue; furthermore, it would be best to avoid the overhead of making copies.
We get around this by storing a pointer to the queue as shown in Figure 12.14.
The implementation is described in the next subsection.

> We use a pointer to a
> queue in the tree
> nodes to avoid copy
> constructor problems.

12.2.2   C++ Implementation

Figure 12.15 shows the header files and the IdNode class (which contains only
public members). An IdNode consists of a String and a pointer to a queue of
integers. The String member Word is declared at line 12: Lines, which is
the pointer to a queue of integers is declared at line 13. Two constructors are provided: The default constructor at line 17 is needed by the binary search tree class;

line 18 gives the declaration for a constructor that initializes an `IdNode` with a `String` and line number. The implementation of this constructor is shown in Figure 12.16. We can see that the `String` component is initialized in the normal way. `Lines` is initialized by dynamically allocating a queue and enqueueing `CurrentLine`. The rest of the `IdNode` class provides the three comparison operators.

```
1  #include <fstream.h>
2  #include <stdlib.h>
3  #include <ctype.h>
4  #include "Bst.h"
5  #include "Queue.h"
6  #include "Iterate.h"
7  #include "String.h"
8
9      // Basic object that will be stored in a search tree
10 struct IdNode
11 {
12     String Word;        // An identifier
13     Queue<int> *Lines; // Lines where it occurs
14
15         // Constructors: default for copy constructor
16         // implies default is accepted for destructor
17     IdNode( ) : Lines( NULL ) { }
18     IdNode( const String & TheWord, int currentLine );
19
20         // Ordering operators
21     int operator<( const IdNode & Rhs ) const
22             { return Word < Rhs.Word; }
23     int operator>( const IdNode & Rhs ) const
24             { return Word > Rhs.Word; }
25     int operator==( const IdNode & Rhs ) const
26             { return Word == Rhs.Word; }
27 };
```

Figure 12.15   `IdNode` class

```
1  // Constructor: Note user must delete the queue themselves
2
3  IdNode::IdNode( const String & TheWord, int CurrentLine )
4                       : Word( TheWord )
5  {
6      Lines = new Queue<int>;
7      Lines->Enqueue( CurrentLine );
8  }
```

Figure 12.16   Constructor for `IdNode`

Two points are important. First, the default copy constructor is in effect, meaning that a shallow copy of Lines is performed. This is needed because, as we have mentioned, we do not want to incur the overhead of duplicating queues. However, this means that we cannot provide a destructor. Each queue is potentially pointed at by more than one Lines member, so providing a destructor could (and, as we will see, in fact would) lead to havoc. Consequently, the queue must be deleted manually, as appropriate.

A shallow copy of Lines is performed. Thus we cannot delete it in the destructor. It must be freed elsewhere.

The Program class shown in Figure 12.17 is similar to the one shown in Figure 11.2, which was part of a balanced symbol program. Many of the member functions were already seen there, and their implementations are not repeated. We do not use derivation, because that would require that we inherit additional data members, such as a stack.

```
1  // Program class interface: evaluate cross-reference
2  //
3  // CONSTRUCTION: with (a) open istream (b) another
4  //       Program object
5  //
6  // ******************PUBLIC OPERATIONS*******************
7  // void GenerateCrossReference( ) --> Name says it all...
8  // ******************ERRORS******************************
9  // Error checking on comments and quotes is performed
10
11 class Program
12 {
13   public:
14     Program( istream & Input ) :
15               CurrentLine( 1 ), InputStream( Input ) { }
16     void GenerateCrossReference( );
17   private:
18         // This is similar to Figure 11.2
19     enum CommentType { SlashSlash, SlashStar };
20     char Ch;                  // Current character
21     int CurrentLine;
22     istream & InputStream;    // Reference to the input stream
23     int NextChar( );
24     void PutBackChar( );
25     void SkipComment( CommentType Start );
26     void SkipQuote( char QuoteType );
27
28         // These are the new private members
29     IdNode Current;
30     String GetString( );
31     int GetNextSymbol( );
32 };
```

Figure 12.17 Class interface for Program

```
1  // Return indicates if Ch can be part of a C++ identifier
2  //
3  static inline int
4  IsIdChar( char Ch )
5  {
6      return Ch == '_' || isalnum( Ch );
7  }
```

Figure 12.18   Routine to test if a character could be part of an identifier

```
1  // Return an identifier read from input stream
2  // First character is already read into Ch
3
4  String
5  Program::GetString( )
6  {
7      static char TmpString[ 256 ];
8      int i;
9
10     for( i = 0; ( TmpString[ i ] = Ch ) && NextChar( ); i++ )
11         if( !IsIdChar( Ch ) )
12         {
13             PutBackChar( );
14             break;
15         }
16
17     TmpString[ ++i ] = '\0';
18
19     return TmpString;    // Automatic conversion will occur
20 }
```

Figure 12.19   Routine to return a `String` from input

The parsing routines are straightforward, though as usual they require lots of effort.

The new parsing routines deal with recognizing an identifier. At line 29 we see that an `IdNode` object is declared; it will store the identifier that is currently being processed. The reason for this is that since we will store a tree of `IdNode` objects, we need an `IdNode` object to pass to the `Find` and `Insert` routines.

A C++ identifier consists of alphanumeric characters and underscores, with the restriction that the first character may not be a digit. Consequently, the routine in Figure 12.18 tests if a character is part of an identifier. The `GetString` routine in Figure 12.19 assumes that the first character of an identifier is already read and is stored in the class data member `Ch`. It repeatedly reads characters until one that is not part of an identifier is seen. At that point we put the character back (at line 13), attach a null terminator to an internal character array (line 17), and then return a `String` (by implicitly calling a `String` constructor).

```
1  // Return next identifier, skipping comments,
2  // string constants, and character constants
3  // Placed identifier in Current.Word and
4  // return 0 only if end of stream is reached
5
6  int
7  Program::GetNextSymbol( )
8  {
9      while( NextChar( ) )
10     {
11         if( Ch == '/' )
12         {
13             if( NextChar( ) )
14                 if( Ch == '*' )
15                     SkipComment( SlashStar );
16                 else if( Ch == '/' )
17                     SkipComment( SlashSlash );
18                 else
19                     PutBackChar( );
20         }
21         else if( Ch == '\\' )
22             NextChar( );
23         else if( Ch == '\'' || Ch == '"' )
24             SkipQuote( Ch );
25         else if( !isdigit( Ch ) && IsIdChar( Ch ) )
26         {
27             Current.Word = GetString( );
28             return 1;
29         }
30     }
31     return 0;         // End of file
32 }
```

Figure 12.20   Routine to fill `Current.Word` with the next identifier

GetNextSymbol, shown in Figure 12.20 is similar to the routine in Figure 11.6. The difference is that here, at line 25, if the first character of an identifier is seen, we fill Current.Word with the identifier.

With all of the supporting routines written, we can discuss the main member function, GenerateCrossReference, which is shown in Figure 12.21. Line 6 declares a binary search tree of IdNode objects. Lines 9 to 19 process the source file. At line 11 a Find is performed for each identifier to see if it has already been seen. By using a constant reference to store the result of the Find we avoid making any copies. If the Find is successful, then at line 15 we can enqueue the current line onto the corresponding queue.[1] Otherwise, we have a new identifier. In that case, we add it to the search tree at line 17.

The result of the Find is accessed by a constant reference to avoid a copy. If the item is found, we add to the referenced queue.

---

1. Note that this does not violate the fact that ThisNode is a constant, because none of ThisNode's members change; the Lines member still points at the same queue.

```
1  // Output the cross reference
2
3  void
4  Program::GenerateCrossReference( )
5  {
6      SearchTree<IdNode> TheIdentifiers;
7
8          // Insert identifiers into the search tree
9      while( GetNextSymbol( ) )
10     {
11         const IdNode & ThisNode =
12                         TheIdentifiers.Find( Current );
13
14         if( TheIdentifiers.WasFound( ) )
15             ThisNode.Lines->Enqueue( CurrentLine );
16         else
17             TheIdentifiers.Insert(
18                         IdNode( Current.Word, CurrentLine ) );
19     }
20
21         // Iterate through search tree and output
22         // identifiers and their line number
23     InOrder<IdNode> Itr = TheIdentifiers;
24
25     for( Itr.First( ); +Itr; ++Itr )
26     {
27         const IdNode & ThisNode = Itr( );
28
29             // Print identifier and first line where it occurs
30         cout << ThisNode.Word << ": " <<
31                             ThisNode.Lines->GetFront( );
32         ThisNode.Lines->Dequeue( );
33
34             // Print all other lines on which it occurs
35         while( !ThisNode.Lines->IsEmpty( ) )
36         {
37             cout << ", " << ThisNode.Lines->GetFront( );
38             ThisNode.Lines->Dequeue( );
39         }
40         cout << '\n';
41
42             // Deallocate the queue
43         delete ThisNode.Lines;
44     }
45 }
```

Figure 12.21   Main cross-reference algorithm

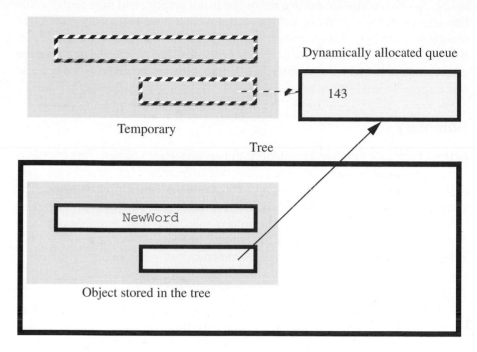

Figure 12.22   The object in the tree is a copy of the temporary; after the insertion is complete, the destructor is called for the temporary

Recall that the `Insert` member function needs an `IdNode` object. Consequently, we create a temporary unnamed `IdNode` by calling the constructor in Figure 12.16. A new `IdNode` will be placed in the search tree by calling the `IdNode` copy constructor. This means that in the `IdNode` that is physically in the search tree, the `String` member is a copy, as is the `Lines` pointer. This is illustrated in Figure 12.22. This line of code is the reason that we cannot `delete` the queue object in a destructor: immediately after the insertion, the `IdNode` destructor is called for the temporary object. As written now, this means that the temporary's `String` member is destroyed (which is fine because the copy has been made), but the queue is not. If the destructor deleted the queue, then the `Lines` pointer for the `IdNode` in the search tree would be pointing at garbage.

Once we have built the search tree, we merely iterate through it using an inorder traversal. To do this, we use the `Inorder` class described in Section 17.4.2. The iterator visits nodes in the binary search tree in their sorted order. It is used in the same way as `ListItr`. The iterator is declared at line 23, and line 25 uses the standard iteration operators provided by the `InOrder` class. At line 27 we have `ThisNode` be a constant reference to the `IdNode` object that is stored in the current search tree node. We print the word and the first line number

If an item is not found, we create a temporary `IdNode`, enqueue the current line, and insert it into the tree. The tree will store a copy of the temporary.

The output is obtained by an inorder traversal using an iterator class. After a word and its lines are output, the corresponding queue is deleted.

at line 30 (we are guaranteed that the queue is not empty), and then dequeue that line number at line 32. While the queue is not empty, we repeatedly output line numbers in the loop that extends from line 35 to 39. We print out a newline at line 40. At this point, the queue is no longer needed, and we can delete the queue corresponding to `ThisNode` at line 43. A main program is not provided because it is essentially identical to Figure 11.9.

Summary

In this chapter we saw implementations of two important utilities. Text compression is an important technique that allows one to increase both the effective disk capacity and the effective modem speed and is an area of active research. The simple method we have described, namely Huffman's algorithm, typically achieves compression of 25 percent on text files. Other algorithms and extensions of Huffman's algorithm perform better. The cross-referencing problem is a general problem that also has many applications.

Objects of the Game

binary trie A data structure in which a left branch represents 0 and a right branch represents 1. The path to a node indicates its representation. (378)

compression The act of reducing the amount of bits required for data representation. There are actually two phases: the encoding phase (compression) and the decoding phase (uncompression). (378)

cross-reference generator Lists identifiers and their line numbers. It is a common application because it is similar to creating an index. (384)

full tree A tree whose nodes either are leaves or have two children. (379)

Huffman's algorithm An algorithm that constructs an optimal prefix code. It works by repeatedly merging the two minimum-weight trees. (380)

prefix code Code in which no character code is a prefix of another character code. This is guaranteed in a trie if the characters are only in leaves. A prefix code can be decoded unambiguously. (379)

Common Errors

1. In the cross-reference generator, attempting to use a queue instead of a pointer to a queue in the tree node would be erroneous. This is because the queue copy constructor is disabled, and construction of a new node requires a copy constructor.

2. In the cross-reference generator, we deliberately use a shallow copy for the pointer to a queue. It would be a disaster if the tree node class provided a destructor. We must destroy the queue manually to avoid memory leaks.

3. When performing file compression it would be bad to read the input file twice.

4. Using too much memory to store the compression table is a common mistake. This would limit the amount of compression that can be achieved.

On the Internet

The cross-reference generator is available.

    Xref.cpp   Contains the source for the cross-reference generator

Exercises

In Short

12.1. Show the Huffman tree that results from the following distribution of punctuation characters and digits: colon (100), space (605), newline (100), comma (705), 0 (431), 1 (242), 2 (176), 3 (59), 4 (185), 5 (250), 6 (174), 7 (199), 8 (205), 9 (217).

12.2. Most systems come with a compression program. Compress several types of files to determine the typical compression rate on your system. How large do the files have to be to make compression worthwhile?

12.3. What happens if a file compressed using Huffman's algorithm is used to transmit data over a phone line, and a single bit is accidentally lost? What can be done about this?

In Theory

12.4. Prove the correctness of Huffman's algorithm by expanding the following steps:

    a. Show that no node has only one child.

    b. Show that the two least frequent characters must be the two deepest nodes in the tree.

    c. Show that the characters in any two nodes at the same depth can be swapped without affecting optimality.

    d. Use induction: As trees are merged, consider the new character set to be the characters in the tree roots.

12.5. Under what circumstances could a Huffman tree of ASCII characters generate a 2-bit code for some character? Under what circumstances could it generate a 20-bit code?

12.6. Show that if the symbols are sorted by frequency, Huffman's algorithm can be implemented in linear time.

In Practice

12.7. For the cross-reference generator, use a sorted linked list instead of a binary search tree. How does this affect performance?

12.8. The disadvantage of using a queue to store line numbers is that the queue is emptied in the course of this operation. This could be a liability in some cases. Instead of storing the line numbers in a queue, use a linked list. Implement and compare the performance of the following strategies:

a. Replace an `Enqueue` with an insertion at the end of the linked list. A traversal of the list is used.
b. Store both a linked list and a `ListItr` object that refers to the last item in the linked list. The insertion at the end of the linked list should be more efficient than in part a.

12.9. Combine Exercises 12.7 and 12.8 so that the cross-reference generator uses a sorted linked list to store the word information, and the word information consists of a `String`, a list of line numbers, and a `ListItr` to the end of the list.

12.10. If a word occurs twice on a line, the cross-reference generator will list it twice. Modify the algorithm so that duplicates are only listed once.

12.11. Modify the algorithm so that if a word appears on consecutive lines, a range is indicated. For example,

```
if: 2, 4, 6-9, 11
```

Programming Projects

12.12. Implement a complete file compression program. Do not forget to provide a decompression algorithm. You will need to write a `BitStream` class.

```
IX: {Series|()            {2}
IX: {Series!geometric|()  {4}
IX: {Euler's constant}    {4}
IX: {Series!geometric|)}  {4}
IX: {Series!arithmetic|() {4}
IX: {Series!arithmetic|)} {5}
IX: {Series!harmonic|()   {5}
IX: {Euler's constant}    {5}
IX: {Series!harmonic|)}   {5}
IX: {Series|)}            {5}
```

Figure 12.23   Sample input for Exercise 12.13

```
Euler's constant: 4, 5
Series: 2-5
    arithmetic: 4-5
    geometric: 4
    harmonic: 5
```

Figure 12.24   Sample ouput for Exercise 12.13

12.13.   Generate an index for a book. The input file consists of a set of index entries. Each line consists of the string IX:, followed by an index entry name enclosed in braces, followed by a page number that is enclosed in braces. Each ! in an index entry name represets a sublevel. A | (represents the start of a range and a |) represents the end of the range. Occasionally, this will be the same page, and in that case, only output a single page number. Otherwise, do not collapse or expand ranges on your own. As an example, Figure 12.23 shows sample input and Figure 12.24 shows the corresponding output.

12.14.   Implement a spelling checker using a hash table. Assume that the dictionary comes from two sources: an existing large dictionary and a second file containing a personal dictionary. Output all misspelled words and the line numbers on which they occur (keeping track of the misspelled words and their line numbers is identical to generating a cross reference). Additionally, for each misspelled word, list any words in the dictionary that are obtainable by applying any of the following rules:

     a. Add one character

     b. Remove one character

     c. Exchange adjacent characters

References

The original paper on Huffman's algorithm is [3]. Variations on the algorithm are discussed in [2] and [4]. Another popular compression scheme is *Ziv-Lempel encoding*, described in [7] and [6]. It works by generating a series of fixed-length codes. Typically, we would generate 4096 twelve-bit codes that represent the most common substrings in the file. [1] and [5] are good surveys of the common compression schemes.

1. T. Bell, I. H. Witten, and J. G. Cleary, "Modelling for Text Compression," *ACM Computing Surveys* **21** (1989) 557-591.

2. R. G. Gallager, "Variations on a Theme by Huffman," *IEEE Transactions on Information Theory* **IT-24** (1978), 668-674.

3. D. A. Huffman, "A Model for the Construction of Minimum Redundancy Codes," *Proceedings of the IRE* **40** (1952), 1098-1101.

4. D. E. Knuth, "Dynamic Huffman Coding," *Journal of Algorithms* **6** (1985), 163-180.

5. D. A. Lelewer and D. S. Hirschberg, "Data Compression," *ACM Computing Surveys* **19** (1987), 261-296.

6. T. A. Welch, "A Technique for High-Performance Data Compression," *Computer* **17** (1984), 8-19.

7. J. Ziv and A. Lempel, "Compression of Individual Sequences via Variable-Rate Coding," *IEEE Transactions on Information Theory* **IT-24** (1978), 530-536.

Chapter 13

Simulation

An important use of computers is *simulation*. In a simulation the computer emulates the operation of a real system and gathers statistics. As an example, we might want to simulate the operation of a bank with k tellers, to determine the minimum value of k that gives reasonable service time. Using a computer has many advantages. First, the information is gathered without involving real customers. Second, a simulation by computer can be faster than the actual implementation because of the speed of the computer. Third, the simulation can be easily replicated. In many cases, the proper choice of data structues can help us improve the efficiency of the simulation.

In this chapter we will see

- how to simulate a game modeled on the *Josephus problem*
- how to simulate the operation of a computer modem bank

13.1 The Josephus Problem

The *Josephus problem* is the following game: N people, numbered 1 to N, are sitting in a circle. Starting at person 1, a hot potato is passed. After M passes, the person holding the hot potato is eliminated, the circle closes ranks, and the game continues with the person who was sitting after the eliminated person picking up the hot potato. The last remaining person wins. It is common to assume that M is a constant of the game, though a random number generator can be used to change M after each elimination.

The Josephus problem arose in the first century AD, in a cave on a mountain in Israel, where Jewish zealots were besieged by Roman soldiers. The historian Josephus was among them. The zealots voted to form a suicide pact rather than surrender to the Romans, to Josephus' consternation. He suggested the game mentioned here. The hot potato was the sentence of death to the person next to the one who got the potato. Josephus rigged the game to get the last lot and convinced the intended victim that they should surrender. That is how we know about this game; in effect Josephus cheated.[1]

If $M = 0$, then the players are eliminated in order and the last player always wins. For other values of M, things are not so obvious. Figure 13.1 shows that if $N = 5$ and $M = 1$, then the players are eliminated in the order 2, 4, 1, 5. In this case player 3 wins. The steps are as follows:

1. At the start, the potato is at player 1; after one pass it is at player 2.
2. Player 2 is eliminated, player 3 picks up the potato, and after one pass it is at player 4.
3. Player 4 is eliminated, player 5 picks up the potato and passes it to player 1.
4. Player 1 is eliminated, player 3 picks up the potato, and passes it to player 5.
5. Player 5 is eliminated, so player 3 wins.

We will first write a program that simulates, pass for pass, a game for any values of N and M. The running time of the simulation is $O(MN)$, which is acceptable if the number of passes is small. As we can see, however, each step takes $O(M)$ time because it performs M passes. We will show how to implement each step in $O(\log N)$ time, regardless of the number of passes that are performed. The running time of the simulation is $O(N \log N)$.

13.1.1   The Simple Solution

We can represent the players by a linked list and use the iterator to simulate the passing.

The passing stage in the Josephus problem suggests that we represent the players in a linked list. We create a linked list with the elements 1, 2, ... , N inserted in order. We then set an iterator to the front element. Each pass of the potato corresponds to a ++ operation on the iterator. When we are at the last player (currently remaining) in the list, we implement the pass by resetting the iterator to the first element. This action mimics the circle. When we are done passing, we remove the element that the iterator has landed on.

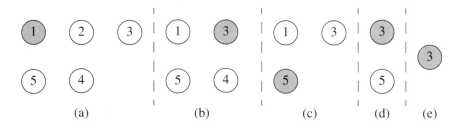

Figure 13.1   The Josephus problem

---

1. Thanks to David Teague for relaying this story.

For reasons that we will see in Chapter 16, it is easier to remove the element after the current position by using the RemoveNext member function. This is reflected by the code in Figure 13.2, where we initialize Current to the last rather than first player. The linked list and iterator are declared at lines 9 and 10, respectively. We construct the initial list by using the loop at lines 14 and 15. The semantics of Insert, as specified in the class interface in Figure 16.7 tell us the insertions are after the iterator's position, and that the result of an insertion is to set the iterator's position to the inserted item. Thus we get the list in the order that we want.

We maintain the iterator at the player prior to the current so that RemoveNext can be applied.

```
1  #include "List.h"
2
3  // Return the winner in the Josephus problem
4  // Linked list implementation
5
6  int
7  Josephus( int People, int Passes )
8  {
9      List<int> L;
10     ListItr<int> P = L;
11     int i;
12
13         // Construct the list
14     for( i = 1; i <= People; i++ )
15         P.Insert( i );
16
17         // Play the game;
18         // Note: P is always one player before
19     while( People-- != 1 )
20     {
21         for( i = 0; i < Passes; i++ )
22         {
23             P++;                // Advance
24             if( !+P )           // If we just went past last player
25                 P.First( );// then go back to the first
26         }
27
28         if( !P.RemoveNext( ) ) // Remove the next player
29         {
30                 // RemoveNext fails if P is last item
31             P.Zeroth( );    // So set P to zeroth item
32             P.RemoveNext( );// In order to remove first player
33         }
34     }
35
36     P.First( );              // Get first (and only) player
37     return P( );             // Return player's number
38  }
```

Figure 13.2   Linked list implementation of Josephus problem

In Figure 13.2, the code at lines 21 to 33 plays one step of the algorithm by passing the potato (lines 21 to 26) and then eliminating a player (lines 28 to 33). This is done until the test at line 19 tells us that only one player remains. At that point we go to the remaining player by calling the `First` member function at line 36 (recall that during most of the algorithm, the iterator is before the logically current player), and then accessing and returning the player's number at line 37.

The running time is O(MN), but memory management routines cause large increases in the running time when M is 1 or 2. You may need to comment out `delete`.

It is easy to see that the running time of this routine is $O(MN)$ because this is exactly the number of passes that occur during the algorithm. For small M, this is acceptable, although we should mention two things. First, the case $M = 0$ does not yield a running time of $O(0)$; obviously the running time is $O(N)$. One does not merely multiply by zero when trying to interpret a Big-Oh expression. Second, if $M - 2$, you may be very surprised with how slow the algorithm is. The problem is that when items in the linked list are removed, calls to `delete` are made by the linked list class. These calls are generally constant-time operations, but $M = 1$ and $M = 2$ can cause some implementations of the memory management routines to exhibit bad behavior, and in fact, each call to `delete` can take $O(\log N)$ time (where N is the number of previous calls to `new`) using some libraries. Consequently, for $M - 1$, even though the total running time of the algorithm should be $O(N)$, it is actually $O(N \log N)$ for systems with bad memory management implementations. You can verify this by going back to the linked list class and commenting out the appropriate call to `delete`. Does this mean that Big-Oh is a meaningless tool? Not at all; the `delete` can be commented if necessary, and the time bound allows us to suspect that it is the `delete` that needs to be commented out.

13.1.2   A More Efficient Algorithm

If we implement each round of passing in a single logarithmic operation, the simulation will be faster.

A more efficient algorithm can be obtained if we use a data structure that supports accessing the kth smallest item (in logarithmic time). This will allow us to implement each round of passing in a single operation. If we look at Figure 13.1, we can see why. Suppose we have N players remaining, and we are currently at player P from the front. Initially N is the total number of players and P is one. After M passes, a calculation tells us that we will be at player $((P + M) \bmod N)$ from the front, except if that would give us player 0, in which case we go to player N. The calculation is fairly tricky, but the concept is not.

The calculation is tricky because of the circle.

Applying this calculation to Figure 13.1, we see that M is 1, N is initially 5, and P is initially 1. So the new value of P is 2. After the deletion, N is lowered to 4, but we are still at position 2 (as part (b) of the figure suggests). The next value of P is 3 (as shown in part(b)), so the third element in the list is deleted and N is lowered to 3. The next value of P is 4 mod 3, or 1, so we are back to the first player in the remaining list (as shown in part (c)). This is removed and N becomes 2. At this point we add M to P obtaining 2. Since 2 mod 2 is 0, we set P to player N, and thus the last player in the list is the one that is removed. This agrees with part (d). After the remove, N is 1, and we are done.

```
1  #include "Bst.h"
2
3  // Recursively construct a perfectly balanced OrderedSearchTree
4  // by repeated insertions in O( N log N ) time
5
6  void
7  BuildTree( OrderedSearchTree<int> & T, int Low, int High )
8  {
9      int Center = ( Low + High ) / 2;
10
11     if( Low <= High )
12     {
13         T.Insert( Center );
14         BuildTree( T, Low, Center - 1 );
15         BuildTree( T, Center + 1, High );
16     }
17 }
18
19 // Return the winner in the Josephus problem
20 // Search Tree implementation
21
22 int
23 Josephus( int People, int Passes )
24 {
25     OrderedSearchTree<int> T;
26     BuildTree( T, 1, People );
27
28     int Rank = 1;
29     while( People > 1 )
30     {
31         if( ( Rank = ( Rank + Passes ) % People ) == 0 )
32             Rank = People;
33
34         T.Remove( T.FindKth( Rank ) );
35         People--;
36     }
37
38     return T.FindKth( 1 );
39 }
```

Figure 13.3 $O(N \log N)$ solution of Josephus problem

All we need then is a data structure that efficiently supports the FindKth operation and a method of inserting the players sequentially into the data structure. There are several similar alternatives. All of them use the fact that a binary search tree can support the FindKth operation in logarithmic time on average, or logarithmic time in the worst case if we use a sophisticated binary search tree. Consequently, we can expect an $O(N \log N)$ algorithm if we exercise care.

FindKth is supported by an ordered search tree.

The simplest method is to insert the items sequentially into a worst-case efficient binary search tree such as a red black tree, AA tree, or splay tree (these trees are discussed in later chapters). We can then call FindKth and Remove, as appropriate. It turns out that a splay tree is an excellent choice for this application because the FindKth and Insert operations will be unusually efficient and Remove is not terribly difficult to code. We will use an alternative because the implementations of these data structures that are provided in the later chapters leave FindKth as an exercise.

Because we would like to see the algorithm work, we will use the OrderedSearchTree class that supports the FindKth operation and is completely implemented in Section 18.2. It is based on the simple binary search tree, and thus does not have logarithmic worst-case performance but merely average-case performance. Consequently, we cannot merely insert the items sequentially; that would cause the search tree to exhibit its worst case performance.

There are several options. One is to insert a random permutation of $1 \ldots N$ into the search tree. The other is to build a perfectly balanced binary search tree using a class member function. Because a class member would have access to the inner workings of the search tree, this could be done in linear time. This routine is left as Exercise 18.22 when search trees are discussed.

The method we take is to write a recursive routine that inserts items in a balanced order. One can show that by inserting the middle item at the root and recursively building the two subtrees in the same manner, we obtain a balanced tree. The cost of our routine is an acceptable $O(N \log N)$; while not as efficient as the linear-time class routine, it does not adversely affect the asymptotic running time of the overall algorithm. The Remove operations are then guaranteed to be logarithmic. This routine is called BuildTree; it and the Josephus function are then coded as shown in Figure 13.3.

13.2 Event-Driven Simulation

Let us return to the bank simulation problem described in the introduction. Here we have a system where customers arrive and wait on a line until one of k tellers is available. Customer arrival is governed by a probability distribution function, as is the service time (the amount of time to be served once a teller is available). We are interested in statistics such as how long on average a customer has to wait and what percentage of the time tellers are actually servicing requests (if there are too many tellers, some will not do anything for long periods).

With certain probability distributions and values of k, these answers can be computed exactly. However, as k gets larger the analysis becomes considerably more difficult, so it is appealing to use a computer to simulate the operation of the bank. In this way the bank officers can determine how many tellers are needed to ensure reasonably smooth service. Most simulations involve thorough knowledge of probability, statistics, and queueing theory.

13.2.1   Basic Ideas

A discrete event simulation consists of processing events. Here the two events are (a) a customer arriving and (b) a customer departing, thus freeing up a teller.

We can use a probability function to generate an input stream consisting of ordered pairs of arrival and service time for each customer, sorted by arrival time.[2] We do not need to use the exact time of day. Rather we can use a quantum unit, which we will refer to as a *tick*.

The *tick* is the quantum unit of time in a simulation.

We might start a simulation clock at zero ticks. We then advance the clock one tick at a time, checking to see if there is an event. If there is, then we process the event(s) and compile statistics. When there are no customers left in the input stream and all the tellers are free, then the simulation is over. This is a *discrete time-driven simulation*.

A *discrete time-driven simulation* processes each unit of time consecutively. It is inappropriate if the interval between successive events is large.

The problem with this simulation strategy is that its running time does not depend on the number of customers or events (there are two events per customer in this case), but instead depends on the number of ticks, which is not really part of the input. To see why this is important, suppose we changed the clock units to microticks and multiplied all the times in the input by 1,000,000. The result would be that the simulation would take 1,000,000 times longer.

The key to avoiding this problem is to advance the clock to the next event time at each stage. Thus we have an *event-driven simulation*. This is conceptually easy to do. At any point, the next event that can occur is either the arrival of the next customer in the input stream or the departure of one of the customers at a teller. Since all the times when the events will happen are available, we just need to find the event that happens nearest in the future and process that event (setting the current time to the time that the event occurs).

An *event-driven simulation* advances the current time to the next event.

If the event is a departure, processing includes gathering statistics for the departing customer and checking the line (queue) to see if there is another customer waiting. If so, we add that customer, process whatever statistics are required, compute the time when the customer will leave, and add that departure to the set of events waiting to happen.

If the event is an arrival, we check for an available teller. If there is none, we place the arrival on the line (queue); otherwise, we give the customer a teller, compute the customer's departure time, and add the departure to the set of events waiting to happen.

The waiting line for customers can be implemented as a queue. Since we need to find the event *nearest* in the future, it is appropriate that the set of events be organized in a priority queue. The next event is thus an arrival or departure (whichever is sooner); both are easily available. An event-driven simulation is appropriate if the number of ticks between events is expected to be large.

The event set (that is, events waiting to happen) is organized as a priority queue.

---

2. The probability function generates interarrival times (times between arrivals), thus guaranteeing that arrivals are generated in chronological order.

```
 1 User 0 dials in at time 0 and connects for 1 minutes
 2 User 0 hangs up at time 1
 3 User 1 dials in at time 1 and connects for 5 minutes
 4 User 2 dials in at time 2 and connects for 4 minutes
 5 User 3 dials in at time 3 and connects for 11 minutes
 6 User 4 dials in at time 4 but gets busy signal
 7 User 5 dials in at time 5 but gets busy signal
 8 User 6 dials in at time 6 but gets busy signal
 9 User 1 hangs up at time 6
10 User 2 hangs up at time 6
11 User 7 dials in at time 7 and connects for 8 minutes
12 User 8 dials in at time 8 and connects for 6 minutes
13 User 9 dials in at time 9 but gets busy signal
14 User 10 dials in at time 10 but gets busy signal
15 User 11 dials in at time 11 but gets busy signal
16 User 12 dials in at time 12 but gets busy signal
17 User 13 dials in at time 13 but gets busy signal
18 User 3 hangs up at time 14
19 User 14 dials in at time 14 and connects for 6 minutes
20 User 8 hangs up at time 14
21 User 15 dials in at time 15 and connects for 3 minutes
22 User 7 hangs up at time 15
23 User 16 dials in at time 16 and connects for 5 minutes
24 User 17 dials in at time 17 but gets busy signal
25 User 15 hangs up at time 18
26 User 18 dials in at time 18 and connects for 7 minutes
27 User 19 dials in at time 19 but gets busy signal
```

Figure 13.4 Sample output for the modem bank simulation: 3 modems; a dial in is attempted every minute; average connect time is 5 minutes; simulation is run for 19 minutes

13.2.2   Example: A Modem Bank Simulation

The *modem bank* removes the waiting line from the simulation. Thus there is only one data structure.

The main algorithmic item in a simulation is the organization of the events in a priority queue. To focus on this, we will write a very simple simulation. The system we will simulate is a *modem bank* at a university computing center.

A *modem bank* consists of a large collection of modems. For example, Florida International University (FIU) has 96 modems available for students. A modem is accessed by dialing one specific number. If any of the 96 modems are available, then the user will be connected to one of them. However if all modems are in use, then the phone will be busy. Our simulation will model the service provided by the modem bank. The variables are

- The number of modems in the bank
- The probability distribution that governs dial-in attempts
- The probability distribution that governs connect time
- How long the simulation is to be run

```
 1  #include <iostream.h>
 2  #include <limits.h>
 3  #include "BinaryHeap.h"
 4  #include "Random.h"
 5
 6  class Event
 7  {
 8    public:
 9      Event( int Name = 0, long Tm = 0, int Type = DialIn ) :
10          Time( Tm ), Who( Name ), What( Type ) { }
11
12      int operator<( const Event & Rhs ) const
13          { return Time < Rhs.Time; }
14      friend class ModemSim;
15    private:
16      enum { DialIn = 1, Hangup = 2 };
17
18      int Who;          // The number of the User
19      long Time;        // When the event will occur
20      int What;         // DialIn or Hangup
21  };
```

Figure 13.5   Event class used for modem simulation

The modem bank is a simplified version of the bank teller problem because there is no waiting line. Each dial-in is an arrival, and the total time spent once a connection is established is the service time. By removing the waiting line, we remove the need to maintain a queue, and thus we have only one data structure, the priority queue. Exercise 13.14 asks you to incorporate a queue: up to L calls will be queued if all the modems are busy. To simplify matters, we will not compute statistics, but instead list each event as it is processed. We also assume that attempts to connect occur at constant intervals; in an accurate simulation we would model this interarrival time by a random process. Figure 13.4 shows the output of a simulation.

We will list each event as it happens; gathering statistics is a simple extension.

The simulation class requires another class that represents events. The Event class is shown in Figure 13.5. The data members consist of the customer number, the time that the event will occur, and an indication of what type an event (DialIn or Hangup) this is. If this simulation were more complex, with several types of events, we would certainly make Event an abstract base class and derive subclasses from it. We do not do that here because, as we will see, that would complicate things and obscure the basic workings of the simulation algorithm. The Event class contains a constructor and a comparison function that is used by the priority queue. Depending on the particular priority queue that is implemented, we may need additional comparison functions, such as operator>, operator!=, and operator==. The BinaryHeap class needs only the single comparison function that we have defined at line 12. The Event class grants friendship status to the modem simulation class ModemSim so that its internal members can be accessed.

The Event class represents events. In a complex simulation, it would derive all the possible types of events as subclasses. Using inheritance for the Event class would add a host of complications to the code.

```
1  // ModemSim class interface: run a simulation
2  //
3  // CONSTRUCTION: with (a) three parameters: the number of
4  //     modems, the average connect time, and the
5  //     interarrival time or (b) another ModemSim object
6  //
7  // *****************PUBLIC OPERATIONS*********************
8  // Type Run( )            --> Run a simulation
9
10 class ModemSim
11 {
12   public:
13     ModemSim( int Modems, double AvgLen, long CallIntrvl );
14
15         // Run the simulation
16     void Run( long StoppingTime = LONG_MAX );
17   private:
18     Random R;                       // A random source
19     BinaryHeap<Event> EventSet;     // Pending events
20
21         // Basic parameters of the simulation
22     int FreeModems;                 // Number of modems unused
23     const double AvgCallLen;        // Length of a call
24     const long FreqOfCalls;         // Interval between calls
25
26         // Add a call to EventSet at the current time,
27         // and schedule one for Delta in the future.
28     void NextCall( long Delta );
29 };
```

Figure 13.6   ModemSim class interface

```
1  // Constructor for ModemSim
2
3  ModemSim::ModemSim( int Modems, double AvgLen,
4                      long CallIntrvl ) :
5      EventSet( Event( 0 ) ),
6      FreeModems( Modems ),
7      AvgCallLen( AvgLen ),
8      FreqOfCalls( CallIntrvl )
9  {
10     NextCall( FreqOfCalls );  // Schedule first call
11 }
```

Figure 13.7   ModemSim constructor

The modem simulation class, ModemSim, is shown in Figure 13.6. It consists of a host of data members, a constructor, and two member functions. The data members include a random number class R shown at line 18. At line 19 we see that the EventSet is maintained as a BinaryHeap of Event objects. If Event were an abstract base class that derived other classes, then we could not store Event objects in the binary heap (because the subclasses might be larger than the base class). We also could not store pointer to Event objects because comparisons would be based on addresses rather than the Event comparison function. The next alternative is to have a binary heap of references to Event; but that will not compile because, as we will see, the binary heap class dynamically allocates arrays, and it is illegal to declare arrays of references. Thus we would have to construct a PtrToEvent class, as in Figure 4.15, and we would have to dynamically allocate objects in the Event hierarchy. Needless to say, this is a large part of the complications that inheritance would introduce. For complex simulations it would be worth the effort, but not here. The remaining data members are FreeModems, which is initially the number of modems in the simulation but changes as users connect and hangup, and AvgCallLen and FreqOfCalls, which are parameters of the simulation. Recall that a dial-in attempt will be made every FreqOfCalls ticks. The constructor, declared at line 13, and implemented in Figure 13.7 initializes these members and places the first arrival in the EventSet priority queue.

The simulation class consists of only two member functions. First, NextCall, shown in Figure 13.8 adds a dial-in request to the event set. It maintains two static variables: the number of the next user that will attempt to dial in and the time that event will occur. Once again, we have made the simplifying assumption that calls are made at regular intervals; in practice we would use a random number generator to model the arrival stream.

NextCall adds a dial-in request to the event set.

```
1  // Place a new DialIn event into the event queue
2  // Then advance the time when next DialIn event will occur
3  // In practice, we would use a random number to set the time
4
5  void
6  ModemSim::NextCall( long Delta )
7  {
8      static long NextCallTime = 0;
9      static int UserNum = 0;
10
11     EventSet.Insert( Event( UserNum++, NextCallTime ) );
12     NextCallTime += Delta;
13 }
```

Figure 13.8   NextCall: Place a new DialIn event into the event queue and advance the time when next DialIn event will occur

```
 1  // Run the simulation until Stopping time occurs
 2  // Print output as in Figure 13.4
 3
 4  void
 5  ModemSim::Run( long StoppingTime )
 6  {
 7      static Event E;
 8      long HowLong;
 9
10      while( !EventSet.IsEmpty( ) )
11      {
12          EventSet.DeleteMin( E );
13          if( E.Time > StoppingTime )
14              break;
15
16          if( E.What == Event::Hangup )       // Hang up
17          {
18              FreeModems++;
19              cout << "User " << E.Who << " hangs up at time "
20                  << E.Time << '\n';
21          }
22          else                                // Dial in
23          {
24              cout << "User " << E.Who <<
25                      " dials in at time " << E.Time;
26              if( FreeModems > 0 )
27              {
28                  FreeModems--;
29                  HowLong = R.Poisson( AvgCallLen );
30                  cout << " and connects for " <<
31                          HowLong << " minutes\n";
32                  E.Time += HowLong;
33                  E.What = Event::Hangup;
34                  EventSet.Insert( E );
35              }
36              else
37                  cout << " but gets busy signal\n";
38
39              NextCall( FreqOfCalls ); // Add next arrival event
40          }
41      }
42  }
```

Figure 13.9   Basic simulation routine

Run runs the simulation.

The other member function is Run, which is called to run the entire simulation. Run does most of the work and is shown in Figure 13.9. It is called with a single parameter that indicates when the simulation should end. As long as the event set is not empty, we process events. Note that it should never be empty because at the time we arrive at line 12 there is exactly one dial-in request in the priority queue, plus one hang-up request for every currently connected modem.

Whenever we remove an event at line 12 and it is confirmed to be a dial-in, we generate a replacement dial-in event at line 39. A hang-up event is also generated at line 34 if the dial-in succeeds. Thus the only way to finish the routine is if `NextCall` is set up not to generate an event eventually, or (more likely) by executing the `break` statement at line 14.

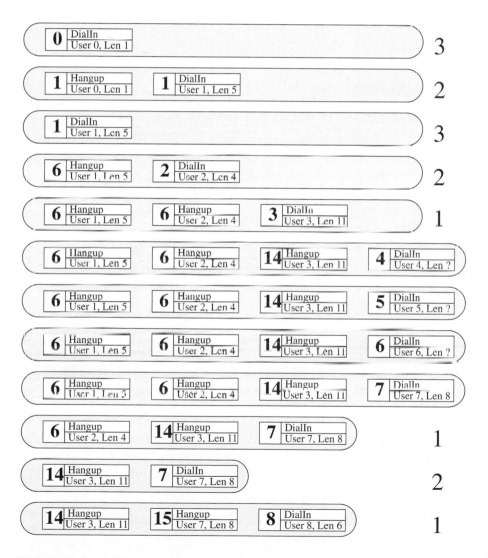

Figure 13.10   Priority queue for modem bank after each step

```
1   // Flimsy main to test ModemSim class
2
3   main( )
4   {
5       int NumModems,
6       long TotalTime;
7       double AvgConnectTime;
8       long DialInFrequency;
9
10      cout << "Enter: number of modems, length of simulation, "
11           << " average connect time, how often calls occur: ";
12
13      cin >> NumModems >> TotalTime >>
14                      AvgConnectTime >> DialInFrequency;
15
16   try
17   {
18      ModemSim S( NumModems, AvgConnectTime, DialInFrequency );
19      S.Run( TotalTime );
20   }
21   catch( ... )
22   {
23      cerr << "Out of memory!!" << endl;
24      exit( 1 );
25   }
26      return 0;
27  }
```

Figure 13.11   Simple `main` to run simulation

A hangup increases `FreeModems`. A dial-in checks to see if a modem is available and if so decreases `FreeModems`.

Let us once again summarize how the various events are processed. If the event is a hang-up, then we increment `FreeModems` at line 18 and print a message at line 19. If the event is a dial-in, we generate a partial line of output that records the attempt, and then, if there are modems available, we connect the user. To do this, we decrement `FreeModems` at line 28, generate a connection time (using a Poisson distribution rather than a uniform distribution) at line 29, print the rest of the output at line 30, and add a hang-up to the event set (lines 32 to 34). Otherwise, there are no modems available and we give the busy signal message. Either way, an additional dial-in event is generated. Figure 13.10 shows the state of the priority queue after each `DeleteMin` for the early stages of the sample output shown in Figure 13.4. The time when each event occurs is shown in boldface, and the number of free modems (if any) are shown to the right of the priority queue. The sequence of priority queue steps is as follows:

1. The first `DialIn` request is inserted
2. After `DialIn` is removed, the request is connected resulting in a `Hangup` and a replacement `DialIn` request

3. A `Hangup` request is processed

4. A `DialIn` request is processed resulting in a connect. Thus both a `Hangup` and `DialIn` event are added (three times)

5. A `DialIn` request fails; a replacement `DialIn` is generated (three times)

6. A `Hangup` request is processed (twice)

7. A `DialIn` request succeeds, `Hangup` and `DialIn` are added.

Once again, if `Event` were an abstract base class, we would expect a procedure `DoEvent` to be defined through the `Event` hierarchy; then we would not need long chains of `if/else` statements. However to access the priority queue, which is in the simulation class, we would need `Event` to store a reference to the simulation class as a data member (initialized at construction time).

A minimal `main` routine is shown for completeness in Figure 13.11. We remark that using a Poisson distribution to model connect time is not appropriate. A better choice would be to use a negative exponential distribution (but the reasons for this are beyond the scope of the text). Additionally, assuming a fixed time between attempts to dial in is also inaccurate. Once again, a negative exponential distribution would be a better model. If we change the simulation to use these distributions, the clock would be represented as a `double`. Exercise 13.11 asks you to implement these changes.

> The simulation uses a poor model. Negative exponential distributions would more accurately model the time between dial-in attempts and total connect time.

Summary

Simulation is an important area of computer science. There are many more complexities involved than can be discussed here. Among other things, the simulation is only as good as the model of randomness, and so a solid background is required in order to know what types of probability distributions are reasonable to assume. Simulation is an important application area for object-oriented techniques.

Objects of the Game

discrete time-driven simulation Processes each unit of time consecutively. It is inappropriate if the interval between successive events is large. (403)

event-driven simulation Advances the current time to the next event. (403)

Josephus problem A hot potato is repeatedly passed, and when passing terminates, the player holding the potato is eliminated. The game continues and the last remaining player wins. (397)

simulation An important use of computers in which the computer emulates the operation of a real system and gathers statistics. (397)

tick The quantum unit of time in a simulation. (403)

Common Errors

1. The most common error in simulation is using a poor model. A simulation is only as good as the accuracy of its random input.
2. Occasionally, as we saw in the linked list implementation of the Josephus problem, delete is expensive. This can be detected by a profiler, and the deletion can be commented out if memory is not scarce.

On the Internet

All the examples in this chapter are available on-line.

Josephus.cpp   Contains both implementations of Josephus and a main
to test them

Modems.cpp   Contains the code for the modem bank simulation

Exercises

In Short

13.1.   If $M = 0$, who wins the Josephus game?

13.2.   Show the operation of the Josephus algorithm with an abstract ordered binary search tree for the case of 7 people with 3 passes. Include a picture of the tree after each deletion.

13.3.   Are there any values of M for which player 1 wins a 30-person Josephus game?

13.4.   Show the state of the priority queue after each of the first ten lines of the simulation depicted in Figure 13.4.

In Theory

13.5.   Let $N = 2^k$ for any integer k. Prove that if M is 1, then player one always wins the Josephus game.

13.6.   Let $J(N)$ be the winner of an N player Josephus game with $M = 1$. Show the following:
a. If N is even, $J(N) = 2J(N/2) - 1$
b. If N is odd and $J(\lceil N/2 \rceil) \neq 1$, then $J(N) = 2J(\lceil N/2 \rceil) - 3$
c. If N is odd and $J(\lceil N/2 \rceil) = 1$, then $J(N) = N$

13.7.   Based on the results in Exercise 13.6, given an algorithm that returns the winner of an N-player Josephus game with $M = 1$. What is the running time of your algorithm?

13.8. Give a general formula for the winner of an N player Josephus game with $M = 2$.

13.9. Using our algorithm for $N = 20$, what is the order of insertion into the `OrderedSearchTree`?

In Practice

13.10. Implement the Josephus algorithm using a queue. Each pass of the potato is a `Dequeue` followed by an `Enqueue`.

13.11. Rework the simulation so that the clock is represented as a double, the time between dial-in attempts is modeled with a negative exponential distribution, and the connect time is modeled with a negative exponential distribution.

Programming Projects

13.12. Implement the Josephus algorithm using splay trees (see Chapter 21) and sequential insertion. (The splay tree class is available online.) Compare the performance with that in the text and with an algorithm that uses a linear-time balanced tree building.

13.13. Rewrite the Josephus algorithm in Figure 13.3 to use a *median heap* (Exercise 6.21). Use a simple implementation of the median heap; the elements are maintained in sorted order. Compare the running time of this algorithm with the time obtained using the `OrderedSearchTree`.

13.14. Suppose FIU has installed a system that queues phone calls when all modems are busy. Rewrite the simulation routine to allow for various-sized queues. Make an allowance for an infinite queue.

13.15. Rewrite the simulation to gather statistics rather than output each event. Then compare the speed of the simulation, assuming several hundred modems and a very long simulation, with some other possible priority queues (some of which are available online), namely

    a. An asymptotically inefficient priority queue representation described in Exercise 6.16.

    b. An asymptotically inefficient priority queue representation described in Exercise 6.17.

    c. Splay trees (see Chapter 21)

    d. Skew heaps (see Chapter 22)

    e. Pairing heaps (see Chapter 22)

Chapter 14

Graphs and Paths

In this chapter we examine the *graph* and show how to solve a particular problem, namely calculation of shortest paths. This is a fundamental problem in computer science because many interesting applications can be modeled by a graph. Computing the fastest route through mass transportation and routing electronic mail through a network of computers are examples of shortest path calculations. We examine variations of the problem that depend on how we interpret the meaning of *shortest* and what kinds of properties the graph has. Shortest path problems are interesting because the algorithms are fairly simple, but they are slow for large graphs unless careful attention is paid to the choice of data structures.

In this chapter we will see

- formal definitions of a graph and its components
- the data structures used to represent a graph
- algorithms to solve several variations of the shortest path problem, with complete C++ implementations

14.1   Definitions

A *graph* $G = (V, E)$ consists of a set of vertices, V, and a set of edges, E. Each edge is a pair (v, w), where $v, w \in V$. Vertices are sometimes referred to as nodes, and edges are sometimes known as arcs. If the edge pair is ordered, then the graph is *directed*. Directed graphs are sometimes referred to as *digraphs*. In a digraph vertex w is *adjacent* to vertex v if and only if $(v, w) \in E$. Sometimes an edge has a third component, known as either a *weight* or a *cost*. In this chapter all graphs will be directed.

A *graph* consists of a set of vertices and a set of edges that connect the vertices. If the edges are ordered, then the graph is *directed*.

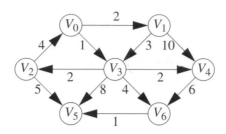

Figure 14.1   A directed graph

w is *adjacent* to v if there is an edge from v to w.

The graph in Figure 14.1 has the following 7 vertices and 12 edges:

$$V = \{V_0, V_1, V_2, V_3, V_4, V_5, V_6\}$$

$$E = \left\{ \begin{array}{l} (V_0, V_1, 2), (V_0, V_3, 1), (V_1, V_3, 3), (V_1, V_4, 10) \\ (V_3, V_4, 2), (V_3, V_6, 4), (V_3, V_5, 8), (V_3, V_2, 2) \\ (V_2, V_0, 4), (V_2, V_5, 5), (V_4, V_6, 6), (V_6, V_5, 1) \end{array} \right\}$$

The following vertices are adjacent to V_3: V_2, V_4, V_5, V_6. We say that for this graph, $|V| = 7$ and $|E| = 12$; here $|S|$ represents the size of set S.

A *path* is a sequence of vertices that are connected by edges.

A *path* in a graph is a sequence of vertices $w_1, w_2, ..., w_N$ such that $(w_i, w_{i+1}) \in E$ for $1 \le i < N$. The *length* of such a path is the number of edges on the path, namely $N - 1$. This is known as the *unweighted path length*. The *weighted path length* is the sum of the costs of the edges on the path. As an example, V_0, V_3, V_5 is a path from vertex V_0 to V_5. The path length is two edges, and the weighted path length is 9. This is the shortest path between V_0 and V_5. However, if the cost is important, then the weighted shortest path between these vertices has cost 8 and is V_0, V_3, V_2, V_5. We allow a path from a vertex to itself. If this path contains no edges, then the path length is 0. This is a convenient way to define an otherwise special case. A *simple path* is a path in which all vertices are distinct, except the first and last can be the same.

A *cycle* in a directed graph is a path that begins and ends at the same vertex and contains at least one edge.

A *cycle* in a directed graph is a path of length at least 1 such that $w_1 = w_N$; this cycle is simple if the path is simple. A *directed acyclic graph*, sometimes referred to by its abbreviation, *DAG*, is a directed graph with no cycles.

An example of a real-life situation that can be modeled by a graph is the airport system. Each airport is a vertex, and two vertices are connected by an edge if there is a nonstop flight between the corresponding airports. The edge could have a weight, representing time, distance, or cost of the flight. Generally, an edge (v, w) would imply an edge (w, v), but it is reasonable to assume that the costs of the edges might be different, since it might take longer (depending on prevailing winds) or cost more (depending on local taxes) to fly in different directions. Naturally, we would like to quickly determine the best flight between any two airports; *best* could mean the path with the fewest number of edges or could be taken with respect to one, or all, of the weight measures. A second example is the routing of electronic mail through computer networks. Vertices represent computers, the edges represent links between pairs of computers, and the edge costs represent communication costs (phone bills per megabytes), delay costs (seconds per megabyte), or combinations of these and other factors.

For most graphs we can expect that there is at most one edge from any vertex v to any other vertex w (this allows one edge in each direction between v and w). Consequently, we expect that $|E| \leq |V|^2$. When most edges are present, we have $|E| = \Theta(|V|^2)$, and the graph is considered *dense*. In most applications the graph is not dense. For instance, in the airport model, we do not expect direct flights between every pair of airports. Instead, we find that a few airports are very well connected and most others have relatively few flights. In a complex mass transportation system involving buses and trains, for any one station we have only a few other stations that are directly reachable and thus represented by an edge. Moreover, in a computer network most computers are attached to a few other local computers. In most cases the graph is relatively *sparse*: $|E| = \Theta(|V|)$, or perhaps slightly more (there is no standard definition of sparse). It is thus most important that the algorithms we develop are efficient for sparse graphs.

> A graph is *dense* if the number of edges is large (generally quadratic). Typical graphs are not dense. Instead they are *sparse*.

14.1.1   Representation

The first thing we must consider is how a graph is represented internally. Let us assume, as the graph in Figure 14.1 suggests, that the vertices are sequentially numbered starting from 0. One simple way to represent a graph is to use a two-dimensional array. This is known as an *adjacency matrix* representation. For each edge (v, w), we set A[v][w] equal to the edge cost; nonexistent edges can be initialized with a logical Infinity. The initialization of the graph seems to require that the entire adjacency matrix be initialized to Infinity, and then, as an edge is encountered, an appropriate entry is set. Under this scenario the initialization takes $O(|V|^2)$. Although it is possible to avoid the quadratic initialization cost (see Exercise 14.3), the fact remains that the space cost is still $O(|V|^2)$, which is fine for dense graphs but completely unacceptable for sparse graphs.

> An *adjacency matrix* represents a graph using quadratic space.

For sparse graphs, a better solution is an *adjacency list* representation. For each vertex, we keep a linked list of all adjacent vertices. The adjacency list representation of the graph in Figure 14.1 is shown in Figure 14.2. Because each edge appears in a list node, the number of list nodes is exactly equal to the number of edges. Consequently, $O(|E|)$ space is used to store the list nodes. Since we have $|V|$ lists, there is also $O(|V|)$ additional space that is required. If we assume that every vertex is in some edge, then the number of edges is at least $\lceil |V|/2 \rceil$, and so we may disregard any $O(|V|)$ terms when an $O(|E|)$ term is present. Consequently, we say that the space requirement is $O(|E|)$, or linear in the size of the graph.

> An *adjacency list* represents a graph using linear space.

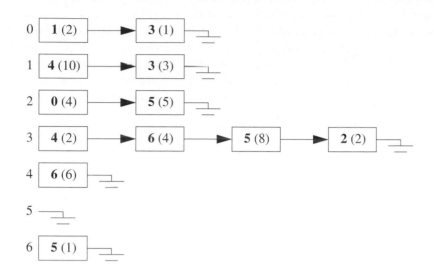

Figure 14.2   Adjacency list representation of graph in Figure 14.1; nodes in list *i* represent vertices adjacent to *i* and the cost of the connecting edge

Adjacency lists can be constructed in linear time from a list of edges.

The adjacency list can be constructed in linear time from a list of edges. We begin by making all the lists empty. When we see an edge $(v, w, c_{v, w})$ we add an entry consisting of w and the cost $c_{v, w}$ to v's adjacency list. The insertion can be anywhere, so it makes sense to do it at the front, in constant time. Consequently, each edge can be inserted in constant time, so the entire adjacency list structure can be constructed in linear time. Note carefully that, when inserting an edge, we do not check to see if it is already present. That cannot be done in constant time (using a simple linked list), and doing the check would destroy the linear-time bound for construction. In most cases this is unimportant. If there are two or more edges of different cost connecting a pair of vertices, any shortest path algorithm will choose the lower-cost edge without resorting to any special processing.

A *dictionary* can be used to map vertex names to internal numbers.

In most real-life applications, the vertices have names, which are unknown at compile time, instead of numbers. Consequently, we must provide a way to transform names to numbers. The easiest way to do this is to provide a *dictionary* in which we store a vertex name and an internal number ranging from 0 to $|V| - 1$ (the number of vertices is determined as the program runs). The internal numbers are assigned as the graph is read. The first number assigned is zero. As each edge is input, we check whether each of the two vertices has been assigned a number by seeing if it is in the dictionary. If so, we use the internal number. Otherwise, we assign to the vertex the next available number and insert the vertex name and number into the dictionary. With this transformation all the graph algorithms will use only the internal numbers. Eventually we will need to output the real vertex names and not the internal numbers, so we must also record, for each internal number, the corresponding vertex name. One way to do this is to keep a string for each vertex. We will use this technique to implement a Graph class. The class and the shortest path algorithms require several data structures, namely a linked list, a queue, a hash table, and a priority queue. The #include directives are shown in Figure 14.3. The queue and priority queue are used in various shortest path calculations. The linked list and hash table are used to represent the graph. In particular, the hash table implements the dictionary.

Before we show the Graph class interface, let us examine Figure 14.4, which shows how our graph will be represented. As indicated in the table labeled Input, we can expect the user to provide a list of edges, one per line. At the start of the algorithm, we do not know the names of any of the vertices, nor how many vertices there are, nor how many edges there are. We use two data structures to represent the graph.

The graph representation uses a `Vector` of structures.

As mentioned earlier, we will maintain a dictionary that will allow us to determine, for any vertex, its internal number. For instance, because D is the first vertex in the input file, it is assigned number 0. C is the second vertex in the input file, so it is assigned number 1. The other data structure is a large table that stores information about all the vertices. As we can see from Figure 14.4, the *Graph table* maintains four pieces of information for each vertex:

- Dist: The length of the shortest path (either weighted or unweighted, depending on the algorithm) from the starting vertex to this vertex. This value is computed by the shortest path algorithm.
- Prev: The previous vertex on the shortest path to this vertex.
- Name: The name corresponding to this vertex. This is established when the vertex is placed into the dictionary and will never change. None of the shortest path algorithms examine this member. It is only used to print a final path.
- Adj: A pointer to a list of adjacent vertices. This is established when the graph is read. None of the shortest path algorithms will change the pointer or the linked list.

```
1  #include <strstream.h>
2  #include <fstream.h>
3  #include <stdlib.h>
4  #include "Vector.h"
5  #include "HashTable.h"
6  #include "List.h"
7  #include "Queue.h"
8  #include "BinaryHeap.h"
```

Figure 14.3   #include directives for Graph class

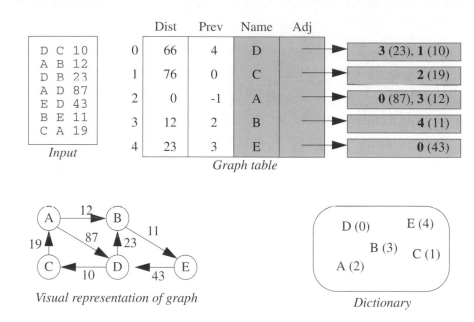

Figure 14.4   Data structures used in a shortest path calculation, with input graph taken from a file: shortest weighted path from A to C is: A to B to E to D to C (cost 76)

A pointer to the adjacency list is used to avoid copying the lists during array doubling.

Let us be more specific. In Figure 14.4 the shaded items are not altered by any of the shortest path calculations. They represent the input graph and do not change unless the graph itself changes (perhaps by addition or deletion of edges at some later point). The items that are not shaded are computed by the shortest path algorithms. Prior to the calculation we can assume they are uninitialized. The only mysterious issue is why Adj is declared as a pointer to a list instead of a list. The reason is that the graph table vector will be resized as needed, and as we recall, this requires that we copy from the old vector to the new vector. Thus, if we were to encounter another vertex and double the vector in Figure 14.4, we would have to allocate a table of size 10 and copy the first five lines of the old table over. We certainly would not want to incur the overhead of making copies of a list (and then destroying the originals), so instead we use a pointer. In this case the array doubling will perform a shallow copy of the Adj pointer, and all will be well.

The algorithms are *single source*: They compute the shortest paths from some start point to all vertices. The Prev member can be used to extract the actual path.

The shortest path algorithms are all *single source*: They assume some starting point and then compute the shortest paths from the starting point to all other vertices. In this example the starting point is A, which by consulting the dictionary, we see is internal number 2. Notice that the shortest path algorithm declares that the shortest path to A is 0. The Prev member allows us to print out the shortest path and not just its length. For instance, by consulting the table, we see that the shortest path from the starting vertex to C (internal number 1) has total cost 76. Obviously the last vertex on this path is C. The vertex on this path that is before C is vertex 0, or D. Before D is vertex 4, which is E. Before E is vertex 3, namely B. Before B is vertex 2, namely A, which is the start vertex. By tracing back through the Prev member, we see that we can construct the shortest path. Although this trace gives the path in reverse order, it is a simple matter to unreverse it. The remainder of this section describes how the shaded part of the graph table is constructed and gives the function that prints out a shortest path, assuming that the Dist and Prev members have been computed. Algorithms for filling in the shortest path are discussed individually.

Figure 14.5 shows the basic item that is placed in the adjacency list, namely an internal vertex number and the edge cost. We will allow the Graph class to have an arbitrary type for the vertex name and another arbitrary (arithmetic) type for the edge costs. Consequently Edge is a templated class. The linked list class uses operator!= to perform a Find operation. Even though we do not use Find, the compiler will complain if operator!= is not declared for Edge. Consequently, we provide a declaration. Note that since we do not actually make a call to it, the body of operator!= need not be provided.

> **The item in an adjacency list is an internal vertex number of the adjacent vertex and the edge cost.**

Class Vertex is shown in Figure 14.6. It is templated with two types. An additional member is provided named Scratch. It has different uses in the various algorithms. Everything else follows from our description above. One warning is in order: On line 7 we must have a space between the two >s that end the template instantiation. Otherwise, the compiler will match the >> token and generate a host of syntax errors.

> **Each entry in the graph table is of (template) type Vertex.**

We are now ready to examine the Graph class interface. The public portion, shown in Figure 14.7, indicates that it is templated. The user can specify a NameType for the vertices (typically a String) and a DistType for the edge costs (typically an int or double).

```
1   // Basic item stored in adjacency list
2
3   template <class DistType>
4   struct Edge
5   {
6                               // First vertex in edge is implicit
7       int Dest;               // Second vertex in edge
8       DistType Cost;          // Edge cost
9
10      Edge( ) { }
11      Edge( int D, DistType C ) : Dest( D ), Cost( C ) { }
12
13      int operator!=( const Edge & Rhs ) const
14              { return Dest != Rhs.Dest; }
15  };
```

Figure 14.5   The basic item stored in an adjacency list

```
 1  // Basic item stored for each vertex
 2
 3  template <class NameType, class DistType>
 4  struct Vertex
 5  {
 6      NameType Name;              // Real name
 7      List< Edge<DistType> > *Adj;     // Adjacent vertices
 8
 9      DistType Dist;        // Cost (after running algorithm)
10      int Prev;             // Previous vertex on shortest path
11      int Scratch;          // Extra variable for use in algorithm
12  };
```

Figure 14.6   Class `Vertex` stores information for each vertex

```
 1  // Graph class interface: evaluate infix expression
 2  // NameType: Must have a hash function, copy constructor,
 3  //      operator=, operator>>, operator<<, zero-parameter
 4  //      constructor
 5  // DistType: Must have conversion from infinity, copy
 6  //      constructor, operator=, operator>>, operator<<,
 7  //      zero parameter constructor, int constructor,
 8  //      +, <, >, ==
 9  //
10  // CONSTRUCTION: with (a) Infinity and optional const char *
11  //      that stores edges in input graph;
12  //      copy constructor is disabled
13  //
14  // *****************PUBLIC OPERATIONS*********************
15  // void AddEdges( NameType V, NameType W, DistType Cvw )
16  //                      --> Add additional edge
17  // int ProcessRequest( )--> Run a bunch of shortest path algs
18  // *****************ERRORS********************************
19  // Some error checking is performed to make sure graph is ok,
20  // parameters to ProcessRequest represent vertices in the
21  // graph, and to make sure graph satisfies properties needed
22  // by each algorithm
23
24  template<class NameType, class DistType>
25  class Graph
26  {
27    public:
28      Graph( DistType Inf, const char *FileName = NULL );
29      ~Graph( );
30
31          // Add additional edges as needed
32      void AddEdge( const NameType & Source,
33                    const NameType & Dest,
34                    DistType Cost );
35      int ProcessRequest( ); // Calculate various shortest paths
```

Figure 14.7   `Graph` class interface (part 1: the public interface)

```
36   private:
37        // Disable copy constructor and copy assignment
38     Graph( const Graph & );
39     const Graph & operator=( const Graph & );
40
41     enum { InitTableSize = 50, NullVertex = -1 };
42
43     const DistType Infinity;    // For initialization
44     HashTable< HashItem<NameType> > VertexMap; // Dictionary
45     Vector<Vertex<NameType,DistType> > Table;   // Graph table
46     int NumVertices;         // Current number of vertices read
47
48        // If Name is an already seen vertex, return its
49        // internal number. Otherwise, add it as a new
50        // vertex, return its new internal number
51     int AddNode( const NameType & VertexName );
52
53        // Add an edge given internal numbers of its vertices
54     void AddInternalEdge( int Source, int Dest,
55                          DistType Cost );
56
57     void ClearData( );   // Initialize the table
58
59        // Read graph from stream requested in constructor
60     void ReadGraph( ifstream & GraphStream );
61
62        // Print the shortest path to DestNode
63        // (specified by its internal number)
64        // PrintPath is the driver routine
65     void PrintPathRec( int DestNode ) const;
66     void PrintPath( int DestNode ) const;
67
68        // Various shortest path algorithms that require
69        // an internal number for start-up
70     void Unweighted( int StartNode );
71     int Dijkstra( int StartNode );
72     int Negative( int StartNode );
73     int Acyclic( int StartNode );
74   };
```

Figure 14.8   Graph class interface (part 2: the private section)

The private section is in Figure 14.8. The copy constructor and copy assign- **Infinity** is pro-
ment operator are disabled at lines 38 and 39, respectively. Some constants are **vided in the Graph**
declared at line 41. Next come the data members. Line 43 stores the value of **constructor.**
Infinity. Since the class is templated, we cannot know what would be reasonable, and thus the class user must provide this value when Graph is constructed.

```
1   template <class NameType, class DistType>
2   Graph<NameType, DistType>::
3   Graph( DistType Inf, const char *FileName ) :
4                         NumVertices( 0 ), Infinity( Inf ),
5                         Table( InitTableSize )
6   {
7       if( FileName != NULL )
8       {
9           ifstream GraphStream( FileName, ios::in );
10          if( GraphStream )
11              ReadGraph( GraphStream );
12          else
13              cerr << "Error opening " << FileName << endl;
14      }
15  }
```

Figure 14.9   Graph constructor

```
1   template <class NameType, class DistType>
2   Graph<NameType, DistType>::~Graph( )
3   {
4       for( int i = 0; i < NumVertices; i++ )
5           delete Table[ i ].Adj;
6   }
```

Figure 14.10   Graph destructor

VertexMap stores the dictionary. We implement the dictionary by using a hash table that stores a HashItem containing both the vertex name and number, but searches based only on the vertex name. This is briefly discussed when we examine the implementation. Some compilers may require the HashItem class declaration to precede the Graph class declaration. Line 45 is the graph table, Table. The number of vertices currently in the table is stored in NumVertices (line 46). The rest of the class provides a host of member functions that perform initialization, add vertices, add edges, print the shortest path, and perform various shortest path calculations. We will discuss each routine when we examine its implementation.

First up is the constructor. Figure 14.9 shows that the constructor provides a value for Infinity, initializes the number of vertices to 0, and initializes Table. An empty dictionary is automatically created. If a file name is provided, then edges are read from it and added to the table by calling ReadGraph. Figure 14.10 shows the destructor that destroys all the dynamically allocated linked lists. It does this at lines 4 and 5.

The dictionary is implemented by using a hash table.

To implement the dictionary, we declare a class named HashItem that will store both the vertex name, Name, and its internal number, Rank. Equality, inequality, and the hash function are performed on the basis of the Name member only. The declarations are shown in Figure 14.11. Using the general hash table framework rather than defining a separate Dictionary class involves a slight amount of additional work (extra copying of NameType objects), but a profiler reveals that the overhead is negligible. The additional work is seen in the routine AddNode, shown in Figure 14.12.

AddNode returns the internal vertex number corresponding to the parameter VertexName. The name of the routine reflects the fact that, if VertexName has not already been seen (indicated by its absence from the dictionary), it is assigned the next available internal number and added to the dictionary, and its entry in the Table vector is initialized. The procedure begins by consulting the hash table. To do this, we first have to create HashV, which is a HashItem object (appropriately instantiated with NameType) at line 10, by initializing it with VertexName (using the appropriate constructor). The construction of HashV represents the overhead of using the general HashTable class rather than a more specific Dictionary class. The net effect is two NameType constructions per edge in the graph, which turns out to be insignificant compared to the other costs already present. Exercise 14.11 asks you to use a direct Dictionary class and compare the running times.

AddNode returns the internal number corresponding to the parameter VertexName. If VertexName has never been seen, it is added to the dictionary and its entry in the Table vector is initialized.

```
1   // The basic entry in the vertex dictionary
2
3   template <class NameType>
4   struct HashItem
5   {
6       NameType Name;
7       int Rank;
8
9       HashItem( ) { }
10      HashItem( const NameType & TheName ): Name( TheName ) { }
11
12      int operator==( const HashItem & Rhs ) const
13          { return Name == Rhs.Name; }
14      int operator!=( const HashItem & Rhs ) const
15          { return Name != Rhs.Name; }
16  };
17
18  // Hash function for HashItem
19  // Calls hash function for NameType
20
21  template <class NameType>
22  unsigned int
23  Hash( const HashItem<NameType> & Key, int TableSize )
24  {
25      return Hash( Key.Name, TableSize );
26  }
```

Figure 14.11   HashItem used to implement the dictionary

```
 1  // Return the internal number for VertexName
 2  // If VertexName is new, then add it to the dictionary
 3  // and add an entry to graph table, doubling if needed
 4
 5  template <class NameType, class DistType>
 6  int
 7  Graph<NameType, DistType>::
 8  AddNode( const NameType & VertexName )
 9  {
10      HashItem<NameType> HashV = VertexName;
11      const HashItem<NameType> & Result=VertexMap.Find( HashV );
12
13      if( VertexMap.WasFound( ) )
14          return Result.Rank;
15
16          // Newly seen vertex
17      HashV.Rank = NumVertices;
18      VertexMap.Insert( HashV );
19
20      if( NumVertices == Table.Length( ) )
21          Table.Double( );
22      Table[ NumVertices ].Name = HashV.Name;
23      Table[ NumVertices ].Adj  = new List< Edge<DistType> >;
24
25      return NumVertices++;
26  }
```

Figure 14.12   AddNode routine returns the internal number for
                    VertexName

```
 1  // Add the edge ( Source, Dest, Cost ) to the graph
 2  // Source and Dest are internal vertex numbers
 3
 4  template <class NameType, class DistType>
 5  void
 6  Graph<NameType, DistType>::
 7  AddInternalEdge( int Source, int Dest, DistType Cost )
 8  {
 9      ListItr< Edge<DistType> > P = *Table[ Source ].Adj;
10      P.Insert( Edge<DistType>( Dest, Cost ) );
11  }
```

Figure 14.13   Add the edge (Source, Dest, Cost) to the graph by
                    inserting into Source's adjacency list; Source and Dest
                    are internal numbers

```
1    // Add the edge ( Source, Dest, Cost ) to the graph
2    // Source and Dest are NameType objects
3
4    template <class NameType, class DistType>
5    void
6    Graph<NameType,DistType>::
7    AddEdge( const NameType & Source,
8             const NameType & Dest, DistType Cost )
9    {
10       AddInternalEdge( AddNode( Source ),
11                        AddNode( Dest ), Cost );
12   }
```

Figure 14.14   Same routine as `AddInternalEdge`, but here `Source` and `Dest` are NameType objects

```
1    // Initialize the graph table prior to running
2    // any shortest path algorithm
3
4    template <class NameType, class DistType>
5    void
6    Graph<NameType, DistType>::ClearData( )
7    {
8        for( int i = 0; i < NumVertices; i++ )
9        {
10           Table[ i ].Dist = Infinity;
11           Table[ i ].Prev = -1;
12           Table[ i ].Scratch = 0;
13       }
14   }
```

Figure 14.15   Routine to initialize the `Table` members for use by the shortest path algorithms

```
1    // Recursive routine to print shortest path to DestNode
2    // after running shortest path algorithm
3
4    template <class NameType, class DistType>
5    void
6    Graph<NameType, DistType>::PrintPathRec( int DestNode ) const
7    {
8        if( Table[ DestNode ].Prev != NullVertex )
9        {
10           PrintPathRec( Table[ DestNode ].Prev );
11           cout << " to ";
12       }
13       cout << Table[ DestNode ].Name;
14   }
```

Figure 14.16   Recursive routine to print the shortest path

```
1  // Driver routine to handle unreachables and print total cost
2  // It calls recursive routine to print shortest path to
3  // DestNode after a shortest path algorithm has run
4
5  template <class NameType, class DistType>
6  void
7  Graph<NameType, DistType>::PrintPath( int DestNode ) const
8  {
9      if( Table[ DestNode ].Dist == Infinity )
10         cout << Table[ DestNode ].Name << " is unreachable";
11     else
12     {
13         PrintPathRec( DestNode );
14         cout << " (cost: " << Table[ DestNode ].Dist << ')';
15     }
16     cout << endl;
17 }
```

Figure 14.17   Routine to print shortest path by consulting the table

```
1  // Read edges from, GraphStream
2  // Checks that each line has at least three components
3
4  template <class NameType, class DistType>
5  void
6  Graph<NameType,DistType>::ReadGraph( ifstream & GraphStream )
7  {
8      const int MaxLineLength = 256;
9      static char OneLine[ MaxLineLength + 1 ];
10     NameType Source, Dest;
11     DistType Cost;
12
13     while( GraphStream.getline( OneLine, MaxLineLength ) )
14     {
15         istrstream LineStream( OneLine, MaxLineLength );
16         if( LineStream >> Source && LineStream >> Dest
17                                  && LineStream >> Cost )
18             AddEdge( Source, Dest, Cost );
19         else
20             cerr << "Bad line: " << OneLine << endl;
21     }
22 }
```

Figure 14.18   Routine to read edges from the `GraphStream` and insert
them into the graph

Once `HashV` is constructed, we can perform a `Find` of the hash table, and
store the return value in `Result`. To avoid further copying, we declare, at line
11, that `Result` is a constant reference. If the `Find` was successful, we can
return the `Rank` member of `Result` and be done. Otherwise, we have a newly

seen vertex. First, at line 17 we assign it an internal number of NumVertices, which represents the next available index into Table (because indices start at 0), and at line 18 we perform an Insert into the hash table. If the graph table Table is full, then it is doubled at line 21. Its real name is stored in the table at line 22, and its adjacency list is dynamically allocated at line 23. Line 25 completes the routine by returning NumVertices (the internal number now assigned to VertexName) and then incrementing NumVertices.

The routine shown in Figure 14.13 adds an edge whose vertices are given by internal numbers. This is a simple routine because all that is needed is to create an Edge<DistType> object with the destination vertex and cost and then insert it into the adjacency list corresponding to the source. The main complexity is the C++ syntax. Line 9 declares that P is a ListItr into the adjacency list corresponding to the source vertex. Note that since Table[Source].Adj is a pointer to a list, we must dereference it. An Edge<DistType> object is then constructed and inserted (at the front). The routine for public use is shown in Figure 14.14. AddEdge adds an edge whose vertices are given by NameType objects. This is another short routine because it merely consults AddNode to get the corresponding internal numbers, and then AddInternalEdge is called.

Edges are added by insertions into the appropriate adjacency list.

The members that are eventually computed by the shortest path algorithm are initialized by the routine ClearData, shown in Figure 14.15. Next comes the routine to print a shortest path after the computation has been performed. As we mentioned earlier, the Prev member can be used to trace back the path. However, this will give the path in reverse order. This is not a problem if we use recursion: the vertices on the path to Dest are the same as those on the path to Dest's previous vertex (on the path) followed by Dest. This strategy translates directly into the short recursive routine shown in Figure 14.16. Of course, it assumes that a path actually exists. PrintPath, shown in Figure 14.17, performs this check first and then prints a message if the path does not exist. Otherwise, it calls the recursive routine and outputs the cost of the path.

ClearData clears out the data members so the shortest path algorithms can begin. PrintPath prints the shortest path after the algorithm has run.

ReadGraph, shown in Figure 14.18 is used to read lines containing edges from a file. We repeatedly read one line of input, assign the line to an istrstream object, and then parse that line.[1] This technique allows us to check that every line has at least the three pieces corresponding to an edge. We could do more work and add code to ensure that there are exactly three pieces of data per line but we prefer to avoid additional complexity.

ReadGraph processes edges in the input file.

The description of the istrstream class indicates that the statement at lines 16 and 17 could be written as

```
if( LineStream >> Source >> Dest >> Cost )
```

However two of our compilers have broken libraries, and operator>> does not return an istrstream object as it should. Consequently, we have rewritten an equivalent expression that does not use the operator>> return value.

istrstream does not behave as advertised.

---

1. istrstream will be replaced by istreamstring in future versions of C++.

```
1  // Prompt user for two vertices and run all shortest path
2  // algorithms between the vertices
3
4  template <class NameType, class DistType>
5  int
6  Graph<NameType, DistType>::ProcessRequest( )
7  {
8      NameType SourceName, DestName;
9      static HashItem<NameType> Source, Dest;
10
11     do
12     {
13         cout << "Enter start node: ";
14         if( !( cin >> SourceName ) )
15             return 0;
16         Source.Name = SourceName;
17         Source = VertexMap.Find( Source );
18     } while( !VertexMap.WasFound( ) );
19
20     do
21     {
22         cout << "Enter destination node: ";
23         if( !( cin >> DestName ) )
24             return 0;
25         Dest.Name = DestName;
26         Dest = VertexMap.Find( Dest );
27     } while( !VertexMap.WasFound( ) );
28
29     Unweighted( Source.Rank );
30     PrintPath( Dest.Rank );
31     if( Dijkstra( Source.Rank ) )
32         PrintPath( Dest.Rank );
33     if( Negative( Source.Rank ) )
34         PrintPath( Dest.Rank );
35     if( Acyclic( Source.Rank ) )
36         PrintPath( Dest.Rank );
37
38     return 1;
39 }
```

Figure 14.19   For testing purposes, `ProcessRequest` calls all the
shortest path algorithms

The remaining routine, besides those that calculate shortest paths, is
`ProcessRequest`. In Figure 14.19 we provide a simple implementation that
prompts for a start vertex and a destination vertex, and then runs four different
shortest path algorithms.

```
1  #include <limits.h>
2  #include <stdlib.h>
3
4  // Simple main to test the graph algorithms
5
6  main( )
7  {
8    try
9    {
10     Graph<String, int> G( INT_MAX, "graph.dat" );
11
12     while( G.ProcessRequest( ) )
13         ;
14   }
15   catch( ... )
16   {
17     cerr << "Out of memory!!" << endl;
18     exit( 1 );
19   }
20     return 0;
21 }
```

Figure 14.20   Simple main

14.1.2   Using a Graph with String Vertices and double Edge Weights

Figure 14.20 shows a very simple main that instantiates a graph object with String as the vertex type and int as the edge cost. The graph is read from the file graph.dat. INT_MAX is defined in <limits.h>. The user must provide a hash function for the String type. See Figure 19.2 for an appropriate hash function.

The Graph class is easy to instantiate and use.

14.2   Unweighted Shortest Path Problem

The *unweighted path length* measures the number of edges. In this section we consider the problem of finding the path between specified vertices that has the shortest unweighted path length.

UNWEIGHTED SINGLE SOURCE SHORTEST PATH PROBLEM
FIND THE SHORTEST PATH (MEASURED BY NUMBER OF EDGES) FROM A DESIGNATED VERTEX S TO EVERY VERTEX.

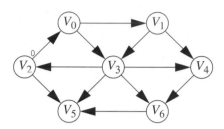

Figure 14.21   Graph after marking the start node as reachable in zero edges

The *unweighted path length* measures the number of edges on a path.

The unweighted shortest path problem is a special case of the weighted shortest path problem (in which all weights are 1). Consequently, we expect that it should have a more efficient solution than the weighted shortest path problem. This turns out to be true, although the algorithms for all the path problems are very similar.

14.2.1   Theory

All variations of the shortest path problem have similar solutions.

To solve the unweighted shortest path problem, we will use the graph in Figure 14.1 with V_2 as the starting vertex S. For now we will concern ourselves with finding the length of all shortest paths, and later on we will see how to maintain the corresponding paths. Immediately, we can tell that the shortest path from S to V_2 is a path of length 0. We can record this information, obtaining the graph in Figure 14.21.

Now we can start looking for all vertices that are a distance 1 away from S. These can be found by looking at the vertices that are adjacent to S. If we do this, we see that V_0 and V_5 are one edge away from S. This is shown in Figure 14.22. Next, we can find vertices whose shortest path from S is exactly 2 by finding all the vertices adjacent to V_0 or V_5 (the vertices at distance 1) whose shortest paths are not already known. This search tells us that the shortest path to V_1 and V_3 is 2. Figure 14.23 shows the progress that has been made so far.

Finally, by examining the vertices adjacent to the recently evaluated V_1 and V_3, we can find that V_4 and V_6 have a shortest path of 3 edges. All vertices have now been calculated. Figure 14.24 shows the final result of the algorithm.

Breadth-first search processes vertices in layers: Those closest to the start are evaluated first. The *eyeball* moves from vertex to vertex and updates distances for adjacent vertices.

This strategy for searching a graph is known as *breadth-first search*. It operates by processing vertices in layers: The vertices closest to the start are evaluated first, and the most distant vertices are evaluated last.

An algorithm to solve the problem is as follows: Let D_i be the length of the shortest path from S to i. We know that $D_S = 0$, and initially $D_i = \infty$ for all $i \neq S$. We maintain a roving *eyeball* that hops from vertex to vertex and is initially at S. If v is the vertex that the eyeball is currently on, then, for all w that are adjacent to v, we set $D_w = D_v + 1$ if $D_w \neq \infty$. This reflects the fact that we can get to w by following a path to v and extending the path by the edge (v, w). Because the eyeball processes the vertices in order of their distance from the start vertex, and the edge adds exactly one to the length of the path to w, we are guaranteed that the first time D_w is lowered from ∞, it will be lowered to the value of the length of the shortest path to w. By the way, this also tells us that the next to last vertex on the path to w is v, so one extra line of code will allow us to store the actual path.

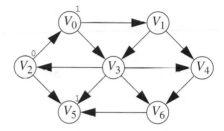

Figure 14.22   Graph after finding all vertices whose path length from the start is 1

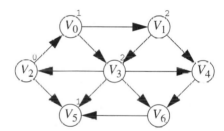

Figure 14.23   Graph after finding all vertices whose shortest path from the start is 2

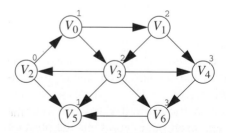

Figure 14.24   Final shortest paths

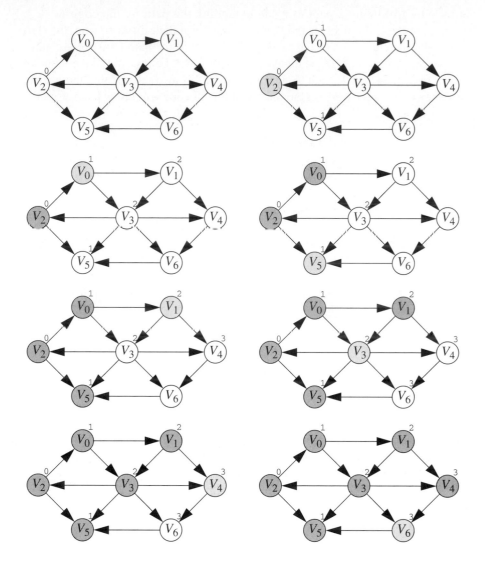

Figure 14.25 How the graph is searched in unweighted shortest path computation

After we have processed all of v's adjacent vertices, we move the eyeball to another vertex u (that has not been visited by the eyeball) such that $D_u \equiv D_v$; if this is not possible, we move to a u that satisfies $D_u = D_v + 1$; if this is not possible, we are done. Figure 14.25 shows how the eyeball visits vertices and updates distances. The lightly shaded node in each stage represents the position of the eyeball. In this picture and those that follow, the stages are shown top to bottom, left to right.

The remaining detail is the data structure. We have two basic issues. First, we have to repeatedly find the vertex at which to place the eyeball. Second, we need to check all w adjacent to v (the current vertex) throughout the algorithm. The second test is easily implemented by iterating through v's adjacency list. Indeed, since each edge is processed once, the total cost of all the iterations is $O(|E|)$. The first test is more challenging: We cannot simply scan through the table looking for an appropriate vertex, because each scan could take $O(|V|)$ time and we need to perform it $|V|$ times. The total cost would thus be $O(|V|^2)$, which is unacceptable for sparse graphs. Fortunately, this is not needed.

All vertices adjacent to v are found by scanning v's adjacency list.

When a vertex w has its D_w lowered from ∞, it becomes a candidate for an eyeball visitation at some point in the future. This is because after the eyeball visits vertices in the current distance group D_v, it will visit the next distance group $D_v + 1$, which is the group containing w. Thus w just needs to wait on line for its turn, and since it clearly need not go before any other vertices that have already had their distances lowered, we see that w needs to be placed at the end of a queue of vertices that are waiting for an eyeball visitation. To select a vertex v for the eyeball, we merely choose the front vertex from the queue. We start with an empty queue, and then to get the ball rolling, we enqueue that start vertex S. Since a vertex is enqueued and dequeued at most once per shortest path calculation, and since queue operations are constant time, the cost of choosing the vertex to select is only $O(|V|)$ *for the entire algorithm.* Thus the cost of the breadth first search is dominated by the scans of the adjacency list and is $O(|E|)$, or linear in the size of the graph.

When a vertex has its distance lowered (which can happen only once), it is placed on the queue so that the eyeball can visit it in the future. The start vertex is placed on the queue when its distance is initialized to zero.

14.2.2   C++ Implementation

Implementation of the unweighted shortest path algorithm is done in the member function Unweighted, shown in Figure 14.26. The code is a line-for-line translation of the algorithm described above. The initialization at lines 10 to 12 makes all the distances infinity, sets D_S to 0, and then enqueues the start vertex. While the queue is not empty, there are vertices for the eyeball to visit. Thus at lines 16 and 17, we move the eyeball to the vertex v that is at the front of the queue. Line 18 iterates over the adjacency list and produces all w that are adjacent to v. The test $D_w \neq \infty$ is performed at line 22; if it is true, then the update $D_w = D_v + 1$ is performed at line 24 along with the update of the Prev member and then enqueueing of w at lines 25 and 26, respectively.

Implementation is much simpler than it sounds. It follows the algorithm description verbatim.

14.3   Positive Weighted Shortest Path Problem

The *weighted path length* of a path is the sum of the edge costs on the path. In this section we consider the problem of finding the weighted shortest path. In the positive weighted shortest path problem, the edges have nonnegative cost, and we want to find the shortest weighted path from some start vertex to all vertices. As we will see, the assumption that edge costs are nonnegative is important

*The *weighted path length* is the sum of the edge costs on a path.*

because it allows a relatively efficient algorithm. The method we describe is known as *Dijkstra's algorithm*. In the next section we will examine a slower algorithm that works even if there are negative edge costs.

POSITIVE WEIGHTED SINGLE SOURCE SHORTEST PATH PROBLEM

FIND THE SHORTEST PATH (MEASURED BY TOTAL COST) FROM A DESIGNATED VERTEX S TO EVERY VERTEX. ASSUME THAT ALL EDGE COSTS ARE NONNEGATIVE.

14.3.1   Theory: Dijkstra's Algorithm

Dijkstra's algorithm solves the weighted shortest path problem.

The weighted shortest path problem is solved in a similar manner as the unweighted problem. However, because of the edge costs, a few things change. We have to examine the following issues:

```
1   // Single source unweighted shortest path algorithm
2
3   template <class NameType, class DistType>
4   void
5   Graph<NameType, DistType>::Unweighted( int StartNode )
6   {
7       int V, W;
8       Queue<int> Q;
9
10      ClearData( );
11      Table[ StartNode ].Dist = 0;
12      Q.Enqueue( StartNode );
13
14      while( !Q.IsEmpty( ) )
15      {
16          V = Q.GetFront( );
17          Q.Dequeue( );
18          for( ListItr<Edge<DistType> > P = *Table[ V ].Adj; +P;
19                                                              ++P )
20          {
21              W = P( ).Dest;
22              if( Table[ W ].Dist == Infinity )
23              {
24                  Table[ W ].Dist = Table[ V ].Dist + 1;
25                  Table[ W ].Prev = V;
26                  Q.Enqueue( W );
27              }
28          }
29      }
30  }
```

Figure 14.26   Unweighted shortest path algorithm, using breadth first search

1. How is D_w adjusted?
2. How do we find the vertex v for the eyeball to visit?

Let us begin by examining how D_w is altered. In solving the unweighted shortest path problem, if $D_w = \infty$, we set $D_w = D_v + 1$ because we lower the value of D_w if vertex v offers a shorter path to w. The dynamics of the algorithm ensure that we need only alter D_w once. We add 1 to D_v because the length of the path to w is one more than the length of the path to v. If we apply this logic to the weighted case, then we should set $D_w = D_v + c_{v,w}$ if this new value of D_w is better than the original value. However, it is no longer guaranteed that D_w is altered only once. Consequently, D_w should be altered if its current value is larger than $D_v + c_{v,w}$ (rather than merely testing against ∞). Put simply, the algorithm decides whether or not it is a good idea to use v on the path to w. The original cost D_w is the cost without using v; the cost calculated above is the cheapest path using v (seen so far).

> We use $D_v + c_{v,w}$ as the new distance and to decide if the distance should be updated.

Figure 14.27 shows a typical situation. Earlier in the algorithm, w had its distance lowered to 8 when the eyeball visited vertex u. However when the eyeball visits vertex v, w needs to have its distance lowered to 6 because we have a new shortest path. This never happened in the unweighted algorithm because all edges add 1 to the path length, so $D_u \leq D_v$ implies $D_u + 1 \leq D_v + 1$, so $D_w \leq D_v + 1$. Here, even though $D_u \leq D_v$, it is still possible that the path to w can be improved by considering v.

> A queue is no longer appropriate to store vertices awaiting an eyeball visit.

Figure 14.27 shows another important point. When w has its distance lowered, it does so only because it is adjacent to some vertex that has been visited by the eyeball. For instance, after the eyeball visits v and processing is complete, the value of D_w will be 6, and the last vertex on the path is an eyeball-visited vertex. Similarly, the vertex prior to v must also be eyeball-visited, and so on. Thus at any point the value of D_w represents *a path from S to w using only vertices that have been visited by the eyeball as intermediate nodes.* This crucial fact tells us the following:

> The distance for unvisited vertices represents a path using only visited vertices as intermediate nodes.

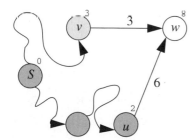

Figure 14.27   Eyeball is at v; w is adjacent; D_w should be lowered to 6

Theorem 14.1   *If we move the eyeball to the unseen vertex with minimum D_i, the algorithm will correctly produce the shortest paths if there are no negative edge costs.*

Proof   *Call each eyeball visit a stage. We prove by induction that, after any stage, the values of D_i for vertices visited by the eyeball is the shortest path and that the values of D_i for the other vertices is the shortest path using only vertices visited by the eyeball as intermediates. Clearly, since the first vertex visited is the start vertex, this statement is correct through the first stage. Assume that it is correct for the first k stages. Let v be the vertex chosen by the eyeball in stage k + 1. Suppose, for the purpose of showing a contradiction, there is a path from S to v of length less than D_v. Clearly this path must go through an intermediate vertex that has not yet been visited by the eyeball. Call the first intermediate vertex on the path not visited by the eyeball u. The situation is shown in Figure 14.28. Clearly the path to u uses only vertices visited by the eyeball as intermediates, so by induction D_u represents the optimal distance to u. Moreover, $D_u < D_v$ because u is on the supposed shorter path to v. This is a contradiction because then we would have moved the eyeball to u instead of v. The proof is completed by showing that all the D_i values remain correct for nonvisited nodes; this is clear by the update rule.*

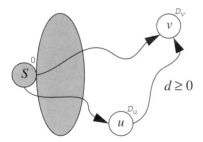

Figure 14.28   If D_v is minimal among all unseen vertices and all edge costs are nonnegative, then it represents the shortest path

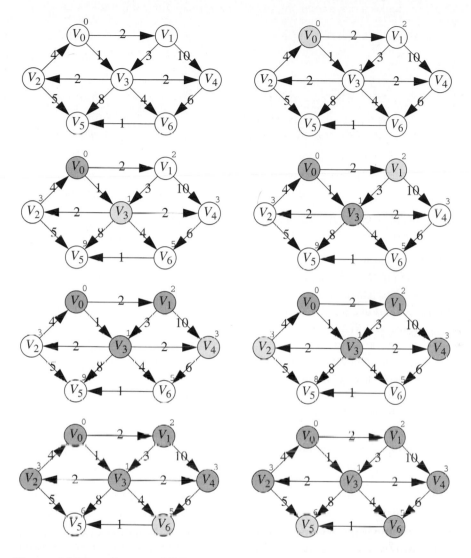

Figure 14.29 Stages of Dijkstra's algorithm

Figure 14.29 shows the stages of Dijkstra's algorithm. The remaining issue is the selection of an appropriate data structure. For dense graphs we can scan down the table looking for the appropriate vertex. As was the case for the unweighted shortest path algorithm, this will take $O(|V|^2)$ time, which is optimal for a dense graph. For a sparse graph we would like to do better.

```
1   // Structure to store in priority queue for Dijkstra's alg
2
3   template <class DistType>
4   struct Path
5   {
6       int Dest;               // W
7       DistType Cost;          // D(W)
8
9       Path( int D = 0, DistType C = 0 ) :
10               Dest( D ), Cost( C ) { }
11
12      int operator<( const Path & Rhs ) const
13          { return Cost < Rhs.Cost; }
14  };
```

Figure 14.30   Basic item stored in the priority queue

The priority queue is an appropriate data structure. The easiest method is to add a new entry consisting of a vertex and a distance to the priority queue every time a vertex has its distance lowered. We can find the new vertex to move to by repeatedly removing the minimum distance vertex from the priority queue until an unvisited vertex emerges.

Certainly, a queue will not work. The fact that we need to find the vertex v with minimum D_v suggests that a priority queue is the method of choice. There are two ways to use the priority queue. One way is to store each vertex in the priority queue, and use the distance (obtained by consulting the graph table) as the ordering function. When we alter any D_w, we must update the priority queue by reestablishing the ordering property. This amounts to a DecreaseKey operation. Matters are complicated by the fact that we need to be able to find the location of w in the priority queue, and maintaining this destroys the sanctity of the priority queue class. However, experiments have shown that this is the fastest way to go, thus pointing to a conflict between the competing goals of speed and software engineering.

We will let software engineering win this time because the difference in running time does not justify the added complexity (at least not for the purposes of this example). Our method will be to insert an object consisting of w and D_w into the priority queue whenever we lower D_w. To select a new vertex v for visitation, we repeatedly remove the minimum item (based on distance) from the priority queue until an unvisited vertex emerges. Because the size of the priority queue could be as large as $|E|$ and there are at most $|E|$ priority queue insertions and deletions, the running time is $O(|E|\log|E|)$. Since $|E| \le |V|^2$ implies $\log|E| \le 2\log|V|$, we have the same $O(|E|\log|V|)$ algorithm that we would have if we used the first method (in which the priority queue size is at most $|V|$).

14.3.2   C++ Implementation

Once again, the implementation follows the description fairly closely.

The object that will be placed on the priority queue is shown in Figure 14.30. As we can see, it consists of w and D_w, and a comparison function defined on the basis of D_w. Figure 14.31 shows the routine Dijkstra that calculates the shortest paths.

Line 8 declares the priority queue PQ. Recall that we must provide a sentinel that is guaranteed to be smaller than or equal to any inserted object. VRec, declared at line 9 will store the result of each `DeleteMin`. As was the case with the unweighted shortest path algorithm, we begin by setting all distances to infinity, setting $D_S = 0$, and placing the start vertex into our data structure.

```
1   // Single source positive weighted shortest path algorithm
2
3   template <class NameType, class DistType>
4   int
5   Graph<NameType, DistType>::Dijkstra( int StartNode )
6   {
7       int V, W;
8       BinaryHeap< Path<DistType> > PQ( Path<DistType>( 0, 0 ) );
9       Path<DistType> VRec;    // Stores the result of a DeleteMin
10
11      ClearData( );
12      Table[ StartNode ].Dist = 0;
13      PQ.Insert( Path<DistType>( StartNode, 0 ) );
14
15      for( int NodesSeen = 0; NodesSeen < NumVertices; NodesSeen++ )
16      {
17          do    // Find an unvisited vertex
18          {
19              if( PQ.IsEmpty( ) )
20                  return 1;
21              PQ.DeleteMin( VRec );
22          } while( Table[ VRec.Dest ].Scratch );
23
24          V = VRec.Dest;
25          Table[ V ].Scratch = 1;    // Mark vertex as being seen
26          for( ListItr<Edge<DistType> > P = Table[ V ].Adj; +P;
27                                                          ++P )
28          {
29              W = P( ).Dest;
30              DistType Cvw = P( ).Cost;
31              if( Cvw < 0 )
32              {
33                  cerr << "Graph has negative edges" << endl;
34                  return 0;
35              }
36              if( Table[ W ].Dist > Table[ V ].Dist + Cvw )
37              {
38                  Table[ W ].Dist = Table[ V ].Dist + Cvw;
39                  Table[ W ].Prev = V;
40                  PQ.Insert( Path<DistType>( W, Table[ W ].Dist) );
41              }
42          }
43      }
44      return 1;
45  }
```

Figure 14.31   Weighted shortest path algorithm: Dijkstra's algorithm

Each iteration of the outermost `for` loop that begins at line 15 puts the eyeball at a vertex v and processes it by examining adjacent vertices w. v is chosen by repeatedly removing entries from the priority queue (at line 21), until we see a vertex that has not been processed. We use the `Scratch` variable to record this: initially `Scratch` is 0, and thus if the vertex is unprocessed, the `while` test will fail at line 22; then when the vertex is processed, `Scratch` is set to 1 (at line 25). The priority queue might be empty, if for instance some of the vertices are unreachable. In that case we can return immediately. The loop at lines 26 to 42 is very much like the unweighted algorithm. The difference is that at line 30 we must extract `Cvw` from the adjacency list entry, we must check that the edge is nonnegative (otherwise, our algorithm could produce incorrect answers), we add `Cvw` instead of 1 at lines 36 and 38, and we `Insert` rather than `Enqueue` at line 40.

14.4   Negative Weighted Shortest Path Problem

Negative edges break Dijsktra's algorithm. An alternative algorithm is needed.

Dijkstra's algorithm requires that edge costs be nonnegative. This is reasonable for most graph applications, but sometimes it is too restrictive. In this section we briefly discuss the most general case.

NEGATIVE WEIGHTED SINGLE SOURCE SHORTEST PATH PROBLEM

FIND THE SHORTEST PATH (MEASURED BY TOTAL COST) FROM A DESIGNATED VERTEX S TO EVERY VERTEX. EDGE COSTS MAY BE NEGATIVE.

14.4.1   Theory

The proof of Dijkstra's algorithm required the condition that edge costs, and thus paths, be nonnegative. Indeed, if the graph has negative edge costs, then Dijkstra's algorithm does not work. The problem is that once a vertex v is processed by the eyeball, it is possible that from some other unprocessed vertex u there is a path back to v that is very negative. In such a case, taking a path from S to u to v is better than going from S to v without using u. Once this happens we would be in trouble: Not only would the path to v be wrong, but the eyeball would have to revisit v because vertices reachable from v may also have the distances affected.

A *negative-cost cycle* makes most, if not all, paths undefined because we can stay in the cycle arbitrarily long and obtain an arbitrarily negative path length.

We have an additional problem to worry about. Consider the graph in Figure 14.32. The path from V_3 to V_4 has cost 2, but a shorter path exists by following the loop V_3, V_4, V_1, V_3, V_4 which has a cost of -3. This path is still not the shortest because we could stay in the loop arbitrarily long. Thus the shortest path between these two points is undefined. This problem is not restricted to nodes in the cycle: The shortest path from V_2 to V_5 is also undefined because there is a way to get into and out of the loop. This loop is known as a *negative-cost cycle*; when one is present in the graph, the shortest paths are not defined. Negative-cost edges by themselves are not necessarily bad; it is the cycles that are. Our algorithm will either find the shortest paths or report the existence of a negative-cost cycle.

A combination of the weighted and unweighted algorithms will solve the problem, but at the cost of a potentially drastic increase in running time. As suggested above, when D_w is altered, we must revisit it at some point in the future. Consequently, we use the queue as was done in the unweighted algorithm, but use $D_v + c_{v,w}$ as the distance measure (as in Dijkstra's algorithm).

> Whenever a vertex has its distance lowered, it must be placed on a queue. This may happen repeatedly for each vertex.

When the eyeball visits vertex v for the ith time, the value of D_v is the length of the shortest weighted path consisting of i or fewer edges. A proof of this is left as Exercise 14.9. Consequently, if there are no negative-cost cycles, a vertex can dequeue at most $|V|$ times, and the algorithm takes at most $O(|E||V|)$ time. Further if a vertex dequeues more than $|V|$ times, we have detected a negative-cost cycle.

> The running time can be large, especially if there is a negative-cost cycle.

14.4.2   C++ Implementation

The implementation of the negative weighted shortest path algorithm is given in Figure 14.33. We make one small change to the algorithm description, namely we do not enqueue a vertex if it is already on the queue. To do this, we use the Scratch member. When a vertex is enqueued, we increment Scratch (at line 36) when it is dequeued, we increment it again (at line 20). Thus Scratch is odd if the vertex is on the queue, and Scratch/2 tells us how many times it has left the queue (and thus explains the test at line 20). When some w has its distance changed, but is already on the queue (because Scratch is odd), we do not enqueue it; however, we add 2 to it to indicate that it logically could have gone on the queue (this may speed the algorithm somewhat in the event of a negative cycle). This is done at lines 36 and 39. The rest of the algorithm uses code that has already been seen in both the unweighted shortest path algorithm (Figure 14.26) and Dijkstra's algorithm (Figure 14.31).

> The tricky part of the implementation is the manipulation of the Scratch variable. We attempt to avoid having any vertex appear on the queue twice at any instant.

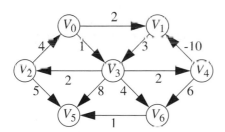

Figure 14.32   Graph with negative cost cycle

```
1   // Single source negative weighted shortest path algorithm
2
3   template <class NameType, class DistType>
4   int
5   Graph<NameType, DistType>::Negative( int StartNode )
6   {
7       int V, W;
8       Queue<int> Q;
9       DistType Cvw;
10
11      ClearData( );
12      Table[ StartNode ].Dist = 0;
13      Q.Enqueue( StartNode );
14      Table[ StartNode ].Scratch++;
15
16      while( !Q.IsEmpty( ) )
17      {
18          V = Q.GetFront( );
19          Q.Dequeue( );
20          if( Table[ V ].Scratch++ > 2 * NumVertices )
21          {
22              cerr << "Negative cycle detected" << endl;
23              return 0;
24          }
25
26          for( ListItr<Edge<DistType> > P = *Table[ V ].Adj; +P;
27                                                          ++P )
28          {
29              W = P( ).Dest;
30              Cvw = P( ).Cost;
31              if( Table[ W ].Dist > Table[ V ].Dist + Cvw )
32              {
33                  Table[ W ].Dist = Table[ V ].Dist + Cvw;
34                  Table[ W ].Prev = V;
35                  // Enqueue only if not already on the queue
36                  if( Table[ W ].Scratch++ % 2 == 0 )
37                      Q.Enqueue( W );
38                  else
39                      Table[ W ].Scratch++; // In effect adds 2
40              }
41          }
42      }
43      return 1;
44  }
```

Figure 14.33   Negative weighted shortest path algorithm; negative edges are allowed

14.5   Path Problems in Acyclic Graphs

An important class of graphs are those without cycles. The shortest path problem is simpler if the graph is acyclic. For instance, we do not have to worry about negative-cost cycles, since there are not any cycles to be found. Thus we consider the following problem:

Directed acyclic graphs **are directed graphs with no cycles. They are an important class of graphs.**

WEIGHTED SINGLE SOURCE SHORTEST PATH PROBLEM FOR ACYCLIC GRAPHS

> *FIND THE SHORTEST PATH (MEASURED BY TOTAL COST) FROM A DESIGNATED VERTEX S TO EVERY VERTEX IN AN ACYCLIC GRAPH. EDGE COSTS ARE UNRESTRICTED.*

14.5.1   Topological Sorting

Before we consider the shortest path problem, we examine a related problem. A *topological order* is an ordering of vertices in a directed acyclic graph, such that if there is a path from u to v, then v appears after u in the ordering. For instance, a graph is typically used to represent the prerequisite requirement for courses at universities. An edge (v, w) indicates that course v must be completed before course w may be attempted. A topological order of the courses is any sequence that does not violate the prerequisite requirements. A *topological sort* finds any topological order.

A *topological sort* orders vertices in a directed acyclic graph such that if there is a path from u to v, then v appears *after* u in the ordering. A graph that has a cycle cannot have a topological order.

It is clear that a topological sort is not possible if a graph has a cycle, since for two vertices v and w on the cycle, there is a path from v to w and w to v. Thus any ordering of v and w would contradict one of the two paths. A graph may have several topological orders, and in most cases any legal ordering will do.

A simple algorithm to perform a topological sort is first to find any vertex v with no incoming edges. We can then print the vertex, and logically remove it, along with its edges, from the graph. Then we apply the same strategy to the rest of the graph. To formalize this, we define the *indegree* of a vertex v as the number of edges (u, v).

The *indegree* of a vertex is the number of incoming edges.

We compute the indegrees of all vertices in the graph. In practice, *logically remove* means that we lower the count of incoming edges for each vertex adjacent to v. Figure 14.34 shows the algorithm applied to an acyclic graph. The indegree is computed for each vertex, and we see that V_2 has indegree zero. Thus it is first in the topological order. If there were several vertices of indegree zero, then we could choose any one of them. When V_2 and its edges are removed from the graph, the indegrees of V_0, V_3, and V_5 are all decremented by 1. Now V_0 has indegree zero, so it is next in the topological order, and V_1 and V_3 have their indegrees lowered. The algorithm continues, and the remaining vertices are examined in the order V_1, V_3, V_4, V_6, and V_5. Once again we state that we do not physically delete edges from the graph; it is just easier to see how the indegree count is lowered by removing edges.

A topological sort can be performed in linear time by repeatedly logically removing vertices with no incoming edges.

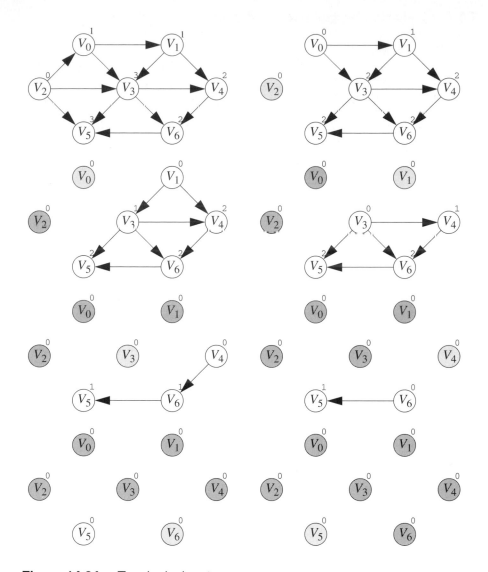

Figure 14.34   Topological sort

The algorithm produces the correct answer and detects cycles if the graph is not acyclic.

The two important issues are correctness and efficiency. Clearly any ordering produced by the algorithm is a topological order. The question is whether every acyclic graph has a topological order, and if so, whether our algorithm is guaranteed to find one. The answer is yes to both questions.

If at any point there are unseen vertices but none of them has indegree equal to zero, then we are guaranteed that there must be a cycle. To see that, pick any vertex A_0. Since A_0 has an incoming edge, let A_1 be the vertex that is connected to A_0. Since A_1 has an incoming edge, let A_2 be the vertex that is connected to A_1. Repeat this N times, where N is the number of unprocessed vertices that are left in the graph. Among $A_0, A_1, ..., A_N$ there must be two identical vertices (because there are N vertices but $N + 1$ A_i's). Tracing backward between those identical A_i and A_j exhibits a cycle.

The algorithm itself can be implemented in linear time by placing all unprocessed indegree zero vertices on a queue. Initially all vertices of indegree zero are placed on the queue. To find the next vertex in the topological order, we merely get and remove the front item from the queue. When a vertex has its indegree lowered to zero, it is placed on the queue. If the queue empties before all vertices have been topologically sorted, then the graph has a cycle. The running time is clearly linear, by the same reasoning used in the unweighted shortest path algorithm.

The running time is linear if a queue is used.

14.5.2   Theory of the Acyclic Shortest Path Algorithm

An important application of topological sorting is its use in solving the shortest path problem for acyclic graphs. The idea is as follows: Have the eyeball visit vertices in topological order.

This idea works because when the eyeball visits vertex v, we are guaranteed that D_v can no longer be lowered, since by the topological ordering rule it has no incoming edges emanating from unvisited nodes. Figure 14.35 shows the stages of the shortest path algorithm using the topological ordering to guide the vertex visitations. Notice that the sequence of vertices visited is not the same as in Dijkstra's algorithm. Also note that vertices visited by the eyeball prior to the eyeball's reaching that start vertex are unreachable from the start vertex and have no influence on the distances of any vertex.

In an acyclic graph, we merely visit vertices in topological order. The result is a linear time algorithm even if there are negative edge weights.

Since we do not need a priority queue, and instead need only incorporate the topological sort into the shortest path computation, we find that the algorithm will run in linear time and will work in the presence of negative edges.

14.5.3   C++ Implementation

The implementation of the shortest path algorithm for acyclic graphs is shown in Figure 14.36. We use a queue to perform the topological sort, and we maintain the indegree information in the `Scratch` member. Lines 14 to 16 compute the indegrees, and at lines 19 to 21 we place any indegree zero vertices onto the queue.

The implementation combines a topological sort calculation and a shortest path calculation. The indegree information is stored in the `Scratch` member. The queue operations are based on `Scratch` being lowered to zero.

We then repeatedly remove a vertex from the queue at lines 25 and 26. Notice that if the queue is empty, the `for` loop will be terminated by the test at line 23, and if this is a premature occurrence because of a cycle, the test at line 46 will fail and an error message will appear (along with a 0 return value) due to lines 49 and 50. Otherwise, the loop at line 28 steps through the adjacency list, and a value of w is obtained at line 30. Immediately we lower w's indegree at line 31, and place it on the queue if it has fallen to zero (at line 32).

Nodes that appear
before *S* in the topo-
logical order are
unreachable.

As we mentioned earlier, if the current vertex v appears prior to S in topological order, then v must be unreachable from S. Consequently, it will still have $D_v \equiv \infty$, and thus cannot hope to provide a path to any adjacent vertex w. We perform a test at line 34, and if this is the case, we do not attempt any distance calculations. This is needed to avoid the possibility of adding a number to infinity, because if infinity is sufficiently large, an overflow could occur producing erroneous results. Otherwise, at lines 37 to 42 we use the same calculations as in Dijkstra's algorithm to update D_w if necessary.

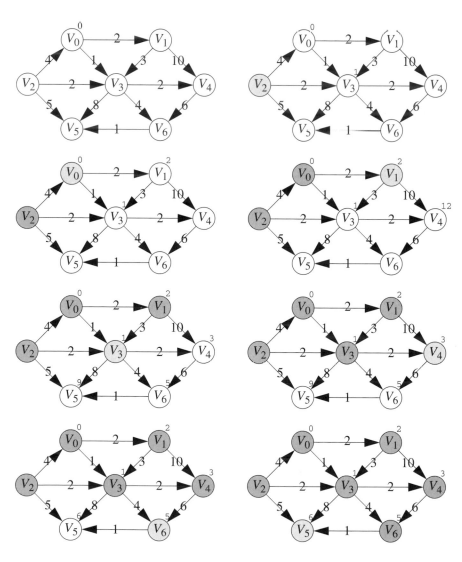

Figure 14.35   Stages of acyclic graph algorithm

```
1   // Single source acyclic weighted shortest path algorithm
2
3   template <class NameType, class DistType>
4   int
5   Graph<NameType, DistType>::Acyclic( int StartNode )
6   {
7       int V, W, Iterations;
8       Queue<int> Q;
9
10      ClearData( );
11      Table[ StartNode ].Dist = 0;
12
13          // Compute indegrees
14      for( V = 0; V < NumVertices; V++ )
15          for( ListItr<Edge<DistType> > P = *Table[ V ].Adj; +P; ++P )
16              Table[ P( ).Dest ].Scratch++;
17
18          // Enqueue vertices of indegree zero
19      for( V = 0; V < NumVertices; V++ )
20          if( Table[ V ].Scratch == 0 )
21              Q.Enqueue( V );
22
23      for( Iterations = 0; !Q.IsEmpty( ); Iterations++ )
24      {
25          V = Q.GetFront( );
26          Q.Dequeue( );
27
28          for( ListItr<Edge<DistType> > P = *Table[ V ].Adj; +P; ++P )
29          {
30              W = P( ).Dest;
31              if( --Table[ W ].Scratch == 0 )
32                  Q.Enqueue( W );
33
34              if( Table[ V ].Dist == Infinity )
35                  continue;
36
37              DistType Cvw = P( ).Cost;
38              if( Table[ W ].Dist > Table[ V ].Dist + Cvw )
39              {
40                  Table[ W ].Dist = Table[ V ].Dist + Cvw;
41                  Table[ W ].Prev = V;
42              }
43          }
44      }
45
46      if( Iterations == NumVertices )
47          return 1;
48
49      cerr << "Graph has a cycle!" << endl;
50      return 0;
51  }
```

Figure 14.36   Shortest path algorithm for acyclic graphs

14.5.4   An Application: Critical Path Analysis

Critical path analysis is used to schedule tasks associated with a project.

An important use of acyclic graphs is *critical path analysis*, which is used to schedule tasks associated with a project. The graph in Figure 14.37 serves as an example. Each vertex represents an activity that must be completed, along with the time it takes to complete the activity. The graph is thus known as an *activity-node graph*, in which vertices represent activities and edges represent precedence relationships. An edge (*v*, *w*) means that activity *v* must be completed before activity *w* may begin. Of course, this implies that the graph must be acyclic. We assume that any activities that do not depend (either directly or indirectly) on each other can be performed in parallel by different servers.

An *activity-node graph* represents activities as vertices and precedence relationships as edges.

This type of graph could be (and frequently is) used to model construction projects, in which several important questions are of interest. First, what is the earliest completion time for the project? We can see from the graph that ten units are required along the path *A*, *C*, *F*, *H*. Another important question is, which activities can be delayed, and by how long, without affecting the minimum completion time? For instance, delaying any of *A*, *C*, *F*, or *H* would push the completion time past ten units. On the other hand, activity *B* is less critical and can be delayed up to two time units without affecting the final completion time.

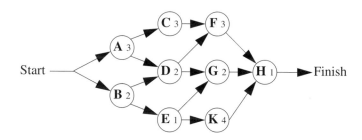

Figure 14.37   Activity-node graph

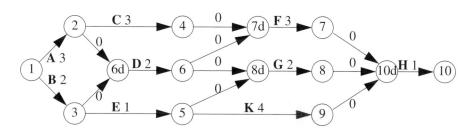

Figure 14.38   Event-node graph

To perform these calculations, we convert the activity-node graph to an *event-node graph*, in which each event corresponds to the completion of an activity and all its dependent activities. Events reachable from a node v in the event-node graph may not commence until after the event v is completed. This graph can be constructed automatically or by hand (from the activity-node graph). Dummy edges and vertices may need to be inserted to avoid introducing false dependencies (or false lack of dependencies). The event-node graph corresponding to the activity graph in Figure 14.37 is shown in Figure 14.38.

To find the earliest completion time of the project, we merely need to find the length of the *longest* path from the first event to the last event. For general graphs the longest path problem generally does not make sense because of the possibility of *positive-cost cycles*, which are the equivalent of negative-cost cycles in shortest path problems. If positive-cost cycles are present, we could ask for the longest simple path, but no satisfactory solution is known for this problem. Fortunately, the event-node graph is acyclic, and thus we need not worry about cycles. It is easy to adapt the shortest path algorithm to compute the earliest completion time for all nodes in the graph. If EC_i is the earliest completion time for node i, then the applicable rules are

$$EC_1 = 0 \text{ and } EC_w = Max_{(v, w) \in E}(EC_v + c_{v, w}).$$

*The **event-node graph** consists of event vertices that correspond to the completion of an activity and all its dependent activities. Edges show what activity must be completed to advance from one vertex to the next. The earliest completion time is the longest path.*

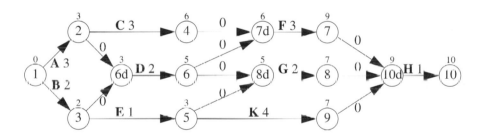

Figure 14.39   Earliest completion times

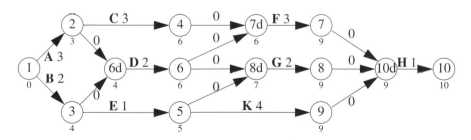

Figure 14.40   Latest completion times

The latest time an event can finish without delaying the project is also easily computable.

Figure 14.39 shows the earliest completion time for each event in our example event-node graph. We can also compute the latest time, LC_i that each event can finish without affecting final completion time. The formulas to do this are

$$LC_N = EC_N \text{ and } LC_v = Min_{(v, w) \in E}(LC_w - c_{v, w}).$$

These values can be computed in linear time by maintaining, for each vertex, a list of all adjacent and preceding vertices. The earliest completion times are computed for vertices by their topological order, and the latest completion times are computed by reverse topological order. The latest completion times are shown in Figure 14.40.

The *slack time* represents the amount of time that an activity can be delayed without delaying overall completion.

The *slack time* for each edge in the event-node graph represents the amount of time that the completion of the corresponding activity can be delayed without delaying the overall completion. It is easy to see that

$$Slack_{(v, w)} = LC_w - EC_v - c_{v, w}$$

Zero slack activities are critical and cannot be delayed. A path of zero-slack edges is the *critical path*.

Figure 14.41 shows the slack (as the third entry) for each activity in the event-node graph. For each node, the top number is the earliest completion time and the bottom number is the latest completion time.

Some activities have zero slack. These are critical activities, which must finish on schedule. There is at least one path consisting entirely of zero-slack edges; such a path is a *critical path*.

Summary

In this chapter we have seen how graphs can be used to model many real-life problems, and in particular how to calculate the shortest path under a wide variety of circumstances. Many of the graphs that occur are typically very sparse, so it is important to choose appropriate data structures to implement them.

For unweighted graphs the shortest path can be computed in linear time using breadth-first search. For positive weighted graphs, slightly more time is needed using Dijkstra's algorithms and an efficient priority queue. For negative weighted graphs, the problem becomes still more difficult. Finally, for acyclic graphs, the problem reverts back to linear time with the aid of a topological sort.

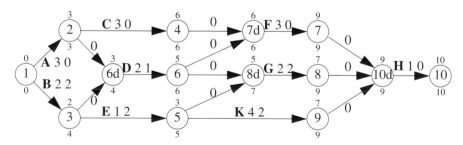

Figure 14.41   Earliest completion time, latest completion time, and slack (additional edge item)

Objects of the Game

activity-node graph Represents vertices as activities and edges as precedence relationships. (450)

adjacency list Represents a graph by using linear space. (417)

adjacency matrix Represents a graph using quadratic space. (417)

adjacent vertex w is adjacent to v if there is an edge from v to w. (416)

breadth-first search Processes vertices in layers: Those closest to the start are evaluated first. The eyeball moves from vertex to vertex and updates distances for adjacent vertices. (432)

critical path analysis Used to schedule tasks associated with a project. (450)

cycle In a directed graph, a path that begins and ends at the same vertex and contains at least one edge. (416)

dense and sparse graphs A graph is dense if the number of edges is large (generally quadratic). Typical graphs are not dense, but are sparse. (417)

Dijkstra's algorithm Solves the positive weighted shortest path problem. (436)

directed acyclic graph (DAG) Directed graphs with no cycles. (445)

direct graph A graph in which edges are ordered pairs of vertices. (415)

edge cost (weight) Third component of an edge that measures cost of traversing the edge. (415)

event-node graph Consists of event vertices that correspond to the completion of an activity and all its dependent activities. Edges show what activity must be completed to advance from one vertex to the next. The earliest completion time is the longest path. (451)

graph Consists of a set of vertices and a set of edges that connect the vertices. (415)

indegree The number of incoming edges of a vertex. (445)

negative-cost cycle Makes most, if not all, paths undefined because we can stay in the cycle arbitrarily long and obtain an arbitrarily negative weighted path length. (443)

path A sequence of vertices connected by edges. (416)

path length The number of edges on a path. (416)

positive-cost cycle In a longest path problem, the equivalent of a negative-cost cycle in a shortest path problem. (451)

simple path A path in which all vertices are distinct, except the first and last can be the same. (416)

single source Describes an algorithm that computes the shortest paths from some start point to all vertices in a graph. (420)

slack time The amount of time that an activity can be delayed without delaying overall completion. (452)

topological sort Orders vertices in a directed acyclic graph such that if there is a path from u to v, then v appears after u in the ordering. A graph that has a cycle cannot have a topological order. (445)

unweighted path length Measures the number of edges on a path. (432)

weighted path length The sum of the edge costs on a path. (435)

Common Errors

1. A common error is failing to check that the input graph satisfies the requisite conditions for the algorithm being used (that is, acyclic or positive weighted).

2. A linked list cannot be used in the `Vertex` structure because its copy constructor is disabled. Even if a copy constructor was enabled for linked lists, we would have to pay excessive costs when the array of `Vertex` structures was expanded.

3. Even though it is never used, `operator!=` must be provided for `Edge`.

4. `istrstream` appears to be broken, and chained input operations are not supported.

5. For `Path`, the comparison function compares the `Cost` member only. If the `Dest` member is used to drive the comparison function, the algorithm may appear to work for small graphs but is incorrect and will give slightly suboptimal answers for larger graphs. It will never produce a path that does not exist, however, making this a difficult error to track down.

6. The shortest path algorithm for negative weighted graphs must have a test for negative cycles; otherwise, it runs forever.

On the Internet

All of the algorithms in this chapter are on-line in one file.

Path.cpp   Contains everything in one file with the simple `main` shown in Figure 14.20

Exercises

In Short

14.1. Find the shortest unweighted path from V_3 to all others in the graph in Figure 14.1.

14.2. Find the shortest weighted path from V_2 to all others in the graph in Figure 14.1.

In Theory

14.3. Show how to avoid quadratic initialization inherent in adjacency matrices while maintaining constant time access of any edge.

14.4. Explain how to modify the unweighted shortest path algorithm so that if there is more than one minimum path (in terms of number of edges), then the tie is broken in favor of the smallest total weight.

14.5. Explain how to modify Dijkstra's algorithm to produce a count of the number of different minimum paths from v to w.

14.6. Explain how to modify Dijkstra's algorithm so that if there is more than one minimum path from v to w, a path with the fewest number of edges is chosen.

14.7. Give an example where Dijkstra's algorithm gives the wrong answer in the presence of a negative edge but no negative-cost cycle.

14.8. Consider the following algorithm to solve the negative weighted shortest path problem: Add a constant c to each edge cost, thus removing negative edges; calculate the shortest path on the new graph; and then use that result on the original. What is wrong with this algorithm?

14.9. Prove the correctness of the negative weighted shortest path algorithm. To do this, show that when the eyeball visits vertex v for the ith time, the value of D_v is the length of the shortest weighted path consisting of i or fewer edges.

14.10. Give a linear time algorithm to find the longest weighted path in an acyclic graph. Does your algorithm extend to graphs that have cycles?

In Practice

14.11. Use a dictionary instead of hash table to implement the vertex map.

14.12. Implement Dijkstra's algorithm using the `DecreaseKey` operation.

14.13. We claim in this chapter that for the implementation of graph algorithms that run on large input, data structures are crucial to ensure reasonable performance. For each of the following instances in which a poor data structure or algorithm is used, provide a Big-Oh analysis of the result, and compare the actual performance with the algorithms and data structures presented in the text. Implement only one change at a time. You should run your tests on a reasonably large and somewhat sparse random graph.

a. When an edge is read, check to see if it is already in the graph.

b. Implement the dictionary by using a sequential scan of the vertex table.

c. Implement the queue by using the algorithm in Exercise 6.13 (this should affect the unweighted shortest path algorithm).

d. In the unweighted shortest path algorithm, implement the search for the minimum cost vertex as a sequential scan of the vertex table.

e. Implement the priority queue by using the algorithm in Exercise 6.16 (this should affect the weighted shortest path algorithm).

f. Implement the priority queue by using the algorithm in Exercise 6.17 (this should affect the weighted shortest path algorithm).

g. In the weighted shortest path algorithm, implement the search for the minimum cost vertex as a sequential scan of the vertex table.

h. In the acyclic shortest path algorithm, implement the search for vertex with indegree zero as a sequential scan of the vertex table.

i. Implement any of the graph algorithms using an adjacency matrix instead of adjacency lists.

Programming Projects

14.14. A directed graph is strongly connected if there is a path from every vertex to every other vertex.

a. Pick any vertex S. Show that if the graph is strongly connected, a shortest path algorithm will declare that all nodes are reachable from S.

b. Show that if the graph is strongly connected, then if the directions of all edges are reversed and a shortest path algorithm is run from S, then all nodes will be reachable from S.

c. Show that the above tests are sufficient to decide if a graph is strongly connected (that is, a graph that passes both tests must be strongly connected).

d. Write a program that checks if a graph is strongly connected. What is the running time of your algorithm?

Explain how each of the following problems can be solved by applying a shortest path algorithm. Then design a mechanism for representing an input, and write a program that solves the problem.

14.15. The input is a list of league game scores (and there are no ties). From this list, if all teams have at least one win and a loss, we can generally "prove," by a silly transitivity argument, that any team is better than any other. For instance, in the six-team league where everyone plays three games, suppose we have the following results: A beat B and C; B beat C and F; C beat D; D beat E; E beat A; F beat D and E. Then we can prove that A is better than F because A beat B who in turn beat F.

Similarly, we can prove that F is better than A because F beat E and E beat A. Given a list of game scores and two teams X and Y, find a proof (if one exists) that X is better than Y, or indicate that no proof of this form can be found.

14.16. A word can be changed to another word by a one-character substitution. Assume that a dictionary of five-letter words exists. Given an algorithm to determine if a word A can be transformed to a word B by a series of one-character substitutions, and if so, outputs the corresponding sequence of words. As an example, `bleed` converts to `blood` by the sequence `bleed, blend, blond, blood`.

14.17. The input is a collection of currencies and their exchange rates. Is there a sequence of exchanges that makes money instantly? For instance if the currencies are X, Y, and Z, and exchange rate is 1 X equals 2 Ys, 1 Y equals 2 Zs, and 1 X equals 3 Zs, then 300 Zs will buy 100 Xs, which in turn will buy 200 Ys, which in turn will buy 400 Zs. We have thus made a profit of 33 percent.

14.18. A student needs to take a certain number of courses to graduate, and these courses have prerequisites that must be followed. Given a list of courses and their prerequisites, and assuming all courses are offered every semester and that the student can take an unlimited number of courses, compute a schedule that requires the minimum number of semesters.

References

The use of adjacency lists to represent graphs was first advocated in [3]. Dijkstra's shortest path algorithm was originally described in [2]. The algorithm for negative edge costs is taken from [1]. A more efficient test for termination is described in [6], which also shows how data structures play an important role in a wide range of graph theory algorithms. The topological sorting algorithm is from [4]. A host of real-life applications of graph algorithms can be found in [5], along with references for further reading.

1. R. E. Bellman, "On a Routing Problem," *Quarterly of Applied Mathematics* **16** (1958), 87-90.

2. E. W. Dijkstra, "A Note on Two Problems in Connexion with Graphs," *Numerische Mathematik* **1** (1959), 269-271.

3. J. E. Hopcroft and R. E. Tarjan, "Algorithm 447: Efficient Algorithms for Graph Manipulation," *Communications of the ACM* **16** (1973), 372-378.

4. A. B. Kahn, "Topological Sorting of Large Networks," *Communications of the ACM* **5** (1962), 558-562.

5. D. E. Knuth, *The Stanford GraphBase*, Addison-Wesley, Reading, MA, 1993.

6. R. E. Tarjan, *Data Structures and Network Algorithms*, Society for Industrial and Applied Mathematics, Philadelphia, PA, 1985.

Part IV: Implementations

Chapter 15

Stacks and Queues

In this chapter we discuss the implementation of the stack and queue data structures. Recall from Chapter 6 that we expect the basic operations to take constant time. For both the stack and queue, there are two basic ways to arrange for constant-time operations. The first is to store the items contiguously in an array, and the second method is to store items noncontiguously in a linked list. We will give implementations for both data structures using both methods. Our code will build on the abstract interfaces given in Chapter 6.

In this chapter we will see

- an array-based implementation of the stack
- an array-based implementation of the queue
- a linked list-based implementation of the stack
- a linked list-based implementation of the queue
- a brief comparison of the two methods
- inheritance used to derive a new data structure, the *double-ended queue*

15.1   Dynamic Array Implementations

In this section we implement the stack and queue using a simple array (and two integers). The resulting algorithms are extremely efficient and also simple to code.

15.1.1   Stacks

As Figure 15.1 shows, a stack can be implemented with an array and an integer. The integer TOS (*top of stack*) provides the array index of the top element of the stack, and thus when TOS is -1, the stack is empty. To Push, we increment TOS and place the new element in the array position TOS. Accessing the top element is thus trivial, and the Pop can be performed by decrementing TOS. In Figure

A stack can be implemented with an array and an integer that indicates the index of the top element.

15.1 we begin with an empty stack, and then show the stack after the following three operations: Push(A), Push(B), and Pop.

Figure 15.2 shows the interface for the array-based Stack class. We implement it as a derived class of the abstract base class AbsStack shown in Figure 6.4. This certainly is not necessary; however, it does have a few advantages. First, the public/private status of the copy constructor is, in effect, inherited. Since the abstract base class disabled copy construction by placing it in the private section, we do not have to redecide the issue. Second, the abstract class took care of the virtual declarations, so once again we do not have to worry about this coding detail. However for more complex classes, things are a little more complicated. Thus, for some of the data structures in future chapters, we will avoid the additional complexity and implement them without inheriting from an abstract class.

The interface specifies three data members: Array, which is dynamically allocated, stores the items in the stack. MaxSize tells us the capacity of Array, and TopOfStack gives the index of the current top of the stack. For an empty stack, this is −1. As mentioned earlier, the copy constructor is effectively disabled, so call by value is disallowed for Stack objects. The constructor for the Stack is specified at line 23. The implementation is given in Figure 15.3. The Stack constructor merely initializes the MaxSize and TopOfStack members and then dynamically allocates the array of elements.

The destructor is shown in the interface at line 24. It merely calls delete[] to deallocate the dynamically allocated Array. Next in the interface is operator=. That operator is used to copy one Stack to an already-constructed second Stack. The implementation is shown in Figure 15.4. Once again there are no new features; we build on our foundation of previously learned concepts. Line 6 checks for the aliasing condition (the assignment A=A), returning immediately if a self-copy is attempted. At lines 10 and 11, we get rid of the old array and use a new, dynamically allocated array. The actual deep copy of the data members is implemented at lines 14 to 17, and a reference to the current object is returned at line 19.

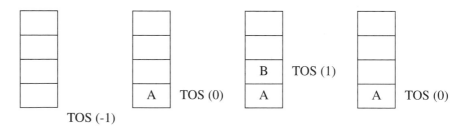

Figure 15.1   How the stack routines work: empty stack, Push(A), Push(B), Pop

```
1  // Stack class interface: array implementation
2
3  // Etype: must have zero-parameter constructor and operator=
4  // CONSTRUCTION: with (a) no initializer;
5  //      copy construction of Stack objects is DISALLOWED
6  // Deep copy is supported
7  //
8  // ******************PUBLIC OPERATIONS*********************
9  // void Push( Etype X ) --> Insert X
10 // void Pop( )          --> Remove most recently inserted item
11 // Etype Top( )         --> Return most recently inserted item
12 // int IsEmpty( )       --> Return 1 if empty; else return 0
13 // int IsFull( )        --> Return 0; stack is never full
14 // void MakeEmpty( )    --> Remove all items
15 // ******************ERRORS*******************************
16 // Predefined exception is propagated if new fails
17 // EXCEPTION is called for Pop or Top on empty stack
18
19 template <class Etype>
20 class Stack : public AbsStack<Etype>
21 {
22   public:
23     Stack( );
24     ~Stack( ) { delete [ ] Array; }
25
26     const Stack & operator=( const Stack & Rhs );
27
28     void Push( const Etype & X );
29     void Pop( );
30     const Etype & Top( ) const;
31     int IsEmpty( ) const { return TopOfStack == -1; }
32     int IsFull( ) const  { return 0; }
33     void MakeEmpty( )    { TopOfStack = -1; }
34   private:
35     // Copy constructor remains disabled by inheritance
36
37     int MaxSize;
38     int TopOfStack;
39     Etype *Array;
40 };
41
42     // Place this at the start of the implementation file
43 static const InitStackSize = 3;
```

Figure 15.2   Stack class interface (array implementation)

```
1  template <class Etype>
2  Stack<Etype>::Stack( ) :
3                     MaxSize( InitStackSize ), TopOfStack( -1 )
4  {
5      Array = new Etype [ MaxSize ];
6  }
```

Figure 15.3   No-parameter constructor for array-based `Stack`

```
1   template <class Etype>
2   const Stack<Etype> &
3   Stack<Etype>::operator=( const Stack<Etype> & Rhs )
4   {
5           // Check for aliasing
6       if( this == &Rhs )
7           return *this;
8
9           // Get some memory
10      delete [ ] Array;
11      Array = new Etype[ Rhs.MaxSize ];
12
13          // Do the copy
14      MaxSize = Rhs.MaxSize;
15      TopOfStack = Rhs.TopOfStack;
16      for( int i = 0; i <= TopOfStack; i++ )
17          Array[ i ] = Rhs.Array[ i ];
18
19      return *this;
20  }
```

Figure 15.4   Copy assignment operator for array-based `Stack`

```
1  template <class Etype>
2  void
3  Stack<Etype>::Push( const Etype & X )
4  {
5      if( TopOfStack + 1 == MaxSize )
6          Array = DoubleArray( Array, MaxSize );
7      Array[ ++TopOfStack ] = X;
8  }
```

Figure 15.5   `Push` member function for array-based `Stack`

The `Stack` member functions are listed in lines 28 to 33 of the interface. Most of these routines have simple implementations. `IsFull`, for example, is always false (as shown in the interface) because we implement array doubling in the `Push` routine. This is shown in Figure 15.5. If it were not for the array doubling, which is a standard exercise that we have seen before,[1] the `Push` routine would be only the single line of code shown at line 7. The remaining routines are equally short, as shown in Figure 15.6.

If there is no array doubling, every operation takes constant time. A Push that involves array doubling will take $O(N)$ time. If this was a frequent occurrence, then we would need to worry. However, it is infrequent because an array doubling involving N elements must be preceded by at least $N/2$ Pushes that do not involve an array doubling. Consequently, we can charge the $O(N)$ cost of the doubling over these $N/2$ easy Pushes, effectively raising the cost of each Push by only a small constant. This technique is known as amortization.

> Recall that array doubling does not affect performance in the long run.

A real-life example of amortization is payment of income taxes. Rather than pay the entire bill on April 15, the government requires that you pay most of your taxes through withholding. The total tax bill is always the same; it is just *when* the tax is paid that varies. The same is true for the time spent in the Push operations. We can charge for the array doubling at the time it occurs, or we can bill each Push operation equally. An amortized bound states that we bill each operation in a sequence for its fair share of the total cost. In our example it means that the cost of array doubling is not excessive at all.

15.1.2 Queues

The easiest way to implement the queue is to store the items in an array with the front item in the front (that is, array index zero) position. If Back represents the position of the last item in the queue, to Enqueue we merely increment Back and place the item there. The problem is that the Dequeue operation is very expensive, because by requiring that the items be placed at the start of the array, we force the Dequeue to shift over all the items one position, after the front item is removed.

> Storing the queue items beginning at the start of any array makes dequeueing expensive.

```
1  template <class Etype>
2  void
3  Stack<Etype>::Pop( )
4  {
5      EXCEPTION( IsEmpty( ), "Can't Pop an empty stack" );
6      TopOfStack--;
7  }
8
9  template <class Etype>
10 const Etype &
11 Stack<Etype>::Top( ) const
12 {
13     EXCEPTION( IsEmpty( ), "Can't Top an empty stack" );
14     return Array[ TopOfStack ];
15 }
```

Figure 15.6   Remaining member functions for array-based Stack

---

1. This form of DoubleArray is discussed in Section 3.5.

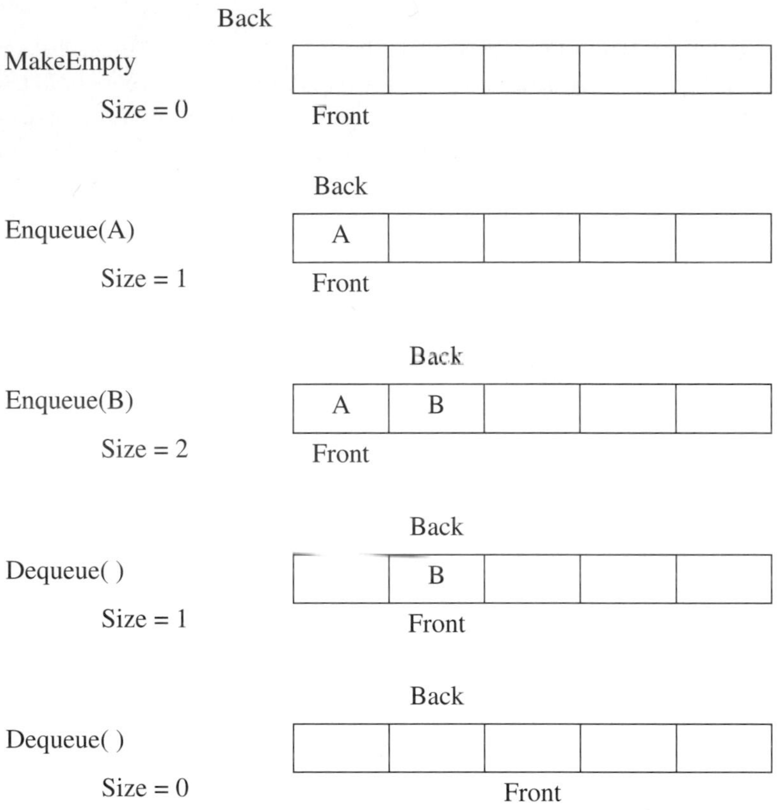

Figure 15.7   Basic array implementation of the queue

A **Dequeue** is imple-
mented by increment-
ing the **Front**
position.

Figure 15.7 shows that to overcome this problem, when a Dequeue is performed, we increment Front rather than sliding over all the elements. When the
queue has one element, both Front and Back represent the array index of that
element. Thus, for an empty queue, Back must be initialized to Front-1.

This implementation assures us that both Enqueue and Dequeue can be
performed in constant time. The fundamental problem with it is shown in the first
line of Figure 15.8. After three more Enqueue operations, we cannot add any
more items, even though the queue is not really full. Array doubling does not
solve the problem because, even if the size of the array is 1000, after 1000
Enqueue operations there is no room in the queue, regardless of its actual size.
Even if 1000 Dequeue operations have been performed, thus abstractly making
the queue empty, we cannot add to it.

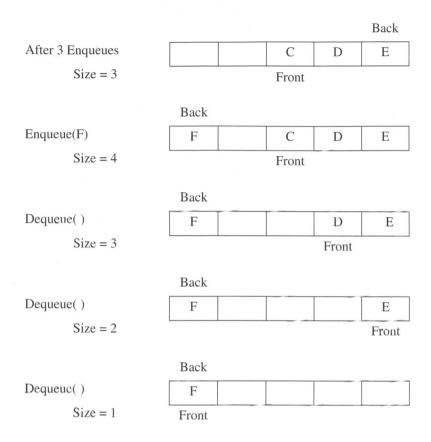

Figure 15.8   Array implementation of the queue with wraparound

As Figure 15.8 shows, however, there is plenty of extra space: All the positions before Front are unused and can thus be recycled. Thus we implement *wraparound*. When either Back or Front reaches the end of the array, we reset it to the beginning. This operation is known as a *circular array implementation*. We only need to double the array when the number of elements in the queue is equal to the number of array positions. To Enqueue(F), we therefore reset Back to the start of the array, and place F there. After three Dequeue operations, Front is also reset to the start of the array.

The interface for the generic Queue class is shown in Figure 15.9. As was the case with the Stack class, the copy constructor is disabled by virtue of being in the private section in the abstract base class. The Queue class has five data members: a dynamically allocated array, its size, the number of items currently in the queue, and the array index of the front and back items.

Wraparound returns to the beginning of the array when the end is reached. Using wraparound to implement the queue is known as a circular array implementation.

```
1  // Queue class interface: array implementation
2  //
3  // Etype: must have zero-parameter and operator=
4  // CONSTRUCTION: with (a) no initializer;
5  //      copy construction of Queue objects is DISALLOWED
6  // Deep copy is supported
7  //
8  // ******************PUBLIC OPERATIONS*********************
9  // void Enqueue( Etype X )  --> Insert X
10 // void Dequeue( )        --> Remove least recently inserted item
11 // Etype Front( )         --> Return least recently inserted item
12 // int IsEmpty( )         --> Return 1 if empty; else return 0
13 // int IsFull( )          --> Return 0; queue is never full
14 // void MakeEmpty( )      --> Remove all items
15 // ******************ERRORS*******************************
16 // Predefined exception is propagated if new fails
17 // EXCEPTION is called for Front or Dequeue on empty stack
18
19 template <class Etype>
20 class Queue : public AbsQueue<Etype>
21 {
22   public:
23     Queue( );
24     ~Queue( ) { delete [ ] Array; }
25
26     const Queue & operator=( const Queue & Rhs );
27
28     void Enqueue( const Etype & X );
29     void Dequeue( );
30     const Etype & GetFront( ) const;
31     int IsEmpty( ) const { return CurrentSize == 0; }
32     int IsFull( ) const  { return 0; }
33     void MakeEmpty( );
34   private:
35     // Copy constructor remains disabled by inheritance
36
37     int MaxSize;
38     int CurrentSize;
39     int Front;
40     int Back;
41     Etype *Array;
42
43     void DoubleQueue( );
44     void Increment( int & X ) const; // Add 1 with wraparound
45 };
46
47 static const InitQueueSize = 3;
```

Figure 15.9   Queue class interface and array implementation

```
1 template <class Etype>         // Add one with wraparound
2 void
3 Queue<Etype>::Increment( int & X ) const
4 {
5     if( ++X == MaxSize )
6         X = 0;
7 }
```

Figure 15.10   Wraparound routine

Two functions are declared in the private section. These functions are used internally by the Queue members but are not made available to the user of the class. One of these functions is the Increment routine. The Increment routine adds one to a parameter passed by reference. Since it implements wraparound, if the result is MaxSize, it is altered to zero. This is shown in Figure 15.10. The other routine is DoubleQueue, which is called if an Enqueue requires a doubling of the array. It is slightly more complex than a simple call to DoubleArray that was used for the Stack class, because the queue items are not necessarily stored starting in array location zero, and thus items must be carefully copied. DoubleQueue is discussed with Enqueue.

If the queue is full, we must implement array doubling carefully.

Many of the public functions are similar to their Stack counterparts, including the constructor, destructor, and copy assignment operator. Figure 15.11 shows the constructor and copy assignment operator. The constructor is not particularly special, except that we must be careful to make sure that we have the correct initial values for both Front and Back. operator= steps through the Queue on the right side and copies each item into the current Queue at lines 22 to 24. The result is copied starting at array position zero; notice the new values of Front and Back at lines 19 and 20. An alternative would have been to copy the entire array, as well as the values of Front and Back. However, we prefer to copy only the elements that are logically in the queue to save time.

The Enqueue and Dequeue routines are shown in Figure 15.12. The basic strategy is simple enough, as illustrated by lines 17 to 19 in the Enqueue routine. DoubleQueue, shown in Figure 15.13, is similar to the Stack doubling routine, except that the copy from the old array to the new array does not start from position zero. We use the same iteration technique that was seen for operator=. The remaining routines are shown in Figure 15.14. They are all short and simple. Once again it should be clear that the queue routines are constant-time operations. The cost of array doubling can be amortized over the sequence of Enqueue operations, in the same way as the Stack.

When we double the queue array, we cannot simply copy the entire array directly.

```
 1  template <class Etype>
 2  Queue<Etype>::Queue( ) : MaxSize( InitQueueSize ),
 3                CurrentSize( 0 ), Front( 0 ), Back( -1 )
 4  {
 5      Array = new Etype [ MaxSize ];
 6  }
 7
 8  template <class Etype>
 9  const Queue<Etype> &
10  Queue<Etype>::operator=( const Queue<Etype> & Rhs )
11  {
12      if( this == &Rhs )
13          return Rhs;
14
15      delete [ ] Array;
16      Array = new Etype [ Rhs.MaxSize ];
17      CurrentSize = Rhs.CurrentSize;
18      MaxSize = Rhs.MaxSize;
19      Front = 0;
20      Back = CurrentSize - 1;
21
22      for( int i = 0, j = Rhs.Front; i < CurrentSize;
23                                      i++, Increment( j ) )
24          Array[ i ] = Rhs.Array[ j ];
25
26      return *this;
27  }
```

Figure 15.11   Copy assignment operator for array-based Queue class

```
 1  template <class Etype>
 2  void
 3  Queue<Etype>::Dequeue( )
 4  {
 5      EXCEPTION( IsEmpty( ), "Queue is empty" );
 6      CurrentSize--;
 7      Increment( Front );
 8  }
 9
10  template <class Etype>
11  void
12  Queue<Etype>::Enqueue( const Etype & X )
13  {
14      if( CurrentSize == MaxSize )
15          DoubleQueue( );
16
17      Increment( Back );
18      Array[ Back ] = X;
19      CurrentSize++;
20  }
```

Figure 15.12   Enqueue and Dequeue for array-based Queue class

```
1  template <class Etype>
2  void
3  Queue<Etype>::DoubleQueue( )
4  {
5      int NewSize  = MaxSize * 2;
6      Etype *Old = Array;
7
8      Array = new Etype[ NewSize ];
9
10     for( int i = 0, j = Front; i < CurrentSize;
11                                      i++, Increment( j ) )
12         Array[ i ] = Old[ j ];
13
14     Front = 0;
15     Back = CurrentSize - 1;
16     MaxSize = NewSize;
17
18     delete [ ] Old;
19 }
```

Figure 15.13   Dynamic expansion for array-based `Queue` class

```
1  template <class Etype>
2  const Etype &
3  Queue<Etype>::GetFront( ) const
4  {
5      EXCEPTION( IsEmpty( ), "Queue is empty" );
6      return Array[ Front ];
7  }
8
9  template <class Etype>
10 void
11 Queue<Etype>::MakeEmpty( )
12 {
13     CurrentSize = 0;
14     Front = 0;
15     Back = -1;
16 }
```

Figure 15.14   Supporting routines for array-based `Queue` class

15.2   Linked List Implementations

An alternative to the contiguous array implementation is using a linked list. Recall from Section 1.8 that in a linked list we store each item in a separate structure; the structure also contains a pointer to the next structure in the list. The advantage of the linked list is that the excess memory is only one pointer per item, whereas a contiguous array implementation uses excess space equal to the number of vacant array items (plus some additional memory during the doubling

The advantage of a linked list implementation is that the excess memory is only one pointer per item. The disadvantage is that the memory allocation is time consuming.

phase). To be competitive with contiguous array implementations, we must be able to perform the basic linked list operations in constant time. We will see that this is easy to do because the changes in the linked list are restricted to the elements at the two ends (front and back) of the list.

15.2.1   Stacks

To implement the stack, the top of the stack is represented by the first item in the list.

The `Stack` class can be implemented as a linked list in which the top of the stack is represented by the first item in the list. This is shown in Figure 15.15. To implement a `Push`, we create a new node in the list and attach it as the new first element. This node can be allocated by a call to `new`. To implement a `Pop`, we merely advance the top of the stack to the second item in the list (if there is one). We should call `delete` on the old first node to avoid memory leaks. An empty stack is represented by an empty linked list. Clearly, each operation is constant time, since by restricting operations to the first node, we have made all calculations independent of the size of the list. All that remains is the C++ implementation.

Figure 15.16 provides the class implementation. Lines 39 to 47 give the type declaration for the nodes in the list. A `StackNode` consists of two data members: `Element` stores the item and `Next` stores a pointer to the next `StackNode` in the linked list. We provide two constructors for `StackNode`. The first can be used to execute

```
StackNode *Ptr1 = new StackNode;
```

and the second can be used for both

```
StackNode *Ptr2 = new StackNode( X );
StackNode *Ptr3 = new StackNode( X, Ptr2 );
```

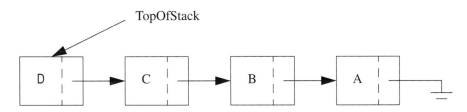

Figure 15.15   Linked list implementation of the stack

```
 1  // Stack class interface: linked list implementation
 2
 3  // Etype: must have zero-parameter and copy constructor
 4  // CONSTRUCTION: with (a) no initializer;
 5  //      copy construction of Stack objects is DISALLOWED
 6  // Deep copy is supported
 7  //
 8  // ******************PUBLIC OPERATIONS*********************
 9  // void Push( Etype X ) --> Insert X
10  // void Pop( )              --> Remove most recently inserted item
11  // Etype Top( )             --> Return most recently inserted item
12  // int IsEmpty( )           --> Return 1 if empty; else return 0
13  // int IsFull( )            --> Return 0; stack is never full
14  // void MakeEmpty( )        --> Remove all items
15  // ******************ERRORS*******************************
16  // Predefined exception is propagated if new fails
17  // EXCEPTION is called for Pop or Top on empty stack
18
19  #include <stdlib.h>
20
21  template <class Etype>
22  class Stack : public AbsStack<Etype>
23  {
24    public:
25      Stack( ) : TopOfStack( NULL ) { }
26      ~Stack( ) { MakeEmpty( ); }
27
28      const Stack & operator=( const Stack & Rhs );
29
30      void Push( const Etype & X );
31      void Pop( );
32      const Etype & Top( ) const;
33      int IsEmpty( ) const   { return TopOfStack == NULL; }
34      int IsFull( ) const    { return 0; }
35      void MakeEmpty( );
36    private:
37      // Copy constructor remains disabled by inheritance
38
39      struct StackNode
40      {
41          Etype Element;
42          StackNode *Next;
43
44          StackNode( ) : Next( NULL ) { }
45          StackNode( const Etype & E, StackNode *N = NULL ) :
46                      Element( E ), Next( N ) { }
47      };
48
49      StackNode *TopOfStack;
50  };
```

Figure 15.16   Interface for linked-list based Stack class

```
 1  template <class Etype>
 2  const Stack<Etype> &
 3  Stack<Etype>::operator=( const Stack<Etype> & Rhs )
 4  {
 5          // Check for aliasing
 6      if( this == &Rhs )
 7          return *this;
 8
 9      MakeEmpty( );
10      if( Rhs.IsEmpty( ) )
11          return *this;
12
13      StackNode *Ptr = new StackNode( Rhs.TopOfStack->Element );
14      StackNode *RhsPtr = Rhs.TopOfStack->Next;
15
16      TopOfStack = Ptr;
17      while( RhsPtr != NULL )
18      {
19          Ptr->Next = new StackNode( RhsPtr->Element );
20          Ptr = Ptr->Next;
21          RhsPtr = RhsPtr->Next;
22      }
23
24      return *this;
25  }
```

Figure 15.17   Copy assignment operator for linked-list-based `Stack` class

The `StackNode` is nested in the private section of the `Stack` class, so it is not visible.

Note that the new type StackNode is nested in the Stack class. This means it is not a type in the normal global scope. This is a good thing because it enforces information hiding: The StackNode is certainly an internal detail of the Stack class. Moreover, by virtue of the private declaration, it is completely invisible to the Stack class users. Not all compilers implement nested class declarations in conjunction with templates. You may need to rework the code by moving the StackNode declaration out of the Stack class. This is clearly a less desirable alternative because it weakens the hiding of information. The Stack itself is represented by a single data member: TopOfStack is a pointer to the first StackNode in the linked list.

The constructor at line 25 tells us that an empty stack is created by setting TopOfStack to NULL. The destructor declared at line 26 calls the member function MakeEmpty to deallocate all the dynamically allocated nodes in the stack. MakeEmpty works by popping the stack until it is empty.

The copy assignment operator is shown in Figure 15.17. Let us discuss how this routine works. At line 6 we check for aliasing and return immediately if it is detected. Otherwise, it is safe to make the current object empty (by popping any elements in the stack). Since the stack is now empty, if the stack on the right side is empty, we can return immediately. This is checked at line 10. Otherwise, we have at least one item to copy. We have `Ptr` point at a newly allocated node that is a copy of the first item in the `Rhs` list at line 13. This item will be the top of the new stack line 16.

A deep copy of `operator=` requires that we step through the second stack and allocate new nodes to be placed in the first stack.

```
1  template <class Etype>
2  void
3  Stack<Etype>::Push( const Etype & X )
4  {
5      TopOfStack = new StackNode( X, TopOfStack );
6  }
7
8  template <class Etype>
9  void
10 Stack<Etype>::Pop( )
11 {
12     EXCEPTION( IsEmpty( ), "Can't Pop an empty stack" );
13
14     StackNode *Old = TopOfStack;
15     TopOfStack = TopOfStack->Next;
16     delete Old;
17 }
18
19 template <class Etype>
20 const Etype &
21 Stack<Etype>::Top( ) const
22 {
23     EXCEPTION( IsEmpty( ), "Can't Pop an empty stack" );
24     return TopOfStack->Element;
25 }
26
27 template <class Etype>
28 void
29 Stack<Etype>::MakeEmpty( )
30 {
31     while( !IsEmpty( ) )
32         Pop( );
33 }
```

Figure 15.18   Simple class members for linked-list-based `Stack`

Note that the **Next** pointer of the last node is **NULL** by virtue of the **StackNode** constructor.

We have `RhsPtr` point at the second item in the `Rhs` list at line 14. We then loop: `RhsPtr` points at a cell containing the next item in the `Rhs` list. `Ptr` points at the last cell in the newly created stack list. Line 17 directs the loop to continue until the `Rhs` list is exhausted. While it is not, we create a new node by using an item in the `Rhs` list and then attach that new node at the end of the new list. The attachment is performed by the assignment to `Ptr->Next` at line 19. We must now update `Ptr` because after this assignment, `Ptr` no longer points to the last node in the new list. This is done at line 21. We also advance to the next node in the `Rhs` list at line 20. When we are done with the loop, everything has been copied over, and we can return. Note carefully that the `Next` pointer for the last node in the list is automatically `NULL`, by virtue of the constructor.

The stack routines are essentially one-liners.

The remaining routines are shown in Figure 15.18. The `Push` operation is essentially one line of code: We allocate a new `StackNode`. A data member contains the item `X` to be pushed. The next pointer for this new node is the original `TopOfStack`. This node then becomes the new `TopOfStack`. All this is done at line 5.

The `Pop` operation is also conceptually simple. After the obligatory test for emptiness, we save a pointer to the node at the top of the stack. We then reset `TopOfStack` to the second node in the list, and call `delete` to remove the popped node. Finally, `Top` and `MakeEmpty` are straightforward routines.

15.2.2   Queues

A linked list in which we maintain a pointer to the first and last item can be used to implement the queue in constant time per operation.

The queue can be implemented by a linked list provided we keep pointers to both the front and back of the list. Figure 15.19 shows the general idea.

The queue routine is almost identical to the stack routine. It is so similar, in fact, that we could derive the `Queue` class from the `Stack` class using private inheritance. We give an independent implementation to make the ideas more clear, and leave the possibility of using inheritance as Exercise 15.11. An easier-to-follow example of inheritance is given in Section 15.4, where we show how to use the `Queue` class to derive an extended set of operations.

The `Queue` class interface is given in Figure 15.20. Nothing is new here, except that we maintain two pointers instead of one. Figure 15.21 shows `operator=`. It is identical to the `Stack operator=`, except for the addition of line 22, assigning to `Back`.

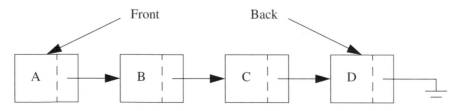

Figure 15.19   Linked list implementation of the queue

```
1   // Queue class interface: linked list implementation
2   //
3   // Etype: must have zero-parameter and copy constructor
4   // CONSTRUCTION: with (a) no initializer;
5   //       copy construction of Queue objects is DISALLOWED
6   // Deep copy is supported
7   //
8   // ******************PUBLIC OPERATIONS********************
9   // void Enqueue( Etype X )--> Insert X
10  // void Dequeue( )        --> Remove least recently inserted item
11  // Etype Front( )         --> Return least recently inserted item
12  // int IsEmpty( )         --> Return 1 if empty; else return 0
13  // int IsFull( )          --> Return 0; queue is never full
14  // void MakeEmpty( )      --> Remove all items
15  // ******************ERRORS*******************************
16  // Predefined exception is propagated if new fails
17  // EXCEPTION is called for Front or Dequeue on empty stack
18
19  #include <stdlib.h>
20
21  template <class Etype>
22  class Queue : public AbsQueue<Etype>
23  {
24    public:
25      Queue( ) : Front( NULL ), Back( NULL ) { }
26      ~Queue( ) { MakeEmpty( ); }
27
28      const Queue & operator=( const Queue & Rhs );
29
30      void Enqueue( const Etype & X );
31      void Dequeue( );
32      const Etype & GetFront( ) const;
33      int IsEmpty( ) const { return Front == NULL; }
34      int IsFull( ) const  { return 0; }
35      void MakeEmpty( );
36    private:
37      // Copy constructor remains disabled by inheritance
38
39      struct QueueNode
40      {
41          Etype Element;
42          QueueNode *Next;
43
44          QueueNode( ) : Next( NULL ) { }
45          QueueNode( const Etype & E, QueueNode *N = NULL ) :
46                      Element( E ), Next( N ) { }
47      };
48
49      QueueNode *Front;
50      QueueNode *Back;
51  };
```

Figure 15.20   Interface for linked-list-based Queue class

```
1  template <class Etype>
2  const Queue<Etype> &
3  Queue<Etype>::operator=( const Queue<Etype> & Rhs )
4  {
5      if( this == &Rhs )
6          return Rhs;
7
8      MakeEmpty( );
9      if( Rhs.IsEmpty( ) )
10         return *this;
11
12     QueueNode *Ptr = new QueueNode( Rhs.Front->Element );
13     QueueNode *RhsPtr = Rhs.Front->Next;
14
15     Front = Ptr;
16     while( RhsPtr != NULL )
17     {
18         Ptr->Next = new QueueNode( RhsPtr->Element );
19         RhsPtr = RhsPtr->Next;
20         Ptr = Ptr->Next;
21     }
22     Back = Ptr;
23
24     return *this;
25  }
```

Figure 15.21   Copy assignment operator for linked-list-based Queue
class

```
1  template <class Etype>
2  void
3  Queue<Etype>::Enqueue( const Etype & X )
4  {
5      if( IsEmpty( ) )
6          Back = Front = new QueueNode( X );
7      else
8          Back = Back->Next = new QueueNode( X );
9  }
10
11 template <class Etype>
12 void
13 Queue<Etype>::Dequeue( )
14 {
15     EXCEPTION( IsEmpty( ), "Queue is empty" );
16
17     QueueNode *Old = Front;
18     Front = Front->Next;
19     delete Old;
20  }
```

Figure 15.22   Enqueue and Dequeue for linked-list-based Queue
class

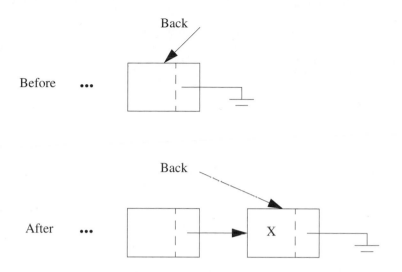

Figure 15.23   Enqueue operation for linked-list-based implementation

Figure 15.22 implements both Enqueue and Dequeue. Dequeue is logically identical to a stack Pop. Enqueue has two cases. If the queue is empty, then we create a one-element queue by calling new and having both Front and Back point at the single node. Otherwise, we create a new node with data value X, attach it to the end of the list, and then reset the end of the list to this new node. This is illustrated in Figure 15.23. Notice that enqueueing the first element is a special case because there is no next pointer to which a new node can be attached. All this is done at line 8 in Figure 15.22. The remaining member functions for the Queue class are identical to the corresponding Stack routines. They are shown in Figure 15.24.

Enqueueing the first element is a special case because there is no next pointer to which a new node can be attached.

15.3   Comparison of the Two Methods

Given a choice, should we use an array-based implementation or a linked-list-based implementation? Both have their advantages. The primary advantage of the array-based version is speed: The operations are extremely fast and avoid the N calls to new and delete that the linked list versions use. Although array doubling does involve calls to new and delete, the number of calls is smaller than log N (because we can only double logarithmically many times). As we discussed, the cost of copying from the old array to the new array can be amortized over the entire sequence of Push or Enqueue operations and is thus very small, unless Etypes are expensive objects to copy. Additionally, the sequential access provided by an array is typically faster than the potential nonsequential access offered by dynamic memory allocation.

The array vs. linked list implementation represents a classic time-space trade-off.

```
 1  template <class Etype>
 2  const Etype &
 3  Queue<Etype>::GetFront( ) const
 4  {
 5      EXCEPTION( IsEmpty( ), "Queue is empty" );
 6      return Front->Element;
 7  }
 8
 9  template <class Etype>
10  void
11  Queue<Etype>::MakeEmpty(   )
12  {
13      while( !IsEmpty( ) )
14          Dequeue( );
15  }
```

Figure 15.24   Supporting routines for linked-list-based `Queue` class

The array implementation does have two drawbacks, however. First, we could potentially use three times as much space as the number of data items would suggest. This is because at the point the array is doubled, we need to have memory to store both the old and the new (double-sized) array. For most of the algorithm, the array is between 50 percent and 100 percent full; on average, it is 75 percent full, meaning that for every three items in the array, one spot is empty. The wasted space is thus 33 percent on average. If the items in the array are large, this could be excessive. By comparison, the linked-list-based version used only an extra pointer per item. For large items this is less than the space usage of the array implementation.

In short, the array implementation is preferable for small objects. The linked list implementation is preferable for large objects if space is scarce or if `Etype` copies are so expensive that the cost of array doubling becomes significant.

15.4   Double-Ended Queues

A *double-ended queue* (*deque*) allows access at both ends. Much of its functionality can be derived from the queue class.

We close this chapter by discussing the use of inheritance to derive new data structures. A *double-ended queue* (*deque*) is like a queue, except that access is allowed at both ends. Rather than use the terms `Enqueue` and `Dequeue`, we use `AddFront`, `AddRear`, `RemoveFront`, and `RemoveRear`. Figure 15.25 shows the derived templated class `Deque`. It is unspecified which `Queue` implementation is being implemented; that is a matter of preference. Let us look at some of the basics.

First, the copy constructor is disabled because it was disabled in the `Queue` class. `operator=` is public because it was public in the `Queue` class. Because we have not provided an implementation, it defaults to a member by member application of `operator=`. The only member is the `Queue` aggregate that is inherited, so we get the same semantics as the Queue class. Similarly, the constructor is member-by-member construction, and the destructor is member by member destruction (including the inherited portion, considered as a single member).

Enqueue and Dequeue become disabled for the Deque class by their placement in the private section. GetFront is unchanged from the Queue class and is thus inherited unmodified. AddBack and RemoveFront call the existing Enqueue and Dequeue routines. Note that at line 27, the call to Enqueue is actually a call to the function at line 34, which is the inherited Queue function. We can also use Queue<Etype>::Enqueue(X). The only routines that need to be written are AddFront, RemoveBack, and GetBack. We leave this as Exercise 15.5.

Implementation of the deque is simple using inheritance.

```
 1  // Double ended queue (Deque)class interface:
 2  //
 3  // Etype: must have zero-parameter and appropriate copy
 4  // CONSTRUCTION: with (a) no initializer;
 5  //      copy construction of Deque objects is DISALLOWED
 6  // Deep copy is supported
 7  //
 8  // ****************PUBLIC OPERATIONS********************
 9  // void AddFront( Etype X )  --> Insert X at front
10  // void AddBack( Etype X )   --> Insert X at back
11  // void RemoveFront( )       --> Remove front item
12  // void RemoveBack( )        --> Remove back item
13  // Etype GetFront( )         --> Return front item
14  // Etype GetBack( )          --> Return back item
15  // int IsEmpty( )            --> If empty return 1 else return 0
16  // int IsFull( )             --> Return 0; queue is never full
17  // void MakeEmpty( )         --> Remove all items
18  // ****************ERRORS******************************
19  // Predefined exception is propagated if new fails
20  // EXCEPTION is called for Get or Remove on empty deque
21
22  template <class Etype>
23  class Deque : public Queue<Type>
24  {
25    public:
26      void AddFront( const Etype & X );
27      void AddBack( const Etype & X ) { Enqueue( X ); }
28      void RemoveFront( ) { Dequeue( ); }
29      void RemoveBack( );
30      const Etype & GetBack( ) const;
31      // GetFront is inherited
32    private:
33      // Disable queue functions Enqueue and Dequeue
34      void Enqueue( const Etype & X );
35      void Dequeue( );
36  };
```

Figure 15.25   Double-ended queue class Deque derived from Queue

Summary

This chapter has described the implementation of the stack and queue classes. Both the stack and queue can be implemented by using a contiguous array or a linked list. In each case all operations use constant time. When instantiated with large objects, the array implementation uses more memory but less time than the linked-list version, yielding a classic time vs. space trade-off. For small objects, the array implementation is preferable because it is faster and uses similar amounts of space.

Objects of the Game

circular array implementation Using wraparound to implement a queue. (467)

double-ended queue (deque) Allows access at both ends. Much of its functionality can be derived from the queue class. (480)

wraparound Returns to the beginning of the array when the end is reached. (467)

Common Errors

1. The circular array implementation of the queue is easily done wrong when attempts to shorten the code are used. For instance, do not attempt to avoid using the `Size` member by using `Front` and `Back` to infer the size. Do not use `operator%` to implement the wraparound.

2. In the stack implementation we must save a pointer to the front node prior to adjusting the top of the stack; otherwise, the `delete` does not work. A common error is to `delete` the top node directly and then adjust the top the stack. This generally works because the deleted node's contents are not overwritten (so the `Next` member still points at the new top of stack), but it is unsafe programming.

3. For all of these routines, memory leaks are common programming errors.

4. Using an implementation that does not provide constant time access is a bad error. There is no reason for the inefficiency.

5. Shallow copies can result in errors. Because the abstract base class has disabled the copy constructor, we can leave it disabled by doing nothing. However, we must rewrite `operator=` to perform a deep copy. We can also write a visible copy constructor, but then call by value will be allowed, and the inexperienced class user who forgets to pass using constant references will have a very inefficient program.

6. Old versions of $g++$ have a bug associated with private constant member functions. This might affect `Increment` in Figures 15.9 and 15.10.

7. Not all compilers support nested template classes. You may need to rewrite the linked-list-based `Stack` and `Queue` classes without nested classes to avoid this limitation.

On the Internet

The files listed below are available. Note that no `main` is provided to test them; the test is their use in the applications in Part III.

Stack.h	Contains a `#include` of `StackAr.h`; feel free to use the linked list version instead
Queue.h	Contains a `#include` of `QueueAr.h`; feel free to use the linked list version instead
StackAr.h	Contains the interface for an array-based stack
StackAr.cpp	Contains the implementation of an array-based stack
StackLi.h	Contains the interface for a linked-list-based stack
StackLi.cpp	Contains the implementation of a linked-list-based stack
QueueAr.h	Contains the interface for an array-based queue
QueueAr.cpp	Contains the implementation of an array-based queue
QueueLi.h	Contains the interface for a linked-list-based queue
QueueLi.cpp	Contains the implementation of a linked-list-based queue

Exercises

In Short

15.1. In each of the four implementations, what happens if the alias test in `operator=` is omitted?

15.2. Draw the stack and queue data structures (for both the array and linked list implementations) for each step in the following sequence: *Add*(1), *Add*(2), *Remove*, *Add*(3), *Add*(4), *Remove*, *Remove*, *Add*(5). Assume an initial size of three for the array implementation.

In Practice

15.3. Compare the running times for the array and linked list versions of `Stack`. Use `int` objects.

15.4. Write a `main` that declares and uses a stack of `int` and a stack of `double` simultaneously.

15.5. Complete the implementation of the `Deque` class.

15.6. Rewrite the stack class of your choice to throw an exception when a `Pop` or `Top` is attempted on an empty stack.

15.7.   Rewrite the queue class of your choice to throw an exception when a `Front` or `Dequeue` is attempted on an empty queue.

15.8.   Implement `operator=` for the array-based queue to copy the elements in `Rhs` to the same array positions. Do not do more copies than are necessary.

15.9.   Implement the array-based stack class using a `Vector` class. What are the advantages and disadvantages of this approach?

15.10.   Using a `Vector` to implement an array-based queue class is problematic because the `Resize` command is not quite what is needed. Show how to rearrange the queue elements after the `Resize` operation so that at most half of the elements move. (Even so, this uses more moves than the non-`Vector` implementation.)

Programming Projects

15.11.   Implement the linked-list-based `Queue` class by privately inheriting from the linked-list-based `Stack` class. Make appropriate choices of members to be made protected.

15.12.   An output-restricted double-ended queue supports insertions from both ends but accesses and deletions only from the front.
     a. Use inheritance to derive this new class from the `Queue`.
     b. Use inheritance to derive this new class from the `Deque`.

15.13.   Suppose we would like to add the `FindMin` (but not `DeleteMin`) operation to the stack repertoire.
     a. Use inheritance to derive the new class, and implement `FindMin` as a sequential scan of the stack items.
     b. Do not use inheritance but instead implement the new class as two stacks, as described in Exercise 6.5.

15.14.   Suppose we would like to add the `FindMin` (but not `DeleteMin`) operation to the deque repertoire.
     a. Use inheritance to derive the new class, and implement `FindMin` as a sequential scan of the deque items. As in Exercise 15.11, make appropriate choices of members to be made protected
     b. Do not use inheritance but instead implement the new class as four stacks. If a deletion empties a stack, you will need to reorganize the remaining items evenly.

Chapter 16

Linked Lists

In Chapter 15 we saw that linked lists can be used to store items noncontiguously. For stacks and queues the advantage of linked lists is primarily that they use only an extra pointer per item, which is low overhead for large items. The linked lists used in Chapter 15 were simplified by the fact that all accesses were performed at one of the list's two ends.

In this chapter we will see

- how we allow access to any item using a general linked list
- the general algorithms used for the linked list operations
- how the *iterator class* provides a safe mechanism for traversing and accessing linked lists
- list variations, such as *doubly linked lists* and *circular linked lists*
- how we can use inheritance to derive a *sorted linked list* class

16.1 Basic Ideas

In this chapter we implement the linked list and allow general access (arbitrary insertion, deletion, and find operations) through the list. The basic linked list consists of a collection of dynamically allocated nodes connected together. In a *singly linked list*, each node consists of the data element and a pointer to the next node in the list. The last node in the list has a NULL next pointer. We will assume that the node is given by the following type declaration:

```
struct ListNode
{
    Etype Element;
    ListNode *Next;
};
```

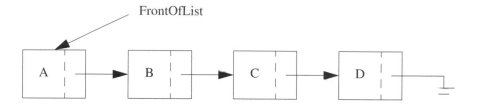

Figure 16.1   Basic linked list

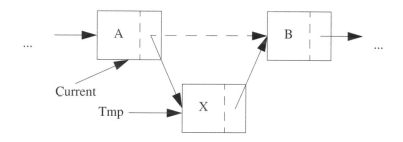

Figure 16.2   Insertion into a linked list: create new node (Tmp), copy in X,
set Tmp's next pointer, set Current's next pointer

The first node in the linked list is accessible by a pointer. This is shown in
Figure 16.1. We can print or search in the linked list by starting at the first item
and following the chain of Next pointers. The two basic operations that we must
be able to perform are insertion and deletion of an arbitrary item X.

**Insertion consists of
splicing a node into the
list and can be accom-
plished with one state-
ment.**

For insertion we must define where the insertion is to take place. If we have
a pointer to some item in the list, the easiest place to insert is immediately after
that item. As an example, Figure 16.2 shows how we insert X after item A in a
linked list. We must perform the following steps:

```
Tmp = new ListNode;        // Get a new Node from the system
Tmp->Element = X;          // Place X in the Element member
Tmp->Next = Current->Next;// X's Next node is B
Current->Next = Tmp;       // A's Next node is X
```

As a result of these statements, the old list … A, B, … now appears as … A, X,
B, … . We can simplify the code if the ListNode has a constructor that initializes the data members directly. In that case, we obtain

```
Tmp = new ListNode( X, Current->Next  ); // Get new node
Current->Next = Tmp;            // A's Next node is X
```

At this point it becomes obvious that `Tmp` is no longer necessary. Thus we have the following one-liner:

```
Current->Next = new ListNode( X, Current->Next );
```

The remove command can be executed in one pointer move. Figure 16.3 shows that to remove item X from the linked list, we set `Current` to be the node prior to X and then have `Current`'s `Next` pointer bypass X. This is expressed by the statement

Removal can be accomplished by bypassing the node. We need a pointer to node prior to the one we want to remove.

```
Current->Next = Current->Next->Next;
```

The list … A, X, B, … now appears as … A, B, … .

A problem with this implementation is that it leaks memory: The node storing X is still allocated but is now unreferenced. By saving a pointer to it first and then calling `delete` after the bypass, we can reclaim the memory:

To avoid leaking, we save a pointer to the node before bypassing it; then we call `delete`.

```
ListNode *DeletedNode = Current->Next;  // Save pointer
Current->Next = Current->Next->Next;    // Bypass the node
delete DeletedNode;                     // Free the memory
```

This summarizes the basics of inserting and removing at arbitrary places in a linked list. The fundamental property of linked lists is that changes to it can be made using only a constant number of data movements. This is a great improvement over an array implementation, because maintaining contiguousness in an array means that whenever an item is added or deleted, all items that follow it in the list must move.

Linked list operations use only a constant number of data movements.

16.1.1 Header Nodes

One problem with the basic description is that it assumes that whenever an item X is removed, there is always some previous item to allow a bypass. Consequently, removal of the first item in the linked list becomes a special case. Similarly, the insert routine does not allow us to insert an item to be the new first element in the list because insertions are restricted to being after some already existing item. What we see is that although the basic algorithm works fine, there are some annoying special cases that need to be dealt with.

Header nodes **allow us to avoid special cases such as insertion of a new first element and removal of the first element.**

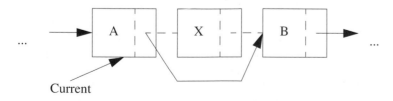

Current

Figure 16.3   Deletion from a linked list

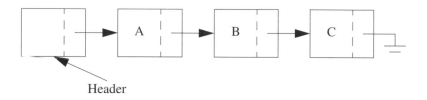

Figure 16.4   Using a header node for the linked list

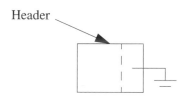

Figure 16.5   Empty list when header node is used

Special cases are always problematic in algorithm design and frequently lead to bugs in the code. Consequently, it is generally preferable to write code that avoids special cases. One way to do that here is to introduce the *header node*.

The header node holds no data but serves to satisfy the requirement that every node have a previous node.

A header node is an extra node in the linked list that holds no data but serves to satisfy the requirement that every node that contains an item have a previous node in the list. The header node for the list A, B, C, D is shown in Figure 16.4. Notice how A is no longer a special case. It can be deleted just like any other node by having `Current` point at the node before it. We can also add a new first element to the list by setting `Current` equal to the header node and calling the insertion routine. By using the header node, we greatly simplify the code. In more complex applications, dummy nodes not only simplify the code but also improve speed because, after all, fewer tests means less time.

The use of a header node is somewhat controversial. Some people argue that avoiding special cases is not sufficient justification for adding fictitious cells; they view the use of header nodes as little more than old-style hacking. Even so, we will use them here precisely because they allow us to show the basic pointer manipulations without obscuring the code with special cases. Whether or not a header should be used is a matter of personal preference. Furthermore, in a class implementation, its use would be completely transparent to the user. We must be careful, however; the printing routine must skip over the header node, as must all searching routines. Moving to the front now means setting the current position to `Header->Next`, and so on. Furthermore, as Figure 16.5 shows, with a dummy header node, a list is empty if `Header->Next` is NULL.

```
1  template <class Etype>
2  int
3  ListSize( const List<Etype> & L )
4  {
5      int Size = 0;
6      for( ListItr<Etype> Itr = L; +Itr; ++Itr )
7          Size++;
8      return Size;
9  }
```

Figure 16.6   Nonmember function that returns the size of a list

16.1.2   Iterator Classes

The typical C strategy identifies a linked list by a pointer to the header node. Each individual item in the list can then be accessed by providing a pointer to the node that stores it. The problem with that strategy is that it is difficult to check for errors. A user could pass a pointer to something that is not a node or to something that is a node but is in a different list. One way to guarantee that this cannot happen is to store a current position as part of the List class. To do this, we add a second data member, Current. Then, since all access to the list goes through the class member functions, we can be certain that Current always represents a pointer to a node in the list, or a pointer to the header node, or NULL.

> By storing a current pointer in the list class, we ensure that access is controlled.

This scheme has a problem: Since there is only one position, the case where two pointers need to access the list independently is left unsupported. A way to avoid this problem is to define a separate *iterator class*. The List class would then not maintain any notion of a current position and would only have member functions that treat the list as a unit, such as IsEmpty, MakeEmpty, and operator=. Routines that depend on knowing where we are in the list would reside in the iterator class. The iterator class maintains a notion of its current position and also the header node for the list it represents (the pointer to the header node can be initialized by the constructor). Access to the list is granted by making the iterator class a friend of the list class.

> The *Iterator class* maintains a current position and performs all routines that depend on knowing the position in the list. The iterator class is a friend of the List class.

One can view each instance of an iterator class as one in which only legal list operations, such as advancing or assignment of a node pointer in its list, are allowed. To see how this works, let us look at a nonmember function that returns the size of a linked list, shown in Figure 16.6.

Itr is declared as an iterator that can access the linked list L. This requires a constructor for ListItr that takes a List as a parameter. Itr is initialized to the first element in L (skipping over the header, of course).

The test +Itr attempts to mimic the test P!=NULL that would be done if P was a normal pointer. That test could be written as P. Since Itr is an iterator object and not an int, we cannot write Itr; we need to define an operator that returns true when the iterator is not logically NULL. The unary + operator seems like the natural choice. Exercise 16.13 suggests an alternative operator. Finally, the expression ++Itr mimics the conventional idiom P=P->Next.

Thus, as long as the iterator class defines a few simple operators, we can iterate over the list in a very natural way. In the next section we see how this is implemented in C++. The routines are surprisingly simple, though the templated syntax can be tedious in places.

16.2   C++ Implementation

We begin the linked list implementation by showing the class interface for the linked list. We inherit from the abstract base class in Section 6.4. The interface for class List is shown in Figure 16.7.

An *incomplete class declaration* is used to inform the compiler of the existence of a friend class.

Lines 17 and 18 represent an *incomplete class declaration*, which informs the compiler that ListItr is a templated class so that the friend declaration at line 33 makes sense. Except for that detail, the interface is straightforward. The ListNode is declared at line 35 to 43 in much the same way that we saw in the discussion of stacks and queue in Section 15.2. We disallow use of the copy constructor by virtue of inheritance and the fact that it is disallowed in the abstract basc class. At line 45 we declare the only data member of the class, namely a pointer to the header node.

The List class is simple because most of the work is pushed into the iterator class.

The constructor at line 24 allocates the header node. We have omitted an error test to avoid complicating the code. The destructor at line 25 calls MakeEmpty to clear the entire list, and then makes one more call to delete the header node. Four member functions are declared: IsEmpty and IsFull are one-liners, while operator= and MakeEmpty are slightly more complex. The List class is simple because most of the work is pushed into the iterator class.

The implementation of MakeEmpty is shown in Figure 16.8. We step through the list continually advancing Ptr to NextNode. Before the advance, we can delete the node that Ptr used to point at. Once we are done, we make the list empty by setting Header's Next pointer to NULL.

Generally, we would also declare an output friend, but as we have seen, we can traverse the list and print everything in it without special privilege if we use the ListItr class. Thus we need not make the output function a friend. Likewise, operator= uses the ListItr class. We defer its implementation until after we discuss the ListItr interface.

The iterator is irrevocably tied to the linked list for which it was constructed.

Figures 16.9 and 16.10 show the interface for ListItr. This is a very interesting class that requires careful attention to detail. The class data members are Header, which is a pointer to the header node, and Current, which is a pointer to the current node. Header is set on construction and can never change. Thus an iterator is irrevocably tied to a single list.

Initially, Current points at the first node, or the header if the list is empty. The default is acceptable for the destructor.

Lines 6 and 7 declare the single constructor. The parameter is a list, and as a result of the construction, Header is set to the list header and Current is set to the first node in the list (skipping the header, of course). If the list is empty, Current will be pointing at the header node because we would expect that the next operation is an Insert. There is no zero-parameter constructor, so an attempt to declare a `ListItr` object without a list initializer will be flagged as a compile-time error. Notice that the `ListItr` does not allocate any memory, so the destructor at line 8 does not have to do anything.

```
1   // List class interface
2   //
3   // Etype: must have zero-parameter and copy constructor
4   //       operator!= must be provided
5   // CONSTRUCTION: with (a) no initializer;
6   //       copy construction of List objects is DISALLOWED
7   // Deep copy is supported
8   // Access is via ListItr class
9   //
10  // *****************PUBLIC OPERATIONS*********************
11  // int IsEmpty( )        --> Return 1 if empty; else return 0
12  // int IsFull( )         --> Return 1 if full;  else return 0
13  // void MakeEmpty( )     --> Remove all items
14  // *****************ERRORS********************************
15  // Predefined exception is propagated if new fails
16
17  template <class Etype>   // Incomplete class declaration
18  class ListItr;           // So friend is visible
19
20  template <class Etype>
21  class List : public AbsList<Etype>
22  {
23    public:
24      List( )  { Header = new ListNode; }
25      ~List( ) { MakeEmpty( ); delete Header; }
26
27      const List & operator=( const List & Rhs );
28
29      int IsEmpty( ) const { return Header->Next == NULL; }
30      int IsFull( )  const { return 0; }
31      void MakeEmpty( );
32
33      friend class ListItr<Etype>;
34    private:
35      struct ListNode
36      {
37          Etype Element;
38          ListNode *Next;
39
40          ListNode( ) : Next( NULL ) { }
41          ListNode( const Etype & E, ListNode *N = NULL ) :
42                  Element( E ), Next( N ) { }
43      };
44
45      ListNode *Header;      // Pointer to a header node
46  };
```

Figure 16.7   Interface for `List` class

```
1  template <class Etype>
2  void
3  List<Etype>::MakeEmpty( )
4  {
5      ListNode *Ptr;
6      ListNode *NextNode;
7
8      for( Ptr = Header->Next; Ptr != NULL; Ptr = NextNode )
9      {
10         NextNode = Ptr->Next;
11         delete Ptr;
12     }
13     Header->Next = NULL;
14 }
```

Figure 16.8   MakeEmpty for List class

```
1  // ListItr class interface; maintains "current position"
2  //
3  // Etype: same restriction as for List
4  // CONSTRUCTION: with (a) List to which ListItr is
5  //     permanently bound or (b) another ListItr
6  // Copying of ListItr objects not supported in current form
7  //
8  // ******************PUBLIC OPERATIONS*******************
9  // void Insert( Etype X )--> Insert X after current position
10 // int Remove( Etype X ) --> Remove X
11 // int Find( Etype X )   --> Set current position to view X
12 // int IsFound( Etype X )--> If X found return 1 else 0
13 // void Zeroth( )  --> Set current position to prior to first
14 // void First( )         --> Set current position to first
15 // void operator++       --> Advance (prefix and postfix)
16 // int operator+( )      --> True if at valid position
17 // Etype operator( )     --> Return item in current position
18 // ******************ERRORS******************************
19 // Predefined exception is propagated if new fails
20 // EXCEPTION is called for illegal access, advance,
21 //     insertion, or First on empty list
```

Figure 16.9   Comment section for ListItr interface

The ListItr class illustrates that the default behavior is not immediately obvious.

Before continuing, let us examine what is happening with ListItr's copy constructor and copy assignment operator. Notice that neither is provided, and neither is disabled in the abstract base class, so it appears that the usual member-by-member defaults apply. Although this is true for the copy constructor, it is not true for operator=, because ListItr contains a constant data member (thus the member-by-member application of operator= fails on the constant data member). Upon reflection, we see that this is correct behavior. Otherwise, a ListItr object that is the target of an assignment could be bound to a different list than it was constructed for. Therefore operator= is in effect disallowed.

Notice how the `const` directive has allowed the compiler to catch what could have been an inconsistent usage. However, a reasonable `operator=` could still be written: we check that the assignment does not attempt to bind the `ListItr` to a different list (by checking the `Header` members of the right and left side), and if so, we can just assign the `Current` member (see Exercise 16.6).

What remains are the member functions. We need to be very careful to document what each function does. For instance, `Insert` adds item `X` into the list immediately following the current position. What if `Current` is NULL? Of course, that is an error. What if we cannot allocate memory for the insertion? Of course, that is an error too. What is the new value of `Current`? In our case, if the insertion is successful, `Current` is set to point at the newly inserted node; otherwise, `Current` is unchanged. For each member function, we document, in the interface, precisely what it does, what errors are possible, and what happens to `Current` (if it is not a constant member function).

Let us discuss the remaining members. `Find` searches for `X`; if `X` is in the list, `Current` is moved to point at the node containing it, and `Find` returns true. Otherwise, `Find` returns false and `Current` is unchanged. `IsFound` searches for `X`, returning true if it is found and false otherwise. It does not alter `Current`. Consequently, it is a constant member function.

`Remove` searches for `X`; if `X` is in the list, it is removed, `Current` is set to point at the header, and `Remove` returns true. Otherwise `Remove` returns false, and `Current` is unchanged. The movement of `Current` is required since we do not want `Current` to point at a node that has already been deleted. Of course, if we prefer, we could always change things so that `Current` is reset only if it had been pointing at the node containing `X` (prior to the call to `Remove`), and is left as is otherwise. This is not bulletproof: There may be two iterators, and one can be left dangling if the other removes a node. A sometimes important routine that is used in Section 13.1, is `RemoveNext`. Its implementation is left as Exercise 16.11.

> This is not bulletproof: there may be two iterators and one can be left dangling if the other removes a node.

Unary `operator+` is used to test if the current position is not NULL. We choose `operator+` because it is the unary operator that seems to make the most sense. It returns true for a "positive result." It does not alter `Current`. `operator()` returns the item in the current position (or an error if the current position is not a node in the list). It does not alter `Current`. `Zeroth` sets `Current` to the header node. It allows insertions at the front of the list. `First` sets `Current` to the first node in the list. If the list is empty, it generates an error. Finally, `operator++` is the pointer advancing operator. We provide both a prefix and postfix form. It sets `Current` to `Current->Next`, assuming of course that `Current` is not NULL. Typically `operator++` returns the old or new value of the object it operates on, depending on whether it is postfix or prefix. However, in this case we have a `void` return type to signify that we do not want to involve this operator in larger expressions. This was required for the technical reason dealing with inheritance and was discussed at the end of Section 4.3.6.

> + means we have not passed the end of the list. ++ is used to advance. The return type is `void` for technical reasons that deal with inheritance.

```
 1  template <class Etype>
 2  class ListItr : public AbsListItr<Etype>
 3  {
 4    public:
 5          // Constructor and Destructor
 6      ListItr( const List<Etype> & L ) : Header( L.Header )
 7          { Current = L.IsEmpty( ) ? Header : Header->Next; }
 8      ~ListItr( ) { }
 9
10      // Insert X after Current position
11      // Errors: Current position is NULL or memory is exhausted
12      // Current: Set to new node on success
13      void Insert( const Etype & X );
14
15      // Set Current position to first node containing X
16      // Returns: 1 if Find is successful, 0 for failure
17      // Current: is unchanged if X is not found
18      int Find( const Etype & X );
19
20      // Returns 1 if X is in the list, 0 otherwise
21      int IsFound( const Etype & X ) const;
22
23      // Remove first occurrence of X; do nothing if not found
24      // Returns: 1 if remove succeeded, 0 otherwise.
25      // Current: is moved to the header if X is deleted
26      int Remove( const Etype & X );
27
28      // Returns 1 if Current is not NULL or Header, 0 otherwise
29      int operator+( ) const
30          { return Current && Current != Header; }
31
32      // Returns the Element in Current node
33      // Errors: Current is not pointing at a node in the list
34      const Etype & operator( ) ( ) const;
35
36      // Set Current to the header node
37      void Zeroth( )     { Current = Header; }
38
39      // Set Current to first node in the list
40      // Errors: List is empty
41      void First( );
42
43      // Set Current to Current->Next; no return value
44      // Errors: Current is NULL on entry
45      void operator++( );
46      void operator++( int ) { operator++( ); }
47    private:
48      List<Etype>::ListNode * const Header;  // List Header
49      List<Etype>::ListNode *Current;        // Current position
50      friend class SortListItr<Etype>;
51  };
```

Figure 16.10   Interface for ListItr class

```
1  template <class Etype>
2  const List<Etype> &
3  List<Etype>::operator=( const List<Etype> & Rhs )
4  {
5      if( this == &Rhs )
6          return *this;
7
8      MakeEmpty( );
9
10     ListItr<Etype> Itr( *this );
11     for( ListItr<Etype> Ritr( Rhs ); +Ritr; Ritr++ )
12         Ptr.Insert( Ritr( ) );
13
14     return *this;
15 }
```

Figure 16.11 Copy assignment operator for the List class, using ListItr to iterate.

```
1  template <class Etype>
2  ostream &
3  operator<<( ostream & Out, const List<Etype> & L )
4  {
5      if( L.IsEmpty( ) )
6          Out << "Empty list";
7      else
8          for( ListItr<Etype> Itr( L ); +Itr; ++Itr )
9              Out << Itr( ) << ' ';
10
11     return Out << '\n';
12 }
```

Figure 16.12 Output nonmember function for List

```
1  template <class Etype>
2  void
3  ListItr<Etype>::Insert( const Etype & X )
4  {
5      EXCEPTION( Current == NULL, "Illegal insertion" );
6      List<Etype>::ListNode *NewNode;
7
8      NewNode = new List<Etype>::ListNode( X, Current->Next );
9      Current = Current->Next = NewNode;
10 }
```

Figure 16.13 Insert routine for ListItr class

```
1   template <class Etype>
2   int
3   ListItr<Etype>::Find( const Etype & X )
4   {
5       List<Etype>::ListNode *Ptr = Header->Next;
6
7       while( Ptr != NULL && Ptr->Element != X )
8           Ptr = Ptr->Next;
9
10      if( Ptr == NULL )
11          return 0;
12
13      Current = Ptr;
14      return 1;
15  }
16
17  template <class Etype>
18  int
19  ListItr<Etype>::IsFound( const Etype & X ) const
20  {
21      List<Etype>::ListNode *Ptr = Header->Next;
22
23      while( Ptr != NULL && Ptr->Element != X )
24          Ptr = Ptr->Next;
25
26      return Ptr != NULL;
27  }
```

Figure 16.14   Find and IsFound routines for ListItr

```
1   template <class Etype>
2   int
3   ListItr<Etype>::Remove( const Etype & X )
4   {
5       List<Etype>::ListNode *Ptr = Header;
6
7       while( Ptr->Next != NULL && Ptr->Next->Element != X )
8           Ptr = Ptr->Next;
9
10      if( Ptr->Next == NULL )
11          return 0;           // Remove fails
12
13          // Bypass and reclaim memory
14      List<Etype>::ListNode *DeletedNode = Ptr->Next;
15      Ptr->Next = Ptr->Next->Next;
16      delete DeletedNode;
17
18      Current = Header;   // Reset Current
19      return 1;
20  }
```

Figure 16.15   Remove routine for ListItr class

```
1  template <class Etype>
2  const Etype &
3  ListItr<Etype>::operator( ) ( ) const
4  {
5      EXCEPTION( Current == Header || Current == NULL,
6              "Illegal access" );
7
8      return Current->Element;
9  }
10
11 template <class Etype>
12 void
13 ListItr<Etype>::First( )
14 {
15     EXCEPTION( Header->Next == NULL, "Empty list" );
16     Current = Header->Next;
17 }
18
19 template <class Etype>
20 void
21 ListItr<Etype>::operator++( )
22 {
23     EXCEPTION( Current == NULL, "Can't advance past end" );
24     Current = Current->Next;
25 }
```

Figure 16.16   Iteration routines for `ListItr` class

We certainly could have added more operators, but this basic set is quite powerful. Some operators, such as `operator--`, are not efficiently supported by this version of the linked list; variations on the linked list that allow constant-time implementation of that and other operators are discussed later in this chapter. For now, let us see how the `ListItr` class can be used to implement `operator-` and `operator<<` for the `List` class.[1]

> The `--` operator is not efficiently supported. A doubly linked list is used if this is a liability.

Figure 16.11 shows how the copy assignment operator for `List` is implemented. At line 5 we test for aliasing, and return immediately if the test is successful. Otherwise, we call `MakeEmpty` to clear out the current list. We then declare a `ListItr` (`Itr`) for the current list, and a second `ListItr` (`Ritr`) for `List Rhs`. At the start, `Itr` points at the header (because its list is empty), and `Ritr` points at the first node in `Rhs`. We repeatedly call `Insert` to add items from `Rhs` into the current list, by executing the standard iteration code at lines 11 and 12. Since the current position in the current list is always the last inserted node, the new list is constructed as an exact copy of `Rhs`. In virtually identical manner, Figure 16.12 uses the iteration operators to output the contents of linked list `L`.

> The copy assignment operator for a linked list can be implemented by using two iterators.

---

1. Under g++ 2.6, it appears that you need to provide an already instantiated function declaration so that the compiler will find the template match. An example for a list of integers is:
   `ostream & operator<<( ostream & Out, const List<int> & L );`

Many of the routines would be one-liners if it were not for the error checks.

Now that we have seen what the `ListItr` interface looks like and how it is used, we can do the implementation of its member functions. Figure 16.13 shows the body of `Insert`. As we have seen earlier, if we did not have to do error checking, this could be a one-line routine. The error check adds a line and we elected to use a temporary for clarity. Still, this is a small piece of code. The most difficult part is the annoying syntax: `ListNode` must be preceded by the `List` class scope, which in turn must be instantiated with `Etype`.

Short circuiting is used in the `Find` routine at line 7 and in the similar part of the `Remove` routine.

The `Find` routine is shown in Figure 16.14. Here we step down the list until either we get to the `NULL` pointer that is past the end of the list, or we find a match. Note carefully that the order of tests at line 7 matters because we are taking advantage of short circuiting. The `IsFound` routine, also shown in Figure 16.14 uses exactly the same logic.

Similarly, the `Remove` routine shown in Figure 16.15 searches for the item `X`; at the end of the loop, `Ptr` points to either the node prior to the one containing `X` or the last node if `X` is not found. The removal then proceeds using the algorithm described earlier. The remaining routines are shown in Figure 16.16. They are all short routines that would be one line, except for the error tests.

16.3 Doubly Linked Lists and Circular Linked Lists

Doubly linked lists allow bidirectional traversal by storing two pointers per node.

As we mentioned in Section 16.2, the singly linked list does not efficiently support some important operations. For instance, although it is easy to go to the front of the list, it is time consuming to go to the end. Although we can easily advance via `operator++`, implementing `operator--` cannot be done efficiently with only a `Next` pointer. In some applications this might be critical. For instance, when designing a text editor, we maintain the internal image of the file as a linked list of lines. We certainly want to be able to move up just as easily as down, to insert both before and after a line rather than just after, and to be able to get to the last line quickly. A moment's thought suggests that to implement this efficiently, we should have each node maintain two pointers: one to the next node in the list and one to the previous node. Then, to make everything symmetric, we should have not only a dummy header but also a dummy tail. This is the so called *doubly linked list*. Figure 16.17 shows the doubly linked list representing A, B. As we can see, each node now has two pointers (`Next` and `Prev`), and searching and moving can easily be performed in both directions. Obviously, there are some important changes.

Symmetry demands that we use both a `Head` and `Tail` and that we support roughly twice as many operations.

First, an empty list now consists of a `Head` and `Tail` connected together, as shown in Figure 16.18. Notice, by the way, that `Head->Prev` and `Tail->Next` are not needed in the algorithms and are not even initialized. The test for emptiness is now

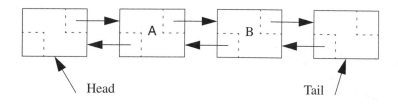

Figure 16.17   Doubly linked list

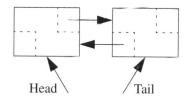

Figure 16.18   Empty doubly linked list

```
Head->Next == Tail
```
or
```
Tail->Prev == Header
```

We no longer use NULL to decide if an advance has taken us past the end of the list. Instead, we have gone past the end if Current is either Head or Tail (recall that we can go in either direction). operator-- can be implemented by
```
Current = Current->Prev;
```

Before describing some of the additional operations that are available, let us see how the insertion and removal operations change. Naturally, we can now do both InsertBefore and InsertAfter. Twice as many pointer moves are involved for InsertAfter with doubly linked lists as compared to the singly linked list. If we write each statement explicitly, we obtain

When we advance past the end of the list, we now hit the **Tail** *node instead of* **NULL**.

Insertion and removal involve twice as many pointer changes, compared to a singly linked list.

```
NewNode = new Node( X );
NewNode->Prev = Current;            // Set X's Prev pointer
NewNode->Next = Current->Next;      // Set X's Next pointer
NewNode->Prev->Next = NewNode;      // Set A's Next pointer
NewNode->Next->Prev = NewNode;      // Set B's Prev pointer
Current = NewNode;
```

As we saw earlier, the first two pointer moves can be collapsed into the new. The pointer changes (in order *a, b, c, d*) are illustrated in Figure 16.19.

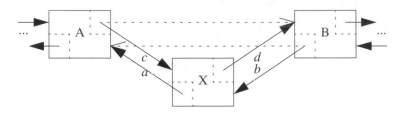

Figure 16.19 Insertion into a doubly linked list by getting new node and then changing pointers in order indicated

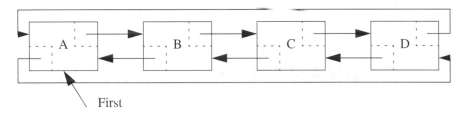

Figure 16.20 Circular doubly linked list

Remove can proceed from the current node because we can obtain the previous node instantly.

Figure 16.19 can also be used to guide us in the removal algorithm. Unlike the singly linked list, we can remove the current node because we will have the previous node available to us automatically. Thus to `Remove X` in Figure 16.19, we have to change `A`'s `Next` pointer and `B`'s `Prev` pointer. The basic moves are

```
OldNode = Current;
OldNode->Prev->Next = OldNode->Next;// Set A's Next pointer
OldNode->Next->Prev = OldNode->Prev;// Set B's Prev pointer
delete OldNode;
Current = Header;
```

To do a complete doubly linked list implementation, we need to decide what operations will be supported. It is reasonable to expect that there will be twice as many operations as in the singly linked list. Each individual procedure will be very similar to the linked list routines; only the dynamic operations involve additional pointer moves. Moreover, for many of the routines, the code is dominated by error checks. While some of the checks will change (for instance, we do not test against `NULL`), they certainly do not become any more complex. We leave the class implementation as a project for Exercise 16.20.

In a *circular linked list*, the last cell's next pointer points to the first. This is useful when wraparound matters.

A popular convention is to create a *circular linked list*, in which the last cell keeps a pointer back to the first. This can be done with or without a header. Typically, it is done without a header, since the header's main purpose is to ensure that every node has a previous node, and this is already true for a nonempty circular linked list. We would maintain a pointer to the first node, but this would not be the same as a dummy node. We can use circular linked lists and doubly linked lists simultaneously, as shown in Figure 16.20. The circular list is useful in cases where we want searching to allow wraparound, as is the case for some text editors. Exercise 16.22 asks you to implement a circular doubly linked list.

16.4   Sorted Linked Lists

Sometimes it is desirable to keep the items in the linked list arranged in sorted order. The fundamental difference between a *sorted linked list* and an unsorted linked list is the insertion routine. Indeed, we can obtain a sorted list class by simply altering the insertion routine from our already written list class. Since the Insert routine is part of the ListItr class, it stands to reason that we should have a new derived class SortListItr, based on ListItr. This is shown in Figure 16.21. The code there is straightforward and uses two ListItr objects to traverse down the corresponding list until the correct insertion point is found. At that point we can apply the ListItr Insert routine. To declare the ListItr objects, we must know which List they refer to. This is done by storing a reference to the List in the SortListItr private section. This reference is initialized when the ListItr is constructed.

We can maintain items in sorted order by deriving a SortListItr class from ListItr.

There are several design issues that can be addressed here; some reflect clear deficiencies and are left as Exercise 16.23. First of all, do we really need to use the ListItr in the new Insert routine? The answer is no if we are willing to go back to the ListItr class and make its data members protected instead of private. However some (including Bjarne Stroustrup) argue that private is a better mechanism than protected, and that when possible it is better to avoid protected. Furthermore, choosing protected requires knowing that another class will want to use the base class members; sometimes this is not obvious when the base class is written, and thus we have to go back and make changes (if the source code is available). Finally, protected allows all derived classes to have access, not just the one you might intend. The benefit, of course, is that sometimes access to members in the base class is absolutely essential for efficiency.

There are a host of design issues that should be considered.

We have had to add a data member TheList to the derived class in order to use the ListItr. This suggests that perhaps the ListItr should have stored the name of the list (in a reference object) that initializes it, instead of the less informative Header node; in this case it would be reasonable to place this reference in the protected section, since it is a constant reference.

A problem with inheritance is that the base class might not be properly set up for inheritance because it is hard to predict what might be derived from it. If a class is not set up for inheritance, we have to go back and make changes.

A deficiency of our scheme is that any list can be accessed by both a ListItr and SortListItr; thus we have no guarantee that the SortListItr is working on a sorted list. We can rectify the situation by adding an extra private data member to the List class that specifies whether the list is sorted or unsorted. This data member would be initialized by the first call to Insert and subsequent calls to Insert would verify that we are not mixing the two types.

```
1  // ListItr class interface; maintains "current position"
2  //
3  // Etype: same restrictions as List plus operator< is needed
4  // CONSTRUCTION: with (a) List to which ListItr is permanently
5  //      bound or (b) another ListItr
6  // Copying of ListItr objects is not supported in current form
7  //
8  // *****************PUBLIC OPERATIONS*********************
9  // void Insert( Etype X )--> Insert X in sorted order
10 // int Remove( Etype X ) --> Remove X
11 // int Find( Etype X )   --> Set current position to view X
12 // int IsFound( Etype X )--> Return 1 if X found else return 0
13 // void Zeroth( )    --> Set current position to prior to first
14 // void First( )        --> Set current position to first
15 // void operator++      --> Advance (both prefix and postfix)
16 // int operator+( )     --> True if at valid position in list
17 // Etype operator( )    --> Return item in current position
18 // *****************ERRORS********************************
19 // Predefined exception is propagated if new fails
20 // EXCEPTION is called for illegal access, advance,
21 //      or First on empty list.
22
23 template <class Etype>
24 class SortListItr : public ListItr<Etype>
25 {
26   public:
27     SortListItr( const List<Etype> & L ) :
28            ListItr<Etype>( L ), TheList( L ) { }
29     ~SortListItr( ) { }
30
31         // Everything is same except Insert
32     void Insert( const Etype & X );  // Insert in sorted order
33   private:
34     const List<Etype> & TheList;
35 };
36
37 template <class Etype>
38 void
39 SortListItr<Etype>::Insert( const Etype & X )
40 {
41     ListItr<Etype> Prev = TheList;
42     ListItr<Etype> Curr = TheList;
43
44     for( Prev.Zeroth( ); +Curr && Curr( ) < X; ++Curr )
45         ++Prev;
46
47     Prev.Insert( X );
48     Current = Prev.Current;
49 }
```

Figure 16.21   A sorted linked list pointer class in which insertions are
restricted to sorted order

Summary

In this chapter we have implemented linked lists using an iterator class. An iterator class can be viewed as a mechanism for achieving safe pointers. Our iterator class ListItr is a friend of our List class. Any operation that depends in any way on positioning in the list is defined in the ListItr class. The List class defines only operations that view the list as an entity (for example, IsEmpty). The ListItr class maintains a notion of a current position that is updated by advancing, searching, inserting, and even removing in the list. We also examined variations of the linked list including doubly linked lists. The doubly linked list allows bidirectional traversal of the list. Finally, we saw how easy it is to derive a sorted linked list class from the basic linked list class.

Objects of the Game

circular linked list Linked list in which the last cell's next pointer points to the first. This is useful when wraparound matters. (500)

doubly linked list Allows bidirectional traversal by storing two pointers per node. (498)

header node An extra node in the linked list that holds no data but serves to satisfy the requirement that every node have a previous node. Header nodes allow us to avoid special cases such as insertion of a new first element and removal of the first element. (487)

incomplete class declaration Used to inform the compiler of the existence of a friend class. (490)

iterator class Maintains a current position and performs all routines that depend on knowing the position in the list. The iterator class is a friend of the List class. (489)

sorted linked list Used to maintain items in a linked list in sorted order. A SortListItr class is derived from ListItr. (501)

Common Errors

1. The most common linked list error is splicing in nodes incorrectly when performing an insertion. This is especially tricky with doubly linked lists.

2. When a header node is used, the list header must be deleted in the destructor.

3. Member functions should not be allowed to dereference a NULL pointer. We use EXCEPTION to test this case.

4. When several iterators access a list simultaneously, problems can result. For instance, what if one iterator deletes the node that the other iterator

is about to access? Solving these types of programs requires additional work.

5. Shallow copies result in an error. Because the abstract base class has disabled the copy constructor, we can leave it disabled by doing nothing. However, we must rewrite `operator=` to perform a deep copy. We can also write a visible copy constructor, but then call by value will be allowed, and the inexperienced class user who forgets to pass using constant references will have a very inefficient program.

6. The `ListItr operator=` is disabled by default because `ListItr` contains a constant data member. Thus, if we try to copy `ListItr` objects, we would get a compile time error. If we want, we can rewrite it to allow copying when the source and target `ListItr` refer to the same list.

7. Forgetting the incomplete class declaration can lead to undefined members being reported at link time.

8. A common error is calling `delete` at the wrong time during `Remove` or `MakeEmpty`.

On the Internet

The linked list class, including the sorted linked list is available.

List.h	Contains the interface for the list and iterator classes
List.cpp	Contains the implementation advertised in `List.h`

Exercises

In Short

16.1. In Figure 16.14, why do we not use the member function `First` at lines 5 and 21?

16.2. Draw an empty linked list when the header implementation is used.

16.3. Draw an empty doubly linked list that uses both a header and a tail.

In Theory

16.4. Give an algorithm to print a singly linked list in reverse, using only constant extra space. This implies that you cannot use recursion. Can this be done if the routine is a constant member function?

16.5. `First` is illegal on empty lists, but `Zeroth` followed by `operator++` is not. Discuss whether or not this is consistent and what the ramifications are of allowing identical behavior for both these cases.

In Practice

16.6.   Implement `operator=` for the `ListItr` class.

16.7.   Add the routine `RemoveNext` to the `ListItr` class. `RemoveNext` removes the item after the current position. How are errors handled?

16.8.   Look ahead in a `ListItr` object requires application of `operator++`, which in turn advances in the list. In some cases it may be preferable to look at the next item in the list, without advancing to it. Write the member function with the declaration below to facilitate this in a general case. The binary `operator+` returns a `ListItr` that corresponds to K positions ahead of `Current`.

```
const ListItr & operator+( unsigned int K ) const;
```

16.9.   Explain what will happen to the member added in Exercise 16.8 when the `SortListItr` class is derived from `ListItr`.

16.10.   Modify `Remove` in the `ListItr` class so that all occurrences of X are removed.

16.11.   Add the routine `RemoveNext` to the `ListItr` class. `RemoveNext` removes the item after the current position. How are errors handled?

16.12.   Modify `MakeEmpty` to use `RemoveNext`. `MakeEmpty` should be greatly simplified.

16.13.   An alternative to `operator+` (that tests if the current position is within the list) is to write a type conversion operator as shown below. Discuss the benefits and liabilities of this approach and provide an implementation.

```
operator int( ) const;
```

16.14.   Derive a `Stack` class from the `List` class.

16.15.   Derive a `Queue` class from a doubly linked `List` class. Why doesn't derivation from a singly linked list class work?

16.16.   For the `ListItr` class, replace the calls to `EXCEPTION` with code that throws an exception.

16.17.   Implement `operator--` for singly linked lists. Notice that it will take linear time.

16.18.   Sometimes we would like to update an entry that is already in the linked list. One way to do this is to have `operator()` return a non-constant reference.

a. Discuss the advantages and problems of allowing this.

b. Implement a constant reference return `operator()` and a non-constant reference return `operator()` simultaneously. *Hint*: Make one a constant member function and the other a nonconstant member.

16.19.   Implement the linked list without the header node.

Command	Function
`1`	Go to the top
`a`	Add text after current line until . on its own line is seen
`d`	Delete current line
`dr num num`	Delete several lines
`f name`	Change name of the current file (for next write)
`g num`	Go to a numbered line
`h`	Get help
`i`	Like append, but add lines before current line
`m num`	Move current line after some other line
`mr num num num`	Move several lines as a unit after some other line
`n`	Toggle whether line numbers are displayed
`p`	Print current line
`pr num num`	Print several lines
`q!`	Abort without write
`r name`	Read and paste another file into the current file
`s text text`	Substitute text with other text
`t num`	Copy current line to after some other line
`tr num num num`	Copy several lines to after some other line
`w`	Write file to disk
`x!`	Exit with write
`$`	Go to the last line
`-`	Go up one line
`+`	Go down one line
`=`	Print current line number
`/ text`	Search forward for a pattern
`? text`	Search backward for a pattern
`#`	Print number of lines and characters in file

Figure 16.22   Commands for editor in Exercise 16.21

Programming Projects

16.20. Implement a doubly linked list class. Include

    a. `MoveToHead` and `MoveToTail` functions

    b. `First` and `Last` functions

    c. `operator--` in both prefix and postfix forms

    d. `InsertBefore` and `InsertAfter` functions

    e. `FindFirst` and `FindLast` functions (the search begins from the front and end, respectively)

    f. `RemoveFirst` and `RemoveLast` functions

16.21. Write a line editor. The command syntax is similar to the UNIX line editor *ed*. The internal copy of the file is maintained as a linked list of lines. To be able to go up and down in the file, you will maintain a doubly linked list. Most commands are represented by a one-character string. Some are two characters and require an argument (or two). A structure contains this information; it should be easy to parse the input if you use the array of structures. Support the commands lines in Figure 16.22.

16.22. Implement a circular doubly linked list.

16.23. Redesign `List`, `ListItr`, and `SortListItr` to

    a. Keep a reference to the `List L`

    b. Not allow interleaving of `SortListItr` and `ListItr Insert` commands

16.24. If the order that items in a list are stored is not important, then we can frequently speed searching with the following heuristic known as *move to front*: Whenever an item is accessed, move it to the front of the list. The reason this usually is an improvement is that frequently accessed items will tend to migrate toward the front of the list, while less frequently accessed items will migrate toward the end of the list. Consequently the most frequently accessed items tend to require the least searching. Implement the move-to-front heuristic for linked lists.

16.25. The primary disadvantage of linked lists is the overhead of memory management calls. We can mitigate this problem by maintaining memory ourselves. Implement a templated `MyMem` class. `MyMem` should maintain an array of nodes for use by the linked list routines. The `List` and `ListItr` classes would then call `MyMem<Etype>.NEW` and `MyMem<Etype>.DELETE` to gain access to these nodes. Initially, all positions except position 0 are available for allocation by `NEW`. The `MyMem` class maintains a list of available positions by chaining these nodes in a linked list, with position 0 as a header. This is called the freelist. Thus initially, position 0's `Next` node would be 1, 1's `Next` would be 2, etc., until we see the last position's `Next` is 0 (logically `NULL`). To satisfy a `NEW` request, we merely return the index of the first element in the freelist, and then remove that element from the freelist. Thus the first `NEW` would return 1, and the freelist would be 2, 3, 4, … (with 0 as the eternal header). A second `NEW` would return 2, and the freelist would be 3, 4, … . When space is exhausted, `MyMem` would implement a doubling of the array to get additional nodes. To implement `DELETE`, we merely place the node at the front of the freelist. Thus `DELETE(1)` makes the freelist 1, 3, 4, … . Notice that the freelist is logically a stack. Implement the class `MyMem` whose interface is shown in Figure 16.23.

16.26.   Write routines `Union` and `Intersect` that return the union and intersection of two linked lists. Assume that the input lists are sorted.

```
1 template <class Etype>
2 class MyMem
3 {
4   public:
5         // Constructor: called once per program
6     MyMem( int MaxSize = 100 );
7
8         // Destructor
9     ~MyMem( ) { delete [ ] MyMemSpace; }
10
11    // NEW returns index in MyMemSpace of an available node
12    // Node is the first on the freelist, skipping position 0
13    // If none exists, double the array
14    // If double fails, return 0
15    int NEW( const Etype & E, int N = 0 );
16    int NEW( );
17
18    // Add MyMemSpace[P] to the freelist
19    void DELETE( int P );
20  private:
21        // The basic object that is being allocated
22    struct MyMemNode
23    {
24        Etype Element;
25        int Next;
26    };
27
28    MyMemNode *MyMemSpace;   // The array of MyMemNode objects
29    int SpaceSize;           // The size of the array
30 };
```

Figure 16.23   `MyMem` class for Exercise 16.25

Chapter 17

Trees

The *tree* is a fundamental structure in computer science. Almost all operating systems store files in trees or treelike structures. In addition to this application, trees are also used in compiler design, text processing, and searching algorithms. The latter application is discussed in the next chapter.

In this chapter we will see

- a definition of a general tree and a discussion of how it is used in a file system
- an examination of the *binary tree*
- how tree operations are implemented using recursion
- how a tree is traversed nonrecursively

17.1   General Trees

We can define trees in two ways: nonrecursively and recursively. The nonrecursive definition is the more direct technique, so we begin with it. The recursive formulation allows us to write simple algorithms to manipulate trees.

Trees can be defined nonrecursively as a set of nodes and directed edges that connect them.

17.1.1   Definitions

Recall from Chapter 6 that a *tree* consists of a set of nodes and a set of directed edges that connect pairs of nodes. Throughout this book, we consider only rooted trees. A rooted tree has the following properties:

- One node is distinguished as the root.
- Every node c, except the root, is connected by an edge from exactly one other node p. p is c's *parent*, and c is one of p's *children*.
- There is a unique path from the root to each node. The number of edges that we must follow is the path length.

Parents and children are naturally defined. A directed edge connects the *parent* to the *child*.

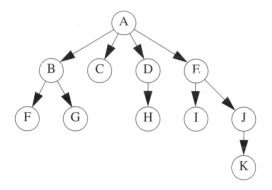

Figure 17.1   A tree

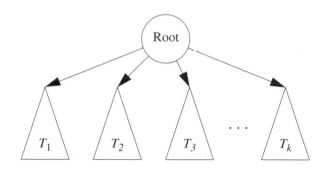

Figure 17.2   Tree viewed recursively

Leaves have no children.

Figure 17.1 illustrates a tree. The root node is *A*. *A*'s children are *B*, *C*, *D*, and *E*. Because *A* is the root, it has no parent. All other nodes have parents. For instance, *B*'s parent is *A*. Some nodes have no children. These nodes are called *leaves*. The leaves in this tree are *C*, *F*, *G*, *H*, *I*, and *K*. The length of the path from *A* to *K* is three (edges). The length of the path from *A* to *A* is zero edges.

The *depth* of a node is the length of the path from the root to it. The *height* of a node is the length of the path from the node to the deepest leaf.

A tree with *N* nodes must have *N* − 1 edges because every node except the parent has an incoming edge. The *depth* of any node in a tree is the length of the path from the root to it. Thus the depth of the root is always 0, and the depth of any node is 1 more than the depth of its parent. The *height* of a node is the length of the path from the node to the deepest leaf. Thus the height of *E* is 2. The height of any node is 1 more than the height of its maximum-height child. The height of a tree is equal to the height of the root.

Nodes with the same parent are *siblings*; thus B, C, D, and E are all siblings. If there is a path from node *u* to node *v*, then *u* is an *ancestor* of *v*, and *v* is a *descendant* of *u*. If $u \neq v$, then *u* is a *proper ancestor* of *v* and *v* is a *proper descendant* of *u*. The *size* of a node is equal to the number of descendants it has (including the node itself). The size of B is 3, and the size of C is 1. The size of a tree is equal to the size of the root.

> The *size* of a node is equal to the number of descendants it has (including the node itself).

An alternate definition of the tree is recursive: A tree either is empty or it consists of a root and zero or more nonempty subtrees $T_1, T_2, ..., T_k$, each of whose roots are connected by an edge from the root. In some instances (most notably the *binary trees* discussed later), we may allow some of the subtrees to be empty. This view of the tree is illustrated in Figure 17.2.

17.1.2   Implementation

One way to implement a tree would be to have in each node, in addition to its data, a pointer to each child of the node. However, since the number of children per node can vary so greatly and is not known in advance, it might be infeasible to make the children direct links in the data structure, because there would be too much wasted space. The solution is simple: Keep the children of each node in a linked list of tree nodes. Thus each node keeps two pointers: one to its leftmost child (if it is not a leaf), and a second pointer to its right sibling (if it is not the rightmost sibling). This type of implementation is called the *first child/next sibling method* and is illustrated in Figure 17.3. Arrows that point downward are FirstChild pointers. Arrows that go left to right are NextSibling pointers. NULL pointers are not drawn because there are too many. In this tree, node B has both a pointer to a sibling (C) and a pointer to a leftmost child (F), while some nodes have only one of these pointers, and some have neither. Given this representation, it is a straightforward exercise to implement a tree class that is hinted at by the interface in Figure 6.15.

> General trees can be implemented using the *first child/next sibling method*. This requires two pointers per item.

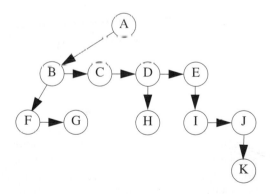

Figure 17.3   First child/next sibling representation of tree in Figure 17.1

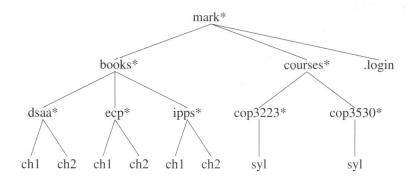

Figure 17.4   UNIX directory

17.1.3   An Application: The UNIX File System

File systems use tree-like structures.

There are many applications for trees. One of the popular uses is the directory structure in many common operating systems, including UNIX, VAX/VMS, and DOS. Figure 17.4 is a typical directory in the UNIX file system. The root of this directory is `mark`. (The asterisk next to the name indicates that `mark` is itself a directory). `mark` has three children, `books`, `courses`, and `.login`, two of which are themselves directories. Thus `mark` contains two directories and one regular file. The filename `mark/books/dsaa/ch1` is obtained by following the leftmost child three times. Each `/` after the first indicates an edge; the result is a pathname. If the path begins at the root of the entire file system, rather than at an arbitrary directory inside the file system, then we have a full pathname; otherwise, we have a relative pathname (to the current directory). This hierarchical file system is very popular because it allows users to organize their data logically. Furthermore, two files in different directories can share the same name, because they must have different paths from the root and thus have different full pathnames. A directory in the UNIX file system is just a file with a list of all its children,[1] so the directories can be traversed using an iteration scheme implied by the abstract class in Figure 6.15; that is, we can sequentially iterate over each child. Indeed, on some systems, if the normal command to print a file is applied to a directory, then the names of the files in the directory can be seen in the output (along with other non-ASCII information).

The directory structure is most easily traversed by using recursion.

Suppose we would like to list the names of all the files in a directory (including its subdirectories). Our output format will be that files of depth d will have their names indented by d tab characters. A simple algorithm to do this is given in Figure 17.5. Output for the directory in Figure 17.4 is shown in Figure 17.6.

---

1. Each directory in the UNIX file system also has one entry (.) that points to itself, and another entry (. .) that points to the parent of the directory. This introduces a cycle. Thus, technically, the UNIX file system is not a tree but is treelike.

```
1 void
2 FileSystem::ListAll( int Depth = 0 )
3 {
4     PrintName( Depth );      // Print the name of the object
5     if( IsDirectory( ) )
6         for each file C in this directory (for each child)
7             C.ListAll( Depth + 1 );
8 }
```

Figure 17.5   Routine to list a directory and its subdirectories in a hierarchical file system

```
mark
        books
                dsaa
                        ch1
                        ch2
                ecp
                        ch1
                        ch2
                ipps
                        ch1
                        ch2
        courses
                cop3223
                        syl
                cop3530
                        syl
        .login
```

Figure 17.6   The directory listing for tree in Figure 17.4

We assume the existence of the class FileSystem and two member functions, PrintName and IsDirectory. PrintName outputs the current FileSystem object indented by Depth tab stops; IsDirectory tests if the current FileSystem object is a directory, returning true if it is. Given that, the recursive routine ListAll is easily written. We need to pass it the parameter Depth, indicating the current level in the directory relative to the root. ListAll is started with Depth equal to 0, to signify no indenting for the root. This depth is an internal bookkeeping variable and is hardly a parameter that a calling routine should be expected to know about. Thus the default value of 0 is provided for Depth.

The logic of the algorithm is simple to follow. The current object is printed out, with appropriate indentation. If the entry is a directory, then we process all the children recursively, one by one. These children are one level deeper in the tree and thus must be indented an extra tab stop. We make the recursive call using `Depth+1`. It is difficult to imagine a simpler piece of code that performs what appears to be a very difficult task.

In a *preorder traversal*, work at a node is performed before work at its children. The traversal takes constant time per node.

This algorithmic technique is known as a *preorder tree traversal*. In a preorder traversal, work at a node is performed before (*pre*) its children are processed. In addition to being a compact algorithm, the preorder traversal is meritorious because it is a linear-time algorithm. We will discuss why later in this chapter.

In a *postorder traversal*, work at a node is performed after work at its children. The traversal takes constant time per node.

Another common method of traversing a tree is the *postorder tree traversal*. In a postorder traversal, the work at a node is performed after (*post*) its children are evaluated. As an example, Figure 17.7 represents the same directory structure as Figure 17.4. The numbers in parentheses represent the number of disk blocks taken up by each file. Since the directories are themselves files, they also use disk blocks (to store the names and information about their children). Suppose we would like to compute the total number of blocks used by all files in the tree. The most natural way to do this is by finding the total number of blocks contained in all of the children (which may be directories that must be evaluated recursively): `books` (41), `courses` (8) and `.login` (2). The total number of blocks is then the total in all the children plus the blocks used at the root (1), namely 52. The routine `Size` in Figure 17.8 implements this strategy. If the current `FileSystem` object is not a directory, `Size` merely returns the number of blocks it uses. Otherwise, the number of blocks in the current directory is added to the number of blocks (recursively) found in all of the children. To illustrate the difference between postorder traversal and preorder traversal, Figure 17.9 shows how the size of each directory (or file) is produced by the algorithm. Once again, the running time is linear. We will have much more to say about tree traversals in Section 17.4.

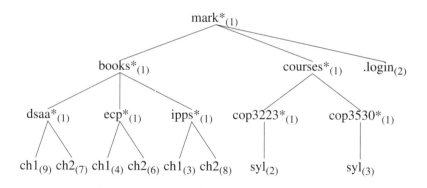

Figure 17.7   UNIX directory with file sizes

```
 1  int
 2  FileSystem::Size( )
 3  {
 4      int TotalSize = SizeOfThisFile( );
 5
 6      if( IsDirectory( ) )
 7          for each file C in this directory (for each child)
 8              TotalSize += C.Size( );
 9
10      return TotalSize;
11  }
```

Figure 17.8   Routine to calculate the total size of all files in a directory

			ch1	9
			ch2	7
		dsaa		17
			ch1	4
			ch2	6
		ccp		11
			ch1	3
			ch2	8
		ipps		12
	books			41
			syl	2
		cop3223		3
			syl	3
		cop3530		4
	courses			8
	.login			2
mark				52

Figure 17.9   Trace of the Size function

17.2   Binary Trees

A *binary tree* is a tree in which no node can have more than two children. Because there are only two children, we can name them Left and Right. The recursive definition is that a binary tree is either empty or consists of a root, a left tree, and a right tree. The left and right trees may themselves be empty. We will use the recursive definition several times in the design of binary tree algorithms. Binary trees have many important uses, two of which are illustrated in Figure 17.10.

A binary tree has no node with more than two children.

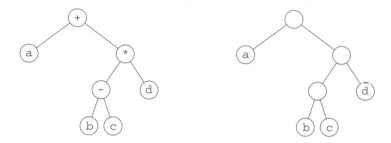

Figure 17.10   Uses of binary trees: left is an expression tree and right is a Huffman coding tree

```
 1  // BinaryNode class interface; stores a node in a tree
 2  //
 3  // Etype: must have copy constructor and operator=
 4  // CONSTRUCTION: with (a) no parameters, or (b) an Etype,
 5  //     or (c) an Etype, left pointer, and right pointer
 6  // Copying of BinaryNode objects is allowed
 7  //
 8  //   *****************PUBLIC OPERATIONS*********************
 9  // BinaryNode *GetLeft( ) --> Return pointer to left child
10  // BinaryNode *GetRight( )--> Return pointer to right child
11  // Etype GetItem( )        --> Return item in node
12  // void SetItem( Etype X )--> Set item in node to X
13  // void SetLeft( BinaryNode *L ) -->  Set left pointer to L
14  // void SetRight( BinaryNode *R )-->  Set right pointer to R
15  // int Size( )             --> Return size of subtree at node
16  // int Height( )           --> Return height of subtree at node
17  // void PrintPostOrder( ) --> Print a postorder tree traversal
18  // void PrintInOrder( )   --> Print an inorder tree traversal
19  // void PrintPreOrder( )  --> Print a preorder tree traversal
20  // BinaryNode *Duplicate( )      --> Return a duplicate tree
21  // *****************ERRORS********************************
22  // Predefined exception is propagated if new fails
```

Figure 17.11   `BinaryNode` class interface (part 1)

Expression trees are one example of the use of binary trees. They are central data structures in compiler design.

One use of the binary tree is in the expression tree, which is a central data structure in compiler design. The leaves of an expression tree are operands, such as constants or variable names, and the other nodes contain operators. This particular tree is binary because all of the operations are binary; although this is the simplest case, it is possible for nodes to have more than two children (and in the case of unary operators, only one child). We can evaluate an expression tree T by applying the operator at the root to the values obtained by recursively evaluating the left and right subtrees. In our case, this yields the expression `(a+((b-c)*d))`. The construction of expression trees and their evaluation is the topic of Section 11.2.

A second use of the binary tree is the Huffman coding tree, which is used to implement a simple but relatively effective data compression algorithm. Each symbol in the alphabetic is stored at a leaf. Its code is obtained by following the path to it from the root. A left link corresponds to a 0, and a right link to a 1. Thus b is coded as 100. Construction of the optimal tree (that is, the best code) is discussed in Section 12.1.

Other uses of the binary tree are in binary search trees, which allow logarithmic time insertions and accesses of items, and priority queues, which support the access and deletion of the minimum in a collection of items. Several efficient implementations of priority queues use trees, as discussed in Chapters 20 to 22.

An important use is in other data structures, notably the binary search tree and priority queue.

```
23  #include <stdlib.h>
24
25  template <class Etype>
26  class BinaryNode
27  {
28    public:
29        // Constructors and destructors
30      BinaryNode( ) : Left( NULL ), Right( NULL ) { }
31      BinaryNode( const Etype & E ) :
32            Element( E ), Left( NULL ), Right( NULL ) { }
33      BinaryNode( const Etype & E, BinaryNode *L,BinaryNode *R )
34            : Element( E ), Left( L ), Right( R ) { }
35      ~BinaryNode( ) { }
36
37        // Access members
38      const BinaryNode *GetLeft( )  const  { return Left; }
39      const BinaryNode *GetRight( ) const  { return Right; }
40      const Etype & GetItem( )        const  { return Element; }
41      void SetItem( const Etype & E )     { Element = E; }
42      void SetLeft( BinaryNode *L )  { Left = L; }
43      void SetRight( BinaryNode *R ) { Right = R; }
44
45        // Some recursive routines
46      int Size( const BinaryNode *T )    const,
47      int Height( const BinaryNode *T )  const;
48
49        // Print tree traversal starting at this node
50      void PrintPostOrder( ) const;
51      void PrintInOrder( )   const;
52      void PrintPreOrder( )  const;
53
54        // Duplicate
55      BinaryNode *Duplicate( ) const;
56    private:
57      Etype Element;        // The data in the node
58      BinaryNode *Left;    // Left subtree
59      BinaryNode *Right;   // Right subtree
60  };
```

Figure 17.12   BinaryNode class interface (part 2)

```
 1  // BinaryTree class interface; stores a binary tree
 2  //
 3  // Etype: must have copy constructor and operator=
 4  //   CONSTRUCTION: with (a) no parameters or
 5  //      (b) another BinaryTree
 6  // Deep copy of BinaryTree objects is supported
 7  //
 8  //   ******************PUBLIC OPERATIONS********************
 9  // BinaryNode *GetRoot( ) --> Return pointer to root
10  // void PrintPostOrder( ) --> Print a postorder tree traversal
11  // void PrintInOrder( )   --> Print an inorder tree traversal
12  // void PrintPreOrder( )  --> Print a preorder tree traversal
13  // int IsEmpty( )         --> Return 1 if empty; else return 0
14  // void MakeEmpty( )      --> Make an empty tree
15  // void Merge( Etype Root, BinaryTree L, BinaryTree R )
16  //                        --> Construct a new tree
17  //   ******************ERRORS********************************
18  // Predefined exception is propagated if new fails
19  // Error message printed for illegal merges
```

Figure 17.13   BinaryTree class interface (part 1)

Figures 17.11 and 17.12 give the class interface for BinaryNode. Lines 57 to 59 tell us that each node consists of a data item plus two pointers. Three constructors are provided. Line 30 is the zero-parameter constructor. Line 31 is used to construct a BinaryNode given an item. In both of these constructors, the left and right pointers are set to NULL. The third constructor, shown at line 33, initializes all the data members of the BinaryNode; notice that our constructors require initialization of both pointers or neither pointer. The default destructor is acceptable for our purposes; we explicitly declare it at line 35.

Many of the BinaryNode routines are recursive. The BinaryTree members use the BinaryNode routines on the Root.

Access to the private data members is allowed through the functions declared at lines 38 to 43. These types of functions are known as *accessor functions*. The Duplicate function, declared at line 55, is used to replicate a copy of the tree rooted at the current node. The routines Size and Height, declared at lines 46 and 47, compute the named properties for the node pointed at by a parameter. These routines are implemented in Section 17.3. We also provide, at lines 50 to 52, routines that print out the contents of a tree rooted at the current node using various recursive traversal strategies. Tree traversals are discussed in Section 17.4. Why do we pass a parameter for Size and Height but use the current object for the traversals and Duplicate? The answer is that there is no particular reason; it is a matter of style, and we have decided to show both styles. We will see in the implementations that the difference amounts to when the required test for a NULL tree is performed.

The BinaryNode class is implemented separately from the BinaryTree class.

In this section we will describe the implementation of the BinaryTree class. We provide a separate class, BinaryNode, to simplify implementation of some of the recursive routines. The alternative is to nest BinaryNode inside of BinaryTree (some older compilers have not implemented templated nested classes, so this might not even be an option for everyone). Additionally, we make a decision that appears to complicate the code: We do not make `BinaryTree` a friend of `BinaryNode`. Instead, we require `BinaryTree` class members to call functions in `BinaryNode` to access the node's private data members. It turns out that this is only a minor inconvenience.

The `BinaryTree` class interface is shown in Figures 17.13 and 17.14. For the most part, the routines are simple to implement because they call `BinaryNode` functions. Line 51 declares the only data member, a pointer to the root node. We disable the copy constructor at line 53 and at line 55 declare an internal function `FreeTree` that `deletes` all the nodes in the tree. `FreeTree` is called by several members, including the destructor.

The only data member in the `BinaryTree` class is a pointer to the root node.

```
20  template <class Etype>
21  class BinaryTree
22  {
23    public:
24          // Constructors and Destructors
25      BinaryTree( ) : Root( NULL ) { }
26      BinaryTree( const Etype &RootItem )
27              { Root = new BinaryNode<Etype>( RootItem ); }
28      ~BinaryTree( ) { FreeTree( Root ); }
29
30      const BinaryNode<Etype> *GetRoot( ) const { return Root; }
31
32          // Recursive traversals, with printing
33      void PrintPreOrder( ) const
34              { if( Root ) Root->PrintPreOrder( );  }
35      void PrintInOrder( ) const
36              { if( Root ) Root->PrintInOrder( );    }
37      void PrintPostOrder( ) const
38              { if( Root ) Root->PrintPostOrder( ); }
39
40          // Emptiness
41      void MakeEmpty( )        { FreeTree( Root ); Root = NULL; }
42      int IsEmpty( )  const    { return Root == NULL; }
43
44          // Copy trees.
45      const BinaryTree & operator= ( const BinaryTree & Rhs );
46
47          // Combine T1 and T2
48      void Merge( const Etype & RootItem,
49              BinaryTree & T1, BinaryTree & T2 );
50    private:
51      BinaryNode<Etype> *Root;
52          // Disable copy constructor
53      BinaryTree( const BinaryTree & );
54          // Called by destructor
55      void FreeTree( BinaryNode<Etype> *T );
56  };
```

Figure 17.14   `BinaryTree` class interface (part 2)

```
1 template <class Etype>
2 const BinaryTree<Etype> &
3 BinaryTree<Etype>::operator=( const BinaryTree<Etype> & Rhs )
4 {
5     if( this != &Rhs )
6     {
7         FreeTree( Root );
8         if( Rhs.Root )
9             Root = Rhs.Root->Duplicate( );
10    }
11
12    return *this;
13 }
```

Figure 17.15   Copy assignment operator for binary tree classes

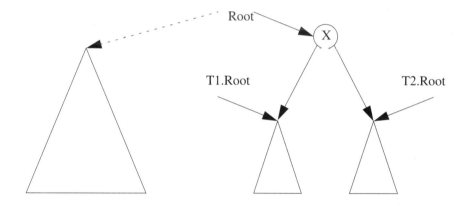

Figure 17.16   Result of a naive `Merge` operation

Two constructors are provided: The one at line 25 creates an empty tree, while the other at line 26 creates a one-node tree. As we mentioned before, the destructor, shown at line 28, calls `FreeTree` to reclaim all dynamically allocated memory. A function is provided at line 30 to provide access to the root node. Routines to traverse the tree are declared at lines 33 to 37. They apply a `BinaryNode` member function to the `Root`, after verifying that the tree is not empty. An alternate traversal strategy that can be implemented as a nonmember, nonfriend is *level order traversal*. All these traversal routines are discussed in Section 17.4. Routines to make an empty tree and test for emptiness are given, with their inline implementations, at lines 41 and 42, respectively. Two routines remain in the interface.

The copy assignment operator is declared at line 45. It is implemented in Figure 17.15. After testing for aliasing at line 5, we call `FreeTree` at line 7 to reclaim the memory. At line 9 we call the `Duplicate` member function to get a copy of Rhs's tree and assign the result as the root of the tree. Notice the test at line 8. Before we can apply the `BinaryNode` member to the node pointed at by the `Root`, we must verify that the `Root` is not NULL. As usual, `operator=` returns a constant reference to the current object; this is done at line 12.

Before we can apply the `BinaryNode` member to the node pointed at by the `Root`, we must verify that the `Root` is not NULL.

The last function in the interface is the `Merge` routine. `Merge` uses two trees, T1 and T2, and an element to create a new tree, with the element at the root and the two existing trees as left and right subtrees. In principle, this is a one-line routine:

`Merge` is a one-line routine in principle. However we must also handle aliasing, avoid memory leaks, make sure that a node is not in two trees, and do error checking.

```
Root = new BinaryNode<Etype>( RootItem, T1.Root, T2.Root );
```

If things were always this simple, programmers would be unemployed. Fortunately for our careers, there are a host of complications. Figure 17.16 shows the result of the simple one-line `Merge`. Two problems become apparent:

- The nodes that `Root` used to point at are now unreferenced, and thus we have a memory leak.
- Nodes in T1 and T2's trees are now in two trees (their original trees and the merged result). This sharing is a problem because when the destructor for T1 is called, it will `delete` nodes in the merged tree too, possibly resulting in erroneous behavior; furthermore, when the merged tree's destructor is called, it will attempt to `delete` nodes that are already deleted, almost certainly resulting in a disaster.

The solution to our problems is simple in principle. We can avoid the memory leak by calling `FreeTree` on the original tree. All we need to do is save a pointer to the `Root` before calling new. We can ensure that nodes do not appear in two trees by setting T1.Root and T2.Root to NULL after the `Merge`.

Memory leaks are avoided by calling `FreeTree` on the original tree. We set the original trees' root to NULL so each node is in one tree.

Complications ensue when we consider some possible calls that contain aliasing:

```
T1.Merge( X, T1, T2 );
T2.Merge( X, T1, T2 );
T1.Merge( X, T3, T3 );
```

The first two cases are similar; we consider only the first. A picture of the situation is shown in Figure 17.17. If we call `FreeTree` for the original tree, we will destroy part of the merged tree. Thus, when we detect an aliasing condition, we do not call `FreeTree`. A second problem is harder to see unless you are careful drawing the picture. Because T1 is an alias for the current object, T1.Root and Root are aliases. Thus, after the call to new, if we execute T1.Root=NULL, we change Root to the NULL pointer, too. Consequently, we need to be very careful with the aliases for these cases.

If an input tree is aliased to the output tree, we must be very careful.

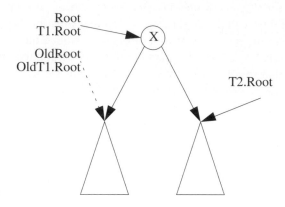

Figure 17.17   Aliasing problems in the `Merge` operation; `T1` is also the current object

```
 1  // Merge routine for BinaryTree class
 2  // Forms a new tree from RootItem, T1 and T2
 3  // Does not allow T1 and T2 to be the same
 4  // Correctly handles other aliasing conditions
 5
 6  template <class Etype>
 7  void
 8  BinaryTree<Etype>::Merge( const Etype & RootItem,
 9                BinaryTree<Etype> & T1, BinaryTree<Etype> & T2 )
10  {
11      if( T1.Root == T2.Root && T1.Root != NULL )
12          cerr << "LeftTree==RightTree; Merge aborted" << endl;
13      else
14      {
15          BinaryNode<Etype> *OldRoot = Root;  // Save old root
16
17              // Allocate new node
18          Root = new BinaryNode<Etype>( RootItem, T1.Root,
19                                              T2.Root );
20
21              // Deallocate nodes in the original tree
22          if( this != &T1 && this != &T2 )
23              FreeTree( OldRoot );
24
25              // Ensure that every node is in one tree
26          if( this != &T1 )
27              T1.Root = NULL;
28          if( this != &T2 )
29              T2.Root = NULL;
30      }
31  }
```

Figure 17.18   `Merge` routine for `BinaryTree` class

```
1  // Return a pointer to a node that is the root of
2  // a duplicate of the tree rooted at the current node
3
4  template <class Etype>
5  BinaryNode<Etype> *
6  BinaryNode<Etype>::Duplicate( ) const
7  {
8      BinaryNode<Etype> *Root =
9                  new BinaryNode<Etype>( Element );
10
11     if( Left != NULL )          // If there's a left subtree
12         Root->Left = Left->Duplicate( );  // Duplicate; attach
13     if( Right != NULL )         // If there's a right subtree
14         Root->Right = Right->Duplicate( );// Duplicate; attach
15
16     return Root;                           // Return resulting tree
17  }
```

Figure 17.19   Routine to return a copy of the tree rooted at the current node

The third case must be disallowed: It would place all the nodes that are in tree T3 in two places in T1. However, if T3 represents an empty tree, the third case should be allowed. All in all, we got a lot more than we bargained for. The resulting code is shown in Figure 17.18. What used to be a one-line routine has gotten quite large.

If the two input trees are aliases, we should disallow the operation, unless the trees are empty.

17.3   Recursion and Trees

Because trees can be defined recursively, it is not surprising that many tree routines are most easily implemented by using recursion. We will provide recursive implementations for almost all the remaining BinaryNode and BinaryTree members. The resulting routines are amazingly compact.

Recursive routines are used for Size, Duplicate, and FreeTree.

Let us begin with the Duplicate member of the BinaryNode class. Since it is a BinaryNode member, we are assured that the tree we are duplicating is not empty. The recursive algorithm is then simple: Allocate a new node with the same data member as the current root; then attach a left tree by calling Duplicate recursively and attach a right tree by calling Duplicate recursively. In both cases we make the recursive call after checking that there is a tree to copy. This description is coded verbatim in Figure 17.19.

Because Duplicate is a BinaryNode member function, we make recursive calls only after testing that the subtrees are not NULL.

Next we code FreeTree. There is a slight difference between FreeTree and Duplicate, because FreeTree is a member of the BinaryTree class. FreeTree receives a pointer to the root of the tree. However, this pointer might be NULL. Consequently, we must test for NULL first. This does however, make it unnecessary to test against NULL prior to making the recursive call (although it can be argued that it would be more efficient to do so, as shown in Exercise

Since FreeTree is not a BinaryNode member, the parameter T might be NULL. We thus test for it at the start of the routine and do not test prior to a recursive call.

17.10). To delete all the nodes in a tree, we delete (recursively) all the nodes in the left subtree, then the nodes in the right subtree (again, recursively), and finally the root. This is shown in Figure 17.20. Two points: The delete of T must be done last, but the order of the two recursive calls is not important. Second, the type conversions at lines 7 and 8 are needed because GetLeft and GetRight return constant pointers, and FreeTree wants a nonconstant pointer. We cannot change FreeTree to accept a constant pointer because delete must have a nonconstant pointer.

```
1  template <class Etype>
2  void
3  BinaryTree<Etype>::FreeTree( BinaryNode<Etype> *T )
4  {
5      if( T != NULL )
6      {
7          FreeTree( (BinaryNode<Etype> *) T->GetLeft( ) );
8          FreeTree( (BinaryNode<Etype> *) T->GetRight( ) );
9          delete T;
10     }
11 }
```

Figure 17.20 Routine to delete all nodes in tree rooted at T

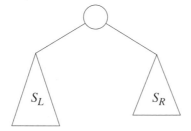

Figure 17.21 Recursive view used to calculate the size of a tree: $S_T = S_L + S_R + 1$

```
1  template <class Etype>
2  int
3  BinaryNode<Etype>::Size( const BinaryNode<Etype> *T ) const
4  {
5      if( T == NULL )
6          return 0;
7      else
8          return 1 + Size( T->Left ) + Size( T->Right );
9  }
```

Figure 17.22 Routine to compute the size of a node

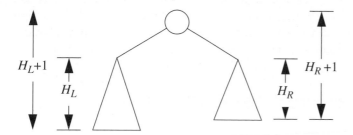

Figure 17.23   Recursive view of node height calculation: $H_T = \text{Max}(\ H_L+1,$
$H_R+1\ )$

```
1  template <class Etype>
2  int
3  BinaryNode<Etype>::Height( const BinaryNode<Etype> *T ) const
4  {
5      if( T == NULL )
6          return -1;
7      else
8          return 1 + Max( Height( T->Left ), Height( T->Right ) );
9  }
```

Figure 17.24   Routine to compute the height of a node

The next function we write is the `Size` routine in class `BinaryNode`. **`Size` is easily implemented recursively after a picture is drawn.** `Size` returns the size of the tree rooted at a node pointed at by T, which is passed as a parameter. If we draw the tree recursively as shown in Figure 17.21, we see that the size of a tree is equal to the size of the left subtree plus the size of the right subtree plus 1 (because the root counts as a node). A recursive routine requires a base case that can be solved without recursion. The smallest tree that `Size` might have to handle is the empty tree (if T is NULL) and the size of an empty tree is clearly 0. We should verify that the recursion produces the correct answer for a tree of size 1, and indeed it is easy to see that it does. The result is implemented in Figure 17.22.

The final recursive routine in this section calculates the height of a node in the tree. This is difficult to do nonrecursively but is trivially implemented recursively, once we draw the picture. Figure 17.23 shows a tree viewed recursively. **`Height` is also easily implemented recursively. The height of an empty tree is –1.** Suppose the left subtree has height H_L and the right subtree has height H_R. Any node that is d levels deep with respect to the root of the left subtree is $d + 1$ levels deep with respect to the root of the entire tree. The same holds for the right subtree. Thus the path length of the deepest node in the original tree is 1 more than its path length with respect to the root of its subtree. If we compute this value for both subtrees, the maximum of these two values plus 1 is the answer we want. What about the base case? Once again, we might be presented with an empty tree. The obvious answer that an empty tree has height 0 is wrong. This is because a single-node tree has height 0 (a leaf always has height 0). To make the recursive formula work for single-node trees, we define the height of an empty tree to be −1. Thus a leaf has two subtrees of height −1, so its height is correctly declared to be 0. The routine that results is shown in Figure 17.24.

17.4   Tree Traversal: Iterator Classes

Throughout this chapter we have seen how recursion can be used to implement the binary tree member functions. When recursion is applied, we compute information about not only a node but also all of its descendants. We say then that we are traversing the tree. Two popular traversals that have already been seen are the preorder and postorder traversal.

```
1  template <class Etype>
2  void
3  BinaryNode<Etype>::PrintPreOrder( ) const
4  {
5      cout << Element << '\n';          // Node
6      if( Left != NULL )
7          Left->PrintPreOrder( );       // Left
8      if( Right != NULL )
9          Right->PrintPreOrder( );      // Right
10 }
11
12
13 template <class Etype>
14 void
15 BinaryNode<Etype>::PrintPostOrder( ) const
16 {
17     if( Left != NULL )                // Left
18         Left->PrintPostOrder( );
19     if( Right != NULL )               // Right
20         Right->PrintPostOrder( );
21     cout << Element << '\n';          // Node
22 }
23
24
25 template <class Etype>
26 void
27 BinaryNode<Etype>::PrintInOrder( ) const
28 {
29     if( Left != NULL )                // Left
30         Left->PrintInOrder( );
31     cout << Element << '\n';          // Node
32     if( Right != NULL )               // Right
33         Right->PrintInOrder( );       // Right
34 }
```

Figure 17.25   Routines to print nodes in preorder, postorder, and inorder

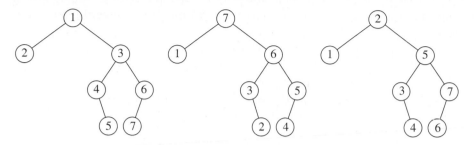

Figure 17.26   Preorder, postorder, and inorder visitation routes

In a preorder traversal the node is processed, and then its children are processed recursively. The Duplicate routine is an example of a preorder traversal because the root is created first, then a left subtree is copied recursively, and then a right subtree is copied recursively.

In a postorder traversal the node is processed after both children are processed recursively. We have seen three examples of this: the functions Size, Height, and FreeTree. In all cases information about a node (for instance, its size or height) can only be obtained after the corresponding information is known for its children. In FreeTree, a node is deleted only after its children are recursively deleted.

A third common recursive traversal is the *inorder traversal*. In an inorder traversal we recursively process the left child, then process the current node, and then recursively process the right child. This mechanism is used to generate an algebraic expression corresponding to an expression tree. For example, in Figure 17.10 the inorder traversal yields (a+((b-c)*d)).

In an *inorder traversal*, we process the current node in between recursive calls.

Figure 17.25 illustrates routines that print the nodes in a binary tree using each of the three recursive tree traversal algorithms. Figure 17.26 shows the order that nodes are visited for each of the three strategies. The running time of each algorithm is linear. In all cases each node is output exactly once. Consequently, the total cost of an output statement over any traversal is $O(N)$. Because of this, we see that each if statement is also executed at most once per node, for a total cost of $O(N)$. The total number of function calls made (which involves the constant work of the internal run-time stack pushes and pops) is likewise once per node, or $O(N)$. Thus the total running time is $O(N)$.

Simple traversal using any of these strategies takes linear time.

Must we use recursion to implement the traversals? The answer is clearly no, since as we discussed in Section 7.3, recursion is implemented by using a stack. Thus we could keep our own stack. The result is generally a somewhat faster program because we can place only the essentials on the stack rather than have the compiler place an entire activation record. The difference in speed between a recursive and nonrecursive algorithm is very dependent on the platform. In many cases the speed improvement does not justify the effort involved in removing recursion. Even so, it is worth knowing how to do it just in case your platform is

We can traverse nonrecursively by maintaining the stack ourselves.

one that would benefit from recursion removal and also because seeing how a program is implemented nonrecursively can sometimes make the recursion clearer.

```
1  // TreeIterator class interface; maintains "current position"
2  //
3  // Etype: same restrictions as for BinaryTree
4  // CONSTRUCTION: with (a) Tree to which iterator is bound
5  // All copying of TreeIterator objects is DISALLOWED
6  //
7  //   ******************PUBLIC OPERATIONS*********************
8  //      First two are not virtual, last two are pure virtual
9  // int operator+( )      --> True if at valid position in tree
10 // Etype operator( )     --> Return item in current position
11 // void First( )         --> Set current position to first
12 // void operator++       --> Advance (prefix)
13 //   ******************ERRORS*******************************
14 // EXCEPTION is called for illegal access or advance
15
16 template <class Etype>
17 class TreeIterator
18 {
19   public:
20     TreeIterator( const BinaryTree<Etype> & TheTree ) :
21         T( TheTree ), Current( NULL ) { }
22     virtual ~TreeIterator( ) { }
23
24     virtual void First( ) = 0;
25     int operator+( ) const { return Current != NULL; }
26     const Etype & operator( ) ( ) const;
27     virtual void operator++( ) = 0;
28   protected:
29     const BinaryTree<Etype> & T;
30     const BinaryNode<Etype> *Current;
31   private:
32         // Disable copy constructor and assignment
33     TreeIterator( const TreeIterator & ) { }
34     const TreeIterator & operator=( const TreeIterator & );
35 };
36
37 template <class Etype>
38 const Etype &
39 TreeIterator<Etype>::operator( ) ( ) const
40 {
41     EXCEPTION( Current == NULL, "Illegal access!" );
42     return Current->GetItem( );
43 }
```

Figure 17.27　　Tree iterator abstract base class

We will write three iterator classes, in the spirit of the linked list. Each will allow us to go to the first node, advance to the next node, test if we have gone past the last node, and access the current node. The ordering that nodes are accessed is determined by the type of traversal. We will also implement a *level order traversal*. In a level order traversal, nodes are visited top to bottom, left to right. Level order traversal is inherently nonrecursive and in fact uses a queue instead of a stack. It turns out to be very similar to the preorder traversal.

An iterator class allows step-by-step traversal.

Figure 17.27 provides an abstract base class for tree iteration. Each iterator will store a reference to the tree and an indication of the current node. These are declared at lines 29 and 30, respectively, and initialized in the constructor. They are protected to allow the derived classes access to them. Copy construction and assignment are disabled at lines 33 and 34. Four functions are declared at lines 24 to 27. operator+ and operator() are invariant over the hierarchy, and so an implementation is provided. The pure virtual functions First and operator++ must be provided by each type of iterator.

The base tree iterator class has a subset of the functions seen in the linked list iterator. Each type of traversal is represented by a derived class.

17.4.1   Postorder Traversal

The postorder traversal is implemented by using a stack to store the current state. The top of the stack will represent the node that we are visiting at some instant in the postorder traversal. However, we may be at one of three places in the algorithm:

Postorder traversal maintains a stack that stores nodes that have been visited but whose recursive call is not yet complete.

1. About to make a recursive call to the left subtree
2. About to make a recursive call to the right subtree
3. About to process the current node

Consequently, each node will be placed on the stack three times during the course of the traversal. If a node is popped from the stack a third time, we can mark it as the current node to be visited.

Each node will be placed on the stack three times: The third time off, it is declared visited. The other times, we simulate a recursive call.

Otherwise, the node is being popped for either the first time or the second time. In that case it is not yet ready to be visited, and so we push it back onto the stack and simulate a recursive call. If the node was popped for a first time, we need to push the left child onto the stack (if it exists); otherwise, the node was popped for a second time, and we push the right child onto the stack (if it exists). In any event, we then pop the stack, applying the same test. Notice that when we pop the stack, we are simulating the recursive call to the appropriate child, and if the child does not exist and thus was never pushed onto the stack, then when we pop the stack, we pop the original node again.

Eventually, either the process pops a node for the third time or the stack empties. In the latter case we have iterated over the entire tree. We initialize the algorithm by pushing a pointer to the root onto the stack. An example of how the stack is manipulated is shown in Figure 17.28.

When the stack is empty, every node has been visited.

Let us trace through the postorder traversal. We initialize the traversal by pushing the root a onto the stack. The first pop visits a. This is a's first pop, so it is placed back on the stack, and we push its left child, b, onto the stack. Next b is popped. Since it is b's first pop, it is placed back on the stack. Normally, b's left child would then be pushed, but b has no left child, so nothing is pushed. Thus the next pop reveals b for the second time. b is placed back on the stack, and its right child, d, is pushed on the stack. The next pop produces d for the first time. Thus d is pushed back on the stack. No other push is performed since d has no left child. Thus d is popped for the second time. It is then pushed back, but since it has no right child, nothing else is pushed. Thus the next pop yields d for the third time. Therefore, d is marked as a visited node. The next node popped is b, and since this is b's third pop, it is marked visited.

Continuing, we see that a is popped for the second time. It is pushed back on the stack along with its right child, c. Next c is popped for the first time, so it is pushed back, along with its left child e. Now e is popped, pushed, popped, pushed, and finally popped for the third time (this is typical for leaf nodes). Thus e is marked as a visited node. Next c is popped for the second time. It is pushed back onto the stack, but since it has no right child, it is immediately popped for the third time and marked as visited. Finally, a is popped for the third time and marked as visited. At this point the stack is empty, and the postorder traversal terminates.

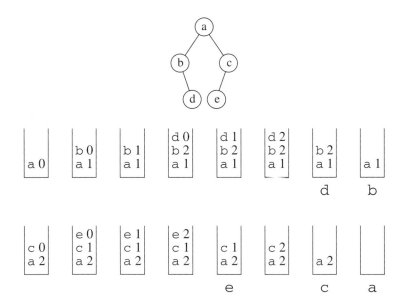

Figure 17.28   Stack states during postorder traversal

```
1  // PostOrder class interface; maintains "current position"
2  //
3  // Etype: same restrictions as for BinaryTree
4  // CONSTRUCTION: with (a) Tree to which iterator is bound
5  // All copying of PostOrder objects is DISALLOWED
6  //
7  // ******************PUBLIC OPERATIONS*********************
8  // Same as TreeIterator
9  // ******************ERRORS*******************************
10 // EXCEPTION is called for illegal access or advance
11
12 template <class Etype>
13 struct StNode
14 {
15     const BinaryNode<Etype> *Node;
16     int TimesPopped;
17     StNode( const BinaryNode<Etype> *N = 0 )
18             : Node( N ), TimesPopped( 0 ) { }
19 };
20
21 template <class Etype>
22 class PostOrder : public TreeIterator<Etype>
23 {
24   public:
25     PostOrder( const BinaryTree<Etype> & TheTree );
26     ~PostOrder( ) { }
27
28     void First( );
29     void operator++( );
30   protected:
31     Stack< StNode<Etype> > S;
32 };
33
34 template <class Etype>
35 PostOrder<Etype>::
36 PostOrder( const BinaryTree<Etype> & TheTree ) :
37                 TreeIterator<Etype>( TheTree )
38 {
39     S.Push( StNode<Etype>( T.GetRoot( ) ) );
40 }
41
42 template <class Etype>
43 void
44 PostOrder<Etype>::First( )
45 {
46     S.MakeEmpty( );
47     if( T.GetRoot( ) )
48         S.Push( StNode<Etype>( T.GetRoot( ) ) );
49     operator++( );
50 }
```

Figure 17.29   Interface for PostOrder class (complete class except for operator++)

```
1   template <class Etype>
2   void
3   PostOrder<Etype>::operator++( )
4   {
5       if( S.IsEmpty( ) )
6       {
7           EXCEPTION( Current == NULL, "Advanced past end" );
8           Current = NULL;
9           return;
10      }
11
12      StNode<Etype> Cnode;
13
14      for( ; ; )
15      {
16          Cnode = S.Top( );
17          S.Pop( );
18
19          if( ++Cnode.TimesPopped == 3 )
20          {
21              Current = Cnode.Node;
22              return;
23          }
24
25          S.Push( Cnode );
26          if( Cnode.TimesPopped == 1 )
27          {
28              if( Cnode.Node->GetLeft( ) )
29                  S.Push(StNode<Etype>(Cnode.Node->GetLeft()));
30          }
31          else  // Cnode.TimesPopped == 2
32          {
33              if( Cnode.Node->GetRight( ) )
34                  S.Push(StNode<Etype>(Cnode.Node->GetRight()));
35          }
36      }
37  }
```

Figure 17.30 `operator++` for `PostOrder` iterator class

An StNode stores a pointer to a node and a count that tells how many times it has already been popped.

The `PostOrder` class itself is directly implemented from the algorithm described above. The interface is shown in Figure 17.29. The `StNode` structure represents the objects that are placed on the stack. It contains a pointer to a node and an integer that stores the number of times the item has been popped from the stack. The `StNode` structure is always initialized to reflect the fact that it has not yet been popped from the stack.

```
1  // InOrder class interface; maintains "current position"
2  //
3  // Etype: same restrictions as for BinaryTree
4  // CONSTRUCTION: with (a) Tree to which iterator is bound
5  // All copying of InOrder objects is DISALLOWED
6  //
7  // *****************PUBLIC OPERATIONS*********************
8  // Same as TreeIterator
9  // *****************ERRORS********************************
10 // EXCEPTION is called for illegal access or advance
11
12 template <class Etype>
13 class InOrder : public PostOrder<Etype>
14 {
15   public:
16     InOrder( const BinaryTree<Etype> & TheTree )
17            : PostOrder<Etype>( TheTree ){ }
18     void operator++( );
19 };
20
21 template <class Etype>
22 void
23 InOrder<Etype>::operator++( )
24 {
25     if( S.IsEmpty( ) )
26     {
27         EXCEPTION( Current == NULL, "Advanced past end" );
28         Current = NULL;
29         return;
30     }
31
32     StNode<Etype> Cnode;
33
34     for( ; ; )
35     {
36         Cnode = S.Top( );
37         S.Pop( );
38
39         if( ++Cnode.TimesPopped == 2 )
40         {
41             Current = Cnode.Node;
42             if( Cnode.Node->GetRight( ) )
43                 S.Push( StNode<Etype>( Cnode.Node->GetRight( ) ) );
44             return;
45         }
46             // First time through
47         S.Push( Cnode );
48         if( Cnode.Node->GetLeft( ) )
49             S.Push( StNode<Etype>( Cnode.Node->GetLeft( ) ) );
50     }
51 }
```

Figure 17.31   Complete InOrder iterator class

```
1  // PreOrder class interface; maintains "current position"
2  //
3  // Etype: same restrictions as for BinaryTree
4  //   CONSTRUCTION: with (a) Tree to which iterator is bound
5  // All copying of PreOrder objects is DISALLOWED
6  //
7  //   *****************PUBLIC OPERATIONS*****************A*******
8  // int operator+( )       --> True if at valid position in tree
9  // Etype operator( )      --> Return item in current position
10 // void First( )          --> Set current position to first
11 // void operator++        --> Advance (prefix)
12 // *****************ERRORS*********************************
13 // EXCEPTION is called for illegal access or advance
14
15 template <class Etype>
16 class PreOrder: public TreeIterator<Etype>
17 {
18   public:
19     PreOrder( const BinaryTree<Etype> & TheTree );
20     ~PreOrder( ) { }
21
22     void First( );
23     void operator++( );
24   protected:
25     Stack< const BinaryNode<Etype> * > S;
26 };
27
28 template <class Etype>
29 PreOrder<Etype>::
30 PreOrder( const BinaryTree<Etype> & TheTree ) :
31         TreeIterator<Etype>( TheTree )
32 {
33     S.Push( T.GetRoot( ) );
34 }
35
36 template <class Etype>
37 void
38 PreOrder<Etype>::First( )
39 {
40     S.MakeEmpty( );
41     if( T.GetRoot( ) )
42         S.Push( T.GetRoot( ) );
43     operator++( );
44 }
```

Figure 17.32   `PreOrder` class interface plus all members except
`operator++`

The `PostOrder` class is derived from `TreeIterator`. It adds an internal stack to the inherited members. The `PostOrder` class is initialized by initializing the `TreeIterator` members and then pushing the root onto the stack. This is illustrated in the constructor at lines 34 to 40. `First` is implemented by clearing the stack, pushing the root, and then calling `operator++`.

Figure 17.30 implements `operator++`. It follows the outline almost verbatim. Line 5 tests for an empty stack; if the stack is empty, we have completed the iteration and can set `Current` to `NULL` and return. Otherwise, we repeatedly perform stack pushes and pops until an item emerges from the stack for a third time. When this happens, the test at line 19 is successful, and we can return. Otherwise, at line 25 we push the node back onto the stack (note that the `TimesPopped` component has already been incremented at line 19). We then implement the recursive call. If the node was popped for the first time and it has a left child, then its left child is pushed onto the stack. Likewise, if the node was popped for a second time and it has a right child, then its right child is pushed onto the stack. Note that in either case, the construction of the temporary `StNode` object implies that the pushed node goes on the stack with zero pops.

Eventually, the `for` loop terminates because some node will be popped for the third time. Note that over the entire iteration sequence, there can be at most $3N$ stack pushes and pops. This is another way of establishing the linearity of a postorder traversal.

> `operator++` is the complicated routine; the code follows the earlier description almost verbatim.

17.4.2   Inorder Traversal

The inorder traversal is the same as the postorder traversal except that a node is declared visited after it is popped a second time. Prior to returning, the iterator pushes the right child (if it exists) onto the stack, so that the next call to `operator++` can continue by traversing the right child. Because this is so similar to a postorder traversal, we derive the `InOrder` class from `PostOrder` (even though an IS-A relationship does not exist). The only change is the minor alteration to `operator++`. The new class is shown in Figure 17.31.

> Inorder traversal is similar to postorder except that, when a node is popped for the second time, it is declared visited.

17.4.3   Preorder Traversal

The preorder traversal is the same as the inorder traversal except that a node is declared visited after it is popped the first time. Prior to returning, the iterator pushes the right child onto the stack and then the left child. Note the order: We want the left child to be processed before the right child, so we must push the right child first and the left child second.

We could derive the `PreOrder` class from `InOrder` or `PostOrder`, but doing so would be wasteful because the stack no longer needs to maintain a count of the number of times an object has been popped. Consequently, the `PreOrder` class is derived directly from `TreeIterator`. The resulting interface, constructor, and `First` routine is shown in Figure 17.32.

> Preorder is the same as postorder, except that a node is declared visited the first time it is popped, and the right and then left children are pushed prior to the return.

```
 1  template <class Etype>
 2  void
 3  PreOrder<Etype>::operator++( )
 4  {
 5      if( S.IsEmpty( ) )
 6      {
 7          EXCEPTION( Current == NULL, "Advanced past end" );
 8          Current = NULL;
 9          return;
10      }
11
12      Current = S.Top( );
13      S.Pop( );
14      if( Current->GetRight( ) )
15          S.Push( Current->GetRight( ) );
16      if( Current->GetLeft( ) )
17          S.Push( Current->GetLeft( ) );
18  }
```

Figure 17.33   `PreOrder` iterator class `operator++`

Popping only once allows some simplifications.

The interface adds, at line 25, a stack of pointers to tree nodes to the `TreeIterator` data members. The constructor and `First` member functions are similar to what we have already seen. As illustrated by Figure 17.33, `operator++` is simpler: We no longer need a `for` loop. As soon as node is popped at line 12, it becomes the current node. We then push the right child and left child if they exist.

17.4.4   Level Order Traversals

In a *level order traversal*, nodes are visited top to bottom, left to right. Level order traversal is implemented by using a queue. The traversal is *breadth first*.

We close by implementing a *level order traversal*. The level order traversal processes nodes starting at the root and going top to bottom, left to right. The name derives from the fact that we output level 0 nodes (the root), level one nodes (roots children), level two nodes (grandchildren of the root), and so on. A level order traversal is implemented by using a queue instead of a stack. The queue stores nodes that are yet to be visited. When a node is visited, its children are placed at the end of the queue, to be visited after the nodes that are already in the queue. It is easy to see that this guarantees that nodes are visited in level order. The `LevelOrder` class shown in Figures 17.34 and 17.35 looks very much like the `PreOrder` class. The only difference is that we use a queue instead of a stack, and we enqueue the left child and then the right child, as opposed to the other way.

The level order traversal implements a more general technique known as *breadth-first search*. An example of this in a more general setting is illustrated in Section 14.2.

```
1  // LevelOrder class interface; maintains "current position"
2  //
3  // Etype: same restrictions as for BinaryTree
4  // CONSTRUCTION: with (a) Tree to which iterator is bound
5  // All copying of LevelOrder objects is DISALLOWED
6  //
7  // ******************PUBLIC OPERATIONS*********************
8  // int operator+( )      --> True if at valid position in tree
9  // Etype operator( )     --> Return item in current position
10 // void First( )         --> Set current position to first
11 // void operator++       --> Advance (prefix)
12 // ******************ERRORS*******************************
13 // EXCEPTION is called for illegal access or advance
14
15 template <class Etype>
16 class LevelOrder : public TreeIterator<Etype>
17 {
18   public:
19     LevelOrder( const BinaryTree<Etype> & TheTree );
20     ~LevelOrder( ) { }
21
22     void First( );
23     void operator++( );
24   private:
25     Queue< const BinaryNode<Etype> * > Q;
26 };
27
28 template <class Etype>
29 LevelOrder<Etype>::
30 LevelOrder( const BinaryTree<Etype> & TheTree ) :
31            TreeIterator<Etype>( TheTree )
32 {
33     Q.Enqueue( T.GetRoot( ) );
34 }
35
36 template <class Etype>
37 void
38 LevelOrder<Etype>::First( )
39 {
40     Q.MakeEmpty( );
41     if( T.GetRoot( ) )
42         Q.Enqueue( T.GetRoot( ) );
43     operator++( );
44 }
```

Figure 17.34   LevelOrder iterator class interface and most members

```
1   template <class Etype>
2   void
3   LevelOrder<Etype>::operator++( )
4   {
5       if( Q.IsEmpty( ) )
6       {
7           EXCEPTION( Current == NULL, "Advanced past end" );
8           Current = NULL;
9           return;
10      }
11
12      Current = Q.GetFront( );
13      Q.Dequeue( );
14      if( Current->GetLeft( ) )
15          Q.Enqueue( Current->GetLeft( ) );
16      if( Current->GetRight( ) )
17          Q.Enqueue( Current->GetRight( ) );
18  }
```

Figure 17.35   `operator++` for `LevelOrder` iterator class

Summary

This chapter discusses the *tree* and in particular, the *binary tree*. We saw how trees are used to implement the file systems on many computers and also some other applications, such as expression trees and coding, that are more fully explored elsewhere. Algorithms that work on trees make heavy use of recursion. We examined three recursive traversal algorithms – preorder, postorder, and inorder – and saw how they can be implemented nonrecursively. We also examined the level order traversal, which forms the basis for an important searching technique known as breadth-first search. In the next chapter we will examine another fundamental use of trees, namely the *binary search tree*.

Objects of the Game

accessor functions Functions that allow access to private data members. (518)

ancestor and **descendant** If there is a path from node *u* to node *v*, then *u* is an ancestor of *v*, and *v* is a descendant of *u*. (511)

binary tree A tree in which no node can have more than two children. A convenient definition is recursive. (515)

child and **parent** Parents and children are naturally defined. A directed edge connects the parent to the child. (509)

depth The length of the path from the root to a node. (510)

first child/next sibling method A general tree implementation in which each node keeps two pointers per item: One to the leftmost child (if it is not a leaf), and a second to its right sibling. (511)

height The length of the path from a node to the deepest leaf. (510)

inorder traversal A type of traversal in which we process the current node in between recursive calls. (527)

leaf Tree node that has no children. (510)

level order traversal A type of traversal in which nodes are visited top to bottom, left to right. Level order traversal is implemented by using a queue. The traversal is breadth first. (536)

postorder traversal A type of traversal in which work at a node is performed after work at its children. The traversal takes constant time per node. (514)

preorder traversal A type of traversal in which work at a node is performed before work at its children. The traversal takes constant time per node. (514)

proper ancestor and **proper descendant** On a path from node u to node v, if $u \neq v$ then u is a proper ancestor of v, and v is a proper descendant of u. (511)

siblings Nodes with the same parents. (511)

size The size of a node is the number of descendants it has (including the node itself). (511)

tree Defined nonrecursively, a tree is a set of nodes and directed edges that connect them. Trees are naturally defined recursively as either empty of consisting of a root and zero or more non-empty subtrees. (509)

Common Errors

1. Allowing a node to be in two trees simultaneously will cause an error because the node will be double-deleted.

2. Failing to check for empty trees is a common error. If this is part of a recursive algorithm, then it is likely that the program will crash.

3. A common error when working with trees is thinking iteratively instead of recursively. Design algorithms recursively first; convert them to iterative algorithms if appropriate.

On the Internet

Many of the examples discussed in this chapter are explored in Chapter 18, which discusses binary search trees. Consequently, the only code available is for the iterator classes. The `BinaryNode` class that they refer to is the one in Figure 18.5, so the iterator classes do not need to use the accessor functions.

Iterate.h   The interfaces for the entire `TreeIterator` hierarchy

Iterate.cpp   The implementation of the `TreeIterator` hierarchy

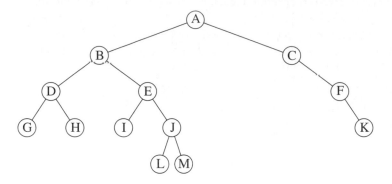

Figure 17.36   Tree for Exercises 17.1 and 17.2

```
1  void
2  MysteryPrint( const BinaryNode<char> * T )
3  {
4      if( T != NULL )
5      {
6          cout << T->Element << '\n';
7          MysteryPrint( T->Left );
8          cout << T->Element << '\n';
9          MysteryPrint( T->Right );
10         cout << T->Element << '\n';
11     }
12 }
```

Figure 17.37   Mystery program for Exercise 17.3

Exercises

In Short

17.1.   For the tree in Figure 17.36,

   a. Which node is the root?
   b. Which nodes are leaves?
   c. What is its depth?
   d. Give the result of a preorder, postorder, inorder, and level order traversal.

17.2.   For each node in the tree of Figure 17.36,

   a. Name the parent node.
   b. List the children.
   c. List the siblings.

      d. Compute the height.

      e. Compute the depth.

      f. Compute the size.

17.3. What is output by the program in Figure 17.37 for the tree in Figure 17.28?

17.4. Show the stack operations when an inorder and preorder traversal is applied to the tree in Figure 17.28.

In Theory

17.5. Show that the maximum number of nodes in a binary tree of height H is $2^{H+1} - 1$.

17.6. A *full node* is a node with two children. Prove that in a binary tree, the number of full nodes plus 1 is equal to the number of leaves.

17.7. How many NULL children are there in a binary tree of N nodes? How many are in an M-ary tree of N nodes?

17.8. Suppose a binary tree has leaves $l_1, l_2, ..., l_M$ at depth $d_1, d_2, ..., d_M$, respectively. Prove that $\sum_{i=1}^{M} 2^{-d_i} \leq 1$ and determine when equality is true. (This is known as Kraft's inequality).

In Practice

17.9. Write efficient functions (give Big-Oh running time) that take a pointer to a binary tree root T and compute the following:

      a. The number of leaves in T

      b. The number of nodes in T that contain one non-NULL child

      c. The number of nodes in T that contain exactly two non-NULL children

17.10. Implement some of the recursive routines with tests that ensure a recursive call is not made on a NULL subtree. Compare the running time with identical routines that defer the test until the first line of the recursive function.

17.11. Rewrite the iterator class to throw an AccessError exception when any of the following occurs: Applying First to an empty tree; applying ++ when Current is already NULL; accessing the data in a tree node when Current is NULL.

Programming Projects

17.12. A binary tree can be generated automatically for desktop publishing by a program. This could be done by assigning an (x,y) coordinate to each tree node, drawing a circle around each coordinate, and connecting each non-root node to its parent. Assume that you have a binary tree stored in memory and that each node has two extra data members to store the coordinates.

a. The x coordinate can be computed by assigning the inorder traversal number. Write a routine to do this for each node in the tree.

b. The y coordinate can be computed by using the negative of the depth of the node. Write a routine to do this for each node in the tree.

c. In terms of some imaginary unit, what will the dimensions of the picture be? How can you adjust the units so that the tree is always roughly two-thirds as high as it is wide?

d. Prove that using this system, no lines cross, and that for any node X, all elements in X's left subtree appear to the left of X, and all elements in X's right subtree appear to the right of X.

e. Can both coordinates be computed in one recursive function?

f. Write a general-purpose tree-drawing program that will convert a tree into the following graph-assembler instructions (circles are numbered in the order they are drawn):

```
Circle( X, Y );// Draw circle with center ( X,Y )
DrawLine( i, j ); // Connect circle i to circle j
```

g. Write a program that reads graph-assembler instructions and outputs the tree to your favorite device.

17.13. If you are running on a UNIX system, implement the *du* command.

Chapter 18

Binary Search Trees

For large amounts of input, the linear access time of linked lists is prohibitive. In this chapter we look at an alternative to the linked list, the *binary search tree*. The binary search tree is a simple data structure that can be viewed as extending the binary search algorithm to allow insertions and deletions. The running time for most operations is $O(\log N)$ on average. Unfortunately, the worst-case time is $O(N)$ per operation.

In this chapter we will see

- what the basic binary search tree is
- how to add order statistics (that is, the FindKth operation)
- three different ways to eliminate the bad worst case (namely the *AVL tree, red black tree*, and *AA-tree*)
- how searching a large database can be quickly implemented using the *B-tree*

18.1 Basic Ideas

The *binary search tree* is a binary tree that satisfies the search order property: For every node X in the tree, the values of all the keys in the left subtree are smaller than the key in X, and the values of all the keys in the right subtree are larger than the key in X. In Figure 18.1 the left tree is a binary search tree, but the right tree is not (because key 8 does not belong in the left subtree of key 7). The binary search tree property implies that all the elements in the tree can be ordered in a consistent manner (indeed, an inorder traversal yields the items in sorted order). The property also does not allow duplicate items. We could easily allow duplicate keys. It is generally better to store different records having identical keys in a secondary structure. If the records are exact duplicates, it is better to allow one record and keep a count of the number of duplicates.

> For any node in the *binary search tree*, all smaller-keyed nodes are in the left subtree, and all larger-keyed nodes are in the right subtree. Duplicates are not allowed.

Figure 18.1   Two binary trees (only the left tree is a search tree)

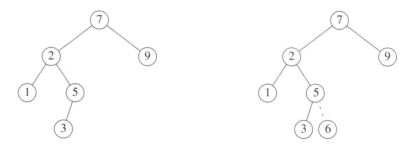

Figure 18.2   Binary search trees before and after inserting 6

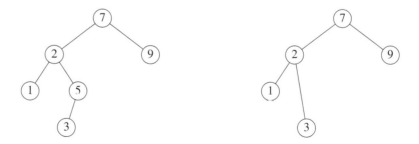

Figure 18.3   Deletion of node 5 with one child, before and after

18.1.1   The Operations

Find is performed by repeatedly branching either left or right, depending on the result of a comparison.

For the most part, the operations on a binary search tree are simple to visualize. We can perform a Find operation by starting at the root and then repeatedly branching either left or right, depending on the result of a comparison. For instance, to find 5 in the binary search tree in Figure 18.1, we start at 7 and go left. This takes us to 2, so we go right. This takes us to 5, and so 5 is found. To find 6, we would follow the same path. When we were at 5, we would go right and encounter a NULL pointer. Thus 6 is not found. Figure 18.2 shows that 6 can be inserted at the point at which the unsuccessful search terminates.

The binary search tree efficiently supports the FindMin and FindMax operations. To perform a FindMin, we start at the root and repeatedly branch left as long as there is a left child. The stopping point is the smallest element. FindMax is similar, except that branching is to the right. Notice that the cost of all the operations is proportional to the number of nodes on the search path. We will show later that this tends to be logarithmic but can be linear in the worst case.

FindMin is performed by following left nodes as long as there is a left child. FindMax is similar.

The hardest operation is Remove. Once we have found the node to be deleted, we need to consider several possibilities. The problem is that the removal of a node may disconnect parts of the tree. We must be careful to reattach the tree and maintain the binary search tree property. We would also like to avoid making the tree unnecessarily deep because, as we have already mentioned, the depth of the tree affects the running time of the tree algorithms.

Remove is difficult because nonleaf nodes hold the tree together, and we do not want to disconnect the tree.

If the node is a leaf, its removal will not disconnect the tree, thus it can be deleted immediately. If the node has only one child, the node can be removed after its parent adjusts a pointer to bypass the node. An illustration of this is shown in Figure 18.3 with the removal of node 5. Notice that this means that RemoveMin and RemoveMax are easy, because the affected nodes are either leaves or have only one child. Note that the root is a special case because it does not have a parent. However, when we implement the Remove member, we will see that the special case is handled automatically.

If a node has one child, it can be removed by having its parent bypass it. The root is a special case because it does not have a parent.

The complicated case deals with a node with two children. The general strategy is to replace the key of this node with the smallest key in the right subtree (which is easily found as mentioned earlier) and then remove that node (which is now logically empty). The second Remove is easy because, as we just remarked, the minimum node in a tree does not have a left child. Figure 18.4 shows an initial tree and the result of removing node 2. We replace the node with the smallest node (3) in its right subtree and then remove 3 from the right subtree. Notice that in all cases, removing a node does not make the tree deeper.

A node with two children is replaced by using the smallest key in the right subtree; then an alternate removal is performed.

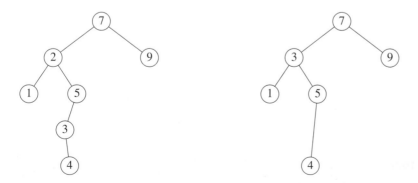

Figure 18.4 Deletion of node 2 with two children, before and after

18.1.2   C++ Implementation

We use a single
BinaryNode class
for all trees in this
chapter. We make
everything in it public
to simplify the code.

In principle, the binary search tree is easy to implement. To keep the C++ features from clogging up the code, we will make a few simplifications. First, Figure 18.5 shows the BinaryNode class. We could try to inherit the class from Section 17.2, but we quickly see that things start to get messy because of privacy. Reuse is nice, but at some point practicality must take over. Thus everything is public in the new BinaryNode class. Because we want to be able to use the same declarations for the more advanced binary search trees discussed later in this chapter, we include two additional class members at lines 10 and 11. They are not used in the implementation in this section. Of course we could omit them and attempt to use inheritance later on, but once again, that obscures the basics too much.

The BinaryNode class contains the usual list of data members (the item and two pointers) plus the additional data members used later. We provide several forms for construction. There are two important details. First, as mentioned above, BinaryNode is a struct, meaning that all of the data members are public. We do this to avoid writing accessor functions. This allows accesses to the tree but is considerably easier for exposition purposes than the alternatives of nesting the class or making the members private.

```
1   #include <stdlib.h>
2
3   template <class Etype>
4   struct BinaryNode
5   {
6       Etype Element;        // The data in the node
7       BinaryNode *Left;     // Left child
8       BinaryNode *Right;    // Right child
9
10      int Size;             // Node's size (used for order stats)
11      int BalancingInfo;    // Information used for balancing
12
13      BinaryNode( ) : Left( NULL ), Right( NULL ),
14          Size( 1 ), BalancingInfo( 1 ) { }
15
16      BinaryNode( const Etype & E ) : Element( E ),Left( NULL ),
17          Right( NULL ), Size( 1 ), BalancingInfo( 1 ) { }
18
19      BinaryNode( const Etype & E, BinaryNode *L,BinaryNode *R )
20          : Element( E ), Left( L ), Right( R ), Size( 1 ),
21          BalancingInfo( 1 ) { }
22
23      ~BinaryNode( ) { }
24  };
```

Figure 18.5   The node class for the binary search tree

```
1  // SearchTree class interface
2  //
3  // Etype: must have zero-parameter and copy constructor,
4  //      and must have operator<
5  // CONSTRUCTION: with (a) no initializer
6  // All copying of SearchTree objects is DISALLOWED
7  //
8  // ******************PUBLIC OPERATIONS*********************
9  // void Insert( Etype X )  --> Insert X
10 // void Remove( Etype X )  --> Remove X
11 // Etype Find( )           --> Return item that matches X
12 // int WasFound( )         --> Return 1 if last Find succeeded
13 // int IsFound( Etype X )  --> Return 1 if X would be found
14 // Etype FindMin( )        --> Return smallest item
15 // Etype FindMax( )        --> Return largest item
16 // void RemoveMin( )       --> Remove minimum item
17 // int IsEmpty( )          --> Return 1 if empty; else return 0
18 // void MakeEmpty( )       --> Remove all items
19 // ******************ERRORS********************************
20 // Predefined exception is propagated if new fails
21 // ItemNotFound returned on various degenerate conditions
22
23 template <class Etype>
24 class SearchTree
25 {
26   public:
27     SearchTree( ) : LastFind( NULL ), Root( NULL ) { }
28     ~SearchTree( ) { FreeTree( Root ); }
29
30     // Insert: If X already present, do nothing
31     // Return 1 if successful
32     int Insert( const Etype & X )
33         { return Insert( X, Root ); }
34
35     // Routines to return minimum/maximum item in tree
36     // If tree is empty, return ItemNotFound
37     const Etype & FindMin( ) const
38         { const BinaryNode<Etype> *P = FindMin( Root );
39           return P ? P->Element : ItemNotFound; }
40
41     const Etype & FindMax( ) const
42         { const BinaryNode<Etype> *P = FindMax( Root );
43           return P ? P->Element : ItemNotFound; }
44
45     // Return item X in tree
46     // If X is not found, return ItemNotFound
47     // Result can be checked by calling WasFound
48     const Etype & Find( const Etype & X )
49         { return ( LastFind = Find( X, Root ) ) ?
50                     LastFind->Element : ItemNotFound; }
```

Figure 18.6   SearchTree class interface (part 1)

The `Root` data member points at the root of the tree, or `NULL` if the tree is empty. The data member `ItemNotFound` is used so that we have something to return when a search fails.

The class interface for `SearchTree` is shown in Figures 18.6 and 18.7. The principal data member is the pointer to the root of the tree, `Root`. However, we need other data members because of the following problem: If we perform a search and return the item found, what do we do when the search fails? Clearly, we have to return something. For stacks and queues, this is an error condition. For linked lists we used an iterator class that maintained the current position; a second member function tested to see if the current position represented a successful search. Combining these ideas, we do the following for search trees:

1. We set `LastFind` to point at the node that results from the last `Find` operation, or `NULL` if the `Find` was unsuccessful. `LastFind` is a class member and is declared at line 75.

2. We return `ItemNotFound` for unsuccessful searches. `ItemNotFound` is another class member and is declared at line 76.

This certainly is not the only way to go.

The public class functions will call hidden private routines. Additionally, we should have used virtual functions, but instead leave this as Exercise 18.7.

Next in the interface are the copy constructor and copy assignment operator. For simplicity we have disabled both. `operator=` could be easily implemented, as shown in Figure 17.15. Next we have seven functions that operate on a node passed as a parameter. We saw this general technique in Chapter 17. The idea is that the publicly visible class routines call these hidden routines and pass `Root` as a parameter. These hidden routines do all the work. Two details: First, at line 73, we use `protected` rather than `private` because we will derive another class from `SearchTree` later in the chapter. Although we should, we do not use virtual functions because the resulting code would be hard to read. Deciding which function to declare virtual is left as Exercise 18.7.

The destructor calls `FreeTree`. Most of the interface is straightforward.

The rest of the `SearchTree` class interface is a straightforward listing of the member functions with inline implementations that call the hidden functions. The constructor, declared at line 27, merely sets the two data pointers to `NULL`. The destructor at line 28 calls `FreeTree` (which has the same implementation as the routine in Figure 17.20). The publicly visible members are listed with description at lines 30 through 71.

`Insert` adds `X` into the current tree by calling the hidden `Insert` with `Root` as an additional parameter. It returns true if the insertion succeeds and false if does not. Failure would occur if `X` was already in the tree or if the request for a new node failed during the insertion. `FindMin`, `FindMax`, and `Find` return the minimum, maximum, or named item (respectively) from the tree. If the item is not found because the tree is empty or the named item is not present, then `ItemNotFound` is returned. For `Find`, `LastFind` is set. `WasFound` can be used to test if the `Find` was successful. `IsFound` calls the hidden `Find` routine and returns either true or false. It does not set `LastFind`, and it does not incur the overhead of returning an `Etype` object.

RemoveMin removes the minimum item from the tree, returning true as long as the tree is not empty. Remove removes a named item X from the tree and returns true if the tree is not empty and X is in the tree prior to the call to Remove. MakeEmpty and IsEmpty are the usual standard fare.

```
51      // Return true if X is in tree
52      int IsFound( const Etype & X )
53          { return Find( X, Root ) != NULL; }
54
55      // Return true if last call to Find was successful
56      int WasFound( ) const
57          { return LastFind != NULL; }
58
59      // Remove X from the tree and return true if successful
60      int Remove( const Etype & X )
61          { return Remove( X, Root ); }
62
63      // Remove minimum item from the tree;
64      // Return true if successful
65      int RemoveMin( )
66          { return RemoveMin( Root ); }
67
68      // MakeEmpty tree, and test if tree is empty
69      void MakeEmpty( )
70          { FreeTree( Root ); Root = NULL; }
71      int IsEmpty( ) const
72          { return Root == NULL; }
73    protected:
74      BinaryNode<Etype> *Root;
75      const BinaryNode<Etype> *LastFind;
76      Etype ItemNotFound;  // Used for returns of not found
77
78          // Disable all copying
79      SearchTree( const SearchTree & );
80      const SearchTree & operator=( const SearchTree & );
81
82          // Simple recursive routine
83      void FreeTree( BinaryNode<Etype> *T );
84      int Insert( const Etype & X, BinaryNode<Etype> * & T );
85      int Remove( const Etype & X, BinaryNode<Etype> * & T );
86      int RemoveMin( BinaryNode<Etype> * & T );
87
88      const BinaryNode<Etype> *
89             FindMin( const BinaryNode<Etype> *T ) const;
90      const BinaryNode<Etype> *
91             FindMax( const BinaryNode<Etype> *T ) const;
92      const BinaryNode<Etype> * Find( const Etype & X,
93                  const BinaryNode<Etype> *T ) const;
94    };
```

Figure 18.7   SearchTree class interface (part 2)

```
 1  // Internal Find routine for SearchTree:
 2  // Return pointer to node
 3  // containing X or NULL if X is not found
 4
 5  template <class Etype>
 6  const BinaryNode<Etype> *
 7  SearchTree<Etype>::
 8  Find( const Etype & X, const BinaryNode<Etype> * T ) const
 9  {
10      while( T != NULL )
11          if( X < T->Element )
12              T = T->Left;
13          else
14          if( T->Element < X )
15              T = T->Right;
16          else
17              return T;      // Match
18
19      return NULL;          // Not found
20  }
```

Figure 18.8   Find operation for binary search trees

```
 1  // Internal FindMin and FindMax for SearchTree:
 2  // Return pointer to node containing minimum/maximum
 3  // or NULL if tree is empty
 4
 5  template <class Etype>
 6  const BinaryNode<Etype> *
 7  SearchTree<Etype>::
 8  FindMin( const BinaryNode<Etype> * T ) const
 9  {
10      if( T != NULL )
11          while( T->Left != NULL )
12              T = T->Left;
13
14      return T;
15  }
16
17  template <class Etype>
18  const BinaryNode<Etype> *
19  SearchTree<Etype>::
20  FindMax( const BinaryNode<Etype> * T ) const
21  {
22      if( T != NULL )
23          while( T->Right != NULL )
24              T = T->Right;
25
26      return T;
27  }
```

Figure 18.9   FindMin and FindMax for binary search trees

As is typical of most data structures, the `Find` operation is easier than `Insert`, and `Insert` is easier than `Remove`. Figure 18.8 illustrates the `Find` routine. As long as a NULL pointer has not been reached, we either have a match or need to branch left or right. The code implements this algorithm quite succinctly. Notice the order of the tests. It is crucial that the test against NULL be performed first; otherwise, the indirection `T->Element` would be illegal. The remaining tests are arranged with the least likely case last.

It seems at first glance that statements such as `T=T->Left` change the root of the tree. This is not the case because T is passed by value. Note carefully that this has nothing to do with the `const` in the function declaration. It is the call-by-value mechanism that matters here. In the initial call, T is simply a *copy* of `Root`. Although T changes, `Root` does not. The calls to `FindMin` and `FindMax` are even simpler because branching is unconditionally in one direction. These routines are shown in Figure 18.9. Notice how we carefully handle the case of an empty tree.

The `Insert` routine is shown in Figure 18.10. Here we use recursion to simplify the code. A nonrecursive implementation is also possible; we will see the technique when we discuss red black trees later in this chapter. The basic algorithm is simple. If the tree is empty, we can create a one-node tree. The test is performed at line 10, and the new node is allocated at line 12. We return true if the allocation succeeded (an exception is propagated otherwise). Notice carefully that in this case T is passed by reference (at line 7). This means that if the actual argument is Root, then Root will be changed to point at the newly allocated node.

Find is easier than Insert, which in turn is easier than Remove.

Because of call by value, the actual argument (Root) is not changed.

For Insert, we must pass the tree T by reference to effect a change.

```
1   // Internal Insert routine for SearchTree:
2   // Add X into subtree rooted at T and return true
3   // if insert succeeds and false if X is a duplicate
4
5   template <class Etype>
6   int
7   SearchTree<Etype>::
8   Insert( const Etype & X, BinaryNode<Etype> * & T )
9   {
10      if( T == NULL )
11      {
12          T = new BinaryNode<Etype>( X );
13          return 1;
14      }
15      else if( X < T->Element )
16          return Insert( X, T->Left );
17      else if( T->Element < X )
18          return Insert( X, T->Right );
19
20      return 0;   // Do not insert duplicates
21  }
```

Figure 18.10   Recursive `Insert` for `SearchTree` class

```
1  // Internal RemoveMin routine for SearchTree:
2  // Remove minimum item in tree rooted at T
3  // Return false only if tree is empty
4
5  template <class Etype>
6  int
7  SearchTree<Etype>::RemoveMin( BinaryNode<Etype> * & T )
8  {
9      if( T == NULL )
10         return 0;
11     else if( T->Left != NULL )
12         return RemoveMin( T->Left );
13
14     BinaryNode<Etype> *Tmp = T;
15     T = T->Right;
16     delete Tmp;
17     return 1;
18 }
```

Figure 18.11   RemoveMin for SearchTree class

If the tree is not already empty, then we have three possibilities. If the item to be inserted is smaller than the item in node T, then we need to call Insert recursively on the left subtree. If the item is larger than the item in node T, we call Insert recursively on the right subtree. This is coded at lines 15 to 18. Note that we return the result of the recursive Insert, so if the recursive call succeeds, so does the original call. The third case is that the item to insert matches the item in T; in this case we do nothing and return 0.

Because T is passed by reference, the subtree is automatically connected.

An important question to answer is, if the recursive insertion at line 16 changes the root of the left subtree, how can we be sure that the subtree will not be disconnected? The answer is that since the tree is passed by reference, any changes to the root of the left subtree will be reflected in the object T->Left, thus guaranteeing that the tree stays connected. It turns out that the only time this happens is when T->Left is NULL and we add a node in the left subtree. But even if the changes were more general, we would still be safe. The key here is that T->Left at line 16 and T->Right at line 18 are passed by reference. If we wrote the routine nonrecursively, we would have to maintain a pointer to the parent node as we descend the tree.

The remaining routines concern deletion. As we described earlier, the RemoveMin operation is simple because the minimum node has no left child. Thus the removed node merely needs to be bypassed. It may appear that this requires us to keep track of the parent of the current node as we descend the tree. Once again we can avoid the explicit use of a parent pointer by using recursion. The code is shown in Figure 18.11.

If the tree T is empty, then RemoveMin fails. Otherwise, if T has a left child, we recursively remove the minimum item in the left subtree via the recursive call at line 12. If we reach line 14, then we know that we are currently at the minimum node. This means that T is the root of a subtree that has no left child. If we set T to T->Right and then delete the node that T used to point at, then the result is that T is now the root of a subtree that is missing its former minimum element. That is what we do at lines 14 to 16. But doesn't that disconnect the tree? The answer again is no. If T was Root, then, since T is passed by reference, Root is changed to point at the new tree. If T was not Root, then it is P->Left, where P is T's parent at the time of the recursive call. The change to T, being by reference, also changes P->Left. Thus the parent's Left pointer points at T, and the tree is connected. All in all, it is a pretty nifty maneuver – what we have done is maintain the parent in the recursion stack rather than explicitly keep track of it in an iterative loop.

Passing T by reference also works in the Remove routines. In effect we maintain the parent in the recursion stack.

```
1   // Internal Remove routine for SearchTree:
2   // Remove X from tree rooted at T
3   // Return false only if X was not found
4
5   template <class Etype>
6   int
7   SearchTree<Etype>::
8   Remove( const Etype & X, BinaryNode<Etype> * & T )
9   {
10      BinaryNode<Etype> *Tmp;
11
12      if( T == NULL )
13          return 0;
14      else
15      if( X < T->Element )    // Go left
16          return Remove( X, T->Left );
17      else
18      if( T->Element < X )    // Go right
19          return Remove( X, T->Right );
20      else
21      if( T->Left != NULL && T->Right != NULL )  // Two children
22      {
23          // Copy from node to delete into node to keep;
24          // then delete
25          Tmp = (BinaryNode<Etype> *) FindMin( T->Right );
26          T->Element = Tmp->Element;
27          return RemoveMin( T->Right );         // Remove minimum
28      }
29          // One or zero children
30      Tmp = T;
31      T = ( T->Left != NULL ) ? T->Left : T->Right;  // Reroot T
32      delete Tmp;                               // Delete old root
33      return 1;
34  }
```

Figure 18.12   Remove member for SearchTree class

Having used this trick for the simple case, we can then adapt it for the general `Remove` routine. This is shown in Figure 18.12. If the tree is empty, the `Remove` is unsuccessful and we can return 0 at line 13. If we do not have a match, then we can recursively call `Remove` for either the left or right subtree as appropriate. Otherwise, we reach line 21, indicating that we have found the node that needs to be removed.

The `Remove` is tricky coding, but is not too bad if we use recursion. The case for one child, root with one child, and zero children are all handled together at lines 30 to 32.

Recall that if there are two children, we replace the node with the minimum element in the right subtree and then remove the right subtree's minimum. This is coded at lines 25 to 27. Otherwise, we have either one or zero children. We save a pointer to the current node at line 30 so that we can delete it at line 32. If there is a left child, then we set `T` equal to its left child, as would be done in `RemoveMax`. Otherwise, we know there is no left child, and we can set `T` equal to its right child. This is succinctly coded in line 31. In any of these cases, the `Remove` is successful and we return true at line 33. This also covers the leaf case.

There are two points to be made about this implementation. First, during the basic `Insert`, `Find`, or `Remove` operation, we perform two comparisons per node accessed to distinguish among the cases <, =, and >. It turns out that we can get by with only one comparison per node. The strategy is very similar to what was done in the binary search algorithm in Section 5.6. We discuss the technique for binary search trees in Section 18.6.2 when we illustrate the deletion algorithm for AA-trees.

Second, we do not have to use recursion to perform the insertion. In fact, a recursive implementation is probably slower than a nonrecursive implementation. An iterative implementation of `Insert` is discussed in Section 18.5.3 in the context of red black trees.

18.2   Order Statistics

The binary search tree allows us to find either the minimum or maximum element in time that is equivalent to an arbitrary named `Find`. Sometimes it is important to be able to access the Kth smallest element, for an arbitrary K provided as a parameter. It turns out that this is easy to do if we keep track of the size of each node in the tree.

We can implement `FindKth` if we maintain the size of each node as the tree is updated.

Recall from Section 17.1 that the size of a node is the number of its descendants (including itself). Suppose we want to find the Kth smallest element and that K is at least one and at most the number of nodes in the tree. Figure 18.13 shows that there are three possible cases, depending on the relation of K and the size of the left subtree, which is denoted by S_L. If K is equal to $S_L +1$ then the root is the Kth smallest element and we can stop. If K is smaller than or equal to S_L, then the Kth smallest element must be in the left subtree, and we can find it recursively. The recursion is not needed but is meant to simplify the algorithm description. Otherwise, the Kth smallest element is the $(K-S_L-1)$th smallest element in the right subtree and can be found recursively.

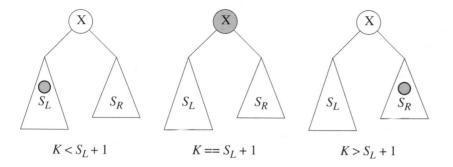

$K < S_L + 1$ $\qquad\qquad$ $K == S_L + 1$ $\qquad\qquad$ $K > S_L + 1$

Figure 18.13 Using the `Size` data member to implement `FindKth`

The main effort is maintaining the node sizes during tree changes. These changes occur in the `Insert`, `Remove`, and `RemoveMin` operations. In principle, this is simple enough. During an `Insert`, each node on the path to the insertion point gains one node in its subtree; thus the size of each node increases by 1. The inserted node has size 1. In `RemoveMin` each node on the path to the minimum loses one node in its subtree; thus the size of each node decreases by 1. During a `Remove` all nodes on the path to the node subjected to the `delete` operation also lose one node in their subtrees. Consequently, we can maintain the sizes at the cost of only a slight amount of overhead.

18.2.1   C++ Implementation

Logically, the only changes required are the adding of `FindKth` and the maintenance of the `Size` data members in `Insert`, `Remove`, and `RemoveMin`. We derive a new class `OrderedSearchTree` from `SearchTree`, the interface for which is shown in Figure 18.14. Let us first examine the new public member functions. The constructor for `OrderedSearchTree` is declared at line 26. It uses the default initialization, meaning that the inherited members are initialized according to the `SearchTree` constructor. The default destructor also applies and is not even listed.

We derive a new class, `OrderedSearchTree`, that supports the order statistic.

The new publicly visible functions `FindKth`, `Insert`, `Remove`, and `RemoveMin`, declared at lines 30, 36, 39, and 42, respectively, call a corresponding hidden member function. We might expect that a routine such as `Insert` at line 36 would not need to be redefined since its body is identical to the `SearchTree` `Insert`. However, if we attempt to inherit the public `Insert`, the call to the hidden `Insert` is scoped to `SearchTree` rather than `OrderedSearchTree`.

We must redefine both the hidden and public update functions.

```
1  // OrderedSearchTree class interface
2  //
3  // Etype: must have zero-parameter and copy constructor,
4  //        and must have operator<
5  // CONSTRUCTION: with (a) no initializer
6  // All copying of OrderedSearchTree objects is DISALLOWED
7  //
8  // ******************PUBLIC OPERATIONS*********************
9  // void Insert( Etype X )  --> Insert X
10 // void Remove( Etype X )  --> Remove X
11 // Etype Find( )           --> Return item that matches X
12 // Etype FindKth( int K )  --> Return Kth smallest item
13 // Etype FindMin( )        --> Return smallest item
14 // Etype FindMax( )        --> Return largest item
15 // void RemoveMin( )       --> Remove minimum item
16 // IsFound( ), WasFound( ), IsEmpty( ), and MakeEmpty( )
17 // are inherited as is
18 // ******************ERRORS********************************
19 // Predefined exception is propagated if new fails
20 // ItemNotFound returned in various degenerate cases
21
22 template <class Etype>
23 class OrderedSearchTree : public SearchTree<Etype>
24 {
25   public:
26     OrderedSearchTree( ) { }
27
28     // Return Kth item in tree
29     // Result can be checked by calling WasFound.
30     const Etype & FindKth( int K ) const
31         { if( Root == NULL ) return ItemNotFound;
32                   else return FindKth( K, Root )->Element; }
33
34     // Add X into the tree. If X already present, do nothing
35     // Return true if insertion was successful
36     int Insert( const Etype & X ){ return Insert( X, Root ); }
37
38     // Remove X from the tree; return true if successful
39     int Remove( const Etype & X ){ return Remove( X, Root ); }
40
41     // Remove minimum item; return true if successful
42     int RemoveMin( )              { return RemoveMin( Root ); }
43   private:
44         // New routines
45     int Insert( const Etype & X, BinaryNode<Etype> * & T );
46     int Remove( const Etype & X, BinaryNode<Etype> * & T );
47     int RemoveMin( BinaryNode<Etype> * & T );
48     const BinaryNode<Etype> *FindKth( int K,
49                       const BinaryNode<Etype> * T ) const;
50     int TreeSize( ) const { return Root ? Root->Size : 0; }
51 };
```

Figure 18.14 OrderedSearchTree class interface

```
 1  // Internal FindKth routine for OrderedSearchTree:
 2  // Return pointer to node containing Kth smallest item
 3  // in tree rooted at T or NULL if K is out of range
 4
 5  template <class Etype>
 6  const BinaryNode<Etype> *
 7  OrderedSearchTree<Etype>::
 8  FindKth( int K, const BinaryNode<Etype> * T ) const
 9  {
10      if( T == NULL )
11          return NULL;
12
13      int LeftSize = T->Left ? T->Left->Size : 0;
14
15      if( K <= LeftSize )
16          return FindKth( K, T->Left );
17      if( K == LeftSize + 1 )
18          return T;
19      return FindKth( K - LeftSize - 1, T->Right );
20  }
```

Figure 18.15   FindKth operation for OrderedSearchTree class

```
 1  // Internal Insert routine for OrderedSearchTree:
 2  // Add X into tree rooted at T and return true
 3  // unless X is a duplicate
 4
 5  template <class Etype>
 6  int
 7  OrderedSearchTree<Etype>::
 8  Insert( const Etype & X, BinaryNode<Etype> * & T )
 9  {
10      if( T == NULL )
11          return ( T = new BinaryNode<Etype>( X ) ) != NULL;
12      else
13      if( X < T->Element )
14          return Insert( X, T->Left ) ? ++T->Size : 0;
15      else
16      if( T->Element < X )
17          return Insert( X, T->Right ) ? ++T->Size : 0;
18      else  // Duplicate -- do nothing
19          return 0;
20  }
```

Figure 18.16   Insert for OrderedSearchTree

The FindKth operation in Figure 18.15 is written recursively, although clearly it need not be. It follows the algorithmic description line for line. The test against NULL at line 10 is necessary because K could be invalid. At line 13 we compute the size of the left subtree. If the left subtree exists, then accessing its

FindKth is easily implemented once the size members are known.

Size member gives the required answer. If the left subtree does not exist, its size can be taken to be zero. Notice that this test is performed after we are sure that T is not NULL.

Insert and Remove are tricky because we do not update the size information if the operation is unsuccessful. We can determine this once the recursive call is complete.

Insert is shown in Figure 18.16. The tricky part is that if the recursive call succeeds, then we want to increment T's Size member and return nonzero; if the recursive call fails, T's Size member is unchanged, and zero is returned. This is reflected by the changes at lines 14 and 17. Since the resulting size is always positive, returning it achieves the effect of returning true. Note that when a new node is allocated by a call to new, the Size member is set to one by the BinaryNode constructor.

Figure 18.17 shows that the same trick can be used by RemoveMin. At line 12, if the recursive call succeeds, we decrement the Size member; by using the postfix operator--, we know that the return in this case is nonzero. If the recursive call fails, we return zero, without lowering Size.

The trickiest operation is Remove. This is shown in Figure 18.18. If the recursive calls to Remove at lines 16 and 19 succeed, we use the same decrementing trick that was performed in RemoveMin. If we get to a node that has two children, then we must replace that node with the minimum in the right subtree and recursively delete from the right subtree. In this case, we can be sure that the tree's size will be lowered, and thus we can update the Size member at line 25. If there is only one child, then the node is bypassed and deleted. There is no need to adjust the Size member.

```
1    // Internal RemoveMin for OrderedSearchTree:
2    // Remove minimum item from tree rooted at T and
3    // return true if tree was not empty prior to removal
4
5    template <class Etype>
6    int
7    OrderedSearchTree<Etype>::RemoveMin( BinaryNode<Etype> * & T )
8    {
9        if( T == NULL )
10           return 0;
11       else if( T->Left != NULL )
12           return RemoveMin( T->Left ) ? T->Size-- : 0;
13
14       BinaryNode<Etype> *Tmp = T;
15       T = T->Right;
16       delete Tmp;
17       return 1;
18   }
```

Figure 18.17   RemoveMin for OrderedSearchTree

```
1   // Internal Remove for OrderedSearchTree:
2   // Remove X from tree rooted at T; return true
3   // if X was found and false otherwise
4
5   template <class Etype>
6   int
7   OrderedSearchTree<Etype>::
8   Remove( const Etype & X, BinaryNode<Etype> * & T )
9   {
10      BinaryNode<Etype> *Tmp = NULL;
11
12      if( T == NULL )
13          return 0;
14      else
15      if( X < T->Element )    // Go left
16          return Remove( X, T->Left ) ? T->Size-- : 0;
17      else
18      if( T->Element < X )    // Go right
19          return Remove( X, T->Right ) ? T->Size-- : 0;
20      else
21      if( T->Left != NULL && T->Right != NULL )   // Two children
22      {
23          Tmp = (BinaryNode<Etype> *) FindMin( T->Right );
24          T->Element = Tmp->Element;
25          T->Size--;
26          return RemoveMin( T->Right );          // Remove minimum
27      }
28          // One or zero children
29      Tmp = T;
30      T = T->Left != NULL ? T->Left : T->Right;
31      delete Tmp;
32      return 1;
33  }
```

Figure 18.18   Remove for OrderedSearchTree class

18.3   Analysis of Binary Search Tree Operations

It is easy to see that the cost of each binary search tree operation (Insert, Find, Remove) is proportional to the number of nodes accessed during the operation. We can thus charge the access of any node in the tree a cost of 1 plus its depth (recall that the depth measures the number of edges on a path rather than the number of nodes). This tells us the cost of a successful search.

> The cost of an operation is proportional to the depth of the last accessed node. This is logarithmic for a well-balanced tree, but could be as bad as linear for a degenerate tree.

Figure 18.19 shows two trees. On the left is a balanced tree of 15 nodes. The cost to access any node is at most four units, and some nodes require fewer accesses. This is exactly analogous to the situation that occurs in the binary search algorithm. We see that if the tree is perfectly balanced, then we have logarithmic access cost.

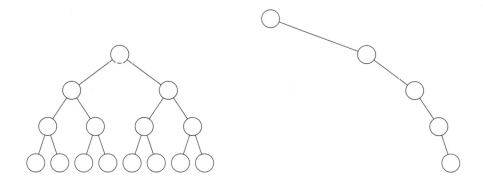

Figure 18.19 Balanced tree on the left has a depth of $\lfloor \log N \rfloor$; unbalanced tree on the right has a depth of $N - 1$

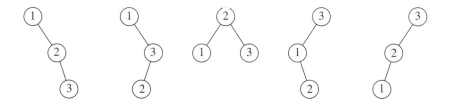

Figure 18.20 Binary search trees that can result from inserting a permutation 1, 2, and 3; the balanced tree in the middle is twice as likely as any other

Unfortunately, we have no guarantee that the tree is perfectly balanced. The second tree in Figure 18.19 is the classic example of an unbalanced tree. Here all N nodes are on the path to the deepest node, so the worst-case search time is $O(N)$. Because the search tree has degenerated to a linked list, we also know that the average time required to search in *this particular instance* is half the cost of the worst case and is also $O(N)$. So we have two extremes: In the best case we have logarithmic access cost, and in the worst case we have linear access cost. What then is the average? Do most binary search trees tend toward the balanced or unbalanced case, or is there some middle ground, such as $\sqrt{N}$? The answer that we will derive is identical to what we saw for quicksort: The average is 38 percent worse than the best case.

On average, the depth is 38 percent worse than the best case. This result is identical to quicksort. We prove in this section that the average depth over all nodes in a binary search tree is logarithmic, under the assumption that each tree is created as a result of random insertion sequences (with no Remove operations). To see what this means, consider the result of inserting three items into an empty binary search tree. Since only their relative ordering is important, we can assume without loss of generality that the three items are 1, 2, and 3. Then there are six possible insertion orders: (1,2,3), (1,3,2), (2,1,3), (2,3,1), (3,1,2), and (3,2,1). We will assume in our proof that each of these insertion orders is equally likely. The binary search trees that can result from these insertions are shown in Figure 18.20. Notice that the tree with root 2 is formed from either the insertion sequence (2,3,1) or the sequence (2,1,3). Thus some trees are more likely than others, and as we will see, it turns out that balanced trees are more likely than unbalanced trees (though this is not evident from the three element case). We begin with the following definition:

DEFINITION: The *internal path length* of a binary tree is equal to the sum of the depths of its nodes.

When we divide the internal path length of a tree by the number of nodes in the tree, we obtain the average depth of a node in the tree. Adding 1 to this average gives the average cost of a successful search in the tree. What we want, therefore, is to compute the average internal path length for a binary search tree, where the average is taken over all (equally probable) input permutations. This is easily done by viewing the tree recursively and using techniques we saw in the analysis of quicksort given in Section 8.6.

> The *internal path length* is used to measure the cost of a successful search.

The internal path length of a binary search tree is approximately $1.38N\log N$, *on average, under the assumption that all permutations are equally likely.*

Theorem 18.1

Let $D(N)$ be the average internal path length for trees of N nodes. $D(1) = 0$. An N-node tree T consists of an i-node left subtree and an $(N-i-1)$-node right subtree, plus a root at depth 0 for $0 \le i < N$. By assumption, each value of i is equally likely. For a given i, $D(i)$ is the average internal path length of the left subtree with respect to its root. In T, all these nodes are one level deeper. Thus the average contribution of the nodes in the left subtree to the internal path length of T is $(1/N)\sum_{i=0}^{N-1}D(i)$ plus 1 for each node in the left subtree. The same holds for the right subtree. We thus obtain the recurrence formula $D(N) = (2/N)\left(\sum_{i=0}^{N-1}D(i)\right) + N - 1$, which is identical to the quicksort recurrence solved in Section 8.6. Thus we obtain an average internal path length of $O(N\log N)$.

Proof

The *external path length* is used to measure the cost of an unsuccessful search.

The insertion algorithm implies that the cost of an insert is exactly equal to the cost of an unsuccessful search, which we will measure by using the *external path length*. In an insertion or unsuccessful search, we eventually reach the test T==NULL. Recall that in a tree of N nodes, there are $N + 1$ NULL pointers. The external path length measures the total number of nodes that are accessed, including the NULL node for each of these $N + 1$ NULL pointers. (The NULL node is sometimes called an *external tree node*, which explains the term *external path length*. As we will see later, it is sometimes convenient to use a sentinel to replace the NULL node.)

DEFINITION: The *external path length* of a binary search tree is the sum of the cost of accessing all $N + 1$ NULL pointers. The terminating NULL node is considered a node for these purposes.

If we divide the average external path length by $N + 1$, we obtain the average cost of an unsuccessful search or insertion. Just as was the case for the binary search algorithm, the average cost of an unsuccessful search is only slightly more than the cost of a successful search. This follows from the following easily proved theorem:

Theorem 18.2	*For any tree T, let IPL(T) be the internal path length of T, and let EPL(T) be its external path length. Then, if T has N nodes,* $EPL(T) = IPL(T) + 2N.$
Proof	*This theorem is proved by induction and is left as Exercise 18.11.*

Random Remove operations do not preserve the randomness of a tree. The effects are not completely understood theoretically, but it appears that they are negligible in practice.

It is tempting to say immediately that these results imply that the average running time of all operations is $O(\log N)$. This is true in practice but has not been established analytically because the assumption used to prove the results above do not take into account the deletion algorithm. In fact, close examination suggests that we might be in trouble with our deletion algorithm because the Remove always replaces a two-child deleted node with a node from the right subtree. This would seem to have the effect of eventually unbalancing the tree and tending to make it left-heavy. It has been shown that if we build a random binary search tree and then perform roughly N^2 pairs of random Insert/Remove combinations, then the binary search trees will have an expected depth of $O(\sqrt{N})$. However it has never been shown that a reasonable number of random Insert and Remove operations (in which the order of Insert and Remove is also random) unbalances the tree in any observable way, and in fact for small search trees, the Remove algorithm seems to balance the tree. Consequently, it is reasonable to assume that for random input, all operations will behave in logarithmic average time, although this has not been proven mathematically. Exercise 18.30 describes some alternate deletion strategies. All of them appear to exhibit degenerate behavior for sufficiently long random sequences.

The most important problem is not the potential imbalance caused by the Remove algorithm, but instead is the fact that if the input sequence is sorted, then the worst-case tree occurs. When this happens, we are in deep trouble: We have linear time per operation (for a series of N operations) rather than logarithmic cost per operation. This is analogous to passing items to quicksort but having bubble sort executed instead. The resulting running time is completely unacceptable. Moreover, it is not just sorted input that is problematic but any input that contains long sequences of nonrandomness. One solution to this problem is to insist on an extra structural condition called balance: No node is allowed to get too deep.

There are several algorithms to implement *balanced binary search trees*. Most are much more complicated than the standard binary search trees, and all take longer on average for insertion and deletion. They do, however, provide protection against the embarrassingly simple cases, and because they are so balanced they also tend to give faster access time. Typically, their internal path lengths are very close to the optimal $N \log N$ rather than $1.38N \log N$, so searching time is roughly 25 percent faster.

> *A balanced binary search tree adds a structure property to guarantee logarithmic depth in the worst case. Updates are slower but accesses are faster.*

18.4   AVL Trees

The first balanced binary search tree was the *AVL tree* (named after its discoverers, Adelson-Velskii and Landis). The AVL tree illustrates the ideas that are thematic for a wide class of balanced binary search trees. The AVL tree is a binary search tree that has an additional balance condition. This balance condition must be easy to maintain and ensures that the depth of the tree is $O(\log N)$. The simplest idea is to require that the left and right subtrees have the same height. Recursion dictates that this idea applies to all nodes in the tree, since each node is itself a root of some subtree. This balance condition ensures that the depth of the tree is logarithmic, but it is too restrictive because it is too difficult to insert new items while maintaining balance. Thus the AVL tree uses a notion of balance that is somewhat weaker but still strong enough to guarantee logarithmic depth.

> *The AVL tree was the first balanced binary search tree. It has historical significance and also illustrates most of the ideas that are used in other schemes.*

18.4.1   Properties

DEFINITION: An *AVL tree* is a binary search tree with the additional balance property that, for any node in the tree, the height of the left and right subtrees can differ by at most 1. As usual, the height of an empty subtree is −1.

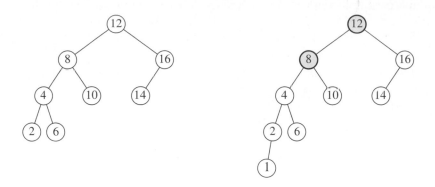

Figure 18.21 Two binary search trees: the left tree is an AVL tree, but the right tree is not (unbalanced nodes are darkened)

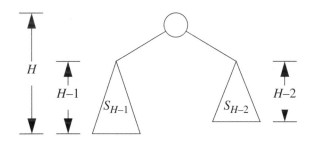

Figure 18.22 Minimum tree of height H

Every node in an AVL tree has subtrees whose heights differ by at most 1. An empty subtree has height –1.

Figure 18.21 shows two binary search trees. The tree on the left satisfies the AVL balance condition and is thus an AVL tree. The tree on the right, which results from inserting 1 using the usual algorithm, is not an AVL tree because the darkened nodes have left subtrees whose heights are 2 larger than their right subtrees. If 13 were inserted using the usual algorithm, then node 16 would also be in violation because the left subtree would have height 1 while the right subtree would have height –1.

The AVL tree has height at most roughly 44 percent greater than the minimum.

The AVL balance condition implies that the tree has only logarithmic depth. To prove this, we need to show that a tree of height H must have at least C^H nodes for some constant $C > 1$. In other words, the minimum number of nodes in a tree is exponential in its height. If so, then the maximum depth of an N item tree is given by $\log_C N$.

An AVL tree of height H has at least $F_{H+3} - 1$ nodes, where F_i is the ith Fibonacci number (see Section 7.3.4).

Theorem 18.3

Let S_H be the size of the smallest AVL tree of height H. Clearly $S_0 = 1$ and $S_1 = 2$. Figure 18.22 shows that the smallest AVL tree of height H must have subtrees of height $H - 1$ and $H - 2$, because at least one subtree has height $H - 1$ and the balance condition implies that subtree heights can differ by at most one. These subtrees must themselves have the fewest number of nodes for their height, so $S_H = S_{H-1} + S_{H-2} + 1$. It is then a simple matter to complete the proof by using an induction argument.

Proof

From Exercise 7.7 we know that $F_i \approx \phi^i / \sqrt{5}$, where $\phi = (1 + \sqrt{5})/2 \approx 1.618$. Consequently, an AVL tree of height H has at least (roughly) $\phi^{H+3}/\sqrt{5}$ nodes. This allows us to conclude that its depth is at most logarithmic. A precise calculation allows us to determine that the height of an AVL tree satisfies

$$H < 1.44\log (N + 2) - 1.328 \qquad\qquad (18.1)$$

so the worst-case height is at most 44 percent more than the minimum possible for binary trees.

As we will see, the depth of an average node in a randomly constructed AVL tree is very close to $\log N$. The exact answer has not yet been established analytically. It is not even known if the form is $\log N + C$ or $(1 + \varepsilon) \log N + C$, for some ε that would be approximately 0.01. Simulations have been unable to convincingly demonstrate that one form is more plausible than the other.

> The depth of a typical node in an AVL tree is very close to the optimal $\log N$.

A consequence of these arguments is that all searching operations in an AVL tree have logarithmic worst-case bounds. The difficulty is that operations that change the tree, such as `Insert` and `Remove`, are not quite as simple as before, because as we can see in Figure 18.21, an insertion (or deletion) can destroy the balance of several nodes in the tree. The balance must then be restored before the operation can be considered complete. We will describe the insertion algorithm and leave deletion for Exercise 18.13.

> An update in an AVL tree could destroy the balance. We must then rebalance before the operation is complete.

The key observation, which also applies for almost all of the balanced search tree algorithms, is that after an insertion, only nodes that are on the path from the insertion point to the root might have their balances altered because only those nodes have their subtrees altered. As we follow the path up to the root and update the balancing information, we may find a node whose new balance violates the AVL condition. We will show how to rebalance the tree at the first (that is, the

> Only nodes on the path from the root to the insertion point can have their balances altered.

deepest) such node, and we will prove that this rebalancing guarantees that the entire tree satisfies the AVL property.

If we fix the balance at the deepest unbalanced node, we will rebalance the entire tree. There are four cases that we might have to fix; two are mirror-images of the other two.

Let us call the node that must be rebalanced X. Since any node has at most two children, and a height imbalance requires that X's two subtrees' heights differ by two, it is easy to see that a violation might occur in four cases:

1. An insertion into the left subtree of the left child of X.
2. An insertion into the right subtree of the left child of X.
3. An insertion into the left subtree of the right child of X.
4. An insertion into the right subtree of the right child of X.

Cases 1 and 4 are mirror-image symmetries with respect to X, as are cases 2 and 3. Consequently, as a matter of theory, there are two basic cases. From a programming perspective, of course, there are still four cases (and numerous special cases).

Balance is restored by tree rotations. A *single rotation* switches the roles of the parent and child while maintaining search order.

The first case, in which the insertion occurs on the "outside" (that is, left-left or right-right), is fixed by a *single rotation* of the tree. A single rotation switches the roles of the parent and child while maintaining search order. The second case, in which the insertion occurs on the "inside" (that is, left-right or right-left) is handled by the slightly more complex *double rotation*. These are fundamental operations on the tree that we will see used several times in balanced tree algorithms. The remainder of this section describes these rotations and proves that they suffice to maintain the balance condition.

18.4.2   Single Rotation

A single rotation handles the outside cases (1 and 4). We rotate between a node and its child. The result is a binary search tree that satisfies the AVL property.

Figure 18.23 shows the single rotation that fixes case 1. The before picture is on the left, and the after is on the right. Let us analyze carefully what is going on. Node k_2 violates the AVL balance property because its left subtree is two levels deeper than its right subtree (the dashed lines are used to mark the levels in this section). The situation depicted is the only possible case 1 scenario that allows k_2 to satisfy the AVL property before the insertion but violate it afterward. Subtree A has grown to an extra level, causing it to be exactly two levels deeper than C. B cannot be at the same level as the new A because then k_2 would have been out of balance *before* the insertion, and B cannot be at the same level as C because then k_1 would have been the first node on the path that was in violation of the AVL balancing condition (and we are claiming that k_2 is).

To ideally rebalance the tree, we would like to move A up one level and C down one level. Note that this is more than the AVL property would require. To do this, we rearrange nodes into an equivalent search tree, as shown in the illustration on the right of Figure 18.23. Here is an abstract scenario: Visualize the tree as being flexible, grab the child node k_1, close your eyes, and shake the tree, letting gravity take hold. The result is that k_1 will be the new root. The binary search tree property tells us that in the original tree $k_2 > k_1$, so k_2 becomes the right child of k_1 in the new tree. A and C remain as the left child of k_1 and right child of k_2, respectively. Subtree B, which holds items that are between k_1 and k_2 in the original tree can be placed as k_2's left child in the new tree and satisfy all the ordering requirements.

As a result of this work, which requires only the few pointer changes shown in Figure 18.24,[1] we have another binary tree that is an AVL tree. This happens because A moves up one level, B stays at the same level, and C moves down one level. k_1 and k_2 not only satisfy the AVL requirements, but they also have subtrees that are exactly the same height. Furthermore, the new height of the entire subtree is *exactly the same* as the height of the original subtree prior to the insertion that caused A to grow. Thus no further updating of the heights on the path to the root is needed, and consequently, *no further rotations are needed.*

One rotation suffices to fix cases 1 and 4 in an AVL tree.

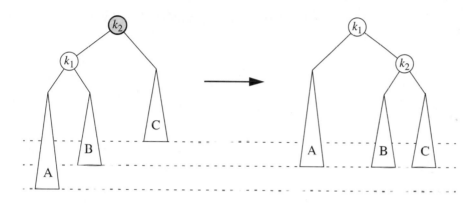

Figure 18.23   Single rotation to fix case 1

```
1   // Rotate binary tree note with left child
2   // For AVL trees, this is a single rotation for case 1
3
4   template <class Etype>
5   BinaryNode<Etype> *
6   RotateWithLeftChild( BinaryNode<Etype> *K2 )
7   {
8       BinaryNode<Etype> *K1 = K2->Left;
9       K2->Left = K1->Right;
10      K1->Right = K2;
11      return K1;
12  }
```

Figure 18.24   Code for single rotation (case 1)

---

1. It would be better if the single and double rotation routines accepted a pointer passed by reference. Recall, however, that the template matching algorithm might not find this as a match. Since these routines are widely used in this chapter, we stick with safe C++ syntax. Note that we could use the more convenient syntax for member functions.

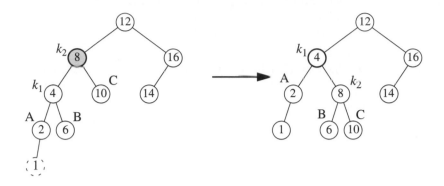

Figure 18.25 Single rotation fixes AVL tree after insertion of 1

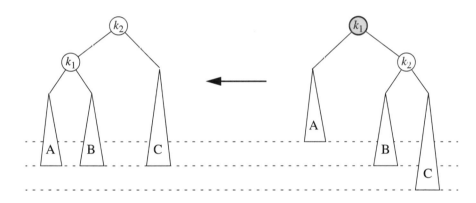

Figure 18.26 Symmetric single rotation to fix case 4

```
 1  // Rotate binary tree note with right child
 2  // For AVL trees, this is a single rotation for case 4
 3
 4  template <class Etype>
 5  BinaryNode<Etype> *
 6  RotateWithRightChild( BinaryNode<Etype> *K1 )
 7  {
 8      BinaryNode<Etype> *K2 = K1->Right;
 9      K1->Right = K2->Left;
10      K2->Left = K1;
11      return K2;
12  }
```

Figure 18.27 Code for single rotation (case 4)

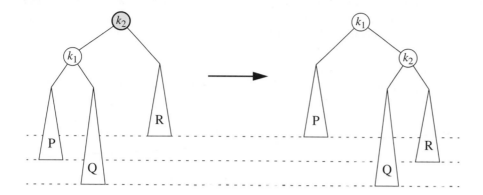

Figure 18.28   Single rotation does not fix case 2

Figure 18.25 shows that after the insertion of 1 into an AVL tree, node 8 becomes unbalanced. This is clearly a case 1 problem because 1 is in 8's left-left subtree. Thus we do a single rotation between 8 and 4, obtaining the tree on the right. As we mentioned earlier, case 4 represents a symmetric case. The required rotation is shown in Figure 18.26, and the code that implements it is shown in Figure 18.27.

18.4.3   Double Rotation

The single rotation has one problem: As Figure 18.28 shows, it does not work for case 2 (or by symmetry, for case 3). The problem is that subtree Q is too deep, and a single rotation does not make it any less deep. The *double rotation* that solves the problem is shown in Figure 18.29.

The fact that subtree Q in Figure 18.29 has had an item inserted into it guarantees that it is not empty. We may assume that it has a root and two (possibly empty) subtrees, so we may view the tree as four subtrees connected by three nodes. We therefore rename the four trees A, B, C, and D. As the diagram suggests, exactly one of tree B or C is two levels deeper than D, but we cannot be sure which one. It turns out not to matter; in Figure 18.29 both B and C are drawn at 1.5 levels below D.

To rebalance, we see that we cannot leave k_3 as the root, and a rotation between k_3 and k_1 was shown in Figure 18.28 not to work, so the only alternative is to place k_2 as the new root. This forces k_1 to be k_2's left child and k_3 to be k_2's right child, and it also completely determines the resulting locations of the four subtrees. It is easy to see that the resulting tree satisfies the AVL property, and as was the case with the single rotation, it restores the height to what it was before the insertion, thus guaranteeing that all rebalancing and height updating is complete.

The single rotation does not fix the inside cases (2 and 3). These cases require a double rotation, involving three nodes and four subtrees.

As an example, Figure 18.30 shows the result of inserting 5 into an AVL tree. We see that a height imbalance is caused at node 8, and that we have a case 2 problem. We perform a double rotation at that node, resulting in the tree on the right.

A double rotation is equivalent to two single rotations.

Figure 18.31 shows that the symmetric case 3 can also be fixed by a double rotation. Finally, we remark that although a double rotation appears complex, it turns out that it is equivalent to the following:

- Rotate between X's child and grandchild.
- Rotate between X and its new child.

The code to implement the case 2 double rotation is compact and is shown in Figure 18.32. The mirror-image code for case 3 is shown in Figure 18.33.

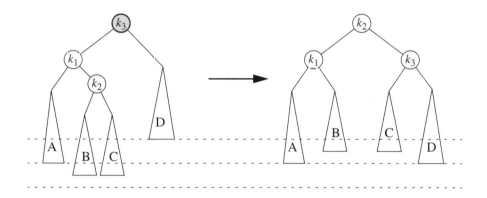

Figure 18.29 Left-right double rotation to fix case 2

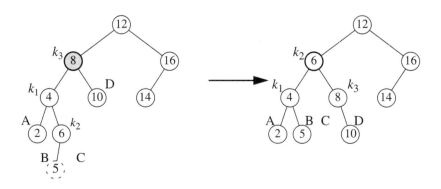

Figure 18.30 Double rotation fixes AVL tree after insertion of 5

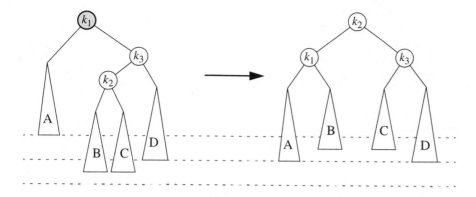

Figure 18.31   Left-right double rotation to fix case 3

```
1  // Double rotate binary tree node: first left child
2  // with its right child; then node K3 with new left child
3  // For AVL trees, this is a double rotation for case 2
4
5  template <class Etype>
6  BinaryNode<Etype> *
7  DoubleRotateWithLeftChild( BinaryNode<Etype> *K3 )
8  {
9      K3->Left = RotateWithRightChild( K3->Left );
10     return RotateWithLeftChild( K3 );
11 }
```

Figure 18.32   Code for double rotation (case 2)

```
1  // Double rotate binary tree node: first right child
2  // with its left child; then node K1 with new right child
3  // For AVL trees, this is a double rotation for case 3
4
5  template <class Etype>
6  BinaryNode<Etype> *
7  DoubleRotateWithRightChild( BinaryNode<Etype> *K1 )
8  {
9      K1->Right = RotateWithLeftChild( K1->Right );
10     return RotateWithRightChild( K1 );
11 }
```

Figure 18.33   Code for double rotation (case 3)

18.4.4 Summary of AVL Insertion

A casual AVL implementation is relatively painless. However, it is not efficient. Better balanced search trees have since been discovered, so it is not worthwhile to implement an AVL tree.

Let us briefly summarize how an AVL insertion is implemented. A recursive algorithm turns out to be the simplest method. To insert a new node with key X into an AVL tree T, we recursively insert it into the appropriate subtree of T (let us call this T_{LR}). If the height of T_{LR} does not change, then we are done. Otherwise, if a height imbalance appears in T, we do the appropriate single or double rotation, depending on X and the keys in T and T_{LR}, and are done (because the old height is the same as the post-rotation height). This recursive description is best described as a casual implementation. For instance, at each node we compare the subtree's heights; in general, it is more efficient to store the result of the comparison in the node rather than maintaining the height information. This avoids repetitive calculation of balance factors. Furthermore, recursion incurs substantial overhead over an iterative version, because in effect we go down the tree and completely back up instead of stopping as soon as a rotation is performed. Consequently, other balanced search tree schemes are used.

18.5 Red Black Trees

A *red black tree* is a good alternative to the AVL tree. The coding details tend to give a faster implementation because a single top-down pass can be used during the insertion and deletion routines.

A historically popular alternative to the AVL tree is the *red black tree*. As on AVL trees, operations on red black trees take logarithmic worst-case time. The main advantage of red black trees is that a single top-down pass can be used during the insertion and deletion routines. This contrasts with an AVL tree in which a pass down the tree is used to establish the insertion point, and a second pass up the tree is used to update heights and possibly rebalance. As a result, a careful nonrecursive implementation of the red black tree is simpler and faster than an AVL tree implementation.

A red black tree is a binary search tree with the following ordering properties:

Consecutive red nodes are disallowed, and all paths have the same number of black nodes.

Red nodes are shaded throughout this chapter.

1. Every node is colored either red or black.
2. The root is black.
3. If a node is red, its children must be black.
4. Every path from a node to a NULL pointer must contain the same number of black nodes.

The depth of a red black tree is guaranteed to be logarithmic. Typically the depth is the same as an AVL tree.

In our discussion of red black trees, we will draw red nodes by shading them. Figure 18.34 shows a red black tree. Every path from the root to a NULL node contains three black nodes.

We can show by induction that if every path from the root to a NULL node contains B black nodes, then there must be at least $2^B - 1$ black nodes in the tree. Furthermore, since the root is black and we may not have two consecutive red nodes on a path, we find that the height of a red black tree is at most $2\log(N+1)$. Consequently, searching is guaranteed to be a logarithmic operation.

The difficulty, as usual, is that operations can change the tree and possibly destroy the coloring properties. This makes insertion difficult and removal especially difficult. We will discuss and implement insertion first and then examine the deletion algorithm.

18.5.1 Bottom-Up Insertion

As we know, a new item is always inserted as a leaf in the tree. If we color a new item black, then we are certain to violate property 4 because we will create a longer path of black nodes. Thus a new item must be colored red. If the parent is black, we are done; thus the insertion of 25 into the tree in Figure 18.34 is trivial. If the parent is already red, then we will violate property 3 by having consecutive red nodes. In this case, we have to adjust the tree to ensure that property 3 is enforced, without introducing a violation of property 4. The basic operations that are used to do this are color changes and tree rotations.

New items must be colored red. If the parent is already red, we must recolor and/or rotate to remove consecutive red nodes.

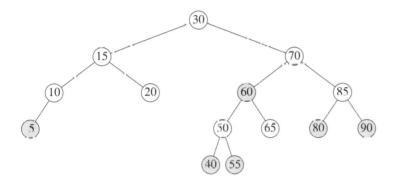

Figure 18.34   Example of a red black tree; insertion sequence is 10, 85, 15, 70, 20, 60, 30, 50, 65, 80, 90, 40, 5, 55)

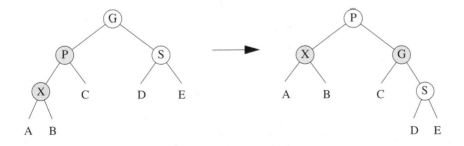

Figure 18.35   If *S* is black, then a single rotation between the parent and grandparent, with appropriate color changes, restores property 3 if *X* is an outside grandchild

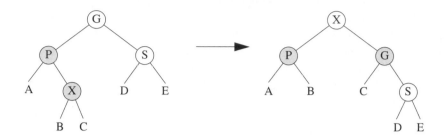

Figure 18.36   If *S* is black, then a double rotation involving *X*, the parent, and the grandparent, with appropriate color changes, restores property 3 if *X* is an inside grandchild

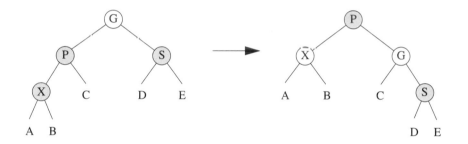

Figure 18.37   If *S* is red, then a single rotation between the parent and grandparent, with appropriate color changes, restores property 3 between *X* and *P*

If the parent's sibling is black, then a single or double rotation fixes things, in the same way as an AVL tree.

There are several cases (each with a mirror-image symmetry) to consider if the parent is red. First, suppose that the sibling of the parent is black (we adopt the convention that NULL nodes are black). This would apply for the insertions of 3 or 8 but not for the insertion of 99. Let *X* be the newly added leaf, *P* be its parent, *S* be the sibling of the parent (if it exists), and *G* be the grandparent. Only *X* and *P* are red in this case; *G* is black because otherwise there would be two consecutive red nodes *prior* to the insertion, in violation of the property 3. Adopting the AVL tree terminology, we say that relative to *G*, *X* can be either an outside or inside node. If *X* is an outside grandchild, then a single rotation of its parent and grandparent along with some color changes will restore the property 3. If *X* is an inside grandchild, then a double rotation along with some color changes suffices. The single rotation is shown in Figure 18.35; the double rotation is shown in Figure 18.36. Even though *X* is a leaf, we have drawn a more general case that allows *X* to be in the middle of the tree. We will use this more general rotation later. Before continuing, let us observe why these rotations are correct. We need to be sure that there are never two consecutive red nodes. In Figure 18.36, for instance, it is easy to see that the only possible instances of consecutive red nodes would be between P and one of its children or between G and C. But A, B, and C must be black; otherwise, there would have been additional property 3 violations in the original tree. In the original tree, there is one black node on the path from the subtree root to A, B, and C, and there are two black nodes on the paths to D and E. It is easy to check that this is still the case after the rotation and recoloring.

So far so good. But what happens if S is red, as is the case when we attempt to insert 79 into the tree in Figure 18.34? Then neither the single nor the double rotation works because both result in consecutive red nodes. In fact, it is easy to see that in this case three nodes must be on the path to D and E, and only one can be black. This tells us that both S and the subtree's new root must be colored red. For instance, the single rotation case that occurs when X is an outside grandchild is shown in Figure 18.37. Although this seems to work, there is a problem: What happens if the parent of the subtree root (that is, X's original great grandparent) is also red? We could percolate this procedure up toward the root until we no longer have two consecutive red nodes or we reach the root (which will be recolored black). But then we would be back to making a pass up the tree, as in the AVL tree.

> If the parent's sibling is red, after we fix things, we will induce consecutive red nodes at a higher level. We would need to iterate up the tree to fix things.

18.5.2   Top-Down Red Black Trees

To avoid the possibility of having to rotate up the tree, we apply a top-down procedure as we are searching for the insertion point. Specifically, we guarantee that when we arrive at a leaf and insert a node, S will not be red. Then we can just add a red leaf and if necessary use exactly one rotation (either single or double). The procedure is conceptually easy.

> To avoid iterating back up the tree, as we descend the tree, we ensure that the siblings parent is not red.

On the way down, when we see a node X that has two red children, we make X red and its two children black. Figure 18.38 shows this color flip. It is easy to see that the number of black nodes on paths below X remains unchanged. However, if X's parent is red, we will introduce two consecutive red nodes. But in this case, we can apply either the single rotation in Figure 18.35 or the double rotation in Figure 18.36. But what if X's parent's sibling is also red? The answer is, *This cannot happen.* If on the way down the tree we see a node Y that has two red children, we know that Y's grandchildren must be black, and since Y's children are also made black, even after the rotation that may occur, we will not see another red node for two levels. Thus when we see X, if X's parent is red, it is not possible for X's parent's sibling to be red also.

> This can be done with color flips and/or rotations

As an example, suppose we want to insert 45 into the tree in Figure 18.34. On the way down the tree, we see node 50, which has two red children. Thus we perform a color flip, making 50 red, and 40 and 55 black. The result is shown in Figure 18.39. However, now 50 and 60 are both red. We perform a single rotation (because 50 is an outside node) between 60 and 70, making 60 the black root of 30's right subtree, and 70 and 50 both red. This is shown in Figure 18.40. We then continue, performing an identical action if we see other nodes on the path that contain two red children. It happens that there are none.

When we get to the leaf, we insert 45 as a red node, and since the parent is black, we are done. The resulting tree is shown in Figure 18.41. Had the parent been red, we would have needed to perform one rotation.

Figure 18.38   Color flip; only if X's parent is red do we continue with a rotation

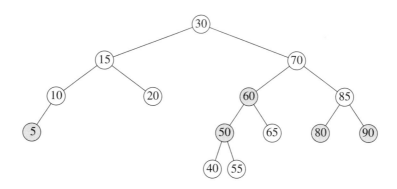

Figure 18.39   Color flip at 50 induces a violation; because it is outside, a single rotation fixes it

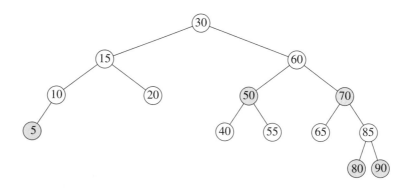

Figure 18.40   Result of single rotation that fixes violation at node 50

As Figure 18.41 shows, the red black tree that results is frequently very well balanced. Experiments suggest that the number of nodes traversed during an average red black tree search is almost identical to the average for AVL trees, even though the red black balancing properties are slightly weaker. The advantage of the red black trees is the relatively low overhead required to perform insertion, and the fact that in practice rotations occur relatively infrequently.

18.5.3   C++ Implementation

An actual implementation is complicated not only by the host of possible rotations but also by the possibility that some subtrees (such as 10's right subtree) might be empty and by the special case of dealing with the root (which among other things, has no parent). To remove special cases, we will use two sentinels:

> **We remove special cases by using a sentinel for the NULL pointer and a pseudo-root. This requires minor modifications of almost every routine.**

- NullNode is used in place of a NULL pointer. NullNode will always be colored black.

- Header will be used as a pseudo-root. It will have key value $-\infty$ and a right pointer to the real root.

Because of this, even basic routines such as IsEmpty need to be altered. Consequently, it does not make sense to inherit from SearchTree. The class interface is thus written from scratch. Its public part is shown in Figure 18.42 and the private section is shown in Figure 18.43. Line 21 reflects the fact that the balancing information used by red black trees is the node color. Recalling that by default the BinaryNode constructor sets this member to one, we see that Black must be one. This is why the enum at line 53 explicitly assigns values to Red and Black. Lines 55 and 56 declare the sentinels that were discussed above. Four pointers, Current, Parent, Grand, and Great, are used in the Insert routine. Their placement in the interface (at lines 59 to 62) indicates that they are essentially global variables, because as we will see, it is convenient to have them shared by Insert and the private routine HandleReorient.

> **On the way down, we maintain pointers to the current, parent, grandparent, and great-grandparent nodes.**

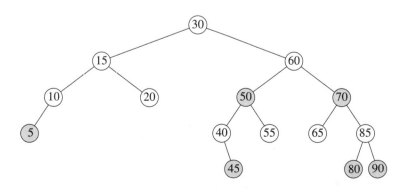

Figure 18.41   Insertion of 45 as a red node

```
 1  // RedBlackTree class interface
 2  //
 3  // Etype: must have zero-parameter and copy constructor,
 4  //      and must have operator<, operator!=, and operator=
 5  // CONSTRUCTION: with (a) Negative Infinity sentinel
 6  // All copying of RedBlackTree objects is DISALLOWED
 7  //
 8  // ******************PUBLIC OPERATIONS********************
 9  // void Insert( Etype X )  --> Insert X
10  // Etype Find( )           --> Return item that matches X
11  // int WasFound( )         --> Return 1 if last Find succeeded
12  // int IsFound( Etype X )  --> Return 1 if X would be found
13  // Etype FindMin( )        --> Return smallest item
14  // Etype FindMax( )        --> Return largest item
15  // int IsEmpty( )          --> Return 1 if empty; else return 0
16  // void MakeEmpty( )       --> Remove all items
17  // ******************ERRORS*******************************
18  // Predefined exception is propagated if new fails
19  // Item in NullNode returned on various degenerate conditions
20
21  #define Color BalancingInfo
22
23  template <class Etype>
24  class RedBlackTree
25  {
26    public:
27      RedBlackTree( const Etype & NegInf );
28      ~RedBlackTree( ) { FreeTree( Header ); delete NullNode; }
29
30      // Add X into the tree; If X already present, do nothing
31      // Return true if insertion was successful
32      int Insert( const Etype & X );
33
34      // Return minimum item in tree
35      // If tree is empty, return undefined
36      const Etype & FindMin( ) const;
37
38      // Return maximum item in tree
39      // If tree is empty, return undefined
40      const Etype & FindMax( ) const;
41
42      // Return item X in tree
43      // If X is not found, return item in NullNode
44      // Result can be checked by calling WasFound
45      const Etype & Find( const Etype & X );
46      int WasFound( ) const { return Current != NullNode; }
47
48      // Routines to make tree empty and test if tree is empty
49      void MakeEmpty( )
50        { FreeTree( Header->Right ); Header->Right = NullNode; }
51      int IsEmpty( ) const { return Header->Right == NullNode; }
```

Figure 18.42   `RedBlackTree` class interface (part 1: public section)

```
52    private:
53      enum { Black = 1, Red = 0 }; // Black==1 for default new
54
55      BinaryNode<Etype> *Header;
56      BinaryNode<Etype> *NullNode;
57
58      // Globals used to traverse down the tree in an insert
59      BinaryNode<Etype> *Current;
60      BinaryNode<Etype> *Parent;
61      BinaryNode<Etype> *Grand;
62      BinaryNode<Etype> *Great;
63
64      void HandleReorient( const Etype & Item );
65      void FreeTree( BinaryNode<Etype> *T );
66
67      // Remove X from the tree; not currently provided
68      int Remove( const Etype & X );
69
70      // Disable operator=
71      const RedBlackTree & operator=( const RedBlackTree & );
72    };
```

Figure 18.43   `RedBlackTree` class interface (part 2: private section)

```
1  // Constructor for RedBlackTree
2
3  template <class Etype>
4  RedBlackTree<Etype>::RedBlackTree( const Etype & NegInf )
5  {
6      NullNode = new BinaryNode<Etype>;
7      Header = new BinaryNode<Etype>( NegInf );
8
9      NullNode->Left = NullNode->Right =
10             Header->Left = Header->Right = NullNode;
11  }
```

Figure 18.44   `RedBlackTree` constructor

All of the remaining routines are similar to their `SearchTree` counterparts except that they have different implementations. `Remove` is placed in the private section because it is unimplemented. Because of the sentinel nodes, there are some minor but important differences. The constructor must be provided with the value of $-\infty$. The destructor, which is shown at line 28, must `delete` the `NullNode` sentinel. Because we have a sentinel, a failed `Find` command can return the element in `NullNode`. This allows a somewhat simpler implementation of the searching operations. `WasFound`, shown at line 46, compares `Current` against `NullNode` rather than NULL. `MakeEmpty` and `IsEmpty`, shown at lines 49 to 51, require using `Header->Right` (rather than the typical `Root`) and `NullNode` (rather than NULL).

```
 1  // Call delete for all nodes in RedBlackTree rooted at T
 2
 3  template <class Etype>
 4  void
 5  RedBlackTree<Etype>::FreeTree( BinaryNode<Etype> * T )
 6  {
 7      if( T != NullNode )
 8      {
 9          FreeTree( T->Left );
10          FreeTree( T->Right );
11          delete T;
12      }
13  }
```

Figure 18.45   FreeTree for RedBlackTree class

```
 1  // Return minimum element in RedBlackTree;
 2  // -Infinity sentinel returned if tree is empty
 3
 4  template <class Etype>
 5  const Etype &
 6  RedBlackTree<Etype>::FindMin( ) const
 7  {
 8      BinaryNode<Etype> *Ptr = Header->Right;
 9
10      while( Ptr->Left != NullNode )
11          Ptr = Ptr->Left;
12
13      return Ptr->Element;
14  }
```

Figure 18.46   FindMin for red black trees; note use of Header and
NullNode

The RedBlackTree constructor is shown in Figure 18.44. It merely allocates the two sentinels and sets all their Left and Right pointers to
NullNode.

**Tests against NULL
are replaced by tests
against NullNode.**

Figure 18.45 shows the simplest change that results from the use of the sentinels. The test against NULL is replaced by a test against NullNode.
FindMin, shown in Figure 18.46, illustrates one advantage that comes with the
sentinels. If the tree is empty, then Header->Right is NullNode. Thus Ptr
will initially point at NullNode in this case. Since NullNode->Left is also
NullNode, the while loop fails immediately, and we return the element in the
NullNode sentinel rather than requiring special tests. FindMin is simple, so
the benefit may not be obvious. For more complicated routines, it is not hard to
see that avoiding numerous special cases can make debugging easier.

The `Find` routine shown in Figure 18.47 uses another common trick. Before we begin the search, we place X in the `NullNode` sentinel. Thus we are guaranteed to match X eventually, even if X is not found. If the match occurs at `NullNode`, we can tell that the item was not found. We will use this trick in the `Insert` procedure. Of course, if copying is expensive, the trick may not be wise. However, it is rare that the cost of a single copy impacts performance greatly.

> **When performing a find, we copy X into the `NullNode` sentinel to avoid extra tests.**

The `Insert` procedure follows directly from our description and is shown in Figure 18.48. The `while` loop encompassing lines 12 to 22 descends the tree and fixes nodes that have two red children by calling `HandleReorient`, as shown in Figure 18.49. To do this, it keeps track of not only the current node but also the parent, grandparent, and great-grandparent. Note that after a rotation, the values stored in the grandparent and great-grandparent are no longer correct. However, we are assured that they will be restored by the time they are next needed.

> **The code is relatively compact given the host of cases and the fact that the implementation is nonrecursive. This is why the red black tree performs well.**

When the loop end either X is found (as indicated by `Current != NullNode`) or X is not found (as indicated by `Current==NullNode`). If X is found, we do not want to continue with the insertion so we return false at line 26. Otherwise, X is not already in the tree, and it needs to be made a child of `Parent`. We attempt to allocate a new node (as the new `Current` node), attach it to the parent, and call `HandleReorient` at lines 27 to 34. Since the insertion was successful, we return true at line 35.

The code used to perform a single rotation is shown in the function `Rotate` in Figure 18.50. Because the resultant tree must be attached to a parent, `Rotate` takes the parent node as a parameter. Rather than keep track of the type of rotation (that is, left or right) as we descend the tree, we pass X as a parameter. Since we expect very few rotations during the insertion, it turns out that it is not only simple but actually faster to do it this way.

> **`Rotate` has four possibilities. The `?:` operator collapses the code, but is logically equivalent to an `if else` test.**

```
 1  // Return element that matches X in a RedBlackTree
 2  // WasFound should test if Current is the NullNode sentinel
 3
 4  template <class Etype>
 5  const Etype &
 6  RedBlackTree<Etype>::Find( const Etype & X )
 7  {
 8      NullNode->Element = X;
 9      Current = Header->Right;
10
11      while( Current->Element != X )
12          Current = X < Current->Element ?
13                      Current->Left : Current->Right;
14      return Current->Element;
15  }
```

Figure 18.47   `RedBlackTree Find`; note use of `Header` and `NullNode`

HandleReorient calls Rotate as necessary to perform either a single or double rotation. Since a double rotation is just two single rotations, we can test if we have an inside case, and if so, do an extra rotation between the current node and its parent (by passing the grandparent to Rotate). In either case we rotate between the parent and grandparent (by passing the great-grandparent to Rotate). This is succinctly code in lines 16 to 18 of Figure 18.49.

```
1  // Insert X into RedBlackTree
2  // Return false if X is a duplicate;
3  // otherwise return true
4
5  template <class Etype>
6  int
7  RedBlackTree<Etype>::Insert( const Etype & X )
8  {
9      Current = Parent = Grand = Header;
10     NullNode->Element = X;
11
12     while( Current->Element != X )
13     {
14         Great = Grand; Grand = Parent; Parent = Current;
15         Current = X < Current->Element ?
16                 Current->Left : Current->Right;
17
18             // Check if two red children; fix if so
19         if( Current->Left->Color == Red &&
20                     Current->Right->Color == Red )
21             HandleReorient( X );
22     }
23
24         // Insert fails if already present
25     if( Current != NullNode )
26         return 0;
27     Current = new BinaryNode<Etype>( X, NullNode, NullNode );
28
29         // Attach to parent
30     if( X < Parent->Element )
31         Parent->Left = Current;
32     else
33         Parent->Right = Current;
34     HandleReorient( X );
35     return 1;
36  }
```

Figure 18.48   Insert routine for RedBlackTree

```
1   // Private routine that is called during an insertion
2   // if a node has two red children
3
4   template <class Etype>
5   void
6   RedBlackTree<Etype>::HandleReorient( const Etype & Item )
7   {
8           // Do the color flip
9       Current->Color = Red;
10      Current->Left->Color = Black;
11      Current->Right->Color = Black;
12
13      if( Parent->Color == Red )        // Have to rotate
14      {
15          Grand->Color = Red;
16          if( Item < Grand->Element != Item < Parent->Element )
17              Parent = Rotate( Item, Grand );// Start dbl rotate
18          Current = Rotate( Item, Great );
19          Current->Color = Black;
20      }
21      Header->Right->Color = Black;     // Make root black
22  }
```

Figure 18.49   `HandleReorient`: called if a node has two red children or when new node is inserted

```
1   // Routine to choose and perform 1 of 4 types of rotations
2
3   template <class Etype>
4   BinaryNode<Etype> *
5   Rotate( const Etype & Item, BinaryNode<Etype> *Parent )
6   {
7       if( Item < Parent->Element )
8           return Parent->Left = Item < Parent->Left->Element ?
9               RotateWithLeftChild( Parent->Left ) :   // LL
10              RotateWithRightChild( Parent->Left );   // LR
11      else
12          return Parent->Right = Item < Parent->Right->Element ?
13              RotateWithLeftChild( Parent->Right )    // RL
14              RotateWithRightChild( Parent->Right );  // RR
15  }
```

Figure 18.50   Routine to perform appropriate rotation

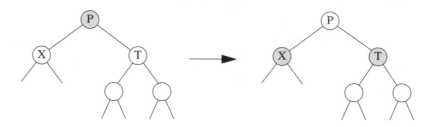

Figure 18.51 *X* has two black children, and both of its sibling's children are black; do a color flip

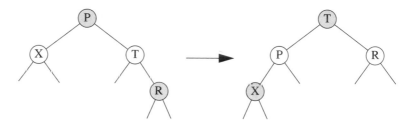

Figure 18.52 *X* has two black children, and the outer child of its sibling is red; do a single rotation

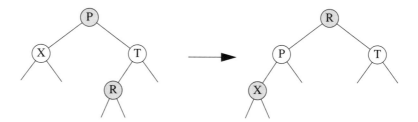

Figure 18.53 *X* has two black children, and the inner child of its sibling is red; do a double rotation

18.5.4   Top-Down Deletion

Deletion in red black trees can also be performed top-down. Needless to say, an actual implementation is fairly complicated because the Remove algorithm for unbalanced search trees is nontrivial in the first place. The normal binary search tree deletion algorithm removes nodes that are leaves or have one child. Recall that nodes with two children are never removed; their contents are just replaced.

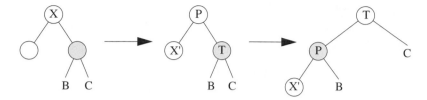

Figure 18.54   *X* is black and at least one child is red; if we fall through to next level and land on a red child, everything is good; if not, we rotate a sibling and parent

If the deleted node is red, then there is no problem. However, if the node that is to be deleted is black, then its removal will violate property 4. The solution to the problem is to ensure that, whenever we are about to delete a node, it is red.

Deletion is fairly complex. The basic idea is to make sure that the deleted node is red.

Throughout this discussion, let *X* be the current node, *T* be its sibling, and *P* be their parent. We begin by coloring the sentinel root red. As we traverse down the tree, we attempt to ensure that *X* is red. When we arrive at a new node, we are certain that *P* is red (inductively, by the invariant we are trying to maintain), and that *X* and *T* are black (because we cannot have two consecutive red nodes). There are two main cases, plus the usual symmetric variants that we omit.

First, suppose that *X* has two black children. There are three subcases, which depend on *T*'s children:

1. *T* has two black children: flip colors (Figure 18.51)
2. *T* has an outer black child: perform a single rotation (Figure 18.52)
3. *T* has an inner black child: perform a double rotation (Figure 18.53)

Examination of the rotations shows that if *T* has two red children, either a single rotation or double rotation will work (so it makes sense to do the single rotation). Notice carefully that if *X* is a leaf, then its two children are black, and so we can always apply one of these three mechanisms to make *X* red.

The second main case is that one of *X*'s children is red. Notice that since the rotations in the first main case always color *X* red, if *X* has a red child, we would introduce consecutive red nodes. Thus we need an alternative solution. In this case we fall through to the next level, obtaining a new *X*, *T*, and *P*. If we are lucky, we will fall onto a red node (we have at least a 50 percent chance that this will happen), making the new current node red. Otherwise, we have the situation shown in Figure 18.54: The current *X* is black, the current *T* is red, and the current *P* is black. We can then rotate *T* and *P*, making *X*'s new parent red; *X* and its new grandparent are black. Now *X* is not yet red, but we are back to the starting point (although one level deeper). This is good enough because it shows that we can iteratively descend the tree. Thus, as long as we eventually reach a node with two black children or land on a red node, we win. This is guaranteed for the deletion algorithm since the two eventual states are:

- X is a leaf. This situation is always handled by the main case since it has two black children.
- X has only one child. If the child is black, the main case applies, and if it is red, we can delete X and make the child black.

Lazy deletion, in which deleted items are merely marked as deleted, is sometimes used. However lazy deletion wastes speace and complicates other routines (see Exercise 18.28).

18.6   AA-Trees

The *AA-tree* is the method of choice when a balanced tree is needed, a casual implementation is acceptable, and deletions are needed.

Because of a host of possible rotations, the red black tree is fairly tricky to code; in particular, the Remove operation is quite challenging. In this section we describe a simple but competitive balanced search tree known as an *AA-tree*. The AA-tree is the method of choice when a balanced tree is needed, a casual implementation is acceptable, and deletions are needed. The AA-tree adds one extra condition to the red black tree: left children may not be red.

This simple restriction greatly simplifies the red black algorithms for two reasons. First, it eliminates about half of the restructuring cases. Second, it simplifies the Remove algorithm by removing an annoying case: If an internal node has only one child, the child must be a red right child, because red left children are now illegal, and a single black child would violate property 4 for red black trees. Thus we can always replace an internal node with the smallest node in its right subtree, and that smallest node will either be a leaf or have a red child that can be easily bypassed and removed.

The *level* of a node in an AA-tree represents the number of left links on the path to the NullNode sentinel.

To simplify the implementation further, we represent balance information in a more direct way. Instead of storing a color with each node, we store its *level*. The level of a node is

- One if the node is a leaf
- The level of its parent, if the node is red
- One less than the level of its parent, if the node is black

The level represents the number of left links on the path to the NullNode sentinel.

A *horizontal link* in an AA-tree is a connection between a node and a child of equal levels. A horizontal link should only go right, and there should not be two consecutive horizontal links.

The result is an *AA-tree*. If we translate the structure requirement from colors to levels, we know that the left child must be one level lower than its parent, and the right child may be zero or one level lower than its parent (but not more). A *horizontal link* is a connection between a node and a child of equal levels. The coloring properties imply

1. Horizontal links are right pointers (because only right children may be red).
2. There may not be two consecutive horizontal links (because there cannot be consecutive red nodes).

3. Nodes at level 2 or higher must have two children.

4. If a node does not have a right horizontal link, then its two children are at the same level.

Figure 18.55 shows a sample AA-tree. The root of this tree is the node with key 30. Searching is done using the usual algorithm. As usual, Insert and Remove are more difficult because the natural binary search tree algorithms may induce a violation of the horizontal link properties. Not surprisingly, it turns out that tree rotations can fix all problems.

18.6.1   Insertion

Insertion of a new item is always done at the bottom level. As usual, this may create problems. In Figure 18.55, insertion of 2 would create a horizontal left link, while insertion of 45 would generate consecutive right links. Consequently, after a node is added at the bottom level, we may need to perform some rotations to restore the horizontal link properties.

Insertion is done by the usual recursive algorithm plus two function calls.

In both cases a single rotation fixes the problem: We remove left horizontal links by rotating between the node and its left child, and we fix consecutive right horizontal links by rotating between the first and second (of the three) nodes joined by the two links. These procedures are called Skew and Split, respectively.

Left horizontal links are removed by a Skew (rotation between a node and its left child); consecutive right horizontal links are fixed by a Split (rotation between a node and its right child).

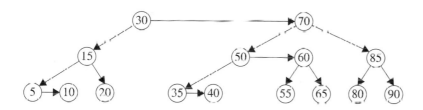

Figure 18.55   AA-tree resulting from insertion of 10, 85, 15, 70, 20, 60, 30, 50, 65, 80, 90, 40, 5, 55, 35

Figure 18.56   Skew is a simple rotation between X and P)

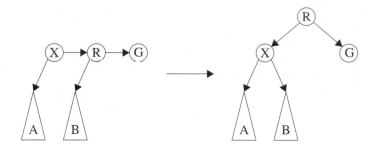

Figure 18.57 `Split` is a simple rotation between `X` and `R`; note that `R`'s level increases

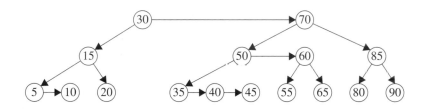

Figure 18.58 After inserting 45 into sample tree; consecutive horizontal links are introduced starting at 35

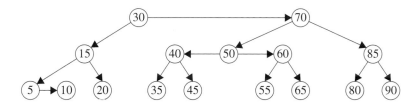

Figure 18.59 After `Split` at 35; introduces a left horizontal link at 50

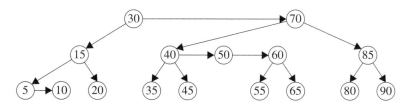

Figure 18.60 After `Skew` at 50; introduces consecutive horizontal nodes starting at 40

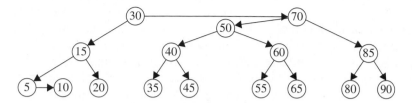

Figure 18.61   After `Split` at 40; 50 is now on the same level as 70, thus inducing an illegal left horizontal link

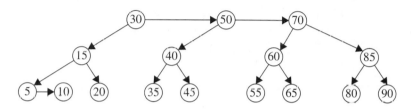

Figure 18.62   After `Skew` at 70; this introduces consecutive horizontal links at 30

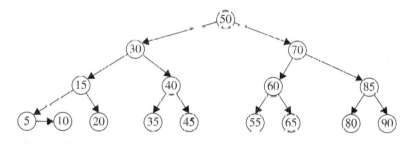

Figure 18.63   After `Split` at 30; insertion is complete

Skew is illustrated in Figure 18.56, and `Split` is illustrated in Figure **Skew precedes**
18.57. A `Skew` removes a left horizontal link but might create consecutive right **Split.**
horizontal links because *P* might be a right horizontal child. Thus we would first
process a `Skew` and then a `Split`. After a `Split`, the middle node increases in
level. This may cause problems for the original parent of *X* by creating either a
left horizontal link or consecutive right horizontal links; both problems can be
fixed by applying the `Skew`/`Split` strategy on the path up toward the root. This
is done automatically if we use recursion, so a recursive implementation of
`Insert` is only two function calls longer than the corresponding unbalanced
search tree routine.

This is a rare algorithm because it is harder to simulate on paper than implement on a computer.

To see the algorithm in action, we show the result of inserting 45 into the AA-tree in Figure 18.55. First, in Figure 18.58 we see that when it is added at the bottom level, consecutive horizontal links form. Skew/Split pairs are applied as necessary from the bottom up toward the root. Thus, at node 35 we see that a Split is needed because of the consecutive horizontal right links. The result of the Split is shown in Figure 18.59. When the recursion backs up to node 50, we see a horizontal left link. Thus we perform a Skew at 50 to remove the horizontal left link (the result is shown in Figure 18.60) and then a Split at 40 to remove the consecutive horizontal right links. The result after the Split is shown in Figure 18.61. The result of the Split is that 50 is on level 3, and is a left horizontal child of 70. Therefore we need to perform another Skew/Split pair. The Skew at 70 removes the left horizontal link at the top level but creates consecutive right horizontal nodes, as shown in Figure 18.62. When the final Split is applied, the consecutive horizontal nodes are removed, and 50 becomes the new root of the tree. The result is shown in Figure 18.63.

18.6.2   Deletion

Deletion is made easier because the one-child case can only occur at level one and we are willing to use recursion.

For general binary search trees, the Remove algorithm is broken down into three cases: The item to be removed is a leaf, has one child, or has two children. For AA-trees we treat the one-child case the same way as the two-child case because the one-child case can only occur at level 1. Furthermore, the two-child case is also easy: The node used as the replacement value is guaranteed to be at level 1, and at worst has only a right horizontal link. Thus everything boils down to being able to delete a level-one node. Clearly this might affect the balance (consider, for instance, the removal of 20 in Figure 18.63).

Let T be the current node, and assume that we are using recursion. If the deletion has altered one of T's children (only the child entered by the recursive call could actually be affected, but for simplicity we do not keep track of it) to two less than T's level, then T's level needs to be lowered also. Furthermore, if T has a horizontal right link, then its right child's level must also be lowered. At this point we could have six nodes on the same level: T, T's horizontal right child R, R's two children, and those children's horizontal right children. Figure 18.64 shows the simplest possible scenario.

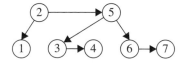

Figure 18.64   When 1 is deleted, all nodes become level 1, introducing horizontal left links

After node 1 is removed, node 2 and thus node 5 become level-one nodes. First we must fix the left horizontal link that is now introduced between nodes 5 and 3. This essentially requires two rotations (one between nodes 5 and 3, and then one between nodes 5 and 4). In this case the current node T is not involved. On the other hand, if a deletion came from the right side, then T's left node could suddenly become horizontal; that would require a similar double rotation (starting at T). To avoid testing all these cases, we just call Skew three times. Once we have done that, two calls to Split suffice to rearrange the horizontal edges.

After a recursive removal, three Skews plus 2 Splits will guarantee rebalancing.

18.6.3   C++ Implementation

The class interface for the AA-tree is shown in Figure 18.65. Much of it duplicates previous tree interfaces. Once again we will use a NullNode sentinel; however, we do not need a pseudoroot. The constructor, which is not shown, allocates NullNode, as was done for red black trees, and has Root point at it. NullNode is at level 0.

The interface and routines are relatively simple (compared to the red black tree)

Insert is shown in Figure 18.66. As we mentioned earlier, it is identical to the recursive binary search tree Insert, except that it adds a call to Skew followed by a call to Split. We can see in Figure 18.67 that Skew and Split are easily implemented using the already existing tree rotations. Finally, Remove is shown in Figure 18.68.

To help us out, we keep two variables, DeletePtr and LastPtr, that have lifetime scope by virtue of their static declaration. When we traverse a right pointer, we adjust DeletePtr; because we call Remove recursively until we reach the bottom (we do not test for equality on the way down), we are guaranteed that if the item to be removed is in the tree, DeletePtr will be pointing at the node that contains it. Notice that this technique can be used in the Find procedure to replace the three-way comparisons done at each node with two-way comparisons at each node plus one extra equality test at the bottom. LastPtr points at the level-one node at which this search terminates. Because we do not stop until we reach the bottom, if the item is in the tree, LastPtr will point at the level-one node that contains the replacement value and must be removed from the tree.

DeletePtr will point at the node containing X (if X is found), or NullNode if X is not found. LastPtr points at the replacement node. We use two-way comparisons instead of three-way comparisons.

After a given recursive call terminates, we are either at level one or we are not. If we are at level one, we can copy the node's value into the internal node that is to be removed; we can then call delete. Otherwise, we are at a higher level, and we need to check if the balance condition has been violated. If so, we restore the balance and then make three calls to Skew and two calls to Split. As we discussed earlier, this guarantees that the AA-tree properties will be restored.

```
1  // AATree class interface
2  //
3  // Etype: must have zero-parameter and copy constructor,
4  //       and must have operator< and operator==
5  //   CONSTRUCTION: with (a) no initializer
6  // All copying of AATree objects is DISALLOWED
7  //
8  // ****************PUBLIC OPERATIONS*********************
9  // Same as SearchTree; omitted for brevity
10 // ****************ERRORS********************************
11 // Predefined exception is propagated if new fails
12 // Item in sentinel node returned for various degenerate cases
13
14 #define Level BalancingInfo
15
16 template <class Etype>
17 class AATree
18 {
19   public:
20     AATree( );
21     ~AATree( ) { FreeTree( Root ); delete NullNode; }
22
23         // Public members are similar to SearchTree members
24     int Insert( const Etype & X ){ return Insert( X, Root ); }
25     int Remove( const Etype & X ){ return Remove( X, Root ); }
26
27     const Etype & FindMin( ) const;
28     const Etype & FindMax( ) const;
29
30     const Etype & Find( const Etype & X );
31     int WasFound( ) const    { return Current != NullNode; }
32
33     void MakeEmpty( )   { FreeTree( Root ); Root = NullNode; }
34     int IsEmpty( ) const    { return Root == NullNode; }
35   private:
36     BinaryNode<Etype> *Root;
37     BinaryNode<Etype> *NullNode;
38
39     // Result of last Find
40     BinaryNode<Etype> *Current;
41
42     void Skew ( BinaryNode<Etype> * & T );
43     void Split( BinaryNode<Etype> * & T );
44
45     void FreeTree( BinaryNode<Etype> *T );
46     int Insert( const Etype & X, BinaryNode<Etype> * & T );
47     int Remove( const Etype & X, BinaryNode<Etype> * & T );
48
49     // Disable operator=
50     const AATree & operator=( const AATree & );
51 };
```

Figure 18.65 Class interface for AA-trees

```
1   // Insert item X into AA-tree rooted at T
2   // Return true unless X is a duplicate
3
4   template <class Etype>
5   int
6   AATree<Etype>::
7   Insert( const Etype & X, BinaryNode<Etype> * & T )
8   {
9       if( T == NullNode )
10      {
11          T = new BinaryNode<Etype>( X, NullNode, NullNode );
12          return 1;
13      }
14      else if( X < T->Element )
15          Insert( X, T->Left );
16      else if( T->Element < X )
17          Insert( X, T->Right );
18      else
19          return 0;
20
21      Skew( T );
22      Split( T );
23      return 1;
24  }
```

Figure 18.66   Insert for AATree class

```
1   // Skew and Split: AA-tree primitives
2
3   template <class Etype>
4   void
5   AATree<Etype>::Skew( BinaryNode<Etype> * & T )
6   {
7       if( T->Left->Level == T->Level )
8           T = RotateWithLeftChild( T );
9   }
10
11  template <class Etype>
12  void
13  AATree<Etype>::Split( BinaryNode<Etype> * & T )
14  {
15      if( T->Right->Right->Level == T->Level )
16      {
17          T = RotateWithRightChild( T );
18          T->Level++;
19      }
20  }
```

Figure 18.67   Skew and Split for AATree class

```
1   // Remove X from AA-tree rooted at T
2   // Return true unless X was not found
3
4   template <class Etype>
5   int
6   AATree<Etype>::
7   Remove( const Etype & X, BinaryNode<Etype> * &  T )
8   {
9       static int ItemFound = 0;
10      static BinaryNode<Etype> *DeletePtr;
11      static BinaryNode<Etype> *LastPtr;
12
13      if( T != NullNode )
14      {   // Search down the tree and set LastPtr and DeletePtr
15          LastPtr = T;
16          if( X < T->Element )
17              Remove( X, T->Left );
18          else
19          {
20              DeletePtr = T;
21              Remove( X, T->Right );
22          }
23          // Remove if at bottom of the tree and X is present
24          if( T == LastPtr )
25          {
26              if( DeletePtr!=NullNode && X==DeletePtr->Element )
27              {
28                  DeletePtr->Element = T->Element;
29                  DeletePtr = NullNode;
30                  T = T->Right;
31                  delete LastPtr;
32                  ItemFound = 1;
33              }
34              else
35                  ItemFound = 0;
36          }
37          // Otherwise, we are not at the bottom; rebalance
38          else if( T->Left->Level < T->Level - 1 ||
39                   T->Right->Level < T->Level - 1 )
40              {
41                  if( T->Right->Level > --T->Level )
42                      T->Right->Level = T->Level;
43                  Skew( T );
44                  Skew( T->Right );
45                  Skew( T->Right->Right );
46                  Split( T );
47                  Split( T->Right );
48              }
49      }
50      return ItemFound;
51  }
```

Figure 18.68   Deletion for AA-tree

18.7   B-Trees

So far we have assumed that we can store an entire data structure in the main memory of a computer. Suppose, however, that we have more data than can fit in main memory, and thus we must have the data structure reside on disk. When this happens, the rules of the game change because the Big-Oh model is no longer meaningful.

The problem is that a Big-Oh analysis assumes that all operations are equal. However, this is not true, especially when disk I/O is involved. Let us be concrete. A 25-MIPS machine allegedly executes 25 million instructions per second. That is pretty fast, mainly because the speed depends largely on electrical properties. On the other hand, a disk is mechanical; its speed depends largely on the time it takes to spin the disk and to move a disk head. Without going into details, we can say that most disks spin at 3600 RPM. Thus in one minute, it makes 3600 revolutions, so one revolution occurs in 1/60 of a second, or 16.7 milliseconds. On average we might expect that we have to spin a disk halfway to find what we are looking for, so if we ignore other factors, we get an access time of 8.3 milliseconds. This is a very charitable estimate; 9 to 13 millisecond access times are more common. Consequently, we see that we can do approximately 120 disk accesses per second. This sounds pretty good, until we compare it with the processor speed. What we have is 25 million instructions equal to 120 disk accesses. Put another way, one disk access is worth about 200,000 instructions. Of course, everything here is a rough calculation, but the relative speeds are pretty clear: Disk accesses are incredibly expensive. Furthermore, processor speeds are increasing at a much faster rate than disk speeds (disk sizes are increasing quite fast). What we see is that we are willing to do lots of calculations just to save a disk access. In almost all cases, it is the number of disk accesses that will dominate the running time. Thus, if we halve the number of disk accesses, the running time will halve.

Let us see how the typical search tree performs on disk. Suppose we want to be able to access the driving records for citizens in the state of Florida. We will assume that we have 10,000,000 items, that each key is 32 bytes (representing a name), and that a record is 256 bytes. We assume this does not fit in main memory. Let us also assume that we are 1 of 20 users on a system (so we have 1/20 of the resources). Thus in one second we can execute a million instructions or perform six disk accesses.

The unbalanced binary search tree is a disaster: in the worst case, it has linear depth, and thus could require 10,000,000 disk accesses. On average, a successful search would require $1.38 \log N$ disk accesses, and since $\log 10000000 \approx 24$, we see that an average search requires 32 disk accesses, or five seconds. In a typical randomly constructed tree, we would expect that a few nodes are three times as deep; these would require about 100 disk accesses, or 16 seconds. A red black tree is somewhat better: the worst case of $2 \log N$ is unlikely to occur, and the typical case is very close to $\log N$. Thus a red black tree would use about 25 disk accesses on average, requiring four seconds.

When data is too large to fit in memory, then the number of disk accesses becomes important. A disk access is unbelievably expensive compared to a typical computer instruction.

Even logarithmic performance is unacceptable. We need to perform searches in three or four accesses. Updates can take slightly longer.

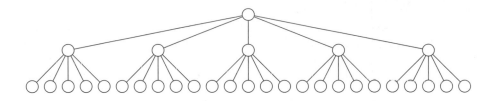

Figure 18.69   Five-ary tree of 31 nodes has only three levels

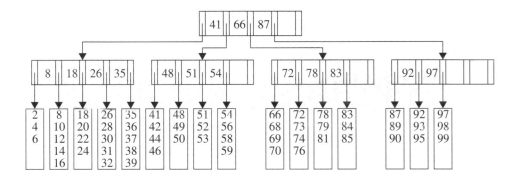

Figure 18.70   B-tree of order 5

An *M-ary search tree* allows *M*-way branching. As branching increases, the depth decreases.

We want to reduce the number of disk accesses to a very small constant, such as three or four. We are willing to write complicated code to do this because machine instructions are essentially free, so long as we are not ridiculously unreasonable. It should probably be clear that a binary search tree will not work, since the typical red black tree is close to optimal height. We cannot go below $\log N$ using a binary search tree. The solution is intuitively simple: If we have more branching, we have less height. Thus, while a perfect binary tree of 31 nodes has five levels, a five-ary tree of 31 nodes has only three levels, as shown in Figure 18.69. An *M-ary search tree* allows *M*-way branching. As branching increases, the depth decreases. Whereas a complete binary tree has height that is roughly $\log_2 N$, a complete *M*-ary tree would have height that is roughly $\log_M N$.

We can create an *M*-ary search tree in much the same way as a binary search tree. In a binary search tree, we need one key to decide which of two branches to take. In an *M*-ary search tree, we need $M - 1$ keys to decide which branch to take. To make this scheme efficient in the worst case, we need to ensure that the *M*-ary search tree is balanced in some way. Otherwise, like a binary search tree, it could degenerate into a linked list. Actually, we want an even more restrictive balancing condition: We do not want an *M*-ary search tree to degenerate to even a binary search tree, because then we would be stuck with $\log N$ accesses.

One way to implement this is to use a *B-tree*. We will describe the basic B-tree; many variations and improvements are known, and an implementation is somewhat complex because there are quite a few cases. However, it is easy to see that in principle it guarantees only a few disk accesses.

A B-tree of order M is an M-ary tree with the following properties:

1. The data items are stored at leaves.
2. The nonleaf nodes store up to $M - 1$ keys to guide the searching; key i represents the smallest key in subtree $i + 1$.
3. The root is either a leaf or has between 2 and M children.
4. All nonleaf nodes (except the root) have between $\lceil M/2 \rceil$ and M children.
5. All leaves are at the same depth and have between $\lceil L/2 \rceil$ and L children, for some L.

An example of a B-tree of order 5 is shown in Figure 18.70. Notice that all nonleaf nodes have between three and five children (and thus between two and four keys); the root could possibly have only two children. Here we have $L = 5$; it happens that L and M are the same in this example, but this is not necessary. Since L is five, each leaf has between three and five data items. Requiring nodes to be half full guarantees that the B-tree does not degenerate into a simple binary or ternary tree. As we mentioned, there are various definitions of B-trees that change this structure in mostly minor ways, but this definition is one of the popular forms.

Each node represents a disk block, so we choose M and L based on the size of the items that are being stored. As an example, suppose that one block holds 8192 bytes. In our Florida example, each key uses 32 bytes. In a B-tree of order M, we would have $M - 1$ keys, for a total of $32M - 32$ bytes plus M pointers. Since each pointer is essentially a number of another disk block, we can assume that a pointer is four bytes. Thus the pointers use $4M$ bytes. The total memory requirement for a nonleaf node is thus $36M - 32$. The largest value of M for which this is no more than 8192 is 228. Thus we would choose $M = 228$. Since each data record is 256 bytes, we would be able to fit 32 records in a block. Thus we would choose $L = 32$. We are guaranteed that each leaf has between 16 and 32 data records and that each internal node (except the root) branches in at least 114 ways. Since there are 10,000,000 records, there are at most 312,500 leaves. Consequently, in the worst case, leaves would be on the fourth level. In more concrete terms, the worst-case number of accesses is given by approximately $\log_{M/2} N$, give or take 1 (for example, the root and the first level could be cached in main memory, and so over the long run disk accesses would be needed only for the third and deeper levels).

The remaining issue is how to add and remove items from the B-tree. We will sketch the ideas involved, pointing out that many of the themes that we have seen before recur.

The *B-tree* is the most popular data structure for disk-bound searching.

The B-tree has a host of structure properties.

Nodes must be half full. This guarantees that we do not degenerate into a simple binary or ternary tree.

We choose the maximum M and L that allow a node to fit in one disk block.

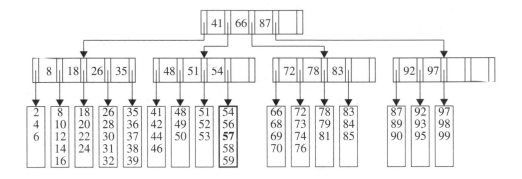

Figure 18.71 B-tree after insertion of 57 into tree in Figure 18.70

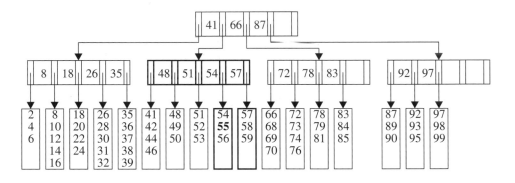

Figure 18.72 Insertion of 55 in B-tree in Figure 18.71 causes a split into two leaves

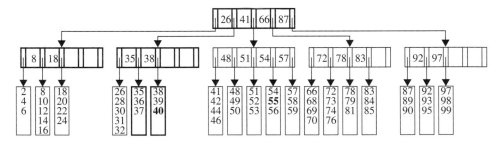

Figure 18.73 Insertion of 40 in B-tree in Figure 18.72 causes a split into two leaves and then a split of the parent node

We begin by examining insertion. Suppose we want to insert 57 into the B-tree in Figure 18.70. A search down the tree reveals that it is not already in the tree. We can add it to the leaf as a fifth child. Note that we may have to reorganize all the data in the leaf to do this, but the cost is negligible when compared to the disk access, which in this case also includes a disk write.

If the leaf contains room for a new item, we insert it and are done.

Of course, that was relatively painless because the leaf was not already full. Suppose we now want to insert 55. As we can see in Figure 18.71, we have a problem: The leaf where 55 wants to go is already full. The solution is simple: Since we now have $L + 1$ items, we split them into two leaves. We are guaranteed that both leaves will have the minimum number of data records needed. We form two leaves with three items each. We require two disk accesses to write these leaves and another disk access to update the parent. Note that in the parent, both keys and pointers change, but they do so in a controlled way that is easily calculated. The resulting B-tree is shown in Figure 18.71. Although splitting nodes is time consuming because it requires at least two additional disk writes, it is a relatively rare occurrence. If L is 32, for example, then when a node is split, two leaves with 16 and 17 items, respectively, are created. For the leaf with 17 items, we can perform 15 more insertions without another split. Put another way, for every split, there are roughly $L/2$ nonsplits.

If the leaf is full, we can insert a new item by splitting the leaf and forming two half-empty nodes.

The node splitting in the previous example worked because the parent did not have its full complement of children. But what would happen if the parent was already full? Suppose, for example, that we insert 40 into the B-tree in Figure 18.72. We must split the leaf containing the keys 35 through 39 and now 40 into two leaves. But this would mean that the parent has six children, and it is allowed only five. The solution is to split the parent. This result is shown in Figure 18.73. When the parent is split, we must update the values of the keys and also its parent, thus incurring an additional two disk writes (so this insertion costs five disk writes). However, once again, the keys change in a very controlled manner, although the code is certainly not simple because of a host of cases.

Node splitting creates an extra child for the leaf's parent. If the parent already has a full number of children, then we split the parent.

When a nonleaf node is split, as is the case here, its parent gains a child. What if the parent already has reached its limit of children? Then we continue splitting nodes up the tree until either we find a parent that does not need to be split or we reach the root. Notice that this idea was seen in bottom-up red black trees and AA-trees. If we split the root, then we have two roots. Obviously, this is unacceptable, but we can create a new root that has the split roots as its two children. This is why the root is granted the special two-child minimum exemption, and it is the only way that a B-tree gains height. Needless to say, splitting all the way up to the root is an exceptionally rare event, because a tree with four levels indicates that the root has been split three times throughout the entire sequence of insertions (assuming no deletions have occurred). In fact, splitting of any non-leaf node is also quite rare.

We may have to continue splitting all the way up the tree (though this is unlikely). In the worst case, we split the root, thus creating a new root with two children.

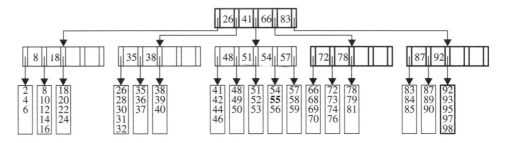

Figure 18.74 B-tree after deletion of 99 from Figure 18.73

There are other ways to handle the overflowing of children. One technique is to put a child up for adoption should a neighbor have room. To insert 29 into the B-tree in Figure 18.73, for example, we could make room by moving 32 to the next leaf. This technique requires a modification of the parent because the keys are affected, but it tends to keep nodes more full and saves space in the long run.

We can perform deletion by finding the item that needs to be removed and removing it. The problem is that if the leaf it was in had the minimum number of data items, then it is now below the minimum. We can rectify the situation by adopting a neighboring item, if the neighbor is not itself at its minimum. If it is, then we can combine with the neighbor, forming a full leaf. Unfortunately, this means that the parent has lost a child. If this causes the parent to fall below its minimum, then it follows the same strategy, and this procedure could percolate up all the way to the root. The root cannot have just one child (and even if it was allowed, it would be silly). If a root is left with one child as a result of the adoption process, then we remove the root, making its child the new root of the tree. This is the only way for a B-tree to lose height. For example, suppose we want to remove 99 from the B-tree in Figure 18.73. Since the leaf has only two items, and its neighbor is already at is minimum of three, we combine into a new leaf of five items. As a result, the parent has only two children. However, it can adopt from a neighbor because the neighbor has four children. As a result, both have three children. The result is shown in Figure 18.74.

> Deletion works in reverse: if a leaf loses a child, it may need to combine with another leaf. Combining of nodes may continue all the way up the tree, though this is unlikely. In the worst case, the root loses one of its two children. In that case, we delete the root, and use the other child as the new root.

Summary

Binary search trees are of great importance in algorithm design. They support almost all the useful operations, and the logarithmic average cost is very small. Nonrecursive implementations of search trees are somewhat faster, but the recursive versions are sleeker, more elegant, and easier to understand and debug. The problem with search trees is that their performance depends heavily on the input being random. If this is not the case, the running time increases significantly, to the point where search trees become expensive linked lists.

We saw several ways to deal with this problem. All involve restructuring the tree to ensure that some sort of balance holds at each node. The restructuring is achieved through tree rotations that preserve the binary search tree property. For these trees the cost of a search is typically less than in an unbalanced binary search tree because the average node tends to be closer to the root. The insertion and deletion costs, however, are typically higher. The balanced variations differ in how much coding effort is involved in implementing operations that change the tree.

The classic scheme is the AVL tree in which, for every node, the heights of its left and right subtrees can differ by at most 1. The practical problem with AVL trees is that it involves a large number of different cases, making the overhead of each insertion and deletion relatively high. Two other alternatives were examined. The first was the top-down red black tree. Its primary advantage is that rebalancing can be implemented in a single pass down the tree, rather than the traditional pass down and back up. This leads to simpler code and faster performance than the AVL tree. The second is the AA-tree, which is similar to the bottom-up red black tree. Its primary advantage is a relatively simple recursive implementation of both insertion and deletion. Both of these structures use sentinel nodes to eliminate annoying special cases.

Use an unbalanced binary search tree only if you are sure that the data are reasonably random or the amount of data is relatively small. Use the red black tree if you are concerned about speed (and are not too concerned about deletion). Use the AA-tree if you want an easy implementation with more than acceptable performance. Use the B-tree when the data are too large to store in main memory.

In Chapter 21 we will examine another alternative, the *splay tree*. This is a very interesting alternative to the balanced search tree that is also simple to code and very competitive in practice. In the next chapter we examine the hash table, which is a completely different method that is used to implement searching operations.

Objects of the Game

AA-tree The method of choice when a balanced tree is needed, a casual implementation is acceptable, and deletions are needed. (586)

AVL tree A binary search tree with the additional balance property that, for any node in the tree, the height of the left and right subtrees can differ by at most 1. As the first balanced search tree, it has historical significance, and it also illustrates most of the ideas that are used in other schemes. (563)

balanced binary search tree Adds a structure property to guarantee logarithmic depth in the worst case. Updates are slower but accesses are faster than the binary search tree. (563)

binary search tree For any node in the binary search tree, all smaller-keyed nodes are in the left subtree, and all larger-keyed nodes are in the right subtree. Duplicates are not allowed. (543)

B-tree The B-tree is the most popular data structure for disk-bound searching. There are many variations of the same idea. (597)

double rotation Equivalent to two single rotations. (570)

external path length The sum of the cost of accessing all external tree nodes in a binary tree. Measures the cost of an unsuccesful search. (562)

external tree node The NULL node. (562)

horizontal link In an AA-tree, a connection between a node and a child of equal levels. A horizontal link should only go right, and there should not be two consecutive horizontal links. (586)

internal path length The sum of the depths of the nodes in a binary tree. Measures the cost of a successful search. (561)

lazy deletion Marks items as deleted. (586)

level The level of a node in an AA-tree represents the number of left links on the path to the NullNode sentinel. (586)

M-ary tree Allows M-way branching. As branching increases, the depth decreases. (596)

red black tree A good alternative to the AVL tree because a single top-down pass can be used during the insertion and deletion routines. The coding details tend to give a faster implementation. (572)

single rotation Balance is restored by tree rotations. A single rotation switches the roles of the parent and child while maintaining search order. (566)

Skew and **Split** Left horizontal links are removed by a Skew, which causes a rotation between a node and its left child. Consecutive right horizontal links are fixed by a Split, which causes a rotation between a node and its right child. (587)

Common Errors

1. Using an unbalanced search tree when the input sequence is not random will give poor performance.

2. The Remove operation is very tricky to code correctly, especially for a balanced search tree.

3. Lazy deletion is a good alternative to the standard Remove, but we must then change other routines, such as FindMin.

4. Code for balanced search trees is almost always error-prone.

5. Passing a pointer to a tree by value is wrong for Insert and Remove. The pointer must be passed by reference.

On the Internet

All of the code in this chapter is available online. Notice that the online version of BST.h uses virtual functions; these were omitted in the text to conserve space.

BinNode.h	Contains the interface for class BinaryNode
BinNode.cpp	Contains the implementation of the class BinaryNode
Bst.h	Contains the interface for class SearchTree
Bst.cpp	Contains the implementation of the class SearchTree
Ordered.h	Contains the interface for class OrderedSearchTree
Ordered.cpp	Contains the implementation of the class OrderedSearchTree
RedBlack.h	Contains the interface for class RedBlackTree
RedBlack.cpp	Contains the implementation of the class RedBlackTree
AATree.h	Contains the interface for class AATree
AATree.cpp	Contains the implementation of the class AATree

Exercises

In Short

18.1.   Show the result of inserting 3, 1, 4, 6, 9, 2, 5, 7 into an initially empty binary search tree. Then show the result of deleting the root.

18.2.   Draw all binary search trees that can result from inserting permutations of 1, 2, 3, 4. How many trees are there, and what are the probabilities of each tree occurring if all permutations are equally likely?

18.3.   Draw all AVL trees that can result from inserting permutations of 1, 2, and 3. How many trees are there, and what are the probabilities of each tree occurring if all permutations are equally likely?

18.4.   Repeat Exercise 18.3 for four elements.

18.5.   Show the result of inserting 2, 1, 4, 5, 9, 3, 6, 7 into an initially empty AVL tree. Then show the result for a top-down red black tree.

18.6.   Repeat Exercises 18.3 and 18.4 for a red black tree.

18.7.   The binary search tree class does not use virtual functions even though it should. Which functions need to be declared virtual?

18.8.   What happens if, in Figure 18.9, the first parameter is Binary-Node<Etype>* & T (that is, T is passed by reference)? Be specific.

18.9.   What happens if, in Figure 18.10, the second parameter is merely BinaryNode<Etype>* T (that is, T is not passed by reference)? Be specific.

18.10.   An alternative to the WasFound mechanism in the tree classes is to throw an ItemNotFound exception.What are the advantages and disadvantages of using exceptions this way?

In Theory

18.11.   Prove Theorem 18.2.

18.12.   Show the result of inserting items 1 through 15 in order into an initially empty AVL tree. Generalize this (with proof) to show what happens when items 1 through $2^k - 1$ are inserted into an initially empty AVL tree.

18.13.   Give an algorithm to perform Remove in an AVL tree.

18.14.   Prove that the height of a red black tree is at most approximately $2\log N$, and give an insertion sequence that achieves this bound.

18.15.   Show that every AVL tree can be colored as a red black tree. Do all red black trees satisfy the AVL tree property?

18.16.   Prove that the algorithm for deletion in an AA-tree is correct.

18.17.   Suppose the Level data member in an AA-tree is represented by an eight-bit unsigned integer. What is the smallest AA-tree that would overflow the Level member at the root?

18.18.   A B*-tree of order M is a B-tree in which each interior node has between $2M/3$ and M children. Leaves are similarly filled. Describe a method to perform insertion into a B*-tree.

In Practice

18.19.   Implement Find, FindMin, and FindMax recursively.

18.20.   Implement FindKth nonrecursively, using the same technique as you would for a nonrecursive Find.

18.21.   An alternative representation that allows the FindKth operation is to store in each node the value of 1 plus the size of the left subtree. Why might this be advantageous? Rewrite the OrderedSearchTree to use this representation.

18.22.   Write a binary search tree member function that takes two keys, Low and High, and prints all elements X that are in the range specified by Low and High. Your program should run in $O(K + \log N)$ average time, where K is the number of keys printed. Thus if K is small, you should be examining only a small part of the tree. Use a hidden recursive function, and do not use an inorder iterator. Bound the running time of your algorithm.

18.23. Write a binary search tree member function that takes two integers `Low` and `High` and constructs an optimally balanced `Ordered-SearchTree` containing all integers between `Low` and `High`, inclusive. All leaves should be at the same level (if the tree size is one less than a power of two) or on two consecutive levels. *Your routine should take linear time.* Test your routine by using it to solve the Josephus problem (Section 13.1).

18.24. The routines to perform double rotations are inefficient because they perform unnecessary pointer moves. Rewrite them to avoid calls to the single rotation routine.

18.25. Give a nonrecursive top-down implementation of an AA-tree. Compare the implementation with the text's for simplicity and efficiency.

18.26. Write the `Skew` and `Split` procedures recursively, so that only one call of each is needed for `Remove`.

18.27. If the insertion into or removal from the AA-tree fails recursively, then there is no need to rebalance the tree. Rework the algorithm to include this observation.

Programming Projects

18.28. Redo the binary search tree class to implement lazy deletion. Note carefully that this affects all the routines; especially challenging are `FindMin` and `FindMax`, which must now be done recursively.

18.29. Implement the binary search tree to use only one comparison per level for `Find`, `Insert`, and `Remove`.

18.30. Write a program to evaluate empirically the following strategies for removing nodes with two children. Which strategy gives the best balance, and which takes the least CPU time to process an entire sequence of operations?
a. Replace with the largest node, X, in T_L and recursively remove X.
b. Alternately replace with the largest node in T_L or the smallest node in T_R, and recursively remove the appropriate node.
c. Replace with the largest node in T_L or the smallest node in T_R (recursively remove the appropriate node), making the choice randomly.

18.31. Write the `Remove` routine for red black trees.

18.32. Implement the ordered search tree operations for the balanced search tree of your choice.

18.33. Implement a B-tree that works in main memory.

18.34. Implement a B-tree that works for disk files.

References

More information on binary search trees, and in particular the mathematical properties of trees, can be found in the two books by Knuth [18 and 19].

Several papers deal with the theoretical lack of balance caused by biased deletion algorithms in binary search trees. Hibbard's paper [16] proposed the original deletion algorithm and established that one deletion preserves the randomness of the trees. A complete analysis has been performed only for trees with three nodes [17] and four nodes [3]. Eppinger's paper [10] provided early empirical evidence of nonrandomness, and the papers by Culberson and Munro [7 and 8] provide some analytical evidence (but not a complete proof for the general case of intermixed insertions and deletions). The claim that the deepest node in a random binary search tree is three times deeper than the average node is proved in [11]; the result is by no means simple.

AVL trees were proposed by Adelson-Velskii and Landis [2]. A deletion algorithm can be found in [19]. Analysis of the average costs of searching an AVL tree is incomplete, but some results are contained in [20]. The top-down red black tree algorithm is from [15]; a more accessible description can be found in [21]. An implementation of top-down red black trees without sentinel nodes is given in [12]; this provides a convincing demonstration of the usefulness of `NullNode`. The AA-tree is based on the symmetric binary B-tree discussed in [4]. The implementation shown in the text is adapted from the description in [1]. A host of other balanced search trees can be found in [13].

B-trees first appeared in [5]. The implementation described in the original paper allows data to be stored in internal nodes as well as leaves. The data structure we have described is sometimes known as a B^+-tree. Information on the B^*-tree, described in Exercise 18.18, can be found in [9]. A survey of the different types of B-trees is presented in [6]. Empirical results of the various schemes are reported in [14]; a C++ implementation can be found in [12].

1. A. Andersson, "Balanced Search Trees Made Simple," *Proceedings of the Third Workshop on Algorithms and Data Structures* (1993), 61-71.

2. G. M. Adelson-Velskii and E. M. Landis, "An Algorithm for the Organization of Information," *Soviet Math. Doklady* **3** (1962), 1259-1263.

3. R. A. Baeza-Yates, "A Trivial Algorithm Whose Analysis Isn't: A Continuation," *BIT* **29** (1989), 88-113.

4. R. Bayer, "Symmetric Binary B-Trees: Data Structure and Maintenance Algorithms," *Acta Informatica* **1** (1972), 290-306.

5. R. Bayer and E. M. McCreight, "Organization and Maintenance of Large Ordered Indices," *Acta Informatica* **1** (1972), 173-189.

6. D. Comer, "The Ubiquitous B-tree," *Computing Surveys* **11** (1979), 121-137.

7. J. Culberson and J. I. Munro, "Explaining the Behavior of Binary Search Trees under Prolonged Updates: A Model and Simulations," *Computer Journal* **32** (1989), 68-75.

8. J. Culberson and J. I. Munro, "Analysis of the Standard Deletion Algorithm in Exact Fit Domain Binary Search Trees," *Algorithmica* **5** (1990) 295-311.

9. K. Culik, T. Ottman, and D. Wood, "Dense Multiway Trees," *ACM Transactions on Database Systems* **6** (1981), 486-512.

10. J. L. Eppinger, "An Empirical Study of Insertion and Deletion in Binary Search Trees," *Communications of the ACM* **26** (1983), 663-669.

11. P. Flajolet and A. Odlyzko, "The Average Height of Binary Search Trees and Other Simple Trees," *Journal of Computer and System Sciences* **25** (1982), 171-213.

12. B. Flamig, *Practical Data Structures in C++*, John Wiley, New York (1994).

13. G. H. Gonnet and R. Baeza-Yates, *Handbook of Algorithms and Data Structures,* 2d ed., Addison-Wesley, Reading, MA, 1991.

14. E. Gudes and S. Tsur, "Experiments with B-tree Reorganization," *Proceedings of ACM SIGMOD Symposium on Management of Data* (1980), 200-206.

15. L. J. Guibas and R. Sedgewick, "A Dichromatic Framework for Balanced Trees," *Proceedings of the Nineteenth Annual IEEE Symposium on Foundations of Computer Science* (1978), 8-21.

16. T. H. Hibbard, "Some Combinatorial Properties of Certain Trees with Applications to Searching and Sorting," *Journal of the ACM* **9** (1962), 13-28.

17. A. T. Jonassen and D. E. Knuth, "A Trivial Algorithm Whose Analysis Isn't," *Journal of Computer and System Sciences* **16** (1978), 301-322.

18. D. E. Knuth, *The Art of Computer Programming: Volume 1: Fundamental Algorithms*, 2d ed., Addison-Wesley, Reading, MA, 1973.

19. D. E. Knuth, *The Art of Computer Programming: Volume 3: Sorting and Searching*, Addison-Wesley, Reading, MA, 1973.

20. K. Melhorn, "A Partial Analysis of Height-Balanced Trees under Random Insertions and Deletions," *SIAM Journal on Computing* **11** (1982), 748-760.

21. R. Sedgewick, *Algorithms in C++*, Addison-Wesley, Reading, MA, 1992.

Chapter 19

Hash Tables

In Chapter 18 we discussed the binary search tree, which allows various operations on a set of elements. In this chapter we discuss the *hash table*, which supports only a subset of the operations allowed by binary search trees. The implementation of hash tables is frequently called *hashing*. Hashing is a technique used to perform insertions, removes, and finds in constant average time. Unlike the binary search tree, the average-case running time of hash table operations is based on statistical properties rather than the expectation of random-looking input. This improvement is obtained at the expense of a loss of ordering information among the elements; operations such as FindMin and FindMax and the printing of the entire table in sorted order in linear time are not supported. Consequently, the hash table and binary search tree have somewhat different uses and performance properties.

In this chapter we will see

- several methods of implementing the hash table
- analytical comparisons of these methods
- some applications of hashing
- hash tables compared with binary search trees

19.1   Basic Ideas

The *hash table* supports the retrieval or deletion of any named item, so what we are implementing is a dictionary. We would like to be able to support the basic operations in constant time, just as was done for the stack and queue. Since the accesses are much less restricted, this seems like an impossible goal: Surely when the size of the dictionary increases, searches in the dictionary should take longer. However, this is not necessarily the case.

The hash table is used to implement a dictionary in constant time per operation.

Suppose, for example, that all the items are 16-bit unsigned integers, ranging from 0 to 65,535. A simple array can be used to implement each operation as follows. First, we initialize an array A that is indexed from 0 to 65,535 with all 0s. To perform `Insert(i)`, we execute `A[i]++`. Note that `A[i]` represents the number of times that `i` has been inserted. To perform `Find(i)`, we check that `A[i]` is not 0. To perform `Remove(i)`, we make sure it is found, and if so, execute `A[i]--`. The time for each operation is clearly constant. There is the overhead of the array initialization, but this is a constant amount of work (65,536 assignments).

There are two problems with this solution. First, suppose we have 32-bit integers instead of 16-bit integers. Then the array A must hold 4 billion items; this is impractical. Second, if the items are not integers but instead are strings (or something even more generic), then they cannot be used to index an array.

The second problem is not really a problem at all. Just as a number 1234 is a collection of digits 1, 2, 3, and 4, the string `"junk"` is a collection of characters `'j'`, `'u'`, `'n'`, and `'k'`. Notice that the number 1234 is just $1 \cdot 10^3 + 2 \cdot 10^2 + 3 \cdot 10^1 + 4 \cdot 10^0$. In Section 12.1 we mention that a character can typically be represented in 7 bits as a number between 0 and 127. Since a character is basically a small integer, we can interpret a string as an integer; one possible representation is `'j'` $\cdot 128^3 +$ `'u'` $\cdot 128^2 +$ `'n'` $\cdot 128^1 +$ `'k'` $\cdot 128^0$. This allows the simple array implementation seen earlier.

The problem with this strategy is that the integer representation we have described generates huge integers: On an ASCII machine, the representation for `"junk"` yields 224229227, and longer strings generate much larger representations. This brings us back to the first problem: How do we avoid using an absurdly large array?

This is done by using a function that maps large numbers (or strings interpreted as numbers) into smaller, more manageable numbers. The function that maps an item into a small index is known as the *hash function*. If X is an arbitrary integer, then `X%TableSize` generates a number between 0 and `TableSize-1` suitable for indexing into an array of size `TableSize`. If S is a string, we can convert S to a large integer X using the method suggested above and then apply the mod operator (`operator%`) to get a suitable index. Thus, if `TableSize` is 10000, `"junk"` would be indexed to 9227. In Section 19.2 we discuss implementation of the hash function for strings in detail.

The use of the hash function introduces a complication: It is possible that two different items hash out to the same position. This can never be avoided because there are many more items than positions. When this happens we say that a *collision* has occurred. There are many ways to quickly resolve the collision. We investigate three of the simplest methods: *linear probing*, *quadratic probing*, and *separate chaining*. Each method is simple to implement but yields different performance, depending on how full the array is.

```
1   // Acceptable hash function
2
3   unsigned int
4   Hash( const String & Key, int TableSize )
5   {
6       unsigned int HashVal = 0;
7
8       for( int i = 0; i < Key.Length( ); i++ )
9           HashVal = ( HashVal * 128 + Key[ i ] ) % TableSize;
10
11      return HashVal;
12  }
```

Figure 19.1   First attempt at a hash function implementation

```
1   // A good hash function that is used in the online code
2
3   unsigned int
4   Hash( const String & Key, int TableSize )
5   {
6       unsigned int HashVal = 0;
7
8       for( int i = 0; i < Key.Length( ); i++ )
9           HashVal = ( HashVal << 5 ) ^ Key[ i ] ^ HashVal;
10
11      return HashVal % TableSize;
12  }
```

Figure 19.2   Faster hash function that takes advantage of allowed
                   overflow

19.2   Hash Function

Computing the hash function for strings has a subtle complication. The conversion of S to X generates an integer that is almost certainly larger than the machine can store conveniently. This is because $128^4 = 2^{28}$, which is only a factor of 16 from the largest unsigned integer on a 32-bit machine. Consequently, we cannot expect to compute the hash function by directly computing powers of 128. Instead, we use the following observation: A general polynomial

$$A_3 X^3 + A_2 X^2 + A_1 X^1 + A_0 X^0 \tag{19.1}$$

can be evaluated as

$$(((A_3) X + A_2) X + A_1) X + A_0 \tag{19.2}$$

```
 1  // A poor hash function when TableSize is large;
 2
 3  unsigned int
 4  Hash( const String & Key, int TableSize )
 5  {
 6      unsigned int HashVal = 0;
 7
 8      for( int i = 0; i < Key.Length( ); i++ )
 9          HashVal += Key[ i ];
10
11      return HashVal % TableSize;
12  }
```

Figure 19.3   Bad hash function if `TableSize` is large

By using a trick, we can evaluate the hash function efficiently and without overflow.

Notice that in Equation 19.2 we avoid computation of X^i directly. This is good for three reasons. First, it avoids a large intermediate result, which as we saw earlier will overflow. Second, the calculation in Equation 19.2 involves only three multiplications and three additions; an N-degree polynomial is computed in N multiplications and additions. This compares favorably with the computation in Equation 19.1. Third, the calculation proceeds left to right (A_3 corresponds to 'j', A_2 to 'u', and so on, and X is 128).

There still is an overflow problem: Since the result of the calculation is still the same, it is likely to be too large. However, we only need the result taken mod `TableSize`. By applying the `operator%` after each multiplication (or addition),[1] we can make sure that the intermediate results remain small. The hash function that results is shown in Figure 19.1. An annoying feature of this hash function is that the mod computation is expensive. Because overflow is allowed (and its results are consistent on a given platform), we can make the hash function somewhat faster by performing a single mod operation immediately prior to the return. Unfortunately, the repeated multiplication by 128 would tend to shift the early characters left, out of the answer. To alleviate this situation, we slightly alter the hash function in the following ways:

1. We multiply by 32 instead of 128. This slows down the shifting of early characters.
2. We use the << operator for efficiency, even though the compiler should know the optimization.
3. We use the exclusive or ^ instead of addition.
4. We use the exclusive or on an additional `HashVal` to try to avoid losing the early characters.

The result is shown in Figure 19.2. This is not necessarily the very best function possible, and it is certainly true that in some applications (for example, if long strings are involved) we may want to tinker with it, but generally speaking it is

---

1. Section 7.4 discusses the properties of the mod operation.

pretty good. Note that it is crucial that `HashVal` be `unsigned`. Otherwise, the overflow could introduce negative numbers. Also note that the result obtained by allowing overflow and doing a final mod is not the same as performing the mod after every step; thus we have slightly altered the hash function. This is not a problem.

It is worth remarking that while speed is an important consideration in designing a hash function, we also want to make sure that the hash function distributes the keys equitably. Consequently, we must be careful not to take our optimizations too far. As an example, consider the hash function in Figure 19.3. It simply adds up the characters in the keys and returns the result mod `Table-Size`. What could be simpler? The answer is that little could be simpler. The function is easy to implement and computes a hash value very quickly. However, if `TableSize` is large, the function does not distribute the keys well. For instance, suppose that `TableSize` is 10,000. Suppose all keys are eight or fewer characters long. Since a `char` is an integer between 0 and 127, the hash function can only assume values between 0 and 1016 (127*8). This is certainly not an equitable distribution. Any speed gained by the quickness of the hash function calculation will be more than offset by the effort taken to resolve what we expect will be a larger than expected number of collisions.

> The hash function must be simple to compute but also distribute the keys equitably. If there are too many collisions, the performance of the hash table will suffer dramatically.

Finally, we remark that zero is a possible result of the hash function, so hash tables are indexed starting at zero.

> The table runs from 0 to `TableSize-1`.

19.3   Linear Probing

Now that we have a hash function, we need to decide what to do when a collision occurs. Specifically, if X hashes out to a position that is already occupied, where do we place it? The simplest possible strategy is *linear probing*: searching sequentially in the array until we find an empty cell. The search wraps around from the last position to the first, if necessary. Figure 19.4 shows the result of inserting the keys 89, 18, 49, 58, and 9 into a hash table when linear probing is employed. We assume a hash function that returns the key X mod the size of the table. Figure 19.4 includes the result of the hash function.

> In *linear probing*, collisions are resolved by sequential scanning on an array (with wraparound) until an empty cell is found.

The first collision occurs when 49 is inserted; it is put in the next available spot, namely spot 0, which is open. Then 58 collides with 18, 89, and 49 before an empty spot is found three slots away in position 1. The collision for element 9 is resolved in a similar manner. As long as the table is large enough, a free cell can always be found, but the time to do so can get quite large. For example, if there is only one free cell left in the table, we may have to search the entire table to find it, and on average we would expect to have to search half the table to find it. This is far from the constant time per access that we are hoping for. On the other hand, we expect that if the table is kept relatively empty, then insertions should not be so costly. This will be discussed soon.

```
Hash( 89, 10 ) = 8
Hash( 18, 10 ) = 8
Hash( 49, 10 ) = 9
Hash( 58, 10 ) = 8
Hash(  9, 10 ) - 9
```

	After Insert 89	After Insert 18	After Insert 49	After Insert 58	After Insert 9
0			49	49	49
1				58	58
2					9
3					
4					
5					
6					
7					
8		18	18	18	18
9	89	89	89	89	89

Figure 19.4   Linear probing hash table after each insertion

The Find follows the same probe sequence as the Insert.

The Find algorithm merely follows the same path as the Insert algorithm. If it reaches an empty slot, the item we are searching for is not found; otherwise, it finds the match eventually. For example, to find 58, we start at slot 8 (as indicated by the hash function). We see an item, but it is the wrong one, so we try slot 9. Again, we have an item, but it is the wrong one, so we try slot 0 and then slot 1 until a match is found. A Find for 19 would try slots 9, 0, 1, and 2, before finding the empty cell in slot 3. Thus 19 is not found. A C++ implementation would require that we maintain an extra data member to allow us to distinguish between an occupied and an empty cell.

We must use lazy deletion.

Actually, we need more: Standard deletion cannot be performed because, much like a binary search tree, an item in the hash table not only represents itself but also connects other items. Thus, if we removed 89 from the hash table, virtually all of the remaining Find operations would fail. Consequently, we implement lazy deletion, marking items as deleted from the table. This is recorded as the third possibility in the extra data member. We thus have either Empty, Active, or Deleted.

19.3.1   Naive Analysis of Linear Probing

To estimate the performance of linear probing, we will make two assumptions:

1. The hash table is large.
2. Each probe in the hash table is independent of the previous probe.

Assumption 1 is completely reasonable; otherwise, we would not be bothering with a hash table. Assumption 2 tells us that if the fraction of the table that is full is λ, then each time we examine a cell, the probability that it is occupied is also λ, independent of any previous probes. Independence is an important statistical property that greatly simplifies the analysis of random events. Unfortunately, as we discuss in Section 19.3.2, the assumption of independence is not only unjustified but also erroneous. Thus the naive analysis we perform is incorrect. Even so, it is helpful because it tells us what we can hope to achieve if we are more careful about how collisions are resolved. As we mentioned earlier, the performance of the hash table depends on how full the table is. Its fullness is given by the load factor:

> **DEFINITION:** The *load factor* of a probing hash table is the fraction of the table that is full. We denote the load factor by λ. The load factor ranges from 0 (empty) to 1 (completely full).

We can now give a simple but incorrect analysis of linear probing.

If independence of probes is assumed, the average number of cells that are examined in an insertion using linear probing is $1/(1-\lambda)$.

Theorem 19.1

For a table with load factor λ, the probability of any cell being empty is $1-\lambda$. Consequently, the expected number of independent trials required to find an empty cell is $1/(1-\lambda)$.

Proof

Let us explain the proof of Theorem 19.1 in more concrete terms. If the probability of some event occurring is p, then on average $1/p$ trials are required until the event occurs, if the trials are independent. For example, the expected number of coin flips until a heads occurs is two, and the expected number of rolls of a single six-sided die until a four occurs is six. This assumes independence.

19.3.2   What Really Happens: Primary Clustering

Consider what happens when independence does not hold. For example, suppose that a head is always followed by a tail. Then for the first toss, the probability of a head is still 0.5. For the second toss, the probability of a head is likewise 0.5. However, the probability of a head on the second toss given that the first toss yielded a tail is 1. The average number of coin tosses required to see a head is now 1.5: half the time it takes one toss, and half the time it takes two. Since the odds of success increase after a failure, the expected number of trials until success has gone down. If the odds of success were to decrease after a failure, then the expected number of trials until success would go up. This is exactly what happens in linear probing.

Let us consider the following analogy. Suppose we have an airport parking garage with many entrances, and the garage is 5 percent empty, meaning that 1 in 20 spaces is available. Does this mean that we can expect to find an empty space among the first 20 we see after entering? The answer is obviously no, as anyone whose been to an airport can attest. Because the closest spaces are the most popular, all of the empty spaces tend to be on the top levels far from the entrance. In other words, in a parking garage, the empty spaces are not uniformly distributed. In fact, we expect to see large groups of empty spaces in the farthest reaches of the parking garage, and huge clusters of cars with no empty spaces toward the entrances of the garage. Moreover, any of the few empty spaces that are near the front are quickly gobbled up, thus joining the clusters together.[2]

To quantify this, let us look at the extreme situation shown in Figure 19.4. The next item that is inserted could hash into one of ten values (from 0 to 9). Five of these values result in an immediate insertion. Since the table is half full, this is exactly what we expect: a 50 percent chance of success. However, if the first probe finds an occupied cell, things get bad. If we hash to position two, we insert in two total tries, position one allows insertion in three tries, position zero inserts in four tries, position nine inserts in five tries, and position eight in six tries. Thus the average cost of an insertion into the hash table in Figure 19.4 is (1+1+1+1+1+2+3+4+5+6)/10 = 2.5, not 2. You might think that this example is unfair because there are so many collisions at positions 8 and 9. Actually it is not, as we will see later.

Another way to look at the situation is to consider a real estate analogy. At the time we are trying to insert into the hash table in Figure 19.4, there are five available locations. Locations four through seven are "undesirable": only items that hash directly to slots will insert there. On the other hand, location three is very "desirable": any item that hashes to 8, 9, 0, 1, 2, or 3 will wind up in location three. Thus location three is in demand, while the other locations are not. In the real estate analogy, properties in a high demand area become expensive to

---

2. This is not quite the same as hashing because each entrance corresponds to an initial probe in the hash table. It is more typical of a full table with a very poor hash function rather than a good hash function. Even so, it illustrates the issue of nonindependence.

buy. We can see that this is true here. In the real estate analogy, once the expensive price is paid, property values for adjacent lots increase. Again this is true here: After location three is full, location four becomes even more in demand, and the average insertion cost increases even more than would be expected from just an increase in table load factor.

In hashing, this phenomenon is known as *primary clustering*. In primary clustering we get blocks of occupied cells. Any key that hashes into this cluster will require excessive attempts to resolve the collision, and then it will add to the cluster. In primary clustering not only do items that collide because of identical hash functions cause degenerate performance, but also an item that collides with an alternate location for another item causes bad performance. The mathematical analysis that is required to take this into account is complex but has been solved. The following theorem can be proved:

> The effect of *primary clustering* is that large clusters of occupied cells form, making insertions into the cluster expensive (and then the insertion makes the cluster larger).

The average number of cells that are examined in an insertion using linear probing is roughly $(1 + 1 / (1 - \lambda)^2) / 2$.

Theorem 19.2

The proof is beyond the scope of the text. See [6].

Proof

For a half-full table we obtain 2.5 as the average number of cells examined during an insertion. This is almost the same as the naive analysis indicated. The main difference occurs as λ gets close to 1. For instance, if the table is 90 percent full, then $\lambda = 0.9$. The naive analysis suggests that ten cells would have to be examined. This is a lot, but is not completely out of the question. However, by applying Theorem 19.2 we see that the real answer is that roughly 50 cells need to be examined, and that is excessive (especially since this is only an average, and thus some insertions must be worse).

> Primary clustering is a problem at high load factors. For half-empty tables, the effect is not disastrous

19.3.3   Analysis of the `Find` Operation

The cost of an insertion can be used to bound the cost of a `Find`. We distinguish between two types of `Find` operations: the unsuccessful `Find` and the successful `Find`. An unsuccessful search is easy to analyze: The sequence of slots that are examined for an unsuccessful search of X is exactly the same as would be examined to `Insert` X. Thus, we have an immediate answer for the cost of an unsuccessful `Find`.

> An unsuccessful search costs the same as an insertion.

For successful searches, things are slightly more complicated. In Figure 19.4 we have a table with $\lambda = 0.5$. Thus the average cost of an insertion is 2.5. The average cost to `Find` the newly inserted item would then be 2.5, no matter how many insertions follow. The average cost to find the first item inserted into the

> The cost of a successful search is an average of the insertion costs over all smaller load factors.

table is always 1.0 probes. Thus, in a table with $\lambda = 0.5$, some searches are easy and some are hard. In particular the cost of a successful search of X is equal to the cost of inserting X at the time X was inserted. To find the average time to perform a successful search in a table with load factor λ, we must compute the average insertion cost by averaging over all of the load factors leading up to λ. With this groundwork we can compute the average search times for linear probing:

Theorem 19.3   *The average number of cells that are examined in an unsuccessful search using linear probing is roughly $(1 + 1/(1-\lambda)^2)/2$. The average number of cells that are examined in a successful search is approximately $(1 + 1/(1-\lambda))/2$.*

Proof   *The cost of an unsuccessful search is the same as the cost of an insertion. For a successful search, we compute the average insertion cost over the sequence of insertions. Since the table is large, we can compute this average by evaluating $S(\lambda) = \frac{1}{\lambda}\int_{x=0}^{\lambda} I(x)\, dx$. In other words, the average cost of a successful search for a table with load factor λ is equal to the cost of an insertion into a table of load factor x, averaged from load factors 0 through λ. From Theorem 19.2, we can derive the following equation:*

$$
\begin{aligned}
S(\lambda) &= \frac{1}{\lambda}\int_{x=0}^{\lambda} \frac{1}{2}\left(1 + \frac{1}{(1-x)^2}\right) dx \\
&= \frac{1}{2\lambda}\left(x + \frac{1}{(1-x)}\right)\Bigg|_{x=0}^{\lambda} \\
&= \frac{1}{2\lambda}\left(\left(\lambda + \frac{1}{(1-\lambda)}\right) - 1\right) \\
&= \frac{1}{2}\left(\frac{2-\lambda}{1-\lambda}\right) \\
&= \frac{1}{2}\left(1 + \frac{1}{1-\lambda}\right)
\end{aligned}
$$

We can apply the same technique to obtain the cost of a successful Find under the assumption of independence (by using $I(x) = 1/(1-x)$ in Theorem 19.3). We find that if there is no clustering, the average cost of a successful Find for linear probing would have been $-\ln(1-\lambda)/\lambda$. If the load factor is 0.5, then we see that the average number of probes for a successful search using linear probing is 1.5, whereas the nonclustering analysis suggests 1.4 probes. Notice that this average is not dependent on any ordering of the input keys; it only depends on the fairness of the hash function. Note also that even with good hash functions, there are bound to be some longer probe sequences and some shorter probe sequences that contribute to the average. For instance, there are certain to be some sequences of length four, five, and six even in a hash table that is half empty. Determining the expected longest probe sequence is a challenging calculation. Primary clustering not only makes the average probe sequence longer but also makes a long probe sequence more likely to occur. The main problem with primary clustering, therefore, is that performance degrades severely for insertion at high load factors, and some of the longer probe sequences typically encountered (that is, those at the high end of the average) are made more likely to occur.

To reduce the number of probes, we would need a collision resolution scheme that avoids primary clustering. Notice, however, that if the table is half empty, then removing the effects of primary clustering would save only a half of a probe on average for an insertion or unsuccessful search and one-tenth of a probe on average for a successful search. Even though we might expect to reduce the probability of seeing a somewhat lengthier probe sequence, the fact remains that *linear probing is not a terrible strategy*. Since it is so easy to implement, any method we use to remove primary clustering must be of comparable complexity; otherwise, we will expend too much time in the course of saving only a fraction of a probe. One such method is *quadratic probing*.

19.4   Quadratic Probing

Quadratic probing is a collision resolution method that eliminates the primary clustering problem of linear probing. Quadratic probing derives its name from the use of the formula $F(i) = i^2$ to resolve collisions. Specifically, if the hash function evaluates to H, and if a search in cell H is inconclusive, then we try cells $H + 1^2$, $H + 2^2$, $H + 3^2$, $H + 4^2$, ..., $H + i^2$ (employing wraparound) in sequence. This differs from the linear probing strategy of searching $H + 1$, $H + 2$, $H + 3$, $H + 4$, , $H + i$.

Quadratic probing examines cells 1, 4, 9, and so on away from the original probe point.

Figure 19.5 shows the table that results when quadratic probing is used instead of linear probing for the same insertion sequence as Figure 19.4. When 49 collides with 89, the first alternative attempted is one cell away. This cell is empty, so 49 is placed there. Next 58 collides at position 8. The cell at position 9 (which is one away) is tried, but another collision occurs. A vacant cell is found at the next cell tried, which is $2^2 = 4$ positions away *from the original hash position*. Thus 58 is placed in cell 2. The same thing happens for 9. Notice carefully that the alternative locations for items that hash to position 8 and the alternative locations for the items that hash to position 9 are not the same. The long probe sequence to insert 58 did not affect the subsequent insertion of 9. This is in contrast to what happened with linear probing.

Remember that it is a quadratic number of positions from the original probe point.

```
Hash( 89, 10 ) = 8
Hash( 18, 10 ) = 8
Hash( 49, 10 ) = 9
Hash( 58, 10 ) = 8
Hash(  9, 10 ) = 9
```

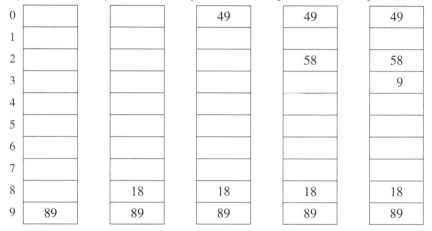

Figure 19.5   Quadratic probing hash table after each insertion (note that the table size is poorly chosen because it is not a prime number)

There are a few details that we need to consider before we write code:

- In linear probing, each probe tries a different cell. Does quadratic probing guarantee that when a cell is tried, we have not already tried it during the course of the current access? Does quadratic probing guarantee that when inserting X, if the table is not full X, will be inserted?

- Linear probing is easily implemented. Quadratic probing appears to require multiplication and mod operations. Does this apparent added complexity make quadratic probing impractical?

- What happens (in both linear probing and quadratic probing) if the load factor gets too high? Can we dynamically expand the table as is typical of other array based data structures?

If the table size is prime and the load factor is no larger than 0.5, then all probes will be to different locations, and an item can always be inserted.

Fortunately, there is relatively good news on all fronts. If the table size is prime and the load factor never exceeds 0.5, we are assured that we can always place a new item X and that no cell is probed twice during an access. However, for this guarantee to hold, we need to ensure that the table size is a prime number. For completeness, Figure 19.6 shows a routine that generates prime numbers. It uses the algorithm in Figure 9.7 (a more complex algorithm is not warranted).

If quadratic probing is used and the table size is prime, then a new element can always be inserted if the table is at least half empty. Furthermore, in the course of the insertion, no cell is probed twice.

Theorem 19.4

Let M be the size of the table, and assume that M is an odd prime greater than 3. We show that the first $\lfloor M/2 \rfloor$ alternative locations are distinct. Two of these locations are $H + i^2 (\mod M)$ and $H + j^2 (\mod M)$, where $0 < i, j \le \lfloor M/2 \rfloor$. Suppose, for the sake of contradiction, that these two locations are the same, but $i \neq j$. Then

Proof

$$H + i^2 \equiv H + j^2 (\mod M)$$
$$i^2 \equiv j^2 (\mod M)$$
$$i^2 - j^2 \equiv 0 (\mod M)$$
$$(i-j)(i+j) \equiv 0 (\mod M)$$

Since M is prime, it follows that either $i - j$ or $i + j$ is divisible by M. Since i and j are distinct and their sum is smaller than M, neither of these possibilities can occur. Thus we obtain a contradiction. It follows that the first $\lfloor M/2 \rfloor$ alternatives are all distinct and, along with the original probe, guarantee that an insertion must succeed if the table is at least half empty.

```
1  // Find next prime > N; assume N >= 5
2
3  int
4  NextPrime( int N )
5  {
6      if( N % 2 == 0 )
7          N++;
8
9      for( ; !IsPrime( N ); N += 2 )
10         ;
11
12     return N;
13 }
```

Figure 19.6   Routine used by quadratic probing to find a prime greater than or equal to *N*

If the table is even one more than half full, the insertion could fail (although this is extremely unlikely). Actually, the failure of an insertion is really not an issue because we would be doing so many probes. Recall that we are expecting to perform an insertion in roughly 2 or 2.5 probes; failure to insert in a table of size 100,000 would imply 50,000 probes. Even so, if we keep the table size prime and the load factor below 0.5, we have a guarantee of success for the insertion. If the table size is not prime, the number of alternate locations can be severely reduced. As an example, if the table size were 16, then the only alternate locations would be at distances 1, 4, or 9 away from the original probe point. Once again, this is not really an issue: Although we would not have a guarantee of $\lfloor M/2 \rfloor$ alternatives, we would usually have more than we would expect to need. However, it is best to play it safe and use the theory to guide us in selecting parameters. Furthermore, it has been shown empirically that prime numbers tend to be best for hash tables because they tend to remove some of the nonrandomness that is occasionally introduced by the hash function.

Quadratic probing can be implemented without multiplications and mod operations. Because it does not suffer from primary clustering, it outperforms linear probing in practice.

The second important consideration is efficiency. Recall that for a load factor of 0.5, removing primary clustering only saves 0.5 probes for an average insertion and 0.1 probes for an average successful search. We do get some additional benefits: It becomes significantly less likely that we encounter a long probe sequence. However, if it takes twice as long to perform a probe using quadratic probing, it is hardly worth the effort. Linear probing is implemented with a simple addition (by one), a test to see if wraparound is needed, and a very rare subtraction (if we need to do the wraparound). The formula for quadratic probing suggests that we need to do an addition by 1 (to go from $i-1$ to i), a multiplication (to compute i^2), another addition, and then a mod operation. Certainly this appears to be much too expensive a calculation to be practical. However, we have the following trick:

Theorem 19.5   *Quadratic probing can be implemented without expensive multiplications and divisions.*

Proof   *Let H_{i-1} be the most recently computed probe (H_0 is the original hash position), and let H_i be the probe we are trying to compute. Then we have*

$$H_i = H_0 + i^2 (\bmod M)$$

$$H_{i-1} = H_0 + (i-1)^2 (\bmod M)$$

(19.3)

If we subtract the two equations in Equation 19.3, we obtain

$$H_i - H_{i-1} = i^2 - (i-1)^2 (\bmod M)$$

$$H_i = H_{i-1} + 2i - 1 (\bmod M)$$

(19.4)

Proof (continued)

Equation 19.4 tells us that we compute the new value H_i from the previous value H_{i-1} without squaring i. Although we still have a multiplication, the multiplication is by 2, which is a trivially implemented bit shift on most computers. What about the mod operation? That too is not really needed because the expression $2i - 1$ must be smaller than M. Therefore, if we add it to H_{i-1}, the result will either still be smaller than M (in which case we do not need the mod) or it will be just a little bit larger than M (in which case we can compute the mod equivalent by subtracting M).

Theorem 19.5 shows that we can compute the next position to probe using an addition (to increment i), a bit shift (to evaluate $2i$), a subtraction by one (to evaluate $2i - 1$), another addition (to increment the old position by $2i - 1$), a test to see if wraparound is needed, and a very rare subtraction to implement the mod operation. The difference is thus a bit shift, a subtraction by 1, and an addition per probe. This is likely to be less than the cost of doing an extra probe if complex keys (such as strings) are involved.

The final detail we need to consider is dynamic expansion. If the load factor exceeds 0.5, we want to double the size of the hash table. This raises a few issues. First, how hard will it be to find another prime number? The answer is that prime numbers are easy to find: We expect to have to test only $O(\log N)$ numbers until we find a number that is prime. Consequently, the routine in Figure 19.6 is very fast: Since the primality test takes at most $O(N^{1/2})$ time, we expect that the search for a prime number takes at most $O(N^{1/2}\log N)$ time. This is much less than the $O(N)$ cost of transferring the contents of the old table to the new.

> **Expand the table as soon as the load factor reaches 0.5. This process is known as rehashing. Always double to a prime number. Prime numbers are easy to find.**

Once we allocate a larger array, do we just copy everything over? The answer is most definitely no. The new array implies a new hash function, so we cannot use the old array positions. Thus we have to examine each element in the old table, compute its new hash value, and insert into the new hash table. This process is known as *rehashing*. In the next section we will see that rehashing is easy to implement in C++.

> **When expanding, we reinsert into the new table using the new hash function.**

19.4.1   C++ Implementation

We are now ready to give a complete C++ implementation of a quadratic probing hash table. We will use a templated class. We assume that the user has provided an appropriate hash function of the form

```
unsigned int Hash( const Etype & X, int TableSize );
```

> **The user must provide an appropriate hash function, copy assignment operator, and equality and inequality operators for the instantiated `Etype`.**

for each instantiated type. We require that `operator=` and a copy constructor be defined for `Etype`. The code can be reworked to avoid copy construction, but `operator=` is a necessity. Finally, we assume that `operator==` and `operator!=` are defined for `Etype`. We derive our class from the abstract class `AbsHashTable` in Figure 6.21. The class interface is shown in Figures 19.7 and 19.8. Let us describe each feature in some detail.

```
1  // HashTable class interface
2  //
3  // Etype: must have zero-parameter and copy constructor,
4  //        operator= and operator!=
5  // CONSTRUCTION: with (a) no initializer
6  // Copy construction of HashTable objects is DISALLOWED
7  // Deep copy is supported
8
9  //   ******************PUBLIC OPERATIONS********************
10 // int Insert( Etype X ) --> insert X
11 // int Remove( Etype X ) --> Remove X
12 // Etype Find( )          --> Return item that matches X
13 // int WasFound( )        --> Return 1 if last Find succeeded
14 // int IsFound( Etype X ) --> Return 1 if X would be found
15 // int IsEmpty( )         --> Return 1 if empty; else return 0
16 // int IsFull( )          --> Return 1 if full;  else return 0
17 // void MakeEmpty( )      --> Remove all items
18 //   ******************ERRORS*******************************
19 // Predefined exception is propagated if new fails
20
21 template <class Etype>
22 class HashTable : public AbsHashTable
23 {
24   public:
25     enum KindOfEntry { Active, Empty, Deleted };
26
27     HashTable( );
28     ~HashTable( ) { delete [ ] Array; }
29     const HashTable & operator=( const HashTable & Rhs );
30
31     int Insert( const Etype & X );
32     int Remove( const Etype & X );
33     const Etype & Find( const Etype & X );
34     int IsFound( const Etype & X ) const
35     int WasFound( ) const;
36     int IsEmpty( ) const; // Return 1 if empty: Exercise 19.17
37     int IsFull( ) const { return 0; }   // Return 1 if full
38     void MakeEmpty( );
```

Figure 19.7   Class interface for quadratic probing hash table (part 1)

```
39    private:
40      struct HashEntry
41      {
42          Etype Element;              // The item
43          KindOfEntry Info;           // Active, Empty, or Deleted
44
45          HashEntry( ) : Info( HashTable<Etype>::Empty ) { }
46          HashEntry( const Etype & E, KindOfEntry i = Empty ) :
47              Element( E ), Info( i ) { }
48      };
49
50      enum { DefaultSize = 11 };
51      int ArraySize;        // The size of this array
52      int CurrentSize;      // The number of occupied slots
53      int LastFindOK;       // True if the last search succeeded
54      HashEntry *Array;     // The array of elements
55
56          // Some internal routines
57      void AllocateArray( );
58      unsigned int FindPos( const Etype & X ) const;
59    };
```

Figure 19.8   Class interface for quadratic probing hash table (part 2)

The hash table will consist of an array of structures; each structure stores an item and a data member that tells us that the entry is either empty, active, or deleted. We use the enumerated type KindOfEntry, declared at line 25, for that purpose. It is placed in the public section because at least one compiler complains at line 45 if it is private. The array is declared at line 54, and the size of the array is declared at line 51. We need to keep track of the number of items in the hash table (including elements marked as deleted); this is stored in CurrentSize, which is declared at line 52. Finally, the class variable LastFindOK is used to record whether or not the last Find operation succeeded. Although the user could test if the parameter to Find matches the return value from Find, in many cases it would be preferable to have a computationally simple test. Alternatives include passing a second parameter to Find that can be set to indicate success or failure, or making use of the exception mechanism.

The rest of the class interface contains declarations for the hash table routines. The Find operation returns the element found in the search for X and sets LastFindOK to true. If X is not found, the return value is whatever was contained in the empty position that terminates the search. Find sets LastFindOK to 0 when this happens. The routine WasFound can be used to determine if a Find was successful. The routine IsFound performs a search but only returns an indication of whether or not the element was found. It avoids the overhead of returning an Etype object.

The general layout is similar to the binary search tree routines.

```
1   // Allocate the hash table array
2
3   template <class Etype>
4   void
5   HashTable<Etype>::AllocateArray( )
6   {
7       Array = new HashEntry[ ArraySize ];
8   }
9
10
11  // HashTable constructor
12
13  template <class Etype>
14  HashTable<Etype>::HashTable( ) : ArraySize ( DefaultSize )
15  {
16      AllocateArray( );
17      CurrentSize = 0;
18  }
19
20
21  // Clear the hash table
22
23  template <class Etype>
24  void
25  HashTable<Etype>::MakeEmpty( )
26  {
27      CurrentSize = 0;
28      for( int i = 0; i < ArraySize; i++ )
29          Array[ i ].Info = Empty;
30  }
31
32
33  // Deep copy of the hash table
34
35  template <class Etype>
36  const HashTable<Etype> &
37  HashTable<Etype>::operator=( const HashTable<Etype> & Rhs )
38  {
39      if( this != &Rhs )
40      {
41          delete [ ] Array;
42          ArraySize = Rhs.ArraySize;
43          AllocateArray( );
44          for( int i = 0; i < ArraySize; i++ )
45              Array[ i ] = Rhs.Array[ i ];
46          CurrentSize = Rhs.CurrentSize;
47      }
48
49      return *this;
50  }
```

Figure 19.9   Hash table initialization and copy assignment operator

The hash table initialization routines and the copy assignment operator are shown in Figure 19.9. There is nothing special going on here. The searching routines are shown in Figure 19.10. They use the private member function FindPos, shown later, to implement quadratic probing. FindPos is the only place in the entire code that depends on quadratic probing. We see that the Find routines are then simple to implement. An element is found if the result of FindPos is an active cell (since if FindPos stops on an active cell, there must be a match). Similarly, the Remove routine shown in Figure 19.11 is short. We check if FindPos takes us to an active cell; if so the cell is marked deleted. Otherwise, we return.

Most routines are just a few lines of code because they call FindPos to perform quadratic probing.

```
1   // Return item in hash table that matches X
2   // Success can be tested by WasFound
3
4   template <class Etype>
5   const Etype &
6   HashTable<Etype>::Find( const Etype & X )
7   {
8       unsigned int CurrentPos = FindPos( X );
9
10      LastFindOK = Array[ CurrentPos ].Info -- Active;
11      return Array[ CurrentPos ].Element;
12  }
13
14
15  // Test if X is in the hash table
16
17  template <class Etype>
18  int
19  HashTable<Etype>::IsFound( const Etype & X ) const
20  {
21      unsigned int CurrentPos = FindPos( X );
22
23      return Array[ CurrentPos ].Info == Active;
24  }
25
26
27  // Return true if last Find operation was successful
28
29  template <class Etype>
30  int
31  HashTable<Etype>::WasFound( ) const
32  {
33      return LastFindOK;
34  }
```

Figure 19.10   Find routines for quadratic probing hash table

```
1   // Remove X from hash table
2   // Return true if X was removed; false otherwise
3
4   template <class Etype>
5   int
6   HashTable<Etype>::Remove( const Etype & X )
7   {
8       unsigned int CurrentPos = FindPos( X );
9
10      if( Array[ CurrentPos ].Info != Active )
11          return 0;
12
13      Array[ CurrentPos ].Info = Deleted;
14      return 1;
15  }
```

Figure 19.11   Remove routine for quadratic probing hash table

Most of Insert is concerned with rehashing if the table is (half) full.

The insertion routine is shown in Figure 19.12. At line 9 we call FindPos. If X is found, we return immediately at line 13; otherwise, FindPos gives the place to insert X. The insertion is performed at line 16. We adjust CurrentSize at line 17 and return unless a rehash is in order. Thus the remaining code implements rehashing.

Lines 22 and 23 save a pointer to the original table and its size. We then create a new, double-sized, empty hash table at lines 26 to 28. Finally, we scan through the original array and Insert any active elements into the new table. The Insert will use the new hash function (since ArraySize has already been adjusted) and will automatically resolve all collisions. We can be sure that the recursive call to Insert (at line 33) does not force another rehash. Alternatively, we could replace line 33 with two lines of code surrounded by braces (see Exercise 19.15). We call delete at line 36 to reclaim the original array.

Quadratic probing is implemented in FindPos. It uses the previously described trick to avoid multiplications and mods.

So far nothing we have done depends on quadratic probing. Figure 19.13 implements FindPos, which finally deals with the quadratic probing algorithm. We keep searching the table until either we find an empty cell or we find a match. Lines 14 through 16 directly implement the methodology described in Theorem 19.5.

19.4.2   Analysis of Quadratic Probing

In *secondary clustering*, elements that hash to the same position will probe the same alternate cells. It is a minor theoretical blemish.

Quadratic probing has not yet been mathematically analyzed. Although quadratic probing eliminates primary clustering, elements that hash to the same position will probe the same alternate cells. This is known as *secondary clustering*. Once again, the independence of successive probes cannot be assumed. Secondary clustering is a slight theoretical blemish. Simulation results suggest that it generally causes less than an extra one half probe per search, and that this is only true for high load factors.

```
1   // Insert X into hash table
2   // Return false if X is a duplicate; true otherwise
3   // Rehash automatically as needed
4
5   template <class Etype>
6   int
7   HashTable<Etype>::Insert( const Etype & X )
8   {
9       unsigned int CurrentPos = FindPos( X );
10
11          // Do not insert duplicates
12      if( Array[ CurrentPos ].Info == Active )
13          return 0;
14
15          // Insert X as active
16      Array[ CurrentPos ] = HashEntry( X, Active );
17      if( ++CurrentSize  < ArraySize / 2 )
18          return 1;
19
20          // REHASHING CODE
21          // Save old table
22      HashEntry *OldArray = Array;
23      int OldArraySize = ArraySize;
24
25          // Create a new double-sized, empty table
26      CurrentSize = 0;
27      ArraySize = NextPrime( 2 * OldArraySize );
28      AllocateArray( );
29
30          // Copy table over
31      for( int i = 0; i < OldArraySize; i++ )
32          if( OldArray[ i ].Info == Active )
33              Insert( OldArray[ i ].Element );
34
35          // Recycle OldArray
36      delete [ ] OldArray;
37      return 1;
38  }
```

Figure 19.12   Insertion routine for quadratic probing hash table, including rehashing code

There are techniques that eliminate secondary clustering. The most popular of these is *double hashing*, in which a second hash function is used to drive the collision resolution. Specifically, we probe at a distance $Hash_2(X)$, $2Hash_2(X)$, and so on. The second hash function must be carefully chosen (for example, it should *never* evaluate to 0), and we need to make sure that all cells can be probed. A function such as $Hash_2(X) = R - (X \bmod R)$, with R a prime smaller than M, will generally work well. Double hashing is theoretically interesting because it can be shown to use essentially the same number of probes as the purely random analysis of linear probing would imply. However, it is some-

Double hashing is a hashing technique that does not suffer from secondary clustering. A second hash function is used to drive the collision resolution.

what more complicated to implement than quadratic probing and, as we see, requires careful attention to some details.

There seems to be no good reason not to use a quadratic probing strategy, unless the overhead of maintaining a half-empty table is burdensome. This would be the case if the items that are being stored were very large. However, this case is solvable, since we can store pointers to items instead of items themselves.

19.5   Separate Chaining

Separate chaining is a space-efficient alternative to quadratic probing in which we maintain an array of linked lists. It is less sensitive to high load factors. It exhibits some of the trade-offs seen in the array vs. linked list stack implementations.

A popular alternative to quadratic probing is *separate chaining*. In separate chaining hashing, we maintain an array of linked lists: $L_0, L_1, ..., L_{M-1}$. The hash function tells us which list to insert an item X, and then when performing a Find, which list contains X. The idea is that although searching a linked list is a linear operation, if the lists are sufficiently short, the search time will be very fast. In particular, suppose the load factor, which is N/M, is λ. Note that for separate chaining, the load factor is not bounded by 1.0. Then the average list has length λ, making the expected number of probes for an insertion or unsuccessful search λ. The expected number of probes for a successful search is $1 + \lambda/2$. This is because a successful search must occur in a nonempty list, and in such a list we expect to have to traverse halfway down the list. The relative cost of successful and unsuccessful searches is unusual in that if $\lambda < 2$, successful searches are more expensive than unsuccessful searches. This makes sense, however, because many unsuccessful searches encounter an empty linked list.

```
1   // Routine to resolve collisions and locate
2   // Cell that must contain X if X is found
3
4   template <class Etype>
5   unsigned int
6   HashTable<Etype>::FindPos( const Etype & X ) const
7   {
8       unsigned int i - 0;          // The number of failed probes
9       unsigned int CurrentPos = Hash( X, ArraySize );
10
11      while( Array[ CurrentPos ].Info != Empty &&
12             Array[ CurrentPos ].Element != X )
13      {
14          CurrentPos += 2 * ++i - 1;    // Compute the ith probe
15          if( CurrentPos >= ArraySize ) // Implement the mod
16              CurrentPos -= ArraySize;
17      }
18
19      return CurrentPos;
20  }
```

Figure 19.13   Routine that finally deals with quadratic probing

A typical load factor is 1.0; a lower load factor does not significantly enhance performance but costs extra space. The appeal of separate chaining is that performance is not affected by a moderately increasing load factor, and thus rehashing can be avoided. For languages that do not allow dynamic array expansion, this is a significant consideration. Furthermore, the expected number of probes for a search is less than in quadratic probing, particularly for unsuccessful searches.

For separate chaining a reasonable load factor is 1.0. A lower load factor does not significantly improve performance, while a moderately higher load factor is acceptable and can save space.

We can implement separate chaining using our already existing linked list classes. However, since the header node adds space overhead and is not really needed, if space were at a premium, we could pass on reusing components and instead implement a simple stacklike list. The coding effort turns out to be remarkably light. We also see that the space overhead is essentially one pointer per node plus an additional pointer per list; in the case that the load factor is 1.0, this is two pointers per item. This could be important if the size of an item is large; in this case we have the same trade-offs that were seen when we discussed the array and linked list implementations of stacks.

Summary

Hash tables can be used to implement the `Insert` and `Find` operations in constant average time. It is especially important to pay attention to details such as load factor when using hash tables; otherwise, the constant time bounds are not meaningful. It is also important to choose the hash function carefully when the key is not a short string or integer. Pick an easily computable function that distributes well.

For separate chaining the load factor is typically close to 1, although performance does not significantly degrade unless the load factor becomes very large. For quadratic probing the table size should be prime and the load factor should not exceed 0.5. Rehashing should be used for quadratic probing to allow the table to grow and maintain the correct load factor. This is important if space is tight and it is not possible just to declare a huge hash table.

We can also use binary search trees to implement `Insert` and `Find` operations. Although the resulting average time bounds are $O(\log N)$, binary search trees also support routines that require order and are thus more powerful. Using a hash table, we cannot efficiently find the minimum element nor extend to allow computation of an order statistic. We cannot search efficiently for a string unless the exact string is known. A binary search tree could quickly find all items in a certain range; this is not supported by hash table. Furthermore, the $O(\log N)$ bound is not necessarily that much more than $O(1)$, especially since no multiplications or divisions are required by search trees.

Use a hash table instead of a binary search tree if you do not need order statistics and are worried about nonrandom inputs.

On the other hand, the worst case for hashing generally results from an implementation error, whereas sorted input can make binary search trees perform poorly. Balanced search trees are quite expensive to implement, so if no ordering information is required and there is any suspicion that the input might be sorted, then hashing is the data structure of choice.

Hashing applications are abundant.

Hashing applications are abundant. Compilers use hash tables to keep track of declared variables in source code. The data structure is known as a *symbol table*. Hash tables are the ideal application for this problem because only Insert and Find operations are performed. Identifiers are typically short, so the hash function can be computed quickly. Notice that in this application, most searches are successful.

Another common use of hash tables is in programs that play games. As the program searches through different lines of play, it keeps track of positions it has seen by computing a hash function based on the position (and storing its move for that position). If the same position reoccurs, usually by a simple transposition of moves, the program can avoid expensive recomputation. This general feature of all game-playing programs is known as the *transposition table*. We discussed this in Section 10.2, where we implement a tic-tac-toe algorithm.

A third use of hashing is in online spelling checkers. If misspelling detection (as opposed to correction) is important, an entire dictionary can be prehashed, and words can be checked in constant time. Hash tables are well suited for this because it is not important to alphabetize words; printing out misspellings in the order they occurred in the document is certainly acceptable.

This completes our discussion of basic searching algorithms. In the next chapter, we examine the binary heap, which implements the priority queue and thus supports efficient access of the minimum item in a collection of items.

Objects of the Game

collision Occurs in a hash table when two or more items hash out to the same position. This problem is unavoidable because there are more items than positions. (610)

double hashing A hashing technique that does not suffer from secondary clustering. A second hash function is used to drive the collision resolution. (629)

hashing The implementation of hash tables to perform insertions, removes, and finds. (609)

hash function Converts the item into an integer suitable to index an array where the item is stored. If the hash function were one to one, we could access the item by its array index. Since the hash function is not one to one, several items will collide at the same index. (610)

hash table Used to implement a dictionary in constant time per operation. (609)

linear probing A way to avoid collisions by sequentially scanning the array until an empty cell is found. (613)

load factor The number of elements in a hash table divided by the size of the hash table array. In a probing hash table, the load factor ranges from 0 (empty) to 1 (full). In separate chaining, it can be greater than 1. (615)

lazy deletion Required in probing hash tables; marks elements as deleted instead of physically removing them. (614)

primary clustering A problem in linear probing that affects performance. Large clusters of occupied cells form, making insertions into the cluster expensive (and then the insertion makes the cluster larger). (617)

quadratic probing A collision resolution method that examines cells 1, 4, 9, and so on, away from the original probe point. (619)

secondary clustering Occurs when elements hash to the same position and probe the same alternate cells. It is a minor theoretical blemish. (628)

separate chaining A space-efficient alternative to quadratic probing in which we maintain an array of linked lists. It is less sensitive to high load factors. It exhibits some of the trade-offs seen in the array vs. linked list stack implementations. (630)

Common Errors

1. The hash function returns an `unsigned int`. Since intermediate calculations allow overflow, the local variable should also be unsigned to avoid risking an out-of-bounds return value.

2. The performance of a probing table degrades severely as the load factor approaches 1.0. Do not let this happen. Rehash when the load factor reaches 0.5.

3. The performance of all hashing methods depends on using a good hash function. A common error is providing a poor function.

On the Internet

The quadratic probing hash table is available for your perusal.

Hash.h   Contains the `HashTable` class interface
Hash.cpp   Contains the implementation of `HashTable`

Exercises

In Short

19.1.   What are the array indices for a hash table of size 11?

19.2.   What is the appropriate probing table size if the number of items in the hash table is 10?

19.3.   Explain how deletion is performed in both probing and separate chaining hash tables.

19.4.   What is the expected number of probes for both successful and unsuccessful searches in a linear probing table with load factor 0.25?

19.5.   Given input { 4371, 1323, 6173, 4199, 4344, 9679, 1989 } a fixed table size of 10, and a hash function $H(X) = X\bmod 10$, show the resulting

    a. Linear probing hash table

    b. Quadratic probing hash table

    c. Separate chaining hash table

19.6.   Show the result of rehashing the probing tables in Exercise 19.5. Rehash to a prime table size.

19.7.   What are the difficulties involved in using a `Vector` to store the hash table?

19.8.   The `IsEmpty` routine has not been written. Can we implement it by returning the expression `CurrentSize==0`?

In Theory

19.9.   An alternative collision resolution strategy is to define a sequence, $F(i) = R_i$, where $R_0 = 0$ and $R_1, R_2, ..., R_{M-1}$ is a random permutation of the first $M - 1$ integers (recall that the table size is M).

    a. Prove that under this strategy, if the table is not full, then the collision can always be resolved.

    b. Would this strategy be expected to eliminate primary clustering?

    c. Would this strategy be expected to eliminate secondary clustering?

    d. If the load factor of the table is λ, what is the expected time to perform an insertion?

    e. Generating a random permutation using the algorithm in Section 9.4 involves a large number of (expensive) calls to a random number generator. Give an efficient algorithm to generate a random-looking permutation that avoids calling a random number generator.

19.10.   If rehashing is implemented as soon as the load factor reaches 0.5, then when the last element is inserted, the load factor is at least 0.25 and at most 0.5. What is the expected load factor? In other words, is it true or false that the load factor is 0.375 on average?

19.11. When the rehashing step is implemented, we must use $O(N)$ probes to reinsert the N elements. Give an estimate for the number of probes (that is, N or $2N$ or something else). *Hint*: Compute the average cost of inserting into the new table. These insertions vary from load factor 0 to load factor 0.25.

19.12. Using certain assumptions, the expected cost of an insertion into a hash table with secondary clustering is given by $1/(1-\lambda) - \lambda - \ln(1-\lambda)$. Unfortunately, this formula is not accurate for quadratic probing. However, assuming that it is,

 a. What is the expected cost of an unsuccessful search?
 b. What is the expected cost of a successful search?

19.13. A quadratic probing hash table is used to store 10,000 String objects (using the String class implemented in Section 2.6). Assume that the load factor is known to be 0.4 and that the average string length is 8 bytes (not including the null terminator).

 a. What is the hash table size?
 b. How much memory is used to store the 10,000 String objects?
 c. How much memory is used to store the remaining (uninitialized) String objects?
 d. How much additional memory is used by the hash table?
 e. What is the total memory used by the hash table?
 f. What is the space overhead?

In Practice

19.14. Implement linear probing. Only FindPos changes.

19.15. For the probing hash table, implement the rehashing code without making a recursive call to Insert.

19.16. Experiment with a hash function that examines every other character in a string. Is this a better choice than the one in the text?

19.17. Modify the class so that the IsEmpty operation can be supported in constant time.

19.18. Modify the deletion algorithm so that if the load factor goes below $1/8$, then a rehash is performed to yield a table half as large. An extra data member must be maintained. Why?

Programming Problems

19.19. Find yourself a large online dictionary. Choose a table size that is twice as large as the dictionary. Apply the hash function described in the text to each word, and store a count of the number of times each position is hashed to. You will get a distribution: Some percentage of the positions will not be hashed to, some will be hashed to once, some twice, and so on. Compare this distribution with what would occur for theoretical random numbers. This is discussed in Section 9.3.

19.20. Perform simulations to compare the observed performance of hashing with the theory. Declare a probing hash table. Insert 10,000 randomly generate integers into the table, and count the average number of probes used. This is the average cost of a successful search. Repeat the test several times for a good average. Run it for both linear probing and quadratic probing, and do it for final load factors 0.1, 0.2, ..., 0.9. Always declare the table so no rehashing is needed. Thus, the test for 0.4 load factor would declare a table of size approximately 25,000 (adjusted to be prime).

19.21. Compare the time required to perform successful searches and insertions into a separate chaining table with load factor 1 and a quadratic probing table with load factor 0.5. Run it for simple integers, strings, and also complex records in which the search key is a string.

19.22. A BASIC program consists of a series of statements, each of which is numbered in ascending order. Control is passed by use of a *goto* or *gosub* and a statement number. Write a program that reads a legal basic program and renumbers the statements so that the first starts at number *F* and each statement has a number *D* higher than the previous statement. You may assume an upper limit of *N* statements, but the statement numbers in the input might be as large as a 32-bit integer. Your program must run in linear time.

References

Despite the apparent simplicity of hashing, much of the analysis is quite difficult, and there are still many unresolved questions. There are also many interesting theoretical issues, which generally attempt to make it unlikely that worst-case possibilities of hashing arise.

An early paper on hashing is [11]. A wealth of information on the subject, including an analysis of closed hashing with linear probing can be found in [6]. Double hashing is analyzed in [5] and [7]. Yet another collision resolution scheme is coalesced hashing, as described in [12]. An excellent survey on the subject is [8]; [9] contains suggestions, and pitfalls, for choosing hash functions. Precise analytic and simulation results for all of the methods described in this chapter can be found in [4]. Yao [13] has shown that uniform hashing, in which no clustering exists, is optimal with respect to cost of a successful search.

If the input keys are known in advance, then perfect hash functions, which do not allow collisions, exist [1]. Some more complicated hashing schemes, for which the worst case depends not on the particular input but on random numbers chosen by the algorithm, appear in [2] and [3]. These schemes guarantee that only a constant number of collisions occur in the worst case (though construction of a hash function can take a long time in the unlikely case of bad random numbers), and are useful for implementing tables in hardware.

One method of implementing Exercise 19.9 is described in [10].

1. J. L. Carter and M. N. Wegman, "Universal Classes of Hash Functions," *Journal of Computer and System Sciences* **18** (1979), 143-154.

2. M. Dietzfelbinger, A. R. Karlin, K. Melhorn, F. Meyer auf def Heide, H. Rohnert, and R. E. Tarjan, "Dynamic Perfect Hashing: Upper and Lower Bounds," *SIAM Journal on Computing* (to appear).

3. R. J. Enbody and H. C. Du, "Dynamic Hashing Schemes," *Computing Surveys* **20** (1988), 85-113.

4. G. H. Gonnet and R. Baeza-Yates, *Handbook of Algorithms and Data Structures*, 2d ed., Addison-Wesley, Reading, MA, 1991.

5. L. J. Guibas and E. Szemeredi, "The Analysis of Double Hashing," *Journal of Computer and System Sciences* **16** (1978), 226-274.

6. D. E. Knuth, *The Art of Computer Programming, Vol 3: Sorting and Searching*, Addison-Wesley, Reading, MA, 1973.

7. G. Lueker and M. Molodowitch, "More Analysis of Double Hashing," *Proceedings of the Twentieth ACM Symposium on Theory of Computing* (1988), 354-359.

8. W. D. Maurer and T. G. Lewis, "Hash Table Methods," *Computing Surveys* **7** (1975), 5-20.

9. B. J. McKenzie, R. Harries, and T. Bell, "Selecting a Hashing Algorithm," *Software-Practice and Experience* **20** (1990), 209-224.

10. R. Morris, "Scatter Storage Techniques," *Communications of the ACM* **11** (1968), 38-44.

11. W. W. Peterson, "Addressing for Random Access Storage," *IBM Journal of Research and Development* **1** (1957), 130-146.

12. J. S. Vitter, "Implementations for Coalesced Hashing," *Information Processing Letters* **11** (1980), 84-86.

13. A. C. Yao, "Uniform Hashing Is Optimal," *Journal of the ACM* **32** (1985), 687-693.

Chapter 20

A Priority Queue: The Binary Heap

The priority queue is a fundamental data structure that allows access to only the minimum item. In this chapter we discuss one implementation of the priority queue data structure, the elegant *binary heap*. The binary heap supports insertion of new items and deletion of the minimum item in logarithmic worst-case time. It uses no pointers (except in the context of dynamic memory allocation) and is simple to implement.

In this chapter we will see

- the basic properties of the binary heap
- how the `Insert` and `DeleteMin` operations can be performed in logarithmic time
- linear-time heap construction algorithm
- a C++ implementation is provided
- an easily implemented sorting algorithm, *heapsort*, that runs in $O(N \log N)$ time but uses no extra memory
- how heaps can be used to implement external sorting

20.1   Basic Ideas

As we discussed in Section 6.8, the priority queue supports access and deletion of the minimum item. These are the `FindMin` and `DeleteMin` operations, respectively. We could use a simple linked list, performing insertions at the front in constant time, but then finding and/or deleting the minimum would require a linear scan of the list. Alternatively, we could insist that the list be always kept sorted; this makes access and deletion of the minimum cheap, but then insertions would be linear.

A linked list or array will require that some operation use linear time.

An unbalanced binary search tree does not have good worst case. A balanced search tree requires lots of work.

Another way of implementing priority queues is to use a binary search tree. This gives an $O(\log N)$ average running time for both operations. However, a binary search tree is a poor choice because the input is typically not sufficiently random. We could use a balanced search tree, but the structures we saw in Chapter 18 are cumbersome to implement, leading to sluggish performance in practice. (In Chapter 21, however, we will see a data structure, the *splay tree*, that has been shown empirically to be a good alternative in some situations.)

The priority queue has properties that are a compromise between a queue and a binary search tree.

Because the priority queue supports only some of the search tree operations, we know it should not be more expensive to implement than a search tree. On the other hand, the priority queue is more powerful than a simple queue because we can implement a queue using a priority queue as follows: Insert each item with an indication of its insertion time; then a `DeleteMin` on the basis of minimum insertion time implements a `Dequeue`. Consequently, it is reasonable to expect an implementation that has properties that are a compromise between a queue and a search tree. This is realized by the *binary heap*, which

- can be implemented using a simple array (like the queue)

- supports `Insert` and `DeleteMin` in $O(\log N)$ worst-case time (a compromise between the binary search tree and the queue)

- supports `Insert` in constant average time and `FindMin` in constant worst-case time (like the queue)

The *binary heap* is the classic method used to implement priority queues.

Like the balanced search tree structures in Chapter 18, the binary heap has two properties: a structure property and an ordering property. As with balanced search trees, an operation on a binary heap can destroy one of the properties, so a binary heap operation must not terminate until both properties are in order. This turns out to be simple to do. In this chapter we will use the term *heap* to refer to the binary heap.

20.1.1   Structure Property

The heap is a *complete binary tree*. This allows representation using a simple array and guarantees logarithmic depth.

Since the only structure that we know gives dynamic logarithmic time bounds is the tree, it seems natural that the heap should organize its data as a tree. Since we would like the logarithmic bound to be a worst-case guarantee, it follows that the tree should be balanced.

A *complete binary tree* is a tree that is completely filled, with the possible exception of the bottom level, which is filled from left to right. The distinguishing feature of the complete binary tree is that there are no missing nodes in the tree. An example of a complete binary tree of ten items is shown in Figure 20.1. Had the node *J* been a right child of *E*, the tree would not be complete because there would be a missing node.

The complete tree has a number of properties that are very useful. First, the height (longest path length) of a complete binary tree of N nodes is at most $\lfloor \log N \rfloor$, because a complete tree of height H has between 2^H and $2^{H+1} - 1$ nodes. This implies that we can expect logarithmic worst-case behavior if we restrict changes in the structure to one path from the root to a leaf.

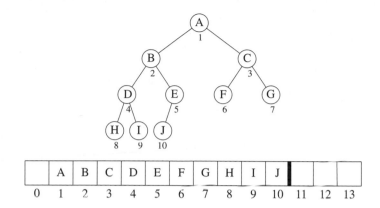

Figure 20.1   A complete binary tree and its array representation

Equally important is the observation that in a complete binary tree, Left and Right pointers are not needed. As shown in Figure 20.1, we can represent a complete binary tree by storing its level-order traversal in an array. We place the root in position 1 (position 0 is left vacant for a reason to be discussed later). We also need to maintain an integer that tells us how many nodes are currently in the tree so that we can distinguish a child node from a NULL equivalent. Then for any element in array position i, we see that its left child can be found in position $2i$. If this position extends past the number of nodes that are in the tree, then we know that the left child does not exist. Similarly, the right child is located immediately after the left child in position $2i + 1$. We again test against the actual tree size to make sure the child exists. Finally, the parent is in position $\lfloor i/2 \rfloor$. Notice that every node has a parent except the root. If the root were to have a parent, the calculation would place it in position 0. Thus we reserve position 0 as a place to put a dummy item that can serve as the root's parent. We will see that this simplifies one of the operations.

> **The parent is in position $\lfloor i/2 \rfloor$, the left child is in $2i$, and the right child in $2i + 1$.**

Using an array to store a tree is known as an *implicit representation*. As a result of this representation, not only are pointers not required, but also the operations required to traverse the tree are extremely simple and likely to be very fast on most computers. The heap structure will consist of an array (of Etype) and an integer representing the current heap size. To allow dynamic array expansion, we will slightly modify this in the C++ implementation.

> **Using an array to store a tree is known as an *implicit representation*.**

Throughout this chapter we will draw the heaps as trees to make the algorithms much easier to visualize. The implementation of these trees will use an array. You may be wondering why we do not use the implicit representation for all search trees. Some of the problems are sketched in Exercise 20.8.

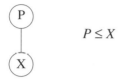

Figure 20.2 Heap order property

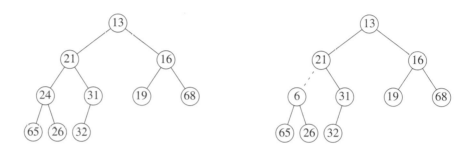

Figure 20.3 Two complete trees (only the left tree is a heap)

20.1.2 Heap-Order Property

The *heap order property* states that, in a heap, the item in the parent is never larger than the item in a node.

The property that allows operations to be performed quickly is the *heap order property*. Since we want to be able to find the minimum quickly, it makes sense that the smallest element should be at the root. If we consider that any subtree should also (recursively) be a heap, then any node should be smaller than all of its descendants. Applying this logic, we arrive at the heap order property.

> **HEAP ORDER PROPERTY**
>
> *IN A HEAP, FOR EVERY NODE X WITH PARENT P, THE KEY IN P IS SMALLER THAN OR EQUAL TO THE KEY IN X.*

The root's parent can be stored in position 0 and given a value of negative infinity.

The heap order property is illustrated in Figure 20.2. In Figure 20.3 the tree on the left is a heap, but the tree on the right is not (the dashed line shows the violation of heap order). Notice that the root does not have a parent; in the implicit representation, we can place the value $-\infty$ in position zero to remove this special case when we implement the heap. By the heap order property, we see that the minimum element can always be found at the root. Thus we see that FindMin is a constant time operation. *Max heaps* support access of the maximum *instead* of the minimum. Minor changes can be used to implement max heaps.

```
1   // BinaryHeap class interface
2   //
3   // Etype: must have zero-parameter constructor and operator=;
4   //     must have operator<
5   // CONSTRUCTION: with (a) Etype representing negative infinity
6   // Copy construction of BinaryHeap objects is DISALLOWED
7   // Deep copy is supported
8   //
9   // ******************PUBLIC OPERATIONS*********************
10  // void Insert( Etype X )  --> Insert X
11  // Etype FindMin( )        --> Return smallest item
12  // void DeleteMin( )       --> Remove smallest item
13  // void DeleteMin( Etype & X )  --> Same, but put it in X
14  // int IsEmpty( )          --> Return 1 if empty; else return 0
15  // int IsFull( )           --> Return 1 if full;  else return 0
16  // void MakeEmpty( )       --> Remove all items
17  // void Toss( Etype X )    --> Insert X (lazily)
18  // void FixHeap( )         --> Reestablish heap order property
19  // ******************ERRORS***************************
20  // Predefined exception is propagated if new fails
21  // EXCEPTION is called for FindMin or DeleteMin when empty
22
23  template <class Etype>
24  class BinaryHeap
25  {
26    public:
27          // Constructor, destructor, and copy assignment
28      BinaryHeap( const Etype & MinVal );
29      ~BinaryHeap( ) { delete [ ] Array; }
30      const BinaryHeap & operator=( const BinaryHeap & Rhs );
31
32          // Add an item maintaining heap order
33      void Insert( const Etype & X );
34
35          // Add an item but do not maintain order
36      void Toss( const Etype & X );
37
38          // Return minimum item in heap
39      const Etype & FindMin( );
40
41          // Delete minimum item in heap
42      void DeleteMin( );
43      void DeleteMin( Etype & X );
44
45          // Reestablish heap order (linear-time function)
46      void FixHeap( );
47
48          // Test if empty, if full, and make empty
49      int IsEmpty( ) const { return CurrentSize == 0; }
50      int IsFull( ) const  { return 0; }
51      void MakeEmpty( )    { CurrentSize = 0; }
```

Figure 20.4   BinaryHeap class interface (part 1: public section)

```
52    private:
53      enum { DefaultSize = 10 };
54
55      int MaxSize;        // Number of elements that can be stored
56      int CurrentSize;    // Number of elements currently stored
57      int OrderOK;        // Zero if heap order is not guaranteed
58      Etype *Array;       // The dynamically allocated array
59
60          // Disable copy constructor
61      BinaryHeap( const BinaryHeap & )
62
63          // Internal routines
64      void PercolateDown( int Index );
65      void GetArray( int NewMaxSize );  // Allocate Array
66      void CheckSize( );                // Used for Toss and Insert
67    };
```

Figure 20.5   BinaryHeap class interface (part 2: private section)

20.1.3   Allowed Operations

Now that we have settled on the representation, we can start writing code. We already know that our heap will support the basic Insert, FindMin, and DeleteMin operations, and the usual IsEmpty and MakeEmpty. We will also add some additional operations. Figure 20.4 shows the public section of the class interface and illustrates some of these additional member functions. Figure 20.5 contains the private section of the class interface.

Toss will add an item but, unlike Insert, it does not guarantee that heap order is maintained. It is useful if we intend to add many items prior to needing access to the minimum.

Let us begin by examining the public member functions. The constructor, destructor, and copy assignment operator are declared at lines 28 to 30. The Insert function is declared at line 33. It adds a new item X into the heap, performing the necessary operations to maintain the heap order property. Line 36 adds a new function, Toss. The Toss function adds a new item X into the heap but does not guarantee that heap order is maintained. Why would we ever want to Toss an item into the heap? The answer is that Toss is a much easier operation than Insert. Of course, as soon as we do a Toss operation, we do not have a heap anymore, so we cannot expect a FindMin or DeleteMin to work. For instance, if we Toss in the new minimum, we have no guarantee that it will be placed at the root (indeed we expect it will not). Consequently, Toss seems like a stupid idea.

FixHeap reinstates the heap order. Because FixHeap is expensive, its use is only justified if there are many Toss operations between accesses of the minimum.

The reason it is not is that there are many applications for which we can Toss in many items before the next DeleteMin occurs. In that case, we do not need to have heap order in effect until the DeleteMin occurs. The FixHeap operation, declared at line 46 reinstates the heap order, no matter how messed up the heap is. It works in linear time. Thus, for instance, if we need to place N items in the heap before the first DeleteMin, it is more efficient to do N Tosses and one FixHeap than N Insert operations. However, we will not use Toss in place of only a few Insert operations.

The remaining operations are as expected. FindMin is declared at line 39 and returns the minimum item in the heap. We provide two forms of DeleteMin: The one at line 43 passes the minimum item back by reference, and the other form does not. The usual IsEmpty, IsFull, and MakeEmpty are provided, with body, at lines 49 to 51.

Once we process a Toss operation, the user cannot perform a FindMin or DeleteMin without an immediately preceding FixHeap. Rather than trust the user to make this call, we maintain a data member OrderOK, which is set to false when a Toss creates a heap order violation. Figure 20.6 shows that FindMin checks to see if the heap order is satisfied. If it is not, a call to FixHeap is automatically made to reinstate the property. Notice that this means that FindMin is not a constant member function. This is why we have not derived the BinaryHeap class from AbsPrQueue.

The remaining data members are the usual suspects: a dynamically allocated array, and integers that record the current heap size and the maximum heap size. The constructor, shown in Figure 20.7, initializes these sizes and sets the heap order as true. It then allocates the array by calling GetArray at line 7. After the array is allocated, the sentinel is placed in position 0, at line 8. The user must provide MinVal as a parameter to the constructor. The body for GetArray is one line of code and is shown in Figure 20.8.

```
1   // Return minimum item in the heap
2   // Call FixHeap first if necessary
3
4   template <class Etype>
5   const Etype &
6   BinaryHeap<Etype>::FindMin( )
7   {
8       EXCEPTION( IsEmpty( ), "Binary heap is empty" );
9
10      if( OrderOK == 0 )
11          FixHeap( );
12      return Array[ 1 ];
13  }
```

Figure 20.6 The FindMin routine

```
1   // Constructor for BinaryHeap
2
3   template <class Etype>
4   BinaryHeap<Etype>::BinaryHeap( const Etype & MinVal ) :
5           MaxSize( DefaultSize ), CurrentSize( 0 ), OrderOK( 1 )
6   {
7       GetArray( MaxSize );
8       Array[ 0 ] = MinVal;
9   }
```

Figure 20.7 Constructor for BinaryHeap

```
1  // Routine to allocate the heap array
2
3  template <class Etype>
4  void
5  BinaryHeap<Etype>::GetArray( int NewMaxSize )
6  {
7      Array = new Etype [ NewMaxSize + 1 ];
8  }
```

Figure 20.8   Allocate `Array` (called by constructor and during array doubling)

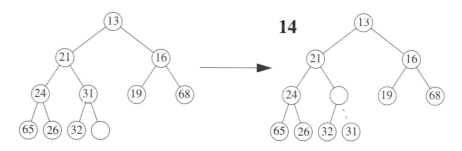

Figure 20.9   Attempt to insert 14, creating the hole and bubbling the hole up

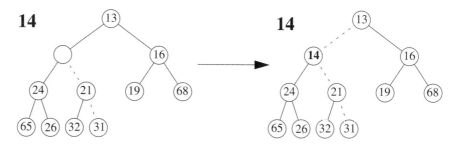

Figure 20.10   The remaining two steps to insert 14 in previous heap

20.2   Implementation of the Basic Operations

The heap order property looks promising so far since easy access to the minimum is provided. We must now show that we can efficiently support `Insert` and `DeleteMin` in logarithmic time. We will see that it is easy (both conceptually and practically) to perform the two required operations. All the work involves ensuring the heap order property is maintained.

20.2.1   Insert

To insert an element X into the heap, we must first add a node to the tree. The only option is to create a hole in the next available location; otherwise, the tree will not be complete, and we would violate the structure property. If X can be placed in the hole without violating heap order, then we do so and are done. Otherwise, we slide the element that is in the hole's parent node into the node, thus bubbling the hole up toward the root. We continue this process until X can be placed in the hole. Figure 20.9 shows that to insert 14, we create a hole in the next available heap location. Inserting 14 into the hole would violate the heap order property, so 31 is slid down into the hole. This strategy is continued in Figure 20.10 until the correct location for 14 is found.

Insertion is implemented by creating a hole at the next available location and then *percolating* it *up* until the new item can be placed in it without introducing a heap order violation with the hole's parent.

This general strategy is known as a *percolate up*; the new element is percolated up the heap until the correct location is found. The routine `CheckSize`, shown in Figure 20.11 will double the array if necessary. Figure 20.12 shows the routines that add items into the heap. The `Toss` routine is short; it just adds the new element X in the next available location. If a heap order violation results, `OrderOK` is set to false. `Insert` implements the percolate up using a very tight loop. The `for` loop that begins at 31 increments the current size and sets the hole to the newly added node. We iterate as long as the item in the parent node is larger than X. Line 32 moves the item in the parent down into the hole, and then the third expression in the `for` loop moves the hole up to the parent. When the loop terminates, line 33 places X into the hole. The sentinel in position zero guarantees that the `for` loop will terminate.

Insert uses the sentinel to avoid a special case at the root.

```
1  // If heap is full, double heap array
2
3  template <class Etype>
4  void
5  BinaryHeap<Etype>::CheckSize( )
6  {
7      if( CurrentSize == MaxSize )
8      {
9          Etype *Old = Array;
10         GetArray( MaxSize * 2 );
11         for( int i = 0; i <= MaxSize; i++ )
12             Array[ i ] = Old[ i ];
13         delete [ ] Old;
14         MaxSize *= 2;
15     }
16 }
```

Figure 20.11   Private member function `CheckSize` doubles `Array` if necessary

```
1   // Add X into the heap without maintaining order
2
3   template <class Etype>
4   void
5   BinaryHeap<Etype>::Toss( const Etype & X )
6   {
7       CheckSize( );
8       Array[ ++CurrentSize ] = X;
9       if( X < Array[ CurrentSize / 2 ] )
10          OrderOK = 0;
11  }
12
13
14  // Insert X into heap and if heap order is being maintained,
15  // percolate X up as needed
16
17  template <class Etype>
18  void
19  BinaryHeap<Etype>::Insert( const Etype & X )
20  {
21      if( OrderOK == 0 )
22      {
23          Toss( X );
24          return;
25      }
26
27      CheckSize( );
28
29          // Percolate up
30      int Hole = ++CurrentSize;
31      for( ; X < Array[ Hole / 2 ]; Hole /= 2 )
32          Array[ Hole ] = Array[ Hole / 2 ];
33      Array[ Hole ] = X;
34  }
```

Figure 20.12   Toss and Insert member functions

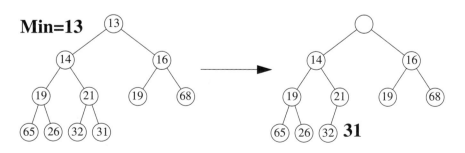

Figure 20.13   Creation of the hole at the root

The time to do the insertion could be as much as $O(\log N)$ if the element to be inserted is the new minimum. This is because it will be percolated up all the way to the root. On average, the percolation terminates early; it has been shown that 2.6 comparisons are required on average to perform the `Insert`, so the average `Insert` moves an element up 1.6 levels.

Insertion takes constant time on average but logarithmic time in the worst case.

20.2.2 DeleteMin

`DeleteMin`s are handled in a similar manner as insertions. As we have seen, finding the minimum is easy; the hard part is removing it. When the minimum is removed, a hole is created at the root. Since the heap now becomes one smaller, the structure property tells us that the last element node must be eliminated. Figure 20.13 shows the situation: The minimum item is 13, the root has a hole, and the former last item needs to be placed into the heap somewhere.

Deletion of the minimum involves placing the former last item in a hole that is created at the root. The hole is *percolated down* the tree through minimum children until the item can be placed without violating the heap order property.

If the last item can be placed in the hole, we would be done. This is impossible, unless the size of the heap is two or three, because elements at the bottom are larger than elements on the second level. We must play the same game that was done for insertion: put some item in the hole and then move the hole. The only difference is that for the `DeleteMin`, we will be moving down the tree. To do this, we find the smaller child of the hole, and if that child is not larger than the item we are trying to place, then we move the child into the hole, thus pushing the hole down one level. In Figure 20.14 we place the smaller child (14) into the hole, sliding the hole down one level. We repeat this again, placing 19 into the hole and creating a new hole one level deeper. We then place 26 in the hole and create a new hole on the bottom level. Finally, we are able to place 31 in the hole, as shown in Figure 20.15. It is easy to see that this is a logarithmic operation in the worst case. This process is known as a *percolate down*. Not surprisingly, the percolation rarely terminates more than one or two levels early, so the operation is logarithmic on average, too.

`DeleteMin` is logarithmic in both the worst and average case.

Figure 20.16 shows the two `DeleteMin` methods. We let the zero parameter `DeleteMin` call the one parameter `DeleteMin` in order to avoid rewriting the tests for emptiness and heap order. These tests are automatically done by the call to `FindMin` at line 7. The real work is done in `PercolateDown`, which is shown in Figure 20.17. The code shown there is similar in spirit to the percolation up in the `Insert` routine. Because there are two children rather than one parent, the code is a bit more complicated. `PercolateDown` takes a single parameter that tells where the hole is to be placed. The item in the hole is then moved out, and the percolation begins. For `DeleteMin`, `Hole` will be position 1. The `for` loop at line 10 terminates when there is no left child. The third expression moves the hole to the child. The smaller child is found at lines 13 to 15. Notice that we have to be careful because the last node in an even-sized heap is an only child; we cannot always assume that there are two children. This is why we have the first test at line 13.

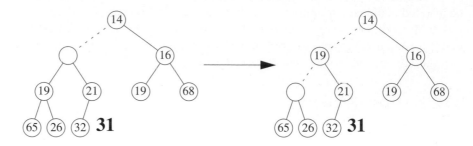

Figure 20.14   Next two steps in `DeleteMin`

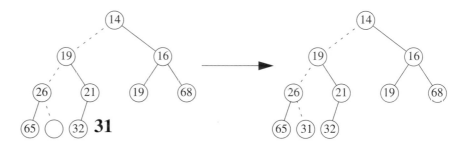

Figure 20.15   Last two steps in `DeleteMin`

```
1   // Delete the minimum item and place it in X
2
3   template <class Etype>
4   void
5   BinaryHeap<Etype>::DeleteMin( Etype & X )
6   {
7       X = FindMin( );
8       Array[ 1 ] = Array[ CurrentSize-- ];
9       PercolateDown( 1 );
10  }
11
12
13  // Delete the minimum item
14
15  template <class Etype>
16  void
17  BinaryHeap<Etype>::DeleteMin( )
18  {
19      Etype X;
20      DeleteMin( X );
21  }
```

Figure 20.16   `DeleteMin` methods

```
 1  // Private member to percolate down in the heap
 2
 3  template <class Etype>
 4  void
 5  BinaryHeap<Etype>::PercolateDown( int Hole )
 6  {
 7      int Child;
 8      Etype Tmp = Array[ Hole ];
 9
10      for( ; Hole * 2 <= CurrentSize; Hole = Child )
11      {
12          Child = Hole * 2;
13          if( Child != CurrentSize &&
14                      Array[ Child + 1 ] < Array[ Child ] )
15              Child++;
16          if( Array[ Child ] < Tmp )
17              Array[ Hole ] = Array[ Child ];
18          else
19              break;
20      }
21      Array[ Hole ] = Tmp;
22  }
```

Figure 20.17   PercolateDown method used for DeleteMin and FixHeap

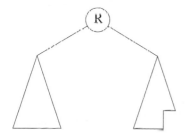

Figure 20.18   Recursive view of the heap

20.3   FixHeap: Linear Time Heap Construction

The FixHeap operation takes a complete tree that does not have heap order and reinstates it. We want this to be a linear time operation, since N insertions could be done in $O(N \log N)$ time. We expect that $O(N)$ is attainable because N successive insertions takes a total of $O(N)$ time on average, based on the result stated at the end of Section 20.2.1. N successive insertions do more work than we require, since they maintain heap order after every insertion. We only need heap order at one instant.

FixHeap can be done in linear time by applying a percolate down routine to nodes in reverse level order.

```
1  // Linear time FixHeap member
2
3  template <class Etype>
4  void
5  BinaryHeap<Etype>::FixHeap( )
6  {
7      for( int i = CurrentSize / 2; i > 0; i-- )
8          PercolateDown( i );
9      OrderOK = 1;
10 }
```

Figure 20.19   Implementation of linear time `FixHeap` method

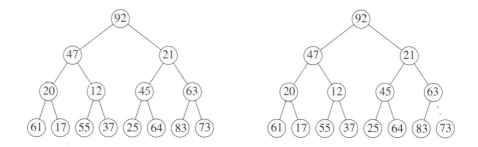

Figure 20.20   Initial heap (left); after `PercolateDown(7)` (right)

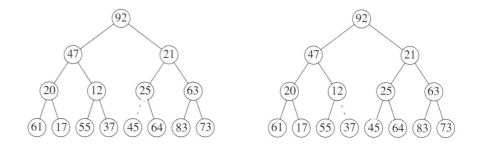

Figure 20.21   After `PercolateDown(6)` (left); after `PercolateDown(5)` (right)

    The easiest abstract solution is obtained by viewing the heap as a recursively defined structure, as shown in Figure 20.18: We would recursively call `FixHeap` on the left and right subheaps. At that point we are guaranteed that we have heap order established everywhere except the root. We can establish heap order everywhere by calling `PercolateDown` for the root. The recursive routine works by guaranteeing that when we apply `PercolateDown(i)`, all descendants of i have been processed by their own call to `Percolate`, recursively. The recursion, however, is not necessary as soon as we make the following observation: If we call `PercolateDown` on nodes in reverse level order, then at the point `PercolateDown(i)` is processed, all descendants of node i will have been processed by a prior call to `PercolateDown`. This leads to an incredibly simple algorithm for `FixHeap`, which is shown in Figure 20.19. Notice that `PercolateDown` on a leaf need not be performed. Thus we start at the highest numbered nonleaf node.

The first tree in Figure 20.20 is the unordered tree. The seven remaining trees in Figures 20.20 through 20.23 show the result of each of the seven `PercolateDown` operations. Each dashed line corresponds to two comparisons: one to find the smaller child and one to compare the smaller child with the node. Notice that there are only 10 dashed lines in the entire algorithm corresponding to 20 comparisons. (There could have been an 11th.)

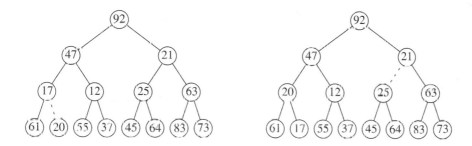

Figure 20.22   After `PercolateDown(4)` (left); after
`PercolateDown(3)` (right)

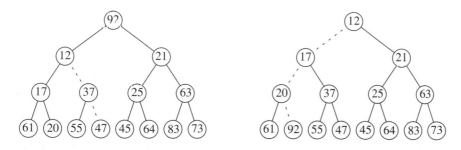

Figure 20.23   After `PercolateDown(2)` (left); after
`PercolateDown(1)` and `FixHeap` terminates (right)

The linear time bound can be shown by computing the sum of the heights of all the nodes in the heap.

To bound the running time of `FixHeap`, we must bound the number of dashed lines. This can be done by computing the sum of the heights of all the nodes in the heap, which is the maximum number of dashed lines. We expect a small number because half of the nodes are leaves and have height zero, another quarter of the nodes have height one, and thus only a quarter of the nodes (those not already counted in the first two cases) can contribute more than one unit of height. In particular, there is only one node that contributes the maximum height of $\lfloor \log N \rfloor$.

We prove the bound for perfect trees by using a marking argument.

To obtain the linear time bound for `FixHeap`, we need to establish that the sum of the heights of the nodes of a complete binary tree is $O(N)$. This is shown in Theorem 20.1. We prove the bound for perfect trees by using a marking argument.

Theorem 20.1   *For the perfect binary tree of height H containing $N = 2^{H+1} - 1$ nodes, the sum of the heights of the nodes is $N - H - 1$.*

Proof   *We use a tree marking argument (a more direct brute force calculation could also be done, as in Exercise 20.10. For any node in the tree that has some height h, we will darken h tree edges as follows: We go down the tree by traversing the left edge and then only right edges. Each edge that is traversed is darkened. As an example, we consider a perfect tree of height 4. Nodes that have height 1 have their left edge darkened, as shown in Figure 20.24. Next nodes of height two have a left edge and then a right edge darkened on the path from the node to the bottom. This is shown in Figure 20.25. In Figure 20.26 three edges are darkened for each node of height three: the first left edge leading out of the node and then the two right edges on the path to the bottom. Finally, in Figure 20.27 we see that four edges are darkened: the left edge leading out of the root and the three right edges on the path to the bottom. We can see the following two facts: (1) No edge is ever darkened twice, and (2) every edge except those on the right path is darkened. Since there are $(N-1)$ tree edges (every node has an edge coming into it except the root) and H edges on the right path, the number of darkened edges is $N - 1 - H$, proving the theorem.*

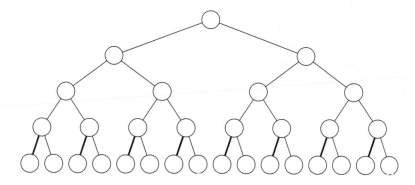

Figure 20.24   Marking of left edges for height one nodes

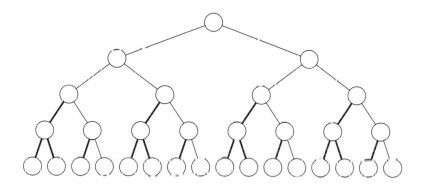

Figure 20.25   Marking of first left and subsequent right edge for height two nodes

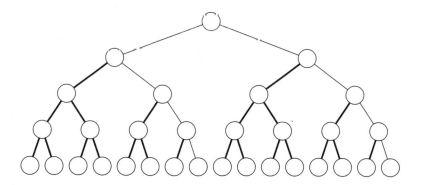

Figure 20.26   Marking of first left and subsequent two right edges for height three nodes

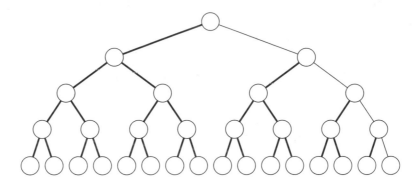

Figure 20.27   Marking of first left and subsequent right edges for height 4 node

A complete binary tree is not a perfect binary tree, but the result we have obtained is an upper bound on the sum of the heights of the nodes in a complete binary tree. Since a complete binary tree has between 2^H and $2^{H+1} - 1$ nodes, this theorem implies that the sum is $O(N)$. A more careful argument establishes that the sum of the height is $N - v(N)$, where $v(N)$ is the number of 1s in the binary representation of N. A proof of this is left as Exercise 20.12.

20.4   Advanced Operations: `DecreaseKey` and `Merge`

In Chapter 22 we will examine priority queues that support two additional operations. The `DecreaseKey` operation lowers the value of an item in the priority queue. The item's position is presumed known. In a binary heap this is easily implemented by percolating up until heap order is re-established. However we must be careful, since by assumption each item's position is being stored separately. All items involved in the percolation have their positions altered. The `DecreaseKey` operation is useful in implementing graph algorithms (for example, Dijkstra's algorithm, seen in Section 14.3).

`Merge` combines two priority queues. Because the heap is array-based, the best we can hope to achieve with a merge is to copy the items in the smaller heap into the larger heap and perform some rearrangements. Even so, this will take at least linear time per operation. If we use general trees with nodes connected by pointers, we will see that we can reduce the bound to logarithmic cost per operation. Merging has uses in advanced algorithm design.

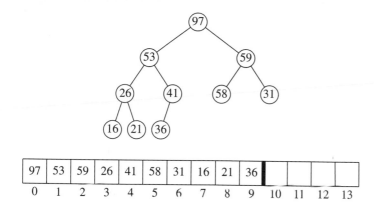

97	53	59	26	41	58	31	16	21	36				
0	1	2	3	4	5	6	7	8	9	10	11	12	13

Figure 20.28   (Max) Heap after `FixHeap` phase

20.5   Internal Sorting: Heapsort

The priority queue can be used to sort N items as follows:

1. Insert every item into a binary heap.
2. Extract every item by calling `DeleteMin` N times. The result is sorted.

A priority queue can be used to sort in $O(N \log N)$ time. An algorithm that is based on this idea is *heapsort*.

Using the observation of the previous section, this is more efficiently implemented as follows:

1. `Toss` each item into a binary heap.
2. Apply `FixHeap`.
3. Call `DeleteMin` N times; the items will exit the heap in sorted order.

Step 1 takes linear time total. Step 2 takes linear time. In step 3, each call to `DeleteMin` takes logarithmic time, so N calls takes $O(N \log N)$ time. Consequently, we have an $O(N \log N)$ worst-case sorting algorithm, which is as good as can be achieved by a comparison-based algorithm, as we discussed in Section 8.8. One problem with the algorithm as it stands now is that sorting an array requires the use of the binary heap data structure, which itself carries the overhead of an array. It would be preferable to emulate the heap data structure on the array that is input, rather than going through the heap class apparatus. We will assume for the rest of this discussion that this is what will be done.

However, even though we do not use the heap class directly, we still seem to need a second array because we have to record the order that items exit the heap equivalent in a second array and then copy that ordering back into the original array. The memory requirement is doubled, which could be critical in some applications. Notice that the extra time spent copying the second array back to the first is only $O(N)$, so unlike mergesort, the extra array does not affect the running *time* significantly. The problem is space.

A clever way to avoid using a second array makes use of the fact that, after each DeleteMin, the heap shrinks by one. Thus the cell that was last in the heap can be used to store the element that was just deleted. As an example, suppose we have a heap with six elements. The first DeleteMin produces A_1. Now the heap has only five elements, so we can place A_1 in position six. The next DeleteMin produces A_2. Since the heap will now only have four elements, we can place A_2 in position five.

Using this strategy, after the last DeleteMin the array will contain the elements in *decreasing* sorted order. If we want the array in the more typical *increasing* sorted order, we can change the ordering property so that the parent has a larger key than the child. Thus we have a *max heap*. As an example, suppose we want to sort the input sequence 59, 36, 58, 21, 41, 97, 31, 16, 26, 53. After the items are tossed into the max heap and FixHeap is applied, we obtain the arrangement shown in Figure 20.28.

Figure 20.29 shows the heap that results after the first DeleteMax. As we can see, the last element in the heap is 21; 97 has been placed in a part of the heap array that is technically no longer part of the heap.

Figure 20.30 shows that, after a second DeleteMax, 16 becomes the last element. Now only eight items remain in the heap. The maximum element that was removed, 59, is placed in the dead spot of the array. After seven more DeleteMax operations, the heap will represent only one element, but the elements left in the array will be sorted in increasing order.

The implementation of heapsort is simple because the basic operations follow the heap operations. There are three minor differences. First, since we are using a max heap, we need to switch the comparisons from > to <. Second, we can no longer assume that there is a sentinel position 0. This is because all our other sorting algorithms store data at position 0, and we must assume that HeapSort will be no different. Although the sentinel is not needed anyway, since there are no percolate up operations, its absence affects calculations of the child and parent: For a node in position i, the parent is in position $(i-1)/2$, the left child is in position $2i + 1$, and the right child is next to the left child. Third, PercolateDown needs to be informed of the current heap size (which is lowered by one in each iteration of DeleteMax). We leave the implementation of PercolateDown as Exercise 20.19. Assuming that we have written PercolateDown, then HeapSort is easily expressed as shown in Figure 20.31.

20.6 External Sorting

So far all the sorting algorithms we have examined require that the input fit into main memory. There are, however, applications for which the input is much too large to fit into memory. This section will discuss *external sorting* algorithms, which are designed to handle very large inputs.

20.6.1   Why We Need New Algorithms

Most of the internal sorting algorithms take advantage of the fact that memory is directly accessible. Shellsort compares elements A[i] and A[i-Gap] in one time unit. Heapsort compares A[i] and A[Child=i*2] in one time unit. Quicksort, with median-of-three pivoting, requires comparing A[First], A[Center], and A[Last] in a constant number of time units. If the input is on a tape, then all these operations lose their efficiency because elements on a tape can be accessed only sequentially. Even if the data is on a disk, there is still a practical loss of efficiency because of the delay required to spin the disk and move the disk head.

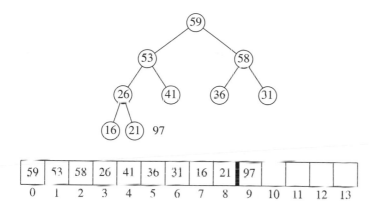

Figure 20.29   Heap after first DeleteMax

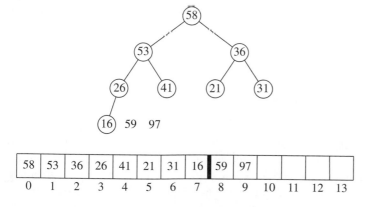

Figure 20.30   Heap after second DeleteMax

```
1  // HeapSort: sort first N items in array A
2  // Etype: must have copy constructor, operator=, and
3  //        whatever comparison routines are used by PercolateDown
4
5  template <class Etype>
6  void
7  HeapSort( Etype A[ ], int N )
8  {
9          // FixHeap
10     for( int i = ( N - 1 ) / 2; i >= 0; i-- )
11         PercolateDown( A, i, N );
12
13     for( int j = N - 1; j >= 1; j-- )
14     {
15             // DeleteMax
16         Swap( A[ 0 ], A[ j ] );
17         PercolateDown( A, 0, j - 1 );
18     }
19  }
```

Figure 20.31   HeapSort routine

A1	81	94	11	96	12	35	17	99	28	58	41	75	15
A2												
B1												
B2												

Figure 20.32   Initial tape configuration

To see how slow external accesses really are, we could create a random file that is large but not too big to fit in main memory. When we read the file in and sort it using an efficient algorithm, the time it takes to sort the input is certain to be insignificant compared to the time to read the input, even though sorting is an $O(N \log N)$ operation (or worse for Shellsort), and reading the input is only $O(N)$.

20.6.2   Model for External Sorting

We assume sorts are performed on tape. Only sequential access of the input is allowed.

The wide variety of mass storage devices makes external sorting much more device dependent than internal sorting. The algorithms that we will consider work on tapes, which are probably the most restrictive storage medium. Since access to an element on tape is done by winding the tape to the correct location, tapes can be efficiently accessed only in sequential order (in either direction).

We will assume that we have at least three tape drives to perform the sorting.

We need two drives to do an efficient sort; the third drive simplifies matters. If only one tape drive is present, then we are in trouble: Any algorithm will require $\Omega(N)$ tape accesses.

20.6.3   The Simple Algorithm

The basic external sorting algorithm uses the merge routine from mergesort. Suppose we have four tapes A1, A2, B1, and B2, which are two input and two output tapes. Depending on the point in the algorithm, the A and B tapes are either input tapes or output tapes. Suppose the data is initially on A1. Suppose further that the internal memory can hold (and sort) M records at a time. The natural first step is to read M records at a time from the input tape, sort the records internally, and then write the sorted records alternately to B1 and B2. We will call each set of sorted records a *run*. When this is done, we rewind all the tapes. Suppose we have the same input as our example for Shellsort. Then the initial configuration is shown in Figure 20.32. If $M = 3$, then after the runs are constructed, the tapes will contain the data as shown in Figure 20.33.

The basic external sort uses repeated two-way merging. Each sorted group is a *run*; as a result of a pass, the length of the runs doubles, and eventually only a single run remains.

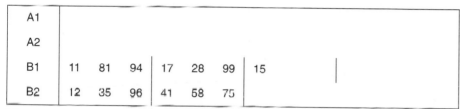

A1							
A2							
B1	11	81	94	17	28	99	15
B2	12	35	96	41	58	75	

Figure 20.33   Distribution of length 3 runs onto two tapes

A1	11	12	35	81	94	96	15
A2	17	28	41	58	75	99	
B1							
B2							

Figure 20.34   Tapes after first round of merging (run length = 6)

A1												
A2												
B1	11	12	17	28	35	41	58	75	81	94	96	99
B2	15											

Figure 20.35   Tapes after second round of merging (run length = 12)

A1	11	12	15	17	28	35	41	58	75	81	94	96	99
A2													
B1													
B2													

Figure 20.36   Tapes after third routine of merging

Now B1 and B2 contain a group of runs. We take the first runs from each tape and merge them, writing the result, which is a run twice as long, onto A1. Then we take the next runs from each tape, merge these, and write the result out to A2. We continue this process, alternating output to A1 and A2 until either B1 or B2 is empty. At this point, either both are empty or there is one (possibly short) run left. In the latter case, we copy this run onto the appropriate tape. We rewind all four tapes, and repeat the same steps, this time using the A tapes as input and the B tapes as output. This will give runs of length $4M$. We continue this process until we get one run of length N, at which point the run represents the sorted arrangement of the input. Figure 20.34, Figure 20.35, and Figure 20.36 shows how this process works for our sample input.

Consequently we need $\lceil \log(N/M) \rceil$ passes over the input before we have one giant run.

The algorithm will require $\lceil \log(N/M) \rceil$ passes, plus the initial run-constructing pass. For instance, if we have 10 million records of 128 bytes each, and four megabytes of internal memory, then the first pass will create 320 runs. We would then need nine more passes to complete the sort. This formula correctly tells us that our example requires $\lceil \log(13/3) \rceil$, or three more passes.

20.6.4   Multiway Merge

K-way merging reduces the number of passes. The obvious implementation uses $2K$ tapes.

If we have extra tapes, then we can expect to reduce the number of passes required to sort our input. We do this by extending the basic (two-way) merge to a K-way merge.

Merging two runs is done by winding each input tape to the beginning of each run. Then the smaller element is found and placed on an output tape, and the appropriate input tape is advanced. If there are K input tapes, this strategy works the same way; the only difference is that it is slightly more complicated to find the smallest of the K elements. We can find the smallest of these elements by using a priority queue. To obtain the next element to write on the output tape, we perform a `DeleteMin` operation. The appropriate input tape is advanced, and if the run on that input tape is not yet completed, we `Insert` the new element into the priority queue. Figure 20.37 shows how the input from the previous example is distributed onto three tapes. Figures 20.38 and 20.39 show the two passes of three-way merging that complete the sort.

A1						
A2						
A3						
B1	11	81	94	41	58	75
B2	12	35	96	15		
B3	17	28	99			

Figure 20.37   Initial distribution of length 3 runs onto three tapes

A1	11	12	17	28	35	81	94	96	99
A2	15	41	58	75					
A3									
B1									
B2									
B3									

Figure 20.38   After one round of three-way merging (run length = 9)

A1										
A2										
A3										
B1	11	12	15	17	28	35	41	58	75	81	94	96	99
B2										
B3										

Figure 20.39   After two rounds of three-way merging

After the initial run construction phase, the number of passes required using K-way merging is $\lceil \log_K(N/M) \rceil$, because the runs get K times as large in each pass. For our example, the formula is verified because $\lceil \log_3 13/3 \rceil = 2$. If we have ten tapes, then $K = 5$, and for the large example in the previous section, 320 runs would require $\log_5 320 = 4$ passes.

	Run	**After**						
	Const.	**T3+T2**	**T1+T2**	**T1+T3**	**T2+T3**	**T1+T2**	**T1+T3**	**T2+T3**
T1	0	13	5	0	3	1	0	1
T2	21	8	0	5	2	0	1	0
T3	13	0	8	3	0	2	1	0

Figure 20.40   Number of runs using polyphase merge

20.6.5   Polyphase Merge

The *polyphase merge* implements a *K*-way merge with *K*+1 tapes.

The *K*-way merging strategy developed in the last section requires the use of $2K$ tapes. This could be prohibitive for some applications. It is possible to get by with only $K + 1$ tapes. The technique is known as *polyphase merging*. As an example, we show how to perform two-way merging using only three tapes.

Suppose we have three tapes, T1, T2, and T3, and an input file on T1 that will produce 34 runs. One option is to put 17 runs on each of T2 and T3. We could then merge this result onto T1, obtaining one tape with 17 runs. The problem is that since all the runs are on one tape, we must now put some of these runs on T2 to perform another merge. The logical way to do this is to copy the first eight runs from T1 onto T2 and then perform the merge. This has the effect of adding an extra half pass for every pass we do. The question is, can we do better?

The distribution of runs affects performance. The best distribution is related to the Fibonacci numbers.

An alternative method is to split the original 34 runs unevenly. Suppose we put 21 runs on T2 and 13 runs on T3. We could then merge 13 runs onto T1 before T3 was empty. We could then rewind T1 and T3 and merge T1, with 13 runs, and T2, with 8 runs, onto T3. We could then merge 8 runs until T2 was empty, which would leave 5 runs left on T1 and 8 runs on T3. We could then merge T1 and T3, and so on. Figure 20.40 shows the number of runs on each tape after each pass.

The original distribution of runs makes a great deal of difference. For instance, if 22 runs are placed on T2, with 12 on T3, then after the first merge, we obtain 12 runs on T1 and 10 runs on T2. After another merge, there are 10 runs on T1 and 2 runs on T3. At this point the going gets slow because we can merge only two sets of runs before T3 is exhausted. Then T1 has 8 runs and T2 has 2 runs. Again we can merge only 2 sets of runs, obtaining T1 with 6 runs and T3 with 2 runs. After three more passes, T2 has two runs, and the other tapes are empty. We must copy one run to another tape, and then we can finish the merge.

It turns out that the first distribution we gave is optimal. If the number of runs is a Fibonacci number F_N, then the best way to distribute them is to split them into two Fibonacci numbers F_{N-1} and F_{N-2}. Otherwise, it is necessary to pad the tape with dummy runs in order to get the number of runs up to a Fibonacci number. We leave the details of how to place the initial set of runs on the tapes as an exercise. We can extend this to a K-way merge, in which we need Kth order Fibonacci numbers for the distribution. The Kth order Fibonacci number is defined as the sum of the K previous Kth order Fibonacci number, as shown in the following equation:

$$F^{(K)}(N) = F^{(K)}(N-1) + F^{(K)}(N-2) + \ldots + F^{(K)}(N-K)$$

$$F^{(K)}(0 \le N \le K-2) = 0$$

$$F^{(K)}(K-1) = 1$$

20.6.6   Replacement Selection

The last item we will consider is construction of the runs. The strategy we have used so far is the simplest possible: We read as many elements as possible and sort them, writing the result to a tape. This seems like the best approach possible until we realize that as soon as the first element is written to the output tape, the memory it used becomes available for another element. If the next element on the input tape is larger than the element we have just output, then it can be included in the run.

Using this observation, we can give an algorithm for producing runs. This technique is commonly referred to as *replacement selection*. Initially M elements are read into memory and placed in a priority queue, using `Toss` operations, followed by a single `FixHeap`. We perform a `DeleteMin`, writing the smallest element to the output tape. We read the next element from the input tape. If it is larger than the element we have just written, we can add it to the priority queue by an `Insert`. Otherwise, it cannot go into the current run. Since the priority queue is smaller by one element, we can store this element in the dead space of the priority queue until the run is completed and use this element for the next run. Storing an element in the dead space is exactly what was done in heapsort. We continue doing this until the size of the priority queue is zero, at which point the run is over. We start a new run by rebuilding a new priority queue, using all the elements in the dead space and a `FixHeap` operation.

> The length of the runs that we initially construct can be larger than the amount of available main memory if we are clever. This technique is commonly referred to as *replacement selection*.

Figure 20.41 shows the run construction for the small example we have been using, with $M = 3$. Elements that are reserved for the next run are shaded. Elements 11, 94, and 81 are placed using `FixHeap`. Element 11 is output, and the 96 that is next is placed in the heap by an insertion because it is larger than the 11. Element 81 is output next. The next element read is 12. Since 12 is smaller than the 81 just output, it cannot be included in the current run. Thus it is placed in the heap dead space. The heap now logically contains only 94 and 96. After they are output, we have only dead space elements, so we construct a heap and begin run 2. In this example, replacement selection produces only three runs, compared with the five runs obtained by sorting. Because of this, a three-way merge finishes in one pass instead of two. If the input is randomly distributed, replacement selection can be shown to produce runs of average length $2M$. For our large example, we would expect 160 runs instead of 320 runs, so a five-way merge would still require four passes. In this case, we have not saved a pass, although we might if we get lucky and have 125 runs or less. Since external sorts take so long, every pass saved can make a significant difference in the running time.

As we have seen, it is possible for replacement selection to do no better than the standard algorithm. However, the input is frequently nearly sorted to start with, in which case replacement selection produces only a few abnormally long runs. This kind of input is common for external sorts and makes replacement selection extremely valuable.

Summary

In this chapter we have seen an elegant implementation of the priority queue. The binary heap requires no pointers and uses only constant extra space, yet it supports the basic operations in logarithmic worst-case time. The heap leads to a popular sorting algorithm, *heapsort*. Exercises 20.24 and 20.25 ask you to compare the performance of heapsort with quicksort. Generally speaking, heapsort is slower than quicksort, but it is certainly simpler to implement. Finally, we saw that priority queues are important data structures for external sorting.

This completes the implementation of the fundamental and classic data structures. In Part V we will examine more sophisticated data structures. We begin with the splay tree, which is a binary search tree that has some remarkable properties.

	3 Elements in Heap Array			Output	Next Item
	Array[1]	Array[2]	Array[3]		Read
	11	94	81	11	96
	81	94	96	81	12
Run 1	94	96	12	94	35
	96	35	12	96	17
	17	35	12	End of Run	Rebuild Heap
	12	35	17	12	99
	17	35	99	17	28
	28	99	35	28	58
Run 2	35	99	58	35	41
	41	99	58	41	75
	58	99	75	58	End of Tape
	99		75	99	
			75	End of Run	Rebuild Heap
Run 3	75			75	

Figure 20.41   Example of run construction

Objects of the Game

binary heap The classic method used to implement priority queues. The binary heap has two properties: a structure property and an ordering property. (640)

complete binary tree A tree that is completely filled and has no missing nodes. The heap is a complete binary tree, which allows representation using a simple array and guarantees logarithmic depth. (640)

external sorting Used when the data are too large to fit in main memory. (658)

FixHeap operation Takes a complete tree that does not have heap order and reinstates it. Can be done in linear time by applying a percolate down routine to nodes in reverse level order. (651)

heap order property In a (min) heap, the item in the parent is never larger than the item in a node. (642)

heapsort A priority queue can be used to sort in $O(N \log N)$ time. An algorithm that is based on this idea is heapsort. (657)

implicit representation Using an array to store a tree. (641)

max heap Supports access of the maximum instead of minimum. (642)

multiway merge K-way merging reduces the number of passes. The obvious implementation uses $2K$ tapes. (662)

percolate down Deletion of the minimum involves placing the former last item in a hole that is created at the root. The hole is percolated down the tree through minimum children until the item can be placed without violating the heap order property. (649)

percolate up Insertion is implemented by creating a hole at the next available location and then percolating it up until the new item can be placed in it without introducing a heap order violation with the hole's parent. (647)

polyphase merge Implements a K-way merge with $K + 1$ tapes. (664)

replacement selection The length of the runs that are initially constructed can be larger than the amount of available memory. If we can store M objects in main memory, then we can expect runs of length $2M$. This technique is commonly referred to as replacement selection. (665)

run The basic external sort uses repeated two-way merging. Each sorted group is a run; as a result of a pass, the length of the runs doubles, and eventually only a single run remains. (661)

Toss operation Adds an item but, unlike Insert, it does not guarantee that heap order is maintained. It is useful if we intend to add many items prior to needing access to the minimum. (644)

Common Errors

1. The binary heap requires a sentinel in position 0. A common error is instantiating with an inappropriate sentinel, or writing the class that forgets to install the sentinel.

2. The most tricky part of the binary heap is the percolate down case, when only one child is present. Since this is a rare occurrence, it is difficult to spot an incorrect implementation.

3. The heap order property must be restored prior to obtaining a minimum element if a Toss has relaxed it.

4. For heapsort, since the data begins in position 0, the children of node i are in positions $2i + 1$ and $2i + 2$.

On the Internet

The code to implement the BinaryHeap is available in two files:

Heap.h   Contains the class interface for BinaryHeap
Heap.cpp   Contains the implementation for the BinaryHeap class

Exercises

In Short

20.1. Describe the structure and ordering properties of the binary heap.

20.2. In a binary heap, for an item in position i, where are the parent, left child, and right located?

20.3. Show the result of inserting 10, 12, 1, 14, 6, 5, 8, 15, 3, 9, 7, 4, 11, 13, and 2, one at a time, into an initially empty heap. Then show the result of using the linear time FixHeap algorithm instead.

20.4. Where could the 11th dashed line in Figures 20.20 to 20.23 have been?

20.5. A max heap supports Insert, DeleteMax, and FindMax (but not DeleteMin or FindMin). Describe in detail how max heaps can be implemented.

20.6. Show the result of the heapsort algorithm after the initial construction and then two DeleteMax operations on the input in Exercise 20.3.

20.7. Is heapsort a stable sort (that is, if there are duplicates, do the duplicate items retain their initial ordering among themselves)?

In Theory

20.8. A complete binary tree of N elements uses array positions 1 to N.

a. Suppose we have a binary tree that has two extra levels (that is, it is very slightly unbalanced). How large must the array be?

b. Suppose we have a binary tree that has one node at depth $2 \log N$. How large must the array be?

c. Suppose we have a binary tree that has one node at depth $4.1 \log N$. How large must the array be?

d. Suppose we have the worst-case binary tree. How large must the array be?

20.9. We want to find the maximum item in the heap.

a. Show that it must be at one of the leaves.

b. Show that there are exactly $\lceil N/2 \rceil$ leaves.

c. Show that we must examine every leaf.

20.10. We would like to prove Theorem 20.1 by using a direct summation.

a. Show that there are 2^i nodes of height $H - i$

b. Write the equation for the sum of the heights using part a.

c. Evaluate the sum in part b.

20.11. Verify that the sum of the heights of a perfect binary tree satisfies $N - v(N)$, where $v(N)$ is the number of ones in the binary representation of N.

20.12. Prove the bound in Exercise 20.11 using an induction argument.

20.13. For heapsort, we know that $O(N \log N)$ comparisons are used in the worst case. Derive the leading term (that is, decide if it is $N \log N$, $2N \log N$, $3N \log N$, and so on).

20.14. Show that there are inputs that force every PercolateDown in heapsort to go all the way to a leaf. *Hint*: Work backward.

20.15. A *d-heap* is an implicit data structure that is like a binary heap, except that nodes have d children. A *d-heap* is thus more shallow than a binary heap, but finding the minimum child requires examining d children instead of two. With this in mind, what is the running time (in terms of d and N) of the Insert and DeleteMin operations for a *d*-heap?

20.16. A *min max heap* is a data structure that supports both DeleteMin and DeleteMax at logarithmic cost. The structure is identical to the binary heap. The min max heap order property is that for any node X at even depth, the key stored at X is the smallest in its subtree, while for any node X at odd depth, the key stored at X is the largest in its subtree. The root is at even depth.

a. Draw a possible min max heap for the items 1, 2, 3, 4, 5, 6, 7, 8, 9, 10. Note that there are many possible heaps.

b. How do we find the minimum and maximum elements?

c. Give an algorithm to insert a new node into the min max heap.

d. Give an algorithm to perform DeleteMin and DeleteMax.

e. Give an algorithm to perform FixHeap in linear time.

20.17. The 2-D heap is a data structure that allows each item to have two individual keys. DeleteMin can be performed with respect to either of these keys. The 2-D heap order property is that for any node X at even depth, the item stored at X has the smallest key #1 in its subtree, while for any node X at odd depth, the item stored at X has the smallest key #2 in its subtree.

a. Draw a possible 2-D heap for the items (1,10), (2,9), (3,8), (4,7), (5,6).

b. How do we find the item with minimum key #1?

c. How do we find the item with minimum key #2?

d. Give an algorithm to insert a new item into the 2-D heap.

e. Give an algorithm to perform DeleteMin with respect to either key.

f. Give an algorithm to perform FixHeap in linear time.

20.18. A *treap* is a binary search tree in which each node stores an item, two pointers, and a randomly assigned priority that is generated when the node is constructed. The nodes in the tree obey the usual binary search tree order but must also maintain heap order with respect to the priorities. The treap is a good alternative to the balanced search trees because balance is now based on the random priorities, rather than the items. Thus the average case results for binary search trees are applicable.

a. Prove that a collection of distinct items each of which has a distinct priority can only be represented by one treap.

b. Show how to perform insertion into a treap, using a bottom-up algorithm.

c. Show how to perform insertion into a treap, using a top-down algorithm.

d. Show how to perform deletion from a treap.

In Practice

20.19. Write the routine `PercolateDown` with the declaration shown below. Remember that the max-heap starts at position 0, not position 1.

```
void
PercolateDown( Etype A[ ], int Index, int Size );
```

20.20. Modify the `BinaryHeap` class to throw an `Underflow` exception when a `FindMin` or `DeleteMin` is attempted on an empty priority queue.

20.21. Implement the `BinaryHeap` using a `Vector` object.

20.22. We would like to derive `BinaryHeap` from `AbsPrQueue`. This exercise asks you to examine some possibilities. See what happens on your compiler when you attempt the following solutions (note that compilers will behave differently).

a. Use the simplest inheritance mechanism and make no arrangements to deal with the inconsistency between the `FindMin` in the abstract base class and derived class.

b. Add a constant member version of `FindMin` to the derived class, but do not supply a body.

c. Add a constant member version of `FindMin` to the derived class that prints an error message if it gets called.

d. Add a constant member version of `FindMin` to the derived class that calls the nonconstant member version with

```
return ( ( BinaryHeap * ) this )->FindMin( )
```

Programming Projects

20.23. Write a program to compare the running time of *N* `Toss` operations followed by a `FixHeap` versus *N* separate `Inserts`. Run your program for sorted, reverse sorted, and random inputs.

20.24. Implement both heapsort and quicksort and compare their performance on both sorted inputs and random inputs. Use different types of data for the tests.

20.25. Consider the following strategy for `PercolateDown`: We have a hole at node *X*. The normal routine is to compare *X*'s children and then move the child up to *X* if it is larger (in the case of a (max)heap) than the element we are trying to place, thereby pushing the hole down; we stop when it is safe to place the new element in the hole. The alternative strategy is to move elements up and the hole down as far as possible without testing whether the new cell can be inserted. This would place the new cell in a leaf and probably violate heap order. To fix the heap order, percolate the new cell up in the normal manner. The expectation is that the percolation up will be only one or two levels on average. Write a routine to include this idea, and compare the running time with a standard implementation of heapsort.

20.26. Implement an external sort.

References

The binary heap was first described in the context of heapsort in [8]. The linear-time FixHeap algorithm is from [4]. Precise results on the number of comparisons and data movements used by heapsort in the best, worst, and average case are given in [7]. Advanced priority queue implementations are discussed in Chapter 21 and Chapter 22. External sorting is discussed in detail in [6]. Exercise 20.15 is solved in [5]. Exercise 20.16 is solved in [2]. Exercise 20.17 is solved in [3]. Treaps are described in [1].

1. C. Aragon and R. Seidel, "Randomized Search Trees," *Proceedings of the Thirtieth Annual Symposium on Foundations of Computer Science* (1989), 540-545.

2. M. D. Atkinson, J. R. Sack, N. Santoro, and T. Strothotte, "Min-Max Heaps and Generalized Priority Queues," *Communications of the ACM* **29** (1986), 996-1000.

3. Y. Ding and M. A. Weiss, "The k-d Heap: An Efficient Multi-dimensional Priority Queue," *Proceedings of the Third Workshop on Algorithms and Data Structures* (1993), 302-313.

4. R. W. Floyd, "Algorithm 245: Treesort 3," *Communications of the ACM* **7** (1964), 701.

5. D. B. Johnson, "Priority Queues with Update and Finding Minimum Spanning Trees," *Information Processing Letters* **4** (1975), 53-57.

6. D. E. Knuth, *The Art of Computer Programming. Volume 3: Sorting and Searching*, Addison-Wesley, Reading, MA, 1973.

7. R. Schaffer and R. Sedgewick, "The Analysis of Heapsort," *Journal of Algorithms* **14** (1993), 76-100.

8. J. W. J. Williams, "Algorithm 232: Heapsort," *Communications of the ACM* **7** (1964), 347-348.

Part V: Advanced Data Structures

Chapter 21

Splay Trees

In this chapter we describe a remarkable data structure known as the *splay tree*. The splay tree supports all the binary search tree operations but does not guarantee $O(\log N)$ worst-case performance. Instead, its bounds are *amortized,* meaning that although individual operations can be expensive, any sequence of operations is guaranteed to behave as if each operation in the sequence exhibited logarithmic behavior. Because this is a weaker guarantee than what is provided by balanced search trees, we find that only the data and two pointers per node are required for each item and that the operations are somewhat simpler to code. As we will see, the splay tree has some other interesting properties.

In this chapter we will see

- descriptions of the concepts of amortization and self-adjustment
- the basic bottom-up splay tree algorithm and a proof that it has logarithmic amortized cost per operation
- how splay trees can be implemented using a top-down algorithm, a complete splay tree implementation (including deletion algorithm)
- comparison between splay trees and other data structures

21.1   Self-adjustment and Amortized Analysis

Although balanced search trees provide logarithmic worst-case running time per operation, they have several limitations:

- Balanced search trees require storing an extra piece of balancing information per node.
- They are complicated to implement, and as a result insertions and deletions are expensive and potentially error-prone.
- We do not win when easy inputs occur.

Let us examine the consequences of each of these deficiencies. First, we see that balanced search trees require an extra data member. Although in theory this can be as little as a single bit (as in the red black trees), in practice the space overhead might not be quite so insignificant. There are two reasons for this. First, when allocating memory for a structure, the compiler must satisfy certain machine restrictions. For instance, on most machines, a 4-byte integer (or pointer) can only be stored at a memory location that is divisible by 4. The compiler must allocate memory in a structure so that an array of structures satisfies all alignment requirements. In general this means that a structure may contain holes in which no data is stored. In our case a structure that consists of an integer data member, two pointers, and a bit to store the color will be stored in 16 bytes rather than 12 bytes and a bit. The memory that the bit field takes becomes unusable for any other purpose; in our case the single bit has added 33 percent to the memory requirements.

Actually, there are some circumstances where things could be worse. This depends on how `new` and `delete` are implemented. On some systems, including some compilers that run on the UNIX operating system, memory is allocated in chunks that are powers of two. This means that a single bit could double the storage requirements or leave it unaffected, depending on whether it causes the total space requirement to cross a power of 2. For instance, in our case 16 bytes are used whether or not an extra color bit is used. However, if we wanted to maintain an ordered search tree in which a 4-byte size is also stored, then the storage requirement that used to be 16 bytes becomes 16+ bytes and is rounded up to 32. These are the so-called binary buddy systems.

The real problem is that the extra data members add complications that we can live without.

In an age where machines' memories are becoming huge, one must ask if worrying about memory is such a large issue. The answer in most cases is probably not, except that maintaining the extra data members requires more complex code and tends to lead to longer running times and more errors. Indeed, it is difficult to tell if the balancing information for a search tree is correct, since errors will only lead to an unbalanced tree. If one case is slightly wrong, it might be difficult to spot the errors. Thus, as a practical matter, algorithms that allow us to remove some complications without sacrificing performance deserve serious consideration.

The *90-10 rule* states that 90 percent of the accesses are to 10 percent of the data items. Balanced search trees do not take advantage of this.

The balanced search trees have a second feature that seems improvable: Their worst-case, average-case and best-case performance are essentially identical. As an example, suppose we perform a `Find` operation for some item X. While it is reasonable to expect that the cost of the `Find` is logarithmic, it is also reasonable to expect that if we perform an immediate second `Find` for X, the second access ought to be cheaper than the first. In a red black tree, this is not true. We would also expect that if we perform an access of X, Y, and then Z, then a second set of accesses for the same sequence would be easy. This is important because of the *90-10 rule*: Empirical studies suggest that in practice 90 percent of the accesses are to 10 percent of the data items. Consequently, we want to get easy wins for the 90 percent case.

The 90-10 rule has been used for many years in disk I/O systems. A *cache* stores in main memory the contents of some of the disk blocks. The hope is that when a disk access is requested, the block can be found in the main memory cache and save the cost of an expensive disk access. Of course, only relatively few disk blocks can be stored in memory. Even so, by storing the most recently accessed disk blocks in the cache, large improvements in performance are observed because many of the same disk blocks are accessed over and over again.

21.1.1   Amortized Time Bounds

We are asking for a lot: We want to avoid balancing information and we want to be able to take advantage of the 90-10 rule. Naturally we expect that we might have to give up some feature of the balanced search tree.

The trade we can make is to sacrifice the logarithmic worst-case performance. Since we are hoping not to maintain balance information, this seems inevitable. However, we cannot accept the typical performance of an unbalanced binary search tree. There is, however, a reasonable compromise: $O(N)$ time for a single access may be acceptable as long as it does not happen too often. In particular, if any M operations (starting with the first operation) take a total of $O(M \log N)$ worst-case time, then the fact that some operations are expensive might be inconsequential. When we can show a worst-case bound for a sequence of operations that is better than the corresponding bound that is obtained by considering each operation separately, we say that the running time is *amortized*. In the preceding example, we have logarithmic amortized cost: Some single operations may take more than logarithmic time, but we are guaranteed compensation by some cheaper operations that occur earlier in the sequence.

Amortized analysis bounds the cost of a sequence of operations and distributes this cost evenly to each operation in the sequence.

Let us remark that amortized bounds are not always acceptable. Specifically, if a single bad operation is too time-consuming, then we really do need worst-case bounds rather than amortized bounds. However, in many cases a data structure is used as part of an algorithm, and only the total amount of time used by the data structure in the course of running an algorithm is important.

We have already seen one example of an amortized bound. When we implement array doubling in a stack or queue, we see that the cost of a single operation can be either constant if no doubling is needed or $O(N)$ if it is. However, for any sequence of M stack or queue operations, the total cost is guaranteed to be $O(M)$, meaning that we have constant amortized cost per operation. The fact that the array doubling step is expensive is inconsequential because its cost can be distributed to a host of earlier inexpensive operations.

21.1.2   A Simple Self-adjusting Strategy (That Does Not Work)

In a binary search tree, we cannot expect to store the frequently accessed items in a simple table: The caching technique benefits from the great discrepancy between main memory and disk access times. Since the cost of an access in a binary search tree is proportional to the depth of the accessed node, we can attempt to restructure the tree by moving frequently accessed items toward the root. Although this costs extra time during the first Find operation, it could be worthwhile in the long run.

The *rotate-to-root strategy* rearranges a binary search tree after each access to move frequently accessed items closer to the root.

The easiest way to move an item toward the root is continually to rotate it with its parent until it becomes a root node. Then, if the item is accessed a second time, the second access is cheap. Even if a few other operations intervene before the item is reaccessed, we expect that it will remain close to the root and thus will be quickly found. We call this the *rotate-to-root strategy*. An application of the rotate-to-root strategy to node 3 is shown in Figure 21.1.[1]

The rotate-to-root strategy is good if the 90-10 rule applies. It can be very bad when it does not.

The result of the rotation is that future accesses of node 3 are cheap (for awhile). Unfortunately, in the process of moving node 3 up two levels, nodes 4 and 5 have each moved down a level. This means that if we do not have a 90-10 rule, it is possible for a long sequence of bad accesses to occur. As a result the rotate-to-root rule will not have logarithmic amortized behavior, which is likely to be unacceptable. We can illustrate a bad case as follows:

Theorem 21.1 *There are arbitrarily long sequences for which M rotate-to-rule accesses use $\Theta(MN)$ time.*

Proof *Consider the tree formed by inserting the keys 1, 2, 3, … , N into an initially empty tree. It is easy to verify that this gives a tree consisting of only left children. This is not bad since the time to construct the tree is only $O(N)$ total. As illustrated in Figure 21.2, each newly added item is made a child of the root, and then only one rotation is needed to place it at the root. The bad part, as shown in Figure 21.3, is that accessing the node with key 1 takes N units of time. After the rotations are complete, access of the node with key 2 takes $N-1$ units of time. The total for accessing the N keys in order is $\sum_{i=1}^{N} i = \Theta(N^2)$. After they are accessed, the tree reverts to its original state and we can repeat the sequence. Thus we have an amortized bound of only $\Theta(N)$.*

---

1. An insertion counts as an access. Thus an item would always be inserted as a leaf and then immediately rotated to the root. An unsuccessful search counts as an access on the leaf at which the search terminates.

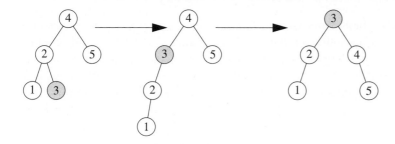

Figure 21.1   Rotate-to-root strategy applied when node 3 is accessed

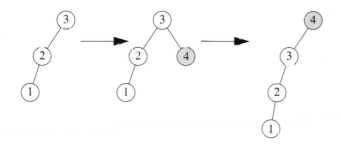

Figure 21.2   Insertion of 4 using rotate-to-root

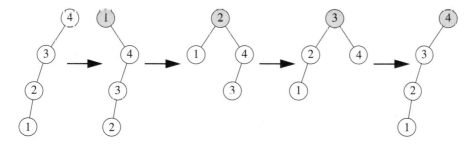

Figure 21.3   Sequential access of items takes quadratic time

21.2   The Basic Bottom-Up Splay Tree

In a basic *bottom-up splay tree*, items are rotated to the root using a slightly more complicated method than simple rotate-to-root.

Achieving logarithmic amortized cost seems impossible because when we move an item to root via rotations, other items are pushed deeper. It would seem that there would always be some very deep nodes if no balancing information is maintained. Amazingly, there is a simple fix to the rotate-to-root strategy that allows the logarithmic amortized bound to be obtained. The resulting rotate-to-root strategy is known as *splaying,* and its implementation leads to the basic *bottom-up splay tree.*

The splaying strategy is similar to rotate-to-root with only one subtle difference. We will still rotate bottom up along the access path (later we will see a top-down strategy). Let X be a nonroot node on the access path on which we are rotating. If the parent of X is the root of the tree, we merely rotate X and the root as shown in Figure 21.4. This is the last rotation along the access path and places X at the root. Note that this is exactly what would be done in the rotate-to-root algorithm. This is a *zig* case.

The *zig* and *zig-zag* cases are identical to rotate-to-root.

Otherwise, X has both a parent P and a grandparent G, and there are two cases plus symmetries to consider. The first case is the so called *zig-zag* case, which corresponds to the inside case for AVL trees. Here X is a right child and P is a left child (or vice versa). We perform a double rotation, exactly like an AVL double rotation, as shown in Figure 21.5. Notice that since a double rotation is the same as two bottom-up single rotations, this case is no different than what is done in rotate-to-root. In Figure 21.1 the splay at node 3 is a single zig-zag rotation.

The *zig-zig* case is unique to the splay tree.

The final case is the *zig-zig* case, which is the outside case for AVL trees. Here X and P are either both left children or both right children. In that case we transform the tree on the left of Figure 21.6 to the tree on the right. Observe that this is different from what rotate-to-root does. Rotate-to-root rotates between X and P and then between X and G. The zig-zig splay rotates between P and G and then X and P.

Splaying has the effect of roughly halving the depth of most nodes on the access path, while increasing by at most two the depth of a few other nodes.

The change in the zig-zig case seems quite minor, and it is surprising that it matters. To see the difference that splaying makes over rotate-to-root, let us consider the sequence that gave the poor results in Theorem 21.1. Once again we insert keys 1, 2, 3, ... , N into an initially empty tree in linear total time and obtain an unbalanced left-child-only tree. However, the result of a splay is somewhat better, as shown in Figure 21.7. After the splay at node 1, which takes N node accesses, a splay at node 2 will take only roughly $N/2$ accesses, rather than $N - 1$ accesses. Splaying not only moves the accessed node to the root but also has the affect of roughly halving the depth of most nodes on the access path (some shallow nodes are pushed down at most two levels). A subsequent splay at node 2 will bring nodes to within $N/4$ of the root, and this is repeated until the depth becomes roughly $\log N$. In fact a complicated analysis shows that what used to be a bad case for the rotate-to-root algorithm is a good case for splaying: sequential access of the N items in the splay tree takes a total of only $O(N)$

time. Thus we win on easy input. In Section 21.4 we show by subtle accounting that there are no bad access sequences.

21.3   Basic Splay Tree Operations

As we mentioned earlier, after each access we perform a splay operation. Let us describe the specifics. When an insertion is performed, we perform a splay. As a result, the newly inserted item becomes the root of the tree. Otherwise, we could spend quadratic time constructing an N item tree.

After an item is inserted as a leaf, it is splayed to the root.

Figure 21.4   Zig case (normal single rotation)

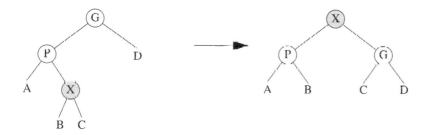

Figure 21.5   Zig-zag case (same as a double rotation); symmetric case omitted

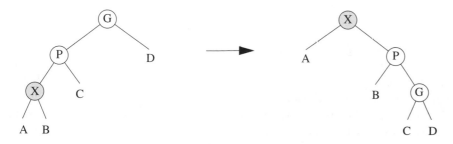

Figure 21.6   Zig-zig case (this is unique to the splay tree); symmetric case omitted

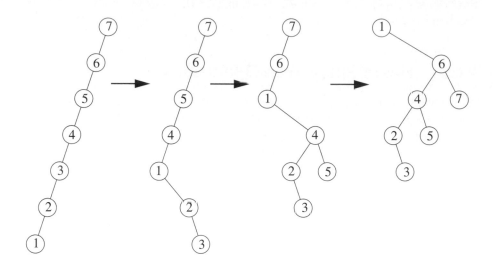

Figure 21.7   Result of splaying at node 1 (three zig-zigs and a zig)

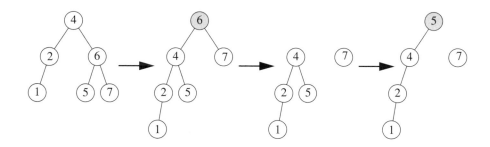

Figure 21.8   The Remove operation applied to node 6: First 6 is splayed to the root, leaving two subtrees; a FindMax on the left subtree is performed, raising 5 to the root of the left subtree; then the right subtree can be attached (not shown)

All searching operations incorporate a splay.

For the Find we splay at the last node that is accessed during the search. If the search is successful, then the node that is found will be splayed and become the new root. If the search is unsuccessful, then the last node that was accessed prior to reaching the NULL pointer is splayed and becomes the new root. This behavior is necessary. Otherwise, we could repeatedly perform a Find for 0 in the initial tree in Figure 21.7 and use linear time per operation. Likewise, operations such as FindMin and FindMax also perform a splay after the access.

The interesting operations are the deletions. Recall that the `DeleteMin` and `DeleteMax` are important priority queue operations. With splay trees these operations become simple. We can implement the `DeleteMin` as follows. First perform a `FindMin`. This brings the minimum item to the root, and by the binary search tree property, there is no left child. We can use the right child as the new root and delete the node containing the minimum. Similarly, `DeleteMax` can be implemented by calling `FindMax`, setting the root to the post-splay root's left child, and deleting the post-splay root.

Even the `Remove` operation is simple. To perform deletion, we access the node that is to be deleted. This puts the node at the root. If it is deleted, we get two subtrees L and R (left and right). If we find the largest element in L using a `DeleteMax` operation, then its largest element will be rotated to L's root, and L's root will have no right child. We can finish the `Remove` by making R the right child of L's root. An example of the `Remove` operation is shown in Figure 21.8.

The cost of the `Remove` operation is two splays. All other operations cost one splay. Thus we need to analyze the cost of a series of splay steps. In the next section we show that the amortized cost of a splay is at most $3 \log N + 1$ single rotations. Among other things, this means that we do not have to worry about the fact that the remove algorithm described above is biased. The splay tree's amortized bound guarantees that any sequence of M splays will use at most $3M \log N + M$ tree rotations, and consequently any sequence of M operations starting from an empty tree will take a total of at most $O(M \log N)$ time.

> Deletion operations are much simpler than usual. They also incorporate a splaying step (sometimes two).

21.4 Analysis of Bottom-Up Splaying

The analysis of the splay tree algorithm is complicated because each splay can vary from a few rotations to $O(N)$ rotations. Furthermore, unlike balanced search trees, each splay changes the structure of the tree. In this section we prove that the amortized cost of a splay is at most $3 \log N + 1$ single rotations. The splay tree's amortized bound guarantees that any sequence of M splays will use at most $3M \log N + M$ tree rotations, and consequently any sequence of M operations starting from an empty tree will take a total of at most $O(M \log N)$ time.

> The analysis of the splay tree is very complicated and is part of a much larger theory of amortized analysis.

To prove this bound, we will introduce an accounting function known as a *potential function*. The potential function is not maintained by the algorithm but rather is merely an accounting device that will aid us in establishing the required time bound. Its choice is not obvious and is the result of a large amount of trial and error.

> The *potential function* is an accounting device used to establish the required time bound.

For any node i in the splay tree, let $S(i)$ be the number of descendants of i (including i itself). The potential function is the sum, over all nodes i in the tree T, of the logarithm of $S(i)$. Specifically, we write

$$\Phi(T) = \sum_{i \in T} \log S(i)$$

To simplify the notation, we let $R(i) = \log S(i)$. This makes

$$\Phi(T) = \sum_{i \in T} R(i)$$

$R(i)$ represents the *rank* of node i. We restate that neither the ranks nor the sizes are maintained by the splay tree algorithms (unless, of course, order statistics are needed). Let us make a few observations before continuing. First, the rank of the root is $\log N$. Second, when performing a zig rotation, only the ranks of the two nodes involved in the rotation change. When performing a zig-zig or a zig-zag rotation, only the ranks of the three nodes involved in the rotation change. Third, a single splay consists of some number of zig-zig or zig-zag rotations followed by perhaps one zig rotation. Each zig-zig or zig-zag can be counted as two single rotations.

Let X be the node that is splayed to the root. Let r be the total number of rotations performed during the splay. Let Φ_i be the potential function of the tree immediately after the ith splay. Φ_0 is the potential prior to the zeroth splay.

Theorem 21.2   *If the ith splay operation uses r_i rotations, $\Phi_i - \Phi_{i-1} + r_i \leq 3\log N + 1$.*

Before proving the theorem, let us see what it means. The cost of M splays can be taken as $\sum_{i=1}^{M} r_i$ rotations. If the M splays are consecutive (that is, no insertions or deletions intervene), then we know that the potential of the tree after the ith splay is the same as prior to the $(i+1)$th splay. Thus we can use Theorem 21.2 M times to obtain the sequence of equations in Equation 21.1.

$$\Phi_1 - \Phi_0 + r_1 \leq 3\log N + 1$$
$$\Phi_2 - \Phi_1 + r_2 \leq 3\log N + 1$$
$$\Phi_3 - \Phi_2 + r_3 \leq 3\log N + 1 \qquad \textbf{(21.1)}$$
$$\cdots$$
$$\Phi_M - \Phi_{M-1} + r_M \leq 3\log N + 1$$

These equations telescope, so if we add them all together, we obtain

$$\Phi_M - \Phi_0 + \sum_{i=1}^{M} r_i \leq (3\log N + 1) M \qquad \textbf{(21.2)}$$

which bounds the total number of rotations as

$$\sum_{i=1}^{M} r_i \leq (3\log N + 1) M - (\Phi_M - \Phi_0)$$

Now we want to consider what happens when insertions are intermingled with finds. It is worth observing that the potential of an empty tree is 0. When a node is inserted into the tree as a leaf, then prior to the splay the potential of the tree increases by at most log N (we will prove this below). If r_i rotations are used for an insertion, and if the potential prior to the insertion is Φ_{i-1}, then after the insertion the potential will be at most $\Phi_{i-1} + \log N$, and after the splay that moves the inserted node to the root, the new potential will satisfy

$$\Phi_i - (\Phi_{i-1} + \log N) + r_i \le 3\log N + 1$$
$$\Phi_i - \Phi_{i-1} + r_i \le 4\log N + 1 \tag{21.3}$$

Thus, if there are F finds and I insertions, and if Φ_i represents the potential after the ith operation, then since each find is governed by Theorem 21.2 and each insertion is governed by Equation 21.3, the telescoping logic tells us that

$$\Sigma_{i=1}^{M} r_i \le (3\log N + 1)\, F + (4\log N + 1)\, I - (\Phi_M - \Phi_0) \tag{21.4}$$

Furthermore, before the first operation the potential is 0, and since it can never be negative, we know that $\Phi_M - \Phi_0 \ge 0$. Consequently, we obtain

$$\Sigma_{i=1}^{M} r_i \le (3\log N + 1)\, F + (4\log N + 1)\, I \tag{21.5}$$

thus showing that the cost of any sequence of finds and insertions is at most logarithmic per operation. Since a deletion is equivalent to two splays, we can see that it too is logarithmic. Thus we must prove the two dangling claims, namely Theorem 21.2 and the fact that an insertion of a node adds at most log N to the potential. Both theorems are proven by using telescoping arguments. Let us take care of the insertion claim first.

Insertion of the Nth node into a tree as a leaf adds at most log N to the potential of the tree.   ***Theorem 21.3***

The only nodes whose ranks are affected are those on the path from the inserted leaf to the root. Let $S_1, S_2, \ldots, S_k$ be their sizes prior to the insertion, and note that $S_k = N - 1$. Note that $S_1 < S_2 < \ldots < S_k$. Let $S'_1, S'_2, \ldots, S'_k$ be the sizes after the insertion. Clearly, $S'_i \le S_{i+1}$ for $i < k$, since $S'_i = S_i + 1$. Consequently, $R'_i \le R_{i+1}$. The change in potential is thus   ***Proof***

$$\Sigma_{i=1}^{k} (R'_i - R_i) \le R'_k - R_k + \Sigma_{i=1}^{k-1} (R_{i+1} - R_i) \le \log N - R_1 \le \log N.$$

To prove Theorem 21.2, we break each splay step into its constituent zig, zig-zag, and zig-zig parts and establish a bound for the cost of each type of rotation. By telescoping these bounds, we obtain a bound for the splay. Before continuing, we need a technical theorem:

Theorem 21.4   *If $a + b \leq c$, and a and b are both positive integers, then*
$$\log a + \log b \leq 2\log c - 2.$$

Proof   *By the arithmetic-geometric mean inequality, we know $\sqrt{ab} \leq (a + b)/2$. Thus $\sqrt{ab} \leq c/2$. Squaring both sides gives $ab \leq c^2/4$, and then taking logarithms of both sides proves the theorem.*

We are now ready to prove Theorem 21.2.

21.4.1   Proof of the Splaying Bound

First, if the node to splay is already at the root, then there are no rotations and there is no potential change. Thus the theorem is trivially true, and we may assume that there is at least one rotation. Let X be the node that is involved in the splay. We need to show that if r rotations are performed (a zig-zig or zig-zag counts as two rotations), then r plus the change in potential is at most $3\log N + 1$. Let Δ be the change in potential caused by any of the splay steps zig, zig-zag, or zig-zig. Let $R_i(x)$ and $S_i(x)$ be the rank and size of any node x immediately before a splay step, and let $R_f(x)$ and $S_f(x)$ be the rank and size of any node x immediately after a splay step. We will show the following bounds:

For a zig step that promotes node X, $\Delta \leq 3(R_f(X) - R_i(X))$, while for the other two steps, $\Delta \leq 3(R_f(X) - R_i(X)) - 2$. When we add these bounds over all steps that comprise a splay, the sum telescopes to the desired bound. We prove each of these bounds separately, and then complete the proof of Theorem 21.2 by applying a telescoping sum.

Theorem 21.5   *For a zig step, $\Delta \leq 3(R_f(X) - R_i(X))$*

Proof   *As we mentioned earlier, the only nodes whose ranks change in a zig step are X and P. Consequently, the potential change is $R_f(X) - R_i(X) + R_f(P) - R_i(P)$. Examining Figure 21.4, we see that $S_f(P) < S_i(P)$; thus it follows that $R_f(P) - R_i(P) < 0$. Consequently, the potential change satisfies $\Delta \leq R_f(X) - R_i(X)$. Since $S_f(X) > S_i(X)$, it follows that $R_f(X) - R_i(X) > 0$, so we obtain $\Delta \leq 3(R_f(X) - R_i(X))$.*

The zig-zag and zig-zig steps are more complicated because three nodes have their ranks affected. First we prove the zig-zag case.

For a zig-zag step, $\Delta \le 3(R_f(X) - R_i(X)) - 2$ ***Theorem 21.6***

As before we have three changes, so the potential change is given by   ***Proof***

$$\Delta = R_f(X) - R_i(X) + R_f(P) - R_i(P) + R_f(G) - R_i(G)$$

From Figure 21.5 we see that $S_f(X) = S_i(G)$, *so their ranks must be equal. Thus we obtain*

$$\Delta = -R_i(X) + R_f(P) - R_i(P) + R_f(G)$$

We also see that $S_i(P) \ge S_i(X)$. *Consequently,* $R_i(P) \ge R_i(X)$. *Making this substitution and rearranging terms gives*

$$\Delta \le R_f(P) + R_f(G) - 2R_i(X) \tag{21.6}$$

From Figure 21.5 we see that $S_f(P) + S_f(G) \le S_f(X)$. *If we apply Theorem 21.4, we obtain* $\log S_f(P) + \log S_f(G) \le 2\log S_f(X) - 2$, *and by the definition of rank, this becomes*

$$R_f(P) + R_f(G) \le 2R_f(X) - 2 \tag{21.7}$$

Substituting Equation 21.7 into Equation 21.6, we obtain

$$\Delta \le 2R_f(X) - 2R_i(X) - 2 \tag{21.8}$$

As was the case for the zig rotation, $R_f(X) - R_i(X) > 0$, *so we can add it to the right side of Equation 21.8, and factor, obtaining the desired*

$$\Delta \le 3(R_f(X) - R_i(X)) - 2$$

Finally, we prove the bound for the zig-zig case:

Theorem 21.7	*For a zig-zig step,* $\Delta \le 3(R_f(X) - R_i(X)) - 2$

Proof   *As before we have three changes, so the potential change is given by*

$$\Delta = R_f(X) - R_i(X) + R_f(P) - R_i(P) + R_f(G) - R_i(G)$$

From Figure 21.6 we have $S_f(X) = S_i(G)$, *and thus their ranks must be equal. Thus we obtain*

$$\Delta = -R_i(X) + R_f(P) - R_i(P) + R_f(G)$$

We also can obtain $R_i(P) > R_i(X)$ *and* $R_f(P) < R_f(X)$. *Making this substitution and rearranging terms gives*

$$\Delta < R_f(X) + R_f(G) - 2R_i(X) \qquad\qquad (21.9)$$

From Figure 21.6 we see that $S_i(X) + S_f(G) \le S_f(X)$, *so by applying Theorem 21.4, we obtain*

$$R_i(X) + R_f(G) \le 2R_f(X) - 2 \qquad\qquad (21.10)$$

Rearranging Equation 21.10, we obtain

$$R_f(G) \le 2R_f(X) - R_i(X) - 2 \qquad\qquad (21.11)$$

When we substitute Equation 21.11 into Equation 21.9, we obtain

$$\Delta \le 3(R_f(X) - R_i(X)) - 2$$

Now that we have established bounds for each of the splaying steps, we can finally complete the proof of Theorem 21.2.

Proof (of Theorem 21.2)   *Let $R_0(X)$ be the rank of X prior to the splay. Let $R_i(X)$ be X's rank after the ith splaying step. Prior to the last splaying step, all splaying steps must be zig-zags or zig-zigs. Suppose there are k such steps. Then the total number of rotations performed at that point is 2k. The total potential change is $\sum_{i=1}^{k}(3(R_i(X) - R_{i-1}(X)) - 2)$. This sum telescopes to $3(R_k(X) - R_0(X)) - 2k$. At this point, the total number of rotations plus the total potential change is bounded by $3R_k(X)$, since the 2k term cancels,* *and the initial rank of X is not negative. If the last rotation is a zig-zig or a zig-zag, then a continuation of the telescoping sum gives a total of 3R(root). Notice that here, the -2 in the potential increase cancels the cost of two rotations. On the other hand, this does not happen in the zig, so we would get a total of 3R(root)+ 1. Since the rank of the root is log N, we have that in the worst case, the total number of rotations plus the change in potential during a splay is at most $3\log N + 1$.*

Proof (of Theorem 21.2, continued)

The proof of the splay tree bound, while complex, does illustrate a few interesting points. First, we see that apparently the zig-zig case is the most expensive, since it contributes a leading constant of three, while the zig-zag contributes two. We also see that the proof would fall apart if we tried to adapt it to the rotate-to-root algorithm. This is because, in the zig case, the number of rotations plus the potential change is $R_f(X) - R_i(X) + 1$. The 1 at the end does not telescope out, so we would not be able to show a logarithmic bound. This is fortunate, since we already know that a logarithmic bound would be incorrect.

The technique of amortized analysis is very interesting, and some general principles have been developed to formalize the framework. Check out the references if you would like more details.

21.5   Top-Down Splay Trees

A direct implementation of the bottom-up splay strategy requires a pass down the tree to perform an access and then a second pass back up the tree. This can be done either by maintaining parent pointers, by storing the access path on a stack, or by using a clever trick to store the path using the pointers in the accessed nodes. Unfortunately, all these methods require a substantial amount of overhead, and we must handle a host of special cases. As we saw in Section 18.5, it is better to implement search tree algorithms using a single top-down pass, and we can use dummy nodes to avoid special cases. In this section we describe a *top-down splay tree* that maintains the logarithmic amortized bound. The top-down procedure is faster in practice and uses only constant extra space. It is the method recommended by the inventors of the splay trees.

As is the case for red black trees, *top-down splay trees* are more efficient in practice than their bottom-up counterparts.

The basic idea behind the top-down splay tree is that as we descend the tree in our search for some node *X*, we must take the nodes that are on the access path, and move them and their subtrees out of the way. We must also perform some tree rotations to guarantee the amortized time bound.

At any point in the middle of the splay, we have a current node *X* that is the root of its subtree; this is represented in our diagrams as the middle tree. Tree *L* stores nodes that are less than *X*; similarly, tree *R* stores nodes that are larger than *X*. Initially, *X* is the root of *T*, and *L* and *R* are empty. As we descend the tree two

We maintain three trees during the top down pass.

levels at a time, we encounter a pair of nodes. Depending on whether these nodes are smaller than X or larger than X, they are placed in L or R along with subtrees that are not on the access path to X. Thus we can maintain the invariant that the current node on the search path is always the root of the middle tree. When we finally reach X, we can then attach L and R to the bottom of the middle tree, and as a result X will have been moved to the root. The issue then is how nodes are placed into L and R and how the reattachment is performed at the end. This is what the trees in Figure 21.9 are illustrating. As is customary, three symmetric cases are omitted.

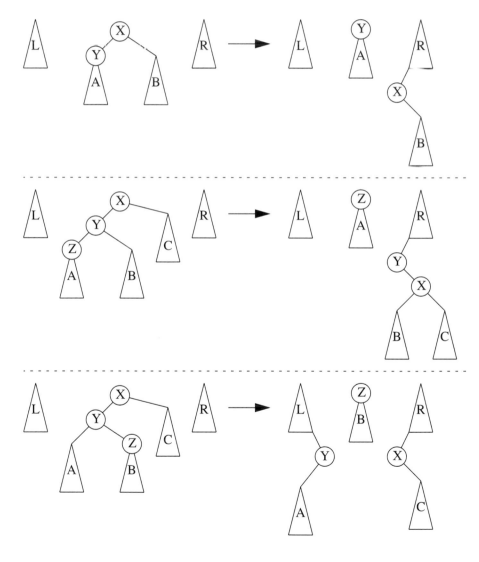

Figure 21.9 Top-down splay rotations: zig (top), zig-zig (middle), and zig-zag (bottom)

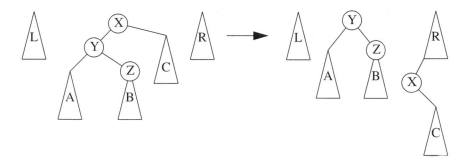

Figure 21.10   Simplified top-down zig-zag

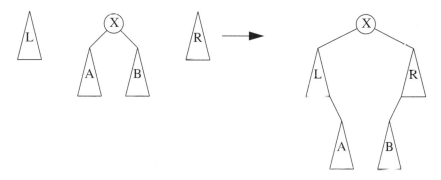

Figure 21.11   Final arrangement for top-down splaying

In all the pictures X is the current node, Y is its child, and Z is a grandchild, should an applicable node exist. The precise meaning of the term *applicable* will be made clear when we discuss the zig case.

If the rotation should be a zig, then the tree rooted at Y becomes the new root of the middle tree. X and subtree B are attached as a left child of the smallest item in R; X's left child is logically made NULL.[2] As a result, X is the new smallest element in R, thus making future attachments easy.

Note carefully that Y does not have to be a leaf for the zig case to apply. If the item we are searching for is found in Y, a zig case will apply even if Y has children. A zig case also applies if we are searching for an item that is smaller than Y and Y has no left child, even if Y has a right child, and also for the symmetric case.

For the zig-zig case, we have a similar dissection. The crucial point is that a rotation between X and Y is performed. The zig-zag case brings the bottom node

---

2. In the code that we write, the smallest node in R does not have a NULL left pointer because it is not needed.

Z to the top of the middle tree, and attaches subtrees X and Y to R and L, respectively. Note that Y is attached to, and then becomes, the largest item in L.

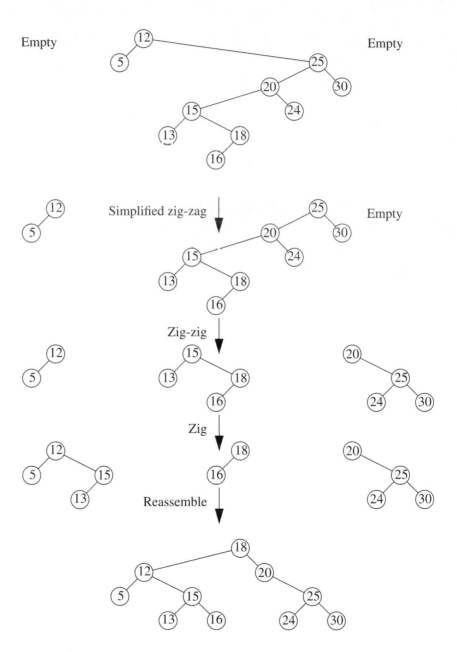

Figure 21.12 Steps in top-down splay (accessing 19 in top tree)

```
1  // SplayTree class interface
2  //
3  // Etype: must have zero-parameter and copy constructor
4  //      and must have operator< and operator==
5  // CONSTRUCTION: with (a) no initializer
6  // All copying of SplayTree objects is DISALLOWED
7  //
8  // *****************PUBLIC OPERATIONS*********************
9  // void Insert( Etype X ) --> Insert X
10 // void Remove( Etype X ) --> Remove X
11 // Etype GetRoot( )       --> Return item in root
12 // int IsFound( Etype X ) --> Return 1 if X would be found
13 // int IsEmpty( )         --> Return 1 if empty; else return 0
14 // void MakeEmpty( )      --> Remove all items
15 // *****************ERRORS********************************
16 // Predefined exception is propagated if new fails
17 // Item in NilNode returned for Find on empty tree
18
19 template <class Etype>
20 class SplayTree
21 {
22   public:
23     SplayTree( );
24     ~SplayTree( ) { FreeTree( Root ); delete NilNode; }
25
26     // Add X into the tree. If X already present, do nothing.
27     // Return true if insertion was successful
28     int Insert( const Etype & X );
29
30     // Remove X from tree; Return 1 if X was found
31     int Remove( const Etype & X );
32
33     // IsFound returns true id X is found and splays to root
34     // GetRoot can be used to see what is there
35     int IsFound( const Etype & X ) { Splay( X, Root );
36         return Root != NilNode && Root->Element == X; }
37     const Etype & GetRoot( ) const { return Root->Element; }
38
39     // Make the tree empty, and test if tree is empty
40     void MakeEmpty( ) { FreeTree( Root ); Root = NilNode; }
41     int IsEmpty( ) const { return Root == NilNode; }
42   private:
43     BinaryNode<Etype> *NilNode;
44     BinaryNode<Etype> *Root;
45
46     void FreeTree( BinaryNode<Etype> *T );
47     void Splay( const Etype & X, BinaryNode<Etype> * & T );
48         // Disable copying
49     SplayTree( const SplayTree & );
50     const SplayTree & operator=( const Splay Tree & );
51 };
```

Figure 21.13   Top-down splay tree class interface

```
1  // Construct for SplayTree
2
3  template <class Etype>
4  SplayTree<Etype>::SplayTree( )
5  {
6      NilNode = new BinaryNode<Etype>;
7      NilNode->Left = NilNode->Right = Root = NilNode;
8  }
```

Figure 21.14   Splay tree constructor

The zig-zag step can be simplified somewhat because no rotations are performed. Instead of making *Z* the root of the middle tree, we make *Y* the root. This is shown in Figure 21.10. This simplifies the coding because the action for the zig-zag case becomes identical to the zig case. This would seem advantageous because testing for a host of cases is time-consuming. The disadvantage is that by descending only one level, we have more iterations in the splaying procedure.

Eventually the three trees are reassembled into one.

Once we have performed the final splaying step, then *L*, *R*, and the middle tree are arranged to form a single tree, as shown in Figure 21.11. Note carefully that the result is different from bottom-up splaying. The crucial fact is that the $O(\log N)$ amortized bound is preserved (see Exercise 21.3).

An example of the simplified top-down splaying algorithm is shown in Figure 21.12. We attempt to access 19 in the tree. The first step is a zig-zag. In accordance with a symmetric version of Figure 21.10, we bring the subtree rooted at 25 to the root of the middle tree, and attach 12 and its left subtree to *L*.

Next we have a zig-zig: 15 is elevated to the root of the middle tree, and a rotation between 20 and 25 is performed, with the resulting subtree being attached to *R*. The search for 19 then results in a terminal zig. The middle's new root is 18, and 15 and its left subtree are attached as a right child of *L*'s largest node. The reassembly, in accordance with Figure 21.11, terminates the splay step.

21.6   Implementation of Top-Down Splay Trees

The splay tree class interface is shown in Figure 21.13. To eliminate annoying special cases, we maintain a `NullNode` sentinel. The sentinel is allocated and initialized in the constructor, as shown in Figure 21.14.

Figure 21.15 shows the member function for insertion of an item `X`. A new node (`NewNode`) is allocated, and if the tree is empty, a one-node tree is created. Otherwise, we splay around `X`. If the data in the tree's new root is equal to `X`, then we have a duplicate. In this case, we do not want to insert `X`. Prior to the return at line 36, we would normally call `delete` to avoid a memory leak. Rather than calling `delete` for the newly allocated node, we use a `static` local variable so that the next call to `Insert` can avoid calling `new`.

```
1    // Insert X into splay tree
2    // Return false if X is a duplicate; true otherwise
3
4    template <class Etype>
5    int
6    SplayTree<Etype>::Insert( const Etype & X )
7    {
8        static BinaryNode<Etype> *NewNode = NULL;
9
10       if( NewNode == NULL )
11           NewNode = new BinaryNode<Etype>( X );
12
13       if( Root == NilNode )
14       {
15           NewNode->Left = NewNode->Right = NilNode;
16           Root = NewNode;
17       }
18       else
19       {
20           Splay( X, Root );
21           if( X < Root->Element )
22           {
23               NewNode->Left = Root->Left;
24               NewNode->Right = Root;
25               Root->Left = NilNode;
26               Root = NewNode;
27           }
28           else if( Root->Element < X )
29           {
30               NewNode->Right = Root->Right;
31               NewNode->Left = Root;
32               Root->Right = NilNode;
33               Root = NewNode;
34           }
35           else     // Already in the tree
36               return 0;
37       }
38
39       NewNode = NULL;    // So next Insert will call new
40       return 1;
41   }
```

Figure 21.15   Top-down splay tree insertion

If the new root contains a value that is larger than X, then the new root and its right subtree become a right subtree of NewNode, and the root's left subtree becomes a left subtree of NewNode. Similar logic applies if the new root contains a value smaller than X. In either case, NewNode is assigned to Root to indicate that it is the new root. Then we make NewNode NULL at line 39 so the next call to Insert will call new.

```
1  // Remove X from splay tree
2  // Return true if X was found; false otherwise
3
4  template <class Etype>
5  int
6  SplayTree<Etype>::Remove( const Etype & X )
7  {
8      BinaryNode<Etype> *NewTree;
9
10     if( !IsFound( X ) )
11         return 0;
12
13         // If X is found, it will be at the root
14     if( Root->Left == NilNode )
15         NewTree = Root->Right;
16     else
17     {
18         // Find the maximum in the left subtree
19         // splay it to root, and then attach right child
20         NewTree = Root->Left;
21         Splay( X, NewTree );
22         NewTree->Right = Root->Right;
23     }
24     delete Root;
25     Root = NewTree;
26     return 1;
27 }
```

Figure 21.16   Top-down splay tree deletion

Figure 21.16 shows the deletion algorithm for splay trees. It is indeed rare that a deletion procedure is shorter than the corresponding insertion procedure. All that remains is the top-down splaying routine.

Our implementation, shown in Figure 21.17, will use a header with left and right pointers to contain eventually the roots of the left and right trees. Since these trees are initially empty, a header is used to correspond to the min or max node of the right or left tree, respectively, in this initial state. This way the code can avoid checking for empty trees. The first time the left tree becomes non-empty, the right pointer will get initialized and will not change in the future; thus it will contain the root of the right tree at the end of the top-down search. Similarly, the left pointer will eventually contain the root of the right tree.

Before the reassembly at the end of the splay, Header.Left and Header.Right point at *R* and *L*, respectively (this is not a typo – follow the pointers). Except for this detail, the code is relatively straightforward. Note that we are using the simplified top-down splay.

```
1   // Top-down splay routine
2   // Last accessed node becomes the new root
3
4   template <class Etype>
5   void
6   SplayTree<Etype>::
7   Splay( const Etype & X, BinaryNode<Etype> * & T )
8   {
9       BinaryNode<Etype> *LeftTreeMax;
10      BinaryNode<Etype> *RightTreeMin;
11      BinaryNode<Etype> Header;
12
13      Header.Left = Header.Right = NilNode;
14      LeftTreeMax = RightTreeMin = &Header;
15
16      // Copy X to NilNode to guarantee match
17      NilNode->Element = X;
18
19      for( ; ; )
20          if( X < T->Element )
21          {
22              if( X < T->Left->Element )
23                  T = RotateWithLeftChild( T );
24              if( T->Left == NilNode )
25                  break;
26                  // Link Right
27              RightTreeMin->Left = T;
28              RightTreeMin = T;
29              T = T->Left;
30          }
31          else if( T->Element < X )
32          {
33              if( T->Right->Element < X )
34                  T = RotateWithRightChild( T );
35              if( T >Right == NilNode )
36                  break;
37                  // Link Left
38              LeftTreeMax->Right = T;
39              LeftTreeMax = T;
40              T = T->Right;
41          }
42          else    // Found X
43              break;
44
45      LeftTreeMax->Right = T->Left;
46      RightTreeMin->Left = T->Right;
47      T->Left = Header.Right;
48      T->Right = Header.Left;
49  }
```

Figure 21.17   Top-down splay algorithm

21.7   Comparison of the Splay Tree with Other Search Trees

The implementation in the previous section suggests that splay trees are not as complicated as red black trees, and almost as simple as AA-trees. Are they worth using? The answer has yet to be resolved completely, but it seems that if the access patterns are nonrandom, then splay trees perform very well in practice and furthermore, some properties relating to its performance can be proven analytically. Nonrandom accesses include those that follow the 90-10 rule, as well as several special cases such as sequential access, double-ended access, and apparently access patterns that are typical of priority queues during some types of event simulations. The exercises ask you to examine this in more detail.

However, splay trees are not perfect. One problem is that the Find operation is expensive because of the splay. Consequently when access sequences are random and uniform, splay trees do not do as well as other balanced trees.

Summary

This chapter described the splay tree, which is a modern alternative to the balanced search tree. Splay trees have several remarkable properties that can be proven, including their logarithmic cost per operation. Other properties are suggested in the exercises. Some studies have suggested that splay trees can be used for a wide range of applications because of their apparent ability to adapt to easy access sequences.

The next chapter describes two priority queues that, like the splay tree, have poor worst-case performance but good amortized performance. One of these, the pairing heap, seems to be an excellent choice for some applications.

Objects of the Game

90-10 rule States that 90 percent of the accesses are to 10 percent of the data items. Balanced search trees do not take advantage of this. (676)

amortized analysis Bounds the cost of a sequence of operations and distributes the cost evenly to each operation in the sequence. (677)

bottom-up splay tree A tree in which items are rotated to the root using a slightly more complicated method than simple rotate-to-root. (680)

potential function An accounting device used to establish the required time bound. (683)

rank In the splay tree analysis, the logarithm of a node's size. (684)

rotate-to-root strategy Rearranges a binary search tree after each access to move frequently accessed items closer to the root. (678)

splaying A rotate-to-root strategy that allows the logarithmic amortized bound to be obtained. (680)

top-down splay tree More efficient in practice than its bottom-up counterpart, as was the case for red black trees. (689)

zig and **zig-zag** The zig and zig-zag cases are identical to rotate-to-root. Zig is used when X is a child of the root, and zig-zag when X is an "inside node." (680)

zig-zig The zig-zig case is unique to the splay tree. It is used when X is an "outside node." (680)

Common Errors

1. A splay must be performed after every access, even unsuccessful ones, or else the performance bounds are not valid.
2. The code is tricky.
3. Because `Find` adjusts the data structure (and is thus not a constant member), the splay tree interface is not entirely compatible with the other search trees.

On the Internet

The splay tree class is available on line.

Splay.h   Contains the header file for the splay tree class
Splay.cpp   Contains the implementation for the splay tree class

Exercises

In Short

21.1.   Show the result of inserting 3, 1, 4, 5, 2, 9, 6, 8 into a

   a. bottom-up splay tree
   b. top-down splay tree

21.2.   Show the result of deleting 3 from the splay tree in Exercise 21.1 for both the bottom-up and top-down versions.

In Theory

21.3.   Prove that the amortized cost of a top-down splay is $O(\log N)$.

21.4.   Prove that if all nodes in a splay tree are accessed in sequential order, the resulting tree consists of a chain of left children.

21.5.   Suppose that in an attempt to save time, we splay on every second tree operation. Does the amortized cost remain logarithmic?

21.6. Nodes 1 through $N=1024$ form a splay tree of left children.

a. What is the internal path length of the tree (exactly)?

b. Calculate the internal path length after each of `Find(1)`, `Find(2)`, `Find(3)` when a bottom-up splay is performed.

21.7. By changing the potential function, it is possible to prove different bounds for splaying. Let the weight function $W(i)$ be some function assigned to each node in the tree, and let $S(i)$ be the sum of the weights of all nodes in the subtree rooted at i, including i itself. The special case $W(i) = 1$ for all nodes corresponds to the function used in the proof of the splaying bound. Let N be the number of nodes in the tree and let M be the number of accesses. Prove the following two theorems:

a. The total access time is $O(M + (M + N)\log N)$.

b. If q_i is the total number of times that item i is accessed, and $q_i > 0$ for all i, then the total access time is $O(M + \sum_{i=1}^{N} q_i \log(M/q_i))$.

In Practice

21.8. Implement a priority queue class using the splay tree.

21.9. Modify the splay tree to support order statistics.

Programming Projects

21.10. Compare empirically the simplified top-down splay that is implemented in Section 21.6 with the original top-down splay discussed in Section 21.5.

21.11. Unlike balanced search trees, splay trees incur overhead during a `Find` operation that can be undesirable if the access sequence is sufficiently random. Experiment with a strategy that splays on a `Find` operation only once a certain depth d is traversed in the top-down search. The splay does not move the accessed item all the way to the root, but rather to the point at depth d where the splaying is started.

21.12. Compare empirically a top-down splay tree priority queue implementation with a binary heap. Use three input models:

a. Random insertions and `DeleteMin` operations

b. Insert and `DeleteMin` operations corresponding to an event-driven simulation

c. Insert and `DeleteMin` operations corresponding to Dijkstra's algorithm

References

The splay tree is described in the paper [3]. The concept of amortized analysis is discussed in the survey paper [4] and also in greater detail in [5]. A comparison of splay trees and AVL trees is given in [1]. [2] shows that splay trees perform well in some types of event-driven simulations.

1. J. Bell and G. Gupta, "An Evaluation of Self-Adjusting Binary Search Tree Techniques," *Software-Practice and Experience* **23** (1993), 369-382.

2. D. W. Jones, "An Empirical Comparison of Priority-Queue and Event-Set Implementations," *Communications of the ACM* **29** (1986), 300-311.

3. D. D. Sleator and R. E. Tarjan, "Self-adjusting Binary Search Trees," *Journal of the ACM* **32** (1985), 652-686.

4. R. E. Tarjan, "Amortized Computational Complexity," *SIAM Journal on Algebraic and Discrete Methods* **6** (1985), 306-318.

5. M. A. Weiss, *Data Structures and Algorithm Analysis in C++*, Benjamin/Cummings Publishing Co., Redwood City, CA (1994).

Chapter 22

Merging Priority Queues

In this chapter we examine priority queues that support an additional operation, Merge. The Merge operation, which is important in advanced algorithm design, combines two priority queues into one (and logically destroys the originals). We represent the priority queues as general trees. This makes the DecreaseKey operation somewhat simpler too, which is important in some applications.

In this chapter we will see

- a discussion of the *skew heap*, which is a mergeable priority queue implemented with binary trees
- a discussion of the *pairing heap*, which is a mergeable priority queue that is based on the *M*-ary tree. The pairing heap appears to be a practical alternative to the binary heap even if the Merge operation is not needed.

22.1 The Skew Heap

The *skew heap* is a binary tree with heap order. There is no structural constraint on the tree so, unlike the heap or the balanced binary search trees, we have no guarantee that the depth of the tree is logarithmic. The skew heap is thus somewhat similar to the splay tree.

The *skew heap* is a heap-ordered binary tree. There is no balancing condition, but it supports all operations in logarithmic amortized time.

22.1.1 Merging Is Fundamental

If a heap-ordered, structurally unconstrained binary tree is used to represent a priority queue, then merging becomes the fundamental operation. This is because we can perform other operations as follows:

- H.Insert(X): Create a one-node tree containing X and merge that tree into the priority queue.

- H.FindMin( ): Return the item at the root.
- H.DeleteMin( ): Delete the root and merge its left and right subtrees.
- H.DecreaseKey(P, NewVal): Assuming that P is a pointer to a node in the priority queue, we can lower P's key value appropriately and then detach P from its parent. This yields two priority queues that can be merged together. Note carefully that P does not change as a result of this operation (in contrast to the equivalent operation in a binary heap).

DecreaseKey is implemented by detaching a subtree from its parent and then using Merge.

We only need to show how to implement merging; the other operations become trivial. The DecreaseKey operation is typically important in some advanced applications. One illustration was seen in Section 14.3 where we discussed Dijkstra's algorithm for shortest paths in a graph. The DecreaseKey operation is not used in our implementation because of the complications of maintaining the position of each item in the binary heap. In a merging heap, the position can be maintained as a pointer to the tree node, and unlike the binary heap, the position never changes.

In this section we will discuss one implementation of a mergeable priority queue that uses a binary tree, the skew heap. First we will show that if we are not concerned with efficiency, it is easy to merge two heap-ordered trees. Next, we will discuss a simple modification (the skew heap) that avoids the obvious inefficiencies in the original algorithm. Finally, we will prove that the Merge operation for skew heaps is logarithmic in an amortized sense, and comment on the practical significance of this result.

22.1.2   Simplistic Merging of Heap-Ordered Trees

Two trees are easily merged recursively.

Assume we have two heap-ordered trees, H_1 and H_2, that need to be merged. Clearly, if either of the two trees is empty, the other tree is the result of the merge. Otherwise, to merge the two trees, we compare their roots. We recursively merge the tree with the larger root into the right subtree of the tree with the smaller root.[1]

The result is that right paths are merged. We must be careful not to create unduly long right paths.

Figure 22.1 shows that the effect of this recursive strategy is that the right paths of the two priority queues are merged to form the new priority queue. All nodes on the right path retain their original left subtree, and only nodes on the right path are touched. It is worth remarking that the example shown in Figure 22.1 is in fact unattainable by only insertions and merges, since as we have just mentioned, left children cannot be added by a merge. The practical effect is that what seems to be a heap-ordered binary tree is in fact an ordered arrangement consisting only of a single right path, and thus all operations take linear time.

Fortunately, a simple modification ensures that the right path is not always long.

---

1. Clearly either subtree could be used. We use the right for simplicity.

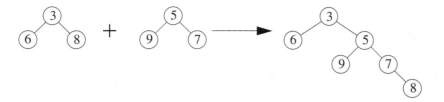

Figure 22.1   Simplistic merging of heap-ordered trees; right paths are merged

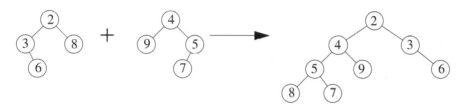

Figure 22.2   Merging of skew heap; right paths are merged, and the result is made a left path

22.1.3   The Skew Heap: A Simple Modification

The merge in Figure 22.1 creates a temporary merged tree. A simple modification is as follows: Prior to completion of a merge, we swap the left and right children for every node in the resulting right path of the temporary tree. Once again, only those nodes that were on the original right paths will be on the right path in the temporary tree, and as a result of the swap, as shown in Figure 22.2, these nodes will then form the left path of the resulting tree. When a merge is performed this way, the heap-ordered tree is a *skew heap*.

To avoid the problem of unduly long right paths, after a Merge we make the resulting right path a left path. Such a merge results in a skew heap.

A recursive viewpoint is as follows: Let *S* be the tree with the smaller root, and let *R* be the other tree.

1. If one tree is empty, the other can be used as the merged result.
2. Otherwise, let *Temp* be the right subtree of *L*.
3. Make *L*'s left subtree its new right subtree.
4. Make the result of the recursive merge of *Temp* and *R* the new left subtree of *L*.

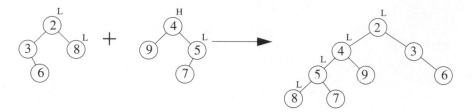

Figure 22.3   Change in heavy/light status after a merge

The result of the child swapping is that we expect that the length of the right path will not be unduly large all of the time. For instance, if we merge a pair of long-right-path trees, those nodes involved in the path will not reappear on a right path for quite some time in the future. While it is still possible to obtain trees with the property that every node appears on a right path, this can only be done as a result of a large number of relatively inexpensive merges. In the next section we prove this rigorously by establishing that the amortized cost of a merge operation is only logarithmic.

22.1.4   Analysis of the Skew Heap

Suppose we have two heaps, H_1 and H_2, and there are r_1 and r_2 nodes on their respective right paths. Then the time to perform the merge is proportional to $r_1 + r_2$. When we charge one unit for each node on the right paths, the cost of the merge is proportional to the number of charges. Since the trees have no structure, it is possible that all the nodes in both trees lie on the right path, and this would give a $\Theta(N)$ worst-case bound to merge the trees (Exercise 22.4 asks you to construct an example). We will show that the amortized time to merge two skew heaps is $O(\log N)$.

As was the case with the splay tree, the proof is done by introducing a potential function that cancels the varying cost of skew heap operations. We want the potential function to increase by a total of $O(\log N) - (r_1 + r_2)$, so that the total of the merge cost and potential change is only $O(\log N)$. If the potential is minimal prior to the first operation, then applying the telescoping sum guarantees that the total spent for any M operations is $O(M \log N)$, as was the case with the splay tree.

What is needed is some sort of potential function that captures the effect of skew heap operations. Finding such a function is quite challenging, but once one is found, the proof is relatively short.

DEFINITION: A node p is *heavy* if the size of p's right subtree is larger than the size of p's left subtree, and *light* otherwise. (A node is light if its subtrees have equal size.)

In Figure 22.3, prior to the merge, nodes 3 and 4 are heavy. After the merge, only node 3 is heavy. Three facts are easily shown. First, as a result of a merge, only nodes on the right path can have the heavy/light status changed, because no other nodes have their subtrees altered. Second, a leaf is light. Third, the number of light nodes on the right path of an N node tree is at most $\lfloor \log N \rfloor + 1$, because the right child of a light node has less than half the size of the light node itself, and the halving principle applies. The additional $+1$ is a result of the leaf being light. With these preliminaries, we can now prove the following:

The potential function is the number of heavy nodes. Only nodes on the merged path have their heavy/light status changed, and the number of light nodes on a right path is logarithmic.

Let H_1 and H_2 be two skew heaps with N_1 and N_2 nodes, respectively, and let N be their combined size (that is, $N_1 + N_2$). Suppose the right path of H_1 has l_1 light nodes and h_1 heavy nodes, for a total of $l_1 + h_1$, while the right path of H_2 has l_2 light nodes and h_2 heavy nodes, for a total of $l_2 + h_2$. Define the potential as the total number of heavy nodes in the collection of skew heaps. Then the merge costs at most $2\log N + (h_1 + h_2)$, but the change in potential is at most $2\log N - (h_1 + h_2)$.

Theorem 22.1

The cost of the merge is merely the total number of nodes on the right paths, $l_1 + l_2 + h_1 + h_2$. Since the number of light nodes is logarithmic, we have $l_1 \le \lfloor \log N_1 \rfloor + 1$ and $l_2 \le \lfloor \log N_2 \rfloor + 1$. Thus $l_1 + l_2 \le \log N_1 + \log N_2 + 2 \le 2\log N$, where the last inequality follows from Theorem 21.4. The merge cost is thus at most $2\log N + (h_1 + h_2)$. The bound on the potential change follows from the fact that only the nodes involved in the merge can have their heavy/light status changed, and from the fact that any heavy node on the path must become light, because its children are swapped. Even if all the light nodes became heavy, the potential change would still be limited to $l_1 + l_2 - (h_1 + h_2)$, and using the same argument as before, this is at most $2\log N - (h_1 + h_2)$.

Proof

The amortized cost of the skew heap is at most $4\log N$ for `Merge`, `Insert`, *and* `DeleteMin`.

Theorem 22.2

Proof   *Let Φ_i be the potential in the collection of skew heaps immediately following the ith operation. Note that $\Phi_0 = 0$, and $\Phi_i \geq 0$. An insertion creates a single node tree whose root is by definition light and thus does not alter the potential prior to the resulting merge. A* `DeleteMin` *discards the root prior to the merge, so it cannot raise the potential (and may in fact lower it). We need only consider the merging costs. Let c_i be the cost of the merge that occurs as a result of the ith operation. Then $c_i + \Phi_i - \Phi_{i-1} \leq 4\log N$, and by telescoping over any M operations, we have $\sum_{i=1}^{M} c_i \leq 4M\log N$, since $\Phi_M - \Phi_0$ is not negative.*

Finding a useful potential function is the most difficult part of the analysis.

The skew heap is a remarkable example of a simple algorithm with an analysis that is not obvious. The analysis, however, is simple to perform once the appropriate potential function is identified. Unfortunately, there is still no general theory that allows one to decide on a potential function. Typically, many different functions are tried before a usable one appears.

A nonrecursive algorithm should be used because of the possibility that we could run out of stack space.

One comment is in order: Although the initial description of the algorithm uses recursion and recursion provides the simplest code, it cannot be used in practice. This is because the linear worst-case time for an operation could cause an overflow of the procedure stack when the recursion is implemented. Consequently, a nonrecursive algorithm must be used. Rather than explore those possibilities, we will discuss an alternative data structure that is slightly more complicated. This data structure has not been completely analyzed but seems to perform well in practice.

22.2   The Pairing Heap

The *pairing heap* is a heap-ordered *M*-ary tree with no structural constraints. Its analysis is not complete, but it appears to perform well in practice.

The *pairing heap* is a structurally unconstrained heap-ordered *M*-ary tree. It has the property that all operations except deletion take constant worst-case time. Although `DeleteMin` could take linear worst-case time, it can be shown that any *sequence* of pairing heap operations has logarithmic amortized performance. It is conjectured that even better performance is guaranteed, namely that all operations except for `DeleteMin` have constant amortized cost, while `DeleteMin` has logarithmic amortized cost. However, this is open.

The pairing heap is stored using a left child/right sibling representation. A third pointer is used for `DecreaseKey`.

Figure 22.4 shows an abstract pairing heap. The actual implementation uses a left child/right sibling representation discussed in earlier chapters. The `DecreaseKey` operation, as we will see, requires that each node contain an additional pointer. A node that is a leftmost child contains a pointer to its parent; otherwise, the node is a right sibling and contains a pointer to its left sibling. This representation is shown in Figure 22.5, where the darkened line indicates that two pointers (one in each direction) connect pairs of nodes.

22.2.1   Pairing Heap Operations and Theory

In principle, the basic operations are simple. This is why the pairing heap performs well in practice. To merge two pairing heaps, we make the heap with the larger root the new first child of the heap with the smaller root. Insertion is a special case of merging. To perform a DecreaseKey, we lower the value of the requested node. Because we are not maintaining parent pointers for all nodes, we do not know if this will violate the heap order. Thus we detach the adjusted node from its parent and complete the DecreaseKey by merging the two pairing heaps that result. In Figure 22.5 we see that detaching a node from its parent means that we remove it from what is essentially a linked list of children. So far we are in great shape: Every operation we have described takes constant time. However, we are not so lucky when it comes to DeleteMin.

> Merging is simple: Attach the larger-root tree as a left child of the smaller-root tree. Insertion and decreasing are also simple.

To perform a DeleteMin, we must remove the root of the tree, creating a collection of heaps. If there are c children of the root, then combining these heaps into one heap requires $c - 1$ merges. This tells us that if there are lots of children of the root, the DeleteMin will cost lots of time. If the insertion sequence is 1, 2, ..., N, then it is easy to see that 1 will be at the root and all the other items will be in nodes that are children of the root. Consequently, the DeleteMin will be $O(N)$. The best we can hope to do is to arrange the merges so that we do not have repeatedly expensive DeleteMin operations.

> DeleteMin is expensive because the new root could be any of the c children of the old root. We need $c-1$ merges.

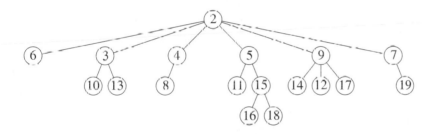

Figure 22.4   Abstract representation of sample pairing heap

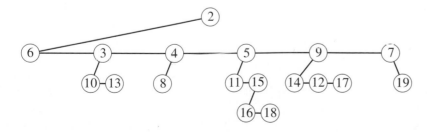

Figure 22.5   Actual representation of pairing heap in Figure 22.4; dark line represents a pair of pointers that connect nodes in both directions

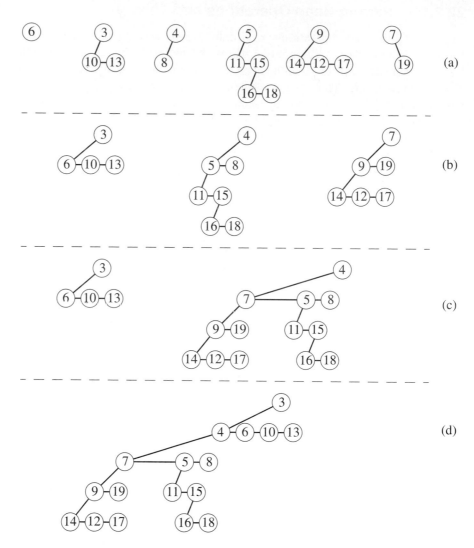

Figure 22.6   Recombination of siblings after a DeleteMin; in each merge the larger root tree is made the left child of the smaller root tree: (a) the resulting trees; (b) after the first pass; (c) after the first merge of the second pass; (d) after the second merge of the second pass

```
1  // PairHeap class interface
2  // Etype: must have zero-parameter constructor,
3  //      copy constructor, operator=, and operator<
4  // CONSTRUCTION: with (a) Etype representing negative infinity
5  // All copying of PairHeap objects is DISALLOWED
6  //
7  // ******************PUBLIC OPERATIONS*********************
8  // PairNode *Insert( Etype X ) --> Insert X; return position
9  // void DeleteMin( )        --> Remove smallest item
10 // Etype FindMin( )         --> Return smallest item
11 // void DeleteMin( Etype & X )
12 //                      --> Remove smallest item, put it in X
13 // int IsEmpty( )           --> Return 1 if empty; else return 0
14 // int IsFull( )            --> Return 1 if full;  else return 0
15 // void MakeEmpty( )        --> Remove all items
16 // void DecreaseKey( PairNode *P, Etype NewValue )
17 //                      --> Lower value of item at P
18 // ******************ERRORS********************************
19 // Predefined exception is propagated if new fails
20 // EXCEPTION is called for FindMin or DeleteMin when empty
21 // Error message for DecreaseKey with higher value
22
23 #include <stdlib.h>
```

Figure 22.7 The description of the `PairingHeap` class interface

The simplest and most practical of the many variants that have been proposed is *two-pass merging*. We first scan merging pairs of children from left to right.[2] After the first scan, we have half as many trees to merge. We then perform a second scan, right to left. At each step we merge the rightmost tree remaining from the first scan with the current merged result. As an example, if we have children c_1 through c_8, the first scan performs the merges c_1 and c_2, c_3 and c_4, c_5 and c_6, c_7 and c_8. As a result we obtain d_1, d_2, d_3, and d_4. We perform the second pass by merging d_3 and d_4; d_2 is then merged with that result, and then d_1 is merged with the result of that merge, completing the DeleteMin. Figure 22.6 shows the result of a DeleteMin on the pairing heap in Figure 22.5.

The order in which the pairing heap subtrees are merged is important. The simplest algorithm is two-pass merging.

Other merging strategies are possible. For instance, we can place each subtree (corresponding to a child) on a queue, repeatedly dequeue two trees, and then enqueue the result of merging them. After $c-1$ merges, only one tree remains on the queue, and this is the result of the DeleteMin. However, using a stack instead of a queue is a disaster because it is possible that the root of tree that results could have $c-1$ children; if this occurs in a sequence, the DeleteMin operation will have linear amortized cost per operation rather than logarithmic. Exercise 22.8 asks you to construct such a sequence.

Several alternatives have been proposed. Most are indistinguishable, but using a single left-to-right pass is a bad idea.

2. We must be careful if there are an odd number of children. When that happens, we merge the last child with the result of the rightmost merge to complete the first scan.

```
1  // Basic node in a pairing heap
2  template <class Etype>
3  struct PairNode
4  {
5      Etype Element;
6      PairNode *LeftChild;
7      PairNode *NextSibling;
8      PairNode *Prev;
9
10     PairNode( const Etype & E ) : Element( E ),
11       LeftChild( NULL ), NextSibling( NULL ), Prev( NULL ) { }
12 };
13
14 template <class Etype>
15 class PairHeap
16 {
17   public:
18     PairHeap( ) : Root( NULL ), CurrentSize( 0 ) { }
19     ~PairHeap( ) { FreeTree( Root ); }
20
21         // Add an item maintaining heap order; return position
22     PairNode<Etype> *Insert( const Etype & X );
23
24         // Return minimum item in heap
25     const Etype & FindMin( ) const;
26
27         // Delete minimum item in heap
28     void DeleteMin( );
29     void DeleteMin( Etype & X );
30
31         // Lower the value of a key in node given by P
32     void DecreaseKey( PairNode<Etype> *P,
33                         const Etype & NewVal );
34         // The usual suspects
35     int IsEmpty( ) const { return CurrentSize == 0; }
36     int IsFull( ) const   { return 0; }
37     void MakeEmpty( )    { CurrentSize = 0; FreeTree( Root ); }
38   private:
39     PairNode<Etype> *Root;
40     int CurrentSize;   // Number of elements currently stored
41
42     PairHeap( const PairHeap & );        // Disable all copying
43     const PairHeap & operator=( const PairHeap & Rhs );
44
45         // Internal routines
46     void CompareAndLink( PairNode<Etype> * & First,
47                         PairNode<Etype> *Second );
48     PairNode<Etype> *CombineSiblings(
49                         PairNode<Etype> *FirstSibling );
50     void FreeTree( PairNode<Etype> *T );
51 };
```

Figure 22.8   Pairing heap class interface and `PairNode`

```
1  // Return minimum item in pairing heap
2
3  template <class Etype>
4  const Etype &
5  PairHeap<Etype>::FindMin( ) const
6  {
7      EXCEPTION( IsEmpty( ), "Pairing heap is empty" );
8      return Root->Element;
9  }
```

Figure 22.9   FindMin member for pairing heap

```
1   // Insert X into pairing heap
2   // Return a pointer to the inserted node
3
4   template <class Etype>
5   PairNode<Etype> *
6   PairHeap<Etype>::Insert( const Etype & X )
7   {
8       PairNode<Etype> *NewNode = new PairNode<Etype>( X );
9
10      CurrentSize++;
11      if( Root == NULL )
12          Root = NewNode;
13      else
14          CompareAndLink( Root, NewNode );
15
16      return NewNode;
17  }
```

Figure 22.10   Insert routine for the pairing heap

22.2.2   Implementation of the Pairing Heap

The functionality of the PairHeap is described in Figure 22.7 and the PairHeap class interface is shown in Figure 22.8. The basic node of a pairing heap is also shown in Figure 22.8 and consists of an item and three pointers. Two of these pointers are the left child and next sibling. The third pointer is Prev, which points at a parent if the node is a first child or a left sibling otherwise. The data members are a pointer to the root node (Root), plus an integer that represents the current number of items in the heap. This member is used to simplify the DecreaseKey operation. The interface is very much like the BinaryHeap class. We do not include a Merge class member; it is straightforward to implement and is left as Exercise 22.11.

The Prev data member points to either a left sibling or a parent.

One notable difference is that FindMin is a constant member function because Toss is no longer needed. A second difference is that Insert returns a pointer to the newly allocated node for use by DecreaseKey. Also, operator= has been disabled (Exercise 22.10 asks you to explain why).

Insert returns a pointer to the new node for use by DecreaseKey.

FindMin is coded in Figure 22.9. Since the minimum is at the root, this routine is easily implemented. Insert, shown in Figure 22.10, creates a one-node tree and merges it with the Root to obtain a new tree. As we mentioned earlier, it returns a pointer to the newly allocated node. Notice that we must handle the special case of an insertion into an empty tree.

DeleteMin is implemented as a call to CombineSiblings.

Figure 22.11 implements the two DeleteMin routines. If the pairing heap is empty, we have an error. Otherwise, at line 9 we save a pointer to the root (so it can be deleted at line 17). After saving the value in the root, we make a call to CombineSiblings at line 15 to merge the root's subtrees and set the result to the new root. If there are no subtrees, we merely set Root to NULL at line 13. Both Insert and DeleteMin adjust CurrentSize appropriately.

```
1  // Delete minimum item in pairing heap; place result in X
2
3  template <class Etype>
4  void
5  PairHeap<Etype>::DeleteMin( Etype & X )
6  {
7      EXCEPTION( IsEmpty( ), "Pairing heap is empty!" );
8
9      PairNode<Etype> *OldRoot = Root;
10
11     X = Root->Element;
12     if( Root->LeftChild == NULL )
13         Root = NULL;
14     else
15         Root = CombineSiblings( Root->LeftChild );
16
17     delete OldRoot;
18     CurrentSize--;
19 }
20
21
22 // Delete minimum item in pairing heap
23
24 template <class Etype>
25 void
26 PairHeap<Etype>::DeleteMin( )
27 {
28     static Etype Ignored;   // To avoid repeated constructions
29     DeleteMin( Ignored );
30 }
```

Figure 22.11 DeleteMin members for pairing heap

```
1   // Change value of key stored at node
2   // pointed at by P to NewVal; NewVal must
3   // be smaller than originally stored value
4
5   template <class Etype>
6   void
7   PairHeap<Etype>::
8   DecreaseKey( PairNode<Etype> *P, const Etype & NewVal )
9   {
10      if( P->Element < NewVal )
11          cerr << "DecreaseKey called with larger value!\n";
12      else
13      {
14          P->Element = NewVal;
15          if( P != Root )
16          {
17                  // Splice P out of its list of children
18              if( P->NextSibling != NULL )
19                  P->NextSibling->Prev = P->Prev;
20              if( P->Prev->LeftChild == P )
21                  P->Prev->LeftChild = P->NextSibling;
22              else
23                  P->Prev->NextSibling = P->NextSibling;
24              P->NextSibling = NULL;
25
26              CompareAndLink( Root, P );
27          }
28      }
29  }
```

Figure 22.12   The DecreaseKey member for pairing heaps

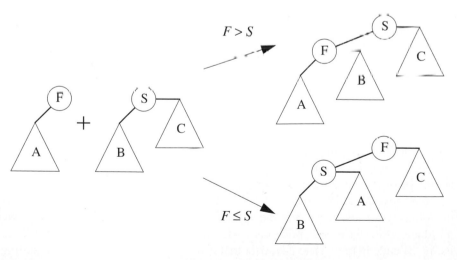

Figure 22.13   CompareAndLink merges two trees

```
1   // This is the basic operation to maintain order
2   // Links First and Second together to satisfy heap order
3   // First is set to the resulting tree
4   // First is assumed not NULL
5   // First->NextSibling MUST be NULL on entry
6
7   template <class Etype>
8   void
9   PairHeap<Etype>::CompareAndLink( PairNode<Etype> * & First,
10                                   PairNode<Etype> *Second )
11  {
12      if( Second == NULL )
13          return;
14      if( Second->Element < First->Element )
15      {
16          // Attach First as leftmost child of Second
17          Second->Prev = First->Prev;
18          First->Prev = Second;
19          First->NextSibling = Second->LeftChild;
20          if( First->NextSibling != NULL )
21              First->NextSibling->Prev = First;
22          Second->LeftChild = First;
23          First = Second;   // Second becomes new root
24      }
25      else
26      {
27          // Attach Second as leftmost child of First
28          Second->Prev = First;
29          First->NextSibling = Second->NextSibling;
30          if( First->NextSibling != NULL )
31              First->NextSibling->Prev = First;
32          Second->NextSibling = First->LeftChild;
33          if( Second->NextSibling != NULL )
34              Second->NextSibling->Prev = Second;
35          First->LeftChild = Second;
36      }
37  }
```

Figure 22.14   CompareAndLink routine

DecreaseKey is implemented in Figure 22.12. First, notice that if the new value is larger than the original, then we might destroy the heap order. There is no way to know without examining all the children, and since there may be a large number of children, it would be inefficient to do so. Thus we assume that it is always an error to attempt to increase the key using the DecreaseKey member. (Exercise 22.9 asks you to describe an algorithm for IncreaseKey.) After performing this test, we lower the value in the node. If the node is the root, we are done. Otherwise, we splice the node out of the list of children that it is in, using the code in lines 18 to 24. After that is done, we merely merge the resulting tree with the root.

```
1    // CombineSiblings assumes that FirstSibling is not NULL.
2
3    template <class Etype>
4    PairNode<Etype> *
5    PairHeap<Etype>::
6    CombineSiblings( PairNode<Etype> *FirstSibling )
7    {
8        if( FirstSibling->NextSibling == NULL )
9            return FirstSibling;
10
11           // Allocate the array
12       Vector<PairNode<Etype> * > TreeArray( CurrentSize );
13
14           // Store the subtrees in an array
15       int NumSiblings;
16       for( NumSiblings = 0; FirstSibling; NumSiblings++ )
17       {
18           TreeArray[ NumSiblings ] = FirstSibling;
19           FirstSibling->Prev->NextSibling = NULL; // break links
20           FirstSibling = FirstSibling->NextSibling;
21       }
22       TreeArray[ NumSiblings ] = NULL;
23
24       // Combine the subtrees two at a time, going left to right
25       int i;
26       for( i = 0; i + 1 < NumSiblings; i += 2 )
27           CompareAndLink( TreeArray[ i ], TreeArray[ i + 1 ] );
28
29           // j has the result of the last CompareAndLink.
30           // If an odd number of trees, get the last one
31       int j = i - 2;
32       if( j == NumSiblings - 3 )
33           CompareAndLink( TreeArray[ j ], TreeArray[ j + 2 ] );
34
35           // Now go right to left, merging last tree with
36           // next to last. The result becomes the new last.
37       for( ; j >= 2; j -= 2 )
38           CompareAndLink( TreeArray[ j - 2 ], TreeArray[ j ] );
39
40       PairNode<Etype> *Result = TreeArray[ 0 ];
41       return Result;
42   }
```

Figure 22.15   The heart of the pairing heap algorithm; implementing a two-pass merge to combine all the siblings, given the first sibling

The two remaining routines are CompareAndLink, which combines two trees, and CombineSiblings, which combines all the siblings, given the first sibling. Figure 22.13 shows how two subheaps are combined. The procedure is generalized to allow the second subheap to have siblings (this is needed for the second pass in the two-pass merge). As we mentioned earlier, the subheap with the larger root is made a leftmost child of the other subheap. The code is shown in Figure 22.14. Notice that we have several instances in which a pointer is tested against NULL before accessing its Prev data member; this suggests that perhaps it would be useful to have a NullNode sentinel that was customary in the advanced search tree implementations. We leave this as Exercise 22.15.

Finally, Figure 22.15 implements CombineSiblings. We use the vector TreeArray to store the subtrees. In the worst case we could have $N - 1$ siblings, so the vector uses CurrentSize to determine its capacity. We begin by separating the subtrees and storing them in TreeArray, using the loop at lines 16 to 21. Assuming we have more than one sibling to merge, we make a left to right pass at lines 26 and 27. The special case in which we have an odd number of trees is handled at lines 31 to 33. We finish the merging with a right to left pass at lines 37 and 38. Once we are done, the result is stored in array position 0. We can save the pointer so it can be returned after the dynamically allocated array is deleted.

As a practical matter, dynamically allocating and deallocating the Vector can be unduly expensive and is probably not always needed. It may be better to use a static Vector object that can be resized as needed. This is left as Exercises 22.12 and 22.18.

22.2.3   Application: Dijkstra's Shortest Weighted Path Algorithm

DecreaseKey is an improvement for Dijkstra's algorithm on instances in which there are lots of calls to it.

As an example of how the DecreaseKey operation is used, we rewrite Dijkstra's algorithm, previously seen in Section 14.3. Recall that at any point we are maintaining a priority queue of DistType objects, ordered by the Dist data member. For each vertex in the graph, we really need only one DistType object in the priority queue at any instant, but for convenience we had many. In this section we will rework the code so that if a vertex w has its distance lowered, then its position in the priority queue is found, and a DecreaseKey operation is performed for its corresponding DistType object.

The new code is shown in Figure 22.16. The changes are all relatively minor. First, at line 8 we declare that PQ is a pairing heap rather than a binary heap. We also maintain a Vector HeapPositions of pointers to pairing heap nodes. Initially, all the pointers are NULL (lines 14 and 15). Whenever an item is inserted into the pairing heap, we make an entry into the HeapPositions array. This occurs at lines 18 and 43. The algorithm itself is simplified: Now we merely call DeleteMin as long as the pairing heap is not empty, rather than repeatedly calling DeleteMin until an unseen vertex emerges. Consequently, we no longer need the Scratch data member. Compare lines 21 to 25 with the corresponding code in Figure 14.31. All that remains is the updates after line 36 indicate that a change is in order. If the vertex has never been placed in the priority queue, we insert it for the first time, updating the HeapPositions array. Otherwise, we merely call DecreaseKey at line 45.

```
1   // Dijkstra's algorithm for shortest paths, using pairing heap
2
3   template <class NameType, class DistType>
4   int
5   Graph<NameType, DistType>::Dijkstra( int StartNode )
6   {
7       int V, W;
8       PairHeap< Path<DistType> > PQ;
9       Path<DistType> VRec;
10          // An array to store pairing heap position
11      Vector< PairNode< Path<DistType> > * >
12                              HeapPositions( NumVertices );
13      ClearData( );
14      for( int i = 0; i < NumVertices; i++ )
15          HeapPositions[ i ] = NULL;
16
17      Table[ StartNode ].Dist = 0;
18      HeapPositions[ StartNode ] =
19          PQ.Insert( Path<DistType>( StartNode, 0 ) );
20
21      while( !PQ.IsEmpty( ) )
22      {
23          PQ.DeleteMin( VRec );
24
25          V = VRec.Dest;
26          for( ListItr< Edge<DistType> > P = *Table[ V ].Adj;
27                                          +P; ++P )
28          {
29              W = P( ).Dest;
30              DistType Cvw = P( ).Cost;
31              if( Cvw < 0 )
32              {
33                  cout << "Graph has negative edges\n";
34                  return 0;
35              }
36              if( Table[ W ].Dist > Table[ V ].Dist + Cvw )
37              {
38                  Table[ W ].Dist = Table[ V ].Dist + Cvw;
39                  Table[ W ].Prev = V;
40
41                  Path<DistType> NewVal( W, Table[ W ].Dist );
42                  if( HeapPositions[ W ] == NULL )
43                      HeapPositions[ W ] = PQ.Insert( NewVal );
44                  else
45                      PQ.DecreaseKey( HeapPositions[ W ], NewVal );
46              }
47          }
48      }
49      return 1;
50  }
```

Figure 22.16   Dijkstra's algorithm using the pairing heap and
                    DecreaseKey

Whether the binary heap implementation of Dijkstra's algorithm is faster than the pairing heap implementation depends on several factors. One study, detailed in the references, suggests that the pairing heap is slightly better than the binary heap when both are carefully implemented. The results depend heavily on the coding details as well as the frequency of `DecreaseKey` operations. More studies are needed to decide when the pairing heap is suitable in practice.

Summary

This chapter describes two data structures that support merging and are efficient in the amortized sense. Both are simple to implement because they lack a rigid structure property. The pairing heap seems to have practical utility, but its complete analysis remains an intriguing open problem.

The next chapter, which is the last chapter, describes a new data structure that is used to maintain disjoint sets. It also has a remarkable amortized analysis.

Objects of the Game

Pairing heap A heap-ordered M-ary tree with no structural constraints. Its analysis is not complete, but it appears to perform well in practice. (708)

Skew heap A heap-ordered binary tree. There is no balancing condition, but it supports all operations in logarithmic amortized time. (703)

Two-pass merging The order in which the pairing heap subtrees are merged is important. The simplest algorithm is two-pass merging. Subtrees are merged in pairs in a left-to-right scan. Then a right-to-left scan is performed to finish the merging. (711)

Common Errors

1. A recursive implementation of the skew heap cannot be used in practice because the depth of the recursion could be linear.
2. It is easy to lose track of the `Prev` pointers in the skew heap.
3. Tests to make sure pointers are not `NULL` must be done throughout.
4. When performing a merge, a node may not reside in two pairing heaps. Otherwise, it will be double-deleted.

On the Internet

The pairing heap class is available.

Pair.h	The class interface for the pairing heap
Pair.cpp	The implementation for the pairing heap

Exercises

In Short

22.1.   Show the result of a skew heap built from the following insertion sequences:

a. 1, 2, 3, 4, 5, 6, 7
b. 4, 3, 5, 2, 6, 7, 1

22.2.   Show the result of a pairing heap built from the following insertion sequences:

a. 1, 2, 3, 4, 5, 6, 7
b. 4, 3, 5, 2, 6, 7, 1

22.3.   For each heap in Exercises 22.1 and 22.2, show the result of two `DeleteMin` operations.

In Theory

22.4.   Give a sequence of operations that lead to a `Merge` requiring linear time to show that the logarithmic amortized bound for skew heap operations is not a worst-case bound

22.5.   Show that both the `DecreaseKey` and `IncreaseKey` operations can be supported by skew heaps in logarithmic amortized time.

22.6.   Describe a linear-time `FixHeap` algorithm for the skew heap.

22.7.   Show that by storing the length of the right path for each node in the tree, it is possible to impose a balancing condition that yields logarithmic worst-case time per operation. Such a structure is known as a *leftist heap*.

22.8.   Show that using a stack to implement the `CombineSiblings` operation for pairing heaps is bad by constructing a sequence that has linear amortized cost per operation.

22.9.   Describe how to implement `IncreaseKey` for pairing heaps.

22.10.   Why is `operator=` disabled for pairing heaps?

In Practice

22.11.   Add the public `Merge` member function to the pairing heap class. Make sure that a node appears in only one tree.

22.12.   Use a static `Vector` class that is resized as necessary to store the `TreeArray` in `CombineSiblings`.

22.13. Modify the `PairingHeap` class to throw an `Underflow` exception when a `FindMin` or `DeleteMin` is attempted on an empty pairing heap.

Programming Problems

22.14. Implement a nonrecursive version of the skew heap.

22.15. Implement the pairing heap with a `NullNode` sentinel.

22.16. Implement the queue algorithm for `CombineSiblings` and compare its performance with the two-pass algorithm in the text.

22.17. If the `DecreaseKey` operation is not supported, parent pointers are not necessary. Implement the pairing heap without parent pointers, and compare its performance with the binary heap and/or skew heap and/or splay tree.

22.18. Implement the pairing heap by managing memory yourself, as described in Exercise 16.25. Compare the performance of Dijkstra's algorithm using both types of pairing heaps with the performance using binary heaps. You will need to construct an appropriate model for a random graph (which in itself is not a trivial task).

References

The *leftist heap* [1] was the first efficient mergeable priority queue. It is the worst-case variant of the skew heap suggested in Exercise 22.7. Skew heaps are described in [5]. The skew heap paper contains solutions to Exercises 22.4 and 22.5.

[2] describes the pairing heap and proves that using two-pass merging, the amortized cost of all operations is logarithmic. It is still open whether this bound is tight. In particular, there is some evidence in [6] that the amortized cost of all operations except `DeleteMin` is actually constant, while the amortized cost of the `DeleteMin` is logarithmic, so that any sequence of D `DeleteMin` and I other operations takes $O(I + D\log N)$ time. On the other hand, there is also evidence that this might not be the case [4]. A data structure that does achieve this bound, but is too complicated to be practical, is the *Fibonacci heap* [3]. It is hoped that the pairing heap is a practical alternative to the theoretically interesting Fibonacci heap. Leftist heaps and Fibonacci heaps are discussed in [7].

A comparison of various priority queues in the setting of solving the minimum spanning tree problem (discussed in Section 23.2.1) using a method very similar to Dijkstra's algorithm is given in [4].

1. C. A. Crane, "Linear Lists and Priority Queues as Balanced Binary Trees," *Technical Report STAN-CS-72-259,* Computer Science Department, Stanford University, Palo Alto, CA, 1972.

2. M. L. Fredman, R. Sedgewick, D. D. Sleator, and R. E. Tarjan, "The Pairing Heap: A New Form of Self-adjusting Heap," *Algorithmica* **1** (1986), 111-129.

3. M. L. Fredman and R. E. Tarjan, "Fibonacci Heaps and Their Uses in Improved Network Optimization Algorithms," *Journal of the ACM* **34** (1987), 596-615.

4. B. M. E. Moret and H. D. Shapiro, "An Empirical Analysis of Algorithms for Constructing a Minimum Spanning Tree," *Proceedings of the Second Workshop on Algorithms and Data Structures* (1991), 400-411.

5. D. D. Sleator and R. E. Tarjan, "Self-adjusting Heaps," *SIAM Journal on Computing* **15** (1986), 52-69.

6. J. T. Stasko and J. S. Vitter, "Pairing Heaps: Experiments and Analysis," *Communications of the ACM* **32** (1987), 234-249.

7. M. A. Weiss, *Data Structures and Algorithm Analysis in C++*, Benjamin/Cummings Publishing Co., Redwood City, CA (1994).

Chapter 23

The Disjoint Set Class

In this chapter we describe an efficient data structure to solve the equivalence problem. The data structure is simple to implement. Each routine requires only a few lines of code. The implementation is also extremely fast, requiring constant average time per operation. This data structure is also very interesting from a theoretical point of view because its analysis is extremely difficult; the functional form of the worst case is unlike any we have yet seen.

In this chapter we will see

- two simple applications of the disjoint set class
- how the disjoint set class can be implemented with minimal coding effort
- how to increase the speed of the disjoint set class using two simple observations
- an analysis of the running time of a fast implementation of the disjoint set class

23.1 Equivalence Relations

A *relation R* is defined on a set S if for every pair of elements (a, b), $a, b \in S$, $a \, R \, b$ is either true or false. If $a \, R \, b$ is true, then we say that a is related to b.

An *equivalence relation* is a relation R that satisfies three properties:

- *Reflexive*: $a \, R \, a$ is true for all $a \in S$
- *Symmetric*: $a \, R \, b$ if and only if $b \, R \, a$
- *Transitive*: $a \, R \, b$ and $b \, R \, c$ implies that $a \, R \, c$

A *relation* is defined on a set if every pair of elements is either related or is not. An *equivalence relation* is reflexive, symmetric, and transitive.

Electrical connectivity, where all connections are by metal wires, is an equivalence relation. The relation is clearly reflexive, as any component is connected to itself. If a is electrically connected to b, then b must be electrically connected to a, so the relation is symmetric. Finally, if a is connected to b and b is connected to c, then a is connected to c.

Likewise, connectivity through a bidirectional network forms equivalence classes of connected components. However, if the connections in the network are directed (that is, a connection from v to w does not imply one from w to v), then we do not have an equivalence relation because the symmetric property does not hold. As an example, suppose town a is related to town b if it is possible to travel from a to b by taking roads. This relationship is an equivalence relation if the roads are two-way.

23.2   Dynamic Equivalence

Given an equivalence relation, which is indicated by the symbol $\sim$, the natural problem is to decide for any a and b if $a \sim b$. If the relation is stored as a two-dimensional array of boolean variables, then of course, this can be done in constant time. The problem is that the relation is usually not explicitly, but rather implicitly, defined.

As an example, suppose the equivalence relation is defined over the five-element set $\{a_1, a_2, a_3, a_4, a_5\}$. Then there are 25 pairs of elements, each of which is either related or not. However, the information that $a_1 \sim a_2$, $a_3 \sim a_4$, $a_1 \sim a_5$, and $a_4 \sim a_2$ are all related implies that all pairs are related. We would like to be able to infer this quickly.

The *equivalence class* of an element *x* in set *S* is the subset of *S* that contains all the elements that are related to *x*. The equivalence classes form *disjoint sets*.

The *equivalence class* of an element $x \in S$ is the subset of S that contains all the elements that are related to x. Note that the equivalence classes form a partition of S: Every member of S appears in exactly one equivalence class. To decide if $a \sim b$, we need only to check whether a and b are in the same equivalence class. This provides our strategy to solve the equivalence problem.

The input is initially a collection of N sets, each with one element. This initial representation is that all relations (except reflexive relations) are false. Each set has a different element, so that $S_i \cap S_j = \varnothing$; such sets are called *disjoint sets*.

The basic operations needed for disjoint set manipulation are `Union` and `Find`.

There are two permissible operations. The first is `Find`, which returns the name of the set (that is, the equivalence class) containing a given element. The second operation adds relations. If we want to add the pair (a,b) to the list of relations, then we first see if a and b are already related. This is done by performing `Find`s on both a and b and checking whether they are in the same equivalence class. If they are not, then we apply `Union`.[1] This operation merges the two equivalence classes containing a and b into a new equivalence class. From a set point of view, the result is to create a new set $S_k = S_i \cup S_j$, destroying the originals and preserving the disjointness of all the sets. The data structure to do this is frequently known as the disjoint set *Union/Find data structure*. We use the

---

1. Union is the traditional name for this operation, which is unfortunate because `union` is a keyword in C++.

term *Union/Find algorithm* to mean a processing of *Union/Find* requests using the disjoint set data structure.

The algorithm is *dynamic* because, during the course of the algorithm, the sets can change via the Union operation. The algorithm must also operate *online*: When a Find is performed, it must give an answer before continuing. Another possibility would be an *offline* algorithm. Such an algorithm would be allowed to see the entire sequence of Union and Find requests. The answer it provides for each Find must still be consistent with all the Unions that were performed up until the Find, but the algorithm can give all its answers after it has seen *all* the questions. The difference is similar to the difference between taking a written exam (which is generally offline because you only have to give the answers before time expires) and taking an oral exam (which is online because you must answer the current question before proceeding to the next question).

> In an *online algorithm* an answer must be provided for each query before viewing the next query.

Notice that we do not perform any operations comparing the relative values of elements but merely require knowledge of their location. For this reason we can assume that all elements have been numbered sequentially starting from 0 and that the numbering can be determined easily by some hashing scheme.

> The set elements are numbered sequentially starting from 0.

23.2.1   Application: Minimum Spanning Trees

A *spanning tree* of an undirected graph G is a tree formed from graph edges that connect all the vertices of G. Notice that, unlike the graphs in Chapter 14, an edge (u, v) in G is identical to an edge (v, u). The cost of a spanning tree is the sum of the costs of the edges in the tree; the *minimum spanning tree* problem asks for the spanning tree of minimum cost. A minimum spanning tree exists if and only if G is connected. As we will see, testing a graph's connectivity can be done as part of the minimum spanning tree computation.

> The *minimum spanning tree* is a connected subgraph of G that spans all vertices at minimum total cost.

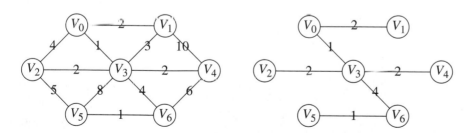

Figure 23.1   A graph G (left) and its minimum spanning tree

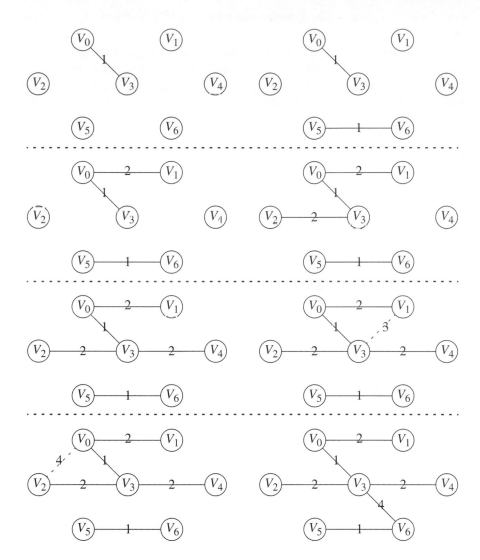

Figure 23.2 Kruskal's algorithm after each edge is considered

In Figure 23.1 the graph on the right is a minimum spanning tree of the graph on the left (it happens to be unique, but this is unusual if the graph has many edges of equal cost). Notice that the number of edges in the minimum spanning tree is $|V| - 1$. The minimum spanning tree is a *tree* because it is acyclic, it is *spanning* because it covers every edge, and it is *minimum* for the obvious reason. If we need to wire a house with a minimum of cable (and we are not allowed to add junctions), then we need to solve a minimum spanning tree problem, where each vertex is an object that is to be added to the wiring network, and each edge is the cost of a direct connection. (If we can add junctions at arbitrary places, then we have the Steiner tree problem, which is much more difficult to solve. Among other things, it can be shown that if the cost of a connection is proportional to the Euclidean distance, then the minimum spanning tree is at most 15 percent more expensive than the minimum Steiner tree.)

A simple algorithm, commonly known as *Kruskal's algorithm*, is used to continually select edges in order of smallest weight and accept an edge into the tree if it does not cause a cycle. Formally, Kruskal's algorithm maintains a forest – a collection of trees. Initially, there are $|V|$ single-node trees. Adding an edge merges two trees into one. When the algorithm terminates, there is only one tree, and this is the minimum spanning tree.[2] By counting the number of accepted edges, we can determine when the algorithm should terminate.

Kruskal's minimum spanning tree algorithm is used to select edges in increasing cost, adding an edge to the tree if it does not create a cycle.

Figure 23.2 shows the action of Kruskal's algorithm on the graph in Figure 23.1. The first five edges are all accepted because they do not create cycles. The next two edges, (v_1, v_3) (of cost 3) and then (v_0, v_2) (of cost 4), are rejected because each would create a cycle in the tree. The edge that is considered afterward is accepted, and since it is the sixth edge in a seven-vertex graph, we can terminate the algorithm.

It is simple enough to order the edges for testing: We can sort them at a cost of $|E|\log|E|$ and then step through the ordered array of edges. Alternatively, we can construct a priority queue of $|E|$ edges and repeatedly obtain edges by calling DeleteMin. Although the worst-case bound is unchanged, using a priority queue is sometimes better because Kruskal's algorithm tends to test only a small fraction of the edges on random graphs. Of course, in the worst case, it is always possible that all the edges must be tried. For instance, if there were an extra vertex v_8 and edge (v_5, v_8) of cost 100, all the edges would have to be examined. In this case a quicksort at the start would be faster. In effect the choice between a priority queue and an initial sort is a gamble on how many edges are likely to be examined.

The edges can be sorted, or a priority queue can be used.

More interesting is the issue of how we decide whether an edge (u, v) should be accepted or rejected. Clearly adding the edge (u, v) will cause a cycle if (and only if) u and v are already connected in the current spanning forest. Thus we merely maintain each connected component in the spanning forest as a disjoint set. Initially, each vertex is in its own disjoint set. If u and v are in the same disjoint set, as determined by two Finds, the edge is rejected because u and v are already connected. Otherwise, the edge is accepted, and a Union is performed on the two disjoint sets containing u and v, in effect, combining the connected components. This is what we want because once edge (u, v) is added to the spanning forest, if w was connected to u and x was connected to v, then x and w must be connected and thus belong in the same set.

The test for cycles is done by using a Union/Find data structure.

---

2. If the graph is not connected, the algorithm will terminate with more than one tree; each tree represents a minimum spanning tree for each connected component of the graph.

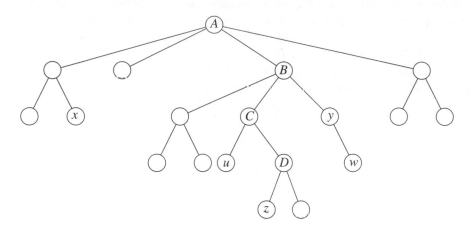

Figure 23.3 The nearest common ancestor for each request in the pair sequence (x, y), (u, z), (w, x), (z, w), (w, y), is *A*, *C*, *A*, *B*, and *y*, respectively

23.2.2 Application: The Nearest Common Ancestor Problem

One illustration of the Union/Find data structure is the offline *nearest common ancestor* (NCA) problem.

OFFLINE NEAREST COMMON ANCESTOR PROBLEM
GIVEN A TREE AND A LIST OF PAIRS OF NODES IN THE TREE, FIND THE NEAREST COMMON ANCESTOR FOR EACH PAIR OF NODES.

NCA **is important in graph algorithms and computational biology.**

As an example, Figure 23.3 shows a tree with a pair list containing five requests. For the pair of nodes *u* and *z*, node *C* is the nearest ancestor of both. (*A* and *B* are also ancestors, but they are not the closest.) The problem is offline because we can see the entire request sequence prior to providing the first answer. This is an important graph theory problem that also has applications in the field of computational biology (where the tree represents evolution).

A postorder traversal can be used to solve the problem.

The algorithm works by performing a postorder tree traversal. When we are about to return from processing a node, we examine the pair list to see if there are any ancestor calculations to be performed. If *u* is the current node, (u, v) is in the pair list, and we have already finished the recursive call to *v*, then we have enough information to determine $NCA(u, v)$.

To understand how this algorithm works, let us examine Figure 23.4. We are about to finish the recursive call to D. All nodes that are shaded have been visited by a recursive call, and except for the nodes on the path to D, all the recursive calls have already finished. We mark a node after its recursive call is complete. If v is marked, then $NCA(D, v)$ is some node on the path to D. The *anchor* of a visited (but not necessarily marked) node v is the node on the current access path that is closest to v. In Figure 23.4, p's anchor is A, q's anchor is B, and r is unanchored because it has yet to be visited; we can argue that r's anchor is r at the point that r is first visited. As Figure 23.4 shows, each node on the current access path is an anchor (of at least itself). Furthermore, the visited nodes form equivalence classes: Two nodes are related if they have the same anchor, and we can regard each unvisited node as being in its own class. Now, suppose once again that (D, v) is in the pair list. Then we have three cases:

> The *anchor* of a visited (but not necessarily marked) node v is the node on the current access path that is closest to v.

- v is unmarked, so we have no information to compute $NCA(D, v)$. However, when v is marked, we will be able to determine $NCA(v, D)$.

- v is marked but not in D's subtree, so $NCA(v, D)$ is v's anchor.

- v is in D's subtree, so $NCA(v, D) = D$; notice that this is not a special case because v's anchor is D.

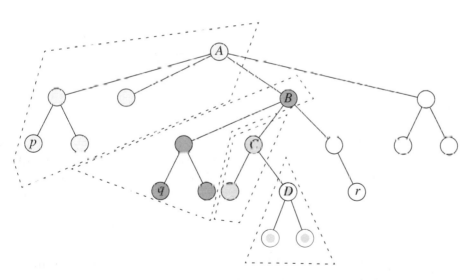

Figure 23.4   The sets immediately prior to the return from the recursive call to D; D is marked as visited and $NCA(D, v)$ is v's anchor to the current path

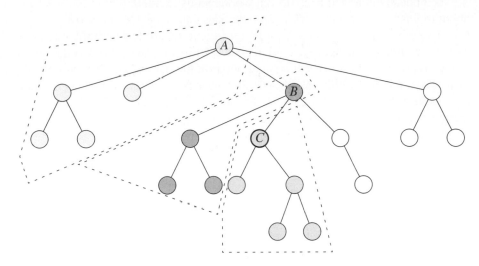

Figure 23.5   After the recursive call from *D* returns, we merge the set anchored by *D* into the set anchored by *C* and then compute all *NCA*(*C*, *v*) for nodes *v* that are marked prior to completing *C*'s recursive call

The Union/Find algorithm is used to maintain the sets of nodes with common anchors.

All that remains is to make sure that at any instant we can determine the anchor of any visited node. This is easily done using the Union/Find algorithm. After a recursive call returns, we call `Union`. For instance, after the recursive call to *D* in Figure 23.4 returns, all nodes in *D* have their anchor changed from *D* to *C*. The new situation is shown in Figure 23.5. Thus we need to merge the two equivalence classes into one. At any point we can obtain the anchor for a vertex *v* by a call to a disjoint set `Find`. Because `Find` returns a set number, we use an array `Anchor` to store the anchor node corresponding to a particular set.

The pseudocode is compact.

A pseudocode implementation of the nearest common ancestor algorithm is shown in Figure 23.6. As we mentioned earlier, the `Find` operation generally assumes that elements of the set are 0, 1, ... , $N - 1$, so we store a preorder number in each tree node in a preprocessing step that computes the size of the tree. Although an object-oriented approach might attempt to incorporate a mapping into the `Find`, perhaps by using a dictionary, in this case it would be computationally inefficient. We also assume that we have an array of lists to store the nearest common ancestor requests. List *i* stores the request for tree node *i*. With those details taken care of, the code is remarkably short.

```
1  // Nearest Common Ancestors algorithm
2  //
3  // Preconditions (and global objects):
4  //    1. Union/Find structure is initialized
5  //    2. All nodes are initially unmarked
6  //    3. Preorder numbers are already assigned in Num member
7  //    4. Each node can store its marked status
8  //    5. List of pairs is globally available
9
10 DisjSets S( TreeSize );            // Union/Find
11 Vector<Node *> Anchor( TreeSize ); // Anchor node for each set
12
13 // main makes the call NCA( Root )
14 // after required initializations
15
16 NCA( Node *u )
17 {
18     Anchor[ S.Find( u->Num ) ] = u;
19
20     // Do postorder calls
21     for( each child v of u )
22     {
23         NCA( v );
24         S.Union( S.Find( u->Num ), S.Find( v->Num ) );
25         Anchor[ S.Find( u->Num ) ] = u;
26     }
27
28     // Do NCA calculation for pairs involving u
29     u->Marked = True;
30     for( each v such that NCA( u, v ) is required )
31         if( v->Marked == True )
32             cout << "NCA(" << u << ", " << v << " is " <<
33                         Anchor[ S.Find( v->Num ) ];
34 }
```

Figure 23.6   Pseudocode for nearest common ancestors problem

When a node u is first visited, it becomes the anchor of itself as in line 18 of Figure 23.6. It then recursively processes its children v by making the call at line 23. After each recursive call returns, the subtree is combined into u's current equivalence class, and we make sure that the anchor is updated at lines 24 and 25. When all the children have been processed recursively, we can mark u as processed at line 29 and finish by checking all *NCA* requests involving u at lines 30 to 33.[3]

---

3. Strictly speaking u should be marked at the last statement, but marking it earlier handles the annoying request *NCA(u, u)*.

23.3   The Quick-Find Algorithm

Having seen the uses of the Union/Find data structure, we now lay the groundwork for its efficient implementation. There are two basic strategies to solve the Union/Find problem. One ensures that the Find instruction can be executed in constant worst-case time, and the other ensures that the Union can be executed in constant worst-case time. It has recently been shown that both cannot be done simultaneously in constant worst-case (or even amortized) time.

The first approach is called the *Quick-Find algorithm*. For the Find operation to be fast, we could maintain, in an array, the name of the equivalence class for each element. Then Find is a simple constant time lookup. Suppose we want to perform Union(a, b). Suppose that a is in equivalence class i and b is in equivalence class j. Then we can scan down the array, changing all i's to j's. Unfortunately, this scan takes linear time. Thus a sequence of $N-1$ Union operations (the maximum, since then everything is in one set) would take quadratic time. In the typical case in which the number of Finds is subquadratic, this is clearly unacceptable.

One idea is to keep all the elements that are in the same equivalence class in a linked list. This saves time when updating, because we do not have to search through the entire array. This by itself does not reduce the asymptotic running time, because it is still possible to perform $\Theta(N^2)$ equivalence class updates over the course of the algorithm.

If we also keep track of the size of the equivalence classes, and when performing a Union we change the name of the smaller class to the larger, then the total time spent for N Unions is $O(N \log N)$. The reason for this is that each element can have its equivalence class changed at most $\log N$ times, since every time its class is changed, its new equivalence class is at least twice as large as its old (so the doubling principle applies).

Using this strategy, any sequence of at most M Find and $N-1$ Union operations takes at most $O(M + N \log N)$ time. If M is linear (or slightly nonlinear), this is still an expensive solution, and furthermore, it is a bit messy since we must maintain linked lists. In the next section, we will examine a solution to the Union/Find problem that makes Union easy but Find hard. This alternative approach is the *Quick-Union algorithm*. Even so, the running time for any sequence of at most M Find and $N-1$ Union operations is only negligibly more than $O(M + N)$ time, and furthermore, only a single array of integers is used.

23.4   The Quick-Union Algorithm

Recall that the Union/Find problem does not require that a Find operation return any specific name, just that Finds on two elements return the same answer if and only if they are in the same set. One idea might be to use a tree to

represent a set, since each element in a tree has the same root. Thus the root can
be used to name the set.

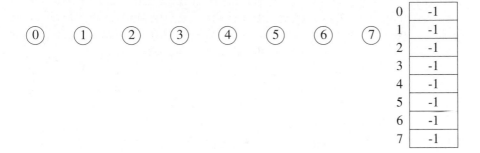

Figure 23.7   Forest and its eight elements, initially in different sets

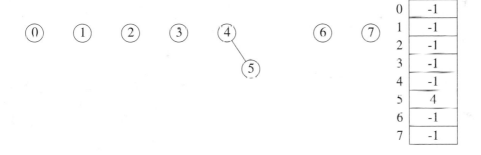

Figure 23.8   Forest after Union of trees with roots 4 and 5

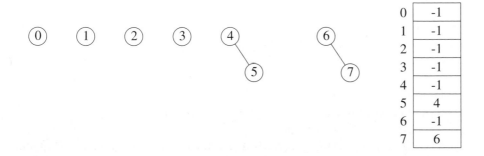

Figure 23.9   Forest after Union of trees with roots 6 and 7

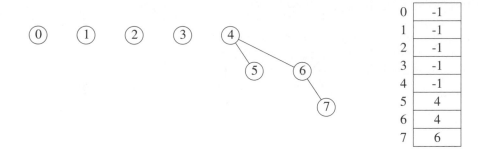

Figure 23.10   Forest after Union of trees with roots 4 and 6

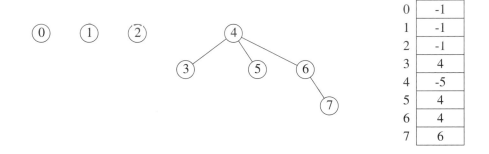

Figure 23.11   Forest formed by union-by-size, with size encoded as a negative number

A tree is represented by an array of integers representing parent nodes. The set name of any node in a tree is the root of a tree.

We will represent each set by a tree (a collection of trees is known as a *forest*). The name of a set is given by the node at the root. Our trees are not necessarily binary trees, but their representation is easy because the only information we need is a parent pointer. Thus we only need an array of integers: Each entry P[i] in the array represents the parent of element i, and we can use −1 as a parent to indicate a root. Figure 23.7 shows the forest and the array that represents it.

Union is constant time.

To perform a Union of two sets, we merge the two trees by making the root of one tree point to the root of the other. It should be clear that this operation takes constant time. Figures 23.8, 23.9, and 23.10 represent the forest after each of Union(4, 5), Union(6, 7), and Union(4, 6), where we have adopted the convention that the new root after Union(x, y) is x.

A `Find` on element *x* is performed by returning the root of the tree containing *x*. The time to perform this operation is proportional to the number of nodes on the path from *x* to the root. The `Union` strategy outlined above makes it possible to create a tree such that every node in the tree is on the path to *x*, resulting in a worst-case running time of $\Theta(N)$ per `Find`. Typically (as we saw in the two applications), the running time is computed for a sequence of *M* intermixed instructions. In the worst case, *M* consecutive operations could take $\Theta(MN)$ time.

The cost of a `Find` depends on the depth of the accessed node and could be linear.

Quadratic running time for a sequence of operations is generally unacceptable. Fortunately, there are several ways of easily ensuring that this running time does not occur.

23.4.1 Smart Union Algorithms

The `Union`s above were performed rather arbitrarily, by making the second tree a subtree of the first. A simple improvement is always to make the smaller tree a subtree of the larger, breaking ties by any method; we call this approach *union-by-size*. The three `Union`s in the preceding section were all ties, so we can consider that they were performed by size. If the next operation is `Union(3, 4)`, then the forest in Figure 23.11 will form. Had the size heuristic not been used, a deeper forest would have been formed (three nodes rather than one would have been one level deeper).

We can prove that if the `Union` operation is done by size, the depth of any node is never more than log *N*. To see this, note that a node is initially at depth 0. When its depth increases as a result of a `Union`, it is placed in a tree that is at least twice as large as before. Thus its depth can be increased at most log *N* times. (We used this argument in the quick-find algorithm in Section 23.3.) This implies that the running time for a `Find` operation is $O(\log N)$, and a sequence of *M* operations takes at most $O(M\log N)$. The tree in Figure 23.12 shows the worst tree possible after 16 `Union`s and is obtained if all `Union`s are between equal-sized trees. (The worst-case trees are known as binomial trees, and have other applications in advanced data structures.)

Union-by-size guarantees logarithmic finds.

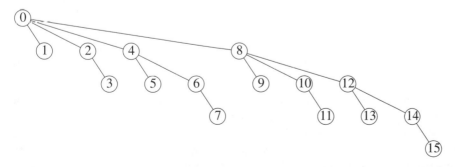

Figure 23.12   Worst-case tree for *N*=16

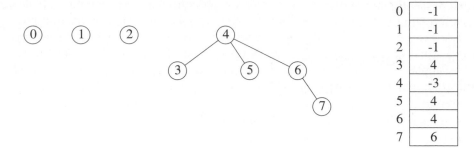

0	-1
1	-1
2	-1
3	4
4	-3
5	4
6	4
7	6

Figure 23.13   Forest formed by union-by-height, with height encoded as a negative number

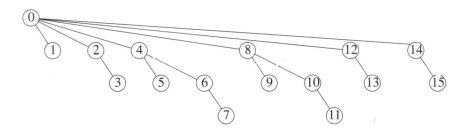

Figure 23.14   Path compression resulting from a `Find(14)` on the tree in Figure 23.12

Instead of storing –1 for roots, the negative of the size is stored.

To implement this strategy, we need to keep track of the size of each tree. Since we are really just using an array, we can have the array entry of the root contain the *negative* of the size of the tree, as shown in Figure 23.11. Thus the initial representation of the tree using all –1s is reasonable. When a Union is performed, we check the sizes; the new size is the sum of the old. Thus union-by-size is not at all difficult to implement and requires no extra space. It is also fast on average because when random Unions are performed, generally very small (usually one-element) sets are merged with large sets throughout the algorithm. Mathematical analysis of this is quite complex, and the references provide some pointers to the literature.

Union-by-height also guarantees logarithm finds.

An alternative implementation that also guarantees logarithmic depth is *union-by-height*. We keep track of the height of the trees instead of the size and perform Unions by making the shallow tree a subtree of the deeper tree. This is an easy algorithm, since the height of a tree increases only when two equally deep trees are joined (and then the height goes up by 1). Thus union-by-height is a trivial modification of union-by-size. Since heights start at 0, we store the negative of the number of nodes on the deepest path, rather than the height. This is shown in Figure 23.13.

23.4.2   Path Compression

The Union/Find algorithm, as described so far, is quite acceptable for most cases. It is very simple and linear on average for a sequence of M instructions. However, the worst case is still unappealing, particularly because it is not obvious that a sequence of Union operations that occurs in some particular application (such as the nearest common ancestors problem) is random (in fact for certain trees, it is far from random). Consequently, we seek a better bound for the worst case of a sequence of M operations. It seems that there are probably no more improvements possible to the Union algorithm, since the worst case is achievable when identical trees are merged. The only way to speed the algorithm up, without reworking the data structure entirely, is to do something clever on the Find operation.

The clever operation is known as *path compression*. Clearly, after we perform a Find on x, it would make sense to change x's parent pointer to point at the root. That way, a second Find on x or any item in x's subtree will be easier. There is no need to stop there, however. We might as well change the parent pointers for all nodes on the access path. The effect of path compression is that *every* node on the path from x to the root has its parent changed to the root. Figure 23.14 shows the effect of path compression after Find(14) on the generic worst tree in Figure 23.12. With an extra two pointer moves, nodes 12 and 13 are now one position closer to the root, and nodes 14 and 15 are now two positions closer. Thus the fast future accesses on the nodes will pay (we hope) for the extra work to do the path compression. Note that subsequent Unions push the node deeper.

> **Path compression makes every accessed node a child of the root until another Union occurs.**

When Unions are done arbitrarily, path compression is a good idea because there is an abundance of deep nodes, and these are brought near the root by path compression. It has been proven that when path compression is done in this case, a sequence of M operations requires at most $O(M \log N)$ time, so path compression by itself guarantees logarithmic amortized cost for the Find operation.

> **Path compression guarantees logarithmic amortized cost per operation.**

Path compression is perfectly compatible with union-by-size, and thus both routines can be implemented at the same time. Path compression is not entirely compatible with union-by-height, because path compression can change the heights of the trees. It is not at all clear how to recompute them efficiently. The answer is do not. Then the heights stored for each tree become estimated heights (sometimes known as *ranks*), but this is not a problem. The resulting algorithm is *union-by-rank*. As we will see in Section 23.6, the combination of a smart union rule and path compression gives an almost linear guarantee on the running time for a sequence of M operations.

> **Path compression and a smart union root guarantee essentially constant amortized cost per operation (that is, a long sequence can be executed in almost linear time).**

```
1  // DisjSets class interface: maintain disjoint sets
2  //
3  // CONSTRUCTION: with (a) int representing number of initial
4  //      sets, or (b) no parameters (DefaultSize is used).
5  // All copying of DisjSets objects is DISALLOWED
6  //
7  // ****************_***PUBLIC OPERATIONS*********************
8  // void Union( int Root1, int Root 2 )
9  //                      --> Merge two sets
10 // int Find( int X )    --> Return set containing X
11 // *****************ERRORS*********************************
12 // Predefined exception is propagated if new fails
13 // Very little error checking is performed otherwise
14
15 class DisjSets
16 {
17  public:
18     // Constructor and destructor
19     DisjSets( int NumElements = DefaultSize );
20     ~DisjSets( ) { delete [ ] Array; }
21
22     // Member functions
23     void Union( int Root1, int Root2 );
24     int Find( int X );
25  private:
26     enum { DefaultSize = 10 };
27
28     int *Array;
29     int Size;
30
31     DisjSets( DisjSets const & Value );   // Disabled
32     const DisjSets & operator = ( DisjSets const & Value );
33 };
```

Figure 23.15   Disjoint sets class interface

23.5   C++ Implementation

Disjoint sets are relatively simple to implement.

The class interface for a disjoint sets class is given in Figure 23.15; the implementation is shown in Figure 23.16. We have omitted error checks to avoid obscuring the algorithmic details. A robust program would, of course, have to check for errors. Without error checks, the entire algorithm is amazingly short.

In our routine Union is performed on the roots of the trees. Sometimes the operation is implemented by passing any two elements and having the Union perform the Find to determine the roots.

The interesting procedure is Find. After the Find is performed recursively, Array[X] is set to the root and is then returned. Since this happens recursively, all nodes on the path will have their entries set to the root.

```
1   // Constructor for DisjSets
2
3   DisjSets::DisjSets( int NumElements )
4   {
5       Size = NumElements;
6       Array = new int [ Size ];
7       for( int i = 0; i < Size; i++ )
8           Array[ i ] = -1;
9   }
10
11
12  // Union two disjoint sets using the height heuristic
13  // For simplicity, we assume Root1 and Root2 are distinct
14  // And represent set names
15
16  void
17  DisjSets::Union( int Root1, int Root2 )
18  {
19      if( Array[ Root2 ] < Array[ Root1 ] ) // Root2 is deeper
20          Array[ Root1 ] = Root2;         // Make Root2 new root
21      else
22      {
23          if( Array[ Root1 ] == Array[ Root2 ] )
24              Array[ Root1 ]--;           // Update height if same
25          Array[ Root2 ] = Root1;         // Make Root1 new root
26      }
27  }
28
29
30  // Perform a Find with path compression
31  // Error checks omitted again for simplicity
32
33  int
34  Disj_Sets::Find( int X )
35  {
36      if( Array[ X ] < 0 )
37          return X;
38      else
39          return Array[ X ] = Find( Array[ X ] );
40  }
```

Figure 23.16   Complete implementation of a disjoint sets class with shabby error checking

23.6   Worst Case for Union-by-Rank and Path Compression

When both heuristics are used, the algorithm is almost linear in the worst case. Specifically, the time required to process a sequence of at most $N - 1$ Union operations and M Find operations in the worst case is $\Theta(M\alpha(M, N))$ (provided $M \geq N$), where $\alpha(M, N)$ is a functional inverse of Ackerman's function which is defined below:[4]

$$A(1, j) = 2^j \qquad\qquad j \geq 1$$

$$A(i, 1) = A(i - 1, 2) \qquad\qquad i \geq 2$$

$$A(i, j) = A(i - 1, A(i, j - 1)) \qquad i, j \geq 2$$

From this, we define

$$\alpha(M, N) = \min \{ i \geq 1 \mid (A(i, \lfloor M / N \rfloor) > \log N) \}$$

Ackerman's function grows very quickly, and its inverse is essentially at most 4.

You might want to compute some values, but for all practical purposes, $\alpha(M, N) \leq 4$, which is all that is really important here. For instance, for any $j > 1$, we have

$$A(2, j) = A(1, A(2, j - 1))$$

$$= 2^{A(2, j - 1)}$$

$$= 2^{2^{2^{2^{\cdots}}}}$$

where the number of twos in the exponent is j. $F(N) = A(2, N)$ is commonly known as a single-variable *Ackerman's function*. The single-variable inverse of Ackerman's function, sometimes written as $\log^* N$, is the number of times the logarithm of N needs to be applied until $N \leq 1$. Thus, $\log^* 65536 = 4$, because $\log \log \log \log 65536 = 1$. $\log^* 2^{65536} = 5$, but keep in mind that 2^{65536} has more than 20000 digits. $\alpha(M, N)$ grows even slower than $\log^* N$. For instance, we see that $A(3, 1) = A(2, 2) = 2^{2^2} = 16$. Thus for $N < 2^{16} = 65536$, $\alpha(M, N) \leq 3$. Further, since $A(4, 1) = A(3, 2) = A(2, A(3, 1)) = A(2, 16)$, which is two raised to a power of 16 stacked twos, we know that in practice, $\alpha(M, N) \leq 4$. However, $\alpha(M, N)$ is not a constant when M is slightly more than N, so the running time is not linear.[5]

In the remainder of this section, we will prove a slightly weaker result. We will show that any sequence of $M = \Omega(N)$ Union/Find operations takes a total of $O(M \log^* N)$ time. The same bound holds if union-by-rank is replaced with union-by-size. This analysis is probably the most complex in the book and one of the first truly complex analyses ever performed for an algorithm that is essentially trivial to implement. By extending this technique, we can show the stronger bound claimed above.

23.6.1   Analysis of the Union/Find Algorithm

In this section, we establish a fairly tight bound on the running time of a sequence of $M = \Omega(N)$ Union/Find operations. The Union and Find operations may occur in any order, but Union is done by rank and Finds are done with path compression.

---

4. Ackerman's function is frequently defined with $A(1, j) = j + 1$ for $j \geq 1$. The form in this text grows faster; thus the inverse grows more slowly.
5. Notice, however, that if $M = N \log^* N$, then $\alpha(M, N)$ is at most 2. Thus, as long as M is slightly more than linear, the running time will be linear in M.

We begin by establishing some theorems concerning the number of nodes of rank r. Intuitively, because of the union-by-rank rule, there are many more nodes of small rank than of large rank. In particular, there can be at most one node of rank $\log N$. What we would like to do is to produce as precise a bound as possible on the number of nodes of any particular rank r. Since ranks only change when Union operations are performed (and then only when the two trees have same rank), we can prove this bound by ignoring path compression.

In the absence of path compression, when executing a sequence of Union *instructions, a node of rank r must have 2^r descendants (including itself).*

Theorem 23.1

The proof is by induction. The basis $r = 0$ is clearly true. Let T be the tree of rank r with the fewest number of descendants and let x be T's root. Suppose the last Union *x was involved with was between T_1 and T_2. Suppose T_1's root was X. If T_1 had rank r, then T_1 would be a tree of rank r with fewer descendants than T, which contradicts the assumption that T is the tree with the smallest number of descendants. Hence the rank of T_1 is at most $r - 1$. The rank of T_2 is at most the rank of T_1, because of union-by-rank. Since T has rank r and the rank could only increase because of T_2, it follows that the rank of T_2 is $r - 1$. Then the rank of T_1 is also $r - 1$. By the induction hypothesis, each tree has at least 2^{r-1} descendants, giving a total of 2^r and establishing the theorem*

Proof

Theorem 23.1 tells us that if no path compression is performed, then any node of rank r must have at least 2^r descendants. Path compression can change this, of course, since it can remove descendants from a node. However when Unions are performed, even with path compression, we are using the ranks, which are estimated heights. These ranks behave as if there is no path compression. Thus when bounding the number of nodes of rank r, path compression can be ignored.

The number of nodes of rank r is at most $N/2^r$.

Theorem 23.2

Proof   *Without path compression, each node of rank r is the root of a subtree of at least 2^r nodes. No other node in the subtree can have rank r. Thus all subtrees of nodes of rank r are disjoint. Therefore, there are at most $N/2^r$ disjoint subtrees and hence $N/2^r$ nodes of rank r.*

The next theorem seems somewhat obvious, but is crucial in the analysis.

Theorem 23.3   *At any point in the Union/Find algorithm, the ranks of the nodes on a path from a leaf to a root increase monotonically.*

Proof   *The theorem is obvious if there is no path compression. If after path compression, some node v is a descendant of w, then clearly v must have been a descendant of w when only* Union *operations were considered. Hence the rank of v is strictly less than the rank of w.*

There are not too many nodes of large rank, and the ranks increase on any path up toward a root.

Let us summarize the preliminary results. Theorem 23.2 tells us how many nodes can be assigned rank r. Because ranks are assigned only by Unions, which have no idea of path compression, Theorem 23.2 is valid at any stage of the Union/Find algorithm – even in the midst of path compression. Theorem 23.2 is tight, in the sense that it is possible for there to be $N/2^r$ nodes for any rank r. It is slightly loose because it is not possible for the bound to hold for all ranks r simultaneously. While Theorem 23.2 describes the number of nodes in a rank r, Theorem 23.3 tells us their distribution. As one would expect, the rank of nodes is strictly increasing along the path from a leaf to the root.

Pennies are used like a potential function. The total pennies is the total time.

We are now ready to prove the main theorem. Our basic plan is as follows: A Find on any node v costs time proportional to the number of nodes on the path from v to the root. We will charge one unit of cost for every node on the path from v to the root during each Find. To help us count the charges, we will deposit an imaginary penny into each node on the path. This is strictly an accounting gimmick that is not part of the program; it is somewhat equivalent to the use of a potential function in the amortized analysis for splay trees and skew heaps. When the algorithm is over, we will collect all the coins that have been deposited to determine the total cost.

As a further accounting gimmick, we will deposit both American and Canadian pennies. We will show that during the execution of the algorithm, we can deposit only a certain number of American pennies during each `Find` (regardless of how many nodes there are). We will also show that we can deposit only a certain number of Canadian pennies to each node (regardless of how many `Find`s there are). Adding these two totals gives us a bound on the total number of pennies that can be deposited.

> We have both American and Canadian pennies. Canadian pennies account for the first few times a node is compressed; American pennies account for later compressions or noncompressions.

We now sketch our accounting scheme in more detail. We will divide the nodes by their ranks. We will then divide the ranks into rank groups. On each `Find`, we will deposit some American coins into a general kitty and some Canadian coins into specific nodes. To compute the total number of Canadian coins deposited, we will compute the deposits per node. By adding up all the deposits for each node in rank r, we will get the total deposits per rank r. Then we will add up all the deposits for each rank r in group g and thereby obtain the total deposits for each rank group g. Finally, we will add up all the deposits for each rank group g to obtain the total number of Canadian pennies deposited in the forest. Adding this to the number of American coins in the kitty gives us the answer.

As mentioned above, we will partition the ranks into groups. Rank r goes into group $G(r)$, and G will be determined later (to balance the American and Canadian charges). The largest rank in any rank group g is $F(g)$, where $F = G^{-1}$ is the *inverse* of G. The number of ranks in any rank group, $g > 0$, is thus $F(g) - F(g-1)$. Clearly, $G(N)$ is a very loose upper bound on the largest rank group. As an example, suppose that we partitioned the ranks as in Figure 23.17. In this case, $G(r) = \lceil \sqrt{r} \rceil$. The largest rank in group g is $F(g) = g^2$, and observe that group $g > 0$ contains ranks $F(g-1)+1$ through $F(g)$ inclusive. This formula does not apply for rank group 0, so for convenience we will ensure that rank group 0 contains only elements of rank 0. Notice that the groups are made of consecutive ranks.

> Ranks are partitioned into groups; the actual groups are determined at the end of the proof. Group 0 has only rank 0.

As mentioned before, each `Union` instruction takes constant time, as long as each root keeps track of its rank. Thus `Union`s are essentially free, as far as this proof goes.

Group	Rank
0	0
1	1
2	2,3,4
3	5 through 9
4	10 through 16
i	$(i-1)^2$ through i^2

Figure 23.17   Possible partitioning of ranks into groups

When a node is compressed, its new parent will have a higher rank than its old parent.

Each Find takes time proportional to the number of nodes on the path from the node representing the accessed item i to the root. We will thus deposit one penny for each vertex on the path. If this is all we do, however, we cannot expect much of a bound, because we are not taking advantage of path compression. Thus we must use some fact about path compression in our analysis. The key observation is that as a result of path compression, a node obtains a new parent, and the new parent is guaranteed to have higher rank than the old parent.

Rules for American and Canadian deposits.

To incorporate this fact into the proof, we will use the following fancy accounting: For each node v on the path from the accessed node i to the root, we deposit one penny under one of two accounts:

1. If v is the root, or if the parent of v is the root, or if the parent of v is in a different rank group from v, then charge one unit under this rule. This deposits an American penny into the kitty

2. Otherwise, deposit a Canadian penny into the node.

Theorem 23.4

For any Find operation, the total number of pennies deposited, either in the kitty or to a node, is exactly equal to the number of nodes accessed during the Find.

Proof

Obvious.

American charges are limited by the number of different groups. Canadian charges are limited by the size of the groups. We eventually need to balance these costs.

Thus all we need to do is to sum all the American pennies deposited under rule 1 with all the Canadian pennies deposited under rule 2. Before we go on with the proof, let us sketch the ideas. Canadian pennies are deposited into a node when it is compressed and its parent is in the same rank group as the node. Because the node gets a parent of higher rank after each path compression, and because the size of a rank group is finite, eventually the node will obtain a parent that is not in its rank group. Consequently, there are only a limited number of Canadian pennies that can be placed into any node, and this number is roughly the size of the node's rank group. On the other hand, the American charges are also limited, essentially by the number of rank groups. Thus we want to choose the rank groups so they are small (to limit the Canadian charges), but there are not too many (to limit the American charges). We are now ready to fill in the details with a rapid-fire series of theorems.

Over the entire algorithm, the total deposits of American pennies under **Theorem 23.5**
rule 1 amount to $M(G(N)+2)$.

For any Find, *at most two American pennies are deposited because of* **Proof**
the root and its child. By Theorem 23.3, the vertices going up the path are
monotonically increasing in rank, and thus the rank group never
decreases as we go up the path. Since there are at most $G(N)$ *rank*
groups (besides group 0) only $G(N)$ *other vertices can qualify as a rule*
1 deposit for any particular Find. *Thus, during any* Find, *at most*
$G(N)+2$ *American pennies can be placed in the kitty. Thus at most*
$M(G(N)+2)$ *American pennies can be deposited under rule 1 for a*
sequence of M Finds.

For any single node in rank group g, the total number of Canadian pen- **Theorem 23.6**
nies deposited is at most $F(g)$.

If a Canadian coin is deposited into a vertex v under rule 2, v will be **Proof**
moved by path compression and get a new parent of rank higher than its
old parent. Since the largest rank in its group is $F(g)$, *we are guaranteed*
that after $F(g)$ *coins are deposited, v's parent will no longer be in v's*
rank group.

The bound in Theorem 23.6 can be improved by using only the size of the
rank group rather than its largest member. However this does not improve the
bound that is obtained for the Union/Find algorithm. Continuing with our theorems, we have:

The number of nodes, $N(g)$ *in rank group* $g > 0$ *is at most* $N/2^{F(g-1)}$. **Theorem 23.7**

Proof   By Theorem 23.2, there are at most $N/2^r$ nodes of rank r. Summing over the ranks in group g, we obtain

$$N(g) \leq \sum_{r=F(g-1)+1}^{F(g)} \frac{N}{2^r}$$

$$\leq \sum_{r=F(g-1)+1}^{\infty} \frac{N}{2^r}$$

$$\leq N \sum_{r=F(g-1)+1}^{\infty} \frac{1}{2^r}$$

$$\leq \frac{N}{2^{F(g-1)+1}} \sum_{s=0}^{\infty} \frac{1}{2^s}$$

$$\leq \frac{2N}{2^{F(g-1)+1}}$$

$$\leq \frac{N}{2^{F(g-1)}}$$

Theorem 23.8   *The maximum number of Canadian pennies deposited to all vertices in rank group g is at most $NF(g)/2^{F(g-1)}$.*

Proof   *The result follows from a simple multiplication of the quantities obtained in Theorem 23.6 and Theorem 23.7.*

Theorem 23.9   *The total deposit under rule 2 is at most $N\sum_{i=1}^{G(N)} F(g)/2^{F(g-1)}$ Canadian pennies.*

Proof   *Because rank group 0 contains only elements of rank 0, it cannot contribute to rule 2 charges (it cannot have a parent in the same rank group). The bound is obtained by summing the other rank groups.*

Group	Rank
0	0
1	1
2	2
3	3,4
4	5 through 16
5	17 through 65536
6	65537 through 2^{65536}
7	Truly huge ranks

Figure 23.18　Actual partitioning of ranks into groups used in the proof

Thus we have the deposits under rules 1 and 2. The total is

$$M(G(N)+2)+N\sum_{i=1}^{G(N)}F(g)/2^{F(g-1)} \tag{23.1}$$

Now we can specify the rank groups to minimize the bound. Our choice is not quite minimal but is close.

We still have not specified $G(N)$ or its inverse $F(N)$. Obviously, we are free to choose virtually anything we want, but it makes sense to choose $G(N)$ to minimize the bound in the equation above. However, if $G(N)$ is too small, $F(N)$ will be large, hurting the bound. An apparently good choice is to choose $F(i)$ to be the function recursively defined by $F(0) = 0$ and $F(i) = 2^{F(i-1)}$. This gives $G(N) = 1 + \lfloor \log^* N \rfloor$. Figure 23.18 shows how this partitions the ranks. Notice that group 0 contains only rank 0, which we required in the proof of Theorem 23.9. F is very similar to the single-variable Ackerman function, differing only in the definition of the base case. With this choice of F and G, we can complete the analysis:

The running time of the Union/Find algorithm with $M = \Omega(N)$ Finds is $O(M \log^* N)$.　　　***Theorem 23.10***

Plug in the definitions of F and G into Equation 23.1. The total number of American pennies is $O(MG(N)) = O(M\log^* N)$. Since $F(g) = 2^{F(g-1)}$, the total number of Canadian pennies is $NG(N) = O(N \log^* N)$. Since $M = \Omega(N)$, the bound follows.　　　***Proof***

Notice that we have more American pennies than Canadian pennies. The function $\alpha(M, N)$ balances things out, which is why it gives a better bound.

Summary

We have seen a very simple data structure to maintain disjoint sets. When the Union operation is performed, it does not matter, as far as correctness is concerned, which set retains its name. A valuable lesson that should be learned here is that it can be very important to consider the alternatives when a particular step is not totally specified. The Union step is flexible; by taking advantage of this, we are able to get a much more efficient algorithm.

Path compression is one of the earliest forms of self-adjustment, which we have seen elsewhere (splay trees, skew heaps). Its use here is extremely interesting from a theoretical point of view, because it was one of the first examples of a simple algorithm with a not-so-simple worst-case analysis.

Objects of the Game

Ackerman's function Grows very quickly, and its inverse is essentially at most 4. (742)

disjoint set class operations The basic operations needed for disjoint set manipulation are Union and Find. (726)

equivalence classes The equivalence class of an element x in set S is the subset of S that contains all the elements that are related to x. (726)

equivalence relation A relation that is reflexive, symmetric, and transitive. (725)

forest A collection of trees. (736)

Kruskal's algorithm Used to select edges in increasing cost, adding an edge to the tree if it does not create a cycle. (729)

minimum spanning tree A connected subgraph of G that spans all vertices at minimum total cost. It is a fundamental graph theory problem. (727)

nearest common ancestor problem (NCA) Given a tree and a list of pairs of nodes in the tree, find the nearest common ancestor for each pair of nodes. NCA is important in graph algorithms an computational biology. (730)

offline algorithm An algorithm in which the entire sequence of queries are made visible. (727)

online algorithm An algorithm in which an answer must be provided for each query before viewing the next query. (727)

path compression Makes every accessed node a child of the root until another Union occurs. (739)

Quick-Find algorithm Union/Find implementation in which Find is a constant time operation. (734)

Quick-Union algorithm Union/Find implementation in which Union is a constant time operation. (734)

rank In the disjoint set algorithm, the estimated height of a node. (739)

relation Defined on a set if every pair of elements is either related or not. (725)

spanning tree A tree formed by graph edges that connects all the vertices of an undirected graph. (727)

union-by-height Makes tree of smaller height a child of tree of larger height during a Union. (738)

union-by-rank Union-by-height when path compression is performed. (739)

union-by-size Makes smaller tree a child of larger tree during a Union. (737)

Union/Find algorithm Executed by procesing Union/Find operations using Union/Find data structure. (727)

Union/Find data structure Used to manipulate disjoint sets. (726)

Common Errors

1. Union assumes that its parameters are tree roots. Havoc results if they are not. A more careful implementation would perform this test.

2. union is a keyword in C++.

On the Internet

Nothing is available for this chapter. You are on your own.

Exercises

In Short

23.1. Show the result of the following sequence of instructions: *Union*(1,2), *Union*(3,4), *Union*(3,5), *Union*(1,7), *Union*(3,6), *Union*(8,9), *Union*(1,8), *Union*(3,10), *Union*(3,11), *Union*(3,12), *Union*(3,13), *Union*(14,15), *Union*(16,17), *Union*(14,16), *Union*(1,3), *Union*(1,14) when the union operations are performed

    a. arbitrarily

    b. by height

    c. by size

23.2. For each of the trees in the previous exercise, perform a Find with path compression on the deepest node.

23.3. Find the minimum spanning tree for the graph in Figure 23.19.

23.4. Show the operation of the *NCA* algorithm for the data in Figure 23.3.

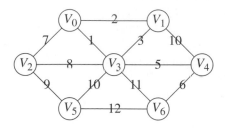

Figure 23.19   A graph *G* for Exercise 23.3.

In Theory

23.5.   Prove that Kruskal's algorithm is correct. Does your proof assume that the edge costs are nonnegative?

23.6.   Show that if Union is performed by height, then the depth of any tree is logarithmic.

23.7.   Show that if all the Unions precede the Finds, then the disjoint set algorithm with path compression is linear, even if the Unions are done arbitrarily. Note that the algorithm does not change, just the performance.

23.8.   Suppose we want to add an extra operation, Remove(X), which removes X from its current set and places it in its own. Show how to modify the Union/Find algorithm so that the running time of a sequence of *M* Union, Find, and Remove operations is still $O(M\alpha(M, N))$.

23.9.   Prove that if Unions are done by size and path compression is performed, the worst-case running time is still $O(M\log^* N)$.

23.10.   Suppose we implement partial path compression on Find(i) by making every other node on the path from i to the root point to its grandparent (where this makes sense). This is known as path halving. Prove that if path halving is performed on the Finds, and either Union heuristic is used, then the worst-case running time is still $O(M\log^* N)$.

In Practice

23.11.   Implement the Find operation nonrecursively. Is there a noticeable difference in running time?

23.12.   Suppose we want to add an extra operation, DeUnion, which undoes the last Union operation not already undone. One way to do this is to use union-by-rank but a compressionless `Find`, and use a stack to store the old state prior to a `Union`. A `DeUnion` can be implemented by popping the stack to retrieve an old state.

a. Why can't we use path compression?

b. Implement the Union/Find/DeUnion algorithm.

Programming Problems

23.13.   Add error checks to the disjoint sets implementation in Figure 23.16.

23.14.   Write a program to determine the effects of path compression and the various union strategies. Your program should process a long sequence of equivalence operations using all of the strategies discussed (including path halving in Exercise 23.10).

23.15.   Implement Kruskal's algorithm.

23.16.   An alternative minimum spanning tree algorithm is due to Prim [12]. It works by growing a single tree in successive stages. We start by picking any node as the root. At the start of a stage, some nodes are part of the tree and the rest are not. In each stage, we add the minimum-cost edge that connects a tree node with a nontree node. An implementation of Prim's algorithm is essentially identical to Dijkstra's shortest path algorithm given in Section 14.3, with an update rule: $d_w = min(d_w, c_{v, w})$ (instead of $d_w = min(d_w, d_v + c_{v, w})$). Also, since the graph is undirected, each edge appears in two adjacency lists. Implement Prim's algorithm, and compare its performance with Kruskal's algorithm.

23.17.   Write a program to solve the offline nearest common ancestor problem for binary trees. Test its efficiency by constructing a random binary search tree of 10,000 elements and performing 10,000 ancestor queries.

References

Representation of each set by a tree was proposed in [8]. [1] attributes path compression to McIlroy and Morris and contains several applications of the Union/Find data structure. Kruskal's algorithm appears in [11], while the alternative discussed in Exercise 23.16 is from [12]. The nearest common ancestor algorithm is described in [2]. Other applications can be found in [15].

The $O(M\log^*N)$ bound is from [9]. Tarjan [13] obtained the $O(M\alpha(M, N))$ bound and showed that the bound is tight. Furthermore, the bound is intrinsic to the general problem and cannot be improved by an alternate algorithm [14]. A more precise bound for $M < N$ appears in [3] and [16]. Various other strategies for path compression and `Union` achieve the same bounds; see

[16] for details. If the sequence of Unions is known in advance, then it is possible to solve the Union/Find problem in $O(M)$ time [7]. This result can be used to show that the offline nearest common ancestor problem is solvable in linear time.

Average-case results for the Union/Find problem appear in [6], [10], [17], and [4]. Results bounding the running time of any single operation (as opposed to the entire sequence) appear in [5].

1. A. V. Aho, J. E. Hopcroft, and J. D. Ullman, *The Design and Analysis of Computer Algorithms*, Addison-Wesley, Reading, MA., (1974).

2. A. V. Aho, J. E. Hopcroft, and J. D. Ullman, "On Finding Lowest Common Ancestors in Trees," *SIAM Journal on Computing* **5** (1976), 115-132.

3. L. Banachowski, "A Complement to Tarjan's Result about the Lower Bound on the Set Union Problem," *Information Processing Letters* **11** (1980), 59-65.

4. B. Bollobas and I. Simon, "Probabilistic Analysis of Disjoint Set Union Algorithms," *SIAM Journal on Computing* **22** (1993), 1053-1086.

5. N. Blum, "On the Single-operation Worst-case Time Complexity of the Disjoint Set Union Problem," *SIAM Journal on Computing* **15** (1986), 1021-1024.

6. J. Doyle and R. L. Rivest, "Linear Expected Time of a Simple Union Find Algorithm," *Information Processing Letters* **5** (1976), 146-148.

7. H. N. Gabow and R. E. Tarjan, "A Linear-time Algorithm for a Special Case of Disjoint Set Union," *Journal of Computer and System Sciences* **30** (1985), 209-221.

8. B. A. Galler and M. J. Fischer, "An Improved Equivalence Algorithm," *Communications of the ACM* **7** (1964), 301-303.

9. J. E. Hopcroft and J. D. Ullman, "Set Merging Algorithms," *SIAM Journal on Computing* **2** (1973), 294-303.

10. D. E. Knuth and A. Schonage, "The Expected Linearity of a Simple Equivalence Algorithm," *Theoretical Computer Science* **6** (1978), 281-315.

11. J. B. Kruskal, Jr., "On the Shortest Spanning Subtree of a Graph and the Traveling Salesman Problem," *Proceedings of the American Mathematical Society* **7** (1956), 48-50.

12. R. C. Prim, "Shortest Connection Networks and Some Generalizations," *Bell System Technical Journal* **36** (1957), 1389-1401.

13. R. E. Tarjan, "Efficiency of a Good but Not Linear Set Union Algorithm," *Journal of the ACM* **22** (1975), 215-225.

14. R. E. Tarjan, "A Class of Algorithms Which Require Nonlinear Time to Maintain Disjoint Sets," *Journal of Computer and System Sciences* **18** (1979), 110-127.

15. R. E. Tarjan, "Applications of Path Compression on Balanced Trees," *Journal of the ACM* **26** (1979), 690-715.

16. R. E. Tarjan and J. van Leeuwen, "Worst Case Analysis of Set Union Algorithms," *Journal of the ACM* **31** (1984), 245-281.

17. A. C. Yao, "On the Average Behavior of Set Merging Algorithms," *Proceedings of the Eighth Annual ACM Symposium on the Theory of Computation* (1976), 192-195.

Appendices

Appendix A

Basic C++

This appendix is the rough equivalent of Chapter 0: a brief summary of the elementary C++ language features that are used throughout the text. Readers who are unfamiliar with C++ should start here. Aggregates (arrays and classes) and pointers are discussed in Chapter 1. C++ details can be found in any C++ language textbook.

A.1   The Environment

How are C++ programs entered, compiled, and run? The answer, of course, depends on the particular platform that hosts the C++ compiler.

On personal computers that run windowing systems, *integrated environments* are available. These user-friendly systems provide editors that allow automatic compilation, linking, and running of programs. When compiler errors are detected, the editor is restarted at the offending line in the source code. Consequently, on these systems each step is as simple as a click of a button.

The other common platform is UNIX. In the simplest scenario a program is entered into a source file whose name ends in an acceptable suffix, using an editor such as *vi*, *emacs*, or *pico*. Acceptable suffixes include .C, .cxx (the x's represent + rotated 45 degrees), and .cpp. The local compiler, typically *g++* or *CC*, compiles the program and generates an executable file named a.out. Options are available to place the executable elsewhere.

For C++ programs, input can come from one of three general places:

- The terminal, which we denote as *standard input*.
- Additional parameters in the invocation of the executable program. These are known as *command-line arguments*.
- A file.

```
 1  // First program
 2  // MW, 4/1/96
 3
 4  #include <iostream.h>
 5
 6  main( )
 7  {
 8      cout << "Is there anybody out there?\n";
 9      return 0;
10  }
```

Figure A.1   Simple first program

Command-line arguments are particularly important for specifying program options. They are discussed in Section A.6.6. C++ provides mechanisms to read and write files portably (usually). This is discussed in Section A.7.2. Many operating systems provide an alternative known as *file redirection*. On UNIX, for instance, the command

```
a.out < inputfile > outputfile
```

automatically arranges things so that any terminal reads are redirected to come from `inputfile`, and terminal writes are redirected to go to `outputfile`.

A.2   The First Program

Let us begin by examining the simple C++ program shown in Figure A.1. First note that the line numbers shown on the left *are not part of the program*; we use them throughout the text for easy reference.

Place the program in the source file `Simple.cpp` (or `Simple.C`, if you prefer). The command

```
CC Simple.cpp
```

will compile the program, and then the command

```
a.out
```

will run it. Alternatively, the command

```
CC Simple.cpp -o Simple
```

will place the executable in a file named `Simple` instead of `a.out`. All compilers come with a host of options, some of which are discussed in other chapters. Check your manual pages for more detailed information.

A.2.1   Comments

C++ has two forms of *comments*. In the first form, which is inherited from C, the token `/*` begins a comment, and `*/` ends the comment. Comments do not nest.

Here is an example:

```
/* This is a
   two line comment */
```

The other form, which is used exclusively throughout the text, is that the token // begins a comment that extends until the end of the line. This is shown on lines 1 and 2 in Figure A.1.

Comments **make code easier for humans to read. C++ has two forms of comments; we use // exclusively.**

Comments exist to make code easier for humans to read. These humans include other programmers who may have to modify or use your code, as well as yourself. A well-commented program is a sign of a good programmer.

A.2.2   #include Statements

In Figure A.1, we see on line 4 the first C++ statement. The *include directive* has the effect of logically reading in another file. In our example the contents of a file named iostream.h are processed as if they had been on line 4 of the source file. The < and > that surround iostream.h, sometimes known as angle brackets, indicate that the file iostream.h does not reside in the current directory but rather in a system directory. Double quotes are used instead of angle brackets to read nonsystem files.

The *include directive* has the effect of logically reading in another file.

The names of included files typically end in .h, although this is not required (and for certain applications, g++ requires the inclusion of .cpp files). The included files may themselves have include directives; thus, unlike comments, include directives nest.

A.2.3   main

A C++ program consists of a collection of interacting functions (functions are described in Section A.6.1). When the program is run, the special function main is invoked. Line 6 signifies that the function main is invoked with no parameters (command-line arguments can be processed by declaring that main is a function that has parameters).

When the program is run, the special function main is invoked.

A.2.4   Return from main

When main terminates, the program is over. The return statement is used to send error codes back to the invoking process. The convention is that a return code of 0 indicates no problem, and a nonzero return is used to indicate errors. We can see that function main returns an object of type int; some programmers explicitly indicate this by placing the word int prior to main. Because this is the default return type in C++, its use is not necessary.

A.2.5   Terminal Output

Ignoring the return statement, the simple program in Figure A.1 consists of a single statement. This statement, shown on line 8 is the output mechanism in C++. Here a constant string is placed on the standard output stream `cout`. Input and output is discussed in more detail in Section A.7. For now we remark that the same syntax is used to perform output for any object, be it integer, floating point, string, or some other type.

A.3   Objects and Declarations

The central paradigm in C++ is the object. C++ defines several types of built-in objects and allows the user great flexibility to define new types of objects, known as classes. In this section, we examine the built-in types, and the basic operations that can be performed on objects.

A.3.1   Declaration and Initialization of Objects

For objects, a *definition* is a declaration that sets aside memory. A simple, nondefining *declaration* merely names an object but does not set aside any memory.

Before we can use any object, we must provide a declaration. There are two terms that are commonly intermixed: *declaration* and *definition*. For objects, a *definition* is a declaration that sets aside memory. A simple nondefining *declaration* merely names an object but does not set aside any memory. We will see the distinction in Section A.6.4 where we have a single object that must be visible across several separately compiled files. One file gives the definition, and the other files merely provide declarations that the definition is provided elsewhere.

Most of our object declarations will be defining declarations, and you can generally assume that unless specified, the use of the term *declaration* for objects refers to a defining declaration.

Having established terminology, we can say that there are three parts of an object definition, one of which is optional. First we must say what kind of an object we are asking for, then we must provide a name for the object. Optionally, we may specify an initial value. If one is not specified, a default mechanism is used (which may include the possibility of an undefined value).

An object is named by using an *identifier*.

An object is named by using an *identifier*. We may use letters, digits, and the underscore character in an identifier, but we may not start with a digit. We may not use reserved words such as `int`, and we should not reuse identifier names unless we know what we are doing (for example, we cannot use `main` as the name of an object).

Here are some examples of declarations:

```
int Num3;                    // Default initialization
int X = 0, Num1 = 0;         // Two objects are declared
double MinimumWage = 4.50;   // Standard initialization
double MaximumWage( 100000.00 );// Alternate initialization
int Num2 = Num1;
```

Objects should be declared near their first use. This is different from C declarations.

A.3.2   Basic Types in C++

The most common of the basic types in C++ is probably the integer. The keyword `int` is used to specify that an object is an integer. The range of integers is machine dependent and, importantly, no checking is performed for overflow. We can find the minimum and maximum integers on a system by examining the values of `INT_MIN` and `INT_MAX` in the standard header file `<limits.h>`.

C++'s *basic types* are integer, floating point, and character.

C++ also allows objects of type `long` or `short`. These may or may not provide integers that use a different number of bits than an `int`. The keyword `unsigned` can also be used to specify that the bit pattern of an integer is to be interpreted as a nonnegative number. This allows a slight extension of the range of representables. Here is what happens on one system (where integers are 16 bits):

```
short           // -32768 to 32767
int             // -32768 to 32767
long            // -2147483648 to 2147483647
unsigned short  // 0 to 65535
unsigned int    // 0 to 65535
unsigned long   // 0 to 4294967293
```

What happens if we mix types? The answer is complicated. Generally speaking, the operation is done in "stronger" type, but be very careful about introducing `unsigned`, because mixing signed and unsigned quantities frequently produces surprising results.

Floating point numbers are represented with the types `float`, `double`, and `long double`. Stick with `double`, because round-off errors tend to accumulate quickly with `float`. Never compare two floating point quantities for equality, precisely because round-off error will generally mean that two floating point quantities are unequal, even if they are logically equal.

The `char` type is used to represent single characters. A `char` typically occupies eight bits. Strings are represented as arrays of characters. C++ does not have a basic boolean type, though it is possible for a programmer to define one. The proposed ANSI C++ library includes a boolean type.

A.3.3   Constant Objects

Integer constants can be represented in either decimal, octal, or hexadecimal notation. Octal notation is indicated by a leading 0; hexadecimal is indicated by a leading 0x or 0X. The following are all equivalent ways of representing the integer 37: 37, 045, 0x25. Octal and hexadecimal integers are not used in this text, but even so, we must be aware of them so that we avoid using leading 0s unless we mean to.

Long integers can be explicitly quantified by using a trailing L. Thus,

```
long X = 1000 * 1000;
```

does not work on 16- bit machines (1000 * 1000 is evaluated in integer math, and the result overflows prior to assignment to X); we would need

```
long X = 1000L * 1000L;
```

The L is not needed for a constant object that is too large to fit in an int:

```
long X = 100000 * 10;
```

100000 is taken as a long (on the 16-bit machine), and the arithmetic is done using longs because of the mixing rule described previously. Unsigned integers can be explicitly quantified by using a trailing U.

The rules for what constitutes a floating point constant are more complicated. Generally speaking, we can write a floating point number explicitly, as in 3.14, or in scientific notation, as in 6.02e23.

A character constant is represented in a pair of single quotes, as in 'a'; internally, this is interpreted as a small number, but the output routines later interpret the small number as the corresponding character. There are some special sequences, known as *escape sequences*, that are used (for instance, how does one represent a single quote?). The important sequences are '\a', '\n', '\\', '\'', and '\"', which mean the alert (bell), newline character, backslash character, single quote character, and double quote character, respectively. A *string constant* consists of a sequence of characters enclosed by double quotes, as in "Hello\a\n".

The reserved word const is used to indicate that a named object should not be altered, as in

```
const double Pi = 3.1415926535897932;
```

A.3.4   Terminal Input and Output

Basic terminal input and output is accomplished by the operators << and >>. The standard input stream is cin, and the standard output stream is cout. Thus the program in Figure A.2 first prompts the user to type in an integer, then reads the integer, and then outputs the integer that was typed. On line 9 we see that we can chain output operations together: We first output a string, then an integer, and then a character.

```
1  #include <iostream.h>
2
3  main( )
4  {
5      int X;
6
7      cout << "Enter an integer: ";
8      cin >> X;
9      cout << "You entered " << X << '\n';
10     return 0;
11 }
```

Figure A.2   Simple program to illustrate input and output

```
1  #include <iostream.h>
2
3  main( )
4  {
5      int First - 12, Second = 8, Third = 6;
6
7      cout << The ints: " << First << Second << Third << '\n';
8      First = Third;
9      cout << The ints: " << First << Second << Third << '\n';
10     Third += Second;
11     cout << The ints: " << First << Second << Third << '\n';
12     First = Second + Third;
13     cout << The ints: " << First << Second << Third << '\n';
14     First++;
15     ++Second;
16     Third = First++ + ++Second;
17     cout << The ints: " << First << Second << Third << '\n';
18
19     return 0;
20 }
```

Figure A.3   Simple program to show operators

```
The ints: 12 8 6
The ints: 6 8 6
The ints: 6 8 14
The ints: 22 8 14
The ints: 23 9 14
The ints: 24 10 33
```

Figure A.4   Output of program in Figure A.3

There is one problem with the program: what if the user does not enter an integer? To handle that case, we would need to check for errors and print an error message. Error messages are generally sent to the error stream `cerr` instead of `cout`. More details about this are given in Section A.7.

A.3.5   Expressions and Simple Statements

A basic unit in C is the expression. A constant or object by itself is an expression, as are combinations of constants and objects with operators. The remainder of this section describes some of the operators available in C++. An expression followed by a semicolon is a simple statement. In Section A.4 we examine other types of statements (and a few additional operators).

A.3.6   Assignment Operators

A simple C++ program is shown in Figure A.3. The program does nothing in particular except demonstrate a few basics. The output of the program is shown in Figure A.4. C++ uses = for assignment. On line 8 the object `First` is assigned the value of the object `Third` (which at that point is 6). As is common with virtually all programming languages, subsequent changes to the value of `Third` do not affect `First`.

C++ provides a host of assignment operators, including =, +=, -=, *=, and /=.

In addition to the basic *assignment operator*, several other assignment operators are available, as indicated on line 10. The += operator adds the value on the right side (of the += operator) to the object on the left side. Thus `Third` is incremented from its value of 6 before line 9, to a value of 14. C++ provides various other assignment operators, such as -=, *=, and /=, which alter the object on the left side of the operator.

Assignment operators not only assign to an object but also form an expression that itself has a value. Thus the expression X=5 not only assigns X the value 5 but also evaluates to 5. This allows the expression to be used as part of a larger expression, as in Y=X=5 (which works because assignment operators are processed from right to left).

A.3.7   Binary Arithmetic Operators

C++ provides several binary arithmetic operators, including +, -, *, /, and %.

Line 12 in Figure A.4 illustrates a *binary arithmetic operator* that is typical of all programming languages. The values of `Second` and `Third` are added, and the resulting value is assigned to `First`. `Second` and `Third` remain unchanged. Besides the addition operator +, there are a host of other operators in C++. The ones found in typical use are -, *, /, and %, which are used for subtraction, multiplication, division, and remainder, respectively. Integer division returns only the integral part and discards any remainder. How this is done when there are negative numbers is unspecified.

As is typical, addition and subtraction have the same precedence, and this precedence is lower than the precedence of the group consisting of the multiplication, division, and mod operators. All of these operators associate from left to right (so 3–2–2 evaluates to –1). All operators have precedence and associativity; the complete table is provided in Appendix B. Generally speaking, the precedence and associativity rules make sense, though there are a few instances in which the precedence and associativity is either poorly chosen or misleading. Parentheses can always be used when the precedence rules would give the wrong meaning.

A.3.8   Unary Operators

In addition to binary operators, which require two operands, C++ provides *unary operators*, which require only one operand. The most familiar of these is the unary minus. Thus –X returns the negative of X. In the interest of fair play and equality, C++ also provides a unary plus operator; we use unary plus for a ListPtr object that we define when we examine linked lists in Chapter 16.

Several unary operators are defined, including – and +.

In addition to the unary minus and plus operators, C++ provides operators to add and subtract 1 from an object. The most benign use of the feature is shown on lines 14 and 15 of Figure A.3. In both cases the *autoincrement operator ++* adds 1 to the value of the object. In C++, however, an operator applied to an object yields an expression that has a value. Although it is guaranteed that the object will be incremented before the execution of the next statement, the question arises: What is the value of the autoincrement expression if it is used in a larger expression?

Autoincrement and autodecrement add and subtract 1, respectively. The operators are ++ and – –. There are two forms, prefix and postfix.

In this case the placement of the ++ is crucial. The semantics of ++X is that the value of the expression is the new value of X, while for X++ the value of the expression is the original value of X. This feature is shown in line 16 of Figure A.3 (and the last two lines of output in Figure A.4). First and Second are both incremented by 1, and Third is obtained by adding the original value of First with the incremented value of Second.

The postfix form of autoincrement (X++) associates from left to right and has highest precedence; it is in a general group of postfix operators that includes the function call operator and a postfix autodecrement operator. The prefix form associates from right to left, and is in the same group as the general class of unary operators that includes a prefix autodecrement and the unary plus and minus operators. These operators are immediately below postfix in strength of precedence.

Expressions such as A+A++ produce undefined results in C++ (because the compiler is free to adjust A at any point it pleases). Thus if the value of an object is altered in an expression, one must exercise some caution. With reasonable restraint, this is not a problem.

A.3.9   Type Conversions

The *type conversion operator* is used to generate a temporary object of a new type. Consider, for instance,

```
double Quotient;
int X=6;
int Y=10;
Quotient = X / Y;      // Probably wrong!
```

The first operation is the division, and since X and Y are both integers, the result is integer division, and we obtain 0. Integer 0 is then implicitly converted to a double so it can be assigned to Quotient. But we intended for Quotient to be assigned 0.6. The solution is to generate a temporary object for either X or Y so that the division is performed using the rules for double. This would be done in any of the following ways:

```
Quotient = double( X ) / double( Y );  // Best
Quotient = double( X ) / Y;            // OK
Quotient = X / double( Y );            // OK
Quotient = ( double ) X / Y;           // C style -- avoid
```

Note that neither X nor Y are changed. An unnamed temporary object is created, and its value is used for the division. The last form is the C style and is best avoided. It works because the type conversion operator has precedence just below the unary operators.

A.3.10   Bitwise Operators

C++ provides *bitwise operators* for the manipulation of integers on a bit-by-bit basis. This allows the packing of several boolean objects into an integral type. The operators are ~ (unary complement), << and >> (left and right shift), & (bitwise AND), ^ (bitwise exclusive OR), | (bitwise OR), and assignment operators corresponding to all these operators except unary complement. Figure A.5 illustrates the result of applying these operators.[1] For the binary bitwise operators, there are corresponding assignment operators. Note that the << and >> tokens that are used for input and output are the same as the bit shift operators. When the left side is a stream object, these operators have different meanings. As we will see, we can define almost any operator as we see fit for new types (that is, classes of) objects that we design.

The precedence and associativity of the bitwise operators are somewhat arbitrary. It is best to use parentheses when working with them.

---

1. Unsigned objects are best for bitwise operators because the results of the bit shifts can be machine dependent for signed objects.

```
// Assume ints are 16 bits
unsigned int A = 3737;      // 0000111010011001
unsigned int B = A << 1;    // 0001110100110010
unsigned int C = A >> 2;    // 0000001110100110
unsigned int D = 1 << 15;   // 1000000000000000
unsigned int E = A | B;     // 0001111110111011
unsigned int F = A & B;     // 0000110000010000
unsigned int G = A ^ B;     // 0001001110101011
unsigned int H = ~G;        // 1110110001010100
```

Figure A.5   Examples of bitwise operators

```
1         // Faculty Profile Fields
2  enum
3  {
4      Sex          = 0x0001, // On If Female
5      Minority     = 0x0002, // On If In A Minority Group
6      Veteran      = 0x0004, // On If Veteran
7      Disabled     = 0x0008, // On If Disabled
8      UScitizen    = 0x0010, // On If Citizen
9      Doctorate    = 0x0020, // On If Holds A Doctorate
10     Tenured      = 0x0040, // On If Tenured
11     TwelveMonth  = 0x0080, // On If On 12 Month Contract
12     Visitor      = 0x0100, // On If Not Permanent Faculty
13     Campus       = 0x0200, // On If Work Is At Main Campus
14
15     Rank         = 0x0c00, // Two Bits To Represent Rank
16     Assistant    = 0x0400, // Assistant Professor
17     Associate    = 0x0800, // Associate Professor
18     Full         = 0x0c00, // Full Professor
19
20     College      = 0xf000, // Represents 16 Colleges
21         ...
22     ArtsScience  = 0x3000, // Arts And Science = College #3
23         ...
24 };
25     // Later in a function initialize Appropriate Fields
26     Tim = ArtsScience | Associate | Campus | Tenured |
27               TwelveMonth | Doctorate | UScitizen;
28
29     // Promote Tim To Full Professor
30     Tim &= ~Rank;        // Turn All Rank Fields Off
31     Tim |= Full;         // Turn Rank Fields On
```

Figure A.6   Packing bits for faculty profiles

Figure A.6 shows how the bitwise operators are used to pack information into a 16-bit integer. This information is maintained by a typical university for a wide variety of reasons, including state and federal mandates. Many of the items require simple yes/no answers and are thus logically representable by a single bit. As Figure A.6 shows, 10 bits are used to represent 10 categories. A faculty member can have one of four possible ranks (assistant, associate, and full professor, as well as nontenure earning), and thus two bits are required. The remaining 4 bits are used to represent one of 16 possible colleges in the university.

Lines 26 and 27 show how `Tim` is represented. Tim is a tenured associate professor in the College of Arts and Science. He holds a Ph.D., is a U.S. citizen, and works on the university's main campus. He is not a member of a minority group, disabled, or a veteran. He is on a 12-month contract. `Tim`'s bit pattern is given by

```
0011 10 1 0 1 1 1 1 0 0 0 0
```

or 0x3af0. This bit pattern is formed by applying the *OR* operator on the appropriate fields.

Lines 30 and 31 show the logic used when Tim is deservedly promoted to the rank of full professor. `Rank` has the two rank bits set to 1 and all the other bits 0:

```
0000 11 0 0 0 0 0 0 0 0 0 0
```

The complement, `~Rank`, is thus

```
1111 00 1 1 1 1 1 1 1 1 1 1
```

Applying a bitwise AND of this and `Tim`'s current setting turns off `Tim`'s rank bits:

```
0011 00 1 0 1 1 1 1 0 0 0 0
```

The result of the bitwise OR operator at line 31 thus makes `Tim` a full professor without altering any other bits:

```
0011 11 1 0 1 1 1 1 0 0 0 0
```

We can find out that Tim is tenured, because `Tim&Tenured` is a nonzero result. We can also find out that Tim is in College #3 by shifting right 12 bits and then looking at the resulting low 4 bits. Notice that parentheses are required. The expression is `(Tim>>12)&0xf`.

A.3.11   The `sizeof` Operator

C++ provides the *sizeof operator* that can be used to determine the number of bytes that are used to store an object. There are two forms. First,

```
sizeof( Type )
```

provides the number of bytes needed to store an object of type `Type`. Thus `sizeof(int)` will evaluate to the number of bytes used to store an `int`, namely 2 or 4 (for most machines). The second form is

```
sizeof Object
```

and provides the number of bytes needed to store `Object`. Typically parentheses are included, even though they are optional. `sizeof` is grouped as a unary operator for the purposes of precedence and associativity.

The *sizeof operator* can be used to determine the number of bytes that are used to store an object.

A.4   Conditional Statements

In this section we examine statements that affect the flow of control, conditional statements and loops. As a consequence, new operators are introduced.

A.4.1   Relational and Equality Operators

The basic test that we can perform on objects is the comparison. We have equality and inequality, and for some objects it makes sense to consider order (that is, less than, greater than, and so on).

In C++ the *equality operators* are `==` and `!=`, `LeftExpr==RightExpr` evaluates to 0 (representing false) if `LeftExpr` and `RightExpr` are not equal. It evaluates to 1 otherwise. In C++, 0 is false, but anything that is not 0 is true. Similarly `LeftExpr!=RightExpr` evaluates to 0 if `LeftExpr` and `RightExpr` are equal, and 1 otherwise. Note that `LeftExpr=RightExpr` is legal C++ and evaluates to the result of an assignment, namely `RightExpr`. Using = instead of == is one of the most common errors in C++.

In C++ the *equality operators* are == and !=.

The *relational operators* are `<`, `<=`, `>`, and `>=`, and these have natural meanings for the built-in types. The relational operators have higher precedence than the equality operators. Both have lower precedence than the arithmetic operators but higher precedence than the assignment operators, so parentheses are frequently unnecessary. All of these operators associate from left to right, but beware that the test `A<B<6` does not check that A is less than B and B is less than 6. Rather, since `A<B` is either 0 or 1, and both of these values are less than 6, in either case the result of the expression will be 1. The next section describes the correct way to perform this test.

The *relational operators* are <, <=, >, and >=.

A.4.2   Logical Operators

C++ provides *logical operators* that are used to simulate the boolean algebra concepts of AND, OR, and NOT. These are sometimes known as *conjunction*, *disjunction*, and *negation*. These operations are represented in by `&&`, `||`, and `!`, respectively. The test in the example above is properly implemented as `A<B && B<6`. The precedence of conjunction and disjunction is sufficiently low that parentheses are not needed. `&&` has higher precedence than `||`, while `!` is grouped with other unary operators. Inputs to the logical operators are 0 for false and nonzero for true. Outputs are 0 for false and 1 for true.

One important rule is that `&&` and `||` are short-circuit operations that guarantee left to right evaluation. *Short circuit evaluation* means that, if the result can be determined by examining the first expression, then the second expression is not evaluated. For instance, in

```
X != 0 && 1/X != 3
```

if `X` is 0, then the first half is false. Automatically the result of the AND must be false, so the second half is not evaluated. As we can see, this is a good thing because division by zero would give erroneous behavior. Short-circuit evaluation allows us to not have to worry about dividing by zero.

A.4.3   The `if` Statement

The `if` statement is the fundamental decision maker. The basic form is

```
if( expression )
    statement
next statement
```

If `expression` evaluates to true, then `statement` is executed; otherwise, it is not. As usual, true means nonzero. When the `if` statement is completed (naturally), control passes to the next statement.

Optionally, we can use an `if-else` statement, as follows:

```
if( expression )
    statement1
else
    statement2
next statement
```

In this case, if `expression` evaluates to true, then `statement1` is executed; otherwise, `statement2` is executed. In either case control then passes to the next statement, as in

```
cout << "1/X is ";
if( X )  // explicit test against zero is redundant
    cout << 1 / X;
else
    cout << "undefined";
cout << '\n';
```

Remember that at most one statement is allowed to be subjected to each of the if and else clauses, no matter how you indent. Here are two mistakes:

```
if( X == 0 );    // ; is null statement (and counts)
    cout << "X is zero\n";
else
    cout << "X is ";
    cout << "not zero\n";  // Two statements no good
```

The first mistake is the ; at the end of the first if. This semicolon by itself counts as the *null statement*; consequently, this fragment won't compile (the else is no longer associated with an if). When that mistake is fixed, we have a logic error: the last line is not part of the else, even though the indenting suggests it is. To fix this problem, we have to use a compound statement, in which we enclose a sequence of statements by a pair of braces:

A semicolon by itself is the *null statement*.

```
if( X == 0 )
    cout << "X is zero\n";
else
{
    cout << "X is ";
    cout << "not zero\n";
}
```

The if statement can itself be the target of an if or else clause, as can other control statements discussed below. In the case of nested if-else statements, an else matches the innermost dangling if. It may be necessary to add braces if that is not the intended meaning.

A.4.4 The while Statement

The *while statement* is one of three basic forms of looping. The syntax is

The *while statement* is one of three basic forms of looping.

```
while( expression )
    statement
next statement
```

Note that, like the if statement, there is no semicolon in the syntax, and if one is present it will be taken as the null statement.

While expression is true, statement is executed; then expression is reevaluated. If expression is initially false, then statement will never be executed. Generally, statement does something that can potentially alter the value of expression; otherwise, the loop could be infinite. When the while loop terminates (normally), control resumes at the next statement.

A.4.5   The `for` Statement

The `while` statement is sufficient to express all repetition. Even so, C++ provides two other forms of looping. The *for statement* is used primarily for iteration. The syntax is

```
for( initialization; test; assignment )
    statement
next statement
```

`initialization`, `test`, and `assignment` are all expressions, and all three are optional. If `test` is not provided, it defaults to the expression 1, which is always true. There is no semicolon after the closing parenthesis.

The `for` statement is executed by first performing the `initialization`. Then, while `test` is nonzero, the following two actions occur: `statement` is performed, and then `adjustment` is performed. If `initialization` and `adjustment` are omitted, then the `for` statement behaves exactly as a `while` statement. The advantage of a `for` statement is clarity: For objects that count (or iterate), it is much easier to see what the range of the counter is. We can see that the following fragment prints the first 100 positive integers:

```
for( int i = 1; i <= 100; i++ )
    cout << i << '\n';
```

Loops nest in the same way as `if` statements. For instance, we can find all small numbers whose sum equals their product (such as 2 and 2, whose sum and product are both 4).

```
for( int i = 1; i <= 10; i++ )
    for( int j = 1; j <= 10; j++ )
        if( i + j == i * j )
            cout << i << ',' << j << '\n';
```

As we will see, however, when we nest loops we can easily create programs whose running times grow quickly.

A.4.6   The `do` Statement

The `while` statement repeatedly performs a test and, if the test is true, executes an embedded statement. One problem is that if the initial test is false, the embedded statement is never executed, and in some cases we would like to guarantee that the embedded statement is executed at least once. The *do statement* is identical to the `while` statement, except that the test is performed after the embedded statement. The syntax is

```
do
    statement
while( expression );
next statement
```

Notice that the do statement includes a semicolon. A typical use of the do statement is the following pseudocode fragment:

```
do
{
    Prompt User;
    Read Value;
} while( Value is no good );
```

The do statement is by far the least frequently used of the three looping constructs. However, when we have to do something repeatedly, a for loop is inappropriate; and when we have to do something at least once, the do statement is the method of choice.

A.4.7   **break** and **continue**

The for and while statements provide for termination before the start of a repeated statement. The do statement allows termination after execution of a repeated statement. Occasionally, we would like to terminate execution in the middle of a repeated (compound) statement. The *break statement*, which is the keyword break followed by a semicolon, can be used to achieve this. Typically, an if statement would precede the break, as in

```
while( ... )
{
    ...
    if( something )
        break;

}
```

The break statement exits the innermost loop only (it is also used in conjunction with the switch statement, described below). If there are several loops that need exiting, a break will not work, and most likely you have poorly designed code.

> **The *break* statement exits the innermost loop or *switch* statement.**

A second problem we would like to handle is that occasionally there are cases where we would like to give up on the current iteration of a repeated statement for the current value and go on to the next iteration. This can be handled by a *continue statement*. Like the break statement, the continue statement includes a semicolon and applies to the innermost loop only. The fragment below prints the first 100 integers, with the exception of those divisible by 10.

> **The *continue* statement goes to the next iteration of the innermost loop.**

```
for( int i = 1; i <= 100; i++ )
{
    if( i % 10 == 0 )
        continue;
    cout << i << '\n';
}
```

Of course, in this example, there are alternatives to the `continue`. The reason it is commonly used is to avoid complicated `if-else` patterns inside loops.

A.4.8   The `switch` Statement

*The **switch** statement is used to select among several small integer values.*

The *switch statement* is used to select among several small integer values. It consists of an expression and a statement that is almost always a compound statement. The (generally compound) statement contains a sequence of statements and a collection of *labels*, which represent possible values of the expression. All the labels must be distinct, and the optional default label, if present, matches any unrepresented label. If there is no applicable case for the `switch` expression, the `switch` statement is over; otherwise, control passes to the appropriate label, and all statements from that point on are executed. A `break` statement may be used to force early termination of the `switch` and is almost always used to separate logically distinct cases. An example of the typical structure is shown in Figure A.7.

```
 1  switch( SomeCharacter )
 2  {
 3    case '(':
 4    case '[':
 5    case '{':
 6      // Code to process opening symbols
 7      break;
 8
 9    case ')':
10    case ']':
11    case '}':
12      // Code to process closing symbols
13      break;
14
15    case '\n':
16      // Code to handle new line character
17      break;
18
19    default:
20      // Code to handle other cases
21      break;
22  }
```

Figure A.7   Layout of a `switch` statement

A.4.9   The Comma Operator

The *comma operator* , is mainly used in the expressions that are part of the `for` statement. The result of `LeftExpr, RightExpr` is that `LeftExpr` is evaluated and then `RightExpr` is evaluated. The value of the entire expression is the value of `RightExpr`. The comma operator has the lowest precedence of all operators. The following is an example of its use:

The *comma operator* , is mainly used in the expressions that are part of the `for` statement.

```
for( i = 0; Sum = 0; i <= N; i++, Sum += N )
    cout << i << '\t' << Sum << '\n';
```

Note that the comma that separates parameters in function calls is not the comma operator. Left to right evaluation of parameters to a function is not guaranteed.

A.4.10   The Conditional Operator

The *conditional operator ?:* is used as a shorthand for simple `if-else` statements. The general form is

The *conditional operator ?:* is used as a shorthand for simple `if-else` statements.

```
TestExpr ? YesExpr : NoExpr
```

`TestExpr` is evaluated first; then either `YesExpr` or `NoExpr` is evaluated, and this is the result of the entire expression. `YesExpr` is evaluated if `TestExpr` is true; otherwise, `NoExpr` is evaluated. The precedence of the conditional operator is just above the assignment operators. This allows us to avoid using parentheses when assigning the result of the conditional operator to an object. As an example, the minimum of `X` and `Y` is assigned to `MinVal` as follows:

```
MinVal = X <= Y ? X : Y;
```

A.4.11   goto

C++ allows gotos; these are occasionally useful for breaking out of deep loops. There is only one goto in the text (see if you can find it), and it is used only for convenience. Generally speaking, it is best to avoid gotos.

A.5   Arrays, Pointers, and Structures

Most examples in this text use arrays, pointers, and structures. See Chapter 1 for a description of this part of the language.

```
 1  int Min( int X, int Y );      // Function declaration
 2
 3  main( )
 4  {
 5      int A = 3, B = 7;
 6
 7      cout << Min( A, B ) << '\n';
 8      return 0;
 9  }
10
11  // Function definition
12  int
13  Min( int X, int Y )
14  {
15      return X < Y ? X : Y;
16  }
```

Figure A.8   Illustration of function declarations, definitions, and calls

A.6   General Layout of a Simple C++ Program

This section describes functions, global declarations, and how these parts of a C++ program are arranged.

A.6.1   Functions

The *function declaration* consists of the name, return type, and parameter list. The *function definition* includes the body.

In C++ a function declaration consists of a name, a (possibly empty) list of parameters, and a return type. Collectively, this defines the interface. The actual code to implement the function, sometimes known as the function body, is formally a compound statement. A *function definition* consists of an interface plus the body. A *function declaration* is the interface followed by a semicolon. When discussing functions, the term *declaration* means function declaration rather than definition. An example of a function declaration, a function definition, and a main routine that uses the function is shown in Figure A.8.

The function name is an identifier (use meaningful names, as usual). When writing the definition, we will place the return type on a separate line. This makes it easier to find the definition because in the definition the function name is at the start of a line, and many text editors allow searches with this restriction.

In *call by value*, the actual arguments are copied into the formal parameters.

The parameter list consists of zero or more *formal parameters*, each with a specified type. When calling a function, the *actual arguments* are (by default) copied into the formal parameters. This is *call-by-value* parameter passing. C++ also allows call by reference. This is discussed in Section 1.8.2. C++ requires that a function declaration (but not necessarily a definition) be visible at the point that a function call is made so that the types of the actual arguments can be checked for consistency against the formal parameters.

The *return statement* is used to send an object back to the caller. If the return type is `void`, then no objects are sent back, and `return;` should be used.

The `return` statement is used to send an object back to the caller.

A.6.2   C++ Extras for Functions

C programmers will be happy to know that C++ provides a few extra goodies for functions. As we have mentioned earlier, call by reference is supported in a more reasonable way than in C.

Overloading of Function Names

Suppose we need to write a routine that returns the index of the maximum element in an array of `ints`. A reasonable function declaration would be

```
unsigned int Max( const int *Array, int N );
```

In C this declaration may be unacceptable if `Max` is already defined. For instance, we may also have

```
int Max( int A, int B );
```

C++ allows the *overloading* of function names. This means that several functions may have the same name as long as their *signature* (that is, their parameter list types) are different. When a call to `Max` is made, the compiler can deduce which of the intended meanings should be applied based on the actual argument list.

Overloading of a function name means that several functions may have the same name as long as their parameter list types are different.

Note that the return type is not included in the signature, and `const` parameters are considered different types than non-`const` parameters.

Default Parameters

C++ allows the user to specify default values for formal parameters. Typically, the default values are included in the function declaration. As an example, the following declaration for `PrintInt` specifies that by default integers should be printed in decimal:

```
void PrintInt( unsigned int N, unsigned int Base = 10 );
PrintInt( 50 );        // Outputs 50
PrintInt( 50, 8 );   // Outputs 62
```

If a default value is specified for a formal parameter, all subsequent formal parameters must have default values too. In the example above, for instance, we could not specify

```
void PrintInt( unsigned int Base = 10, unsigned int N );
```

Consequently, parameters that might be omitted are arranged so that those most likely to assume default values will go last.

A default value can be specified in the function definition instead of the declaration, but this is considered bad practice. A default value cannot be specified more than once.

Inline Functions

In some situations, particularly trivial but frequently called functions, the overhead of making a function call can be significant. In C, this is avoided by preprocessor macros. However preprocessor macros are unsafe because if the parameters are altered, then the macro is not semantically equivalent to the function.

The `inline` directive suggests to the compiler that it should generate code that avoids the overhead of a function call but is nonetheless semantically equivalent. In conjunction with the `const` directive, `inline` makes preprocessor macros mostly unnecessary (except for conditional compilation, as discussed below).

Although the compiler can ignore the suggestion, good compilers realize that careful inline optimization can drastically affect the running time of a program and will thus usually do the right thing.

The `inline` directive should be specified in the function definition rather than the declaration. Note that if an inline function is altered, any source code that calls it must be recompiled. This is not the case for "true" functions and thus represents a severe disadvantage of inline functions. It implies that the body of an inline function must be visible at the time the function is called.

Using Existing C Routines

For the most part, any C routines that we need to use can be compiled by C++. In some cases, however, we may have an already-compiled C library that we want to be available to C++ programs. In that case, because C++ encodes the parameter types in the function names (for purposes of overloading and type checking) and C does not, the linkage will fail.

To use C routines, we must provide the C prototype preceded by `extern "C"`. For instance,

```
extern "C" int IsLeap( int Year );
```

Most C++ implementations provide these types of declarations for the C library routines.

A.6.3   Storage Classes

Objects that are declared inside the body of a function are local variables and can be accessed by name only within the function body. These objects are created when the function body is executed and disappear when the function body terminates. `static` local variables have lifetimes that extend throughout the entire program; they are initialized only once, and the values are retained through successive calls to the function.

Objects declared outside the body of a function are global. In the case of a name conflict between a local variable and a global variable, the local variable wins. To access a global variable in such a case, use the scope resolution operator `::`.

The fundamental rule that concerns all global objects (and global functions) is that they may be declared several times, but they must be defined exactly once. The `extern` keyword is used to indicate a declaration of a global object that does not define it. Thus,

```
int Global = 0;       // Defining declaration (definition)
extern int Global;    // Declaration, not defining
```

A.6.4   Separate Compilation

The convention for separate compilation is that types (including class declarations), declarations, and global declarations are placed in header files that end in `.h`. Function bodies, class bodies, and global definitions are placed in C++ source files that end in `.cpp` (other extensions are also recognized). The source code available by anonymous ftp has several examples of this.

Suppose that we have two C++ source files `Part1.cpp` and `Part2.cpp`. To compile this on a UNIX system, `Part1.cpp` and `Part2.cpp` are separately compiled and then linked with

```
CC -c Part1.cpp Part2.cpp
CC Part1.o Part2.o
```

Then if only `Part1.cpp` changes, the program can be recompiled by

```
CC -c Part1.cpp
CC Part1.o Part2.o
```

This process can be automated by the *make* utility. Other systems have similar mechanisms.

A.6.5   Conditional Compilation

If a `.h` file is read more than once, class declarations may be processed twice, in error. This is avoided by using *conditional compilation* to ensure that the declarations are processed once. The standard idiom is as follows: If the header file is named `Header.h`, we insert at the start of the file

```
#ifndef _Header
#define _Header
```

and at the end of the file we add

```
#endif
```

The first time the file is included, `_Header` is not defined, so the entire header file is processed. On subsequent includes, the `#ifndef` becomes false, so control passes to the `#endif`.

A.6.6   Command-Line Arguments

Command-line arguments are available by declaring `main` with the signature

```
main( int argc, char *argv[ ] )
```

Here `argc` is the number of command-line arguments (including the command name), and `argv` is an array of strings (`char *` objects) that store the command-line arguments. As an example, the program in Figure A.9 implements the `echo` command.

```
1  #include <iostream.h>
2
3  main( int argc, char *argv[ ] )
4  {
5      for( int i = 1; i < argc; i++ )
6          cout << argv[ i ] << ' ';
7      cout << '\n';
8      return 0;
9  }
```

Figure A.9   `echo` command

A.7   Input and Output

Input and output (I/O) in C++ is achieved through the use of streams. The header file `iostream.h` is included for all basic I/O. Although the C library routines (such as `printf` and `scanf`) will also work, their use is strongly discouraged.

The iostream library is very sophisticated and has a host of options. We only examine the most basic uses.

A.7.1   Basic Stream Operations

Four streams are predefined for terminal I/O. They are `cin`, `cout`, `cerr`, and `clog`. `cin` is the standard input, `cout` is the standard output, `cerr` is the standard error, and `clog` is also the standard error. The difference between `clog` and `cerr` is that writes to `clog` are unbuffered.

As we have seen, the stream extraction operator `>>` is used for formatted input, and the stream insertion operator `<<` is used for formatted output. Here is an example:

```
int X;
int Y;

cin >> X >> Y;                          // Read X and then Y
cout << X << Y << ( X + Y ) << '\n'; // Output some stuff
```

Formally, the bit shift operators are overloaded to accept a stream and an object, and a function is present for each type of object; operator overloading guarantees that the correct function is matched. When a new class is built, the class designer can overload the bit shift operator so that objects of the new class can be output as if they were predefined types. Furthermore, because input streams and output streams are of different types, statements such as

```
cin << X;      // Attempt to output into cin
```

will fail at compile time.

Input and output have their respective problems. For input, how do we detect errors? For output, how can we finely control the format?

Errors in the Input

In the example above, what happens if the user does not provide two integers but instead provides a sequence of letters? In that case we have an input error.

Two things happen. First, the result of the expression will be zero, so we can test when we do not get the input that we expect, as in

```
if( cin >> X >> Y )
{
    // Read was ok
}
else
    // Error
```

Additionally, there are member functions that can be applied to an input stream. For example, the expression

```
cin.eof( )
```

returns true if the end-of-file caused a read to fail. The expression

```
cin.fail( )
```

returns true if a format error has occurred. The expression

```
cin.good( )
```

returns true if all is well. Once an error has occurred, it should be cleared after recovery by a call to

```
cin.clear( );
```

Manipulators

We have seen the use of endl in output, as in

```
cerr << "Format error" << endl;
```

endl is a *manipulator*. Its function is to place a newline on the stream and then flush the stream buffer, thus forcing a write. dec, hex, and oct are manipulators used to change the output of integers to decimal, hexadecimal, and octal. Thus

```
cout << 37 << oct << 37 << hex << 37;
cout << 37;    // still hexadecimal
```

outputs 37, 45, 25, and 25. We can include the base (that is, a leading 0 or 0x) in the output by using

```
cout << setiosflags( ios::showbase );
```

The manipulator setw(int TmpFieldWidth) is used to set the field width for the next argument that is placed on the output stream. If the actual width of an object is smaller than the field width allowed, it is right-justified (in that width) by default and filled with padding. We can control what is used as padding characters (the default is blank spaces). For instance, when writing amounts on checks, blank spaces are avoided to discourage fraud. Thus, we might have

```
cout.fill( '*' );      // Pad with *
cout.precision( 2 );   // Two decimal places
cout << setw( 8 ) << 12.49 << '\n';
```

which prints `***12.49`.

There are a host of options available, and of course the library is still in a state of flux. Check a current C++ reference manual for more details.

One-Character-at-a-Time Input and Output

The `put` member function can be used to output a single character. For instance,

```
cout.put( '\n' );
```

outputs a newline character. Similarly, the `get` member function can be used to read a single character (including a white-space character, if that is next in the input stream). It returns zero if the end-of-file causes a failure; otherwise, it returns a reference to the new input stream. Here is an example:

```
char Ch;
if( cin.get( Ch ) )
    cout << "Read " << Ch << '\n';
else
    cout << "End of file encountered\n";
```

Note that there are several different versions of `get`. The `putback` member function is used to undo a `get`. The `peek` member function is used to examine the next character in the input stream without digesting it.

Finally, the routine `getline` can be used to read a line of input. The declaration is

```
istream &
getline( char *Buffer, int Limit, char Delimiter = '\n' );
```

`getline` reads characters from an input stream and forms a null terminated string specified by `Buffer`. Reading stops when either the `Delimiter` is seen or `Limit-1` characters are processed. The `Delimiter` is not included in the string but remains in the input stream (and thus is the next character read).

The usual disclaimer applies: There are many more functions and options than reported here.

A.7.2   Sequential Files

One basic rule of C++ is that everything that works for terminal I/O also works for files. To deal with a file, we associate either an `ifstream` (for input file) or `ofstream` (for output file) object with it. We then use the same syntax as terminal I/O. The header file `fstream.h` should be included. An example that illustrates the basic ideas is shown in Figure A.10.

```
 1  #include <fstream.h>
 2
 3  // Copy from InFile to Outfile
 4
 5  void
 6  Copy( const char *InFile, const char *OutFile )
 7  {
 8          // Cheap check for aliasing
 9      if( strcmp( InFile, OutFile ) == 0 )
10      {
11          cerr << "Input and output files are identical\n";
12          return;
13      }
14
15          // Open input stream
16      ifstream InStream( InFile );
17      if( !InStream )
18      {
19          cerr << "Can't open " << InFile << endl;
20          return;
21      }
22
23          // Open output stream
24      ofstream OutStream( OutFile );
25      if( !OutStream )
26      {
27          cerr << "Can't open " << OutFile << endl;
28          return;
29      }
30
31          // Do the copy
32      while( InStream.get( Ch ) )
33          if( !OutStream.put( Ch ) )
34          {
35              cerr << "Output error!" << endl;
36              return;
37          }
38  }
```

Figure A.10   Copy routine using files

Functions that deal with files should use references to `ostream` and `istream` objects as parameters. An `ofstream` actual argument will match an `ostream &` formal parameter. Also, direct access files are supported, but we will not go into details.

A.7.3   String Streams

For many applications the `>>` operator is not sufficient. For instance, suppose we are expecting to repeatedly read two integers X and Y from an `ifstream` F. Initially, the following logic appears to work:

```
1  const int LineLength = 256;
2  char OneLine[ LineLength ];
3
4  while( !F.getline( OneLine, LineLength ).eof( ) )
5  {
6      istrstream LineStr( OneLine, LineLength );// string stream
7
8      LineStr >> X;        // Read first integer
9      LineStr >> Y;        // Read second integer
10
11     if( LineStr.good( ) )
12     {
13         // Read two integers!!
14     }
15     else
16     {
17         // Error: but no need to issue reset
18     }
19 }
```

Figure A.11   Fragment that illustrates string streams

```
while( F >> X >> Y )
{
    // process two integers
}
```

Unfortunately, this does not catch errors. For instance, files that contain exactly one integer per line will be read without incident (because white space includes the newline character). If we want to insist that every line has at least two integers, we need to read a line at a time and then extract the integers from the line. This is done using the istrstream. The header file strstream.h must be included. An example of typical use is the fragment in Figure A.11.[2]

On line 4 we read a single line of input from the file. A string stream is created at line 6. At lines 8 and 9 we read from the string stream. Notice that the string stream has memory of previous reads. Supposedly we should be able to chain the extraction operators into one statement, but this does not work on a few compilers, so instead we use separate extractions. After we have done the extractions, we can test the stream state.

Notice that we do not need to reset the stream state, because each iteration of the while loop generates a new string stream. To avoid the possibility of extraneous inputs, however, we might want to test that nothing else is left in the string stream. The operations that can be performed on string streams are similar to those that can be performed on general streams. ostrstream objects are used to compose character arrays; but using an ostrstream is a bit more complicated and so it is used less often.

---

2. The proposed standard library replaces istrstream with istringstream.

Objects of the Game

assignment operators C++ provides a host of assignment operators, including =, +=, -=, *=, and /=. (766)

autoincrement (++) and autodecrement (--)operators Add and subtract 1, respectively. There are two forms, prefix and postfix. (767)

basic types C++'s basic types are integer, floating point, and character. (763)

binary arithmetic operators C++ provides several, including +, -, *, /, and %. (766)

bitwise operators Used to manipulate integers on a bit-by-bit basis. This allows the packing of several boolean objects into an integral type. (768)

break statement Exits the innermost loop or switch statement. (775)

comma operator (,) Mainly used in expressions that are part of the for statement. (777)

command-line argument Accessed by two parameters to main. (782)

comments Make code easier for humans to read. C++ has two forms of comments; we use // exclusively. (761)

conditional compilation Used to ensure that header files are processed only once. (782)

conditional operator (?:) Used as a shorthand for simple if-else statements. (777)

continue statement Goes to next iteration of innermost loop. (775)

declaration and definition of a function The function declaration consists of the name, return type, and parameter list. The function definition includes the body. (778)

declaration and definition of an object For an object, a definition is a declaration that sets aside memory. A simple nondefining declaration merely names an object but does not set aside any memory. (762)

do statement A looping construct that guarantees the loop is executed at least once. (774)

equality operators In C++, the equality operators are == and !=. (771)

escape sequences Used to represent certain character constants. (764)

for statement A looping construct that is used primarily for simple iteration. (774)

identifier Used to name an object. (762)

if statement The fundamental decision maker. (772)

include directive Has the effect of logically reading in another source file. (761)

input and output (I/O) Input and output in C++ is achieved through the use of streams. The header file `iostream.h` is included for all basic I/O. Although the C library routines (such as `printf` and `scanf`)will also work, their use is strongly discouraged. The iostream library is very sophisticated and has a host of options. We only examine the most basic uses. (782)

integrated environments Common on PCs; support editing, compiling and debugging in one common environment. (759)

logical operators C++ provides logical operators that are used to simulate the boolean algebra concepts of AND, OR, and NOT. The corresponding operators are `&&`, `||`, and `!`. (772)

`main` When the program is run, the special function `main` is invoked. (761)

null statement Consists of a semicolon by itself. (773)

octal and hexadecimal integer constants Integer constants can be represented in either decimal, octal, or hexadecimal notation. Octal notation is indicated by a leading `0`; hexadecimal is indicated by a leading `0x` or `0X`. (764)

overloading of a function name means that several functions may have the same name as long as their parameter list types are different. (779)

relational operators The relational operators are `<`, `<=`, `>`, and `>=`. (771)

`return` statement Used to send back on object to the caller. (779)

short-circuit evaluation If the result of a logical operator can be determined by examining the first expression, then the second expression is not evaluated. (772)

signature The function name and the parameter list types. The return type is not part of the signature. (779)

`sizeof` operator Used to determine the number of bytes that are used to store an object. (771)

standard input The terminal, unless redirected. There are also streams for standard output and standard error. The basic I/O streams are `cin`, `cout`, `cerr`, and `clog`. (759)

string constant Consists of a sequence of characters enclosed by double quotes. (764)

`switch` statement Used to select among several small integer values. (776)

type conversion operator Used to generate a temporary object of a new type. (768)

unary operators Several unary operators are defined, including unary minus (–) and unary plus (+). (767)

`while` statement One of three basic forms of looping. (773)

Common Errors

1. The most common C++ error is using = instead of ==.

2. Adding unnecessary semicolons gives logical errors because the semi-colon by itself is the null statement. This means that an unintended semicolon immediately following a `for`, `while`, or `if` statement is very likely to go undetected and break your program.

3. Off-by-one errors are especially common in C++.

4. Local variables are not initialized by default. Do not attempt to use the value of an uninitialized variable. Be aware that zero seems to be a common uninitialized value and occasionally gives the appearance of a working program.

5. At compile time C++ detects some instances in which a function that is supposed to return a value fails to do so. But ultimately it is your responsibility to remember.

6. Arithmetic overflow is undetected in C++.

7. Mixing types can produce unexpected results, especially when unsigned quantities are involved. Do not overuse unsigned variables.

8. A leading 0 makes an integer constant octal when seen as a token in source code. So `037` is decimal `31`.

9. Like all languages, floating point numbers are subject to round-off errors. Use `double` instead of `float` to make the effect less pronounced.

10. Multiple side effects in a single statement produced undefined results in some cases. There is a precise rule for this, but in general, keep the code simple, and you will not have problems.

11. Division and mod operations can produce machine independent results when negative numbers are involved. Avoid this.

12. Precedence rules involving some operators (notably the bitwise operators) are counterintuitive. Many errors result from the wrong precedence. For instance, `?:` has lower precedence than `<<`.

13. Use `&&` and `||` for logical operations, `&` and `|` for bitwise operations. Do not mix these up.

14. In C++, 0 is false, nonzero is true. Thus −1 is true.

15. The routines in `ctype.h` return 0 or nonzero, rather than 0 or 1.

16. The `else` clause matches the closest dangling `if`. It is common to forget the braces needed to match the `else` to a distant dangling `if`.

17. When using a `switch` statement, it is common to forget the `break` statement between logical cases. If it is forgotten, control passes through to the next case; generally this is incorrect.

18. An object may be declared several times but defined exactly once. Otherwise, you will get an error.

19. Escape sequences begin with the backslash character \, not the forward slash /.

20. The eof member function returns true only if a read has already failed because the end-of-file was reached. It cannot be used to test if a read is about to fail.

21. Mismatched braces may give misleading answers. Use CheckBalance, which is described in Section 11.1 to check if this is the cause of a compiler error message.

References

Most of the material in this chapter is taken from [1]. See any C++ book for details on the stream library.

1. M. A. Weiss, *Efficient C Programming: A Practical Approach*, Prentice-Hall, Englewood Cliffs, NJ (1995).

Appendix B

Operators

Figure B.1 shows the precedence and associativity of all C++ operators. It also indicates which operators are overloadable. The precedence of `throw` is just above the comma operator.

Category	Examples	Associativity	Overloadable
Scope resolution	:: (unary scope) :: (class scope)	Left to right	No
Postfix	Function ( ) [] -> . ++ --	Left to right	Yes, except
Prefix and unary	sizeof * & ! ~ + ++ -- new delete	Right to left	Yes, except sizeof
Selector	->* .*	Left to right	->* only
Multiplicative	* / %	Left to right	Yes
Additive	+ -	Left to right	Yes
Shift	<< >>	Left to right	Yes
Relational	< <= > >=	Left to right	Yes
Equality	== !=	Left to right	Yes
Boolean AND	&	Left to right	Yes
Boolean XOR	^	Left to right	Yes
Boolean OR	|	Left to right	Yes
Logical AND	&&	Left to right	Yes
Logical OR	||	Left to right	Yes
Conditional	?:	Right to left	No
Assignment	= *= /= %= += -=	Right to left	Yes
Comma	,	Left to right	Yes

Figure B.1   C++ operators listed from highest to lowest precedence

Appendix C

Some Library Routines

This appendix lists some of the library routines that are used in this text.

C.1   Routines declared in `<ctype.h>`

```
int isalnum( int Ch );        // Nonzero if alphanumeric
int isalpha( int Ch );        // Nonzero if alphabetic
int iscntrl( int Ch );        // Nonzero if control character
int isdigit( int Ch );        // Nonzero if 0-9
int isgraph( int Ch );        // Nonzero if graphic
int islower( int Ch );        // Nonzero if lower case
int isprint( int Ch );        // Nonzero if printable
int ispunct( int Ch );        // Nonzero if punctuation
int isspace( int Ch );        // Nonzero if white space
int isupper( int Ch );        // Nonzero if upper case
int isxdigit( int Ch );       // Nonzero if 0-9 or a-f or A-F

int tolower( int Ch );        // Return lower case equivalent
int toupper( int Ch );        // Return upper case equivalent
```

These routines test a character for various properties.

C.2   Constants declared in `<limits.h>`

```
CHAR_BIT   // Bits per bytes

SCHAR_MIN // Smallest value, signed char
SCHAR_MAX // Largest value, signed char
UCHAR_MAX // Smallest value, unsigned char
CHAR_MIN  // Smallest value, char
CHAR_MAX  // Largest value, char

SHRT_MIN  // Smallest value, short
SHRT_MAX  // Largest value, short
USHRT_MAX // Largest value, unsigned short

INT_MIN   // Smallest value, int
INT_MAX   // Largest value, int
UINT_MAX  // Largest value, unsigned int

LONG_MIN  // Smallest value, long
LONG_MAX  // Largest value, long
ULONG_MAX // Largest value, unsigned long
```

C.3   Routines declared in `<math.h>`

```
// Trigonometric functions -- all angles in radians
double sin( double Theta );
double cos( double Theta );
double tan( double Theta );
double asin( double X );   // Result is between +/- Pi/2
double acos( double X );   // Result is between 0 and Pi
double atan( double X );   // Result is between +/- Pi/2

// Hyperbolic functions
double sinh( double Theta );
double cosh( double Theta );
double tanh( double Theta );

// Logarithms and exponents
double exp( double X );    // e to the X
double log( double X );    // log base e
double log10( double X );  // log base 10
double pow( double X, double Y );   // X to the Y
double sqrt( double X );   // Square root

// Miscellaneous
double ceil( double X );   // Ceiling function
double floor( double X );  // Floor function
double fabs( double X );   // Absolute value
```

<math.h> provides routines for mathematical operations. On some UNIX systems you must specify -lm as a last option to the compiler to load these routines. All angles are in radians. Some of the common routines are listed above.

C.4   Routines declared in `<stdlib.h>`

```
    // Program termination
void abort( void );          // Terminate program with SIGABRT
int atexit( void ( *Func )( void ) ); // See below
void exit( int Status );   // Exit program, flush buffers

    // Spawn a command
int system( const char *Command );

    // Get environment variable
char *getenv( const char *Name );
```

`<stdlib.h>` has a host of routines, most of which are remnants of C and are best avoided. These include `malloc` and `free` as well as some generic routines that use old style `void *` parameters instead of templates. We list only those that relate to either program termination or the environment.

`abort` causes the program to terminate by sending signal `SIGABRT`. Unless arrangements are made, this is not considered "normal termination."

The function `exit` terminates a program normally. It is called implicitly when `main` returns. As a result, functions registered with `atexit` are called in reverse order of their registration. Output streams are then closed and flushed, and the program terminates with `Status` passed back to the calling environment.

The result of `system` is that `Command` is passed to the operating system's *command processor* and is run. How this is done is highly system dependent.

`getenv` is used to search for environment variables; again this is highly system dependent. As an example, UNIX users can try the statement

```
cout << "Terminal type is " << getenv( "TERM" ) << '\n';
```

C.5   Routines declared in `<string.h>`

```
    // =, +=, ==, and length for strings
char *strcpy( char *Lhs, const char *Rhs );
char *strcat( char *Lhs, const char *Rhs );
int strcmp( const char *Lhs, const char *Rhs );
size_t strlen( const char *Str );

    // Find character Ch or string Pattern in Str
char *strchr( const char *Str, int Ch );    // First match
char *strrchr( const char *Str, int Ch );   // Last match
char *strstr( const char *Str, const char *Pattern );
```

`<string.h>` has a host of routines that deal with pointers and memory in C; this library is part of C++, but for the most part routines in it should be used only occasionally. The search routines return a pointer to the character that begins match.

Appendix D

Modifications for Exceptions

This appendix describes modifications to the code in the text that can be used if your compiler supports exceptions. We also reiterate what you need to do if your compiler does not support exceptions.

D.1   Exceptions Already Used

As discussed in Chapter 1, the only use of exceptions made in this text deals with the failure of new to allocate memory. If your system supports the most recent C++ proposals, you will want to replace . . . with bad_alloc. If not, see the next paragraph.

   If your system does not support exceptions, you have some other options. This includes g++ users. At the time of this writing, g++ 2.6.2 is the current version and does not support exceptions well. Consequently, the default is to not allow exceptions. If you attempt to compile the code in the text with the option -fhandle_exceptions, it still will not work *even if there are no exceptions caught or thrown.*[1] Consequently, you should not use that option. The compiler will then complain that throw, catch, and try are reserved words. Comment out the try and catch blocks in main. Figure D.1 shows how this is done for the sample program in Figure 1.11. What happens when new fails? On g++, you will get the error message *virtual memory exceeded.* So there's still no point in testing the return from new.

   For other systems, if you elect not to use exceptions, install a new_handler that calls abort. The rest of this appendix describes what we do in the book in preparation for the eventual use of exceptions.

---

1. For many of the classes in the text, the compiler will complain that it cannot destroy partially constructed objects. This happens if a class has another user-defined class object as a data member. This complaint occurs whether or not you try to use the exception features.

```
 1  // Read an unlimited number of ints
 2  // No attempts at error recovery
 3  // Return a pointer to the data, and set ItemsRead
 4
 5  int *
 6  GetInts( int & ItemsRead )
 7  {
 8      int ArraySize = 0;
 9      int InputVal;
10      int *Array = 0;
11
12      ItemsRead = 0;
13      cout << "Enter any number of integers: ";
14      while( cin >> InputVal )
15      {
16          if( ItemsRead == ArraySize )
17          {          // Array doubling code
18              int *Original = Array;
19              Array = new int[ ArraySize * 2 + 1 ] );
20              for( int i = 0; i < ArraySize; i++ )
21                  Array[ i ] = Original[ i ];
22              delete [ ] Original; // Safe if Original is NULL
23              ArraySize *= 2;
24              ArraySize++,
25          }
26          Array[ ItemsRead++ ] = InputVal;
27      }
28      return Array;
29  }
30
31  main( void )
32  {
33      int *Array;
34      int NumItems;
35
36      // The actual code
37  //try                                       // COMMENT OUT
38  //{                                         // COMMENT OUT
39      Array = GetInts( NumItems );
40      for( int i = 0; i < NumItems; i++ )
41          cout << Array[ i ] << '\n';
42  //}                                         // COMMENT OUT
43      // Exception handler; ... used because standard is evolving
44  //catch( ... )                             // COMMENT OUT
45  //{                                         // COMMENT OUT
46  //  cerr << "Out of memory!!" << endl;      // COMMENT OUT
47  //  exit( 1 );                              // COMMENT OUT
48  //}                                         // COMMENT OUT
49      return 0;
50  }
```

Figure D.1   A no-exception version of Figure 1.11 that reads an unlimited number of `int`s and writes them out.

D.2   The routine in the Text: **EXCEPTION**

For the purposes of exposition, in the text we use the routine EXCEPTION with the following definition:

```
void
EXCEPTION( int Condition, const char *ErrorMsg )
{
    if( Condition )
    {
        cerr << ErrorMsg << endl;
        abort( );
    }
}
```

The idea is that calls to the routine EXCEPTION can be replaced by an if and a throw on systems that have exception support.

D.3   The **throw** clause

To illustrate exception handling, we will modify the String class from Section 2.6 to throw exceptions. We will also show how they are caught by writing a simple main. Figure D.2 illustrates the simplest use of exceptions in C++. Here we replace the call to EXCEPTION in Figure 2.29 with a statement that throws an exception. What is being thrown is an object. In this case, we throw an int object. When an object is thrown, control winds back through the calling sequence until a try block is encountered that has an acceptable handler. The handler is specified by a catch statement.

```
1  // operator[ ] throws an int for out of bounds access
2  //     the int is the Index.
3  char
4  String::operator[]( int Index ) const
5  {
6      if( Index < 0 || Index > strlen( Buffer ) )
7          throw( Index );
8      return Buffer[ Index ];
9  }
```

Figure D.2   String operator[] with exception handler (version #1)

```
1  main( )
2  {
3      String S = "junk";
4
5    try
6    {
7      cout << S[ 10 ] << '\n';    // Out of bounds access
8    }
9    catch( int BadIndex )
10   {
11     cerr << "Illegal access: index was " << BadIndex << endl;
12   }
13
14     return 0;
15 }
```

Figure D.3   Simple main to show how an exception is caught

Figure D.3 shows a try block with a catch statement. The try block is used to handle the int exception thrown by operator[]. As soon as the exception is thrown, control passes to the appropriate catch block, the code there is executed, and then the try/catch combination is considered terminated. In our case this takes us to line 14, which is the return statement in main. The exception handler can manipulate the thrown object, as shown on line 11. This is a more general mechanism than specifying . . . to catch any exception.

D.4   Using Inheritance to Describe Exception Hierarchies

Because any object can be thrown, the general exception handling practice is to design a hierarchy of exception handlers. If we place a base class as the parameter for a catch statement, any thrown object of a publicly derived class will be caught.

To illustrate this technique, we design a hierarchy to describe exceptions arising in this book. We name the base class AlgErrors. As shown in Figure D.4, AlgErrors contains a String object that stores the name of the function that threw the exception. This string is initialized by the AlgErrors constructor. A virtual member function ErrMsg is provided to print an error message. By default it prints the name of the throwing function (the type of exception is usually known by the context). Two derived classes are also declared: Underflow (for handling illegal operations on empty stacks, queues, and priority queues) and AccessError (for handling illegal operations on list and tree iterators). The declaration of these classes consists of a single constructor definition. A third derived class is used to implement RangeError for String (and

Vector) objects. Here we add another data member to store the offending index and redefine the ErrMsg function.

Figure D.5 lists the classes that use EXCEPTION to process errors and the functions that are affected. Note that some functions, such as the BinaryHeap DeleteMin, do not call EXCEPTION directly but call a member that calls EXCEPTION.

```
1   // Example of exception mechanism in C++.
2
3   // AlgErrors is a general base class to handle exceptions.
4   // It stores the name of the function that threw the exception
5
6   struct AlgErrors
7   {
8       const String Thrower;
9       AlgErrors( const char *FuncName ) :
10          Thrower( FuncName ) { }
11      virtual void ErrMsg( ) const
12          { cerr << "Exception thrown from " << Thrower << endl; }
13  };
14
15  // Derived classes for different types of exceptions
16
17  // Illegal access or remove in
18  // empty stack, queue, priority queue
19  struct Underflow : public AlgErrors
20  {
21      Underflow( const char *Thrower ) :
22          AlgErrors( Thrower ) { }
23  };
24
25  // Illegal access in lists, iterators, and so on
26  struct AccessError : public AlgErrors
27  {
28      AccessError( const char *Thrower ) :
29          AlgErrors( Thrower ) { }
30  };
31
32  // RangeError: out of bounds in arrays, or lists, and so on
33  struct RangeError : public AlgErrors
34  {
35      int Index;
36      RangeError( const char *FuncName, int Ind ) :
37          AlgErrors( FuncName ), Index( Ind ) { }
38      void ErrMsg( ) const
39          { cerr << "Index=" << Index << ' '; AlgErrors::ErrMsg( ); }
40  };
```

Figure D.4   Exception hierarchy

Class	Exception	Members
Vector	RangeError	operator[]
Stack	Underflow	Top, Pop
Queue	Underflow	Front, Dequeue
ListItr	AccessError	First, Insert, operator(), operator++
TreeIterator	AccessError	First, operator(), operator++
BinaryHeap	Underflow	FindMin, DeleteMin
PairingHeap	Underflow	FindMin, DeleteMin

Figure D.5   The classes that use EXCEPTION

```
1  // operator[] throws a RangeError for out of bounds access
2  char
3  String::operator[]( int Index ) const
4  {
5      if( Index < 0 || Index > strlen( Buffer ) )
6          throw( RangeError( "String::operator[]", Index ) );
7      return Buffer[ Index ];
8  }
```

Figure D.6   String operator[] with exception handler (version #2, uses the hierarchy)

Figure D.6 shows that we now throw a RangeError object, which is initialized with the throwing function's name and the out-of-range index. Note that this is an automatic variable, so it cannot be caught using a constant reference parameter. Thus in Figure D.7 the catch statement uses call by value. Notice that the error handling here is very simple and general: Any of the errors that can arise from our data structures can be caught without a change in code (unless we want to attempt error recovery).[2]

D.5   Exception Specifiers

A problem with the exception-handling mechanism is that the function declarations, which are the only source of information to the user of a class, no longer convey information about what exceptions the implementor may be planning to throw. This makes it hard for the user of the class to set up handlers. To handle this deficiency, C++ allows the addition of the *exception specifier*. The exception

---

2. Since we are using . . . to catch memory errors, and since the first handler that matches is the one that is used, we place the . . . handler after the AlgErrors handler.

specifier can be placed at the end of the function signature to indicate what exceptions might be thrown. This is known as the *throw list*. For instance, in the String class interface, we would modify the declaration of operator[] to include the throw list as follows:

```
char & operator[]( int Index ) const throw( RangeError );
```

The exception specifier is not part of the signature, so the throw list need not be included in the implementation. But it is best to include it for consistency. The newly revised implementation is shown in Figure D.8.

The throw list should include any exceptions that are thrown either directly or indirectly. If the throw list is empty, then no exceptions are expected to be thrown. If the exception specifier is not provided, then any exception may be expected to be thrown. If an unexpected exception (that is, one that is not indicated in the throw list) is thrown, function unexpected is called; it is possible to change the meaning of what happens in this case by using set_unexpected. However, the precise rules are in a state of flux at the time of this writing.

```
1  main( )
2  {
3      String S = "junk";
4
5      try
6      {
7        cout << S[ 10 ] << '\n';      // Out of bounds access
8      }
9      catch( AlgErrors E )
10     {
11       E.ErrMsg( );
12     }
13
14     return 0;
15 }
```

Figure D.7   Simple main to show how an exception is caught

```
1  char
2  String::operator[]( int Index ) const throw( RangeError )
3  {
4      if( Index < 0 || Index > strlen( Buffer ) )
5          throw( RangeError( "String::operator[]", Index ) );
6      return Buffer[ Index ];
7  }
```

Figure D.8   String operator[] with exception handler (version #3, uses the hierarchy)

Index

S

scheduler 206
scope resolution operator : : 50, 60, 781
seed 310
selection of *k*th smallest
    in binary search tree 202, 401–402,
        554–558
    using quickselect 288–291
self-adjusting data structure
    linked list 507
    path compression 739–740
    rotate-to-root strategy 677–679
sentinel
    AA-tree 591
    binary heap 207, 423, 642
    linked list header node 487–488
    pairing heap 722
    priority queue 642
    red black tree 577–584
    splay tree 694
separate chaining 610, 630–631
separate compilation 87, 114, 781
sequential search 168–169
set_unexpected 807
setiosflags 784
shallow copy 37, 387
Shape class 131–138
Shellsort 268–271
    additional increment sequences 303
    basic algorithm 268–269
    implementation 271
    performance 269–271
short 763
short circuit evaluation 772
sibling 511
Sieve of Erastothenes 181
signature 779
simple path 416
simulation 397–411
    See also discrete-event simulation,
        discrete-time simulation, Jo-
        sephus problem
single rotation 566–569
single source algorithm 420
SingleBuffer class 116–117
singly linked list 485

sizeof operator 771
Skew 587–589
skew heap 703–708
    analysis 706–708
    event-driven simulation 413
    linear-time construction 721
    merging 703–706
slack time 452
Smalltalk 140
sorted linked list 501–502
sorting 263–298
    comparison-based 265
    lower bound 267–268, 291–292
    stable 300, 304
    uses of 264–265
    See also external sorting, heapsort,
        indirect sorting, insertion
        sort, mergesort, quicksort,
        Shellsort
sparse graph 417
spelling checker 395, 632
splay tree 675–698
    analysis 683–689
    as priority queue 698
    bottom-up splay 680–683
    deletion 683, 696
    event-driven simulation 413
    Josephus problem 413
    sequential access 699
    top-down 689–697
    vs. balanced search tree 698
splaying 680
Split 587–589
stable sort 300, 304
stack 188–191, 461–465, 471–476
    abstract base class 188–190
    allowed operations 188
    and computer languages 188–191,
        351–373
    array implementation 461–465
    inorder, postorder, preorder traversals
        529–536
    linked list implementation 471–476
    linked list vs. array 479–480
standard error 783
standard input 759, 783
standard output 783